W9-BVU-690

Distorted Mirrors

Distorted Mirrors

AMERICANS

AND THEIR RELATIONS

WITH RUSSIA

AND CHINA

IN THE

TWENTIETH CENTURY

DONALD E. DAVIS
EUGENE P. TRANI

UNIVERSITY OF MISSOURI PRESS
COLUMBIA AND LONDON

Library of Congress Cataloging-in-Publication Data

Davis, Donald E.
  Distorted mirrors : Americans and their relations with Russia and
China in the twentieth century / Donald E. Davis, Eugene P. Trani.
       p.   cm.
  Summary: "Drawing on memoirs, archives, and interviews, Davis
and Trani trace American prejudice toward Russia and China by
focusing on the views of influential writers and politicians over the
course of the twentieth century, showing where American images
originated and how they evolved"—Provided by publisher.
  Includes bibliographical references and index.
  ISBN 978-0-8262-1853-7 (alk. paper)
  1. United States—Relations—Soviet Union.   2. United States—
Relations—China.   3. Soviet Union—Foreign public opinion,
American.   4. China—Foreign public opinion, American.
5. Politicians—United States.   6. Authors, American—United
States—Political activity.   7. United States—Intellectual life—20th
century.   8. Soviet Union—Relations—United States.   9. China—
Relations—United States.   10. Public opinion—United
States—History—20th century.   I. Trani, Eugene P.   II. Title.
  E183.8.S65D385   2009
  973.91—dc22
                                                        2009004941

♾™ This paper meets the requirements of the
American National Standard for Permanence of Paper
for Printed Library Materials, Z39.48, 1984.

Designer: Stephanie Foley
Typesetter: The Composing Room of Michigan, Inc.
Printer and Binder: The Maple-Vail Book Manufacturing Group
Typefaces: Block T and Palatino

The University of Missouri Press expresses its sincere appreciation for
the contribution of the Virginia Commonwealth University Foundation
toward the publication of this book.

For our wives, Mary L. Davis and Lois E. Trani,
with deep appreciation for their forbearance and understanding

contents

foreword

Thomas R. Pickering

In late 1975, I was in Aleppo in northern Syria. A town of great antiquity, it had seen many travelers and invaders come and go. I was visiting in the former category. My guide and friend was Richard Murphy, then my diplomatic colleague serving as U.S. ambassador to Syria. I was ambassador in Jordan. The Murphys were joining us on a camping trip down the Euphrates valley. Richard had been consul in Aleppo before the office had been burned and then closed in 1967 in reaction to the Israeli occupation of the Golan during the Six Days' War. Richard, an accomplished and experienced old hand in the region, knew well many *Halebis,* as Aleppines are called in Arabic, after *Haleb,* the Arabic name for their city.

Two encounters from that time are still fixed in my memory. One of the evenings in Aleppo, we joined at a Syrian club on the heights overlooking the city several local families for dinner. One called themselves Macarpoli, the slightly Grecianized version of the name of the famous Venetian traveler and explorer of the thirteenth century, Marco Polo.

Later we visited the Belgian consul. He lived and did business in the second floor of a khan dating back to the times of Marco Polo. For those not familiar with Middle Eastern names and traditions, a khan is part warehouse and camel stable on the first floor and a hotel and residential rooms and offices on the second. The building itself surrounds the four sides of a large arcaded court. Khans are found all along the caravan trails of the Middle East and central Asia as well as in the large cities. Aleppo has some dozen khans, many of great antiquity. They existed to support the supply lanes leading into and out of China and Russia from the Mediterranean coast. The khan we visited to meet with the Belgian consul and enjoy his hospitality for the evening has a long association with the West, the *Frangis,* or Franks, in Arabic. The Belgian consulate is the lineal descendant of the first Venetian consulate, reported to have been established in the same location at the beginnings of the thirteenth century.

What does all this have to do with the more recent history of U.S.-Chinese and U.S.-Russian relations from the beginnings in the late eighteenth century to the endings of the Cold War? Aleppo is a metaphor in many ways for *Distorted Mirrors*. Besides being firmly astride and serving as a central entrepôt for European trade with central Asia, for China and Russia and Siberia in the Middle Ages and the Renaissance, Aleppo with Marco Polo and the Venetians parallels in its history something of what happened seven and eight centuries later as the United States, China, and Russia opened up to each other. The central features of the eleventh-century European move to the East and the American move to the East or West, depending on your perspective regarding China and Russia, have some major parallels.

Personalities were extremely important in influencing the ideas and reactions of whole generations on the American side. We know less about how significant they were in Moscow and Beijing. We do know that Marco Polo left some legacy of his presence in the China of his age, even if the memory in China is shrouded under the greater movements of imperial politics, war, and change. What also is true is that Marco Polo and his journey made an even greater impact on Europe as it opened its collective eyes and perspectives after a long hibernation in the Dark Ages. So personalities count. From the first Kennan and the China missionaries to the China hands and the Bohlens and Thompsons of the 1930s and '40s, we see the salient impacts on our official and popular understanding of the czarist empire and the Soviet Union and the faltering Chinese empire and the Warlords that were nineteenth- and early-twentieth-century China.

So too commerce and trade made a major impact—arenas where both Venice and Genoa, most often in intensive competition, made themselves felt from the twelfth through the eighteenth centuries in the Arab Muslim and then Turkish Ottoman lands with their special caravan connections with both China and Russia. The United States for large portions of the nineteenth century and into the twentieth became a new trading powerhouse. China, perhaps much more than Russia, attracted Americans with its quality products and fabled markets. Russia was less important in this regard, because America too was rich in raw materials. But the emerging complex relationships that characterized in particular the second half of the twentieth century were heavily influenced by the early days of exploration built around individuals and motivated by, as many were, exploring and exploiting the trading and commercial opportunities. Many of them passed through distorted mirrors as they evolved.

Parallels have value in illustrating underlying trends and activities. Over history some things are repeated, and one has a sense that exploration and trade have been for a long time motivating factors in human endeavors, opening up relationships that over time take on a character and a quality that endure and are difficult to reset rapidly.

The second major lesson is that opportunities for change and changing circumstances work best when catalytic conditions are present. Marco Polo's descent from the deserts of central Asia into China presented one of those catalytic opportunities for both Europeans and the Chinese. However tenuous the caravan trade, Europeans understood much more after Marco Polo about where those goods came from, who made them, and how perhaps to make the trade more valuable and positive. China benefited in a similar way. The process was regularized by Venice and Genoa, establishing early diplomatic and trading presences within the network designed to support such trade, finding their way some distance down the caravan routes to attempt to control if not dominate the rich profits to be made. America in the nineteenth century followed the same approach. Diplomacy came as the commercial process opened up.

What now are the lessons for the first half of the twenty-first century? They are some of the same and perhaps some new.

People are important and continue from earliest times to be significant factors in developing and influencing relations. And exploration continues as before. Not because the geography and people on it are new and need to be understood, but because in other dimensions things are changing more rapidly than ever before, and it requires capable people with a sense of history and the events around them to make sense out of the new events being produced every day by the changing economic and political landscape. They are needed also to provide that the benefits accrue to both sides in ensuring the continuation of tranquillity and prosperity.

There is no substitute for effective diplomacy. The isolated Venetian consulate in Aleppo of the early thirteenth century is a far cry from modern diplomacy supported by the technical marvels of a globalizing world. Yet one is the antecedent of the other, and each depended upon wise leaders, capable people, and clear policy to survive and thrive.

As we look ahead at the next few decades a number of points will be clear in our relations with Russia and China, and indeed in their relations with each other. It is now almost obvious that there will not be a unipolar world in the future. I seriously doubt there was ever a real unipolar moment in the past. Too much of importance that had to be done required the cooperation of others—cooperation that we alone could not absolutely ensure would be forthcoming. China and Russia, along with India, Japan, and in one form or another the European Union, will be the new major players, perhaps with the addition of a few states, such as Brazil. This will not be true "multipolarity" in the sense that all states will be equal in economic and military power and influence. Although the United States for some time in the future will enjoy enormous benefits from its economic strength and military posture, these will not enable or entitle it to have its views automatically prevail on many key issues for most of the time. This new multipolar, or better yet multifaceted, age will require excellent diplomacy leading to strong bilateral relations with and among these major players, on the one hand, as well as new and better-founded institutional relationships to bring them together on key issues, on the other.

Globalization will continue apace, strengthening the need for ties of many types. Relationships will become more interdependent as they become more complex. Science and technology in all of its ramifications will increasingly be the key to progress and stability. But serious efforts will also need to be made through international cooperation, particularly among these lead players, to avoid the perversion of science and technology in areas that affect stability and security across a wide range of actions. These include not just traditional military and normal law-and-order issues but also issues throughout the economy and beyond. Communications and information, nanotechnology, and new developments in biological and related sciences are just a few of the harbingers of change, progress —and challenge.

How should we be dealing with China, Russia, and the others in this new environment? The lessons from *Distorted Mirrors* and other elements of the past history of U.S. relations with China and Russia provide some interesting guideposts for the future.

One of these is clear. Common interests are crucially important to the development of a positive agenda. Without a positive agenda much of the energy in the relationship is quickly exhausted in the exchange of mutual recriminations, which leads to a downward cycle in the relationship. Franklin D. Roosevelt knew this when he opened the door to relations with the Soviet Union in 1933 on the basis of trying to build a positive agenda. Similarly, Richard M. Nixon and Henry A. Kissinger saw the value and indeed the necessity of developing a common agenda from a shared exchange of views on the world outlook of the United States and the People's Republic of China (PRC) in 1971 and 1972. The crucial nature of understanding the history of the relationship and what that brings to the table, both good and bad, as well as the importance attached to personal diplomacy and analysis by those involved in the relationship, have been key to the development of U.S. relations with China and Russia over the past decade and a half in particular.

Looking ahead, we could do a great deal worse than emphasizing a careful bilateral examination of our jointly shared interests and goals with Russia and China. The United States has an important advantage in this regard. Over the years, the Soviet Union and now Russia in particular have looked at the benefits to be enjoyed in joining with the United States in taking the lead in the international community on one or another set of issues. Space, nuclear disarmament, and nonproliferation have been among these important questions.

With regard to China, the joint-leadership part of the paradigm has been less clear. But what was important at the beginning of the relations was that Premier Zhou Enlai shared with Henry Kissinger many elements of a worldview, including their common concern about the dangers posed to both parties by the Soviet Union, and as a result the necessity of banding together to offset that Soviet threat.

Although common, shared views on areas of congruency play a significant role in helping to build stronger and more balanced relations, it is also true that the achievement of some success in the area of common interest can add to the inducement to each side to continue the progress and, most important, to provide an inducement as well to dealing with the negative issues that are almost always part of the relationship. We will not see a time with either country when the negatives will entirely disappear. Our backgrounds and viewpoints, indeed our geostrategic positions, are too different ever to assume there will not be negative questions to be contended with in the relationship. What is important is that we ought to have, and with careful diplomacy can have, positives to offset those negatives, whether they are in the area of human rights, economic differences, or the role and place of democracy in the life of the countries concerned.

Another factor will also be important in solidifying the effort to develop strong bilateral relationships with Russia and China. Again, here the human factor looms large. Over the years our relations with both China and Russia have seen the benefits of a strong leader managing the relationship on both sides. Roosevelt personally assumed a large role, and to the extent that it was complemented, as *Distorted Mirrors* makes clear, it was Stalin who played that role. With regard to China, we must look at Kissinger and Zhou Enlai for the lead, with Mao and Nixon in the van.

In the past decade, the Gore-Chernomyrdin Commission played a similar role in Russia. It was responsible for helping to develop the positive agenda around cooperative projects in many fields, from space to health, agriculture, and cooperative threat reduction. The value of that relationship was that it could muster and marshal cabinet-level participation from each side to ensure that there were high-level authority and accountability for the carrying out of commitments on joint work. Where roadblocks intervened, the two leaders often could step in and work out the necessary compromise. Also, in dealing with important issues such as the withdrawal of ex-Soviet nuclear weapons from the Ukraine, the two could coordinate joint efforts to achieve the objective.

A similar set of arrangements has also been put in place by the Bush administration with respect to at least one crucial part of our relationship with China—economic cooperation. Henry Paulson, secretary of the Treasury, has led from the U.S. side, with a number of Chinese counterparts, the effort to develop closer cooperation in the area of economic policy between Washington and Beijing.

These three factors—shared interests, cooperative projects, and focused high-level leadership on each side—mark an important part of what could be a more successful approach to our bilateral relations with China and Russia in the decades ahead. And strong bilateral relations are a critical component of successful multilateral cooperation across the board. They are the fundamental building blocks of that relationship. I saw this most clearly when in the opening stages of the First Gulf War at the United Nations in the Security Council in 1990, we were able to gain the continuing and consistent support of China and Russia because we enjoyed, with the leadership of President George H. W. Bush and Secretary of State James Baker, a strong mutual commitment to building our bilateral relations. That meant that we had a better basis for multilateral cooperation in the United Nations and elsewhere in meeting crises and challenges.

Over the next two decades, certainly, increasing attention will be paid as well to reformulating some of the institutions for multilateral cooperation. The G8 has had differential success depending on the issues involved and the state of relations among the parties. But what is clear is that the G8 can do a great deal even if it cannot do everything, and it is certainly more obvious now than ever before that India and China need to be fully represented in that body if it is to continue making progress.

What is less sure is that the expanded G8 will be able to address all issues, both economic and political, that deserve the attention of the world's leading states. Also, something will need to be done to provide for broader representation of the world community in such bodies so that smaller developing countries do not get left totally out of the picture. Perhaps, rather than a G16 or a G20, which has been suggested, more variable formulations will need to be adopted. Not all states will need to participate on all issues as much as they might desire to do so. So on some very narrow issues of singular economic importance, perhaps a G3 or G4 would be more appropriate, at least for the consultative process of seeking ways forward, bringing in others at later points as needed and desirable.

History helps us better to understand today and better to avoid the mistakes of the past. The fascinating history of the past two centuries of U.S. relations with China and Russia adds richly to that mix. History too can help us point the way to the future. *Distorted Mirrors* gives a good sense of where we have been on track and where we have gone off course. No two sets of relationships will be more significant for our planet and its survival in the next decades of this century than those between the United States and China and the United States and Russia.

foreword to the russian edition

to be published by Vagrius Publishers, Moscow
September 2009
Vyacheslav Nikonov

Perceptions are no less significant in politics than reality. Myths and stereotypes are even more long-lasting and less subject to change than the destinies of people and nations. Yet perceptions are rooted in reality if one treats reality in terms of concepts and interests.

An awareness of reality that generates perceptions is crucial for understanding the world and for adequate political planning. One can build policies looking into a false mirror, but then the result appears to be wrong and very costly. It is no secret that the world's future in the 21st century will depend largely on relations in the U.S.-China-Russia triangle, and it would be a short-sighted and risky endeavor if we build them in a false mirror mode.

These considerations explain the significance of the magnificent research done by Donald Davis and Eugene Trani, two brilliant historians and good friends, in which they convincingly show why Russia's image in the U.S. is far less attractive than that of China; and that this is the reason for the disproportion in the respective political agendas.

Today one can often hear Americans say that Russia's unfavorable image arises from the fact that it was and remains an authoritarian state. That is close to reality. It is true that Russia has no democratic political tradition; the Russian state under the Tsarist empire and the Soviet system were by no means exemplary in terms of the rule of law, political pluralism or high standards of protecting citizens' rights and freedoms (if, of course, one can name exemplary countries at all). It also is true that democracy in modern

Russia—which is only twenty years old—deserves criticism (although it is worth mentioning that American democracy co-existed with slavery for one hundred years). Yet it does not explain why Americans' perceptions of China are much more favorable, especially if one considers that the imperial, Homindan and Communist regimes in China were far less liberal and democratic than their Russian analogies.

A country's image is a product of many variables, such as history, culture, tradition, geopolitics, geo-economy and current policies. It is important that this refers not to countries which are perceived, but to those who perceive—because an image is always in the eyes of the beholder.

There is no simple answer to the question why Russia looks less attractive for Americans than China. The reason is multifaceted. Yet it is clear that a country's behavior at a certain point in history is of little, if any, importance. If you look at leading U.S. newspapers at the beginning of the 20th, the middle of the 20th or beginning of the 21st century, you will see that the images of both Russia and China in the U.S. mass media and public opinion were constant, or almost unchanged.

Remarkably, Russia encounters problems with the way it is perceived only in the West, while China has similar problems in the East. Why is this? An interesting answer was suggested by a friend of mine, a Canadian diplomat who has lived in Moscow for more than ten years. He believes that the main problem with the perception of Russians by Westerners, above all Anglo-Saxons, lies in the fact that Russians are . . . white. There would no problems if they were green, pink or some other color. In that case the Westerners would say: "They are different"—the way they talk about people from Asia, Africa and other countries where the political regimes may be really appalling. But Russians look like Westerners and are expected to behave likewise and have the same reactions, habits and faith. Yet Russians *are* different, which makes them the most suspicious creatures in the world, and this causes irritation. The Chinese are people of a different culture for Americans; hence the Chinese have the right to a unique identity, originality, and their own traditions—things Russians are denied. U.S. human rights activists would never think of organizing gay parades in Beijing, as they completely contradict the Chinese cultural and religious tradition. But they do attempt to organize them in Moscow, disregarding Russian tradition.

It looks like similar psychological effects have always existed. Davis and Trani maintain that the modern perception of Russia and China by Americans is rooted in the intellectual frameworks laid down in the 1890s by the two outstanding explorers George Kennan and William Woodville Rockhill, who traveled, respectively, across Russia and China. George Kennan's travels were described in the book *Siberia and the Exile System,* and Rockhill's exploration of China was depicted in the book *The Land of the Lamas.*

Why did these undoubtedly talented and truthful writers become interested in such different subjects?

A traveler in a foreign country describes, first of all, things that make it different from his native country. Kennan, who had heard about Tolstoy, Dostoyevsky and Tchaikovsky, visited St. Petersburg, Moscow and other big cities and met with representatives of the Russian elite who had had a European education. Naturally he came to the conclusion that Russians are like people in the West. That is why he did not pay attention to Russia's high level of culture, the achievements of a thousand-year-old civilization, religion, history, traditions and mentality—he just took it all for granted. Yet he saw things that made Russia different from the U.S.: active revolutionaries and terrorists fighting the regime; Siberian exile where the revolutionaries were sent together with criminals; a great number of oppositionist intellectuals who had had a good education in Western literature and sympathized with the revolutionaries; and the country's notorious social inequality. As a result, Kennan limited his travel sketches to descriptions of Russian prisons, while Russia arose before the eyes of the astounded U.S. public as an embodiment of Dante's inferno and an evil empire. Not surprisingly, the socialist revolutionary terrorists who later fled Russia received a very warm welcome in the U.S., where their leader Gregory Gershuni, responsible for the deaths of hundreds of Russian officials and peaceful civilians, was virtually carried by a rapturous mob along the streets of New York.

If Rockhill had limited his picture of China to a description of the country's prisons, it would have looked more atrocious, since the Chinese penitentiary and law-enforcement system differed from the Russian one only in that it was worse. However, Rockhill was not interested in prisons or the system of political criminal investigation in China; and there were no oppositionists or Western-oriented intellectuals there. He saw that China differed from the West in its rich, unique thousand-year-old culture and religions, the Confucian tradition and its peculiar lifestyle. Thus, the American intellectual tradition permitted the Chinese to be different. Russians were denied that.

However, certain perception stereotypes seem to date from much earlier than the 19th century. Historians report that the first-ever coordinated image campaign against Russia, which was initiated by the Vatican, was attempted in the late 16th century when Moscow was at war with the Catholic Livonian Order. This point in history bred an anti-Russian stereotype—as a barbarian threat to religion, which eventually became an integral part of Western mentality and which the U.S. inherited as well.

China emerged in the Western mentality of the 18th century at the time of the "opium wars," which were imposed on China by Great Britain to make the Chinese use drugs grown in India. The events marked the beginning of a gradual decline in the Chinese empire, and it soon became an arena for active, offhand policies by the leading Western powers. China turned into a compliant object of politics. Russia, on the other hand, always remained an obstinate subject, which resolutely defended its sovereignty from external interference. A country dependent on you is much more attractive than the one that is independent.

Ethnic diasporas are another factor that has played an important role in creating the system of mirrors that reflect the world for people in the West, especially in the U.S.—a country of immigrants. The immigration of the Chinese to America was mostly economic in nature: the Chinese would flee their country not to escape the regime, but rather in search of a better life. The Chinese diaspora in the U.S. has been always united, and its members do not feel negative toward their native country. On the contrary, they actively promote its culture, tradition and even national food.

Meanwhile, immigrants coming to the U.S. from the Russian Empire were mainly representatives of ethnic minorities from its western provinces: Poles, people of the Baltics and Jews; they all had an understandably negative attitude toward the metropolis. Those immigrants used America's electoral mechanisms to make the fight for their rights in the Russian Empire an organic part of U.S. foreign policy. This immigration was followed by new waves of immigrants who sought to escape the Soviet regime; for them Russia was associated either with the inferno which they managed to break away from, or a lost—probably forever—paradise.

Once becoming citizens, representatives of different ethnic groups could contribute to the formation of the U.S. political agenda toward their native countries by disseminating information about their history, culture, and politics, as well as describing them in the mass media. For decades the staff of university departments, media editorial offices and departments at diplomatic agencies relating to China would be replenished with Americans who advocated the Rockhill school of thought and with pro-China ethnic Chinese. Meanwhile, Russian academic and political centers operating in the U.S. were dominated by Kennan followers and anti-Russia immigrants—mostly from Eastern Europe, not Russia. This partly explains why China has had an extensive and influential lobby in Washington, while the Russian lobby works against Moscow. Current and former offended Russian citizens who formed this lobby, partially made up of fugitive oligarchs, have repeatedly stated their intention of working toward the overthrow of the incumbent Russian power and named concrete amounts of money directed for that purpose via mass media spin doctors, lobbyist structures and political circles.

It also is true that geopolitics has always been a decisive factor influencing perception. No one loves strong competitors. Throughout the entire century described in this book, the West and the U.S. in particular have had more grounds to treat Russia as their geopolitical rival than China. Only twice during the past century—in February 1917 and in December 1991—did the U.S. applaud Russia and that was when it committed the suicide that resulted in the breakdown of its society and its economic collapse.

The Soviet Union, which had built an alternative social and economic system and declared world Communism as its primary goal, sent a challenge to the entire Western system of values. In this sense, the challenge was truly existential. The bipolar confrontation during the Cold War era turned the Soviet Union and the U.S. into tough competitors on a global scale; the two countries not only perceived each other as competitors, they were actual rivals. As for China, it was viewed as a less significant geopolitical player, and after the Communists came to power in China, it was regarded as a secondary power, a derivative of Soviet might.

Things changed after the breakup of the Soviet Union: the Russian Federation, the country, which yielded to the Soviet Union in all parameters, lost its global ambitions. The U.S. became a domineering superpower in a unipolar world, but it still viewed Russia as an obstacle on its path to global domination. Today Russia is a strong state, which, after a decade of chaos and semi-decay, is intensively reinforcing its economic potential and resuming a foreign policy based on the primacy of its national interests. However, China has a good chance to move into the position of a second world center of power and become a major geopolitical competitor of the U.S. within this century. This tendency already is likely to affect its image in the short run. It would be very difficult for the U.S. to set Russia and China against each other, as relations between the two countries are now at a stage at which they have never been before—and much better than what either of them has with Washington.

At the same time, China is the U.S.'s largest trading partner and this is a double-edged factor in terms of perception. Beijing may both bring into play its U.S. partners to promote its interests and image in the U.S., and also have an allergic response to the U.S. due to economic rivalry and trade wars. Russia and the U.S. are engaged on a smaller scale; they do not have influential business groups that could have a serious impact on the perceptions and politics in Moscow and Washington (although it is worth noting that top managers of U.S. companies working in Russia have a better view of Russia than those who do not work there).

One can talk infinitely about images and perception, but there is one thing of special note. Russia's image may not be good, but the U.S. image in the world is much worse than that of Russia or China.

Moscow believes the best way to improve Russia's image abroad is to make it a normal democratic country that lives in peace with itself and the world—and that is Russia's wish for other countries as well. Russia is definitely better than its image abroad, especially in the U.S.

preface

Other studies have tackled the subject of American views and policies toward Russia and China.[1] Such works examined enduring attitudes, temporary opinions, and policies that arose from selected issues or events. In referring to his own book, historian Peter Filene tried to "go beyond the ephemeral, often atypical appearance to the underlying and motivating intellectual process." He further explained, "By selecting a long time span I hoped to avoid mistaking opinions for attitudes, to discover the motive intellectual forces underlying the flux of transient polemic."[2]

For us, the use of pollsters such as Gallup was unsatisfactory. This was because Gallup did not begin until 1935, and the questionnaires and documents dealt with fleeting, contemporary issues. As another writer pointed out, "public-opinion polls provide no panacea for getting at public opinions, much less for understanding the attitudes and belief systems which underlie them."[3]

We discovered we were dealing with profound cultural likes and dislikes toward Russia and China, similar to ethnic, racial, and gender stereotypes. These cultural stereotypes were almost primitive. At a certain stage of America's development, they became ingrained and difficult to dislodge. Issues or events, even important ones, rarely penetrated to these subterranean cultural feelings. Rather, they rode on the surface of deeper trend lines. Filene believed such perceptions toward Russia, and we may add China, were simply a "symptom of a more general set of attitudes." The historian, he realized, is engaged in a "delicate enterprise of probing or interpreting the verbal surface in order to reach the attitudes concealed beneath."[4]

We believe the selective but representative samples we present of the ways in which these attitudes developed reflect underlying trends starting at a certain moment in America's cultural evolution—a stage when the country emerged from relative continental isolation and began seeking its place in the world. At that moment, stereotypical prejudices formed, though they had been subconsciously building.[5] America's crucial decade for Russia and China was the 1890s.

The relevance of the twentieth century to this study lies in its turning initial distortions by "Siberian" George Kennan and diplomat William Woodville Rockhill of the 1890s into deep-seated and widespread prejudices in the United States. These consisted in Americans distrusting Russia and believing in China. Two important exceptions were during World War II for Russia and Mao's success in China. The twentieth century remains important in the evolution of an American anti-Russian and pro-Chinese sentiment. From our standpoint, the significance of these distortions is their potential bearing on the twenty-first century. If unrestrained prejudices developed in the twentieth century reemerge in the twenty-first, they could have dangerous consequences for America. Perhaps the most worrisome would be the alliance of Russia and China against the United States. Say, for example, American trade with China diminished to a trickle while Russia's need for Chinese products and China's demand for Russian raw materials brought a realization that together they could break America's worldwide hegemony. For argument's sake, let's pick the Orwellian-like year 2084 as a culminating date for such a scenario. America, for the first time since 1919, would dance to the tune of its two great twentieth-century rivals. This reminds us of Paul Kennedy's answer to why the Spanish-American alliance failed—amongst other things, its inability to secure either Britain or France as a partner until the Bourbon alliance of 1756.[6] For now, we leave it to the reader's imagination to draw out further unpleasantries for the United States, and we will return to this theme often.

Our story of twentieth-century distortions comprises a series of tableaux, enlivened by the writings of selected players. Others could have been chosen, but our feisty bunch illustrates key situations and conflicts. The structure of international relations or the clash of civilizations plays a lesser role in our method. Rather, we let our players develop their own stories as illustrations of deeply rooted trends. The following two paragraphs represent a sample of our method.

Russia presented a dilemma for scholar Samuel Harper, who was charmed by czarist Russia but initially rejected Soviet Russia. That difficulty was resolved with the diplomats trained by Robert Kelley in the 1920s in favor of renewing "Siberian" George Kennan's antipathy. Journalist Eugene Lyons sustained that negative impulse when, in a role reversal with Harper, he turned against his own socialist impulses to hate Soviet Russia. American ambassador William C. Bullitt underwent a similar role reversal, disillusioned by the Soviet utopia. President Franklin D. Roosevelt used his second appointment to Moscow, Joseph Davies, to bring Russia into the U.S. orbit, but Stalin chose Hitler. After Germany's invasion of the USSR, it was

Davies who preached that Allied alliances with Stalin could bring victory. Yet the high point in the drama, Yalta, also marked a renewal of those suspicions that had always bedeviled the U.S. relationship, then given currency by the young diplomat George F. Kennan's containment theory and the emergence of the Cold War—wherever the blame for the latter rests. It took President Ronald Reagan to renew FDR's approach and recognize that the "evil empire" no longer existed under Mikhail Gorbachev.

On the Chinese side, President Woodrow Wilson and philosopher John Dewey offered American progressivism to China when it was trapped between tradition and revolution. Journalists Edgar Snow and Teddy White and novelist Pearl Buck fought for a realistic understanding, but failed to educate Americans, who thought of China as an upside-down Shangri-la. World War II brought FDR, Stalin, Churchill, Chiang Kai-shek, General "Vinegar" Joe Stilwell, and the State Department's China Hands into the drama. They failed either to renew Nationalist China or to ally the United States with Mao. It took President Richard Nixon and his national security adviser, Henry Kissinger, as it did with Reagan and Russia, to restore the U.S.-China relationship. America is the benefactor of their work: accommodation with Russia and restoration of goodwill with China. Can this balance be maintained in the twenty-first century, given the history of the twentieth century's distortions? The following summary of this book's chapters offers a trail through the twentieth century's maze of distortions and suggests some of the dangers inherent in the contemporary world.

In the following chapters, arranged in a loose chronological order, the authors will show where American images of Russia and China originated, their evolution, and how they have often helped to sustain a similar foreign policy, generally negative toward Russia and positive toward China. We want to see how certain individuals were some of the primary makers of those perceptions and policies, because of what they saw and learned—or what they thought they saw and learned—be it cabbages or kings or pigs with wings. We lay the basis for this in the book's introduction, "Distortions in the Looking Glass," by examining the thoughts and actions of two persons who helped lay the foundations for American relations with Russia and China in the twentieth century, the elder George "Siberian" Kennan and the "Old China Hand" William Woodville Rockhill. In Part I, "Russia," we take seven chapters with the Russian side of the equation. Chapter 1, "'Soviet Sam' and the Émigrés," analyzes the career of Samuel Harper, one of America's earliest Slavic experts as well as émigré Russian scholars. In Chapter 2, "The Boys from Riga," we deal with Robert F. Kelley's tenure in the State Department and the corps of Russian specialists trained during the twenties in Riga, Latvia. To sustain the popular perceptions of Russia as an "evil empire," in Chapter 3, we look at the journalism of Eugene Lyons and some of his fellow journalists, who criticized Russia. Chapter 4, "Honeymooners," studies American diplomats who first went to Soviet Russia in the thirties. This brings us to a consideration of the unusual relationship of President Franklin D. Roosevelt and Premier Joseph V. Stalin during World War II in Chapter 5, "Chums." In Chapter 6, "Mr. X," we follow the rise of one of Kelley's protégés, George F. Kennan, and his doctrine of containment. The man who turned Kennan's notions of containment into the forceful policy of "rollback" was Paul Nitze, the subject of Chapter 7, "Gray Eminence."

Part II on China also contains seven chapters, starting with Chapter 8, "Missionary Diplomacy," which covers the policies of early-twentieth-century presidents, particularly Woodrow Wilson and the role of American missionaries in China. In Chapter 9, "Pragmatist in China," we take up John Dewey's two years in China and his impact on education there. Chapter 10, "Red Star over China," investigates the life and times of the pro–Red China journalist Edgar Snow. Chapter 11, "The Novelist and the Ambassador," considers the literary works of Pearl S. Buck and the activities of Ambassador Nelson T. Johnson. During World War II, FDR tried to invent a policy for the Far East with the cooperation of Chiang Kai-shek, especially at the wartime conferences in Cairo, the subject of Chapter 12, "The President and the Generalissimo." During this time, Teddy White reported on China for Henry Luce and *Time* magazine, the subject of Chapter 13, "Luce's Man in Chungking." After the communist victory in 1949, the United States had nothing to do with Red China until President Richard Nixon and his national security adviser, Henry Kissinger, again opened the People's Republic of China, which we narrate in Chapter 14, "Gurus." The period of 1949 to 1969, especially the Korean and Vietnam wars, though further angering Americans toward the PRC, could not extinguish the underlying positive feelings, which President Nixon and Henry Kissinger were able to reignite and President Jimmy Carter to fan with his moves toward recognition.

In our closing section, "Old Conclusions, New Beginnings," we study President Ronald Reagan's successful policy in taming Soviet Russia by resurrecting FDR's "chums" policy. We also note how President George H. W. Bush and his national security adviser, Gen. Brent Scowcroft, were able to avert disengagement in 1989 due to the Tiananmen Square insurrection. The president sent Scowcroft and Deputy Secretary of State Lawrence Eagleburger to Beijing. They assured the Chinese leadership that U.S. policy would remain friendly even though public sentiment was hostile. In the "Afterword," we suggest where U.S. attitudes and policies currently are. Here we quote in full Dr. Trani's op-ed piece for the *International Herald Tribune*. Both represent an additional tableau of what has been offered in the text.

• • •

In 1984, after a five-week stay in the People's Republic of China, one of the authors, Eugene P. Trani, was interviewed by the influential Chinese paper *Reference News*, which published the results on May 20, 1984. That interview led him to do an op-ed piece for the *Kansas City Star*, on July 8, 1984.[7] In that article, "China the Friend vs. Russia the Foe: Different Perceptions Can't Help but Affect Shape of Foreign Policy," he first formulated the thesis of this book. Twenty-two years later, his mind had not changed when he did another op-ed for the *International Herald Tribune*.[8] These two articles form the bookends of the present work. The first one is quoted here in full:

> A colleague of mine, who has just ended a teaching assignment in the Soviet Union, sent me a post card in which he said all he could think of as he left Moscow was Martin Luther King's famous line: "Free at last, free at last."
>
> That observation, and my own recent experiences in both Russia and China, called to mind again the vastly different perceptions among Americans of the two largest communist nations in the world—the Union of Soviet Socialist Republics and the People's Republic of China.
>
> When Americans visit Russia, they usually sense deep suspicion on the part of their hosts. Russian waiters, clerks, customs officials, service people, bureaucrats and government officials do make trips to the Soviet Union memorable, but most frequently it is not in a positive sense. American visitors to the Soviet Union also are put off by the number of uniformed personnel, both police and military, whom they see.
>
> In contrast, Americans who visit China usually comment on the great warmth and hospitality with which they are received. Chinese hosts and service people have a knack for making visitors feel truly welcome. Many Americans have left the Soviet Union with a great sense of relief; in fact, at times spontaneous cheers erupt as planes leave the tarmac at the Moscow or Leningrad airports.
>
> By comparison, departures from China are sad, and often Americans leave with the feeling that new friendships will last many years. The point is that lifestyles and traditions cause a great many travelers to feel positive and optimistic about China and negative, suspicious and pessimistic about the Soviet Union.
>
> Neither view is completely accurate. Americans tend to overemphasize problems in the Soviet Union and in Soviet-American relations, and underemphasize potential problems in China and in Chinese-American relations. These current images are part of the reason that America has very different relations with the two major communist nations in the world.
>
> For most Americans the sight of President Reagan in Beijing and Shanghai was not at all unnatural and was a logical step in bettering relations be-

tween these two countries. Given the current state of Soviet-American relations, a comparable visit to Moscow and Leningrad would be considered almost impossible by the majority of Americans.

In general, Americans seem to have warm feelings toward the Chinese people and, despite ingrained prejudices against communist governments, show a degree of interest and sympathy for the leadership of the People's Republic. The same Americans typically harbor negative ideas about the Russian character and are automatically suspicious of anything that comes from the Kremlin.

One must ask why. The question is especially important because these different perceptions cannot help but be reflected in American foreign policy.

Historically, Americans generally have looked favorably on China and unfavorably on Russia: in part, that is because there were extensive early contacts between the peoples of the United States and China and few contacts between the peoples of the United States and Russia. Even before the revolutions that brought communists to power in each country—1917 in Russia and 1949 in China—Americans who visited China greatly outnumbered those who traveled to Russia.

American businessmen, missionaries, educators and philanthropists constituted a small but visible part of the social fabric of pre-revolutionary China. From the time the United States established relations with China in 1784, those Americans sent home impressions that were generally favorable. Over time, a vast literature about the Chinese people and their country grew out of the flow of friendly reports.

In contrast, very few Americans visited Russia before 1917 and those who did experienced little that inspired their sympathy. It could be argued that in the 19th century, Russia was strong enough to resist the participation of foreigners in the important aspects of national life, while China was so weak that foreigners could meddle at will.

Whatever the case, literary images established in the 19th century continued into the 20th century. Best-selling authors like Pearl Buck (*The Good Earth*) generated immeasurable good will toward Chinese people, who were portrayed as simple and happy. Literary accounts about Russia mostly continued to be negative. Even during the 1930s, when many intellectuals in America were caught up in a "Red romance" with the Soviet Union, the prevailing view of Russia was of an unhappy country bedeviled by want and lost personal liberties.

Another reason American perceptions of China and Russia developed so differently may be found in the attitudes of the Chinese and Russians who came to the United States. The Chinese who emigrated in the 19th century and formed the Chinese-American community felt no animosity toward their motherland and, indeed, took much pride in its accomplishments.

At the same time, Russians who came to the United States both before and after the Russian Revolution generally felt themselves to be victims of religious bigotry, political demagoguery or some other inscrutable force. Such national attitudes have persisted. Even today, Chinese-Americans generally are heartened by positive developments and progress in the People's Republic.

The most recent group to come to the United States from Russia, the Jewish immigrants, are severe critics of the Russian government and values and have applauded the American government in every hard-line stance toward the land of their birth.

The nature of the development of Chinese and Russian studies in American universities also has contributed to these different perceptions. Academic programs to study Chinese culture were established, in the main, by Americans whose pleasant experiences in China conditioned them to render sympathetic interpretations. Russian studies, on the other hand, were founded and have long been dominated by a cadre of Russian émigrés critical of developments in the Soviet Union.

For many years the major professor of Chinese history at Harvard University was John K. Fairbank, a scholar who was considered the "dean" of Chinese studies in the United States. He was known for his sympathy for China and his capacity for reporting events from a Chinese perspective. At that same time, Harvard's professor of Russian history was Michael Karpovich, an émigré who served in the Washington Embassy of the last non-Bolshevik Russian government. Mr. Karpovich's anti-Bolshevik convictions were reflected in his interpretations of Russian life and history.

Students at Harvard thus heard pro-Chinese Chinese history and anti-Russian Russian history. The faculty of Chinese and Russian studies programs developed along parallel lines at other major universities. At Yale, for example, Arthur Wright taught Chinese history for many years, while George Vernadsky taught Russian history. When students began to graduate in the image of their mentors and to enter academic, political and diplomatic life, they in turn helped perpetuate pro-Chinese and anti-Russian attitudes in the United States.

Certainly the leaders of Russia and China during the Second World War influenced the images of these two countries. Russia's Josef Stalin, despite his zeal to eliminate the fascist foe, was viewed by many Americans as a "blood-thirsty dictator" who executed his opponents. Stalin's image, which became even worse when the allies found themselves unable to work out arrangements for a viable peace after 1945, generated further negative feelings among Americans toward the Soviet Union.

In contrast, Chiang Kai-shek, in some ways no less a dictator than Stalin, enjoyed an image in the West as a democrat and facilitator in a nation striving to become modern. The characteristics of Chiang Kai-shek (only a few people suspected graft and inability to enforce reforms) were easily attributed to all of China.

To be sure, there is one overriding factor that historically has fashioned

America's negative image of Russia and the Soviet Union; that is the anti-Semitism that has long been practiced in that country. There is no comparable influence in Chinese-American relations.

Given the significance of American relations with these countries, it is important that Americans from every walk of life understand these perceptions and the influences that have helped formulate them, and do everything possible to bring about more of a balance in our treatment toward these countries. Seemingly, the mirror image of these perceptions is shared by the Chinese and the Russians, with most Chinese favorably disposed to the United States and most Russians very suspicious of America.

For those who would like to see how Russians and Chinese have viewed America, we have added two online-only appendixes: the first by Professor Alla Porshakova of the Moscow State Linguistic University deals with Russia, and the second by Professor Jin Guangyao of Fudan University in Shanghai takes up China. Both may be found at http://press.umsystem.edu/spring2009/davis.trani/appendix.htm.

acknowledgments

This book has been nearly thirty years in the making, beginning with Gene Trani's Fulbright Scholarship in 1981 at Moscow State University, where Gene taught American history. Years later, with Gene's sabbaticals at St. John's College at the University of Cambridge in 1998 and 2007 and at Lincoln College in Oxford in 2005, the authors developed the book's conceptual framework, and we have enjoyed another coauthorship on an important subject.

We wish to thank our colleagues whose considerable expertise was invaluable: Professor Jin Guangyao, professor of history, Fudan University, Shanghai; Professor Boris Shiriaev, professor and chair, Department of North American Studies, School of International Relations, St. Petersburg State University; Professor Alla Porshakova, professor of history at Moscow State Linguistic University; Professor Judyth Twigg, a political science professor of Russian government at Virginia Commonwealth University; and Professor John Herman, VCU's professor of Chinese history. Professors Porshakova and Guangyao are the authors of the appendixes to this book, which are available on the University of Missouri Press's web site.

We also want to thank Margaret Acquarulo and Kathy Honsharuk for their thorough, diligent help in editing and organizing the final manuscript, and we would also like to acknowledge the two anonymous outside readers for the press who helped us think more generally about our subject matter. We have included some of their suggestions.

Our deep appreciation is extended to the Johnson family for allowing us to use Ambassador Johnson's papers in our research, and for depositing the papers in VCU's Cabell Library.

We wish to thank our mentor and brilliant professor, Dr. Robert Ferrell, for a lifetime of support. To our editor, Beverly Jarrett, we extend our deepest gratitude, for her support and tireless efforts in the publication of this manuscript.

To our spouses, Lois E. Trani and Mary L. Davis, we once again express our profound devotion and thanks.

Distorted Mirrors

introduction
Distortions in the Looking Glass

Two American adventurers journeyed into the unknown. Each spun his expedition's tale in books, articles, and speeches. They enchanted their public with stories from forbidden lands. Each persuaded politicians to create looking-glass worlds from his images. These two exceptional explorers were "Siberian" George Kennan, who made Russia synonymous with oppression, and "old China hand" William Woodville Rockhill, who identified Cathay as the "Land of the Lamas." A serendipity: both wayfarers published their extraordinary books—Kennan's *Siberia and the Exile System* and Rockhill's *Land of the Lamas*—in 1891 and both by the Century Company.

●　●　●

George Kennan first journeyed through northeastern Siberia from 1865 to 1867 as part of the Russian-American Telegraph Expedition to connect a line from a cable under the Bering Sea and across Eurasia. Though that project never came to fruition, Kennan was fascinated with Russia, learned the language, and embarked on a series of lectures, thrilling audiences with his adventures. When his sympathetic pictures of Siberia and czarism came under attack by William Armstrong, inspector of consulates during President Ulysses Grant's administration, Kennan resolved to return to Russia to make a thorough investigation of the exile system.

Kennan's book affected American views by distorting them from sympathetic or neutral to negative. Kennan had changed from Russophile to Russophobe. The adventurer, after two years in Siberia to research his book, now saw czarism with disdain but exonerated ordinary Russians. He proclaimed czarism's barbarity, for it had created and maintained inhumane, unjust penal colonies; they were Russia's version of Dante's hell. Siberian exile poisoned the entire nation.

Kennan's new interpretation raised public awareness of U.S. diplomacy toward Russia. The first fruit was in President Theodore Roosevelt's anti-Russian diplomacy at the Portsmouth Peace Conference settling the Russo-

Japanese War in 1905. Kennan's prejudice transformed Russia in the minds of his compatriots from benign to beneath contempt.[1]

Kennan's analysis had begun in 1885 and ended two years later in the Siberian city of Tiumen. Depressing data and his eyewitness accounts confirmed for him czardom's cruelty and injustice. Tiumen's holding prison held four times the number designed for it, resulting in poor sanitary conditions. Hospital conditions were unspeakable. "Never before in my life had I seen faces so white, haggard, and ghastly as those that lay on the gray pillows in these hospital cells." Authorities admitted conditions were bad. The average death rate stood at almost 30 percent, so high it was not found anywhere outside Russia in the civilized world. Crowded convict barges were unhealthy. From Tiumen, Kennan wrote several letters to R. Smith, president of the Century Company, on Siberia's condition. In one he described his change from apologist to critic of the penal program and the Russian government: "I must frankly say, [this is] the worst prison I have ever seen, and if the places where they keep the exiles generally farther on in Siberia, are as bad as this one, I shall have to take back some things that I have said and written about the exile system. The Tiumen forwarding prison comes nearer to an Inferno than anything I have ever seen."[2] Kennan's conversion from optimist to pessimist about czarist Russia began here.

By July 4, 1885, Kennan and his artist-photographer friend George Frost had reached Omsk and traveled to Semipalatinsk. It was here that Kennan and Frost had their first glance of political exiles. Those camps shattered his former views—views gained from his 1865–1867 trip. His former 1860s ideas of "nihilists"—a term for all dissidents—did not match the reality of his 1880s investigations. Nihilists were more reasonable and better educated, hardly fanatical, and had more character than he had pictured.[3] An exile said, "Every one of them [the exiles], I think, would lay down his arms, if the Tsar would grant to Russia a constitutional form of government and guarantee free speech, a free press, and freedom from arbitrary arrest, imprisonment and exile."[4]

When he left the Altai mountain region, Kennan claimed, "I am sparing neither expense nor labor nor hardship in *The Century*'s service. I am not yet half through, but I think I can now safely promise you the best most accurate and most trustworthy description of Siberia and the life of the Siberian exiles that has ever been written—at least in our language." He made good on that promise. Advocacy was another matter. The Altai was where political exiles enjoyed the most freedom, and they "opened to me the whole 'nihilist' and political exile world." Kennan extracted from them their notes to others and more than seven hundred prisoner résumés. "With these letters of introduction and this list I defy the Government to prevent me from making a thorough study not only of the life of political exiles but of the inner history of the whole Russian revolutionary movement." Even before he left Tomsk for eastern Siberia, his most "long-cherished opinions with regard to nihilists and the working of the exile system had been completely overthrown."[5]

Kennan's study reached its peak in the dreaded Irkutsk mines, places reserved for the worst offenders. Inmates refused to take the czar's oath of allegiance, and the czar punished them by extending their terms by ten more years. On Kennan's way to Kara, he met Ekaterina Breshkovskaia, future "little grandmother" of Russia's 1917 Revolution. She told him that even if exiles and their children died there, it would not be in vain. "Interviews with such political exiles—and I met many in the Trans-Baikal—were to me more bracing tonic than medicine," he remarked. Prison accommodations at Verkhni Udinsk, even according to a Russian authority, were worse than those provided dogs.[6]

Smith wrote him, "If the expedition is going to cost more than we estimated, it is also going to be of much more importance than we supposed —you will be glad to learn that the great prosperity of the Century Co. remains unabated, and that we are securing for the magazine such contributions as will continue no doubt to give it the widest circulation and secure for your reports from this expedition, the largest audience." If that were not enough, R. W. Gilder, the Century Company's editor, said, "You seem to be doing the subject in the most thorough and unprejudicial manner, and none of us doubt that the result will be not only interesting but of use to the world. The *Century* has several very important schemes, which are not yet known to the public. Yours is the most valuable."[7] Century counted on his sensationalism; he did not disappoint them.

Studying penal servitude of political offenders now became Kennan's special goal. He did it secretly, as everywhere guards scrutinized him. At Kara he met a previously known convict, Nathalie Armfeldt, serving a fourteen-year prison sentence, deprived of her civil rights and then exiled to Siberia forever. She told Kennan "ghastly stories of cruelty, suffering, insanity, and suicide." The warden discovered this sortie. When confronted by him, Kennan pretended ignorance of restrictions but owned up to an awareness of probable limits. Fearing searches of his prisoners' letters given him to send homeward, he destroyed them. "The risk of keeping them," he wrote, "had become too great to be justifiable." He erased, or put into cipher, names he had stored in his notebooks. "I was not put upon my word of honor, I was not searched, and I might have carried those letters safely to their destination, as I afterward carried many others."[8]

On his way north from Kiatcha, he stopped at Selenginsk and met more political exiles, equally excluded and sentenced. Police considered them the most dangerous class of conspirators, and they were sentenced by military courts.[9] Kennan's mind irreversibly changed. The adventurer pondered inadequacies of czarist reform projects where people and commissions did nothing: if you wanted explanations, you inquired; if you went to the Ministry of the Interior, if you persisted at the Council of the Empire, if you hounded special commissions, only new schemes resulted. The whole administrative nightmare revolved slowly until it sucked reform out of sight.[10] Kennan's disillusionment was complete. The only path forward was destruction of the autocracy. Finally back at Tiumen, he and Frost took a week's rest. Smith congratulated him, "You have done a most heroic thing, and your letters, if you will permit us to use them in our own way from time to time, as your magazine articles appear, will show this to the world, and will be such an advertisement of the magazine papers as no one could in cold blood . . . sit down and write."[11]

Kennan's book refuted the notion of an antigovernment party as a homogenous "gang of wrong-headed malcontents, visionary enthusiasts, fanatical assassins who would be imprisoned in any civilized state [but rather] Russian political exiles [are] entitled to our sympathy." He based this on personal meetings with more than five hundred exiles, many government officials, and relevant literature. The resulting publication became an instantaneously popular classic. Nihilism could not be applied to any antigovernment party. There were leftists from liberals to terrorists. Nihilism was a reproach used to discredit "all persons who were not satisfied with the existing order." The term could be used for regicides like Sergei Nechaiev, who aimed to kill not only the czar and his family but any bureaucrats. Yet Kennan called for his imprisonment in European Russia with all the others as a substitute for Siberian exile. Russia's Siberian system had to be abolished.[12]

Although other travelers, most notably Isabel Hapgood, had discovered popular ignorance or religious fervor, humor or hospitality in Russia, they and the public generally accepted Kennan's effort to remake Russia. The *Chicago Tribune* wrote, "The *Century* takes on more and more the character of a reviewer. In it, the history of our times is more fairly set forth than in any other magazine. The *Century* articles on Russia by George Kennan are attracting the attention of the civilized world." If criticized, Kennan would reply, "I know more about the exile system than any man in the Russian Prison department . . . and if I could get before a court of justice with power to summon and protect witnesses I would prove a state of affairs that would disgrace the Russian Government in the eyes of the whole civilized world and make Alexander III blush with shame under his clothes!"[13]

Americans were also exasperated. Kennan had, almost single-handedly, changed the image of Russia. America's looking glass had portrayed a docile Russian bear. After Kennan, it reflected a menacing Siberian tiger. Russia was despotic, maintaining a cruel prison system. Czarism should be overturned by a liberal democratic revolution. Kennan was entitled to his opinion, his distortion, if you will, buttressed by two years of research. He was free to spread his gospel, but was it any of his business to prescribe medicine for his self-proclaimed patient? His compatriot, the Sinologist William Woodville Rockhill, also would prescribe medicine for his Chinese patient.

• • •

William Rockhill, explorer, Orientalist, and diplomat, first journeyed into deepest China, starting in Peking during December 1888.[14] Unlike Kennan, his influence was to be much more toward policy making than popular images. By February 1889, he had left China proper, entered the Kokonor steppe, and headed toward Tibet. He then realized Lhasa could be entered only secretly, as getting permission was futile. He disguised himself in Chinese costume, hoping to be mistaken for one of China's minorities. Rockhill trudged by opium dens, "singsong girlies," and "red rag" convicts in his Mongolian fur cap, gown, and shaven head and face. "At last, some six months after leaving Peking, and less than 400 miles from his goal, Rockhill knew he was beaten, for he did not have enough money to continue towards Lhasa." He made another try, got within 110 miles of Lhasa, and was turned back by hostile Tibetans. He had been warned along the way that if he advanced to Lhasa, he and his party would be killed. Lhasa was the Forbidden City, the Shangri-la of Buddhism. Nevertheless, he had penetrated extensively into this forbidden land. His adventurous tale earned him a gold medal from the Royal Geographical Society.[15]

Rockhill finished *Land of the Lamas: Notes of a Journey through China, Mongolia, and Tibet* in 1891 and, like Kennan, wrote articles for *Century* magazine. These made interesting reading for specialists, explorers, and the curious. He wrote his friend Alfred E. Hippisley, "I have been wildly going over my notes. Gilder, of the *Century* magazine, has asked me to write three or four articles for them and though I extremely dislike writing for the magazine reading public, the price he has offered me for my work compelled me to accept for I must try to pay for my voyage now." He tried reentering the State Department, where he had previously served in the American legations to China and Korea, even if it meant assignment to Korea: "So be it, rather a cycle of Cathay or Korea than fifty years of America for me."[16] But in 1893, Rockhill accepted appointment as the State Department's chief clerk and subsequently became minister to Greece.

Rockhill the explorer became Rockhill the diplomat and as such made his greatest contribution. Here he exercised profound influence as the architect of America's open-door policy toward China. That happened when John Hay assumed his duties as secretary of state in late 1898. Since he had no Far Eastern adviser, he brought his friend Rockhill, then minister to Greece, to Washington. Arriving in D.C. the following spring, Rockhill reviewed Chinese affairs. His friend Alfred Hippisley, a longtime bureaucrat in the Imperial Chinese Customs Service, was there on leave. According to one author, he advised Rockhill that "the United States [should] approach the other European powers and get from each of them an assurance that they would not interfere with treaty ports in their spheres of influence (that is, with ports where the Imperial Maritime Customs Service had its establishments) and that the Chinese treaty tariff should apply without discrimination to all merchandise entering their respective spheres of influence."[17] Impressed with this advice, he recommended it to Hay, who wrote back, "am more than ready to act." Rockhill composed a paper referring to Hippisley's memorandum. President William H. McKinley endorsed it. A series of notes, all drafted by Rockhill and issued by Hay, proclaimed the open door: no power would interfere with treaty ports, vested interests, or spheres of influence; the Chinese treaty tariff would apply to all merchandise; harbor and railroad fees would be equal.

The following year Hay made a second effort, qualitatively different from the first. This effort, Hay's Circular, was also initiated and crafted by Rockhill. It maintained the "Chinese territorial and administrative entity" by standing against further partitioning. "The idea of preserving Chinese territorial and administrative entity, in itself a somewhat ambitious policy, gave way almost unconsciously to the idea of a downright guarantee of Chinese territory."[18]

These two features of Rockhill's career—writer and diplomat—anchored America's enduring sympathy for China, its mystery and potential.[19] This suave Far Eastern diplomat and image maker should not be underestimated. Rockhill, acting through Hay, had become author and originator of America's long-standing views of China, much the way Kennan had toward Russia.[20] To further his image of China and policy toward China, Rockhill—as well as President Theodore Roosevelt and his circle—sided with Japan as China's guardian and champion of U.S. and Chinese interests against imperialism.

Rockhill's open-door modus vivendi and his cardinal doctrine embedded in Hay's Circular remain lasting tributes to his influence. Like Kennan's contributions, his too became permanent features of American diplomacy. By the age of forty, he was America's leading Orientalist and explorer of inner Asia. By fifty, he was the greatly respected member of TR's "Tennis Cabinet." When Rockhill unexpectedly passed away at sixty-one, TR wrote his widow, "Your husband was one of those men who rendered literally invaluable public service of a kind so unusual that it was never fully appreciated by his fellow countrymen."[21] This praise makes necessary a more detailed explanation of Rockhill's diplomatic career.

For Kennan and his followers, Russia remained an evil empire. For Rockhill and his successors, China would be the object of selfless interest, the Shangri-la of America's good purposes. Never mind that neither country asked or wished for such condescensions. Kennan had quarreled with many over Russia's image. Rockhill had met TR through his Bostonian Brahmin friends and had convinced all of them of America's Asian mission. For example, in the mid-1890s historian Henry Adams dropped a note to Rockhill, "Roosevelt breakfasts with me Friday at twelve p.p.c and wants you to come with a tender spirit. Try and do without your diplomates for an hour." When Rockhill rose from third assistant secretary to assistant secretary of state, TR said, "I never wish to see you leave the State Department until you go to China as minister."[22] He saw to that in 1906. TR wrote Rockhill that he and a few others had made resolute efforts to keep him on as first secretary because he was a person "no sensible man would dream of dispensing with." TR feared a Republican victory would put Rockhill out, as he was a part of the Democratic Cleveland administration. After the Republican Party's victory, however, Rockhill tried to get himself appointed as minister to China. His supporters failed. Instead, E. H. Conger became minister, and Rockhill went off as minister to Greece, Romania, and Serbia.[23]

In September 1898, McKinley replaced Secretary of State William R. Day, John Sherman's brief substitute, with John Hay. Henry Adams confessed to Rockhill, "Hay needs help badly. He has no one to rely upon, and the Cabinet as far as I know, is a heavy load to carry. I can conceive of no foreign policy likely to satisfy anybody, but that is only one difficulty. He is surrounded by embarrassments of all sorts, and although I think he will get through them, I don't yet know how many friends he can carry with him." Hay came home from London, probably passing Day and his Spanish-American War peace commissioners on their way to Madrid, "without the faintest idea of his position. What sort of control or direction is exercised by anyone at Washington is a mystery. . . . State Dept. is probably as chaotic and headless as the War Dept." Hay turned to Rockhill: "There are many things I would like to say to you, and to get your views upon, but in the hurry of departure this is impossible." Hay was just then leaving London to assume his new duties in Washington. The chaos in the State Department proved to be Rockhill's opportunity. TR wrote, "The country ought to have him, and yet the country is so blind that it does not see the good that he can do."[24]

Rockhill entered the debate in August 1899; this was the critical month.

He made that daring assertion that lifted the discussion to a new level by setting the stage for Hay's Circular of the following July.[25] Rockhill suggested he already had thought further about spheres of influence and shared Hippisley's and his own views with Hay, who "wrote to me the other day [August 7] that he was fully awake to the great importance of what you and I had said to him, and that he is more than ready to act, 'but the senseless prejudices in certain sections of the Senate and people compel us to move with caution.'" Then came Rockhill's daring assertion: "I can not, however, think that, at the present stage, it will be sufficient for this country to insist that no discrimination shall apply to any of our merchandise entering the various spheres of interest. We must go much farther than that. Our action, to my mind, should be such that the very vague assurances given by Great Britain, Russia, and other powers as to their desire to *maintain and insure the integrity* of the Chinese Empire should be expressed in much stronger terms and assume tangible shape." Rockhill dismissed others expressing different opinions on the subject as having a "most superficial view of the country and practically no knowledge of its racial and administrative peculiarities." His explorations, command of the languages, and books had, like Kennan's, uniquely secured that knowledge for him. "Nine-tenths of their information are second hand; but, notwithstanding that, they are the ones who carry weight at home." He and Hippisley had to "keep pegging away at it [and he had] embodied the substance of your two letters in a memorandum to the State Dept., which may prove of some use." He sent extracts of Hippisley's letters to Assistant Secretary of State Alvey Adee.[26]

By August 24, 1899, Hay recognized Rockhill's breakthrough and wrote him, "I am taking a good deal for granted—your presence in Washington —your leisure, and your inclination to give us a *coup d'epaul*." Adee sent the Secretary Rockhill's letter with long extracts of Hippisley's letters. Rockhill wrote Hippisley about doing an article for *Forum* or *North American Review*. He had spotted John Barrett's article, which seemingly related to their ideas. This route appeared only probable, because "it seems to me that this is at the present time the very best thing we can do, for there is no one here at Washington to whom one can talk, and public opinion must be stirred up." If published, he planned a second dealing with reform. He noted, "China is, and will remain, the one absorbing subject."[27] Rockhill enclosed his memorandum, dated August 28, and sent it to Hay.

It was from this memorandum that Hay composed the open-door notes of September 6, 1899—first to Germany, Russia, and Great Britain, then to Japan, Italy, and France. Rockhill depicted swift change in Washington, especially Hay's readiness to go with a limited approach—the three points (noninterference in spheres of influence, the Chinese tariff applied to all merchandise, equality of harbor-railroad fees)—for the immediate time being and to reserve Rockhill's corollary for later. It came on July 3, 1900: "My project of publishing our views on the policy of the United States in China has been nipped in the bud," Rockhill related, "as I have been requested by the Secretary of State, to submit the project to him on the steps which should be taken by the United States at once to insure our commercial interests. I have embodied the substance of your remarks in it."[28]

Since the memo was going to the president, it had to come from Rockhill to avert more explanations. Rockhill wrote his friend Hippisley, "I have, and shall again whenever I can, show that I am but your mouthpiece."[29] In a belabored and restricted sense, he was. Otherwise, Rockhill created America's seemingly selfless efforts to protect China's territorial integrity. America's moral shield, he assumed, would save China.

Nowhere had Rockhill directly advocated China's democratization or a revolution to wipe out its oriental venality, as Kennan had for Russia. Nor had he suggested American force to keep the open door opened. Japan would play that vital role. Kennan also favored Japan as a balancer to Russian ambitions. However, both Kennan and Rockhill had distorted Russia's and China's image in America: Russia emerged as an evil empire, an empire needing liberal democracy. China was a Shangri-la requiring only America's good intentions.

Given the various impacts of these two formidable figures, it only remained for the views and policies of a small number of influential academics, writers, journalists, diplomats, and politicians to set America's long-term trends in the twentieth century. On the Russian side, Samuel Harper was one of the earliest.

part I
Russia

Among our portraits, an almost straight line of negativity runs from "Siberian" George Kennan to Ambassador William C. Bullitt. The only positives along that axis are President Wilson's embrace of the Provisional Government, Samuel Harper's reconciliation with Bolshevism, and Bullitt's initial enthusiasm for cooperation. There were others not studied here who fought for recognition of Soviet Russia—well-known protagonists such as former Red Cross worker Ray Robins and businessman Alexander Gumberg. Although they were aided in the Senate by the powerful voice of William E. Borah (R-ID), their cause remained in the minority. In the country, suspicion and downright hostility reigned. Harper remained bitter until he made his peace in 1926. Then, Sam became "Soviet Sam." Robert F. Kelley, the State Department's Russian whiz kid, relentlessly opposed the Soviets. He instilled this attitude in his protégés—Loy Henderson, George F. Kennan, Charles "Chip" Bohlen—whom he trained in Riga, Latvia. Journalists were, with certain exceptions like Walter Duranty, kept from Moscow until the Soviets allowed them there by the late 1920s. Eugene Lyons, one of them, used his socialist connections to gain entry. He even managed to get an important interview with Stalin. However, he came to see the worker's paradise as a dystopia.

FDR pushed official recognition of the USSR through in 1933. Yet what interested us here was the persistence of what came to be known as the "Riga Axioms," the attitude developed by Kelley and his boys. Whatever successes at accommodation FDR achieved, especially during World War II, his so-called Yalta Axioms, resistance to them continued nevertheless. FDR purged the State Department to no avail. That fear and suspicion again gained impetus after the president's death. Its champions were George F. Kennan and America's high priest of the Cold War, Paul H. Nitze. Whatever accommodation FDR had achieved was lost. This, of course, is not to say that Stalin and his successors were blameless. It does reveal that deep undercurrents of popular opinion against Russia remained. From the end of the Cold War to today, each side—Riga versus Yalta—still contends. The real question is whether the prevailing twentieth-century attitude will gain ascendancy in the twenty-first century.

1

"Soviet Sam" and the Émigrés

Charles Crane, a Chicago industrialist, took Sam Harper's father, president of the University of Chicago, to Russia in 1900. Crane donated a special fund for Russian studies at the university, and the two men introduced Russian into Chicago's curriculum. Sam Harper wrote, "Little attention was being given in American universities to the analysis of events, historical or contemporary, east of the line of Vienna." Crane urged Harper to study Russian, and he did under Paul Boyer at the School of Oriental Languages in Paris from 1902 to 1904. Russia was, Harper remarked, "considered the land of bombs, Cossack knouts, pogroms, and other terrors."[1] This was because of what was widely known as "Kennanitis." But a new generation of Slavicists started with Sam Harper. The field was turning academic and professional. Like Kennan and Rockhill, Harper was influential in two ways: first, through his writings and lectures; second, because of his close ties to the State Department.

• • •

Harper made his first of many trips to Russia in February 1904.[2] American interest in Russia renewed because of World War I. Harper made three trips there from 1915 to 1918, the first in 1915, a second as adviser to Ambassador David R. Francis in 1916, and the third one as a consultant to the Root Mission, sent by President Woodrow Wilson in 1917, under Senator Elihu Root (R-NY), to encourage Russia's continued participation in World War I.[3] In 1916, he reported on a rise in anti-Semitism; Russians welcomed Americans only "of the right kind." Harper said of Francis, former governor of Missouri, "I have been seeing more of the governor these last weeks. He is very energetic, very clear on most points, and has shown a kindly friendly attitude toward Russia, which is realized and appreciated."[4] Harper spent 1915 observing Russia's war effort and studying people's organizations such as the Union of Zemstvos (land organizations), Union of Municipalities, war industry, and cooperative committees. In

March 1917, after the liberal March Revolution, journalist Milton Browner interviewed Crane and Harper. He reported their thought that it was a "political, not social [revolution, and the] Russian people want the country solidly behind the army to win this war." Crane observed, "The people as a whole form one of the purest democracies in the world." Browner pressed them, "But how can you expect so much from an ignorant, illiterate, moujik [peasant] nation?" Harper responded, "Another mistaken notion. . . . The zemstvos have for years, in connection with the national government, [worked on] the education of the people." This distortion—that the Russian peasant was somehow an intuitive democrat—Harper shared with Kennan.[5] Browner's challenge, passed over by Crane and Harper, was also ignored by almost everyone else.

Harper was as happy as any Russian liberal, and he began campaigning for Russia's new Provisional Government, especially after America entered the war in April. The State Department asked him to draft a memo on the revolution, assessing members of the new government. The revolutionaries, Harper reported, carried on nonviolently. The new ministers were outstanding. He extended these evaluations on a broader scale as a popular lecturer. In them, he suggested that the last stage of Russia's political development had arrived and a final victory over the German-led Central Powers would follow.[6]

Students demanded Harper's classes. Invitations to discuss Russia poured in. He received letters from a wide assortment of people, expressing concern about whether the new government could fight to the finish. Harper harbored no doubts. He crusaded for the March Revolution. He gave an address as early as March 28, 1917, to the American-Russian Chamber of Commerce in Chicago, where he expressed confidence in Russia's capacity to unify itself behind the liberals.[7] Harper considered political, not social, change essential. The single problem had been czarism. Now it was destroyed, and democracy could be quickly achieved.[8] He denied criticism of this position in a letter to Charles R. Crane: "All is running very smoothly in Russia . . . and the coup is a clear success." Montgomery Schuyler of the *New York Times* lacked confidence in the Provisional Government. "Schuyler could not be persuaded to go to Moscow [in 1916] and talk with Prince Lvov . . . and he would not go near the Duma, and laughed at my enthusiasm for the liberal cause." There was no justification to such skepticism. Socialists would not pose a threat to the Provisional Government, and all of Russian society would work together. In a letter to James Keeley of the *Chicago Herald,* Harper complained about a pessimistic editorial warning of socialist insurgents. Harper believed the soviets—spontaneous workers' organizations—would cooperate with the Provisional Government and act as a loyal opposition.[9]

This March Revolution, Harper believed, created a "new" Russia. Moderates like Paul Miliukov, head of the liberal Cadet Party, would realize their reforming hopes.[10] A good sign of Harper's thinking was his letter to Foreign Minister Miliukov: "It is most interesting to note how many Americans are at last understanding what you explained to them so clearly several years ago, namely, the existence of a Russia to which we could give our fullest sympathy and support." Harper's liberal bias influenced both President Woodrow Wilson and his secretary of state, Robert Lansing. At Assistant Secretary of State Richard Crane's suggestion, Lansing turned to Harper and Richard's father, Charles, for their opinions. Both predicted the Provisional Government would stay strong and continue fighting Germany. Lansing later recalled: "I conferred with several men, who knew Russia and the Russian people, such men as Charles R. Crane, and Professor Samuel N. Harper. . . . I found them optimistic as to the success of the Constitutional Democrats [Cadets] and of their ability to control the situation."[11]

Harper's attitude remained optimistic despite negative rumors current in the American press. He wrote to Jean Jules Jusserand, French ambassador to the United States, "I have become even more optimistic over the situation in Russia." He refused to worry about radicals, who were, he thought, under German influence. He was even glad Germany allowed Vladimir Lenin, the Bolshevik (communist) leader, back to Petrograd.[12] It would not be an exaggeration to say that from March to May 1917, Harper had little conception of the differences existing between the two governments that had spontaneously appeared in the chaos following Czar Nicholas II's abdication, the Petrograd Soviet and the Provisional Government: "The program of the new government made no mention of the war, but there was no need to mention it, for the assumption was the war was to be prosecuted with great vigor—such a policy having been one of the chief reasons for the Revolution, for liberals, and for moderate socialists."[13]

After recognizing the Provisional Government on March 20, 1917, President Woodrow Wilson sent the Root Mission to assess Russia's military needs against the Germans. The president considered Harper's name, but Lansing believed he lacked political influence. Harper thought he could be helpful to the mission by serving it unofficially. He caught up with the mission after it got to Petrograd in June.[14] Harper wrote a friend, "I can be more useful by not being attached to the Commission. Then I can pick up all sorts of stuff, from my friends, who would not talk to me as frankly were I secretary of Commission."[15] He estimated his role to be "chief political adviser to the ambassador [and that] I seem to be the man the Governor now trusts the most."[16]

Then came Lenin and his Bolshevik party's seizure of power in November. Looking back wistfully on that period, Harper believed that "we Americans were guilty of wishful thinking, grasping at mere details to support our picture." Even Charles Crane had remarked about the popular foundations for the Provisional Government, "cement seems to be running out."[17] Harper hoped "men like [Prince George E.] Lvov and Miliukov and [Alexander] Guchkov will come into their own again."[18]

Later, Harper summed up his evaluation of the 1917 revolutions in an article, "The Spirit of the Russian Revolution." The Bolsheviks were the worst result, because they had played the German card and made peace with them at Brest Litovsk in March 1918. He compared their cynicism and single-mindedness to that of the degenerate aristocrats of previous years. The ouster of some liberals from the government was another negative aspect. The March Revolution was why Russia had remained in the war at all. The imperial regime would have quit and joined the Germans. Russia proved that "extreme socialism is not democracy, and that the internationalism of certain groups is simply another German trick."[19]

Harper regarded the Bolshevik Revolution as a temporary slip in Russia's march toward democratic government. "I am discouraged at the moment though I have not lost faith, that men like Miliukov will be able to take the lead again." He wrote to William Phillips at the State Department, "The Russian situation has been very disheartening these last weeks. . . . I have become very philosophic over it. . . . When will the results of the experiment be evident to the broader masses? Only when they feel, by their own bitter experience. Then the 'sobered' masses will accept the leadership of men like Miliukov." Harper had deferred his teaching duties and stayed in Washington to aid the State Department in evaluating Soviet Russia. The Bolsheviks, for Harper, were intriguers, internationalist in nature, disrupting a government that would be able to return to power on their defeat. He called them clever and favored an unofficial relationship in which the United States might be able to "outwit them."[20]

American interest in Russia peaked after the Brest-Litovsk Treaty when the Soviets made peace with Germany on March 3, 1918. The State Department created a Russian Division, and Harper was made a special attaché, serving part-time until 1922. Beyond translating and interpreting official Russian documents, Harper supported President Wilson's non-recognition policy.[21]

Harper did a series of memorandums for the State Department from 1919 to 1920, giving Bolshevism special treatment. He called the Soviet government a rule of the minority with an initial policy of destroying the old order by civil war and mass terror. The Bolsheviks were to blame for Russia's economic collapse: they had no constructive policy; they wanted only world revolution; elections were rigged for communists; opposition parties were illegal; counterrevolutionaries were shot; a class system determined food rationing; the army was an agent for oppression; only proletarian culture was to be allowed; paper money was an expedient to check economic crisis. Harper reported on administrative collapse, industrial decline, and vast shortages. He pointed to the dangers of the Comintern (Communist International), which fomented foreign revolutions. He portrayed Bolshevism as unredeeming and negative and was sure it would crumble.[22] In another memorandum, Harper made it clear the Bolsheviks had made "many definite demands for the overthrow of the Government of the United States."[23] How similar much of this sounds to the negative conclusions Kennan had previously drawn about czarism.

Harper's major concern was how Americans viewed Bolshevism. Like "Siberian" Kennan, he was also an anti-Bolshevik advocate. He wanted to influence public views and state policy. He scheduled many speaking engagements for the American-Russian League, War Committee of the Union Club, and American Friends of a New Middle Europe. These addresses were enthusiastically received. Harper worked closely with the Federal Bureau of Investigation director, J. Edgar Hoover, and shared in a Senate investigation headed by William King (R-UT). These efforts fanned anti-Bolshevik sentiment.[24] On the subject of diplomatic relations or trade, Harper was negative. As he noted, "When in 1930 in Moscow I had the first of my many talks with [Commissar for Foreign Affairs Maxim] Litvinov, . . . I stated my view that formal recognition would serve no useful purpose for either side unless it were based on common interests and mutual respect."[25]

Secretary of State Charles Evans Hughes and Secretary of Commerce Herbert Hoover by 1922 had schemed to send a technical unit to Russia to study economic conditions. Though President Warren Harding approved, some figured the plan would only strengthen the Bolsheviks, and the administration's enthusiasm cooled, especially that of Hughes.[26] Harper noted that important people were coming increasingly to him for advice, and the "big chief" was delegating "more of his supreme authority to others."[27] Harper had decided during 1919 and 1920 that it was impossible to deal with the Bolsheviks. He believed Russian demoralization ate its way through every phase of activity, and Soviet strength was powerless to stop it. If Bolshevism failed, normalcy would return. "If not by armed effort, this mechanism is bound to be overturned by an explosion from within, made inevitable by those inexorable laws of economic life, which the Bolsheviki have defied and outraged."[28]

He confidently wrote his British academic friend Bernard Pares, "Bolsheviks are very near the end of their rope, but what causes me the most anxiety is the fact that one does not see any compact, constructive group ready to take their place."[29] Frustrated, he returned to teaching in 1921. By

May there was a big reorganization in the State Department because of the coming to power of the Harding administration.[30] Harper made it clear that he was on leave in order "to be out of the politics of the first months of the new administration."[31]

Harper was still vigorously anti-Bolshevik. Yet already in 1922, he was ready to head for Berlin, Riga, and on to Moscow. That did not mean he had gone over to the enemy; rather, "things will have taken such a turn by that date that it would be well to run in, always if I am quite sure that I can get out again."[32] It could not be arranged. DeWitt Clinton Poole, heading the State Department's Russian Division, asked if Harper would not mind helping out informally from time to time and remain official in order to get access to departmental files. Harper agreed. He told the Russian Provisional Government's former ambassador to the United States Boris Bakhmetev that he was "taking life very easily these days" because he did not have to read everything. By April 1923, as he explained to a friend, it was "simply hopeless to try to appeal to Americans these days on the Russian situation except where it is a matter of feeding starving people. . . . Americans will answer you that [they are] sick and tired of these Russian politics, and Bolshevism, and anti-Bolshevism and all the rest of it." He was recovering from a "serious nervous break-down" by carrying teaching and Washington on his shoulders and "studying a purely destructive movement, and taking a negative [sic] attitude toward the subject." He told Pares much the same, but still insisted that Russian "regeneration" was possible if the "microbe" on it was not strengthened.[33] He became a Russian watcher because there would not be a change of policy unless there was a change of administration. His standing with the State Department remained stronger than ever, and he was admitted to its "inner secrets."[34]

The years of waiting and wondering were 1921–1925. Beginning in 1925, however, he was asked by a university colleague to do a study of civics in Soviet Russia.[35] With this, his first visit to Russia since 1917, he began a personal evolution from severe to mild critic of the USSR. He came to be regarded as an apologist for positions held by the Bolsheviks; he eventually got the nickname "Soviet Sam" among his students.[36] Crossing the Russian frontier in mid-July 1926, Harper reemerged at the end of October, having completed his research after gaining wide-ranging impressions of the conditions prevailing there. He spent the rest of the year in Berlin, organizing his research and drafting a memo, "Three Months in the Soviet Union."[37] Harper classified this document as confidential, and it gained no greater exposure than examination by close friends and associates until years later when he included portions of it in his memoirs. It represented his personal impressions of Russian life in contrast to his later and more specific study of civic training in the USSR.

Beginning with the subject most relevant to him, Harper commented on treatment of foreign visitors. He noted some likenesses with prerevolutionary times and many important differences. He was not restricted in his movements, but he was aware of constant observation. He found communist officials helpful but formal. Each was confined to his own particular field. This slowed Harper's research, since officials were unwilling to send his inquiries to other departments. Faced with the task of doing his own legwork, Harper began in earnest. He found civic training a comprehensive effort to educate citizens on how to carry out Marxism-Leninism. He examined both the principles behind this training and their applications by visiting workers' clubs, youth groups, and the Red Army. Much of his time was spent in Moscow, though Harper traveled into the countryside to study the peasantry. There his movements and choice of areas were not restricted.[38]

About living conditions, Harper found them better than expected. The foreign visitors' accommodations were acceptable, although Moscow's finest hotel was reserved only for party members. Daily fare was dull but adequate. Harper was soon introduced to establishments where meals and drinks were of a more continental and pleasing variety. Correspondents familiarized Harper with these semilegal restaurants and watering holes. They told him the government tolerated these establishments, probably for gaining hard currency.

For average Russians, times were hard. A housing shortage existed in large cities, and there were long lines at the markets. Luxury items were in evidence in the shop windows, but few could afford them. Harper found public transportation excellent, though there was not a single private automobile in Moscow. Streetcars were for the general populace, whereas party functionaries sped around in official limousines. The times appeared hard, but he discovered that most Russians considered the twenties prosperous compared with the darkest years of the civil war. Harper was sure that anyone who had not been through those privations would find current conditions less than tolerable.

Harper avoided visiting his old Russian friends unless certain his presence caused them no misfortune. The former liberal intelligentsia existed in a reduced state. Often they held reasonably high positions in the Soviet, but they were carefully monitored. They were certain their status would last only until they were able to pass their particular expertise on to trusted officials. Harper found that economists suffered most among his friends, those in drama and the arts the least. But this was in 1926 and still the heyday of Lenin's New Economic Policy (NEP) of limited capitalism.

Party members did not discuss matters freely and only then referred to official statements in the newspapers. Noncommunists welcomed party rifts. They hoped rifts would lead to a weakening of communist power. At first new oppositions inspired the majority into policies of mild oppression. Noncommunists turned to support Stalin. They thought he represented a more nationalistic tendency and did not firmly believe in world revolution. Harper admitted he followed this line of thinking and subjectively campaigned for Stalin several times among his friends.[39] Watching from the press box at the funeral of Felix Dzerzhinsky, head of the secret police, or Cheka, Harper and his journalist friends noted the tense atmosphere among top Bolsheviks such as Lev Trotsky, Gregory Zinoviev, Lev Kamenev, and Lenin's widow, Nadezhda Krupskaya, who were positioned on a platform below the rostrum from which Joseph Stalin, Vyacheslav Molotov, and other Stalinists surveyed the proceedings.[40]

Harper was sympathetic with efforts of "young communists" politically to remove the old guard headed by Trotsky. He thought these older heroes of the revolution capable only of creating and dispensing propaganda. He further identified a hooligan element neutralizing the efforts of Stalin's group. An important reason Harper took sides was that he found the new younger communist officials willing to make concessions for establishing international relations, especially with the United States. The defeat of Trotsky's group would allow the majority to retreat on matters of nationalization, repudiation of debts, and international revolution. This would fix a more favorable climate for foreign relations, and trade would result.

Harper, returning to Berlin after his research, received a cursory examination by border officials. He promised to send copies of his finished study to various departments within the Soviet government. He was invited to attend a celebration of the ninth anniversary of the revolution at the Soviet embassy in Berlin. On the eve of his departure from Russia, he had heard indirectly that his behavior there had been considered remarkably discreet in view of his record. He left after registering informally for permission to return in the future.[41]

● ● ●

Harper's new opinions of Russia began to enter America's business community, hungry for trade with Soviet Russia. Only a few Americans then saw foreign policy toward Russia in a different light from the Republican administrations of the twenties. One of them, prorecognition senator William E. Borah, thought that political hostility toward the Soviet Union violated American standards of recognition. Russia's stability, for Harper, begged the question of recognition because the Soviets had existed for more than a decade. He recognized that Soviet debt repudiation and confiscations were difficult problems for both sides to overcome. Anticommunists responded to Borah as well as to Harper by saying that America was under no obligation to recognize a nation claiming the right to subvert the U.S. government and deny its debts.[42]

The unanticipated and often unhappy experiences of British and French recognition of the USSR justified America's stance. As Secretary of State Frank B. Kellogg (1925–1929) stated, "Recognition of the Soviet regime [had] not brought about any cessation of interference by the Bolshevik leaders in the internal affairs of any recognizing country, nor [had] it led to the acceptance by them of other fundamental obligations of international relations."[43] Russia sought foreign goodwill by granting economic concessions. The Bolsheviks were willing to negotiate debt payment and compensate for property lost or destroyed but on condition of new, larger loans.[44] Yet Americans rejected this aiding of Soviet power. A compromise seemed unlikely because many congressmen did not trust Russia to compete fairly. After all, they reasoned, Russia also used forced labor. These facts led a group of congressmen and their constituents to ask the Treasury Department to boycott whatever few goods did arrive from Russia. That initiative failed, and distrust remained.[45]

This uneasiness over communist trade and labor policies extended to a fear and foreboding of Bolshevism and uneasiness about Russia. Americans dismissed Bolshevik good faith because, they believed, communists could not be trusted. Assistant Secretary of State William Castle doubted the Bolsheviks would uphold any diplomatic arrangements. Wall Street investor Francis Walsh protested against arrangements with a "worthless" nation. Businessman Robert Durham believed the Russians held no moral obligations to their trade agreements.[46]

American hostility further sharpened over communist propaganda aimed at undermining capitalism and promoting Soviet-style welfare. Soviet propaganda threatened America worldwide. For instance, Russian newspapers made statements discrediting the United States, falsely accusing the country of inciting war between Japan and Russia.[47] Or they also overestimated unemployment in the United States: "When unemployment reached the figure of 3,000,000 in the United States in the early part of 1930 Moscow Wireless dispatches estimated the number at 6,000,000, [and] when the actual number increased to 6,000,000 Moscow's published estimate became 12,000,000."[48] This propaganda sought to convince the Russian masses that their standard of living was superior to Americans. Some may have even believed that American workers were starving.[49]

Though the Bolsheviks promised to stop their propaganda after recognition,[50] Frederick Schuman, a colleague of Harper at the University of Chicago, said that they were "neither willing nor able to abandon a goal which years of prison and exile and martyrdom [had] made [a] central feature of a faith which fills them with an almost religious inspiration." The

Bolsheviks, he continued, were "fighters in a Holy War as truly as ever were the Crusaders of the Middle Ages [and] their exaggerated rhetoric was no mere 'sound and fury,' signifying nothing; it was the expression of their most cherished ideals."[51] Recognition, so the State Department postulated, would come about only because "either the urgent political necessities of the United States made collaboration with Russia a necessity for us or the Russians satisfied our public opinion that there was no longer any actual connection between the Soviet Government and the propaganda directed against the government of the United States."[52]

Representative Hamilton Fish (R-NY) headed a congressional commission investigating communism in the United States. The Fish Commission made efforts to eliminate American communism and continue the Wilsonian quarantine. It believed communist activities even included the destruction of "the souls of little children [through] all kinds of vices [and that] communists corrupted students and teachers."[53] As proof, the commission cited the example of the chairman of the American Communist Party, William Foster, who testified that the party opposed lynching, approved interracial marriage, and believed that violence was necessary to overthrow American capitalism and create communism. The commission drew the conclusion that communism was a conspiracy aimed at destroying the United States.[54] It proposed laws to deport alien communists. Those aliens staying in the country and continuing to propagandize were dangerous and had to be deported. A dissenting minority report argued otherwise: there was no need for hysteria because communism could be met with "economic and social justice."[55]

When Harper returned from Europe, he began his schedule of teaching and studying. To this routine he made one important addition—he resumed an active program of public lecturing. His thinking was that first-hand observations in Russia were a valuable experience that should be passed on. Harper's long-range study made it dubious that he could communicate more than a limited view because of Soviet surveillance of his activities while there. Both the form and the content of his lectures began to reflect a definite change of attitude from Harper's earlier State Department days. He insisted on a minimum of one hour with enough time for questions and answers, believing that anything less was inadequate for presenting a true picture of the Soviet Union. In this period, he was faced with the usual task of correcting misconceptions on the part of his audience about his subject. He refused to engage in discussions where "both sides" were to be presented. His reply to these invitations was that he was a student, not a partisan. This was a change from Harper's previous anti-Bolshevik stand during and after the first years of the revolution.

Harper explained his changing understanding by pointing out that he was first and always a student of Russia, its people and institutions. This was his career, his life's work. He explained that Bolshevism had come to the country he had chosen to study. He had been there before Bolshevism, but since it had come, he would have to study it also.[56] The manner in which Harper now chose to study and publicize the Soviet Union was to present its stated aims, programs, and accomplishments as objectively as possible. Audiences and colleagues reacted negatively. Harper's American audiences expected judgments on the Soviet Union. Were Bolsheviks angels or devils? Was the Soviet system a success or a failure? Harper was unwilling to praise or condemn.

Because of his new approach, some of Harper's associates believed he had gone "soft" on communism. This attitude was noted among his old State Department colleagues, who still supported the official U.S. policy and remained anti-Bolshevik by inclination. One employee of the Eastern European Department, which had replaced the Russian Division, accused Harper of deliberate opportunism. Preston Kumler thought Harper's failure to criticize the Soviet regime was merely a ploy to ensure visa privileges.[57] Harper considered this charge without foundation, saying that he tried only to avoid emotionalism. He added that he had no way of knowing what would please or offend Russians. He described his purpose as understanding, not evaluation. Kumler modified his charge to the point of stating that Harper practiced an unconscious solicitude toward Soviet authorities. Harper stopped correspondence with Kumler.[58] He continued to follow his chosen methods and kept well informed on events in Russia.

Events followed a course that also soothed the anti-Bolshevik tendencies Harper had held. He always had considered Trotsky the most radical and unstable of the Soviet leaders and Stalin the most practical. The censure and exile of Trotsky in 1928 were not unwelcome eventualities in Harper's estimation. Stalin's almost simultaneous announcement of the first Five Year Plan (FYP) excited Harper's interest. Its concentration on internal growth rather than internationalist propaganda was a further reassurance. Any program having as its primary goal building a new Russia was bound to have his support.

His book on Soviet civic training, which was the research purpose of Harper's 1926 trip to Russia, was not completed and published until 1929. Although his editor urged a faster pace, Harper wished to avoid what he called the "toils of undigested impressions."[59] He continued to study Soviet publications to supplement his field research and to guarantee that his study would be current. In his preface, Harper stressed the revolutionary aspect of all Soviet institutions. His study dealt with a system of recent date and one that was changing. Civic training and education had a high priority in the Soviet Union. They were part of the third front of the revolution.

The first two fronts, military and political, were accomplished by 1921. Emphasis passed to this third front.[60]

In accord with the theme of the overall project, *Studies in the Making of Citizens*, Harper began his book with an analysis of Soviet citizenship. He divided the population into economic groups: industrial workers and peasantry, with subdivisions of poor, middle, and rich peasants; party workers or toiling intelligentsia; and the "incompletely slaughtered bourgeoisie." These groups made up the citizenry of the Soviet Union, except for the rich peasants (kulaks) and the bourgeoisie, who were excluded from politics. Finally, members of these groups would progress from the contemptible position of "mere inhabitant" to "stalwart, revolutionary, Communist fighter."

To present a summary of civic training in the Soviet Union, it was necessary to have a knowledge of Soviet institutions to include a discussion of them before he could explore civic training. At the time Harper undertook his study, this was untrammeled ground. The book emerged as a study of most aspects of Soviet institutions, organizations, and media from the view of civic training. Many Sovietologists would later follow his pioneering example after World War II.[61]

He began with a chapter on the single most important institution in the Soviet Union, the communist party. This was one agency he had been unsuccessful in penetrating as deeply as he wished during his trip. Yet he defined three basic principles of party organization: monolithic unity, democratic centralism, and iron discipline. After giving a short history of the party, Harper mentioned the overall theme of his study: tutelage. He explained this as the leadership of the party over the citizenry and party control of civic training. Control was the basic fact of existence in the Soviet Union. Harper brought out the importance of Lenin as founder of an authoritarian party and as the object of a cult as leader of the revolution. The center of this cult was Lenin's mausoleum. He described the impression and effect, even for a foreigner, of touring the mausoleum and viewing the embalmed body of Comrade Lenin.

In the late twenties the structure and operation of the Soviet government were as unknown to Westerners as was the communist party. Harper devoted a chapter to the Soviet state. His observations were that the bureaucratic system had not been removed and the exercise of power remained firmly in the hands of the tightly knit party. There was no question the masses were becoming interested and active through the soviets. Having established the character of the Soviet government and its institutions, Harper turned to the methods and means of Soviet civic training. Beginning with various Soviet publications such as *Pravda* and *Izvestiia*, he examined Soviet museums and excursions, civic celebrations and campaigns, literature, art, drama, radio, cinema, music, and general and political education.

His method of analysis was characterization and description rather than technical and comparative. Harper compiled a list of basic civic activities expected of the citizen in the Soviet state: voting, payment of taxes, subscription to loans, contribution to the defense of the country, and conformity to its laws. He added that the Soviet state was continuing the revolution. Greater citizen participation was expected. The leading civic responsibility of the Soviet citizen was to contribute to building the socialist order. Basic civic duties were given a definite purpose and direction as determined by party leaders. Harper stressed the constant class approach in political activity and the drive toward collectivism as always present in the economic field. He pointed to the great flexibility that was practiced. Soviet officials were always willing to alter their methods to get desired results. They were mindful that Soviet civic training was, like their entire state apparatus, a large-scale and radical experiment. Harper commented on the lack of hesitation in employing techniques of agitation and propaganda, and there was no tendency by officials to reject these direct methods.

Always aware of the continuing aspect of the revolution, Harper believed that the Soviet program of the "citizen in production," with its deliberate and constant planning, would need observation into the future for evaluation of the younger generation of the "Workman-Peasant Government" as this group came into active political life. He wondered how that new generation could be both nationalist and internationalist. Here he contrasted the internationalist character of the original Bolshevik doctrine with the current development of a strong nationalist sentiment in the Soviet Union. He traced this seeming contradiction to civic training. The Soviet citizen was expected to be an internationalist in theory, but in reality this concept took on a distinctively nationalist flavor. He explained that the method used to resolve these opposing doctrines was to foster the notion of the Soviet Union as the homeland of the toilers of the world. This attitude made it possible to justify nationalist policies by representing the Soviet Union as the bastion of world revolution, which was to be defended and expanded. Soviet support of revolution in other countries was a contribution to the security of the system within Russia.[62]

Civic Training in Soviet Russia was met with interest in Russia. I. M. Pavlov reviewed the book in *Izvestiia*. He began with an introduction of Harper as a professor of Russian language and institutions at the University of Chicago. He explained that Americans found it necessary to include such posts within their universities. This was followed by a complimentary summary of Harper's career, which touched on his knowledge of the Russian language and on his many Russian travels. The review referred to Harper's evaluations as "serious, objective, based on personal experience, on the study of an enormous mass of material, and absolutely free from apology but also completely free from malignancy."[63] Despite some criticism—primarily that Harper was a capitalist representative of a bourgeois state—Harper was recognized in Russia as a serious student of the Soviet state. In turn, Harper openly admitted using *Izvestiia*'s review as a general pass during his later travels into Russia.[64] He made five more visits to the USSR during the 1930s.

Following his initial visit in 1926, Harper made trips to the Soviet Union in 1930, 1932, 1934, 1936, and 1939. As in the past, he continued his work at the University of Chicago and did public lecturing. Progressively, through these years, he was looked on as pro-Soviet. In his view, he was presenting the facts, but he did not hide a growing feeling that the Soviet experiment would succeed. His position caused him serious difficulties regarding such events as the Moscow Show Trials and the Nazi-Soviet Nonaggression Pact. Harper described conditions in Russia in 1930 and 1932 as the harshest he had encountered. He considered the first Five Year Plan as an innovative and exciting experiment, though he felt the Russian people were exhausted. In making his evaluations, he insisted that he was devoted to understanding the full significance of Russian events without losing his balance. He admitted being carried away at times by communist claims of progress, while at other times he was forced into cynicism by Soviet methods and achievements. A correct focus was his task.[65]

A lecture Harper gave on Bolshevism in 1930 was an interesting contrast to his earlier attitudes on communism and on the revolution. He began by identifying several types of tyranny the Russian people had to endure in their country: the political tyranny of czarist Russia, the continuing tyranny of illiteracy, the tyranny of great distances, and the tyranny of a severe climate.[66] He explained that the Russian people had always been a little more than equal to these trying tyrannies, but their condition had made them prone to listen to any promise of hope. This attitude accounted for the 1917 revolutions, especially the November Revolution. He said this revolution was a mass protest of a war-weary people, existing in utter material and mental breakdown. The soviets, elective bodies of workers and peasants that had been the product of the March Revolution, became the channel of the November Revolution. A group had been preparing for several years for such an opportunity and provided the leadership. It gave the mass movement direction; its leader was Lenin. Describing the continuance of the thirteen-year revolution, Harper identified the Bolsheviks as excellent psychologists and the world's best propagandists. The hardships, trials, and executions caused by Bolshevik methods were substantially true, but, overall, Harper believed the revolution produced faith and enthusiasm, leading to a betterment of the people and country.[67]

The Soviet constitution of 1936 was welcomed by Harper as another sign of progress and of the goodwill of the Soviet Union toward other nations. In practice, the Soviet electoral system under one-party rule was puzzling to many Westerners. Even more maligned and misunderstood was the term *Soviet democratism*. Harper argued that, for the Soviets, democratism meant participation. The purpose of elections was to bring the party and the people closer together. They were confirmatory rather than contested, and, in the Soviet interpretation, they displayed the moral and political unity of the people.[68] As was the case for most of his statements during these years, Harper presented the Soviet view, even if it was mistaken to be his own endorsement.

Harper defined the Bolsheviks' political purge as a struggle, employing traditional Bolshevik methods to eradicate dissent in the party. Members were being dealt with as communists who had accepted the iron discipline of the party when they joined. They knew that opposition was impossible within its framework. In these terms, it was possible for the Soviets to justify purging and to explain the confessions involved. Dissent was treason in the party. Nevertheless, Harper was sympathetic with these "Old Bolsheviks" only in that they were double victims: victims of the purge and victims of the intrigues of the "pathetic figure in Mexico" (Trotsky). In his memoirs, Harper went so far as to accuse Trotsky of having cooperated with Germany in 1917 against Kerensky; perhaps he was working with Hitler in 1937 against Stalin.[69] In addition, efforts of the "Old Bolsheviks" to oppose Stalin for what they felt was his betrayal of the revolution indirectly served the aims of aggressive fascism. This was true whatever Trotsky's role. Because of these speculations of Harper, Stalin emerged, in Harper's view, as a staunch defender of Leninism. He saved the party from Trotskyism and created a new constitution. The party dissenters were eliminated.[70] Most of this was speculation rather than belief, and Harper speculated privately, away from the lecture circuit, that the ultimate goodness or badness of the purge would be determined by subsequent production statistics.[71]

In a deeper analysis of the purges, Harper divided the process into stages. The first dealt with conspirators and saboteurs, next came ordinary nonpolitical racketeers and chiselers, then innocent bystanders who suffered, and finally a reversal to a purging of the purgers. Harper admitted that it was to Stalin's personal advantage to pare away the "Old Bolsheviks," whittling the possible interpreters of Lenin down to a single spokesman. The process had erupted into a wholesale slashing and left Harper perplexed. One of his greatest complaints was that he had to view these events from a distance, relying only on the Soviet press and fragmentary reports. His confusion at the time was plain in the different ways in which he described the purges. He referred to this as complex, a process that Westerners could not understand. Then he called it a simple trimming of the old tree. Later, he accused the Soviets of a blood purge for revenge.[72]

Dissatisfaction with the Soviet Union in the minds of many Americans was due to the failure to extend trade and Stalin's purges, which Harper observed in 1937–1938. He continued his public appearances and attempted to explain what was happening in Russia, both internally and in its foreign relations. "Soviet Sam" increasingly came to be regarded as an apologist for the positions held by Russian communists.[73] This difficult time for Harper resulted from the fact that he continued to present the Russian position as an objective observer. Harper was caught in the wake of anti-Soviet sentiment sweeping the United States. Initially, he maintained that his policy of presenting a factual picture was not an acceptance of Soviet policy. Explanation was not justification. Later, when the pressure on him to condemn the Russians continued unabated, Harper changed into the role of counterpropagandist. These pressures added to a cataract condition in both eyes and resulted in another psychological breakdown and period of seclusion.

The views that brought on Harper's troubles were seen as pro-Russian. He looked on the Nazi-Soviet partition of Poland as simply implementing the Soviet statement that an advancing army should be met on someone else's territory.[74] He said the Soviet invasion of the Baltic states and Finland was an application of the indirect-action clause of the collective security system. He argued that some Americans supported the same policy, if necessary, in Latin America. Later, he referred to the Winter War—Russia's invasion of Finland—as "Stalin's Blunder" and speculated that Hitler might have egged him on. He contended, though, that Soviet recognition of the Baltic states had always been contingent on the latter's ability to repulse any power that threatened the Soviet Union.

In Harper's view, the Nazi-Soviet nonaggression pact of 1939 had turned out to be exactly that. There was no alliance, no common action or cooperation. The partition of Poland had been two separate actions. Following his belief in the inevitability of a German-Russian war, he held that the chief reason for the pact and for all later Soviet action was preparation of the country and the people for this coming conflict with Germany. After two years "in the doghouse," as Harper put it, he felt justified for his support of Russia against the Nazi invasion in June 1941.[75]

In mid-January 1943, during the height of the alliance between his native land and his adopted land of study, Sam Harper died at the age of sixty-one. Fewer than two weeks later, the turning point of the war occurred—the German surrender at Stalingrad. Harper, with his insight and renewed optimism, had foreseen this Russian victory. He was not allowed that realization, but he did die in the certainty of this great triumph of the Russian people. Throughout his career, he had been close to émigré Russian academics. In important ways, they shared his task of educating Americans about Russia.

•   •   •

American academics had come to see Russia, Soviet Russia, in a negative light. No matter how hard Harper tried to reconcile himself to Stalinist Russia, these negative feelings with him and among his professional colleagues persisted. Other scholars further perpetrated these negative views. Between 1920 and the reestablishment of Russian-American treaty relations in 1933, intellectuals among the Russian émigrés began to exert notable influence on American ideas about Russia. Perhaps those who had helped establish Russian history as a field of professional study were most important; it was they, through their academic alliances, teaching, and writing, who created new and lasting images of Russia in the minds of America's college educated. Then came the hiatus of World War II when collaboration with the USSR was necessary, and a wave of optimism overcame negative thoughts about Russia. The proportion of émigré scholars was unusually high, and historians formed a noticeable group among them. According to a tally in 1927, no fewer than seventy-five émigré historians in Europe and America had published some five hundred works on history in nine languages since 1921. Most of the works were articles (longer studies lacked appeal because the authors were distant from their sources), and most of the scholars had chosen affiliations with universities in Europe.[76] Still, émigré historians played an important part in setting up Russian studies in the United States; indeed, they came to dominate the field.

American universities had been slow to include history, especially of nations other than the United States, among the essential parts of a higher education. In 1880, for example, Harvard employed only three historians, Princeton one, Dartmouth none. The role of founding Russian studies fell to Archibald Cary Coolidge, a Harvard-trained, widely traveled, multilingual Boston Brahmin who chose an academic life at his alma mater. After several years of European study, Coolidge became convinced that Russia's "Eastern" heritage (meaning Byzantine) was the key to understanding its dynamics. In 1894, Coolidge offered Harvard's first history course to include substantial content on Russia. In 1895, he delivered the first paper on a Russian topic at an annual meeting of the American Historical Association. In addition, in 1896 he persuaded Harvard to hire America's first university instructor of Russian language and literature.[77] Crane and Harper quickly followed.

Before World War I, a few other native scholars showed interest, most noticeably, as earlier mentioned, Samuel Harper at the University of Chicago. Still, Archibald Coolidge, who loved Russia but considered its government after 1917 "monstrous and unclean"—as did Harper—trained more than half of the people who were teaching Russian and Eastern European history in America in 1925. There was little available locally to help these early specialists and pioneers. Until 1926, the only Russian history textbook in English was a translation from French, made forty-five years earlier, of parts of Alfred Rambaud's *L'histoire de la Russie depuis les origines jusqu' à nos jours* (The History of Russia since Its Origins until Our Day).[78]

During the 1920s, curriculum reform and the intellectual curiosity of a rapidly growing number of university students created jobs for Russian émigrés.[79] Three Russian Americans in particular—Michael Karpovich at Harvard, George Vernadsky at Yale, and Michael Florinsky at Columbia—set the tone of new scholarship and trained a generation of graduate students, who, in turn, carried the orientation of their mentors deep into the community of educated Americans. That orientation was both antiautocratic and anti-Bolshevist. It held that a great reservoir of humane and democratic sentiment among the Russian people had been stifled, first by the arrogance of the reactionary Right, and then by the doctrinal rigidity of the revolutionary Left. The clear message to American students was that in matters of social and political development, there was not much about Russia to love.

Archibald Coolidge had helped Michael Karpovich (1888–1959) onto the college lecture circuit in 1918 when the native of Russian Georgia found himself out of a job as confidential secretary to Boris A. Bakhmetev, the Provisional Government's last ambassador to the United States. Then in 1927, Coolidge supported Karpovich for a faculty position at Harvard, and by it gave Harvard its first great strength in Russian studies. Karpovich directed more than thirty Ph.D. dissertations in Russian history. Mostly through his students, who included—to name only a few—Richard Pipes, Donald Treadgold, George Fischer, Robert Daniels, Hans Rogger, and Robert Paul Browder, he influenced what educated Americans knew and thought about Russia. Karpovich had been a radical Socialist Revolutionary in his youth, and he had spent a short time in jail. Later, he cast his lot with the more liberal Cadets (Constitutional Democrats). He allegedly refused to make a profession of anticommunism because he believed taking an ideological stand led to bad history. Nevertheless, he glorified the achievements of pre-Soviet Russian history, and, at the same time, he never hid his feeling that the victory of the communists was a catastrophe. He preferred not to lecture on the Soviet period if he could avoid it, for fear, he said, of not being objective.[80] Looking back on what he had learned in graduate school, one of Karpovich's students was certain that in the mind of his mentor, "the gentry world of the period of Alexander I and Nicholas I, for all the imperfections of autocracy and serfdom, . . . was the golden age of Russian civilization [because that period] represented the first great achievement of what may be called Russian humanism." It was the one era, Martin Malia, the student, recalled, about which Karpovich was "just a little sentimental." It pained him to record the decline of that Russian humanistic tradition by talking about the Soviet period.[81]

When Michael Karpovich was a graduate student at Moscow University before the Great War, he became friends with George Vernadsky (1887–1973). Vernadsky left Russia in 1920, spent seven years as an expatriate in Europe, and in 1927 joined the faculty at Yale. Archibald Coolidge had first considered Vernadsky for Harvard's position, but rejected him because of reports about his poor English.[82] Perhaps Vernadsky's greatest influence on America was through the written word, particularly his textbook *A History of Russia*. First published in 1929, five editions later and many years after his death, it was still in print. Vernadsky's monographic works, a series beginning with *Ancient Russia*, set a standard for scholarship in the West.[83] Like Karpovich, Vernadsky told modern Russian history mostly as a story of wrong paths taken, a tale in which the good guys and gals seldom won.

Michael Florinsky (1894–1981), who left Russia after the Bolshevik Revolution, spent the immediate postwar years in London as associate editor to Sir Paul Vinogradov, who was overseeing producing a twelve-volume study of wartime Russia for the Carnegie Endowment for International Peace. The ambitious intent of these studies was "to describe and, where possible, to measure the economic costs of the war and the displacement it caused in the processes of civilization." When Vinogradov died in 1925, Florinsky came to the United States to work with Yale University Press and James T. Shotwell, the Carnegie Endowment's general editor, to complete the work.[84] The self-proclaimed "outspoken critic of the Soviet system" stayed on to finish his Ph.D. at Columbia, to teach there, and to write, eventually, *Russia: A History and an Interpretation*, a two-volume work hailed as "the first comprehensive and yet concise history of Russia which is not a textbook." It had gone through ten editions when Florinsky died in 1981.[85] His study of the prospects for European integration and his book on social and economic policies in totalitarian states are still in print.

Florinsky steadfastly insisted that Russia's revolutionary organizations (Social Democrats and Socialist Revolutionaries) "had in reality little to do with" the overthrow of the imperial regime. Although they carried on some propaganda, he wrote, "it would be entirely unreasonable to ascribe to it an important part in the downfall of the Empire. All the revolutionary leaders were far away from the capital. Lenin was in Switzerland, Stalin in distant Siberia. Trotsky was dividing his time between his office near Union Square, New York City, and his apartment in the Bronx. The imperial

regime was not really overthrown: it collapsed of its own inner weaknesses and flagrant ineptitude." The Bolsheviks survived, he contended, only
because Lenin promised land to the peasants by inviting them to "plunder
what has been plundered." Florinsky saw the Soviet government as "a continuation of a tradition since, perhaps, as early as the twelfth century."[86]

Of the trickle-down effect of Florinsky's scholarship, there seems little
doubt. For instance, even as late as 1985, a commission of America's Soviet scholars investigating the coverage of Russia in American junior high
and high school textbooks was insulted by the failure of several authors
even to get the name right of the founder of the Soviet state. However, those
authors, synthesizers all, obviously had drawn from Michael Florinsky,
who, for many years, explained that Vladimir Ilich Ulianov's pseudonym
was "Nicholas Lenin." Other examiners of Russian-Soviet coverage in
American-authored textbooks for schoolchildren agreed that "a negative
emotional tone is definitely evident either explicitly or implicitly in much
of the content."[87]

These three émigré scholars maintained a cordial contact with former
ambassador Boris Bakhmetev. Bakhmetev had stayed on without portfolio
after the fall of the Provisional Government, and he continued to control the
unexpended portion of the American loan to the Provisional Government
three years into the communist era. He devoted his energies until the mid-
1920s to conditioning and reinforcing American ideas about Russia and
policy toward the Marxist government. He deluged American diplomats
with thoughts that "no one entertains any illusions as to the possibility of
maintaining in Russia . . . a system based on advanced socialistic theories"
and that, in view of the "inevitable failure of the Bolshevik regime," it
would be wrong now to agree to a final settlement on any international
issue in which Russia had a stake. He believed the United States should
safeguard Russian interests in a spirit of "moral trusteeship" and make only
"provisional arrangements subject to reconsideration and adjustment when
Russia comes back."[88]

Bakhmetev, who became a professor of engineering at Columbia University, influenced scholarship through the Humanities Fund he founded
and directed. Karpovich served on the fund's board. The Humanities Fund,
specifying its involvement "not be mentioned to outside parties," paid sub-
ventions to Yale University Press to publish the volumes of Vernadsky's
serial history. By 1942, Bakhmetev was encouraging Karpovich and Vernadsky to work together for the next twelve to fifteen years (with Humanities Fund support) on a master ten-volume account of Russian history. Although that project never fully materialized, Bakhmetev's support to these
and selected other Russian scholars focused attention on some common
ideas, none more important than the nature of the Russian state. They took

their theme from Paul Miliukov, an eminent prewar scholar and for a short term the Provisional Government's minister of foreign affairs. The general features of Russia in the long run, they thought it important to suggest, were European, but different because of backwardness, the slow pace of development, and unique problems and contacts in expansion and defense.[89]

Whatever the differences between early-day scholars of Russia in the United States over the evolution of nation-states, the efficacy of constitutional monarchy or republican government, or the wisdom of various policies, they agreed the Bolsheviks destroyed the potential for a happier life in Russia. Because these scholars trained students to carry on the historical examination of the Soviet Union, they were the forerunners of what has been called the Anglo-American totalitarian school of Sovietology. As the orthodox truth from the late 1940s into the 1960s, this school of thought held that the Bolsheviks were embryonically totalitarian and that "out of the totalitarian embryo would come totalitarianism full-blown."[90] Stephen Cohen notes perceptively that whereas most scholars of China are enamored of its history, culture, and people, "many Sovietologists, on the other hand, seemed to dislike or hate their subject."[91] One can imagine that this sentiment, if not its expression, would please those who were present at creating Russian-Soviet studies. In the twenties and thirties these pioneers were aided by a growing number of experts in the State Department who often shared their views. Their leader was Robert F. Kelley. It was he and his recruits who created a policy toward Russia that has become known as the "Riga Axioms." Its distinguishing characteristic was a deep suspicion of Russia and, even on occasion, the Russian character itself. It became the dominant motif of twentieth-century American attitudes about Russia, however much opponents like Borah and FDR struggled against it. Not even President Ronald Reagan's conversion to accommodation with his declaration that the "evil empire" was no more has been able to put it to rest.

2

The Boys from Riga

The twenties were awkward for Russo-American relations. The United States did not recognize Soviet Russia and, besides, demanded compensations for Bolshevik confiscations of U.S. public and private assets. Commerce continued, but at one's own risk. Without an embassy or consulates, gaining information on communist Russia's national and international developments was usually indirect and circuitous, as Harper had discovered. America's main source of knowledge about the USSR was a "listening post," established at first informally in 1919 at Riga, Latvia's capital, which was initially staffed by "Old Russian Hands" from the now defunct American embassy in Petrograd. The following analysis of the Riga "listening post's" contribution to American understanding and policy toward Russia falls into broad parts: a survey of U.S. perceptions of the New Economic Policy and Stalinist Russia of the 1920s and 1930s; a study of the phases of work of the Riga listening post itself, from its initial data-gathering period, 1919–1828, to its mature analytical phase, 1928–1933; and, finally, from 1933 to 1939, a time of its specialized reporting—focusing on one example—while the newly established Moscow embassy began researching current events.

• • •

The Riga staff's story stretched from President Woodrow Wilson's nonrecognition policy of Soviet Russia in 1920 to the outbreak of World War II in 1939, when it was necessary to close the Riga Legation. Between these two points, America passed through phases, including President Wilson's attorney general A. Mitchell Palmer's Red Scare; Charles Evans Hughes's "business at your own risk"; Herbert Hoover's famine aid by the American Relief Administration (ARA); Soviet-American cultural encounters led by such luminaries as Vladimir Mayakovsky and Theodore Dreiser; recognition in 1933, long championed by Senator William Borah; and attempts at accommodation by Ambassador Joseph E. Davies, 1936–1938.

Amid all of this, Russian and American culture "melded" by "symbiosis." As a leading historian noted, one product was joint discovery of new cultural directions symbolized by the American modern dancer Isadora Duncan, who was active on both sides of the 1917 revolutionary divide. She returned to Moscow in 1921, telling cultural commissar Anatoly Lunacharsky that she was "sick of bourgeois, commercial art." Her romance with peasant-poet Sergei Esenin stirred controversy. They married in 1922 and divorced in 1923. More melding occurred when Nikita Balieff and his *Chauve-Souris* relocated to Paris and New York, becoming a dominant feature of nightlife. Konstantin Stanislavsky brought his Moscow Art Theater to New York City in 1922, and, when in Boston, he signed a contract to publish his autobiography. On Stanislavsky's second tour, President Calvin Coolidge received him at the White House. These exchanges were promoted by Boris Skvirsky, representing the Russian Information Bureau, and Olga Kameneva, head of Moscow's All-Russian Society for Cultural Relations with Foreign Countries. They became official sponsors of *amerikanizm*, the Soviet cultural offensive to gain U.S. diplomatic recognition. A supporter of their efforts was Sherwood Eddy, a Young Men's Christian Association (YMCA) secretary whose yearly study seminars to the USSR began in 1926. Philosopher John Dewey, vice president of the American Society for Cultural Relations with Russia, participated. Dewey met and promoted Joseph Schillinger, the talented Russian jazz musician and composer. Many black jazz musicians went to the USSR, including Sam Wooding and the "Chocolate Kiddies." Soviet composer Dmitri Shostakovich's *amerikanizm* was taken with this Afro-American idiom, writing *Tahiti Trot* and *Golden Age*.

Armand Hammer represented one of the first American business efforts, signing an asbestos concession on October 28, 1921, shortly after conversing with Lenin. He also sent furs and caviar to the United States and formed Alamerico (Allied American Corporation), replaced in 1924 by the Soviet Amtorg (American Trade Corporation). In 1925, he manufactured pencils and by 1928 was disposing of confiscated Russian art. Henry Ford sold ten thousand Fordson trucks in 1925. Nothing much came of railroad magnate Averell Harriman's manganese mine concession started in 1924 and liquidated in 1928. Carpetbaggers hyped such deals in the twenties, especially American Alexander Gumberg and Comrade Boris Skvirsky through his Russian Information Bureau or the Russian-American Chamber of Commerce.

America's curiosity about Russia peaked in the 1930s with the professionalization of Slavic studies, a growing number of U.S. journalists in Moscow, notably Walter Duranty, and the celebrated visits of poets and writers. Perhaps the most famous incidents of cultural exchange were Soviet poet Vladimir Mayakovsky's visit to the United States in 1922–1923 and the American novelist Theodore Dreiser's journey to Russia in 1927–1928. Even the Afro-American writer Langston Hughes went to Moscow, although his projects came to nothing. Others sojourned to Russia until Stalin decreed socialist realism—art furthering the state—and the Great Terror's purges cooled American ardor.[1] Americans at large had missed this rich cross-cultural "melding" because of nonrecognition and, by then, the purges, which further scared them off. The U.S. government itself was largely reduced to what the Riga listening post told it, at least until recognition in 1933 and establishing the U.S. Embassy in 1934. Riga's reports continued negative Russian stereotypes.

A third generation of American experts after "Siberian" Kennan and, then, "Soviet Sam" Harper further distorted images. Robert F. Kelley, who headed the newly created Eastern European Division of the State Department in 1926, and these other specialists forged their expertise first in Russian studies at Paris, Berlin, or Prague, and then practical training at Riga. Kelley's autobiographical sketch stated his own qualifications: bachelor's and master's degrees at Harvard; a year at the Paris School for Oriental Languages with Professor Paul Boyer; army officer from 1917 to 1922, serving in the Baltics; and consular service in Calcutta in 1923, reassigned to the Eastern European Division as chief assistant in 1925 and chief of the division from 1926 to 1936. He described the division's duties: "While refraining from official recognition of the Soviet regime, the Division sought to develop relations between the United States and Russia along the lines calculated to encourage forces and trends in the Soviet Union working counter to the world revolutionary aims and activities of the Communist dictatorship." He went on to point out, "In anticipation of the need of Russian specialists in the future, the Division instituted a special language training course for selected officers of the Foreign Service." His colleague Loy W. Henderson added, "Kelley took the lead in the latter twenties in preparing promising young Foreign Service officers for work in, or connected with, the Soviet Union." That, Henderson stressed, made it "possible to staff our Embassy in Moscow immediately with young officers acquainted with the Russian language, Russian history, and political and economic conditions in the Soviet Union." In a letter to a young scholar, Henderson remarked, "I had a tremendous admiration for him as a man of integrity, a scholar, and a diplomat."[2]

Beyond these remarks, much more has been ascribed to Kelley. Scholar Daniel Yergin claimed Kelley godfathered the "Riga Axioms," which, Yergin believed, embodied a profound pessimism toward Bolshevik totalitarianism: *first*, the Soviet Union was understood to be a world revolutionary state with a foreign policy derived from communist ideology and not Russia's national, or Great Power, interest; *second*, its totalitarian foreign policy had its origins in its communist domestic system, usually referred to as the "Munich analogy" because it was likened to Hitlerite totalitarianism and timetables in pursuing a grand design to destroy the West; *third*, given the first two axioms, it was essential for the United States to exercise extreme caution and vigilance, while avoiding negotiations as much as possible, because they were usually pointless or ended as appeasement; *fourth*, the Soviet Union could be considered a "world bully," that is, even though its foreign policy was camouflaged in ideology, it was driven by sheer power calculations; finally, *five*, there was a far-reaching Soviet plan, derived from its Marxist ideology, with definite objectives.[3]

Another commentator called Kelley the State Department's creator of the hard line toward Soviet Russia where, as chief of the Russian Division, he initiated training policy analysts at the Paris School of Oriental Languages —the place where he and Harper had once studied. Kelley, who served three years as a military attaché in the Baltics, was the one who was "unusual in the belief that Communist rule in Russia was both an unmitigated evil and a permanent reality." The State Department needed officers fluent in Russian who knew Russian history and Bolshevism's background. Kelley sold the department on a program allowing two officers each year, starting with George F. Kennan, the distant cousin of "Siberian" Kennan, to prepare themselves as Russian experts. Both Secretary of State Hughes and his successors, Frank Kellogg and Henry L. Stimson, supported Kelley's program. Much later, Kelley recalled, "I think the program turned out very successfully and not only was successful but was absolutely indispensable to the development of our relations with the Soviet Union in those early years, to the knowledge and study of what was going on."[4]

About the nature of these studies, Kennan reminisced about wanting to work on the Soviet period, and Kelley responded, "No, I don't want you to take those courses. I want you to get the equivalent grounding in Russian history and literature and language as a Russian who had finished one of the Czarist universities before the Revolution would have had." On this point, Kennan remarked, "This was the best advice ever given to me, and it shows with what enlightenment and wisdom this language training was run at that time by Bob Kelley." After fifty years, Kelley's view of the Soviet Union in 1975 remained as it had been in the twenties. The Soviet's three major objectives, then and now, he thought, were to "build up the power and strength of the Soviet state [and] to gain overwhelming military superiority over the United States [and] to extend wherever possible the influence and power of the Soviet Union."[5]

Others thought otherwise. When in 1928 Secretary of State Frank Kellogg invited all nations as signatories to his pact outlawing war, the USSR immediately joined, which left the State Department insisting the Soviet action in no way meant recognition. When the new secretary of state, Henry Stimson, hinted at reconciliation, Kelley told Harper that no changes were in store regarding recognition. Assistant Secretary of State William R. Castle agreed. Prorecognitionist Alexander Gumberg called Kelley the obstacle to recognition in the State Department.[6]

Between 1926 and 1936, Kelley selected seven persons for Russian training; the first six in pairs. George F. Kennan and William Gwynn were coupled; Kennan went to Berlin and Gwynn to Paris. Norris B. Chipman studied in Paris, along with Eric Kuniholm; Charles "Chip" Bohlen and Edward Page also were sent to Paris. Francis B. Stevens was the last and a single who studied in Prague. Generally, after two years of intensive language study, they did a year of practical work at the Riga legation. "The language officers' training," one author concluded, "simply gave them a perspective on Russia which emphasized the negative cultural and social effects of bolshevism and taught them to interpret Soviet policy and behavior in ways appropriate to nonrecognition." Another author was so bold as to write, "Kelley's principal function before 1933 was to find reasons for not recognizing the Soviet Union."[7]

So much for the reclusive and reticent Kelley, indeed, the first gray eminence of the State Department's Sovietologists—a generation removed from "Soviet Sam" Harper and two from "Siberian" Kennan. How much Russian distortion and looking-glass illusion Kelley had may be a mystery. But there was no mystery about Loy Henderson, Kelley's cofounder of the State Department's Soviet Service, who has been called the "leader of this loosely defined but highly influential group [of Riga Boys]."[8]

• • •

If Kelley founded the "Riga Boys" and if Loy Henderson was their ringleader, neither claimed to be such. Yet to the end of Henderson's long and distinguished career, he was clear about Soviet Russia: "I may add that so far as the Cold War is concerned, it seems to me that it began on November 7, 1917, and continued unabated in varying forms up to this moment." That moment was September 1971; he died in 1986.[9]

Because of an arm injury he had suffered as a lad, the army rejected Henderson in 1917. The following year the American Red Cross accepted him and sent Henderson first to France, on to Berlin, and then to Eastern Europe. By August 1919, they commissioned him for service in Riga. He first met Kelley there in that chaotic time when there was a "free corps" army of Germans, Balts, and former Russian prisoners of war (POWs). They mingled and fought Estonians, Latvians, and Lithuanians. There he began relief work and POW repatriation by meeting with Karlis Ulmanis, Latvia's first prime minister, and in Libau with the earl of Caledon and his brother Lord Alexander of Tunis. Col. Edward Ryan invited him to serve on a commission to care for and repatriate Russian POWs in the Baltics. "My decision to accept the colonel's invitation represented," he later wrote, "one of the turning points of my life. From it flowed more than 40 years of work in the foreign field."[10]

Henderson arrived in Riga as Prince Aveloff Bermondt's Iron Division prepared to attack the city. However, former Lettish Rifles repulsed them with British and French naval protection from their fleet guns. He witnessed the Iron Division's rout. He also worked in Mittau and Kaunas by supplying portable hospitals. In January 1920, he returned to Riga and then went to Narva for the antityphus campaign. It was on April 2, 1920, that Henderson first met Soviet diplomats. By September 1921, he had returned to the United States and, on Evan Young's advice, then chief of the Russian Division and former head of the Riga Legation, took and passed the consular examinations. He served in Dublin as vice consul and then was reassigned to the Division of East European Affairs in December 1924.[11]

Henderson acquainted himself with all the Russian documents and printed materials sent from Riga and meticulously collected and cataloged by the East European Division, especially the binder marked "Russian Policy Book." The State Department had resolved to set up a center for the study of Soviet affairs in the Office of the Commissioner of the United States for the Baltic Provinces of Russia. It had been operating unofficially since 1919. In March 1922, more personnel were added. It became America's window on Russia—"a clearing house entrusted with the collection and classification of all the information received." After Latvia's recognition on July 25, 1922, a minister replaced the commissioner, and a separate Russian Section was officially created within the legation under Consul, now First Secretary, David B. Macgowan, and Vice Consul of Career, now Third Secretary, Earl L. Packer, with Hugh S. Martin as special assistant, performing intelligence work. Thus, the legation divided in two: one part serving the Baltics and the other assisting Russian information. At first, it was thought the center was temporary because Bolshevism would soon collapse. "All three had served in an official capacity in Russia following the Russian Revolution of 1917 and had, therefore, acquired some knowledge of communism, and all three spoke Russian."[12]

A sample of the Russian Section's work for the first nine months of 1923 demonstrates an enormous amount performed: "The tabulation showed Macgowan to be responsible for 317 despatches totaling 4,035 pages, Packer for 142 despatches totaling 1,509 pages, and Martin for 147 despatches totaling 819 pages." Most of the pages were translations. Political themes prevailed with economics a runner-up, followed by church persecutions.[13]

Its official existence for seventeen years, 1922–1939, went through three phases: an introductory period from 1922 to 1928, when it was consumed with factual reporting of events through translations; a high point from 1928 to 1933, when analysis and tendencies commanded its attention, especially single subjects; and, finally, a third phase from 1933 to 1939 under the "Old Russian Hand" Felix Cole. During the middle period the three officers were David Macgowan as supervisor with the assistance of Loy Henderson and John A. Lehrs. Lehrs was an American businessman who left Russia in 1919, became an American Relief Administration consultant, and then part of the early Riga listening post. With his Russian fluency, he initially worked on repatriation cases. In 1931–1933, George F. Kennan took over economic matters from Lehrs. "By 1933, the Russian Section had matured and had become a serious scholarly institution." After recognition in late 1933 and the Moscow embassy established by early 1934, the two kept a close liaison, the embassy focusing on current events and the legation on detailed studies. The war in Europe in September 1939 forced the State Department to close the Russian Section. "During the summer," wrote Frederic L. Propas, "the language officers were also instructed in political analysis by Loy W. Henderson, along with Kelley, one of the first experts recruited and trained in State Department Soviet Studies by [Evan] Young in the early 1920s." It was assumed that these language officers "all emerged as hostile observers of the Soviet Union." However, they were not "programmed," he argued, and Kennan and Bohlen became flexible analysts.[14]

The two most famous Riga Boys, George F. Kennan and Chip Bohlen, left interesting commentaries of their Riga years and the training involved as a part of the Kelley-Henderson gang. Kennan recalled being recruited in 1928 to spend twelve to eighteen months in the field at Riga, studying Russia and Russian on the practical side, interspersed with two to three years' postgraduate work in Berlin. Riga he remembered as a "variegated and highly cosmopolitan cultural life." In the summer of 1929, he returned to Berlin. His private language tutors in Riga and Berlin were Russian émigrés. Kennan skipped the third year and went back to Riga, instead of Tallin, as part of the Russian Section. He recalled Kelley as a "taciturn and infinitely discreet bachelor [who] was a graduate of Harvard and the Sorbonne." Kelley was a "scholar by instinct and dedication." Even Foreign Affairs Commissar Maxim Litvinov said that Kelley's files were better than the ones at Moscow's Foreign Office.[15]

Bohlen also remembered Kelley as tall and reticent, but in no way was he "an anti-Soviet crusader." This was a curious comment when most others considered him just that. Because Kelley had done exhaustive research on the Soviet Union, he insisted that emotionalism be avoided and replaced with factual verification and objectivity. As Bohlen noted, "From Moscow's point of view, this attitude was anti-Soviet, but from an American perspective, it was valuable training." About Bohlen's training, he decided on Russia only when he joined the State Department, even though he had done little preparation at Harvard. He was sent to Prague for a practical internship in general diplomatic work and in 1931 was transferred to the École Nationale des Langues Orientales Vivantes in Paris. Kennan had gone to Berlin, as he spoke better German than French, and Bohlen went to Paris, as he was already fluent in French. He, along with Kennan, was chosen by America's first ambassador to Soviet Russia, William C. Bullitt, to help gear up the new U.S. Embassy in Moscow.[16]

Meanwhile, Henderson's study of U.S. policy toward Soviet Russia led him to conclude that the policies of the Harding-Coolidge administrations were similar to those of President Wilson. They shared the same beliefs about the Bolsheviks because Lenin had gained power by trickery, ruled without consent of the governed, systematically interfered in America's internal affairs, refused to recognize obligations assumed by previous Russian governments, and confiscated U.S. properties without compensation. The United States could not recognize the Soviet Union until it stopped revolutionary activity in the United States, restored or compensated U.S. public and private companies for losses due to confiscation, and paid off the debts of previous Russian governments owed the U.S. government, businesses, and private citizens. Naturally, the Soviets rejected the first claim, were willing to negotiate reciprocity on the second, and would try to "do all that was consonant within its own dignity and interest" to renew its U.S. friendship on the remaining. The Soviets tempted U.S. businesses and cultivated sympathizers such as Senator Borah, and they managed through him to get a resolution introduced in May 1923: that the Senate favored recognition. Hearings began in January 1924, and Kelley was sent to the Senate to defend the State Department's position, a "David before the Senate's Goliath," Henderson recollected. Borah insisted that severance was the same as withdrawal of recognition. Kelley pointed out that it was not. "Borah," Henderson recalled, "apparently had not realized that the granting of recognition to a government gave it a status in international law and in domestic courts that could not be taken away by the severance of relations." Kelley also proved overwhelming Soviet interference in U.S. internal affairs.[17] Borah's resolution failed.

About trade, Secretary of State Charles Evans Hughes argued that the Soviet Union would need long-term credits, yet it refused compensations for confiscations, thus losing its credit standing. Companies were free to trade at their own risk. Henderson insisted American policies were based not on antagonism toward Russia or the Russian people but toward a "gang of well-organized, cruel conspirators." The United States stood for an integral Russia, except for Armenia, Poland, and the Baltic states—the latter recognized in July 1922. The division's name changed from Russian Affairs to Eastern European Affairs, and some of the Old Russian Hands, such as DeWitt C. Poole, were replaced by Evan Young's men—Kelley, Packer, and Henderson.[18]

The work of the Division of Eastern European Affairs increasingly consisted mainly of matters on trade, though it gathered information and investigated claims, legal suits, Comintern activities, and changes in Soviet policies that might justify recognition. To preserve American noninvolvement and nonrecognition, it devised a formula: "No action by the United States should be construed as the recognition of a government that we had not as yet recognized unless the action had been taken with the explicit intent to accord recognition." In a statement to Senator Butler, chairman of the Republican National Committee in 1928, Secretary of State Frank B. Kellogg summarized America's policy to Russia: "It would be both futile and unwise to enter into relations with the Soviet Government so long as the Bolshevik leaders persist in aims and practices in the field of international relations which preclude the possibility of establishing relations on the basis of accepted principles governing intercourse between nations."[19]

One of the most important sources of information to promote these aims was the U.S. Legation in Riga. Its library was "almost without parallel outside the Soviet Union." It subscribed to more than fifty Russian newspapers and periodicals, and most arrived there within a couple of days. Diplomats, visitors, reporters, businessmen, and technicians of one sort or another passed through Riga. Much of Henderson's time was spent on Comintern activities and the rest on treaties and agreements the Soviet Union had signed. These studies convinced Henderson by the mid-1920s that the "Soviet Union was pursuing the policy of trying to keep the countries of Western Europe at loggerheads [and] with the aid of German militarists the Soviet policy eventually prevailed." They were, he decided, determined to create chaos and revolution in the outside world so "they could achieve their ultimate objective of a communist world with headquarters in Moscow." This was, of course, the fundamental Riga Axiom. With that in mind, it was necessary to draw up plans to develop a corps of trained specialists. Kelley sent Henderson to Riga for that purpose on May 12, 1927; he was appointed third secretary of the legation. This planner, not one of the Old Russian Hands, became the first of the Riga Boys himself.[20]

Henderson's instructions read, in part, that he was to study Russian matters and prepare himself for future Russian service, especially language.

But all of that was left to the legation's judgment, and its urgent administrative needs, it so happened, soon took priority, leaving Henderson to fit Russian in whenever he could find the time. David Macgowan and John Lehrs continued in this effort with Henderson working as an adjunct to them. He was disappointed, but he understood that only young and still unclassified officers were to be assigned formal study. Officers of the higher grades "would be expected to acquire the qualification expected of specialists while on assignments to Eastern European posts or to the Division of Eastern European Affairs." Appeals to improve the Russian Section in the late twenties met with the response of "no funds available." Though shorthanded, the Russian Section, especially through Macgowan, was profuse in its translations and reporting.[21]

Though their Riga reports were often criticized because they emphasized Soviet shortcomings and panned communist accomplishments, they also served to disclose exaggerated Soviet claims. American experts and journalists understood that they were censored and under wraps for criticizing the USSR, if they ever wished to return there. Henderson's reporting focused on economic developments, especially trade and foreign concessions. He also was asked to prepare reports on Soviet aims, world revolution, and the Red Army. Kelley's protégé was now given over as half-time to the Russian Section in the fall of 1928. Henderson was to be assigned full-time to the Russian Section, soon joined there by Kennan and Landreth Harrison. In 1928, Herbert Hoover became president, with Henry Stimson as his secretary of state. In Russia, Stalin ruled as dictator by 1929. Henderson started a special "Stalin" file, and he was detailed to follow collectivization. Though Henderson again requested a year's leave for special language study, he was once again denied because it was reserved for junior officers such as Landreth Harrison, Norris Chipman, and Bernard Gafler only. When Henderson married a Latvian, the department returned him to Washington for work in the East European Division in January 1931.[22]

Secretary of State Stimson, a friend of Senator Borah, hoped to bring Kelley and the senator together for a long talk. Henderson said the new secretary sincerely believed that if "one would treat the Bolsheviks as gentlemen worthy of trust the Bolsheviks would respond as gentlemen." Henderson was against that notion, and Stimson was preoccupied with the Far East. Henderson's work under Stimson consisted of what he had previously done, although mounting pressure for recognition led the division to prepare pro and con materials. Henderson was especially interested in how the Soviet Union had treated its previous treaty commitments. He also looked into how the Soviet Union interfered internally in the United States; how it paid its international debts and handled nationalization and the confiscations of properties; what were its claims against the United States, that is, funds or properties belonging to previous Russian governments; and what were the rights of diplomats in the Soviet Union and the legal process affecting foreign nationals in the USSR. There were other problems, such as living and working quarters in Russia, contacts with Russian nationals, drugs, medical facilities, transportation, and the dangers of arrest and spying.[23]

· · ·

One of the earliest items sent by the Riga listening post for the secretary of state was from March 1920. The U.S. commissioner to the Baltic provinces of Russia, Evan Young, dealt with Soviet conditions. His report was based on a conversation he had had with an émigré Russian politician, Gregory Alexinsky. The Bolshevik Revolution, Alexinsky thought, intensified capitalism by turning peasants and workers into small landowners and shopkeepers—"under the cloak of communism." Diplomatic relations were impossible with a revolutionary government that would not keep its treaty obligations or sustain popular sympathies. Lenin reigned through terror. He would be overthrown after Russians regained their strength.[24] That outlook dominated the legation's views throughout its existence. The Division of Russian Affairs chief, DeWitt Clinton Poole, a former embassy consular in Moscow, summarized the legation's idea of the Soviet Union in March 1920. He claimed certain disclosures were "essential to an understanding of the Russian situation, especially in its international bearings." These facts were a centralized party with its leaders occupying the chief Soviet and Comintern positions: "The three [party, Soviet, and Comintern] may be distinguished theoretically, in practice they represent a single movement [whose aim was] world-wide revolution." He finished, "Therefore, while the Soviet institution, as such may agree to abstain from subversive propaganda abroad, neither the Russian Communist Party nor the Third International [Comintern] would be bound thereby."[25]

Socioeconomic and political themes, mainly translations, overshadowed the legation's reporting. Soviet internal conditions and Comintern threats initially headed the list. They were soon followed by an extensive Soviet interest in recognition and trade. There were translations from party congresses and conferences, a who's who of Russian officials, with their positions and biographies. These translations ranged over such topics, usually arranged in monthly and yearly reports, as citizenship, foreign affairs, the courts and crime, public health, concessions, foreign loans, youth, party dissensions and the power struggle, and U.S. travelers.

All of this vast reporting, each one usually prefaced with a brief remark by a legation officer, culminated the first period to 1927 in a large summary document, which was chronologically and topically arranged, with an index to people, by the Division of East European Affairs to the State Department, dated June 15, 1927. The introduction explained it as a "compilation of notes and telegrams of the Soviet Government, resolutions of Soviet organs, statements of Soviet officials, and other papers bearing upon the attitude of the Soviet Government towards the United States." It claimed to contain "the most important documents available in the Department relating to this matter." By this time, the Riga Boys were being trained by Kelley to relieve or add to the workloads of the legation's separate Russian Section. It was ready to start its second period from 1928 to recognition in 1933, and a third to 1939. It was at this point that Kelley had made this summary report. Considering its importance, he had five copies printed for the division, a sixth for the Index Bureau, and a seventh for the Riga Legation.[26]

Themes mentioned by Young and Poole were extended by Kelley. He began with the Bolshevik decree of November 8, 1917, calling for an end to World War I and secret diplomacy. However, it was the time from 1920 to 1927 that distinguished the first period of the Riga Legation's work. January 1920 began with the arrest of the Soviet trade representative in the United States, Ludwig A. Martens, as an enemy alien. Though America was not at war with Russia and the Soviet Union had no "unfriendly designs" on the United States, trading problems were the main issue. Restrictions complicated matters. Bolshevik envoy Maxim Litvinov claimed that American travelers in the Soviet Union had to be limited as retaliation due to the persecution of Russian nationals in the United States. By February 1920, Commissar of Foreign Affairs Georgii Chicherin asserted that there was "no intention on the part of Soviets of intervening with American internal affairs." He pressed for a U.S.-Soviet conference to reconcile differences, repeated by Martens, who opposed his deportation. He claimed documents in the Senate hearings were fraudulent. On April 3, 1920, *Izvestiia* argued, "Radical change in the attitude of Americans towards Soviet Russia has taken place."[27]

Litvinov suggested in May 1920 that the Soviet Union wanted the United States to take over all of its "financial burdens," to be concentrated as a single debt, which would eventually be repaid. Russia would have only one creditor rather than many, against which Russia's various raw materials and concessions would serve as securities. But American authorities maintained that Soviet Russia's promises were not kept. About Martens, Litvinov claimed the popularity of his mission caused his expulsion. Despite President Wilson's secretary of state Bainbridge Colby's note declaring nonrecognition, the Soviet Union was willing to enter into de facto trade relations. The Soviet take on Colby was interesting. His friendship would mean American domination of Russia, rather than that of local soviets. The

Soviet Union protested over "charges that the Soviet Government violates its promises." Despite differences of political and social structures, proper, peaceful, and normal relations could be established. By October 1920, the Soviets announced American businessman Frank Vanderlip's concession in Kamchatka as an example of a successful and "mutually advantageous" arrangement with an American capitalist. The Russians excused Martens's deportation as the "product of a panicky state of mind." Panic was governmental, so the Soviets thought, not popular. The Soviet Union was confident of a return to normalcy. As Martens left the United States in January 1921, he claimed the Soviets were always ready to resume normal relations. About Colby, the Soviet Union distrusted the "hollow idealistic phrases of Wilson, but we believe that we can do business with a realistic American businessman like Vanderlip." Harding, they thought, would be more cooperative. Litvinov asked for a resumption of negotiations, but the United States believed the Bolsheviks were returning to capitalism and politicians counseled waiting. Soviet trade representative Leonid Krasin dismissed Secretary of State Charles Evans Hughes's "uncompromising tone [and said the Soviet government] will continue to seek reestablishment of relations with the United States."[28]

Russia protested not being invited to the Washington Naval Conference in July 1921. Yet the Bolsheviks accepted American Relief Administration aid on August 20, 1921. By October, Moscow's party boss, Lev Kamenev, praised its work, saying that even though the United States "commercially and politically is widely separated from us it is the first country to aid us on a large scale." That same October, the Soviet Union called for an international conference to settle its debts and claims against it. Krasin believed in November that U.S. commercial cooperation was essential to Russian reconstruction and that de facto recognition was necessary. The Washington Naval Conference continued to bother the Soviet Union in fear of a united front against it. On November 28, 1921, Lenin renewed the appeal for the United States to "take over Russian debts to other countries and write off similar amounts owed to America by those countries." America would then be Russia's sole creditor. This was especially true since the United States was the only remaining Great Power and, thus, the Soviet Union must come to terms with America. Previous refusals of the United States were due to ignorance, but "Americans will come to know these conditions and their attitude will change." Krasin in January 1922 called on the U.S. consulate in London, seeking full recognition. However, since the United States, in his opinion, had made war on Russia, Soviet counterclaims must be considered. Chicherin recognized the paradox between famine aid and the American government's irreconcilable attitude. He continued, "False information respecting us had so far exercised too strong an influence in the

American political world." It was hoped that journalists could tear down that wall. Using the carrot-and-stick approach, Chicherin offered the possibility of exploiting Siberia, and he reiterated how badly informed Americans were. As to Soviet pledges, Chicherin maintained that the "Soviets have always kept their pledges and always would."

In August 1922, the American ambassador in Berlin discussed with both Krasin and Chicherin the possibility of a technical committee going to Russia to study economic conditions. This resulted in a letter of August 28, 1922, in which Chicherin welcomed trade negotiations with the U.S. government and was willing to send a trade commission or vice versa. The refusal of Americans was just like "schoolboys," and he offered himself to go to the United States to "get to the bottom of America's misunderstanding of Russian affairs." He regretted America's refusal to admit him. The proposal of a committee's exchange, he continued, should be entertained by the United States. Yet groups of American businessmen were welcomed, but with reciprocity. He meant to stress that Soviet-American economic relations were possible only in case America understood that it could not adopt a policy toward Russia of "act as you would at home." Economic relations were equally important to both.[29]

Recognition had support in the U.S. Senate, especially through Senators William Borah (R-ID) and Robert La Follette (R-WI). In January 1923, Chicherin sent a memorandum to Julian E. Gillespie, a member of the special U.S. economic mission at Lausanne, Switzerland: "Chicherin stated that public opinion in the U.S. was prejudiced against Russia." An article in *Izvestiia* by Steklov attacked Secretary of State Hughes's statement to a delegation of the Women's Committee for Recognition of Russia to the effect that a bad Russian economy prevented recognition. Steklov argued that Hughes wanted the internal structure of Russia changed to a bourgeois regime. Differences of political leaders, Steklov insisted, "do not warrant an absence of diplomatic relations."[30] An interview with Krasin revealed that, according to him, there were no problems to gaining an understanding if the United States would only enter negotiations.[31] Col. William N. Haskell, director of the ARA in Russia, while feted at a Moscow banquet was told that the Soviet government "will make the utmost efforts for the establishment of friendship between Russia and America." It was acknowledged that there could be an understanding only on the principles of equality and reciprocity, especially noticing that they supplemented each other economically.[32]

At the end of 1923, *Izvestiia* argued that President Calvin Coolidge had given a recent speech indicating America was ready to "come to an agreement with Soviet Russia." It continued, "The United States is beginning to recognize the importance of Russia's markets and powerful economic groups in the United States are commencing to exert a pressure on the American Government to revise its policy towards the Soviets." Obstacles to an agreement, according to *Izvestiia*'s commentary on Coolidge, were not serious. The question of debts did not play a serious role. On this basis, Chicherin wrote that Coolidge was prepared to enter negotiations assuming three conditions: mutual nonintervention in each other's internal affairs (mutuality), a willingness to negotiate everything, and the negotiations of claims by reciprocity. The Riga Legation then translated articles in *Izvestiia* and *Pravda* of December 22 and 25, 1923, discussing Secretary of State Hughes's reply to Chicherin. They accused Hughes of spreading rumors of the Soviet Union's imminent collapse, refusing to consult others, and forging documents (supposedly Chicherin's) claiming communist propaganda in the United States and paying large sums for them. Once again, *Pravda* insisted there was no connection between the Soviet Union and the Comintern. Any instructions that its president, Gregory Zinoviev, might make to the American Workers' Party had nothing to do with the Soviet government, since he signed them as chief of the Comintern: "The charge that there is a plot of the Soviet government to spread propaganda in the United States subversive to its constitution is nonsense from beginning to end." All these delaying tactics of Hughes to discredit the Soviet Union would fail because Russia could wait. Meanwhile, in the coming U.S. elections, recognition would be an important issue, and it was necessary "in order that commercial relations may be facilitated."[33]

Despite American claims of Russia's debt, money "arbitrarily expended" in the first place, no country except England was repaying its World War I debts, and "we also shall not pay." Zinoviev claimed the U.S. Department of Commerce had calculated the amount besides nationalized enterprises. "But recognition is one thing, and the present action of the bill is another." Yet trade and the problem of the debt became increasingly tied together and important, so much so that Chicherin was willing to get negotiations toward recognition started by discussing the debt question. Trade was rising despite nonrecognition, but there was always the Soviet threat of going elsewhere, even though there were the successes of such organizations as Amtorg and the Soviet Textile Syndicate. "As long as Hughes remains at his post Soviet Russia must consider seriously the advisability of maintaining trade relations with America."[34]

By the beginning of 1925 and into 1926–1927, the twin questions of recognition and normalizing commercial relations dominated reports from Riga. They illustrated the importance the Soviet Union attached to an accommodation with the United States, which it considered the dominant financial and political power in the world. Until Hughes's resignation in the spring of 1925, he was considered the U.S. statesman most irreconcilable to recognition, and increasingly he based his arguments against it on the twin problems of debt and propaganda. As the world's main creditor nation, the United States objected to setting precedents. Russia understood that the "chief cause of American and European hostility is cancellation of Czarist debts." Undersecretary of State William R. Castle even raised the issue of hypothetical loans to Russia after recognition was again on the American agenda. Arguments in favor were that the USSR was stable, its economy was improving, and it offered markets for U.S. goods. Those against, however, feared agricultural competition and propaganda threats. In October, Litvinov called for a full and open discussion of U.S. claims and Russian counterclaims. Stalin insisted in December that the USSR's claims against the United States were greater anyway, that Russia could not revoke the Soviet law on the cancellation of czarist debts, but certain unspecified exceptions might be made. Chicherin continued his "willingness" to discuss all questions.[35]

Soviet arguments in 1926 and 1927, as reported by Riga, began to shift or at least be refined. An editorial from *Ekonomicheskaia Zhizn'* (Economic Life) of January 3, 1926, discussed the "pressure in favor of relations with Soviet Russia being exercised by American businessmen." Wall Street itself began to see opportunities for markets and investments. The big "if" was whether a "definite political agreement" could be reached so a "powerful impulse will be given to the development of trade between them." Walter Duranty of the *New York Times* quoted the Soviet chief of the Concessions Commission, Adolf Joffe, on April 16, 1926, that an "American concessionaire in Russia is as safe as a concessionaire of a country diplomatically related to Soviet Russia." However, Joffe added, if that concessionaire were a former owner in Russia, he must renounce any claims against the USSR. Litvinov, speaking before the Federal Central Executive Committee on April 22, 1926, maintained Soviet readiness to negotiate. Nevertheless, if the United States made recognition dependent on the Soviets repaying former prime minister Alexander Kerensky's loan made by the United States to Russia's Provisional Government in 1917, then the USSR would have to consider counterclaims. Further, on April 30, 1926, the Riga Legation found out from Walter Brown of the ARA that Litvinov had told him the "Soviet Government hesitates to make a flat offer to repay the American debt for fear that it would be 'buying a pig in a poke.'" Yet by the summer of 1926, Duranty reported to the *New York Times* on August 4 and again on September 1 that the Soviet Union was willing to receive a Soviet debt-funding commission. A new subtlety was, "Russia stands ready to pay to the measure of its capacity." Krasin went so far as to say to John Gunther of the *Washington Star* on October 9, "If negotiations are begun, Soviet Russia is willing to acknowledge its debts to the United States and to drop counterclaims." The United States was partly excused from not recognizing the USSR because it did not "realize the political and economic importance of the Soviet regime." It was not until FDR's presidency that his administration recognized the importance of the power equation in balancing Russia with Nazi Germany and imperialist Japan.[36]

Among the various dispatches between 1920 and 1927 when Robert F. Kelley did his summary and had assumed control of the East European Division, there was a scattering of interesting and miscellaneous ones, done monthly and covering assorted topics. A typical one on the political situation titled "Signs of Opposition" was dated December 17, 1924, and submitted by Felix Cole, chief of mission of the American Legation, Riga. In it, he wrote of a troubled political atmosphere, especially referring to the Ukraine, Moldavia, and the city of Kharkov. "There has been," he stated, "considerable evidence in the Moscow press that the 'kulaks' [well-to-do peasants] were becoming bold and defiant, and even voted for others than those nominated by the local 'germ' cell." Nationalism and internationalism, as Soviet policies, did not mix well. Opposition to the Moscow dictatorship required the arrest of certain nationalistic central committee members. He added, "The state of mind of the remainder of the population can be imagined." To enforce the dictatorship, he noted, "the Political Bureau of the Russian Communist Party and the OGPU [Consolidated State Political Administration] have the whip-hand in the Ukraine, as in every part of the Soviet Union." There was a "general detestation and loathing of the Communist dictatorship" that pointed to an approaching emancipation from it. Hatred had turned to contempt and, then, to fear. Cole supported this introduction with four translated articles. This Riga style—starting with an analyst's introduction, followed by a series of translations from the Soviet press—was the typical pattern for the weekly, monthly, and yearly reports.[37]

Cole often delved into various topics such as Soviet administration, the party, its personnel, its congresses and conferences, foreign relations, the military, justice, health, education, and religion—often all of them were the usual points of discussion of these monthly reports. Cole wrote, "Socially dangerous elements" were to be expelled from urban areas. As to party activities, he pointed out the Political Bureau of the Central Committee controlled both internal and external policy, including "its domination over the Communist International and the latter's numerous agencies, engaged in propagating revolution and Communism in other countries." Cole also called attention to purges within the party of "intellectual elements, particularly suspected of opposition to the Party leaders." He likened the Political Bureau's aims to those of Peter the Great, that is, to build up a "reliable administrative machine." In foreign relations, he said that a Soviet delegation to London had presented Britain with a bill of £8 billion sterling for damages the British interventionists caused during the Russian Civil War of 1918–1921. The Comintern trained foreign parties to bore into trade unions and make "preparations for armed uprisings, the seizure of power, the inauguration of Soviets and the enforcement of the dictatorship of the proletariat."[38]

In January 1927, Cole summarized a series of newspaper editorials where Litvinov disclaimed boasts that the Soviets had their hands in revolutionary movements everywhere. Litvinov continued stressing the Soviet desire for diplomatic relations with the United States. Cole wrote, nevertheless, that it was "habitual with Soviet leaders to represent all criticism of themselves as emanating from single persons, or restricted circles." Thus, Britain's Lord Curzon and former secretary of state Hughes were so labeled.[39] The new secretary of state, Frank Kellogg, continued the department's keen interest in reports from Riga.[40] The secretary was particularly anxious about the Comintern's activities and, in this case, its activities in Britain. He was, as well, following trade issues. Riga was sure to feed that appetite.

The head of the Soviet trading company Amtorg, S. G. Bron, in the middle of 1928, told the press of his company's successes, despite anti-Soviet propaganda. Some of these were due to the "enlightenment carried on by the American-Russian Chamber of Commerce." In the translations of Bron's interviews, he was quoted as saying that Amtorg not only traded but also studied American systems of production, organization, work, and technique. Nonrecognition caused the obstacle of unregulated trade and created "a strong trend in favor of the development of direct trade" with the USSR. Credits remained a problem, with short-term ones obtainable but not for the long term. Russian business was so favorable to the United States that of the total $330 million of Soviet trade, only $30 million represented Soviet export to the United States. Especially, U.S. machinery was better, cheaper, and more productive than that purchased elsewhere.[41]

Even with Soviet efforts to improve trade and play down or explain away Comintern activities, Riga continued to be hostile and emphasize the negative side of Soviet life. A very good illustration of this was a remark of Cole in early January 1930. He quoted the great French historian Hippolyte Taine, when he wrote about the Old Regime in France before 1789 and, substituting "Communism" for the "Social Contract," saw some "striking historical analogies to the Soviet Union: the new state commanded all of one's loyalties; the others ceased. The past is destroyed and cursed in favor of a new millennium, of a new man." The second analogy was between the French and Russian peasant. "Individuality gives way to the 'sheep-like habit of being led, of awaiting an impulsion, of turning towards the accustomed center, toward Paris (Moscow), from which his orders have always arrived. Political ignorance and docility are everywhere complete.'"[42]

When American fellow travelers extolled Soviet virtues, they were interviewed and their opinions recorded. Two such sympathizers were Anna Louise Strong and Louis Fischer. Loy Henderson indicated that even though their interviews were "strictly confidential," they refused to criticize the USSR. Strong defended collectivization, especially after Stalin's March 2, 1930, "Dizzy with Success" article, in which he called for a slowing down of collectivization. Fischer complained that the Soviet press was agitational and that official documents did not show the regime's real intentions. The German Foreign Office had the real facts, or, better yet, one should be there. If there—as the Riga Legation could not be—one would realize the truth of accusations in the trials against wreckers, that there was no such thing as slave labor, the Comintern was not the Soviet government, collectivization was making "regular and sound progress," there was no danger of a war in Eastern Europe, and the war scare could be excused as a way of increasing mass enthusiasm "for the economic program and for the improvement of the defenses of the country."[43]

• • •

The work of the Riga Legation reached an apogee in April 1933 with its most brilliant 104-page memorandum, "Notes on Russian Commercial Treaty Procedure," by George F. Kennan. Kennan himself later referred to this "long interpretive report" by suggesting that Russian commercial treaties had done little to ensure "the personal safety of one's nationals in Russia."[44] Kennan's two opening paragraphs determined the rest of his exposition. Capitalist states, he wrote, assumed a commonality of political, economic, and legal principles. They were similar enough to have typical kinds of commercial treaty procedures. From that simple and safe starting point, he leaped to a stunning hypothesis, anticipating many other lines of his later analysis about U.S.-USSR compatibility: "The principles on which the Soviet state is founded are not only at variance but often in direct opposition to those accepted by most other states. The legal status of the individual in Russia, the control of economic activity, the whole foundation of the political and economic life of the state have almost nothing in common with those prevailing in other countries." Since the two systems—capitalist and communist—are at "variance" or are in "direct opposition," then it is only "natural the relations between such a system and other countries should call for a different treaty regulation than that which has grown up between capitalist states." With this opening announcement of basic incompatibility, what other relations, or procedures, he asked, would be at "variance" or in "direct opposition" to each other than just commercial treaties? Would there not be diplomatic relations and the whole notion of accommodation? This memorandum anticipated a later and broader examination such as his "Long Telegram" of 1946 or his "X" article, "The Sources of Soviet Conduct," of 1948.[45]

In this dispatch, however, Kennan restricted himself to the "peculiarities" the Soviet system posed for "ordinary commercial treaty procedure, and to indicate the extent to which existing treaties have not met these peculiarities." Kennan termed stark differences "peculiarities," although he had already labeled them as in "direct opposition." He persisted with the notion that they were the "new conditions presented to the rest of the world by the *peculiar* character of the Russian state. Without exception," he continued, "they regulate commercial relations in a way much more favorable to Russia than to the other contracting parties."[46] These "new conditions" were much more than just "peculiar" or just "more favorable to Russia."

The Soviet Union was class based rather than individually based, meaning its laws offered no protection to foreigners conducting business there. Since the state controlled everything, its trade delegations were monopolies that, under the cover of diplomatic immunity, could do almost anything without restrictions, in disregard to local courts. It could successfully use marketing, purchasing, and political pressure to their full and sovereign advantage. Kennan examined the commercial treaties of Soviet Russia, since its first with Italy (1924) and Germany (1925). He also covered countries having "special arrangements." Nor did the Soviet's extreme realism and reliance on force and self-interest account for the only divergences.[47]

He scrutinized the Soviet state's nature—its constitution and civil law code. Soviet commercial treaties, under their "Rights of Establishment and Protection" clauses, gave foreign nationals the same rights as Soviet citizens, because they had not been fixed by treaty or special laws. These rights were not extensive and, more important, were not inalienable but were "subject to simple legal modification." The courts were "in reality administrative rather than purely legal organs [and thus] Soviet citizens are completely at the mercy of the administrative authorities, and will not be assured the protection of law in the exercise of any civil rights whatsoever." Even if spelled out either in the treaty or in special agreements, Soviet courts were under no pressure, except diplomatic by the states involved, to respect them. An example was the German treaty, whose detailed provisions were still insufficient. So also were the three great principles of traditional commercial treaties: most favored nation (MFN), national treatment, and reciprocity.[48]

Class, not nationality discrimination, existed in the USSR; foreign nationals, anyway, got only what Soviet citizens obtained, "administrative authority." About this kind of reciprocity, Kennan noted, "Foreign governments are often legally powerless to employ against foreigners on their territory methods which the Soviet Government can apply without an instant's hesitation." It would be "helpless in practice to exercise the privileges which it legally enjoys." And when the Germans suggested that their citizens receive treatment "accorded to members of the most favored class," the Russian trade delegation dismissed it as "out of the question." Kennan pointed to various matters from injuries to ownership, from expropriations and personal property rights to transit of goods, and so forth. It was next to impossible for foreign individuals to do business in the USSR by equally competing.[49]

German associations found that only through "special agreements" defining quantity of goods, fixed periods of time for delivery, and specific credit arrangements could they come closer to what they had already granted the Russian trade delegations in their own German territories, that is, the diplomatic status of immunity, exterritoriality, private codes, inviolable property rights, and full economic information. None of these, or even all of them, matched the total sovereignty and monopoly of Soviet trade delegations. The functions of capitalist corporations and Soviet trade delegations were, simply, not the same. Soviet trade delegations executed "functions ordinarily performed by consular and diplomatic officers." On this matter, Kennan inferred, "There can be no satisfactory settlement of this question as long as capitalist states continue to accept missions of the Russian Government which combine both sovereign and non-sovereign functions of the state." If, he speculated, a clear separation of these could be made, much of the confusion might be eliminated. Licensing and tariffs were basically bargaining, not regulatory, tools.[50]

By 1930, foreigners, especially governments, were catching on. Stanley Baldwin, leader of the conservative opposition, in that year spoke in the House of Commons on terminating the Anglo-Russian trade agreement: "Trade is completely in the hands of the Russian Government, and they can effectively exclude British trade, as they already do, by merely placing orders with our competitors instead of with ourselves."[51] Kennan offered a solution to the difficulty that had been tentatively explored by Latvia. That section of his memorandum, "Part VII. The Direct Regulation of Trade," was marked "Confidential."

None of the measures started by private business associations, particularly German, was entirely satisfactory—such as setting minimum or maximum quantities of goods to be imported or exported, the fixed period of time to accomplish this, the terms of credit, or delivery conditions. Kennan emphasized that Russia simply cut down on other nonindustrial imports. Anyway, they were only temporary expedients, never comprehensive enough. Besides, the Soviet government could go over the head of capitalist states to wring better deals from individuals and play one off against the other. On that score, he concluded, "It is sufficient to point out that to allow the Russian Government to deal directly over a long period of time with associations of business men who are more or less dependent on Russia for a good part of their business, means to extend to the Russian Government a potential power of interference in the domestic affairs of the capitalist state in question—a power which can be deprecated only by those who are convinced the attitude of Russia toward the capitalist world is one of the warmest altruism and cordiality."[52]

Countries lacking powerful business associations such as Latvia in 1927 tried regulating trade with Russia by direct means: Latvia granted customs concessions simply on the basis that "trade between the two parties would amount to certain prescribed figures during the years in which the treaty was to be in force." If not met by either party, then one or the other could suspend customs rebates. The Russian trade delegation in Riga, by a separate note, guaranteed Latvian exports to reach treaty figures. As Kennan remarked, "This represents the only example in history of a direct obligation completely limiting the freedom of action of the Russian Government with respect to imports from a foreign country, and stipulating an exact minimum figure for the value of these imports over a number of years." Nevertheless, it was only a note, not a treaty obligation. The agreement, in fact, was broken by the Russian government. Latvia took no sanctions, probably because this "failure was due to political considerations rather than to lack of legal justification." Kennan noted that the whole thing was "absurd" anyway because capitalist states lacked monopolies over trade. Therefore, they could not bind private businesses to buy or sell specific quantities unless they wanted to pass such legislation forcing transactions regardless of market forces. The only real regulatory powers left to capitalist governments lay in stipulating sanctions within the commercial treaty itself, that is, "unless the trade reached a certain minimum figure, sanctions might be applied." These sanctions included ending customs privileges, automatic termination of the entire treaty, a trade boycott, and restricting credit. Such arrangements, Kennan thought, exhausted all the possibilities open in a commercial treaty's procedures. The rest of his memorandum related to various details of commercial navigation within Russia itself.[53]

Kennan had referred to this memorandum in his memoir, but with another emphasis. He had elaborated on the difficulty, if not impossibility, of individual businessmen, corporations, or business associations adequately to deal with a total state trade monopoly. Rather, government restrictions must be utilized in the original trade treaty, which were qualitatively different from a previous reliance on MFN and so forth among capitalist states. Two other aspects in the dispatch drew his attention: arrest and detention of one's nationals in the Soviet Union, and especially the charge of espionage. In the German treaty of 1925, for those arrested, German authorities would be notified within a week, and the arrested would quickly be visited by German consuls. "These clauses represented the furthest the Soviet authorities had ever been willing to go in promising foreign nationals in Russia some protection against arbitrary persecution or intimidation at the hands of the Soviet secret police."[54] But the clauses did not insist on consul visitation alone and in privacy. Russian officials might not be absented, which occurred in the Shakhty Trial in 1928.[55] Kennan jumped to Litvinov's vague statement of 1933 on what constituted espionage, which he quoted fully and remarked that economic espionage could consist of merely "asking for information on these subjects, i.e., statistics, grain crop size, currency issuance, gold production, etc." Even mere acceptance of such information was classified as economic espionage. According to an "advisory opinion" of the Russian delegation of 1925, which Litvinov had quoted, a foreigner who even happened to be told the size of the total grain crop in Russia could be convicted of economic espionage.[56]

Kennan's point was the utter vulnerability of one's nationals while conducting business in the USSR, whereas Russian trade delegates could conduct a "careful examination of the general trends of the German market and of credit and finance conditions in Germany." This was one of the "leading deficiencies of the existing commercial treaties with Russia."[57] In his memoir, Kennan chose to make the case of "personal safety of one's nationals in Russia." The memoir seized on it not only as an indictment of FDR's inattention to "weak verbiage" but as an episode in, as he later put it, "one of the most consistent and incurable traits of American statesmanship—namely, its neurotic self-consciousness and introversion, the tendency to make statements and take actions with regard not to their effect on the international scene to which they are ostensibly addressed but rather to their effect on those echelons of American opinion, congressional opinion first and foremost, to which the respective statesmen are anxious to appeal." Statesmen were eager to look good in the mirror of American opinion. He ridiculed striking these "attitudes before the mirror of domestic political opinion." Litvinov's assurances would not stand in the way of "arrest, prosecution, and police pressures of one sort or another . . . nor would they have provided our government with any adequate legal platform for intervention on behalf of the American, once he had been arrested."[58]

The remainder of the Riga Legation's work until its closing in 1939 tended in this analytical vein, but the important on-site observations shifted to Moscow where the U.S. Embassy was fully established in 1934. There was, for instance, a long report on the Soviet policy toward debt and confiscating property, a subject Kelley abstracted in his report to the secretary of state on July 27, 1933.[59] Reports also continued stressing Comintern activities, especially the Communist movement in the United States.[60] Packer and Kuniholm were in charge of the Russian section from 1936 to 1939. They were responsible for closing the operation when war began in September 1939, particularly in safeguarding the legation's library and archives and terminating the section's employees, where exception was made for their evacuation if they might suffer serious consequences under the Soviets, as well as liquidating properties.[61]

The final stage of the Riga "listening post" dated from opening the Moscow embassy in 1934 to the outbreak of the war in 1939. In that period, the legation was run by Ambassador John Van Antwerp MacMurray and the Russian Section, which Felix Cole had termed a "den of vipers." Moving Riga's operation to Moscow was considered, but lack of space and freedom canceled this choice. Although the legation was responsible for the three Baltic states, most of its work continued to center around gathering intelligence. Dispatches went back to Kelley and his Eastern European Division, though he was purged in 1936 by FDR and sent to Turkey. As Kennan put it, "Kelley was summoned one fine morning to the office of the Under Secretary of State [Sumner Welles] and informed that the Division of Eastern European Affairs was abolished forthwith." His division was "liquidated" and transferred to the Division of Western European Affairs. Its library went to the Library of Congress, and its special files "were to be destroyed." This "curious purge," as Kennan called it, came directly from the White House. Kennan and Bohlen rescued some of the library. Moscow and Riga worked in harmony, and Cole, Lehrs, John Perts, Gwynn, and Page—assisted by eight translators—carried on by doing special topics.[62]

Kennan wrote a fitting epitaph for the Riga work and the "Russian Division" above it, from their beginnings back in 1919 for Riga and 1924 for the Division of Eastern European Affairs until their demise in 1936 and 1939, respectively: "But the division, well-informed as it was, took, as did we, a sharply critical view of Soviet policies and methods, and believed in standing up firmly to the Kremlin on the many issues in dispute, even if it had to be at the cost of a certain amount of open disagreement and unpleasantness."[63] That unpleasantness became the focus of American journalists assigned to the worker's paradise. Eugene Lyons was perhaps the first to emphasize it. Nor was he the last. As late as 1986 and more than fifty years since Lyons left Russia for good, Nicholas Daniloff—a journalist and direct descendant of the Decembrist conspirators of 1825—was ripped off Moscow's streets by the KGB and imprisoned in Lefortovo as an American spy. It would seem to many Americans that little had changed and Lyons had been right all along with all the other naysayers.

3

Assignment in Utopia

When assessing why American opinions of Russia remained negative, it is useful to remark that Russia, whether czarist or commissarial, punished dissidents with imprisonment, exile, and death. Travelers and academics were, overall, almost unanimous in this assessment. Journalists' views were also consistent with this judgment. For example, the Soviet Union was "so villainous" in American perceptions that one journalist thought it hardly mattered what the media reported. Whether true or not, in the 1920s and 1930s journalists enjoyed a unique position reporting on Stalin's Russia and had notable influence on American views and the government policies they helped inspire. Walter Duranty lunched with Franklin Roosevelt, who sought the *New York Times*'s man in Moscow's views on recognition. Eugene Lyons, United Press (UP) correspondent in Moscow, published a bestseller on Russia in the thirties, *Assignment in Utopia*. Among all of the media distortions, Lyons's reporting stands the test of time. In the opinion of Whitman Bassow, later *Newsweek*'s Moscow bureau chief, American views were shaped even "more by what politicians tell them than by what they read and see."[1] But politicians did read what American journalists in Moscow wrote about Russia. Their inside stories remain important tools to discover Russia, even considering their distortions. Today's TV and Web sites make media views even more pervasive.

When Samuel Harper first went to Russia in 1904, he noted that Russians were happy to meet a real American so they could contrast their views against what they considered the "unfriendly specters raised by our belligerent press." Harper was comforted when "Secretary Hay finally and publicly upbraided American newspapermen for their biased treatment of Russia." Harper then realized Americans had a "great deal of prejudice and emotionalism" about Russia. He contributed more positive articles to the *Chicago Tribune* and felt the *New York Sun* correspondent was the best then in Russia. An example of journalistic overkill was when he was back home in 1906 and read in the *Tribune*, which he had represented while in Russia during the 1905 revolution, that "blood flowed in the streets of St. Petersburg."[2]

During World War I, Americans started to realize that events in Russia were important to them. Harper met Philip Sims, who represented the United Press and was sent to establish a permanent office. After the March Revolution, Americans became optimistic about liberal chances in Russia, especially after the United States entered the war in April. In a famous study, Walter Lippmann and Charles Merz drew two major conclusions about the *New York Times*'s coverage of the period of the Provisional Government, March 15, 1917–November 7, 1917: the first was that the difficulties in Russia to July, especially in the army, were not concealed from the careful reader, but the overwhelming tendency of captions and emphasis was "so optimistic as to be misleading"; the second was that from July to November, although the regime's difficulties played a bigger role in reportage, misleading optimism continued. The paper sought a solution to Russia's problems by searching for a "dictator-savior" and placing "mistaken hope" in a rightist coup; it seriously underestimated growing Bolshevik power from July onward.[3] After the Bolsheviks came to power, American journalists played out much of Soviet history negatively, with some of the most notable exceptions being John Reed during 1917–1920 and Walter Duranty from there through the first two Five Year Plans. Otherwise, some well-known sharp critics were Henry Shapiro during World War II and afterward Harrison E. Salisbury from 1949 to 1955, Whitman Bassow and Hedrick Smith, and Nicholas Daniloff during the remainder of the Cold War.

●　●　●

Correspondents in revolutionary Russia, 1917 to 1921, had much to do with shaping American attitudes. Arno Dosch-Fleurot of the *New York World* believed the fundamental purposes of the Bolsheviks and the Allies were essentially the same. His opinions were found daily in the *New York World*, presented with so-called facts, and taken by the public as authoritative. His inferences, derived from his specious sources, fed his worst hopes and fears. After speaking with members of the Root Mission, sent by President Wilson to aid the Provisional Government, Dosch-Fleurot was certain "they had not grasped that the real Government of Russia was the Soviet." He was convinced the mission was nothing more than a well-meaning American gesture but lacking understanding of Russians.[4] Dosch-Fleurot was in close contact with other Americans in Petrograd, including John Reed, future founder of the American Communist Party and author of the classic *Ten Days That Shook the World*.

Throughout the Brest-Litovsk crisis, Dosch-Fleurot returned dispatches predicting the Bolsheviks would not sign a peace treaty with Germany. This speculation turned out to be false. Dosch-Fleurot was friendly with Lev Trotsky, commissar of foreign affairs, who offered the Allies participation in the negotiations. They refused. Dosch-Fleurot reflected Trotsky's hopes against a separate armistice. Before the Bolsheviks took power, Trotsky told Dosch-Fleurot that the Bolsheviks wanted a general peace based on the principle of "no annexations, no indemnities." German militarists were not expected to accept such conditions, claimed Trotsky, and when they refused, the German masses would overthrow their autocratic regime. If a German revolution failed, "then every soldier in the Russian Army will know he is fighting to save the revolution."[5]

Negotiations at Brest between Bolshevik Russia and imperial Germany opened on December 22, 1917, with occasional breaks. The Petrograd Soviet never excluded resistance from its list of possibilities and for some time debated over the correct course of action. In the end, Lenin's policy of peace at all costs won. Most Americans throughout December and January were patient with the Bolsheviks and believed that a restatement of war aims was necessary. Some papers and journals, including the *New Republic, Nation, New York Evening Post, Springfield (Mass.) Republican, Philadelphia Public Register, Des Moines Register, Chicago Daily News,* and *St. Louis Post-Dispatch,* entertained the possibility of a reconsideration of the war's settlement. The *Nation* and the *New Republic* were sane, prudent journals, presenting news on Russia.

Historian Christopher Lasch assumed that throughout the Brest-Litovsk crisis many American papers were conciliatory toward the Bolshevik government, unlike any other period during the war.[6] After signing the Brest treaty, the *New York World* and others presented Russia as giving in to the Germans. This strengthened the position of the growing number of interventionists. The apparent letdown at the end of the Brest negotiations was the fault of overly optimistic editorials in papers such as the *New York World*.

Dosch-Fleurot went so far as to blame Allied diplomacy for the outcome of the Brest crisis. The *New York World* shared this opinion and presented a news headline saying, "Allies Themselves Are to Blame for Russia's Defection."[7] By July 1918, Dosch-Fleurot had become a member of the interventionist camp and thought the Soviets were no longer representative of Russians. Most interventionists believed the Soviets were not representative, but this did not require or justify direct American intervention.

Herbert Bayard Swope also wrote for the *New York World*. Swope had been the *World*'s Washington correspondent and was in contact with Col. William B. Thompson, head of the American Red Cross Mission to Russia.

Swope reported that President Wilson's Fourteen Points speech was a move toward a working agreement with the Soviets, and he predicted the dismissal of Ambassador David R. Francis. According to Swope, the ambassador had misguided the State Department by saying the Bolsheviks did not desire a separate peace and that they really wanted a general peace without annexations or indemnities. According to Lasch, Swope saw that the Bolshevik scheme of things had a kinship with those ideals Wilson had phrased.[8]

William English Walling in the *New York Times* dismissed Swope as ignorant and uninformed. Walling considered Swope's reports as gossip, originating from America's propaganda arm in Russia, Edgar Sisson's Committee on Public Information. He did not consider the influence that Dosch-Fleurot and Thompson had on Swope. Walling went on to say that Swope failed to see that the Wilson administration recognized the Bolsheviks were moving toward a separate "German Peace."[9] Lack of sufficient firsthand experience in witnessing Russian affairs and command of the language had affected interpreting Brest-Litovsk by these journalistic shapers of American opinion.

Another influential source on American perceptions was Moscow correspondent Louis Edgar Browne of the *Chicago Daily News.* Like Dosch-Fleurot, he believed the Allied and Bolshevik causes were essentially the same. His reporting was also based on what he considered to be authoritative sources in Moscow. Browne was an advocate for recognition and support for the Soviet government to bring Russia back into the war.[10] With the knowledge that the Bolsheviks were intent on withdrawal from the hostilities, Browne believed the Wilson administration had better come to grips with that fact. The future of U.S.-Russian relations could become adversely affected if American antagonism persisted.

Isaac Don Levine reported for the *Chicago Tribune* during 1917–1918. Levine's sources were taken from large quantities of various dispatches sent from Petrograd and other capitals of the world to his Chicago office. The March Revolution was a great cause of jubilation for Levine, and he saw the removal of the czarist regime as a step in Russia's struggle for democracy. The conservative *Chicago Tribune* was a paper that presented many hopes for Russian democracy, American style. Before the November Revolution, Levine had called for a redeclaration of war aims by the Allied powers; otherwise, "a clash between the Provisional Government and the masses would be inevitable. . . . The possibility of a new revolution for a while loomed high on the Russian horizon." His reporting of the developments in Russia sometimes opposed the conservative slant that the *Tribune* adopted; this slant clearly favored the Allied cause in the war. Levine recognized Russia's inability to fight any longer after three arduous years against the Central Powers, and he found himself in disagreement with the *Tribune*'s editorial policy of "get in there and fight" toward Russia.[11]

On November 2, 1917, Prime Minister Alexander Kerensky of Russia's Provisional Government granted an interview with the Associated Press (AP) and emphasized the total exhaustion to which Russia had been reduced. Yet the following day the State Department issued an optimistic statement: "Reports from Petrograd by mail and telegraph show that Premier Kerensky and his government, far from yielding to discouragement, are still animated by a strong determination to carry the war through to a victorious completion."[12]

According to Levine, Kerensky was at the point of collapse. The coup that followed, it was hoped, was transitory. Levine differed: "The Allies made their initial blunder when they failed to recognize the new Russia as really new. . . . It looked upon the Allies as strange bedfellows, because of their connection with the old imperialistic Russia. . . . The Russian democracy did not consider itself bound by the Czar's covenants and treaties. . . . The Allies failed to see this fact and deal with it as such." Levine was branded as "pro-Bolshevik" by Walling. Nevertheless, Levine reported further: "Kerensky's government was not overthrown. It fell of itself. It crumbled away like a house built upon the sands."[13]

The election for the Constituent Assembly was held on November 25, 1917. Out of thirty-six million votes cast, only nine million went for the Bolsheviks. Lenin abolished the assembly. In January, Levine severely censored Lenin's act and analyzed the differences between the Soviets and Bolshevik Party. Herbert Croly, editor of the *New Republic*, did not print the story but later incorporated some of it into "The Stakes in Russia," advocating recognition.[14]

Another person reporting for the *New York Times* then was the Englishman Harold Williams, married to the well-known Cadet Ariadna Tyrkova-Williams. He was passionate about Russia, but he revealed limited knowledge about the country. Liberals and conservatives discussed distinctions between Soviets and the Bolsheviks. Williams argued that the soviets were distinctively Bolshevik institutions, and he inferred that they were a form of class tyranny. Dictatorship was not opposed by Williams, but rather a dictatorship of the proletariat. In a letter to Samuel Harper, he wrote, "I think the first stage [in Russia's reconstruction] must be a wise military dictatorship." To hold elections "in the present state of the popular mind [was simply to encourage] adventurers, of whom there are so terribly many."[15] To Williams, such a step was necessary toward Russia's education for democracy.

When Lenin dissolved the Constituent Assembly in January 1918, Williams expressed horror, calling it "a snowstorm, raging full in this fiercest of winters, and it is as though all the powers and the elements of darkness were rushing and roaring in the whirlwind that enwraps this city of doom."[16] Lippmann and Merz criticized Williams's inconsistency. Before the November Revolution, Williams sympathized with Russia; afterward, he was an ultrainterventionist and anti-Bolshevik.[17] Williams became biased in his reporting from Petrograd.

Throughout November 1917, until direct intervention by the Allies the following spring and summer, a key issue for American journalists was whether the Bolsheviks would remain. Most editorials expressed a hope that Bolshevism's demise would quickly come. Russian experts such as Alexander Sakhovsky, a *zemstvo* (Russian land committee) agent, expressed doubt about Bolshevik longevity.[18] Given the unique circumstances in Russia and as a result of its czarist heritage, the Allies pressured Kerensky's government to keep Russia in the war at all costs.

It seemed the only additional question needing to be answered was what would follow the Bolsheviks. They were viewed as transitory. In January 1918, the *Times* ran two items suggesting the Bolsheviks were temporary.[19] If they did what the Allies wanted, they might have some legitimacy. This suggested that subservience to the Allies was what the Bolsheviks stood against. At one instance during the Brest-Litovsk crisis, they almost discarded their anti-Allied stance to obtain Allied aid and prevent a humiliating peace. Trotsky's negotiations and final defiance of the Germans appealed to some Americans, such as Raymond Robins, Thompson's successor as head of the American Red Cross Mission.[20] Once this dream of Russia's return to the war failed with the Petrograd Soviet's vote in favor of immediate peace in 1918, American calls for Bolshevik removal resumed in the *Times*.

News of this period from 1918 to 1920—the years of civil war and intervention—was biased in the hope that Russians would "do their bit" in the war. What Americans did not realize was that Russia was no longer able to contribute toward Germany's defeat. Three years of bloody war had devastated the Russian military machine. Even though some members of the Soviets expressed a desire to fight on, they could not deny overwhelming German military superiority.[21] Correspondents, as a whole, did not emphasize this unavoidable fact, realized by several Americans in Russia; it conflicted with the preferred U.S. policy.[22] As a result, the American public remained unaware of the true state of Russia. The period following Brest showed a radical change in the character of the news and the various persons who reported it. Russia's defeat and Germany's western offensive created panic in the West as an outright and total German victory was feared.

Back in September 1917, John Reed stepped into this cauldron, working for two socialist magazines, the *Masses* and the *New York Call*. He kept a daily diary and collected every scrap of newsprint he could find. With a translator and his own strong Bolshevik sympathies, he was admitted to the Smolny Institute, seat of the Second All-Russian Congress of Soviets, on the night the Bolsheviks seized power. His masterpiece, *Ten Days That Shook the World*, was the inside story, the big scoop. While others filed dispatches, "John Reed alone knew and had talked with the principal players, had mastered the complex politics of the numerous factions, and understood the relations among them."[23] He became more than just a reporter; he converted to communism. On October 17, 1920, he died in Moscow of typhus, contracted while on a speaking tour in Baku, and his ashes were buried in the Kremlin wall. By January 1921, all foreign correspondents had left Soviet Russia and were barred from returning. They were considered enemies and spies.

Foreign reporters and some State Department trainees gathered in Riga, listening to stories from Petrograd, some three hundred miles away. Among them was Walter Duranty, whom the *New York Times* sent there. Duranty was able to scoop a sensational front-page story about an arrested Soviet courier, carrying "seditious documents" to American communists, and that scoop would get him his place as the *New York Times*'s Moscow correspondent. The story turned out to be false and was added grist for the Lippmann and Merz critique of the *Times*. With a famine in Soviet Russia and the American Relief Administration given entry to feed the starving, Duranty was able under the cover of the ARA to join a few others readmitted to Russia. After an absence of almost three years, American newspapers would again have a Moscow dateline.[24]

The small bunch of journalists—Duranty, Floyd Gibbons, George Seldes, James Howe, Francis McCullough, Percy Noel, and Sam and Bella Spewack—were housed at the Savoy Hotel. Gibbons had raced ahead to get the first eyewitness account of the famine by dashing to Samara, an early reporting triumph. Duranty was able to stretch his assignment into a career lasting until 1941 and became the most "influential if controversial" correspondent of the *New York Times*: "He was attacked by conservatives as an apologist for the Kremlin and by liberals and communists as anti-Soviet."[25]

Reporting on Moscow from the press center at the Savoy was difficult. It was like covering a war because the correspondents were closely watched. Sam Spewack was the only American who spoke the language, while the others did what Reed had done and hired translators. Walter Duranty learned Russian by reading newspapers and gained some fluency. Every story written had to be submitted to Narkomindel (the People's Commissariat for International Affairs) for approval before transmission. Konstantin Oumansky was the chief censor, named ambassador to the United States in 1939. Stories were often smuggled out by the diplomatic pouch, disguised as personal letters in their first few paragraphs and never carrying Moscow datelines. Yet travel was usually unrestricted. George Seldes got two scoops, one by asking Y. K. Peters, a Cheka (secret police) official, if 1.7 million "counterrevolutionaries" were killed in the Red Terror of the civil war. When Peters laughed it off, Seldes retorted, "100,000?" Peters replied by suggesting that Seldes "split the difference." Seldes got his Lenin interview in much the same way. Invited to an address given by Lenin in November 1922, someone asked the Bolshevik leader if he spoke English. Answering in poor English, Lenin noted, "I cannot understand you, Americans especially, because you hate the word BOLSHEVISM—so you make BOLSHEVISM the most hated word. After all, there are many interpretations of Karl Marx and BOLSHEVISM is one of them. . . . [W]e adopted the one that Daniel DeLeon started in the Socialist Labor Party." To which Seldes cried out, "That's my father's friend you're talking about!"[26] In 1923, Seldes was expelled from Russia, as Cheka agents discovered his misuse of the ARA's diplomatic pouch for smuggling stories out of Russia.

In 1930, six American journalists remained in Moscow, and they collectively represented the Associated Press, United Press, *New York Times*, *Chicago Daily News*, and *Christian Science Monitor*. Surveillance of them was maintained by the Press Department of Narkomindel. In the mid-1930s, the *New York Herald Tribune*'s Joseph Barnes was assigned to Moscow. Moscow was, in the words of Whitman Bassow, a "correspondent's nightmare—or a dream assignment, depending on the individual's frustration threshold." What Bassow meant was there was much to report, but the censor restricted what could pass through the Press Department. Stalin's government was determined to destroy peasant resistance and, at the same time, conceal the story.[27]

Walter Duranty considered himself the dean of the foreign journalists in Moscow, and, in 1932, he won the Pulitzer Prize for his reporting on Russia. Harper mentioned various other journalists who made up the press corps of Americans in Moscow during the thirties: "Of the newspapermen stationed in Moscow in 1926, I played around particularly with Junius B. Wood, of the *Chicago Daily News*, James Mills, of the Associated Press; and William Henry Chamberlin, of *The Christian Science Monitor*. Wood and Mills were older and more experienced newspapermen than most of the others, and they were covering the Soviet Union as old hands at the game." He liked the Knickerbockers—Laura and Hubert—for their "intellectual keenness." He mentioned that by 1932, two of the younger reporters, Chamberlin and Eugene Lyons of the United Press, were "beginning to go sour." Especially Lyons had gotten cynical. As Harper remarked, "These two were good examples of people who had come over full of enthusiasm, with a set pattern in mind, and who subsequently became the most severe critics—and not always, as previously, the most correct in their criticism."[28] That severe criticism, indeed, the negative attitude that prevailed among most Americans, was best illustrated in the life and times of a single correspondent, Eugene Lyons. Like "Siberian" Kennan and often "Soviet Sam" Harper before him, the more he saw, the more he disliked.

• • •

Eugene Lyons, in his book *Assignment in Utopia*, gave one of the most revealing accounts of his own disillusionment—a syndrome that was soon to be called "the God that failed."[29] It became a widely acclaimed best-seller. It had all started simply enough for Lyons. Though born in Russia, he had come to America as a small boy. Almost as soon as he could think, he believed himself a socialist. From a "Socialist Sunday School," he graduated to "Yepsels," the Young People's Socialist League. When he went to college, the Russian Revolution had become the "harbinger of the Great Change." As he wrote, the Bolshevik Revolution "in the name of the Soviets seemed confirmation of the new era born eight months before." The very day Lyons got out of his army uniform, he wrote his first story for the Workers Defense Union. "My writing was for the cause. Such," he contends, "is the towering egotism of youth, even in its most altruistic poses." The vitality of that altruism sent him to Italy to be, he hoped, the John Reed of the Italian workers in 1920. He failed but returned to champion Nicola Sacco and Bartolomeo Vanzetti, executed in 1927 for supposedly murdering two payroll clerks. In the aftermath of their conviction, he returned from Boston to New York City and cast his lot with the communists. Though he never joined the party, he worked for the Soviet news agency TASS as the editor of the mouthpiece of the Friends of Soviet Russia and their journal, *Soviet Russia Pictorial*. He broke with former friends in the Socialist Party, whom he called "knaves," "liars," and "betrayers." They were nothing short of "deserters" and "renegades."[30]

Now, 1923, the Soviet news agency operated under an agreement with the United Press. When in 1926 the Stalinist faction won out over the Trotskyites, Lyons's office instantly became Stalinist, and he sided with the victorious faction. The post of Moscow correspondent needed filling. Lyons did not succeed in 1926, but in 1927 he received that post. In his acceptance, he believed that he was taking a "post of immense strategic importance in the further service of that cause, and doing so with the whole hearted agreement and understanding of my chiefs in TASS and therefore, presumably, of the Soviet Foreign Office."[31] On December 31, 1927, he set sail for the land of his dreams, reaching Moscow on February 8, 1928. The true believer had arrived and, armed with his altruism, meant through his columns to rid Americans of their misconceptions about the land of the proletarian dictatorship.

Lyons entered as the New Economic Policy was ending. He became part of the noncommunist colony, though his natural impulse was toward it. This meant being ostracized by people whose friendship he had counted on. Despite restrictions, his acquaintances grew. In faraway New York's revolutionary circles, he became known as a capitalist. From the start, he began to notice an important distinction: two different foreigners could visit the USSR and come away with "diametrically opposite impressions." It was those with self-delusions who bothered him. Even among his colleagues, he recognized important differences. For example, Junius Wood ridiculed Soviet Russia, while Walter Duranty was taken for a Soviet enthusiast. At first, Lyons stuck to "ardently partisan" dispatches. Stalin's victory over Trotsky did not mean a swing to the right, as the world assumed. Rather, Stalin "stole Trotsky's thunder" and turned sharply to the left. By the end of 1925, the "Right Opposition" challenged Stalin. Grain quotas fell, and "extraordinary measures" were used, which meant the quotas of grain collections were met by any means; peasants universally opposed these measures.[32]

In trying to report the grain-quota glitch, Lyons found out about the annoying censorship. Correspondents were placed into "friendly" and "unfriendly" groups. Yet he was "distinctly and proudly 'friendly.'" This was because he still "belonged" in the Russian Revolution. Several of his articles on American themes were published in Soviet journals as well as his book *The Life and Death of Sacco and Vanzetti*, which was even published in Russian by the Soviet press. All that would begin to change with his reporting of the first so-called demonstration trials, the Shakhty case, trials that, "year after year, were to bewilder the world with their spectacle of men confessing incredible crimes and embracing death." To his chagrin, charges were not proved, investigations were behind closed doors, and full or partial confessions were already obtained. In other words, the accused were prejudged. In this, the first and a model for all future cases, an "Act of Accusation" described in detail various and sundry sabotages, espionages, grafts, and so forth. These all dissolved into conjecture and hearsay, and international intrigues never developed. The demonstration trials were, for Lyons, great hoaxes where innocence or guilt was of no importance. He concluded that something might be wrong with his "mystical assumption" that the "revolution can do no wrong, since even its crimes are justified by its mystical mandate from History. . . . For me, as for others, it remained a glaring proof of the dangers of immense unrestrained power with its inevitable temptation to use unstinting force where force was least effective."[33]

That "unstinting force," as he called it, was used to its maximum for the collectivization of agriculture during the first Five Year Plan—against all who opposed it or who might be considered as opposing it. Russia's Iron Age was "unrolled tumultuously, in a tempest of brutality." There was to be a new emphasis on "grain factories," socialized through state ownership. Stalin's decision, on October 1, 1928, marked the final emergence of his dictatorship. The "Right," until now tolerated, became a heresy. Lyons remarked that it had taken Stalin six years to destroy the leaders of the "Left Opposition" but only six months to liquidate the leaders of the "Right Opportunists." Now there followed a *chistka* (cleansing) of the ranks. The NEP was considered bourgeois degeneracy, and the *byvshiye* (former people) had to be rooted out. Suspicion also fell on the so-called technical intelligentsia. Many disappeared or became *lishentsi* (disenfranchised people)—without rights or legal standing. Nevertheless, Lyons still discounted the corruption of the Soviet bureaucrats. "Few foreigners in Moscow," he wrote, "outdid the United Press man in the glorification of the new socialist objectives." His theme song continued to be the march of a backward agrarian country toward becoming the leading industrialized society. By substituting the glorious future for a squalid present, he was able for a time to justify the enormous human cost.[34]

A conference of the party officially sanctioned Stalin's ascendancy and the drive to the left in April 1929. So 1929 was termed the *perelom* (break). The party line gained a disciplined hardness, and the party, "without hesitation," Lyons reflected, "doomed millions to extinction and tens of millions to inhuman wretchedness in the mystical delusion of [its] divine mission." Lyons, in fact, substituted "historical" for "divine." He characterized the *perelom* by six principles, which turned such words as *idealism, compassion,* and *love* into insulting epithets: first, the party became sacrosanct; second, Stalin personified the sanctity; third, human life was valueless—only the raw historical stuff was important; fourth, proletarian and poor-peasant parentage attained the highest value; fifth, class was the method of social advance; and sixth, foreign revolutionaries must accept Moscow's leadership or be termed "social fascists." At home, *udarniki* (shock brigadiers) became the pacesetters in the workplace, and the old exploitative measures were reintroduced: piecework, bonuses, docking, and socialist competition —all to fulfill the plan's quotas. An uninterrupted workweek was introduced with every fifth day free for one-fifth of the workers.[35]

Lyons's growing apostasy was noticed, and the word spread by Kenneth Durant, his former employer at the Soviet news agency, TASS, in New York City. Since TASS had an agreement with United Press for acquiring U.S. news, it had been through Durant that Lyons obtained a United Press assignment in Moscow in the first place. In the summer of 1929, there was a

"Great Tourist Invasion" of the USSR. Among the "invaders," Durant came with his pro-Soviet New York City circle of correspondents. The tourist hordes arrived to tell the "whole truth" about Russia in their forthcoming books and articles. Even ordinary Russians resented their "complacent gullibility." Lyons's disillusionment grew by watching these "twittering" foreigners and their "gushing enthusiasm." "To me," he wrote, "there was from the first something obscene in the invasion of smug foreigners in this time of national distress." There were bits of a scavenger element in reporting a nation's wounds and then calling them lovely sacrifices. Only a few of them, he noted, understood that they were "picnicking in a graveyard." Others had already called Lyons a political renegade for writing some sharp criticism, though he had striven for political consistency rather than intellectual integrity. He wrote Durant on the latter's return to America, and Durant's reply was pointed: "The gist of it was that I was an 'ingrate.'" Lyons realized that excommunication was painful, even if his faith had faltered. He was beginning to join the ranks of the two distinguished notables before him, whose faith in one or another Russian government had also faltered, namely, George "Siberian" Kennan and "Soviet Sam" Harper.[36]

Lyons thought the *gosplanners* (state planners) were akin to religious mystics in that they called for ten million tons of pig iron in the plan's fifth year, which they boosted to seventeen million. In actuality, it came in at a little over six million. Likewise, the coal schedule was originally seventy-five million tons and was hiked to ninety million, but only sixty-four million tons were extracted. And so on down the line. About collectivization, the same zeal set one-tenth, then one-fifth, and finally one-half of all farms to be collectivized by 1932. With prodding by the OGPU (State Political Administration) and the Red Army, some rushed to the collectives, but dark references appeared to kulaks (middle-class peasants) and their agents.

Industrialization, basically, rested on successful collectivization. If the so-called kulaks opposed it, then a policy of class war, that is, liquidation, would follow. Nevertheless, Lyons's dispatches paraded the successes of collectivization, though it was an open secret that they were based on "naked force." Clearly, there would be no retreat. On December 27, 1929, Stalin said as much and raised the slogan of "liquidation of the kulaks as a class." Lyons remarked, "It was the signal for the most startling piece of brutality, considering its dimensions, in the annals of revolution." It meant smashing and dispersing between five and ten million peasants "quickly and rapaciously." Previous figures were forgotten as whole areas such as the lower and middle Volga basins and North Caucasus were to be fully collectivized by the end of 1930 and the rest of the country by the end of 1931. Lyons reported, "Hell broke loose in seventy thousand Russian villages" with a vast Red Terror. A population the size of Switzerland or Denmark was stripped of everything and herded into cattle and freight cars and dumped wherever labor was needed in the frozen North or deserts of central Asia. By February 1930, the government announced it had attained 50 percent collectivization and in important grain regions close to 100 percent. The country reacted spontaneously and calamitously by slaughtering livestock and destroying half or more of it. Decreeing the death penalty for such action did not stop it. "The economic losses entailed by the sixty-five days of ferocious compulsion were almost incalculable."[37]

Stalin's hardheaded realism had deprived the revolution at the end of the first FYP of half its cattle and horses, two-thirds of its sheep and goats, and two-fifths of its pigs, most occurring during these sixty-six days between December 27, 1929, and March 2, 1930. On that latter date, Stalin called off the terror with his article in *Pravda*, "Dizzy with Success." In it, he blamed the local officials' zeal for the excesses. Lyons summarized the article: Stalin criticized "r-r-revolutionaries" who thought that they could start collectivization by "pulling down church bells" and socialize by "military force." The Kremlin had, in Lyons's words, "sanctimoniously disavowed responsibility." About two-thirds of so-called paper collectives now collapsed, and the 63 percent mark dropped to 22 percent. Soviet newspapers recognized "great mistakes." This enormous catastrophe marked a watershed for Lyons. "For two years I had been building an intricate structure of justifications for the Soviet regime. Now, without my willing it, the structure began to disintegrate around me." He recalled his "private pledge never to attack the Soviet regime." But did a recital of realities constitute an attack? What if it needed the corrective of public exposure? Was exaggeration of victories and denial of failures to be continued at all costs? At this point, Lyons closed, "I still held in the main to the last alternative." And that was to nurture the socialist fatherland at all costs.[38]

It was now that Lyons got his greatest scoop: he interviewed Stalin, the first such that the Soviet dictator had granted in the past four years. It happened in a curious way. Lyons had written Stalin for an interview back in 1929. Such an interview was the most sought after on earth, according to Lyons. So he tried an "oblique insult." On a suggestion by a friend, Lyons attacked Stalin's vanity in reverse—insult instead of flatter the dictator: "An enormous amount of nonsense about you has been spread throughout the world. Some through ill will, others through ignorance, have depicted you as a taciturn recluse hiding behind the Kremlin walls, unapproachable and scarcely human. Indeed, I saw one item in the press insisting that you did not exist at all, that you were a mere figment of Bolshevik imagination." Was there some truth in such accusations? asked Lyons. An interview, Lyons suggested, would disapprove these notions. Stalin replied:

I am sorry that I cannot at the present time grant your request for an interview. Motives: (a.) interviews do not destroy legends but rather create an unhealthy atmosphere for new sensations and legends; (b.) I have not at the moment free time for an interview.

I ask your pardon for the delay of the answer. There is a lot of work and the matter lay waiting an opportunity for answering.

Respectfully yours,
J. Stalin

Rather than publishing any of this, a worthy story in itself, Lyons ignored section (a.) as "philosophical generalization" and accepted section (b.) "as a concrete undertaking" for an interview in the future. Periodically, Lyons wrote Stalin to remind him of his promise.[39]

On November 23, 1930, Stalin's office rang to tell Lyons that the dictator of the proletariat would talk to him in an hour, at five o'clock. As Lyons told it, "Stalin was about to give the first interview since he had achieved his pinnacle of power." Lyons arrived at the Staraya Ploshchad (Old Square), and the guards and secretaries were awaiting him, ushering him into the antechamber of "the most powerful, most feared, least known human being on the face of the globe." Lyons remarked on the "unmistakable simplicity" of the setting, the "hall-mark . . . of Stalin himself." When called, Stalin met Lyons at his office door, shook hands, offered cigarettes, and stretched out leisurely in his chair. Lyons had asked for only a few minutes, but it now took on the dimensions of an "unhurried social call."[40]

Why had he been selected? Probably his letters for more than a year played a part, but now he was unprepared for a really long interview. Lyons asked for permission to quote Stalin that he had not been assassinated, and Stalin agreed, though he hated to take bread out of the mouths of the Riga correspondents, that is, those not under the Moscow Press Bureau's censorship but living in the sovereign republic of Latvia. The interview ranged over the merits of bourgeois journalism, Soviet-American relations, the FYP, the need for more foreign trade, economic classes in the United States, and a key question: "Are you a dictator?" Stalin answered, "No, I am no dictator. Those who use the word do not understand the Soviet system of government and the methods of the Communist Party. No man or group of men can dictate. Decisions are made by the Party and acted upon by its chosen organs, the Central Committee and the Politburo." The conversation then turned to Stalin's personal life—his wife and three children. Klement Voroshilov, the Red Army chief, had entered the room and took part in the conversation. On this domestic note, the interview broke up. Stalin asked to see the dispatch, and Lyons typed it out then and there. Stalin approved it with only minor corrections or suggestions and wrote on it, "More or less correct, J. Stalin."[41]

The interview appeared Monday morning, November 24, 1930, in the *New York Herald Tribune*. The interview, as reported in the *Tribune*, contains much more information than Lyons chose to put in his book, especially by the editor's placing of headlines and subtitles throughout the article. The main headline banner for that day read: "Stalin Urges U.S. Trade with Soviet in His Only Interview in Four Years." Just above the column by Lyons, the banner read: "Communist Official Says America Must Appreciate Such Advantages; Sees Victory in World." And below that in bold print it read: "Denies Dictatorship; Jests at Death Story." Finally, the last banner read: "Charges Bourgeois Plot to Upset Russia, Doubts If Geneva Arms Parley Will Aid, Disavows Dumping." The article then recounted that Lyons had interviewed Stalin for more than an hour. Stalin said, "If it cannot establish political ties with the United States, the Soviet Union at least desires to strengthen its economic ties with America. An America being a great, wealthy, technically progressive and developed country, must appreciate the advantages of such economic intercourse as much as we do." About debts owed Americans, Stalin remarked that since the United States had suffered the least during World War I, it should be willing to compromise on this issue. When Lyons suggested that this involved a principle of the sanctity of debts and private property, Stalin said, "Since when has the bourgeois placed principle above money?" He added that after the American Revolution and Civil War, the United States repudiated its debts. "And you were right, too." About dumping, Stalin did not take the criticisms seriously. About the charge that he was a "dictator," "Stalin laughingly denied he was the Soviet 'Dictator.'" Persons who gave him that title were ignorant of the Soviet government and the Communist Party. "It was just very funny" was his summary of the dictator title. Of the prospects for world revolution, Stalin answered in two words: "prospects good." On Geneva, he said that "it can't do any harm to participate in the conference." The interview ended when Stalin "personally found a typewriter, ordered tea and sandwiches for this reporter, and apologized for not having received me before this. Interviews don't fit very well into my personal five-year plan," he said. Lyons ended the article with his own observation that though Stalin was the hardest man in the Soviet Union to get an interview with, he "proved to be the easiest of all to talk to." Stalin spoke slowly and with a Georgian accent, using "broad Oriental gestures." His mind, Lyons noticed, "seems automatically to organize its materials into simple forms and in words comprehensive to any one." Lyons ended on this note: "It was hard to recognize in this good-natured man the Stalin whom Nikolai Lenin, dead leader, characterized as 'rude.' He spoke sympathetically and smiled pleasantly."[42]

Lyons noted, "It was front-paged throughout the world . . . as one of the ranking 'scoops' in recent newspaper history." Lyons compared his interview to others and believed his came closest to H. G. Wells in conveying Stalin's "essential humanness and simplicity." Yet ever afterward, Lyons was "overwhelmed with a conviction of failure: why had he neglected to confront Stalin with problems such as the use of terror, suppression, and punishment of heretical opinion; the persecution of scientists and scholars; the distortion of history; the enslavement of workers and peasants; and the faking of statistics? For failing to do this, Lyons was to "reproach myself" for years. "I was," he wrote, "depressed by the feeling of a magnificent opportunity frittered away."[43]

The interview had occurred when, after a six-month pause, a renewal of the collectivization program began. The new harvest was in and the artel-type collective, or *kolkhoz*, where the peasant kept a home, garden plot, and some domestic animals, became the standard. It was regarded as a "glorified cooperative" by "naively rapturous foreigners." The *kolkhoz* was, "in essence, . . . no more socialistic than farms cultivated for the church or the crown in other countries, paying their farmhands on the basis of the crops produced: share cropping for the government." It could not own tractors or other machinery, which were rented to the collective by the Machine Tractor Station in return for 20–30 percent of the crops. All the time, the "rapturous foreigners" continued in the "pleasant illusion that Bolshevism was a new, more gloriously intransigent bohemianism." They forgave occasional excesses. Walter Duranty of the *New York Times* became the greatest apologist, summing up his position in a famous quote: "Your correspondent has been convinced by ten years intimate study of soviet situation that you can't make omelettes without breaking eggs." Then, Lyons commented, whenever anyone wanted to suggest a "tongue-in-cheek reporter playing the game of those in power, he referred to the immortal omelette." Even Lyons fell back on the "price-paid-for-the-future theory" of suffering and terror to adjust his old faith to the new realities. But, by then, there was something "barbarous, ugly, and inhuman" mixed into the socialist future.[44]

As to Lyons's own apologetics, he soon felt more ashamed of them as "mealy mouthed caution." He was coming to believe that he had "somehow betrayed the Russian people by minimizing and concealing their sufferings—that I came consciously to recognize my new viewpoint." He was part of a lush apologetic literature that fed the hope for a more just world. Into the group of apologists, Lyons cast Duranty, Maurice Hindus, Anna Strong, and Louis Fischer—those who privately admitted the truth, even agonized over it, yet no trace of their wounds appeared in their articles and books. The most famous and fatuous of the apologists was George Bernard

Shaw. "The great G.B.S.," Lyons wrote, "was more interested in being seen than in seeing, in being heard than in hearing." Lyons came to understand that Shaw was not taken in but collaborated in the deception, with the world as the dupe. For example, when he judged food in Russia by what was served at the Metropole Hotel, collectivization by a model farm, the OGPU by a colony it ran, and socialism by all the Kremlin yes-men who surrounded him, it all was a "cold and calculated taunting." At its worst, "The lengthening obscenity of ignorant or indifferent tourists, disporting themselves cheerily on the aching body of Russia, seemed summed up in this cavorting old man." What made Shaw's clowning in Russia especially bad was that it contributed to a myth of the worker's utopia. Shaw's behavior was enough, in itself, to turn Lyons from a volunteer propagandist for the Soviet idea to a critic. He increasingly realized the "gaping gulf" between research and application, between planning and reality, that crossed every sphere of Russian life.[45]

The word that symbolized a crucial turning point in Lyons's transformation from a supporter to a detractor of the Bolshevik Revolution was *valuta* (real values). Lyons came to regard the planned torture for *valuta* as the trademark of both Bolshevism and fascism—the "urge to excuse brutality." It was a symptom of "something pathological" in which the "guinea-pig theory" had conquered every instinct. This pathological streak he saw dignified in Bolshevik rhetoric as "firmness." "I saw it reflected in the semi-official apologetics of foreigners who found it in their conscience to treat the vast network of concentration camps as an 'industrial' enterprise and an 'educational institution' without so much as a suspicion that their emotional arteries were hopelessly hardened." It reminded him of Dostoyevsky's imagined torture and murder of a child, made necessary and inevitable in "creating a noble fabric of human destiny." Ivan Karamazov, it will be remembered, asks his brother, Alyosha, whether he would kill an innocent child to create the millennium, to which Alyosha answers no. *Valuta* remained in Lyons's mind as a "counterweight to all the boasts and promises and revolutionary pretensions that filled the press, the billboards, the speeches, and the plans."[46]

Lyons came to recognize that "the first expression of that disrespect for life is a readiness to sacrifice the lives of others." He called it a "postponement, not a solution," for achieving Soviet goals: "I came to believe that its causes lay much deeper, in the very assumptions of the Soviet regime, particularly the assumptions that the sacrifice of human beings did not matter in the achievement of human happiness, that the sacrifice of socialist ethics were of no account in the building of socialism, and—most important and most Russian of all—that anything could be accomplished by brute force."[47]

The growing tragedy of human sacrifice reached its apogee in the "calamitous winter of 1932–33." Agrarian Russia had been shaping up for a disaster of stupendous magnitude, "ranking with the greatest catastrophes in modern times." It occurred in an area declared as 100 percent collectivized and 100 percent kulak liquidated, namely, in the Ukraine and North Caucasus. Apologists later accused the peasants for the famine that killed millions.[48] In response to that accusation, Lyons wrote, "For all the sophistries of wishful thinking 'friends' of the U.S.S.R. and cynical apologists, forty million people can never be either 'innocent' or 'guilty' but rather the creatures of forces beyond their control." Because of this "brimstone and fire" in the Ukraine and North Caucasus, Lyons's lingering scruples against speaking out about Soviet realities were badly shaken up. In January 1933, Lyons got the first scoop on the great "man-made famine" by obtaining the documents from a European journalist "playing ball" with the Soviet leaders, who turned over the papers about three Cossack towns in the Kuban and North Caucasus where all the inhabitants, forty thousand, were thrown into cattle cars and shipped to the Arctic forests as an object lesson. Though Lyons could not get the story past the censors, even though documented, he filed it from Berlin while on a scheduled trip. It was a scoop that horrified the world. But, as he wrote, "My Kuban story, it thus transpired, started the first serious breach in the conspiracy of silence around the famine. The Soviet authorities, I had reason to learn, never forgave me."[49]

About the overall achievement of the first FYP, Lyons infers that in industrial production, it was about half fulfilled and that in agriculture, production actually declined by 20 percent by 1937 against 1913 figures. When all aspects of society were considered by Lyons—industry, agriculture, living standards, housing, costs in life, suffering, and terror—"the Plan must be regarded as one of the most startling failures in all human history."[50]

Witnessing the Metro-Vickers Trial in 1933 confirmed once more for Lyons that "dictatorship under an infallible leader calls for a system of scapegoats." The press corps' concealment of the famine of 1932–1933 further turned Lyons from being an apologist for Stalin. Finally, Ralph Barnes of the *New York Herald Tribune* exposed the magnitude of the famine at the conservative figure of one million victims. That story forced others to admit the truth, especially Duranty and the *New York Times*. Others came forward—American engineer Jack Calder and English journalist Gareth Jones.[51] Even Duranty finally withdrew his previous estimates.

Lyons's "undeviating" stand against the right of the Soviet government to try foreigners accused of crimes within its borders marked his full turn against Bolshevism. No longer was he granted favors by the government. He remarked, "I had shed the last of the veils of political inhibition in searching out the facts behind the formulas. . . . The need for evasions to spare my own feelings had fallen away." With American recognition in 1933 and a story Lyons published on the Soviet confrontation with Japan, Maxim Litvinov, the Soviet foreign minister, was emboldened to demand his recall. His last day in Moscow was January 31, 1934.[52]

• • •

For the remainder of the Soviet period, Bassow concluded, "Perceptions and stereotypes [of Americans were] so ingrained that most Americans will not permit the facts to undermine their prejudices or tightly held opinions." During World War II, restrictions on journalists in Russia were very tight due to the need for military secrecy. Henry Shapiro managed to get an exclusive on the Battle of Stalingrad. Sometimes news was planted and faked as, for instance, the story that Stalin had "struck the bald pate of Marshal Semyon K. Timoshenko" with a champagne bottle at the Teheran Conference in November 1943—a conference Marshal Timoshenko did not attend. Yet the "system created by the Soviets to control the news of the conflict . . . 'was so diabolical that to this day old war correspondents shudder when they recall it.'"[53]

During the Cold War, especially from 1949 to 1956, U.S. correspondents worked under the "most trying and frustrating conditions" since 1921. In a seven-year period from 1946 to 1953, "almost everything millions of readers in the United States and the rest of the world learned about the Soviet Union came from them [Henry Shapiro, UP; Eddy Gilmore and Thomas Whitney, AP; and Harrison Salisbury, the *New York Times*] and Glavlit (Main Administration for Literary Affairs)." Gilmore called this "Moscow Madness." With Stalin's death in 1953, things began to change, especially with Nikita Khrushchev after his 1956 condemnation of Stalin at the Twentieth Party Congress. Then the networks came to Moscow. There was a hunger abroad for film footage of ordinary Russians. Daniel Schorr of CBS News became an "instant" celebrity. In 1961, Khrushchev removed the censorship. Reporters could use their own telephones rather than be required to access the Central Telegraph office. The Cuban missile crisis, the U-2 incident, and Khrushchev's ouster became headlines and major TV coverage stories. As Bassow recalls, "Television's impact on American public opinion" was important, and Russians tried to plant stories.[54] However, détente was still a dangerous period when American reporters could be roughed up, expelled, or killed by Leonid Brezhnev's KGB.

Nicholas Daniloff's case in 1986 was a good example of American overreaction.[55] His tribulations stretched from his KGB arrest on August 30, 1986, to his release from Lefortovo Prison on September 11, 1986; he was allowed to leave Russia on the twenty-ninth. As Moscow's bureau chief for

U.S. News and World Report, he had spent five years there, although he had been there on assignment as the magazine's journalist earlier. Of Russian descent, he spoke the language fluently. That ancestry was especially significant: he was the great-great-grandson of Alexander Frolov, a Decembrist conspirator against Czar Nicholas I who had spent thirty-one years in Siberian exile. Though aware his ancestry had a special place in Russian history, he decided to look seriously into this connection only toward the end of his assignment. As that research neared completion and as he readied to return to the United States, he was arrested and imprisoned as a CIA spy. His imprisonment lasted almost one month, during which his case became a cause célèbre—finally ending on the desks of President Ronald Reagan and party general secretary Mikhail Gorbachev. There it rested until they could reach a compromise settlement: releasing Soviet spy Gennadi Zakharov in exchange for Daniloff—"the first American journalist locked up in a Soviet prison since 1949, when Stalin threw Anna Louise Strong, an American Communist, into the Lubyanka."[56] These were the raw facts. Beyond them, Daniloff wove a fascinating story by comparing his incarceration to that of his ancestor and drawing parallels between czarist and commissarial Russia. They were striking, scattered like gems throughout.

The Soviet Union, like its predecessor, was a land of "complicated rules and regulations that no one keeps if he can possibly get away with it." Like Siberian exile, the KGB's prison was notorious, and its barbarity infamous. Both were states within a state. His grandmother often referred to Russia as "not just a state, but a state of mind." It was "a country of irreconcilable contradictions: generosity, hospitality, and kindness were mixed with slovenliness, cruelty, and stupidity." In the Soviet psyche, like the older Russian one, "resides a feeling of inferiority before the Western world. Officials," wrote Daniloff, "are quick to sense condescension from foreigners and, when pushed, can strike back in petty ways." You could put Reagan's "evil empire" literally into the mouth of Frolov. The old Soviet boast, "Everything is better in our country," had soured to, "It's no worse than elsewhere." There was an inner tension in Russian society itself: "whether the country should turn eastward or westward (or inward, toward isolation, which happened in Stalin's last years)." Daniloff quoted the Marquis de Custine's 1839 remark: "All foreigners are treated like criminals upon arrival in Russia. So many precautions, considered indispensable here but completely disregarded elsewhere, warned me I was on the verge of entering the empire of fear." Daniloff continued, "Not much had changed. The Soviet suspicion of foreigners, the national paranoia about frontiers, are understandable in light of history."[57]

Daniloff's cell mate joked about Lefortovo being the highest building in Moscow because "from the roof you can see all the way to Siberia." Daniloff later reflected about Frolov's following the Siberian exiles' tradition and climbing the snowcapped Sayan mountain Dumnaya Gora (Thoughtful Mountain) to see the Siberian expanse and reflect upon it before entering. He even compared the Decembrists' women, who voluntarily followed their husbands into Siberian exile, with the interrogator's remark that Daniloff's spouse, Ruth, a freelance journalist, was an "aggressive wife." "I was reminded of Nicholas I's annoyance at the wives of the Decembrists when they protested the incarceration of their husbands. Like them, she was a thorn in the side of the authorities, revealing their barbarism to the world." The Reds celebrated that uprising as an "aborted blow against tyranny rather than a failed attempt to introduce Western democracy to Russia." Often, Daniloff would compare his jail conditions to those of Siberian exile, whether under the czars or commissars. In one striking passage, Daniloff reflected after closing a book about the Decembrists he was reading in prison, "How little had changed in Russia. Finding parallels between czarist and Soviet rule became one of my few distractions—that is, as long as I did not allow the similarities to unnerve me. Frolov's misfortune invariably made me wonder if Siberia would be part of my destiny."[58]

His ancestor's interrogation alternated in the book with his own, especially dwelling on Col. Sergei Muravyov-Apostol's famous remark at the botched execution of himself, "Poor Russia! We cannot even hang properly!" Daniloff referred to captivity in Lefortovo as the Decembrist Nikolai Basargin did about Siberia: "You are no longer an inhabitant of this world." Daniloff even thought Lefortovo's commandant, Petrenko, was similar to Frolov's General Leparsky—capable of human decency. When referring to his inquisitor, Colonel Sergadeyev, he explicitly noted comparisons: "He must have realized that I was drawing parallels between my fate and that of the Decembrists. Like most Soviets, Sergadeyev considered the Decembrists' struggle sacred. . . . Any comparison between today and czarist times infuriates Soviet ideologues, who live with the illusion that 1917 marked a total break with the past."[59]

When Daniloff was freed from Lefortovo, he became very accusatory, quoting Mikhail Lermontov's severely critical poem about "unwashed" Russia, a land of slaves, police, pashas, all-seeing eyes, all-hearing ears. One might conclude, as Bassow did, "The Soviet Union has become such a villain in the American psyche that most of us carry a profoundly negative image of the Russians: bad, threatening, mysterious, powerful, anti-American. Although much of this image is rooted in reality, it means that no matter what the media report from Moscow, the fundamental 'bad guy' image will not be affected."[60]

American diplomats frequently came away with a more or less negative picture of Russia as established by numerous travelers, academics, and journalists, most typically represented by Kennan, Harper, and Lyons. The first four ambassadors were William Bullitt, Joseph Davies, Laurence Stein-hardt, and Adm. William H. Standley. All but Davies disliked the USSR. Thus, President Roosevelt found it necessary to work through his special representatives to Moscow—Averell Harriman and Harry Hopkins—men who shared FDR's accommodation policy. The question was: could FDR make a positive policy toward Russia stick in the face of deep-seated dis-trust?

4

Honeymooners

President Franklin D. Roosevelt had two goals in his search for accommodation with the USSR. First, recognition would clarify debts and confiscations, being a means for broadening business ties while bringing Soviet Russia into the antifascist camp. Second, accommodation would result in alliance and, after 1940, an international organization in which Soviet Russia would collaborate to keep peace. FDR's Russian policy achieved some temporary gains and problematical long-term ones. By 1939, with the onset of the Nazi-Soviet Pact and the outbreak of war in Europe, FDR's rush to recognition had so far failed to achieve his two goals. Yet FDR still made efforts for a permanent understanding with the USSR. These were, at best, tactical maneuvers, not always serious initiatives to reverse the Wilsonian doctrine of ignoring the USSR, continued for more than a decade by Republican administrations and reinforced by the State Department's deep-seated negative attitudes toward Russia.[1]

• • •

November 1932 saw Roosevelt's election as U.S. president. He was a man whose liberal views encouraged advocates of recognition, though he had made few remarks on Russian relations. "His position on recognition was so constructed as to give hope to both sides without making false statements to either."[2] Electing a potentially prorecognition president was important if this issue were to succeed.[3]

As his campaign for the presidency heated up in May 1932, what he called his "privy council," later named his "Brain Trust"—Raymond Moley, Rexford G. Tugwell, Adolf A. Berle Jr., Samuel I. Rosenman, Basil "Doc" O'Connor, and Hugh Johnson—advised him of the trade opportunities that recognition might gain.[4] The group urged that FDR study recognition as a serious choice. Roosevelt publicly reviewed the question of Russia in the summer of 1932, calling on Walter Duranty, the *New York Times*'s Pulitzer Prize–winning correspondent in Moscow, to the governor's mansion in Albany.[5] At their luncheon, he inquired about Soviet gold production and whether the Soviets could pay their debts.[6] FDR again acknowledged his interest in Russia in December, after the election, and promised to review the policy of nonrecognition.[7] He was curious about the possibilities offered by trade and the promise Russia held in securing world peace by intimidating aggressive totalitarian states such as Japan. Roosevelt was, perhaps, more interested in peace and strengthening America's international security than in trade, but both issues played a role in his decision to move toward recognition.[8] The president was hesitant to act on the question until he learned whether he had congressional and public support. Frank Freidel, one of FDR's leading biographers, has suggested that what appeared as a "recovery measure came to be a collective security diplomatic move" to offset Japan. At the time, Freidel continued, the Soviets also saw America as a "counterweight to the Japanese."[9] Importantly, almost no one FDR consulted, with the possible exception of Duranty, had any particular expertise when it came to the USSR. On this issue, the president and his advisers were pragmatists, so much so that Roosevelt wanted personally to direct negotiations. He told his close friend and future secretary of the treasury Henry Morgenthau Jr. in mid-1933 that he could "straighten out the whole question." The president, according to Morgenthau, believed the State Department would oppose him, and, therefore, he wanted to bypass their obstructionism.[10]

Robert F. Kelley, who headed the Division of Eastern European Affairs and directed the Russian Section of the State Department during the twenties, was especially opposed to recognition and communism. His protégés, the so-called Riga Boys, were most notably George F. Kennan, Charles E. Bohlen, and Loy W. Henderson. To reemphasize, the Riga Axioms formulated by this group rested on the premise that Soviet behavior was grounded in Marxist ideology and sought world conquest, a position that gained credence because Kennan, Bohlen, Henderson, and others who were part of Kelley's Russian Section disliked and distrusted the Bolsheviks from the outset. Kelley's "bureaucratic genius" ensured an anti-Soviet bias.[11] On the eve of FDR's initiation of recognition talks, Kelley warned Undersecretary of State William Phillips of the "desirability of retaining in our hands one of the most effective weapons we have to obtain from the Soviet Government some measure of conciliation in reaching a solution of outstanding problems,—namely Government financial assistance, in the form of loans or credits, to facilitate American exports to Russia."[12] Assistant Secretary of State R. Walton Moore noted, "After eagerly seeking and obtaining recognition she becomes more indifferent to her obligations than theretofore."[13] As it turned out, ignoring such crucial advice proved deadly.

Though Secretary of State Cordell Hull cautiously favored recognition, his plan was to reach an understanding like Kelley's memorandum and in earlier writing on three questions—"no Soviet interference in our internal affairs; freedom of religion for Americans in Russia; and debt settlement" —before inviting Russian representatives to Washington.[14] Such a lengthy negotiation was not what FDR wanted. At first, working through Morgenthau, contact was made in August with Amtorg, the Soviet trading company. No one there wanted responsibility. As Morgenthau reported, the president asked, what about "bringing this whole Russian question into our front parlor instead of back in the kitchen?"[15] FDR's plan was to approach the Soviets through Boris E. Skvirsky, adviser to the Soviet mission in Washington, the unofficial embassy of the USSR. Now the president decided to bring William C. Bullitt into his scheme and have him contact Skvirsky, carrying out the negotiations directly under the president's supervision.[16]

Bullitt had been none other than Senator Henry Cabot Lodge's cat's paw in helping the Senate defeat President Wilson's Treaty of Versailles in 1919, thus throwing himself into the Democratic Party's political wilderness. Perhaps he had done this out of political spite in having his negotiations with Lenin in 1919 rejected by both Woodrow Wilson and Briton's prime minister, David Lloyd George. His anger at Wilson even led him to a coauthorship with Sigmund Freud of an unflattering study of Wilson's personality. Nonetheless, he cherished a chance to rejoin party politics in some big way. He had kept close to Col. Edward M. House, Wilson's adviser, as a means of reestablishing his ties to the liberal democratic wing of the party. Bullitt kept his deep interest in European affairs, and in the spring of 1932, sensing as Colonel House had that Democrats knew little about contemporary Europe, went on a fact-finding trip there. Both House and journalist Eugene Lyons had surmised that Bullitt, when he reached Moscow, was an unofficial representative for FDR. Russian officials were uncertain why Bullitt had come. After he returned to America, he hoped the colonel would put him in touch with Roosevelt. Nothing happened. Then he approached a common friend, Louis B. Wehle, FDR's Harvard companion and a prominent New York lawyer, who considered Bullitt one of the most knowledgeable experts on Europe. A meeting in Albany for October 5, 1932, was arranged. Roosevelt was pleased with Bullitt's report on European conditions. In early November, FDR wanted more information on the debt question and was willing to send Bullitt to Europe on his own recognizance, beginning his use of personal emissaries. Bullitt started corresponding with Wehle, who made these reports available to the president. Bullitt returned to America in mid-December 1932, after wining and dining with Ramsay MacDonald, Édouard Herriot, and others who renounced defaulting, though public opinion ran high in Europe for canceling the debt. The president gained vastly from Bullitt's personal diplomacy. After a Hyde Park meeting with Hoover's secretary of state, Henry L. Stimson, in January 1933, FDR again asked Bullitt to go to Europe, though press leaks vitiated Bullitt's efforts and he was accused of being a "Colonel House in disguise."[17] The publicity had helped Bullitt, and though he had wanted the French ambassadorship, he stepped out of the way for Jesse Straus, the president of Macy's and a longtime Roosevelt supporter. He was still without an official post, but FDR "enjoyed having ebullient, well-informed 'Bill Bullitt' around."[18]

In the end, it was Raymond Moley who got the "bad boy" of the Wilson administration into FDR's government as a special assistant to the secretary of state, thus not needing Senate approval. It has further been suggested that Bullitt was brought in to work on the recognition problem.[19] Roosevelt now turned to Bullitt to conduct the recognition negotiations, planning to have him first contact Skvirsky. Probably, FDR realized the Russians would interpret Bullitt's leadership in this endeavor as a positive sign.[20] With Hull scheduled for Pan-American talks in Montevideo, Roosevelt asked Bullitt to contact the Russians by getting together with Skvirsky, who relayed to the Soviet government the president's interest in opening negotiations. Roosevelt approved Bullitt's invitation, which was then sent in secret code after Skvirsky promised no public revelations if the Soviets disapproved. Moscow approved. The State Department, naturally, wanted a public invitation to go through it. The president preferred sending a letter directly to Soviet president Mikhail Kalinin. Whereas, on the one hand, Hull had stressed resolving issues on a lower level, on the other hand, Bullitt had pressed for dealing with the top Soviet bureaucracy. Bullitt won. The president's letter calculated that none other than Commissar for Foreign Affairs Maxim Litvinov would go to Washington.[21]

Roosevelt, judging his political support enough, formally began contact with Soviet Russia on October 10, 1933. He sent a letter to Kalinin, showing his wish to receive representatives to explore with them personally all questions outstanding between both countries.[22] Kalinin responded on October 17, telling Roosevelt he would gladly accept the president's proposal to send a representative of the Soviet government to the United States to discuss questions of interest standing between the two countries, "Mr. M. M. Litvinov, People's Commissar for Foreign Affairs, who will come to Washington at a time to be mutually agreed upon."[23] While the commissar traveled to Washington, the State Department conducted surveys of editorial opinion around the country. Undersecretary of State William Phillips reported, "Out of 300 papers there has been during the last thirty days comparatively little editorial comment on the subject." He went on to say that whereas the

Northeast did not "appear to be enthusiastically in favor of recognition, the majority of the Southern and Mid-Western States are in favor of recognition and that the Pacific Coast States are somewhat indifferent."[24] Personal negotiations between Litvinov and the president began on November 8, ending November 16, 1933, formally granting recognition and allowing FDR to avoid any kind of congressional approval whatsoever.

One document, the "gentleman's agreement," remained secret until 1945. In it, besides what had already been agreed to in the Hull-Kelley three-point memorandum and Bullitt's addition about retroactivity, the matter of the debt payment was considered. In this document, the word *loan* instead of *credit* was used. Afterward, Litvinov insisted the United States promised extending credits first, before any debts were paid. Bullitt countered otherwise, but to no use. As one historian on this subject remarked, "The United States Government, by its less than precise action, handed the Soviets a ready-made weapon to brandish in the dispute that followed."[25] Indeed, the entire tenor of the negotiations, as then suggested by Judge R. Walton Moore, assistant secretary of state, was that Litvinov always insisted on "unconditional recognition and then an effort to follow to remove all serious difficulties by negotiations."[26]

FDR appointed William C. Bullitt first ambassador to the USSR on November 17, 1933, the same day he announced recognition. When Bullitt presented his letters of credence to Mikhail Kalinin, the latter revealed the esteem in which the Soviet leadership held Bullitt: "The outstanding role which you personally, Mr. Ambassador, have played in the matter of mutual *rapprochement* of our two countries is well known to the wide public in the Union of Soviet Socialist Republics, and the very fact, therefore, that it was precisely you who were chosen by the President of the United States as the first Ambassador in the USSR, in itself is considered by us as an act of friendship."[27] Bullitt received a royal reception, being met at the railway station by representatives of Litvinov's office. An American flag draped the entrance of the Hotel Nationale in Moscow where he stayed. The ambassador joined the commissar for a private luncheon. At the Bolshoi, Bullitt's presence was announced, and he got a standing ovation. He dined with Marshal Klement Voroshilov, head of the Red Army, at the commander's Kremlin apartment, where they were joined by Molotov, Litvinov, and Stalin, who raised a toast: "To President Roosevelt, who in spite of the mute growls of the Fishes, dared to recognize the Soviet Union."[28]

In an amazing document, Bullitt recounted his sensational reception in the Soviet capital. He had, based on this document, been ridiculed as naive and susceptible to flattery.[29] Yet Bullitt's telling of his first few days in Russia, from December 11 to 21, displayed an acute awareness of what he could promise with assurance and where he had to stop, however much Stalin and company cajoled. They cajoled mightily. He could travel anywhere in the USSR and even with his own airplane. Any government information on economic and social statistics was available to him. Rubles would be exchanged at a fair rate for the U.S. diplomatic staff. Machine tools would be needed from the United States as well as 250,000 tons of steel rails. An "utmost intimacy" of information could be exchanged between America's and the USSR's military and naval men, if desired. Stalin said, "I want you to understand that if you want to see me at any time, day or night, you have only to let me know and I will see you at once." The dictator inquired, was there "anything at all in the Soviet Union that you want?" Bullitt asked for the "property on the bluff overlooking the Moscow River" as a U.S. Embassy site. Stalin replied, "You shall have it." Voroshilov asked for the presence of American military, naval, and air attachés in Moscow. Litvinov came close to asking for American permission for the USSR to join the League of Nations: he wondered "whether the Government of the United States would have any objection to the Soviet Government joining the League of Nations."[30]

Why was the Soviet leadership so forthcoming and, seemingly, compliant? There were two important reasons for which they were expecting, in Molotov's words, "the old friend" to deliver an immediate quid pro quo: chiefly, they were looking for quick American help in dealing with a perceived Japanese threat; second, they wanted large long-term credits. Even Bullitt noted, "It is difficult to exaggerate the cordiality with which I was received by all members of the Government including Kalinin, Molotov, Voroshilov and Stalin." Nevertheless, Bullitt was all hardheaded business: "I repeatedly emphasized to all with whom I talked that the United States had no intention whatsoever of getting into war with Japan but that our participation in any Far Eastern difficulties would be confined to the use of our moral influence to maintain peace." Even that they valued.[31] When Litvinov pressed Bullitt for nonaggression pacts involving the United States, the USSR, China, and Japan, the ambassador "explained to him the difficulties in the way of any such proposal." Litvinov then yielded by admitting, "Anything that could be done to make the Japanese believe that the United States was ready to cooperate with Russia, even though there might be no basis for the belief, would be valuable." Litvinov would settle for an American squadron or even a single warship to pay a visit to Vladivostok. Again, he got nowhere with Bullitt, who replied, "I could not answer that question, but would submit it to my Government."[32] So much for Roosevelt's man going to his friend the president and getting what the Soviets begged for, even if it meant FDR going over the heads of some strong public and congressional opinion.

Probably, the Soviets realized their number-one request was problematical. In addition, recognition might have sufficed anyway, with the special attention given to Bullitt. About the second issue, that of credits, they were not about to give in, however much Bullitt made demands on the issue of the "gentleman's agreement," which had suggested a $150 million repayment for Soviet debts and confiscations, especially given the deflation of the dollar's value due to the Great Depression. In fact, when Bullitt returned home after Litvinov's "tremendous reception" for him, the ambassador met in Washington with the first Soviet ambassador to the United States, Alexander A. Troyanovsky. In an "entirely informal discussion," Bullitt was candid: "I told Mr. Troyanovsky that I considered that a payment by the Soviet Government to the Government of the United States of $150,000,000 was an absolute minimum. I pointed out that the dollar had been devalued to 60 per cent of its former value and that $150,000,000, therefore, represented merely $90,000,000 at the old rate of exchange."[33] None of this hardheaded realism by Bullitt suggested a person easily taken in by Soviet flattery. Rather, the record of Bullitt's tenure as ambassador to the USSR displayed his willingness to sacrifice the flattery and shallow promises of Soviet leadership to get a fair resolution to the debt question.[34]

When Bullitt returned to Moscow in mid-March, he found an impasse. He explained to Cordell Hull that there were "several instances in which the Soviet Government does not seem disposed to carry out understandings between it and the Government of the United States." Litvinov objected to a fair rate of exchange on the purchase of rubles by the embassy staff for "necessary minor expenditures," the promised property on Lenin Hills for the new embassy would not be forthcoming, and, most important, Litvinov insisted, "he had agreed to payment of the Soviet debt only in return for a straight loan to be spent anywhere and not a commercial credit to be utilized in the United States."[35]

Bullitt decided these misunderstandings were the result of "inefficiency" rather than "bad faith," and from now, "understandings with the Soviet Government or representatives thereof should be made in writing or should be confirmed at a later date by a written document."[36] As Beatrice Farnsworth notes, Bullitt held his optimism. Differences could be worked out, as Bullitt told the secretary of state: "I derived the impression that if we maintain our position energetically and forcibly we shall be able to arrive at a solution in large measure satisfactory to us."[37] As Farnsworth points out, "In the months following, the form of payment—whether an outright loan or a credit—became the focus of dispute."[38] Litvinov had "expressed objection to almost every sentence of the draft."[39] He believed that if the debt were paid, every other government would demand payment, and that no government now was paying its war debts. The tone of the conversation was indicated by Bullitt's remark that Litvinov was "vehement in his objection to interest." He drew a clear distinction between "loans" and "credits." "Litvinov took the surprising position that he had not agreed to pay any extra interest or any credits whatever but only on loans to be given to his Government to be used for purchases anywhere." In fact, "Litvinov also objected to the fixing of 10 percent as the amount of additional interest."[40] Farnsworth infers that beyond a poorly worded agreement, Litvinov never expected to pay the debt because all European nations were defaulting.[41]

Nevertheless, 1934 was mostly a year of high hopes and deep disappointments for Bullitt and FDR. So was 1935, even though Bullitt had received Hull's warning that the Johnson bill had just passed the Senate that March and would go to the House of Representatives in April, where it passed in May.[42] As Hull noted, "It prohibits the purchase or sale in the United States of obligations hereafter issued any Government in debt default."[43] In early April, it looked as if Litvinov might settle on a long-term credit, not insisting on a loan. When the question of $100 million was brought up by Bullitt, it was countered by Litvinov, stating that the Kerensky government had "received almost none of the funds [that were used] for the support of themselves [Boris A. Bakhmetev and his treasurer, Sergei Ughet] and various armed attacks on the Soviet Government."[44] By April 7, things had turned nasty. Bullitt maintained that a State Department draft of April 7, calling for a payment of $150 million at 5 percent per annum, would be necessary to waive all claims before recognition. According to Bullitt, this elicited an "angry and adamant" reaction: "He refused to take the State Department draft as a basis of discussion either now or later alleging that it was in absolute contravention of his understanding with the President."[45]

Things seemed deadlocked with Bullitt writing Hull that the Soviets wanted to wriggle out of the problem and intimating they would try to avoid him and go straight to the president. Moore answered: FDR agreed with Bullitt. "We should await further suggestion as to debts which we believe may be expected. If and when that occurs, he may indicate some modifications he is willing to accept. He has entire confidence in you and you are at liberty in your own tactful way to intimate to Litvinoff how the relations of the two countries may be unfortunately affected by failure to agree."[46] Troyanovsky met with Moore and threatened to "go public." Moore cooled him down: "I told him that we are advised that Litvinoff has said that he has spoken his last word, whereupon he stated Litvinoff has cabled him that Bullitt has made a similar remark. Then he authorized me to inform Bullitt that Litvinoff will be very glad to resume the negotiations."[47] Both sides pulled away from the brink in early May. Bullitt begged to meet FDR in Hawaii. FDR put him off with the excuse that Ambassadors Joseph Grew and Nelson Johnson (Japan and China) would have to be invited, and it would have the look of a "Far Eastern Pacific conference and would create such a stir that there might be real discussion and speculation at a time when they want to avoid just that." He asked Bullitt to "write me the real low-down on what happens at your parties with the Russian foreign office at 3 A.M." Bullitt replied. He needed to "know your point of view on this Russian business, and I think it might be worth while for you to have a first hand report from me. I have a feeling that together we might be able to devise a method of settlement." Otherwise, he believed, the "so-called debt negotiations at the moment are hopeless."[48]

The deadlock went into August 1934. Discussions continued with Troyanovsky in Washington to no benefit. Bullitt tried to preserve cordial relations with Litvinov while, he told FDR, building a "backfire in the Kremlin by way of Voroshilov and [Lev] Karakhan." In the end, he believed, "we shall be able to beat down Litvinov's resistance. I do not expect any immediate results."[49] John Wiley, Bullitt's counselor and deputy from 1934 to 1935, wrote his boss on August 16. He did not care what policy was determined because it was a mistake to "waste everybody's time, patience, and good humor . . . to achieve the impossible."[50]

FDR asked R. Walton Moore to persist: "I see no reason why you should not go ahead . . . and try to bring the Russian matter to a conclusion."[51] This was a response to Troyanovsky's efforts to move along by seemingly accepting the $150 million debt and suggesting acceptance of credits.[52] There was no problem with fixing the debt, but Troyanovsky "demands from us an open credit of $1,000,000,000, payable in 20 years, which is equivalent to a straight loan. . . . We can only for the present let the matter ride."[53] Bullitt made an extra effort through Soviet journalist Karl Radek to Stalin, but matters remained the same. The State Department thought that enough concessions had already been made, and Hull stressed that a loan, that is, open credit, was not possible. Now, with Bullitt preparing to return for consultations, the matter, at that moment, seemed dead. At least, that was how Bullitt saw it: "The answer, I think, is that the Russians have had so much success lately that they are feeling exceedingly cocky." The prospects for the harvest were good. An eastern Locarno—small Eastern European countries bound to France by defensive treaties—seemed likely, or at least a French and Czechoslovak alliance to protect Russia's western front from Poland and Germany should the USSR be engaged in a war with Japan in the East. Japan would not attack in either the autumn or spring. By the following summer, the Red Army would be ready. "The maintenance of really friendly and intimate relations with us, therefore, seems to the Russians much less important than it did when Litvinov was in Washington." Only if either a Japanese attack seemed likely or a rapprochement between the United States and Japan occurred would Russia "discover that our demands with regard to debts and claims were most reasonable."[54]

As Bullitt prepared to return home on leave, he made some personal observations about the USSR. He remained upbeat and tried to show Russia's improvements since he first came in 1919. Then, Russia was a mass of starving people fighting the tyrannies of the past under the leadership of fanatics who had replaced Moses by Marx, Christ by Lenin, and Christianity by communism: "The Russia of 1934 still has no greater freedom than under the Czars. It is a nation ruled by fanatics who are ready to sacrifice themselves and everyone else for their religion of communism."[55]

In Bullitt's absence, John Wiley took over the Moscow embassy at a crucial moment. Bullitt had agreed with FDR to select members of his staff personally. Wiley had served him at the London Monetary and Economic Conference in 1933. By this time, Wiley had been stationed in eleven different diplomatic missions, including Warsaw and Berlin. So he was prepared for the calamity: the formal breakdown of the debts and claims negotiations that had taken place on January 31, 1935. In Hull's office, the secretary stated—in the presence of Moore, Kelley, Bullitt, and Troyanovsky—that "he was profoundly disappointed." The United States had gone to the limit to which it could and had made considerable concessions. Because of the position taken by the Soviet government, negotiations seemed to have ended. Troyanovsky agreed and said he had "no proposals to make." Hull announced on February 6 the withdrawal of the naval and air corps attachés, canceling of the consulate general, and reductions in the embassy's personnel.[56]

When diplomacy got to an impasse in 1935, FDR still called Bullitt his "Bill Buddha" and hoped Bill was not being ostracized in Moscow by information givers.[57] By March 1936, Bullitt had become bitter. He referred to Konstantin Oumansky, chief of the press section of Narkomindel (the People's Commissariat for International Affairs) from 1931 to 1936, soon to be counselor of the Soviet Embassy in the United States from 1936 to 1939, and Soviet ambassador from 1939 to 1941, as "that filthy little squirt." By April 1936, Bullitt already had his new assignment as U.S. ambassador to Paris.[58] Bullitt's parting remarks on dealing with the Soviet Union are contained in a series of dispatches from mid-1935 to spring 1936. These constituted his swan song about Stalin's Russia. They explained his frustration with the USSR, but they also were an analysis, embodying both the Riga Axioms and future Cold War thinking of presidents from Truman to Reagan. They reflected some of the same distortions as "Siberian" Kennan and the Riga Boys. Louis Fischer, the well-known pro-Soviet American journalist, had purposely leaked a forthcoming Soviet move to him, and Bullitt saw through it. The journalist told him that the "full congress of the Third

International should be held in Moscow at the end of July or the beginning of August." Would that, Fischer asked, "constitute a violation of Litvinov's pledge" about propaganda? Bullitt did not answer such a hypothetical question. To the ambassador's query, Secretary of State Hull replied that it did. Bullitt questioned Litvinov, who claimed both he and Stalin knew nothing of the Comintern's purpose for meeting in Moscow. Bullitt retorted, "You will have to tell that one to somebody else. You cannot expect me to believe that Stalin knows nothing about the Third International." Litvinov replied, "No, I assure you." Bullitt underlined that "our relations will be so gravely prejudiced that it is impossible to predict the consequences." Litvinov continued his line: "I know nothing about it." Bullitt cautioned Hull to expect any eventuality. With this, in a series of dispatches, Bullitt further speculated "with regard to the present and future policy of the Soviet Union."[59]

Bullitt's first dispatch, dated July 19, 1935, amounted to a pre–George F. Kennan "long telegram" analysis of Soviet foreign policy based on the Riga Axioms. Their overall aim, Bullitt claimed, was to "produce world revolution." Diplomatic relations with friendly nations was only an armistice, never ending in a definitive peace. It was a "happy respite" until the battle could be renewed on favorable terms. The job of the Foreign Office was to "maintain peace everywhere until the strength of the Soviet Union has been built up to such a point that it is entirely impregnable to attack and ready, if Stalin should desire, to intervene abroad." The USSR kept a "finger in every pie" and tried to prevent agreements between European states. It regarded a European war as inevitable, even ultimately desirable. Then, the Red Army would be strong enough to protect fledgling communist states. It hoped for a U.S. war with Japan, preventing simultaneous attacks on it from the East and the West. If a Pacific war followed, the USSR would avoid an alliance until Japan was defeated and then take Manchuria and Sovietize China.[60]

The second dispatch, dated August 21, 1935, counseled a restrained reaction—a model tip for later Cold Warriors—to Soviet provocation: holding the Seventh Comintern Congress in Moscow, with a prominent American contingent headed by Earl Russell Browder, secretary-general; Gil Green, Young Communist League chair; and William Foster, chairman of the Communist Party USA, all subsequently elected to the Comintern's Executive Committee. Bullitt believed the U.S. government was "juridically and morally justified" in severing relations; he cautioned against that action. It would be correct but "inordinately difficult" to restore. An official observation post was desirable for information, protecting Americans, and because "in this decade the Soviet Union either will be the center of attack from Europe and the Far East or will develop rapidly into one of the greatest forces in the world." America should not break relations. Nor should it make written or oral protests. It should explain the USSR's aims to Americans, severely restrict visas to Soviet citizens, and revoke exequaturs —recognition of Soviet consuls in the United States. The president, he recommended, should consider mentioning the nature of the original recognition agreements to unmask the Comintern's Trojan-horse activities forbidden by those agreements. Bullitt advised against withdrawing military attachés or reducing embassy staff. He cautioned FDR to be prepared: "Some sort of violent Soviet reprisal or replay is to be expected." This advice avoided confrontation. FDR did send a note of protest, warning that further infringements would end in serious results. A Soviet response denied any violations. Bullitt reemphasized, "Both the Soviet Government and the Communist International are merely different aspects of Stalin's mind and will." FDR had Hull issue a restatement in a note to the press, and the matter was dropped.[61]

Bullitt's final dispatches, on March 4 and April 20, 1936, dwelled on the nature of any Russian bureaucracies—czarist or commissarial—a description that closely paralleled "Siberian" Kennan's earlier remarks. Bullitt elaborated on how Americans should deal with this Soviet phoenix rising from czarist ashes. Though he called this an "accurate picture of life in Russia in the year 1936," his view was almost the same as that of Minister Neil S. Brown's remarks made in the years 1851–1853, and quoted verbatim by Bullitt, as he noted, except for "inconsequential omissions and for the fact that in three instances the word 'Empire' has been changed to 'Country' and in one instance the word 'Minister' has been changed to 'Ambassador.'"[62] Bullitt insisted it was what he could have and would have written without any changes.

Brown had cataloged Russian bureaucratic failures: secrecy, a distrustful Russian mind, especially "government officials," so ceremonial that nothing was done or things were delayed to oblivion. Russia was a rigorous police system with a state of siege mentality, and having absolute censorship, often capricious, eliminating financial information, the military, and politics from public discussion. Few foreigners were allowed into the country. This was because of a fear of foreign influence on the populace, and was a result of the plots of the antiforeigner party. Russians invented nothing mechanical and built only on borrowed capital; even in the arts, it mimicked foreign genius. No nation needed foreigners more, yet Russia was jealous of them. Even foreign legations were barely tolerated. Ministers and their staffs were "subjected to a system of espionage." Nothing was made public if worth knowing. Display was everything. Most of all, Russians had a "strange superstition that they were destined to conquer the world."[63]

Bullitt's last dispatch explained Stalin. The dictator supported democracies, in Bullitt's view, as a way of planting Trojan horses. If the Trojans came to power, their previous democratic friends would be shot. Bullitt restated what was the fundamental Riga Axiom: "The problem of relations with the Government of the Soviet Union is, therefore, a subordinate part of the problem presented by communism as a militant faith determined to produce world revolution and the 'liquidation,' (that is to say, murder), of all non-believers." Their tool was mass murder, and their beliefs were only to "the Caliph of that faith." They were agents of a foreign power, aiming to destroy liberty and in the process kill millions of Americans, if need be. The Soviet Union's economic power rapidly increased to become self-sufficient. Towns had improved, but not the countryside. All this could be maintained only in a police state: "Russia has always been a police state. It is a police state today." The authority of the Kremlin rested on the army, the vast secret police, and enthusiastic communists. Japan represented its greatest threat, because Germany still needed more preparation. The Soviet bureaucratic machine might break under war stress. Russians were bad bureaucrats; the communist state required exceptional ones.[64] The parallels between czarist and Bolshevik Russia were clear and hence, also, the distortions feeding American distrust from one regime to another.

Friendly relations could never be established with such a government. Relations had to be maintained because of Russia's importance as a Great Power, strategically found between Europe and the Far East. Valuable information could be obtained only by being there. U.S. policy should prevent war, especially if Russia were to win against Japan, and China were then to go communist. If the opposite occurred, China would be subjected to Japan. If war did result, the United States should negotiate so no one was a victor. In Europe, Franco-German hostility should be reconciled. With the USSR, trade should be encouraged, but by direct bargaining. It could be cut off at any moment, so the United States should give the Russians no loans or long-term credits. Their raw materials would increasingly compete, especially oil and grain, but their machinery still needed much improvement. The U.S. government had to know more about the Communist Party USA, that is, how it related to Soviet representatives. Patience was the key to dealing with the Soviet Union. It was still only a potential danger, thus the United States should not expect too much or despair, Bullitt recommended. Be steady toward the Soviet Union by always making the weight of U.S. influence felt, but never threatened. He finished, "Above all, we should guard the reputation of Americans for businesslike efficiency, sincerity, and straightforwardness." Honesty, not spying, was the best policy. It was disarming to them, especially since they knew so little about being honest.[65] No matter how much Bullitt blamed Litvinov for the misunderstandings and tried to thwart him, nothing came of it. Bullitt left Moscow in June 1936, never to return.[66]

Given previous suspicions about Bolshevism that had originated in the Wilson administration, the sixteen-year break in relations upheld by three Republican administrations, and then the rush to recognition, it is no wonder that possibilities for a full rapprochement were not great on both sides. Since the debt issue was an important consideration throughout, it was natural this issue would be a source of dispute. The failure to resolve it can be seen either as the first signal of FDR's gullibility when it came to Stalin and company or as an effort on FDR's part to give Stalin the benefit of the doubt in hopes of future successes. Bullitt indicated that dealing with Stalin was not the same as relations with the duke of Norfolk.[67] After all, the debt was not a strategic concern, as were Germany and Japan. If one follows this line of thought, it is easier to see why FDR and Bullitt eventually fell out, and why FDR was inclined toward his second ambassador to the USSR, Joseph Davies, however much the embassy experts thought him to be "incompetent."[68] It also goes a long way in explaining why those experts had quickly warmed over to Bullitt and remained hostile to his successor.

George F. Kennan, working in the new Moscow embassy, was clear. Bullitt, he said, became "embittered" over the Soviet attitude and soon favored the "hard line toward Moscow, a line which most of us in the embassy wholeheartedly supported but which FDR, caring little about the specific issues involved, had no intention whatsoever of adopting."[69] FDR blamed Bullitt for deteriorating relations. As far as the president was concerned, he "knew nothing about, or cared nothing for, what we had accomplished in building up the embassy at Moscow." Indeed, Kennan came to believe the Moscow ambassadorship, for FDR, was only "another political plum to be handed out in return for campaign contributions."[70]

Recent research proves that Bullitt nixed any deal short of a total diplomatic victory on this issue of a hard line rather than ingratiate himself either to the State Department or to Stalin.[71] Bullitt had become deeply anti-Soviet and sided with the East European Division of the State Department and its champion, Robert F. Kelley. Kelley's "Riga Boys," Loy Henderson, George F. Kennan, Charles Bohlen, and others, had helped to shape Bullitt's negative attitude toward Russia. More important, they influenced Secretary of State Cordell Hull and his second-in-command, Judge R. Walton Moore. Bullitt's opinions increasingly became part of the overall negative American attitude toward Russia.

It was now that FDR decided to purge the East European Division from the State Department. The point man to perform this was Undersecretary of State Sumner Welles, a favorite of the president and the first lady. Hull disliked Welles and hated Eleanor Roosevelt's interference, but it was a chance for the New Dealers to liberalize the State Department. Welles's views on Russia were closer to Kelley's than to FDR's. The administration itself was split into two warring camps on the Soviet Union. On the one side were Kelley and his Riga Boys; on the other were Davies, Welles, Eleanor, and the rest of the left-wing New Dealers. The latter group treated the Riga gang as "reactionary obstructionists," whereas the "Riga-ites" thought of the first lady and her coterie as naive amateurs. The intensity of the struggle peaked in the spring of 1937, and, in June, Welles finally liquidated the division. "He summoned Kelley and told him Eastern Europe no longer existed on the divisional charts of the department, that his job was being abolished, and that he was being transferred to Turkey."[72] This move pleased Davies, who would be busy trying to curry the favor of the Kremlin elite. Naturally, this initiative had to make Henderson uneasy as the chief remaining Riga-ite.

• • •

Roosevelt's second ambassador to the USSR, Joseph E. Davies, arrived in Moscow on January 19, 1937, more than six months after Bullitt had left. Davies was a successful corporation lawyer, an old friend of FDR's, and married to one of the wealthiest women in the world, Marjorie Post Hutton. With few exceptions, diplomats and historians have usually judged the ambassadorship of Davies as a flop and the man himself as a simpleton, knave, or worse. Those exceptions have cautiously credited Davies with following a line demanded by the administration itself: settlement of obligations was more important to the USSR than to the United States, and, therefore, any move to renegotiate was up to the Soviets; there was no hope at stopping Comintern activities; the annual trade treaty could be negotiated; and, last, the ambassador was to evaluate Soviet power, especially, military, economic, and political.[73] After his ambassadorship to Moscow, Davies played an important role in convincing FDR that the Red Army would withstand the Wehrmacht in 1941 and that Lend-Lease would allow Stalin to prevail over Hitler. Those years he spent in Moscow have remained tarnished in the literature as the portrait of a naive American: he was taken in by Soviet flattery, bought off with bargain-priced art, and deceived by the terror, purges, and show trials. These charges, though true to one degree or another, do not penetrate into the real substance of his book *Mission to Moscow*. "The President wanted to find out which side Moscow would support in the event of war between the Western democracies and fascist powers."[74] Why was Davies positively viewed by the public as well as FDR? The president "scratched four words" in his copy of Davies's book's cover: "This book will last."[75] This is because the notion of accommodation with

Russia had gone against the tide of American thought since "Siberian" Kennan's times but now seemed possible.

Three people who served as State Department professionals at the Moscow embassy have left caustic remarks about Ambassador Davies: Third Secretaries George F. Kennan and Charles E. Bohlen and the embassy's second secretary, Loy W. Henderson. Kennan remarked that Davies "drew from the first instant our distrust and dislike. . . . We doubted his seriousness [or] that he shared our own sense of the importance of the Soviet-American relationship [and] that his motives in accepting the post were personal and political and ulterior to any sense of the solemnity of the task itself."[76] According to Kennan, only American journalists in Moscow received his confidence. During the second purge trial, featuring Karl Radek in 1937, Kennan was reduced to fetching sandwiches for the ambassador while Davies exchanged "sententious judgments with the gentlemen of the press concerning the guilt of the victims [and] he placed considerable credence in the fantastic charges leveled at these unfortunate men."[77]

Charles E. Bohlen was less kind. Davies had, according to Bohlen, "gone to the Soviet Union sublimely ignorant of even the most elementary realities of the Soviet system and of its ideology."[78] He swallowed the Soviet line, never understood the purges, and accepted the Soviet version of a conspiracy against the state.[79] Of Davies's only embassy confidant, then military attaché Col. Philip R. Faymonville, Bohlen labeled him as having a "pro-Russian bias."[80] Referring to translating for Davies at the third and last Moscow show trial, Bohlen remarked, "I still blush when I think of some of the telegrams he sent to the State Department about the trial."[81] Bohlen had in mind the following, taken from Davies's March 17, 1938, dispatch to Secretary of State Cordell Hull: "It is my opinion so far as the political defendants are concerned sufficient crimes under Soviet law, among those charged in the indictment, were established by the proof and beyond a reasonable doubt to justify the verdict provided by Soviet criminal statutes."[82] Bohlen claimed that Davies called the trial dignified and "believed in the defendant's guilt."[83] Bohlen qualified this remark by saying that "Davies did express shock over the lack of protection of the defendants' rights."[84]

By 1938, with Kennan gone, Bohlen rose to senior Russian language officer in charge of political reporting. He noted that his tasks were made easier with Davies's departure to become ambassador to Belgium. Further reflecting on Davies, Bohlen remarked, "He was incurably optimistic in his reports to Washington, thereby misleading our government. His dispatches, while containing a good deal of information and shrewd observation, were almost always superficial and heavily slanted."[85] Finally, Bohlen commented on what he called the "incredible movie" of 1943, *Mission to Moscow*.

Two Soviet technicians "helped turn it into one of the most blatantly propagandistic pictures ever screened." He went on to say, "So crude was its propaganda that, even with the nation-wide sympathy for the Russian people, the film was a flop."[86]

The second secretary of the embassy, Loy W. Henderson, had a more balanced view of Davies and, for that matter, Col. Philip R. Faymonville, the embassy's pro-Soviet military attaché, than either Kennan or Bohlen. Faymonville was cool to Bullitt and enthusiastic to Davies. Davies's arrival, of course, had a "marked effect" on the work of the embassy.[87] This difference showed itself in Davies's reports, where he, as well as Faymonville, balanced criticism with "friendly explanations and rationalizations." Both were careful because they feared leaks.[88] Faymonville was known to have "won the confidence of the Soviet authorities and [Davies's friends] urged the ambassador to work closely with him."[89] One way or another, Soviet officials "never lost an opportunity to insinuate that the division [Division of East European Affairs] was primarily responsible for the sad state of American-Soviet relations."[90] They also believed that Davies sympathized with their attempts to buy an American battleship and could put in a good word for them.[91] Davies was, according to Henderson, acutely aware of "bygone campaigns [and was] careful not to enter into acrimonious discussions regarding the violation by the Soviet government of the various pledges."[92] This, he thought, was a wise move, especially with Comintern activities, debts, claims, and credits.[93]

Henderson thought that both Bullitt and Davies were bright and agreeable personalities who could speak and write compellingly. "Davies, however, unlike Bullitt, tended to admire men because they had succeeded in amassing enormous wealth or accumulating great power."[94] He was a practical individual and not concerned when top leaders fell out, or were toppled and killed. Henderson insisted he was attentive to his staff and looked to them for information. He kept within FDR's policy: "It was his intention to do his utmost to convince the Soviet leaders with whom he was to come into contact of his admiration for them, for their objectives, and for the good things that they were doing."[95] Here were the roots of FDR's accommodation policy. Because of this approach, Davies built up for himself —and perhaps FDR—a pro-Soviet reputation in the United States and the USSR.

To be pro-Soviet meant that Davies would have to explain away the purge trials and the terror. Though he did not shirk from the cruelties of the regime, he regarded Stalin with awe. As he exclaimed to Henderson, "I have seen him; I have finally had a talk with him; he is really a fine, upstanding, great man."[96] He was convinced that he had gained the confidence of Stalin and Molotov. This led him to reveal to Henderson that "the president had instructed him that his main mission in Moscow was to win the confidence of Stalin, to be able to talk over Soviet-American relations frankly and personally with Stalin, that he had been striving ever since his arrival in Moscow to carry out this mission, and that just on the eve of his departure he had finally succeeded."[97] Henderson interpreted this meeting as a chance for Stalin to urge Davies to get him the battleship.

Davies was shocked at the trial and execution of the officer corps, many of whom he had not only recently entertained but also given glowing reports of their work to the secretary of state. He worried, according to Henderson, that the picture of Stalin as a "benign, idealistic person that he had been trying to paint for the benefit of the president" might be marred. He defended Stalin: "He is generally considered to be a clean-living, modest, retiring, single-purposed man, with a one-track mind, devoted to communism and the elevation of the proletariat."[98] He did admit the justice system offered no protection for the accused and the rights of the individual. Davies was satisfied "beyond a reasonable doubt" the defendants were guilty of treason.[99]

Davies, following FDR's lead, believed the USSR would become an "extremely great power." He insisted the Soviet Union was friendlier to the United States than to any other nation, and he recommended, "It would appear unwise to change the present status or to consider the discontinuance of diplomatic relations except under some severe provocation." He finished, "There is no doubt of the sincerity and the friendliness of the U.S.S.R. toward the Government of the United States, in marked contrast to a greater degree than to any other nation."[100] Davies left the Soviet Union on June 11, 1938, to take the ambassadorship to Belgium, Europe's premier listening post. His successor, Laurence Steinhardt, did not assume his post until more than a year later when he presented his letters of credence to Kalinin. Meanwhile, chargé d'affaires Alexander Kirk ran the embassy between the tenures of Davies and that of Ambassador Steinhardt. Henderson left Russia on July 2, 1938. He remarked that any Soviet special attention that had been given to certain Americans was "not accompanied by any noticeable relaxation of Soviet practices. . . . Nor was it accompanied by any fundamental changes in the Soviet attitude toward problems that were disturbing American-Soviet relations."[101]

• • •

Alexander Kirk, brought to Moscow to replace Henderson as deputy chief of mission, arrived there in July 1938, and stayed until May 1939. He was transferred to Rome shortly after Ambassador Steinhardt took over. Kirk negotiated the commercial agreement of 1938, an annual affair. According to Henderson, the Moscow embassy never functioned better than under Kirk's experienced eyes. He was known for concise reports, discipline, and high standards.[102] There were two important features of Kirk's work: first, he combined with Stuart Grummon, the first secretary, and Bohlen to send a dispatch on November 25, 1938, clearly against the previous policy of Davies and, therefore, the administration itself: "It may be assumed that the Kremlin does not envisage cordial relations with capitalist governments on any permanent basis but rather as a temporary expedient."[103] Henderson commented, "There were still at the time many Americans in high positions and also many foreigners who thought they might be able to persuade the Soviet government to change its policies."[104] Also, Bohlen retained his embassy position and kept a secret contact in Germany's Moscow embassy in the person of Hans Heinrich Herwarth von Bittenfeld and knew of the coming of the Nazi-Soviet Pact as early as May 1939.[105]

Steinhardt, a lawyer and ardent FDR supporter, had previously served as minister or ambassador to six capitals, including those of Sweden and Peru. Henderson remarked, "There was little doubt that President Roosevelt had a tendency to prefer experienced 'political appointees' to professional Foreign Service officers." Steinhardt was an "energetic, shrewd ambassador who never hesitated to recommend to the department the policies that it should follow."[106] Though he did not speak Russian, he trained for the job, speaking with both Bullitt and Davies. He adopted an attitude of "friendly reserve" toward his Moscow duties, which meant avoiding "gushing flattery." Reciprocity was the key to his policy.[107] Fortunately, the new ambassador had the support of Bohlen, Llewellyn Thompson, Walter Thurston, Charles Thayer, and Angus Ward—with all but Thurston fluent in Russian.[108] Bohlen was apprehensive of Steinhardt, who "knew little of the Soviet Union," was a "smooth New York lawyer," and was "highly egocentric."[109]

Arriving only days before the Nazi invasion of Poland and the Soviet occupation of its eastern section, two problems needed Steinhardt's immediate attention: Americans trapped in Poland and U.S. shipping caught on the high seas by Germans and placed in neutral Soviet ports. He sent Ward to Lvov to solve the Polish problems and appealed to the Soviets to free the impounded American merchant vessel, *City of Flint*. In neither task was much achieved. Most shocking was the Soviet invasion of Finland, where Americans had sentimental attachments. The League of Nations expelled the USSR on December 14, 1939. Anti-Soviet feelings reached a climax, and FDR placed the USSR under a limited "moral embargo" by asking private enterprise to restrain commerce. Added to this was the list of strategic materials and items necessary to build up America's own defenses, like machine tools. Ambassador Konstantin Oumansky objected, to no benefit.

Many influential Americans demanded recalling the ambassador and severing relations. Steinhardt thought both motives to be idle gestures. Given the rising tide of anti-Russian feelings in America, Moscow became increasingly unpleasant. To this, Steinhardt recommended retaliation against Soviet diplomats in America, and FDR tried to comply, though not nearly at the level of a quid pro quo. FDR did stop the export of airplanes, aluminum, oil, technical information, and so forth. Steinhardt's job continued to be getting the ship and crew of the *City of Flint* released from the Soviet port. He felt the Soviet government conspired with Germany to protect their position and the German prize crew. Because of his pressure, the Russians finally complied.[110] Steinhardt was encouraged by stiffening American attitudes.[111]

The ambassador returned to the United States in August 1940 and was well received. U.S.-USSR relations had reached their lowest point: Soviet Russia had taken over the Baltic republics, defeated Finland, and seized parts of Romania and Poland. Molotov summed up the Russian-American friendship: "I shall not dwell on our relations with the United States if only for the reason that there is nothing good that can be said about them."[112] All that was to change dramatically.

FDR hoped that some small concessions might change or separate Russia from Germany. Hull claimed that he sought counsel for this decision. Secretary of War Henry L. Stimson also wanted credit for this change of course to "woo Russia a little."[113] Welles began to hold informal talks with Oumansky. He told the Russian ambassador that "it would be far more constructive and in the better interests of the peoples of the two countries for an effort to be made by both sides, including the Ambassador himself, not to spend time complaining and finding causes to contention."[114] This marked an important turning point. A series of conferences then began between Oumansky and Welles on August 1, 1940. Although Oumansky continued to complain, progress was made. Steinhardt was furious about these talks because they made his reciprocity policy impossible. He called it "appeasement."[115] Steinhardt's reason for his policy was, so it seemed to him, that Molotov's trip to Berlin in November 1940 had brought the two parties closer. That assumption proved mistaken. As the State Department gathered evidence that Hitler was planning to invade Russia, Steinhardt's false interpretation became clear. Hull, especially, pressed to give "less occasion for Soviet officials to feel unkindly toward this Government."[116] Steinhardt was urged to communicate to Molotov that Hitler was planning an attack, which he failed to do unless further instructions were received.[117] Hull and Welles both deferred to Steinhardt's judgment. By the spring of 1941, accommodation had halted. Nothing tangible had been gained, and Steinhardt's hard line was back in force.[118] Steinhardt's victory was short-lived.

Steinhardt had been, at first, convinced the Nazi-Soviet Pact would be long lasting. He changed his mind, but disliked any thawing in U.S.-USSR relations. He disapproved of warning the Soviets of an imminent German attack because they would dismiss this as information designed by the British to undo the Soviet-German relationship. That attack came on June 22, 1941, after repeated warnings by various and sundry—Winston Churchill, communist spy Richard Sorge, and even the German ambassador, Count Werner von der Schulenberg. Hull's reaction was to urge unrestricted aid.[119] Reciprocity was dropped as FDR agreed with Hull. Churchill promised all available aid to Russia. It was an extraordinary chance for Hitler's enemies. FDR wrote to Admiral William Leahy: "Now comes this Russian diversion. If it is more than just that it will mean the liberation of Europe from Nazi domination—and at the same time I do not think we need worry about any possibility of Russian domination."[120]

• • •

Former ambassador Davies claimed the honor of convincing FDR to aid Russia massively.[121] Whether Davies's opinions were crucial or not, Secretary of the Interior Harold Ickes reported that FDR realized it was time to risk helping Russia.[122] Now Harry Hopkins—FDR's alter ego, former Works Progress Administration head, and secretary of commerce—decisively entered the picture. On the eve of the Nazi "drive to the East," Hopkins's eyes caught a report by Gen. Raymond E. Lee, an American army observer in London. The general thought Germany's forces were like lava spewing out of a volcano's mouth, unstoppable at its source but at its farthest, cooling, slowing, stopping. Hopkins heard of Hitler's invasion of Soviet Russia on the night of June 21, Washington time, as he picked it up by shortwave radio. His first thoughts were that Lend-Lease aid to Britain had "paid off" by forcing Hitler to "turn left" and that "he [Hopkins] was instantly compelled to face a new and gigantic problem of aid to Russia" to stop the German "lava" at its farthest extent.[123] Secretary of War Henry L. Stimson as well as the general staff believed Russia would fall in one to three months. During this respite, the Atlantic theater should be strengthened in preparation for renewed German assaults. Britain agreed. Nazi foreign minister Joachim von Ribbentrop boasted, "Russia of Stalin will be erased from the map within eight weeks."[124]

Among the few cautiously optimistic voices were Prime Minister Winston Churchill; his minister of supply, Lord Max A. Beaverbrook; and his ambassador in Moscow, Sir Stafford Cripps. They supported "immediate and unstinted aid for the Soviet Union." Churchill reassured Britain of his consistent opposition to communism: "All this fades away before the spectacle which is now unfolding [and he pledged] all possible help to Russia and the Russian people."[125] Various people urged FDR to do likewise. Herbert Bayard Swope, editor of the *New York World*, pointed out America's opposition to communism yet the need to preserve unity: "We are not for Communism, but we are against all that Hitler stands for."[126] Former ambassador Joseph E. Davies sent Hopkins a memorandum two weeks after Hitler's invasion of Russia. He predicted a tougher Soviet resistance to Hitler than military experts had, even if Moscow, Belarus, and the Ukraine fell. Given timely Allied aid plus Russian determination, Stalin could even win. Davies warned that Hitler might "induce Stalin to consent to an arrangement."[127] After all, he continued, "Stalin is oriental, coldly realistic and getting along in years. It is not impossible that he might again even 'fall' for Hitler's peace and the lesser of two evils."[128] As far as Stalin was concerned, capitalist enemies surrounded Russia. Stalin would pull Allied "chestnuts out of the fire" if they would not be hostile to him after the war. However, "Stalin could find some assurance that regardless of ideological differences the Administration is disinterestedly and without prejudice desirous of aiding them to defeat Hitler."[129] Davies argued that it was not the Soviet intent to project communism to the United States or Europe after the war, nor was it even possible. Davies advocated, "Word ought to be gotten to Stalin direct that our attitude is 'all out' to beat Hitler and that our historic policy of friendliness to Russia still exists."[130]

To study the "respite" granted the British by the Nazi invasion of the USSR, Hopkins set out for Prestwick, Scotland, on July 13, 1941, going straight to Churchill to discuss the new situation and make plans for the forthcoming Atlantic Conference. Britain was becoming a fortress with all manner of Lend-Lease aid and American missions. FDR had appointed Hopkins as an adviser and assistant on Lend-Lease, though Hopkins never had the title of administrator. Yet that was his role for a little more than a year since it had passed Congress. The war in Russia was in its fourth week when Hopkins arrived at Chequers, Churchill's country residence. The Nazi-Soviet war was being followed minutely, and there appeared a faint twinkle in Churchill's eye that the Russians might last the winter. Britain and Russia had already signed an "agreement for joint action [to] render each other assistance and support of all kinds [and that] neither party would negotiate or conclude an armistice or treaty of peace except by mutual agreement." Even so, Stalin seemed unimpressed by British promises.[131]

Meeting at No. 10 Downing Street, Hopkins heard Gen. James E. Chaney mention that the war in the Middle East and the expected invasion of Britain all depended on "how soon the Russians collapsed." Every calculation seemed based on that assumption.[132] The longer Russia held out, the more time would be gained to building up British defenses. Hopkins saw that the scheduled Atlantic Conference, targeted for early August, required detailed knowledge of Russia's situation. No one, even the British military men in Moscow, knew. "Since all deliberations on all phases of the war at that time, including American production and Lend Lease, depended on the question of how long Russia could hold out, Hopkins decided that he should make a quick trip to Moscow and try to get an answer to that question from Stalin himself."[133] Churchill agreed. Hopkins cabled the president on July 25: "Am wondering whether you think it important and useful . . . to make certain the Russians maintain a permanent front. . . . If Stalin could in any way be influenced at a critical time . . . through a personal envoy. I think the stakes are so great that it should be done. Stalin would then know in an unmistakable way that we mean business on a long term supply job."[134] It was unlikely that they had discussed such a trip previously: "Hopkins himself conceived the idea for the trip very suddenly and acted on it immediately."[135] FDR replied on July 26: "Welles and I highly approve Moscow trip and assume you would go in a few days. . . . I will send you a message for Stalin."[136] That cable gave FDR's "authorization for one of the most extraordinarily important and valuable missions of the whole war."[137] Churchill said, "Tell [Stalin] that Britain has but one ambition today, but one desire—to crush Hitler. Tell him he can depend on us."[138] FDR personally wrote to Stalin, "Mr. Hopkins is in Moscow at my request for discussions with you personally . . . on the vitally important question of how we can most expeditiously and effectively make available the assistance which the United States can render to your country. . . . I ask that you treat Mr. Hopkins with the identical confidence you would feel if you were talking directly to me."[139]

On July 28, Hopkins left for Moscow via a PBY Catalina (flying boat) to Archangel, arriving on July 30 in Moscow. Steinhardt took him to meet Stalin at 6:30 P.M. In Hopkins's six hours of conversations with Stalin, plus added talks with Molotov and others, "he had gained far more information about Russia's strength and prospects than had ever been vouchsafed to any outsider. Stalin had certainly taken Roosevelt's request to heart and had reposed complete confidence in Hopkins, and Hopkins for his part left the Kremlin with the profound conviction that Stalin was not talking through his or anyone else's hat. This was indeed the turning point in the wartime relations of Britain and the United States with the Soviet Union."[140]

At the first meeting, Hopkins underlined the need of the anti-Hitlerite coalition's unity, while Stalin stressed the "minimum moral standard" by which nations coexist and said the "'present leaders of Germany knew no such minimum moral standard and that, therefore, they represented an anti-social force in the present world.'"[141] Stalin concluded by noting that the views of the United States, Britain, and Russia coincided. Hopkins proceeded to the questions of urgent short-term and long-term aid, in which Stalin emphasized antiaircraft, machine guns, and aluminum.[142]

On the second day, July 31, Hopkins met with British ambassador Sir Stafford Cripps, Steinhardt, and Molotov, and again at 6:30 P.M. with Stalin. Hopkins made ample notes of this last meeting with the Soviet dictator. In that report, divided into three sections, Stalin first gave a detailed analysis of the current military situation and the urgent needs of the USSR, highlighting antiaircraft guns, aluminum for plane manufacture, rifles, and machine guns. Second, for the long haul, heavy munitions were requested, and he spoke of holding a conference of leaders. The third part, which Hopkins marked for the president only, Stalin "spoke bluntly of the desirability of U.S. entry into the war against Germany."[143]

Steinhardt, no Soviet enthusiast, even remarked with some astonishment that Hopkins was "received promptly by Stalin who granted him very extensive interviews and discussed with a frankness unparalleled in my knowledge in recent Soviet history the subject of his mission and the Soviet position."[144] Hopkins himself evaluated his trip: "Joseph Stalin knew what he wanted, knew what Russia wanted, and he assumed that you knew."[145] According to biographer and playwright Robert E. Sherwood, one of FDR's speechwriters and chief of the overseas branch of the Office of Wartime Information, "Hopkins was a sincere and even aggressive friend of Russia and an intense admirer of Russia's gigantic contribution to the winning of the war. He had nothing but contempt for those jittery Americans who were forever looking for Communists under the bed."[146] Hopkins feared a system that "concentrated such absolute power in one mortal man." He also suspected that "Stalin's power was not so absolute as he had at first imagined." This was because Hopkins suspected the Politburo was "an unseen, incomprehensible and unpredictable but potent influence on Stalin and thus on all Allied long-term policy."[147]

Hopkins left Moscow on August 1, 1941, and the next day he joined Churchill on the great British battleship *Prince of Wales*. The two sailed across the North Atlantic for the rendezvous with Roosevelt at Placentia Bay and their drawing up of the Atlantic Charter. In a sense, Stalin now also had a seat at the table, and Americans again began to view Russia as they had for much of the nineteenth century and during World War I, in a positive light. It was now up to FDR to make good on Hopkins's promises to Stalin. More than that, he saw a chance for lasting accommodation in place of the prevailing fear Americans had specifically for communism and for Russia in general. It was risky, but FDR was a consummate risk taker. The twenty-first century seems ready for such a bold American.

5

Chums

There is a cartoon of Averell Harriman, FDR's friend and Lend-Lease administrator for Britain, and Prime Minister Winston Churchill's confidant and press baron, Lord Max A. Beaverbrook, parachuting into the Kremlin in September 1941. They were following up on the Hopkins mission that promised Western aid to Stalin. It was barely three months after the Nazi invasion had begun on June 22, with German armies poised for a final assault on Moscow. It provides a kind of paradigm for some of the New Dealers who dealt with the USSR: they began enthusiastically and later turned negative. This appeared to be Harriman's first Russian encounter as part of the Harriman-Beaverbrook Mission to ascertain Russian military needs with the Lend-Lease program. However, he had had two earlier business ventures in the 1920s and 1930s. One was with the Soviet Georgian Manganese Company concession from 1925 to 1928, entailing a trip to the USSR in 1926. The other was with the Soviet Russian Finance and Construction Corporation during the 1930s. But the Harriman-Beaverbrook Mission of 1941 initiated a sustained Russian encounter with Soviet leaders, especially during his ambassadorship from 1943 to 1946. All of his Soviet ventures started relatively well but ended in Harriman's discouragement: in 1941, Stalin's predicament was dangerous and American resources potentially vast. As Winston Churchill once remarked over the question of an early mounting of a second front that bringing a "no" to the Kremlin, or something short of Stalin's full request, was "like carrying a large lump of ice to the North Pole."[1] Harriman was not cheered by that prospect, nor was the president, who feared becoming the iceman. As Harriman later said of the previous mission led by Harry Hopkins in July, "There was no alternative and nothing was lost in attempting to support Russia, and a tremendous gain might result if our aid proved effective."[2] Only Stalin's necessity and FDR's willingness had made U.S.-USSR accommodation possible. From the beginning, it was a marriage of convenience.

Harriman and Beaverbrook met Stalin the evening of their arrival, September 28, 1941. Konstantin A. Oumansky was to translate. At Harriman's insistence, Maxim Litvinov served as translator—Harriman did not like Soviet Russia's ambassador to the United States, but he had met Litvinov in 1926 and felt confident in him. The only ones present in their three interviews with Stalin were Molotov, Litvinov, Beaverbrook, and Harriman. Stalin disliked the American and British ambassadors, Laurence A. Steinhardt and Sir Stafford Cripps. Neither was invited. Since they and their staffs were omitted, that created problems. As Harriman noted, "The fact that we did not take our respective missions with us caused me some difficulty, particularly with Admiral William Standley, who had been chief of naval operations, and felt his dignity was slighted."[3] Steinhardt, he recalled, was cordial, though Harriman had little confidence in him and Hopkins had already suggested his recall.

Harriman was anxious to get the job done. He realized the Germans were only a few miles away, though damage from bombing was insignificant, especially compared with London. Moscow itself had changed from his last visit in 1926. Avenues were wider, there were more apartment houses, though shoddy, and automobiles were now on the streets. Things had advanced from "raggedness" to "shoddiness," including the drabness of the people.

About the negotiations, there was a feeling that Stalin held great suspicion toward them, and both embassies believed the Russian war was all but over. Harriman was impressed by Hopkins's optimism and disgusted with Cripps and the American Embassy. Harriman remarked, "It was my job to do a job and I didn't expect to get much help from those who were there and depended very much on the mission that came, who were all substantially in the attitude I was in." In dealing with the Russians, the general view was that one had to "buy the horse twice."[4]

At nine o'clock on the evening of their arrival, Harriman and Beaverbrook were driven directly to the Kremlin and went straight to Stalin's office, where large pictures of Marx, Engels, and Lenin were hanging. Stalin did the talking through Litvinov's translations; Molotov was silent. With notable frankness, Stalin outlined the military situation, disguising nothing. Moscow had to be held. Hitler's mistake, Stalin contended, was in opening three fronts instead of driving straight to Moscow, the nerve center of operations. He spoke of the "tragic cost of the surprise attack" in detail.[5] His needs from America and Britain were significant, especially tanks and armor plate. Immediately, he wanted four thousand tons of barbed wire a month. Past midnight, the first meeting broke up on a positive note of friendly cooperation. As Harriman put it, "There was in the history of the talks, the first evening was marked by frankness on the part of Stalin in stating his position and the expectance of us to be of assistance."[6]

The second meeting on the following evening was quite the opposite: "He seemed to have in mind that the smallness of our offers meant that we wanted the Soviet regime to be destroyed by Hitler."[7] Because Stalin was blunt, that made it possible for Harriman to be just as blunt. Only once did Stalin show any interest in what was being offered. When Harriman suggested giving him five thousand jeeps, they were snapped up. Harriman was unclear whether the nastiness was old-fashioned Russian horse trading, an effort to smoke them out, or that Stalin's associates thought the offers were inadequate. Despite the unpleasantness, Harriman asked for a third meeting.

Then it was all straightforward business, at which Harriman excelled. A list of seventy items the Russians wanted was methodically scrutinized. Stalin added a request for eight to ten thousand trucks a month, noting this was a war of motors and the side with the largest number would win. Beaverbrook, sensing the changed atmosphere, asked whether Stalin was satisfied. The dictator smiled. With the business of aid settled, the conversation turned to larger questions. Harriman, knowing FDR's wishes and intentions, urged Stalin to gain a personal relationship with both Roosevelt and Churchill. Beaverbrook suggested an invitation for Churchill to visit Moscow. The only difficulty arose when Stalin proposed a protocol of the agreements. Though Harriman had no authority to sign anything, a general protocol was arranged. Harriman optimistically assumed that "if personal relations were maintained with Stalin, the suspicion that has existed between the Soviet Government and our two governments might well be eradicated."[8] Harriman noted, "Personal relationships could influence —even if they could not determine—the affairs of nations."[9] Certainly, this was FDR's attitude.

At a final banquet, Harriman had a chance further to gauge the tone of Stalin and Russia. Stalin insisted that it was the former British prime minister Neville Chamberlain's blundering hostility that forced the Nazi-Soviet Pact. Otherwise, a three-way pact with Russia, France, and Britain might have prevented war. In response to Harriman's question about the current military situation, Stalin said Leningrad would withstand the attack, as would the Crimea. The danger was in the Ukraine. He taunted them about an immediate second front.[10] Harriman and Beaverbrook returned home on October 3, 1941. Stalin had left a strong impression on the American envoy as a man of great simplicity and directness who spoke his mind candidly.

Ambassadors Steinhardt and Cripps were ordered to leave Moscow with the diplomatic corps on October 8, 1941. Steinhardt's replacement came as a second thought—a surprise. Adm. William H. Standley had retired from the navy shortly after his sixty-fourth birthday on January 1, 1937, as chief of naval operations (CNO). For a short while, he had done odd jobs for the New York World's Fair, the Electric Boat Company, and the government's Office of Production Management. In September 1941, his successor as CNO, Adm. Harold R. Stark, asked him to escort the Harriman-Beaverbrook Mission to Moscow with the rank of minister in meetings with Soviet naval officers. His job, as with the rest of the mission, was, "in Mr. Harriman's words, 'Give and give and give, with no expectation of any return, with no thought of a *quid pro quo*.' "[11] At three o'clock on October 1, 1941, the First Confidential Protocol between the United States, USSR, and Britain was signed by Harriman, Lord Beaverbrook, and Molotov.[12] Shipments of aid would be to one billion dollars and financed by Lend-Lease, with no interest charged and payments on the principal to begin five years after the war and continued for ten years. Col. Philip R. Faymonville, the former Moscow embassy's military attaché to Ambassador Joseph Davies, was "spot-promoted" to brigadier general and left in Moscow at Hopkins's request as the representative for Lend-Lease aid.

• • •

By early November 1941, Steinhardt had resigned, and Standley accepted the post of ambassador in late February 1942. The new ambassador approached his assignment with misplaced optimism.[13] Standley met Molotov quickly. Stalin kept him waiting about twelve days. Meanwhile, the State Department revoked the authority given to him in Washington: "Under no circumstances, should you take up with Marshal Stalin or Mr. Molotov any of the matters discussed with you prior to your departure from Washington. If either of them brings up those subjects, act as if you have no knowledge of them."[14] Those matters, as the admiral recounted, consisted of the "whole scope of my briefing"—releasing Polish officers, permission for Siberian flights, coordinating intelligence, improving radio communications, releasing U.S. pilots interned in Siberia after bombing runs over Japan, and improving the exchange of technical information. Standley objected. Washington failed to reply. He ignored the suggestion. It was another bad omen because the salty ambassador resented being bypassed. The first such incident was the secrecy surrounding FDR's asking Stalin to send Molotov to Washington, if FDR and Stalin were unable to meet personally. Further annoyances were NKVD (People's Commissariat of Internal Affairs) surveillance and the inability to meet with ordinary citizens.

Standley finally got an audience with Stalin. Beginning with the usual formalities, Standley communicated FDR's wish to meet personally with Stalin the following summer in Alaska or Siberia. Stalin hoped it would happen. The ambassador apologized for the delays in Lend-Lease and mentioned certain obstacles to further cooperation: the need for an air shuttle from Basra to Moscow or Alaska to Siberia. Stalin suggested Greenland to Iceland to Murmansk. Finally, Standley asked that Soviet technicians in the United States be given greater authority. Stalin replied that they bought faulty equipment. Exchange of technical plans got nowhere. The same was true with reverse Lend-Lease, especially raw materials. Here Stalin objected that American contractors did not want Soviet orders. He also brought up the lack of American convoying, which piqued the admiral. Stalin complained about landing U.S. flyers in Siberia and the necessary internment of them to avoid trouble with Japan. The first interview ended. It was the best one Standley ever had. Usually, he spoke with Molotov. Standley wished for "a new and more personalized diplomacy [but] was beginning to realize how naïve I had been."[15]

FDR's personal diplomacy remained the biggest bane to the admiral. Timidity got him nowhere with the Soviets. Standing up to them did. Nevertheless, Standley realized, "Special representative after Big Dignitary come to Russia, leapfrog over my top-hatted head, and follow out the Rooseveltian policy—do not antagonize the Russians, give them everything they want, for, after all, they are killing Germans, they are fighting our battles for us."[16] Even except for unending supplies delivered on time, no matter whatever the difficulty and losses incurred, particularly from German planes and subs operating along the Murmansk route, the top Soviet demand and priority was the second front. To this end, FDR had invited Molotov to Washington in the spring of 1942. The ambassador was not privy to any of this. He was told that Molotov was to negotiate the Second Protocol for Lend-Lease. His real purpose was not revealed: to arrange the second front for 1942.[17] Standley got news of this from a BBC broadcast. Molotov was jubilant, as were the Russian people.

Standley cautioned the State Department. Churchill and Harriman finally came to Moscow to tell Stalin that "there would be no 'Second Front' in France in 1942."[18] Rather than code SLEDGEHAMMER for the second front, there would be GYMNAST, a North African operation. During the four-day visit of the prime minister, Standley was completely left out. Churchill explained the change: "To every statement, Mr. Stalin took exception with undiplomatic bluntness that was almost insulting"—so the admiral learned. By the second day, even TORCH, the final code name for the North African landing, initially exciting Stalin, now turned sour. Molotov called it ambiguous. Stalin's aide-mémoire conveyed deep disappointment because "the refusal . . . inflicts a mortal blow to the whole of the Soviet public opinion . . . and complicates the situation of the Red Army at the front and prejudices the plan of the Soviet Command." Harriman blamed the second day's freeze on the Politburo, not Stalin. As the iceman,

Churchill took a tongue-lashing. In the end, Stalin had to accept it. He was powerless to change it.[19]

Neither Standley nor Col. Joseph Michella, his military attaché, could get any information from newly promoted general Philip Faymonville, now the Lend-Lease representative and later head of the U.S supply mission to Russia. Both Moscow and Washington thwarted the admiral, who disliked Roosevelt's desire to appease the Russians. Standley was angered that the United States never got any credit for its aid. Faymonville refused to play ball with the embassy's staff. When the ambassador reported home, in October 1942, he demanded of Gen. James H. Burns and Hopkins that something be done about Faymonville: "If I return to Moscow as Ambassador," he said, "you'll have to put him under my control. I can't have him running wild around Moscow the way he has been." He concluded, "They [Burns and Hopkins] excused themselves hurriedly and walked away."[20] While in D.C., he complained directly to FDR: "Stop acting like a Santa Claus, Chief [and] let's get something from Stalin in return." Reciprocity was needed. He turned to Hopkins and faulted the system, not Faymonville. Then he moaned about the Republican former presidential candidate Wendell Willkie's Russian junket and all the special deals he made while working without him: "[Willkie] went around me or over my head, his deprecatory remarks before important Russians, and his general disregard and contempt for the office of the Ambassador."[21] FDR said he would do something. Hopkins remained silent. The admiral waited in D.C. for some decisive action. Finally, he visited Hopkins in his office-bedroom in the White House in early December. When Hopkins asked about Standley's return to Moscow, the admiral said, "That depends on you, Harry." He went on: "The President directed that orders be issued to General Faymonville to report to me for duty. I have been informed by Mr. Stettinius that *you* are the only person in Washington who can issue such orders. When those orders have been issued, I will leave for Moscow."[22] Hopkins gave in. Faymonville still always found ways around these orders.[23]

Soon after Standley's return to Moscow, he removed his office from Kuibyshev to Moscow. By then, Stalingrad was liberated. The ambassador loudly complained to reporters, "The Russian authorities seem to want to cover up the fact that they are receiving outside help. Apparently they want their people to believe that the Red Army is fighting this war alone." When told the remark was not off the record, the reporters jumped at the chance to dispatch that comment home. It caused an uproar in American newspapers. Russian officialdom and pro-Soviet supporters in the United States called for his scalp. It was the beginning of the end for Standley's ambassadorship.[24]

Standley had flown in the face of FDR's Russian policy, detailed clearly in a memo of Gen. James H. Burns dated December 1, 1942. As Burns explained, if successful against the Nazis, the USSR would be one of the three most powerful nations. It was urgent that "we should be real friends [and that] Soviet relationships are the most important to us of all countries" except Britain and would give help to defeating Japan after Germany's defeat. Burns's credo, reflecting Hopkins and FDR, was to be generous, not lavish, and loyal, giving easy credits and formulating a peace that would "meet Russia's legitimate concerns."[25] With Burns in Russia in April 1943, avoiding the ambassador and working over his head with Faymonville doing as he pleased, the admiral resigned. In his letter to FDR on April 27, 1943, he asked to be returned to the United States by early October. Between his resignation and actual departure, former ambassador Joseph Davies came again as a special presidential representative. It was the same embarrassment to the ambassador, as with Willkie, all over again. Standley had by now become persona non grata with both Stalin and FDR by the fall of 1943. At the same time, Stalin recalled Ambassadors Ivan Maisky from London and Maxim Litvinov from D.C. A low point had been reached.[26]

The president again held out for Davies to retake the ambassadorship to Moscow. Davies's doctor claimed a Moscow winter would kill him. Hull recommended Harriman, who finally accepted. Harriman was still optimistic about getting along with Stalin. He considered Soviet policy nationalistic, emphasizing security and postwar reconstruction. Besides, he believed Russia's territorial ambitions could be balanced both by its inability to digest Eastern Europe and by its need for a major place in the emerging family of nations. Russia, he then believed, needed U.S. aid in its postwar reconstruction. Harriman wrote Hull, "We cannot . . . assume too much. The essential quality of our relations with the Russians is still patience and forbearance."[27] He thought it was essential to include the Russians in the next military conference, but he reported to the president that "certain doubts which some people have had regarding Soviet intentions are now laid to rest [but also] the character of certain real difficulties that exist has been more sharply defined."[28] On the upside, the Soviets had accepted the Four Power Declaration (adopted at the Moscow Conference of Foreign Ministers of the United States, United Kingdom, USSR, [and China adhering] in October 1943), the Atlantic Charter, the terms of unconditional surrender of the Axis as determined by a European Advisory Commission, and to separate Austria and Germany, but the Polish and Finnish problems remained. It seemed to Harriman, at the start of his ambassadorship, that there was more or less agreement on treating Germany, Russia's western borders, and Iran. Charles Bohlen, then chief of the Russian Desk at the State Department, stressed the West's tacit approval: "The Soviet Union alone would determine its relations with the states bordering on its western frontier." The future of these nations could give rise to misunderstandings.[29]

With all of these forebodings, Harriman presented his credentials to Mikhail Kalinin on October 23, 1943. He had reached Moscow on the eighteenth with his daughter Kathy, Secretary of State Cordell Hull, and Gen. John R. Deane, the new military attaché, Faymonville's replacement. He confided to Molotov that he was empowered to discuss both diplomatic as well as military supply questions, ending for good the Faymonville problem.[30] He told Hull that the United States should promise less rather than more and to allow the embassy wide discretionary powers. Admiral Standley might have approved these new arrangements. Harriman served for two years and three months. During that time, as his daughter said, "Life here at Spaso [the U.S. ambassador's residence] functions at an ever increasing tempo. Ave has almost nightly excursions to the Kremlin, the last one at two a.m., but he's bearing up well."[31]

The first business of Harriman's ambassadorship was to facilitate Hull at the Moscow Foreign Ministers' Conference of October 1943, at which the secretary of state spent sixteen days. Stalin had, initially, proposed the conference as a preparation for the first meeting with FDR and Churchill. Hull's objective was to get the so-called Four Power Declaration, called the Declaration on General Security, accepted and signed. It provided for postwar peace and security, joint action on the surrender and disarmament of enemies, establishment of the United Nations, and arms control in the postwar period. The Russians swallowed this but were not keen on including the Chinese as a signatory with Great Power status. Hull was unable to get Molotov to agree to one further provision: "not to employ their forces within the territories of other states except for the purposes envisaged in this Declaration and after joint consultation and agreement." Molotov objected that the USSR would not give its allies a veto power over its armies in Eastern Europe. "Molotov was willing to *consult* but not to wait for Allied *agreement.*" The Allies had done the same for Italy. As with Hull's insistence on China, Molotov pressed for the second front.[32]

Harriman insisted on giving the Russians a full picture of the entire Western effort, Asian and European, including the plan for OVERLORD, the final code name for the cross-Channel invasion scheduled for 1944. Besides, Harriman's military attaché, General Deane, asked for shuttle bombing—land, refuel, reload, and return—from the USSR, exchanged weather and signal communications, and increased transport flights. The Soviets agreed to all "in principle," though shuttle bombing took until February to initiate. When Molotov referred to Harriman as a tough bargainer, the ambassador replied, "I have come as a friend." Molotov answered, "I intended my remarks to be complimentary." Hull and Harriman called on Stalin, October 25, to offer a Big Three meeting at Teheran. Stalin finally accepted on November 10, 1943. As Harriman cabled FDR, "Plan to remain in Teheran 36 hours, which would give reasonable opportunity for two 3-cornered meetings and for you to see U. J. [Uncle Joe] alone as well." FDR responded to Stalin, "I have therefore decided to go to Tehran as it is of vital importance that you and Mr. Churchill and I should meet. . . . The whole world is watching."[33] Yet Harriman warned FDR about two persistent problems—Germany and Poland. About the former, Russian aims were much tougher, especially about reparations. Concerning the latter, Russia assumed acceptance of the 1941 borders. Stalin was hostile to the Polish government-in-exile. He would take unilateral actions if necessary, and he was determined to avoid any cordon sanitaire. Roosevelt was forewarned and, presumably, forearmed.[34]

Harriman, a neighbor of the Roosevelt's Hyde Park home and longtime friend, probably had as good a fix as anyone on FDR's views toward Soviet Russia and Stalin:

> Now Roosevelt—I can't tell you the exact cut of his mind on when and how he thought the Russians would develop into a more friendly relationship. I think he was thoroughly alive to the fact that they hadn't kept their agreements that they'd made with him, and when he recognized that he was quite bitter about it. . . . [H]e had a singleness of purpose on two sides—one was the war, and he also had a singleness of purpose to do everything he could to try to come to an understanding with Stalin to break down the suspicions that existed and to develop a basis on which the three powers could work together for peace.[35]

About Harry Hopkins, Harriman had this evaluation of giving the Russians everything they wanted: "It was Hopkins' interpretation, because I think that Hopkins believed it so sincerely that he erred on the side of generosity rather than the side of restraint. I think that if Hopkins had been a little tougher, Roosevelt's policy could've erred in detail a little tougher than he was. But . . . I think Hopkins had an influence on that because he so thoroughly agreed with the President's policies."[36] And so it was that Harriman himself followed this line of FDR's. Shortly after FDR's death in early April 1945, even Harriman reconsidered.

• • •

In this spirit, one of accommodation, the president's party left for Teheran from the Cairo meeting with Chiang Kai-shek and Churchill on November 27, 1943. In that first meeting between FDR and Stalin, they got along "famously," as Harriman recollected. The "unlikely partnership between the New York Brahmin and the Georgian Bolshevik" began.[37] Bohlen, who translated for FDR, records that the first words of the president were "I am glad to see you. I have tried for a long time to bring this about."[38] About the subjects discussed at the first meeting, Bohlen's account is the best: the situation on the Russian front; China and Stalin's negative view of Chiang Kai-shek; Syria over Gen. Charles de Gaulle's provisional government there; and both FDR's and Stalin's hostility toward the French general and France, with FDR suggesting a UN trusteeship for Indochina and no Frenchmen participating in a reestablished French government if they had acted in Pétain's (Vichy) government; and agreement not to discuss India. Finally, the Western Allies would make good on their decision at Quebec in the summer of 1943 to "invade France in the spring of 1944." Bohlen's remarks are critical of FDR's comment that the "best solution" for India would be reform from the bottom, on the Soviet line. Bohlen refers to this as a "Soviet method" and as a "striking example of Roosevelt's ignorance about the Soviet Union. He undoubtedly viewed the Bolshevik coup d'etat as a genuine revolution. He did not realize that the Bolsheviks were a minority who seized power during a period of anarchy. The revolution came after the Bolsheviks and not on the demands of the majority of the Russian people."[39]

Harriman, though not present at this first private meeting, remarked that FDR "raised the possibility of giving some portion of the American and British excess merchant fleets to Russia at the war's end." This would be a fine thing, Stalin thought, not only for the Soviet Union but also for the United States and Britain because the Western powers could get a plentiful supply of raw materials in exchange.[40] One author concluded, "Both of legendary charm when they wished to be, Stalin's fondness for Roosevelt was as genuine a diplomatic friendship as he ever managed with any imperialist."[41]

At four o'clock on November 28, 1943, the first plenary session of the Big Three began. FDR presided and proceeded to review the Pacific theater and then turned to the central issue—code OVERLORD for invading northern France for the following spring. Stalin praised Allied successes and proposed Red Army help. FDR asked Stalin about possible Aegean or Adriatic operations, if Turkey entered the war. Stalin replied, "He doubted that neutral Turkey could be brought into the war." The way to get at the heart of Germany, Stalin insisted, was through France.[42] It was unwise to scatter the effort. FDR suggested their military staffs work out a plan for invading southern France as a divisionary movement. Stalin complained that his military staff was not at Teheran, only Voroshilov. Churchill still preferred a Mediterranean operation first. He was outvoted. "Roosevelt winked at Stalin, the start of his gauche flirtation that enhanced the Marshal's position as arbiter of the Grand Alliance."[43] On this wink, the first session ended.

Harriman began to notice that the "Russians were enjoying the unaccustomed informality of their new relationship with Western leaders."[44] Stalin had spotted Hopkins, walked across the room, and shook his hand warmly. At a steak and baked potato dinner hosted by FDR, Stalin again complained about the French, whose ruling class was "rotten to the core." It was "positively dangerous to leave them in possession of their former empire." De Gaulle "acted as though he was the head of a great power." Although Stalin questioned the wisdom of unconditional surrender because it might strengthen German resistance, he favored "dismemberment and the harshest possible treatment to prevent the recrudescence of German militarism."[45] When Churchill raised the Polish question, Stalin shoved it aside by saying that only the Polish frontier should be moved to the Oder River and the USSR should keep the lands up to the Curzon line.

Stalin called on FDR the afternoon of November 29. FDR brought up the shuttle-bombing plan for both Europe and Japan. Stalin said he would consider it. Roosevelt then laid out his plan for a general world organization, consisting of a world assembly, an executive committee, and a third component made up of what he called the Four Policemen—Russia, the United States, Britain, and China. Stalin had doubts and preferred two separate organizations—one for Europe, another for Asia. About Europe, FDR intimated that in any future European war, it would be up to the British and Russians to supply armies, whereas the United States would send only ships and planes.[46] It was also before the second plenary session that Churchill presented Stalin with a sword from King George VI in celebration of the Russian victory at Stalingrad.[47]

Shortly afterward, the second plenary session began on November 29. Gen. Sir Alan Brooke, the British chief of staff, and his American counterpart, Gen. George C. Marshall, explained OVERLORD. FDR commented that no commander was as yet picked. Churchill continued refusing a date for the operation. Stalin "got to his feet and turning to Molotov and Voroshilov, said, 'Let's not waste our time here. We've got plenty to do at the front.' Roosevelt managed to pour unction on troubled waters."[48] Bohlen, on the other hand, reported that Stalin said, "I don't care if it is the 1st, 15th, or 20th, but a definite date is important." Bohlen added that Stalin leaned forward and wanted to ask an "indiscreet question," with his words coming out in an almost matter-of-fact tone: "He never showed any agitation and rarely gestured." Stalin said, "Do the British really believe in Overlord, or are you only saying so to reassure the Russians?"[49] Churchill assured Stalin the conditions agreed to at the Moscow Foreign Ministers' Conference would be met.

Stalin hosted the second night's banquet. The evening passed after some ironic jokes about executing German officers. Bohlen mentioned that Hopkins saw Churchill and told him to lay off on extending the date of OVERLORD. The next morning, November 30, the British agreed to May, and Stalin then announced the Red Army would open a simultaneous offensive. As Bohlen noted, "I was not privy to Roosevelt's talks with Hopkins or with Harriman. But at that time Roosevelt was relying more and more on Hopkins, virtually to the exclusion of others. At Teheran, Hopkins's influence was paramount."[50]

On the morning of November 30, FDR and Churchill met privately with Stalin and the combined chiefs of staff made their plans. At a luncheon, FDR announced the combined chiefs' recommendation: "We will launch Overlord during May, in conjunction with a supporting operation against the south of France on the largest scale that is permitted by the landing craft available at that time." That satisfied Stalin.[51] FDR added that the commander would be named in three or four days. That evening, they celebrated Churchill's sixty-ninth birthday. Britain would relax the Montreaux Convention and allow Russia's naval and merchant ships free access through the Dardanelles, as well as opening the Baltic and the Kiel Canal to all. In the Far East, Dairen would be made a free port. At the dinner, Stalin paid an extraordinary tribute to FDR and the Americans. FDR returned the compliments.

On December 1, at a luncheon hosted by FDR, Churchill pleaded for Soviet leniency toward Finland. Afterward, in a private Stalin and FDR meeting before the final third plenary session, FDR excused himself from discussing the Polish question by pointing out that it would be a touchy issue in the upcoming elections. Though sensitive to the question of the Baltic states, FDR jokingly remarked that the United States would not go to war with the USSR over their independence. Stalin mentioned that instead of an international organization, the UN should be regional. The final plenary session took place that evening. Again, the Polish question arose, and both FDR and Churchill urged Stalin to negotiate with the London Poles. Stalin accepted the Curzon line in exchange for the northern section of East Prussia. FDR presented a dismemberment plan of five separate states for Germany whereas Churchill's had three, and Stalin, not thinking much of either, preferred FDR's plan. Stalin refused any Danubian confederation. Finally, the Big Three signed a brief document guaranteeing Iran's status and a three-power declaration. In it they committed themselves to a peaceful world, free of "tyranny and slavery, oppression and intolerance." It concluded: "We leave here, friends in fact, in spirit and in purpose." Bohlen remarked that the conference "was in an optimistic mood and took off in good spirits for the flight to Cairo."[52]

Bohlen referred to the Teheran Conference as the most successful of the wartime meetings of the Big Three. FDR's message to Stalin of December 3, 1943, confirmed Bohlen's assessment: "I consider the conference to have been a great success, and it was an historic event, I feel sure, in the assurance not only of our ability to wage war together but also to work for the peace to come in utmost harmony."[53] Stalin responded similarly. On December 7, Harriman was able to deliver to Molotov the message that may have erased any lingering Russian doubts—Gen. Dwight D. Eisenhower's appointment to command OVERLORD. Harriman noted what he called an almost "revolutionary change" in the Russian media toward the Western Allies, citing the "historic decisions" of Teheran daily.[54] From then until the next Big Three meeting at Yalta, the year 1944 had its own set of difficulties.

Harriman came home in the spring of 1944 for consultations. By then, he had begun to grow wary of the huge Soviet requests that Hopkins supported. Amid all of this, Stalin remained intransigent on Poland. He would not budge off the Curzon line, failed to relieve the Warsaw uprising, and set up the Lublin committee as the Polish Provisional Government, the so-called Polish Committee for National Liberation. All these things led Harriman to believe Stalin had wanted all along to "establish a Russian sphere of influence extending through Eastern Europe and the Balkans."[55] It was only on September 9, after the Germans had subdued most of the Warsaw uprising, that Stalin helped. Though FDR had made it clear that Churchill's October visit to Moscow did not speak for him, the prime minister had made his "notorious" spheres of influence proposal.[56]

Stalin went to the British Embassy for dinner and in a toast to the absent FDR noted that "he doubted whether Germany could have been defeated without the full weight of the United States on the side of the Allies."[57] There were, however, other items of hope. The Allies had landed in France in June, liberated Paris, and made good progress to the Rhine. Stalin had committed himself to help win the war with Japan three months after Germany's defeat. By December 27, FDR had sent word that he would meet with Stalin and Churchill at Yalta early in 1945. Even Molotov looked forward to a six billion–dollar reconstruction loan from the United States as a long-term credit with no payments during the first nine years. The credit stumbling block of the 1930s, it seemed, had been overcome. The year 1944 had been a mixture of hot and cold running diplomacy in FDR's efforts at accommodation. The litmus test for FDR's accommodation policy now hinged on the success of the Big Three at Yalta and the good health and strength of FDR to make it stick. The president reached Malta, during his trip to the Crimea, on Friday morning, February 2, 1945. He had less than ten weeks to live.[58]

• • •

Whereas the "Riga Axioms" were defined and supported by the institutional base of Russian specialists within the State Department, the so-called Yalta Axioms were more amorphous and lacked an institutional basis. Beyond the president himself and his closest advisers, they had no enthusiastic cheering section. Relying on public opinion could be dicey. Furthermore, the president's Russian policy had determined critics or, at the very least, mildly querulous foes. The Riga Boys, though some were excluded from FDR's diplomatic exile, remained opposed, with the notable exception of Chip Bohlen, who translated for FDR at Teheran and Yalta. Robert Kelley cooled his heels in Ankara, Loy Henderson in Baghdad, and George Kennan in Lisbon. William Bullitt, a Riga convert, warned FDR that Stalin would successfully communize Europe in the wake of Hitler's defeat.[59]

By 1943, according to historian Daniel Yergin, FDR had developed his "grand design." Yalta was to be its verification. The Yalta Axioms rested on accommodating the Soviet Union, but in a realistic way. The basis of "working with" instead of "against" the USSR rested on the "factor of power," within a new world organization. The United Nations would have an upper chamber, or Security Council, consisting of the Great Powers, or Four Policemen—the United States, Great Britain, Soviet Russia, and China (or five with France)—which, acting in concert, would be called on to maintain the peace through force, if necessary. This line of analysis, designating FDR as a realist in contrast to Wilson's idealism, led to understanding the Yalta Conference primarily as gaining Russia's UN adherence along Rooseveltian lines. All remaining issues were of secondary importance to FDR. That is, the Polish and German questions, which occupied most of the time, were of lesser value to FDR. Commentators, both eyewitnesses and others, subtracted the Japanese issue because it was not formally discussed at Yalta and had been informally agreed to previously. Nevertheless, it was also part of FDR's accommodation. He had to give in to Russian requests of a pre–Portsmouth Treaty of 1905 territorial arrangement for Russia, if he was to get Stalin's acquiescence to the UN as well as his participation in the war against Japan. A quid pro quo linked the two issues.

The remaining Yalta Axioms boiled down to treating the USSR as a conventional Great Power, rather than an essentially ideological phenomenon with its own Marxian world plan for domination through the Comintern (dissolved in May 1943). The Riga Axioms had called for avoiding Soviet diplomatic relations. The Yalta Axioms required accommodation through an intimate partnership of personal diplomacy at the highest levels of summitry. FDR recognized that Stalin made the crucial decisions. It was essential to talk directly to him. His approval alone was necessary if anything substantive was to be accomplished. Russia would behave as a Great Power within its own sphere of influence and not as an ideologically driven empire. FDR believed the so-called break of the 1917 Russian Revolution was closing, that is, the gap between communist East and capitalist West was narrowing.[60]

Since summitry also consisted of FDR's personal charm and abilities, the essence of the Yalta Axioms rested on his health, his mental and physical abilities at Yalta to carry out his agenda. Eyewitness accounts of the Yalta negotiations, though they often varied in emphasis, generally agreed FDR was physically well enough and mentally awake to be an effective leader of the conference, one who ably occupied the middle ground while successfully blending the two wings of the negotiations—Churchill and Stalin. The three major British participants—Prime Minister Winston Churchill, his secretary of state for foreign affairs, Anthony Eden, and the Permanent Undersecretary of State for Foreign Affairs Sir Alexander Cadogan—were sometimes skeptical. Churchill made only one direct reference to FDR's health. At the very end of the conference, during the final dinner hosted by the prime minister, he mentioned that the president "seemed very tired."[61] Otherwise, Churchill drew a presidential portrait of an actively engaged person. Eden commented while still at Malta, "President vague and loose and ineffective." He went on to say, "I do not believe that the President's declining health altered his judgment, though his handling of the Conference was less sure than it might have been." He concluded by mentioning, "For those who attributed Roosevelt's decisions to illness, it must be remembered that though the work of the Conference was strenuous enough to keep a man even of Churchill's energy occupied, Roosevelt found time to negotiate in secret, and without informing his British colleague or his Chinese ally, an agreement with Stalin to cover the Far East." That document, Eden believed, was a "discreditable by-product of the Conference."[62]

Cadogan's remarks were negative toward everyone except Stalin. When he first saw FDR at Yalta on February 6, 1945, he wrote in his diary, "He looks rather better than when I last saw him. But I think he is woollier than ever." He further remarked, "The Great Men don't know what they're talking about and have to be educated, and made a bit more tidy in their methods." He criticized Churchill concerning the proposed UN. "I was terrified of what the P.M. might say, as he doesn't know a *thing* about it—he has always refused to look at it—and here he was plunging into debate." As to FDR, "The President has certainly aged." On the eighth, he referred to Churchill as a "silly old man" and accused FDR of having "flapped about." Stalin was a "great man" who showed up "very impressively against the background of the other two ageing statesmen." As to FDR, "The President in particular is very wooly and wobbly. Lord Moran says there's no doubt which of the three will go first." And he was very negative toward Secretary of State Edward Stettinius.[63]

Americans close to FDR made mention of his health. James F. Byrnes, director of war mobilization, noticed while the party was still on the USS *Quincy* heading for Malta, "I was disturbed by his appearance. I feared his illness was not due entirely to a cold."[64] Shortly after their return to Washington, Byrnes remarked how Gen. Lucius D. Clay was "shocked at his appearance." Byrnes excused himself because "I did not realize, as Clay did, the change in his appearance."[65] Adm. William D. Leahy marveled at the president's memory.[66] He handled the "frequent arguments between Churchill and Stalin with great skill."[67] For FDR's health, the admiral wrote about how badly FDR looked in certain official photos: "When these photos were developed and brought to our attention, I heard the only serious comment about Roosevelt's health made by our group during the entire Yalta Conference. There was one photograph in particular in which some of our party thought he looked very ill. He did not appear that way to me. I thought it was simply a poor photograph and that members of our party were unduly alarmed."[68] He evaluated FDR's overall performance at Yalta: "It was my feeling that Roosevelt had conducted the Crimean Conference with great skill and that his personality had dominated the discussions. Since he was the presiding officer, and most of the arguments were between Stalin and Churchill, he played the role of arbiter at many of the daily sessions. The president looked fatigued as we left, but so did we all."[69]

Secretary of State Edward R. Stettinius Jr., who had replaced the aging Hull, reflected on FDR's health and purposes because they were so closely intertwined with the importance of the president's personal diplomacy. The secretary put it this way before the conference as to what FDR confided to him: "If he and the Prime Minister could sit around a conference table again with Marshal Stalin, not only would the war be brought to a speedier conclusion, but plans could also be laid to solve these problems [Poland, Germany, and the UN] and to create the basis for an enduring peace."[70] Stettinius declared, "It was not that President Roosevelt believed that he had a hypnotic influence or that he had a liking for personal diplomacy, but his attitude was based on the solid fact that it was only Marshal Stalin who could make decisions."[71] Stettinius went on to say that FDR had no "illusions" about the Russians, that he fully understood the "dangers and difficulties" in dealing with them.[72] He did have "hopes," but FDR understood the difference: "He did not have the illusion, as his enemies have charged, that world peace could be achieved easily or by appeasing the Soviet Union."[73] And, like Leahy, Stettinius was impressed with FDR's grasp of details.[74] To allay the overly suspicious Russians, FDR was careful to keep them well informed.[75]

Stettinius had noticed that at FDR's inauguration, "It seemed to me that some kind of deterioration in the President's health had taken place between the middle of December and the inauguration on January 20." He emphasized that "at all times from Malta through the Crimean Conference and the Alexandria meeting I always found him to be mentally alert and fully capable of dealing with each situation as it developed. The stories that his health took a turn for the worse either on the way to Yalta or at the Conference are, to the best of my knowledge, without foundation." His ability to deal fully and equally with Churchill and Stalin was the "best answer to these stories."[76] Later, Stettinius added, "Throughout this give-and-take [referring to the UN discussions], his mind functioned with clarity and conciseness, furnishing excellent proof that he was alert and in full command of his faculties."[77] FDR exercised leadership during the conference, as well as being the arbiter and chief conciliator. FDR's ultimate goals were to "maintain the unity of the three Great Powers, to defeat Germany, and then to get them all around a table to work out a world organization."[78] Stettinius maintained, "The pace of the Conference was grueling and by this time [February 10] the President naturally showed fatigue. However, he continued to explain the American position skillfully and distinctly, and he also served as a moderating influence when the discussions became heated."[79]

As to the content of the conference itself, Bohlen, FDR's speechwriter Robert E. Sherwood, and Stettinius gave good accounts. On Saturday, February 3, 1945, FDR and Churchill arrived at the Saki Air Force Base in the Crimea. Stalin got in on Sunday morning. He and Molotov made a personal call on the president at the Livadia palace at four o'clock. According to Chip Bohlen, FDR's translator, they "greeted each other as old friends, and in a sense they were. . . . Smiling broadly, the president grasped Stalin by the hand and shook it warmly. Stalin, his face cracked in one of his rare, if slight, smiles, expressed pleasure at seeing the President again."[80] After discussing the military situation, they both spoke negatively of de Gaulle and the possibility of a French zone in occupied Germany, to be carved out of the British and U.S. zones. At five, they met in the grand ballroom for the first plenary session.

Though weary, FDR presided, while his closest confidant, Harry Hopkins, remained in bed. Hopkins was to lose eighteen pounds while at the conference. The entire three hours were devoted to the eastern and western fronts as reported by the military experts. It should be noted that the eight-day conference had no orderly organization, or fully approved stenographic report. Instead, "issues were brought up, discussed, then shunted off to the Foreign Ministers or military chiefs or just dropped for a few hours." Nevertheless, there were plenary sessions each day at four o'clock and daily morning and afternoon sessions of the diplomatic and military chiefs.[81]

At the first plenary session, on Sunday, February 4, Stalin suggested that Roosevelt should again preside. FDR acted as both arbiter and conciliator. The Big Three and their staffs reviewed the military situation: General A. I. Antonov for the USSR and Gen. George C. Marshall for Britain and the United States, with Sir Charles Portal explaining the air war and Adm. Sir Andrew B. Cunningham detailing the U-boat threat. Churchill once again suggested a Balkan expedition for the Allies, but his proposal was dropped.[82]

Roosevelt hosted a Russian-style dinner, and, as Bohlen reported, "very good humor" prevailed. During informal conversations, the rights of small nations in the UN were discussed. "Stalin had already made known his views that the three big powers, which had borne the brunt of the war, should bear the responsibilities of the peace, and that he was opposed to giving the smaller powers any rights that could in any way contradict the wishes of any great power."[83] In general, there were such moments of "irritation and bitterness" throughout, but the "over-all mood of good feeling continued right to the last dinner, given by Stalin." Even so, Bohlen remarked, "Yalta is undoubtedly the most controversial conference in United States history."[84] Stalin paid an exceptional compliment to FDR: "There was a third man, Roosevelt 'whose country had not been seriously threatened with invasions, but through perhaps a broader conception of national interest, and even though his country was not directly imperiled, had been the chief forger of the instrument which had led to the mobilization of the world against Hitler.'—a reference to Lend-Lease."[85]

The second day, Monday, February 5, the foreign secretaries met for lunch at the Koreis Villa, formerly Count Yusuopov's palace, where Stalin's delegation stayed. Molotov emphasized the Soviet expectations of German reparations, a topic argued back and forth throughout the conference. He also spoke of long-term credits from the United States. The second plenary session met at four o'clock, and Hopkins attended this and the rest of the sessions. It was now that the conferees got serious. Stalin mentioned that he did not object to a French zone in occupied Germany if it were carved out of the U.S. and British zones, thus leaving the Russian zone as constituted. He remained opposed to the French participating in the Allied Control Commission for Germany. At first, FDR agreed with Stalin against the British. Yet at the close of the plenary, FDR was converted, and later concluded that the French should be given a seat on the Control Commission. "At this point, Stalin raised his arms above his head and said, 'Sdaiyous,' which means 'I surrender.'" As Bohlen remarked, "One of the results of Stalin's acceptance was to reinforce Roosevelt's idea that he had great personal influence on the dictator."[86] Stalin wanted to know if occupation zones also meant Germany's ultimate dismemberment, and if Germany was divided, what kind of government each part would have. This would all have to be part of the terms of unconditional surrender. Furthermore, Stalin raised the question of reparations. All agreed to dismemberment, but the details were to be worked out by the foreign secretaries. The surrender terms would not detail this. As to reparations, Russia's ambassador to Britain, Ivan M. Maisky, suggested both in-kind and yearly payments, of which the Soviet Union would receive ten billion dollars of the total. Arguments over Germany's ability to repay ensued, and the whole matter was referred to a reparations commission representing only the Big Three.[87]

At the third plenary session, on Tuesday, February 6, both Churchill and FDR appealed to Stalin's "generosity" concerning Poland. Stalin remained adamant. Roosevelt, though he feared a breach, persisted, suggesting in a letter to Stalin that representative Polish leaders meet then and there to form an interim government and pledge to free elections at the earliest moment. He also reassured Stalin that the United States would "never lend its support in any way to any provisional government in Poland that would be inimical to your interests."[88] The Big Three signed a communiqué avoiding the word *dismemberment,* but decided to include it in the surrender document. It was also at this plenary that Secretary of State Stettinius detailed FDR's plans for a world organization, beginning with voting, and leaning on what had been accomplished at the Dumbarton Oaks Conference the previous August 21 to September 27, 1944: the structure, procedures—especially voting—and aim of preserving world peace and security. The argument over how many votes the USSR should have in the UN Assembly finally, by the end of the conference, boiled down to three, that is, including Byelorussia and Ukraine. The veto had yet to be decided.

At the fourth plenary session, on Wednesday, February 7, Stalin rejected FDR's letter pleading for Poland, in which the president told Stalin he was determined to avoid a breach. Stalin presented a Soviet plan in which the seeds of a compromise appeared. According to this, the Lublin committee would add members of democratic émigré circles and hold free elections as soon as possible. These leaders would be invited to form an interim government of national unity in Moscow. As to the so-called free elections, nothing was mentioned of Allied supervision. Nevertheless, Bohlen concluded: "I do not presume to know what was going on in Roosevelt's mind, but from what he said at Yalta and from his actions there, I feel that he did everything he could to help the Poles."[89] Actually, the Russians pretty well won out on this issue, as the Lublin committee, with some additions from abroad and within Poland, became the "Polish Provisional Government of National Unity." Also at the fourth session, it was decided to give Byelorussia and Ukraine each an assembly vote in the UN and allow France into the Allied Control Commission, as well as that the UN should convene at the earliest moment, April 25, in San Francisco. The voting formula, as it were, included the question of the veto, already drafted at Dumbarton Oaks, to be exercised by the four, or five, if France were included on the UN's council. As to French participation on the Control Commission, Harriman privately conveyed to Stalin FDR's change of mind on the subject, and the marshal "said that since this was the President's decision he would go along with it."[90] On February 10, Stalin signed the Declaration on Liberated Europe, without any argument. The declaration said that there would be consultation among the Big Three regarding the development of democracy in liberated countries.[91]

The fifth plenary session was held on February 8, 1945. Before the plenary, Stalin came to FDR's study for a military discussion and asked about voting in the UN Assembly. The president had agreed to two additional votes for the Soviet Union. As to the military, certain airfields near Budapest were agreed to for Allied bombers. At the plenary, FDR announced his agreement to the additional votes for the USSR. The Big Three accepted the idea that only Associated Nations who declared war on the Axis should be invited to the opening session of the UN. The deadline for doing so was set at March 1, 1945. Also, the borders of the new Poland were discussed, with much of the Curzon line being accepted in the East and the western border to be determined by the foreign ministers after further study.[92]

The sixth plenary, on Friday, February 9, agreed on the Polish formula of including Poles from outside and inside that country to reorganize into the Provisional Government of National Unity, and to hold free and unfettered elections as soon as practicable. It also agreed that German reparations would be about twenty billion dollars, with ten billion, or 50 percent, going to Russia. As to whether trusteeships could be invited to the UN, it would later be considered. Churchill was particularly vexed over this and hotly defended the British Empire. A Declaration on Liberated Europe was adopted that referred strictly to the Atlantic Charter as not applying to the British Empire. The question of war criminals was touched on as well as the military situation.[93]

On Saturday, February 10, the seventh, and last, plenary session was held. Final drafts on reparations and one on Poland were submitted. No sum was mentioned in the former, and the western border of Poland was to be determined later.[94]

Finally, with Churchill absenting himself but signing it, FDR and Stalin came to agreement that the USSR would enter the war against Japan within one to three months after Hitler was defeated. Besides, earlier on February 8, they had settled what was in it for Russia: the southern half of Sakhalin, the Kurile Islands, joint running of the Manchurian and South Manchurian railroads with China, the leasing of Port Arthur, and the internationalization of the port of Dairen. In these arrangements, China was not consulted until later.

Bohlen, who was present throughout and did all of FDR's translating, came to the following conclusion: "Regardless of what was said or not said, written or not written, agreed to or not agreed to at the Yalta Conference, there was nothing that could have prevented the breakup of the victorious coalition and the onset of the Cold War once Stalin set his course." This apparently simple view might be hard to endorse if it had been stated by almost anyone other than a man with the credentials of Bohlen himself.[95] Nevertheless, Bohlen absolves the United States from any responsibility for the Cold War with that remark. Yet American negativism was certainly a contributing factor.

• • •

It was in the first postwar years when mutual alienation between the USSR and the United States renewed. Politicians regarded the U.S. monopoly on atomic weapons as a trump card, capable of guaranteeing to the United States safety in its growing opposition to a former ally. President Truman concluded every meeting on matters of military strategy with the appeal, "We should maintain our superiority." Truman's secretary of state, Dean Acheson, later commented, "A decade and a half later a school of academic criticism has concluded that we overreacted to Stalin, which in turn caused him to overreact to policies of the United States." By then, Moscow had become a dark and sinister place in Stalin's last years. That overreaction marked a watershed in the Cold War.[96]

Both Moscow and Washington may have missed a slim chance to end the Cold War after Stalin's death and avoid wasting enormous resources for three and a half decades. Whatever peace offerings the Kremlin presented, the White House was not buying. President Dwight Eisenhower and Secretary of State John Foster Dulles believed Premier Georgii Malenkov's "peace offensive" was a ruse to wreck Western unity. Malenkov's two statements, made on March 9 and March 15, 1953, shortly after Stalin's death, stressed that there were no issues that they could not resolve peacefully. Eisenhower met Malenkov's challenge with his own two speeches: on April 16 and December 18, 1953. In them, he evaluated Malenkov's new line by proposing that the Soviet Union prove its intentions with deeds, not just words: for example, ending the Korean War, concluding an Austrian State Treaty, and releasing German prisoners of war. Dulles followed Eisenhower by introducing a new doctrine in January 1954: local defense reinforced by massive retaliation. The West's conventional forces, the administration believed, were not an adequate deterrent to Soviet ground forces, unless they rearmed Germany.

Peace initiatives slipped away quickly after the East Berlin insurrection of July 1953 and the Soviet hydrogen bomb test in August. The National Security Council's NSC-162/2 built on Operation Solarium's review of U.S. security policy. It proposed the "capability of inflicting massive retaliatory damage by offensive striking power" as deterrence. Such retaliation required a preponderance of power and eschewed parity. Eisenhower and Dulles viewed "containment" as negative and futile. They instead opted for "rollback": a strategy to force Russia out of Eastern Europe.

The German question also thwarted East-West accommodation. The Secret Service chief (KGB), Lavrentii Beria, asked the Soviet Politburo to abandon socialism in the German Democratic Republic (GDR), a policy, he thought, consistent with Stalin's 1952 note envisioning a "democratic," united, and neutral Germany. His suggestion would have substituted East German leader Walter Ulbricht's "accelerated construction of socialism" with a "new course" of controlled reform. Nevertheless, Stalin's successors feared bargaining away the GDR for a freely elected, neutral, and unified Germany. Their machinations only temporarily stopped West Germany's rearmament and its joining the North Atlantic Treaty Organization. In May 1955, the West formally recognized and received the Federal Republic of Germany into NATO. Meanwhile, the mass exodus from the GDR had not been halted, nor had economic viability for the GDR been attained. Even Winston Churchill had a suggestion—a Locarno-like settlement for Germany guaranteeing its borders—which the West would bargain for at a summit called to end the Cold War. Eisenhower rejected Churchill's proposal.

Eisenhower fixated on psychological warfare and propaganda schemes, especially the discussion of the Cold War's Manichaean discourse of good against evil. Even the "totalitarian model" influenced policy makers. Given these activities just after Stalin's death, a case could be made for dividing the Cold War into two parts: 1947–1953 as "total confrontation" and the period after 1953 as "compelled coexistence."[97]

Domestic postwar problems and tensions also registered forcefully in the Eisenhower-Dulles policy toward Moscow. Eisenhower was convinced the United States was locked in an apocalyptic struggle with the Soviet Union. He described the struggle as a contest between freedom and slavery, lightness and dark, good and evil. For all this, the American government was fully confident in its economic, military, and strategic superiority. Throughout the fifties, this Eisenhower-Dulles orthodoxy persisted, although there were some shifts from liberating to liberalizing the Iron Curtain and from psychological warfare to cultural infiltration. Stalin died in March 1953. The Eisenhower administration never broke with its assumptions about the Soviet threat. The communist victory in China, the Soviet detonation of the atomic bomb, the French failure in Indochina and rejection of the European Defense Community, the Hungarian Revolution of 1956, and U.S. failure to defeat Chinese forces in Korea—all of these events contributed to frustrations and fears, helping explain the single-minded American approach to meeting the communist challenge. Throughout Eisenhower's term, policy toward Russia had as much to do with the mood at home as with events abroad. As in the twenties, the national state of uncertainty over domestic affairs moved many Americans to pursue a rhetorical crusade against a nation whose political and economic system represented a standing challenge. Representatives of America's political establishment as well as the overwhelming majority of historians and publicists strengthened the confidence of America in their belief in the aggressive foreign policy of the USSR. It was, so they thought, directly connected with the Soviet dictatorship.[98]

A main reason that additional cooperation between the former allies became impossible derived from a traditional negativism or distortion toward Russia that was further inflamed by the "totalitarian model" of socialism in the Soviet Union, and anything that did not fit into this scheme was repudiated out of hand. As Hans J. Morgenthau put it, "The Kremlin was perceived as the headquarters of the devil on earth, causing all that was wrong with the world and more particularly, scheming the destruction of the United States." In the "Selected Glossary of Communist Terms," which accompanied a popular textbook by Richard Allen, the word *aggression* was interpreted as "any act, which serves to impede Communist achievement of a goal," and *progressive* was "an adjective used to describe anything which assists the Communist cause, or which injures the interests of the West."[99] The notorious "Red Issue" of *Collier's* published on October 27, 1951, carried a fantasy story inventing a "real" plan to start a nuclear war against the USSR in 1957. The story also fictionalized the possibilities of using Russian Americans and dissidents in the fight against the Soviet state. Another story published then by *U.S. News and World Report* called "Subversive Tactics in the Cold War" said Washington planned organizing the military to kill leading communists. Preserving totalitarianism in the Soviet Union converted Russia into the major culprit of worsening bilateral relations.

The Eisenhower administration practiced a more flexible strategy in its dealings with Moscow than its rhetoric suggested. Nevertheless, it insisted on Soviet conversion to American standards. In 1953, after Moscow called for direct talks with the United States about disputed problems, Eisenhower and Dulles rejected the proposal unless they had prior assurances the Soviet Union would accept several American demands. Among those demands were a peace treaty with Austria, freedom of prisoners of war held from World War II, a Germany united and based on free and secret elections, full independence for Eastern European nations, and arms-limitation agreements. The administration was asking for Soviet conformity to American political assumptions as a precondition for dialogue. The objective, at bottom, was less to enter talks than to insist that the Russians become more like Americans.

Despite this impulse, by the summer of 1955, Eisenhower felt compelled to meet with the leaders of the Soviet Union. Several developments at home and abroad, especially acquiring the H-bomb by both sides, created the belief that discussions would have to be tried. The goal of converting rather than accommodating the Soviet Union remained intact. To emphasize the moral and social differences between the two sides, Eisenhower addressed the nation before he left for Geneva. His message was clear. America, the morally superior nation, would go to Geneva, hoping, with God's help, to convert the Russians to America's way of peace. The three major goals the administration set for itself at Geneva were unification of Germany, militarized and safely within NATO; European security, by which was meant fewer Soviet troops stationed in central Europe and a relaxed Soviet control of Eastern European countries; and a leveling and control of armaments, with the United States retaining unchallenged superiority of, and supervision over, nuclear weapons.[100]

The president suggested an exchange of military blueprints of armed forces and regular aerial inspections to verify their accuracy. Eisenhower told his advisers that since Russia already knew the location of most American installations, this step would benefit Americans more than Russians. Americans knew less about Russian installations than Russians knew about American ones. Premier Nikita Khrushchev's reaction was tough. He called this proposition a transparent espionage device. The American side could hardly expect the Russians to take this seriously. Eisenhower's observations were more revealing of U.S. attitudes than of Russian realities. From the American perspective, the Soviets were not to be bargained with; they were to be converted and won over to the virtues of free elections, independence, disarmament, and peace. Because Soviet intransigence made this impossible, the next best thing was to demonstrate America's moral superiority to peoples everywhere. According to Russian specialists on the United States, Eisenhower played out the dominant mood in America. The country wanted conformity at home and abroad. If the Soviet Union would not abide by American standards of proper behavior in international affairs, it was to be ostracized. Eisenhower's moral indignation toward the USSR in Geneva for refusing to accede to American ideas echoed the moral recriminations toward dissenting opinion at home. The Soviet impression was, and remained, that domestic conformity and orthodoxy set the standard for U.S. policy overseas.[101]

A compulsive American need was to see the Soviets in domestic U.S. terms, and that compulsion continued to dominate the Eisenhower administration's thinking in its second term. A second meeting between Eisenhower and Khrushchev in 1959 illustrated this point. In September, the Soviet prime minister traveled to the United States, where he urged the necessity of détente. When Khrushchev privately declared to Eisenhower that the Soviet Union did not want war, the American president remarked that the attitudes shown at the latest meeting of the foreign ministers gave a contrary impression. Eisenhower told Khrushchev that the big obstacle on the American side in the way of better relations was a matter of national psychology—the need for Americans to believe that the Soviet system did not stand for the destruction of the United States. Yet there was a certain American enthusiasm for Khrushchev.[102]

This negative concept, further developed by George F. Kennan and known as "containment," became a permanent feature of U.S. foreign policy toward the Soviet Union. It contributed much to continuing hostile stereotypes in America's view of Russia, one might say an almost "Kennanization" of America's Russian foreign policy.

It is now necessary to take a small step backward in order to see how FDR's accommodation was already being attacked from within his administration, despite his efforts to rid himself of the Riga Boys.

6

Mr. X

The anonymous Mr. X came into being when Secretary of Defense James V. Forrestal asked the deputy for foreign affairs at the National War College, George Frost Kennan, to revise a paper on dialectical materialism, written by Edward F. Willett. Kennan declined that request but agreed to write an original essay. Kennan presented the first draft of this to the Council on Foreign Relations on January 7, 1947, and, then, at the War College on January 24. In these lectures, Kennan employed a term that he had first used in a lecture back in October 1946: *contain*.[1] He ended his War College address saying, "The problem of meeting the Kremlin in global affairs therefore boils down to this: Its inherent expansive tendencies must be firmly *contained* at all times by counter-pressure which makes it constantly evident that attempts to break through this containment would be detrimental to Soviet interests."[2]

Forrestal found this draft "disappointing" and asked for a revision, to which Kennan, also displeased, agreed. The result, Forrestal thought, was "astonishingly good."[3] Hamilton Fish Armstrong, editor of *Foreign Affairs*, missed the original presentation to the council. He had heard "on every side most enthusiastic accounts of your talk [and asked] whether there is any likelihood that you might be willing to put down your views in the form of an article for *Foreign Affairs*."[4] At first, Kennan demurred because of his State Department connections, but if it were an "anonymous article, or one under a pen name," he might just get permission.[5] After "mulling over" Kennan's letter, Armstrong decided that the "projected article more than outweighs from our point of view the disadvantage of anonymity."[6] Kennan asked for the State Department's permission to publish an anonymous article: "The views which I hold on this topic and which I presented in an informal way to the members of the Council of Foreign Relations were set forth in a more orderly fashion in the article which I prepared for Secretary Forrestal. Now that article has been noted in official circles here, I am wondering whether the Secretary would object to its being published in this manner."[7] After it was cleared for publication on April 8, Byron Dexter of the *Foreign Affairs* staff told Kennan that anonymous articles were usually designated as "'X' or some other letter of the alphabet."[8] And so the "X" persona of George F. Kennan was born.

Armstrong's estimation of Kennan's second draft agreed with Forrestal's: "The piece is awfully well written."[9] Anonymity flew out the window as Kennan's authorship soon leaked to the press. The *New York Times*'s Washington, D.C., bureau chief, Arthur Krock, on July 8, titled his article on it "A Guide to Official Thinking about Russia." Krock dropped further hints about X's identity: "The undisclosed author has stated and analyzed . . . with an authority which may be accounted for by the fact that the thesis is exactly that adopted by the American government after appeasement of the Kremlin proved a failure." He went on to say it was "obviously written by someone who studied the masters of the Soviets for years and at the closest range possible to a foreigner." Krock singled out "containment" as the key to the "X" article and finished by writing, "That is the conclusion of 'X,' whose views closely resemble those marked 'Top Secret' in several official files in Washington."[10] *Life, Newsweek,* and *Reader's Digest* quickly received permission to publish excerpts and reprints over Kennan's name. Mr. X, now known as George F. Kennan, had reached the apogee of his career.[11]

•   •   •

Kennan had returned home from Moscow in 1937 and taken up the Russian Desk in the newly formed European Division of the State Department. Chip Bohlen assumed his place in Moscow. After one year, Kennan was sent to Prague because his views were out of accord with Davies and, therefore, the Roosevelt administration.[12] After Prague, he served in Germany and, then, when war was declared, went to Lisbon, followed by London. In the spring of 1944, while on vacation in the United States, Bohlen introduced him to W. Averell Harriman, who was looking for a minister-counselor to escort him to Moscow where he would assume the ambassadorship. After a seven-year absence, once again Kennan found himself in Moscow, even though he had told Harriman, "I took pains to emphasize, that my views on policy toward the Soviet Union were not exactly those of the administration."[13] In early July, he arrived in Moscow via Teheran.

Kennan wrote Harriman about the need, from the Soviet view, to have spheres of influence. What would the Soviets expect of an international organization, even if they might not join? "We are now faced with the prospect of having our people disabused of this illusion." If so, U.S. policy "would regret to have to make it plain to our public that Russia alone, of all the great powers, was unwilling to submit her future actions to the judgment of international society." Whatever the United States did, it could not admit that such a decision would have domestic repercussions. If so admitted, Russia would hold a "whip hand" over the United States and demand a high price to change its position.[14] Domestic policy should not have any international vibrations. Harriman disagreed. The ambassador believed no U.S. president could survive by turning over Poland without a fight. "And George said: 'Well, that's the trouble. Domestic politics shouldn't have any influence on international affairs.'"[15]

By September, he was able to reflect on the situation in two papers, "Russia—Seven Years Later" and "Russia's International Position at the Close of the War with Germany," both important in evolving the Mr. X persona finally found in the famous "Long Telegram" of February 1946 and the "X" article of July 1947, "The Sources of Soviet Conduct." According to Kennan, his long absence from Moscow gave him a fresh perspective. When he had left in 1937, Russia "was not a happy place." The purges had been "enormously destructive in human values." Only a handful of Old Bolsheviks—those who made the 1917 revolution—had survived, and a "world of new faces" took their places. "Stalin had settled firmly back into the throne of Ivan the Terrible and Peter the Great." Only he set the course for the future. After seven years, after the German invasion had tried Russia's national worth and pulled the regime and people together, it had produced, among other things, "a new sense of national solidarity." But could it put behind it the brutality and poverty of the past?[16]

War losses were balanced by newly acquired territories and populations. Soviet economic life, for all the changes in content, remained the same in form. Reconstruction would take three to four years, with an annual income of twenty billion dollars, using half for consumption and the rest to restore military-industrial production. The standard of living would take longer to recover. The Soviet Union would not necessarily be dependent on the outside world and could, if pressed, manage on its own resources. Credits would interest Russia only if they made possible the importing of things on Stalin's wish list. Paying back credits was not a concern, because the leadership thought it had learned that the West could not afford for Russia to go bankrupt. If there were no credits, then Russia would use its gold and foreign currency reserves and whatever was exported to rebuild.[17]

As for the Soviet Union's spiritual life, Kennan reported mass enthusiasm for Russia's classics and a thirst for knowledge, amusement, and artistic experience. He was impressed with Soviet analytical abilities and the "cult of the past," especially traditional ballet, and in each area a genius for technical perfection. Exact sciences were flourishing; the social sciences were frozen in Byzantine scholasticism. All around was a "vast and pompous despotism," what he termed a "military totalitarian state." It preached capitalistic encirclement and its own program of territorial and political expansion. As long as there had been no second front against Hitler, Stalin needed collaboration with the West; as soon as there was a second front, he could revert to spheres of influence. Stalin himself was isolated and relied on information reaching him from a small circle of advisers. Kennan concluded that Russia remained an enigma to the West, a land living by contradictions. "What is valid in the Russian world is unsettling and displeasing to the American mind." Whoever would seek to understand Russia, therefore, would receive little appreciation for the effort. It would be, thought Kennan, a "lonely pleasure."[18]

In May 1945, Kennan made another attempt at this lonely pleasure by issuing a warning in his report, "Russia's International Position at the Close of the War with Germany." Here he shrewdly analyzed the nature of Soviet power by a people who since 1914, whether at war or peace, had lived for thirty-one years "under martial law and war conditions without respite." The greatest change had come about not from developments within but from without: "disintegration of the power of neighboring peoples."[19] Could Russia turn its conquests into a source of strength rather than weakness? The Soviet state in two decades had repeated much of czardom's history during the past two centuries—in the first ten years of Peter the Great and in the second ten years of Alexander I.

The USSR ruled Eastern Europe, but it commanded over non-Russian peoples and languages and cultures. Its "chauvinism and arrogance," its "naked bluntness," lacked any constructive content—only "discipline and drive." It had behind it no great idea that could inspire the conquered. As for Marxism, it was dated; the Soviets had only short-lived programs such as putting on trial Nazi collaborators and instituting land reform. The power of the secret police held the empire together. Soviet competence was lacking in concentrating human energy. To hold Eastern Europe—ninety-five million people in subservience—"as reluctant members of a Russian security sphere will take probably a greater administrative and police force than was necessary even in normal times, and this last must have numbered in the millions."[20]

For all of its outward external symbols of power, inwardly it was weak to the extent that the "government lost moral dominion over the masses of the Russian population." There were "no longer many illusions among the Russian people as to the moral or spiritual quality of all that the state represents."[21] It could only command loyalty, not inspire it. It needed Western support to bless its domination, grant its legitimacy, and extend material support. The Kremlin would lean on what it supposed Americans had been taught—collaboration, cordiality, and confidence in the Soviet Union as a partner in peace; otherwise, war and catastrophe would result. Such Soviet misconceptions of America were, in Kennan's estimation, "powerful auxiliary" instruments for retaining power in Eastern Europe. In ninety-nine cases out of a hundred, the United States took the initiative for establishing a confident and cordial relationship and was met inevitably by "suspicion, discourtesy, and rebuff." Nevertheless, "they consider that Anglo-Saxon opinion can always be easily appeased in a pinch by a single generous gesture, or even in all probability by a few promising words, and that Western statesmen can always be depended upon to collaborate enthusiastically in this appeasement."[22] The Soviet Union would probably be unable to maintain its dominion in Eastern and central Europe any time the West stood up to it.

Nobody in Moscow believed the West would stand firm, and Russia's global policy rested on that assumption. Indeed, if such persons existed, FDR had wanted them fired in the spring of 1943. Such policies as generosity, sympathy, sincerity, courtesy, and a "genuine Good Neighbor Policy" toward the Soviet Union, wrote FDR, should prevail. If not, he continued, "I desire that the above policies be put into effect at once and that any officials representing this country in Soviet relations who do not accept them fully and give loyal support to them be replaced."[23]

Kennan thought FDR and his New Dealers' approach to be one of either collaboration or outright appeasement, as, for example, at Teheran and Yalta. In this Kennan essay, written only a month after FDR's death, he accused the dead president of teaching the American public that collaboration with Russia is "entirely possible" and that it "depended only on the establishment of the proper personal relationships of cordiality and confidence with Russian leaders."[24] Even the Soviet leaders, in his estimation, saw it as such. Many years later, when looking back at this, Kennan said, "I think that [FDR's] hopes about Russia were largely unrealistic during the wartime period. I don't think FDR was capable of conceiving of a man of such profound iniquity, coupled with enormous strategic cleverness. He had never met such a creature." Kennan continued, "I watched our government making concession after concession to the Soviet government for wartime reasons."[25]

In a 1965 lecture, "The Shattering of the Rooseveltian Dream," Kennan expanded on this theme. That dream consisted of an "entire complex of illusions and calculations and expectations that led Franklin Roosevelt and those associated with him to take, during the Second World War, an unrealistic and unduly hopeful view of the prospects for pleasant and collaborative relations between the western powers and the Soviet Union."[26] At the same time, they neglected serious discussions about a postwar settlement.

There were three components to this dream. First, FDR "never doubted his ability to charm the Soviet leaders and to influence them by his personal touch." Second, there was a "military pro-Sovietism," fearing that "Soviet leaders, if not treated with utmost sympathy and consideration, might abandon the war effort and make a separate peace." This tied in with FDR's "impatience" with the British and his "sentimentality" about the Chinese. These "combined to produce in American governing circles, I am sorry to say, a general feeling that the Americans, the Russians and the Chinese would stand together as the dominant forces of the postwar world." Kennan labeled this a "fatuous dream." The third ingredient was that "nothing seemed more unnecessary or out of place than to try to sit down with the Russians in the middle of the war and to thrash out the sordid problems of borders and political arrangements in the future Europe." A realistic framework might have allowed for the "difficulty of postwar collaboration" to have become clearer "at an earlier date." As a result, the armies would have met farther east, and "Berlin and Prague would almost certainly have been kept within the western orbit." A Soviet occupation and orbit would have been constituted, as they were not dependent on Teheran, Yalta, and Potsdam. They were "part of the price paid" for Soviet collaboration.[27]

• • •

Averell Harriman explained the rapid descent into the Cold War from the time of FDR's death on April 12, 1945, to Kennan's "Long Telegram" of February 22, 1946. He detailed the growing "get tough with Russia" policy. Harriman met President Harry S. Truman five days after FDR's burial. When asked by Truman to "run down the list of urgent problems with the Soviet Union," he said that Russia followed two contradictory policies: cooperating with the West and creating a sphere of influence in Eastern Europe. In his judgment, "standing firm" meant Russia would back down on key issues, as it needed Western economic help in postwar reconstruction.[28] The Russians believed the United States required exporting to the USSR and would offer credits rather than face a postwar depression. "A ridiculous idea, Truman said, interjecting again that he proposed to stand firm. There would be no departures from American principles or traditions to win favor with Stalin." Harriman called Russia's introduction of "secret police methods" the new "barbarian invasion of Europe." Nevertheless, he "still believed the United States could arrive at a workable relationship with the Russians."[29] He was disappointed to hear Truman say he would not proceed with the United Nations if the Russians dropped out. It was revealing that Harriman had rushed back to Washington because he feared that Truman did not understand what FDR at the end finally did understand, that "Stalin is breaking his agreements." Harriman also made his views known around Washington for the "selective application of the *quid pro quo* treatment."[30]

Molotov arrived in Washington on his way to San Francisco for the opening of the United Nations. Truman's first meeting with Soviet Foreign Minister Vyacheslav M. Molotov went smoothly, but at their second meeting, after the president had been briefed and decided over Secretary of War Henry L. Stimson's objections to use "brutal frankness," he told Molotov the "Soviets should carry out the Yalta decisions on Poland." Molotov complained, "I have never been talked to like that in my life." The president replied, "Carry out your agreements and you won't get talked to like that."[31] Harriman, shocked, believed Truman had given Molotov an excuse to tell Stalin that Roosevelt's policy was being abandoned. In San Francisco, Harriman informed reporters that Stalin was not living up to his agreements. Although some supported Harriman's claim, others such as Alexander Uhl of *PM* magazine disapproved: "Two of Harriman's listeners, Raymond Gram Swing and Walter Lippmann, were so shocked that they got up and left the room."[32] This was, perhaps, the earliest suggestion of Lippmann's rejection of the future Mr. X "containment" thesis. They objected to Harriman's remark: "We must recognize that our objectives and the Kremlin's objectives are irreconcilable." Harriman's friend and press secretary later related that his boss had bucked the "pro-Russian climate of the times. The press found it extraordinary and somewhat inexplicable, he said, that this rich man could have spent so much time in the Soviet Union and yet somehow failed to see its essential virtues."[33] Harriman returned to Moscow. The coming round of the press corps to Harriman's view, from the Yalta Axioms to the Riga Axioms, was important to the future success of Kennan's containment thesis.

In early May, even Secretary of State Edward R. Stettinius Jr. in a press conference registered America's "great concern" over disintegrating Russian relations and especially the Polish problem. When Bohlen and Harriman returned to Washington, Bohlen suggested sending Harry Hopkins, FDR's confidant, to Moscow to talk with Stalin as a possible last-minute reprieve. Harriman prodded Truman for this and for a face-off in a tripartite meeting at Potsdam with the Big Three.[34] Many irritants stood in the way. Truman had ended Lend-Lease abruptly, prematurely, and then reversed himself. To revive FDR's vision, Truman even sent former ambassador Davies on a special mission to Churchill to convince him that he was being too hard on the Russians. "Davies told Churchill that his recent warnings against the spread of Communism in Europe, and the threat of Soviet domination, put him in the same camp as Hitler and Goebbels." Imagine how stunned Churchill was.[35] To Davies's suggestion that Truman meet Stalin before Churchill and somewhere else in Europe, Churchill refused—all three must meet "simultaneously and on equal terms."[36]

Hopkins met Stalin for the first of six meetings, beginning on May 26, 1945. As Harriman said, "Each remarkable for its extraordinary candor and rare good feeling." Even though greeted as an old friend, Hopkins was blunt: "The real reason Truman had sent him, Hopkins said, was that so many Americans were disturbed or alarmed over the trend of relations with Russia." Deteriorations in popular support arose over a "sense of bewilderment at our inability to solve the Polish question." Stalin blamed British conservatives friendly to Polish exiles who tried to resurrect the cordon sanitaire. At the second meeting, Stalin "put all his grievances on the table." He began complaining about inviting Argentina to the United Nations, though that country had not declared war on Germany until hostilities ended, contrary to Yalta. Why should France be a member of the Reparations Commission, conceived as a three-power body at Yalta? There was the premature curtailment of Lend-Lease, though hastily corrected by Truman. Stalin had requested one-third of the German fleet and merchant vessels the West had captured. Hopkins assured Stalin that they would be handed over. Stalin believed the Americans acted as if they no longer needed Russia. Parenthetically, this Russian attitude has persisted to the present, as once expressed by the Russian Federation president, Vladimir Putin.[37]

At their fourth and fifth meetings, Poland again surfaced. Stalin did not object to a parliamentary system, but he did reject freeing fourteen Poles who were supposed Nazi collaborators. They had to stand trial. He did agree to include émigré Poles in the new government whose formation was soon to be discussed in Moscow. Stalin consented to dismembering Germany and establishing the Allied Control Council. About Korea, Stalin accepted China's temporary trusteeship. Russia would begin its war against Japan on August 8. China should be a single country, not divided by the communists and Kuomintang (KMT). Manchuria would be nominally under Chinese sovereignty. They also settled the veto in the Security Council by Stalin dropping his demand of the right to veto "not only enforcement action by the Security Council but also its agenda." Andrei Gromyko, Russia's ambassador to the United States, had been as stubborn as was Molotov on this point, but Stalin waved it off as unimportant. However successful Hopkins had been, according to Harriman, the visit gained only a respite, a "breathing dividend."[38]

It was at this stage that Truman cleaned house by replacing FDR's top administrators. In early July, Hopkins resigned. Tom Clark replaced Francis Biddle as attorney general; Robert Hannegan took Frank Walker's place as postmaster general; Clinton Anderson became secretary of agriculture, replacing Claude Wickard; Lewis Schwellenbach succeeded Francis Perkins at the Department of Labor. Most important, Stettinius resigned, and James F. Byrnes took over as secretary of state. It was the "Byrnes gang" that accompanied Truman to Potsdam in July—Ben Cohen, Jimmy Dunn, and H. Freeman "Doc" Matthews. As Harriman put it, "I was not alone in being ignored."[39]

Before leaving government, Hopkins persuaded Truman to pull back U.S. troops from the Soviet zone according to the London arrangement. Churchill had urged Truman not to withdraw by some three hundred miles. It was feared the Russians would not pull back in Austria if the United States refused in Germany. Meanwhile, the London Poles arrived in Moscow and quickly obtained a more broadly based representation from the Lublin Poles. This encouraged Truman to recognize the new Polish Provisional Government of National Unity. Churchill followed suit. T. V. Soong, also visiting Moscow now, got Stalin to recognize Chiang Kai-shek's Nationalist government's sovereignty over Manchuria. With those talks in progress, Truman arrived in Berlin on July 15.[40]

The Russians, with no conclusions having yet been reached on reparations, were busy denuding their zone of anything useful. The Potsdam Conference, what Churchill called "Terminal," had a full palette, but Churchill was replaced in an election by the Labour Party's Clement Atlee, who arrived on July 28. Only Stalin remained of the "Big Three." The first agreement reached was to form a Council of Foreign Ministers, including France and China. It would draft peace treaties for all but Germany, which would not have a treaty until a German government could be formed. Until then, the Allied Control Council would rule, with coordination of each zone's governance in Berlin. A bargain was struck on reparations: each occupier could take freely from its own zone, but the Russians were to get added reparations from Western zones in exchange for food and coal from the East. Molotov asked for two billion dollars, but got only 15 percent in exchange for food and materials plus 10 percent in free reparations apart from what he obtained from the Russian zone. Few deliveries were carried out because Russia failed to send matching quantities of coal and food.[41]

On July 16, Truman received word that the first A-bomb had been successfully tested. He told Stalin on the twenty-fourth. According to Harriman, "The idea of using the bomb as a form of pressure on the Russians never entered the discussions at Potsdam." It was later learned that the "Russians were in possession of the salient facts about our development of the bomb before Potsdam."[42] Truman issued the Potsdam Declaration, calling on Japan's unconditional surrender; a refusal would mean "prompt and utter destruction." Japan refused. The bomb was dropped on Hiroshima on August 5. Soong saw Stalin on August 7, when Stalin now demanded

Dairen as well as Port Arthur and the seizure of Japanese properties in Manchuria. Truman objected. Harriman appealed, in Truman's name, for easing Soviet demands on the Chinese; Stalin replied that Manchurian ports and railroads had been built by Russia. Even so, the Chinese got a half-interest. On August 9, the Russians declared war on Japan and quickly invaded Manchuria.[43]

Now the Soviet initiative in the Far East began. Molotov requested a "combined" Far Eastern command with veto power over selecting a supreme commander, and he even asked if it were conceivable that there might be two supreme commanders: Gen. Douglas MacArthur and Marshal Alexander M. Vasilievsky. Harriman told Molotov that these suggestions were "absolutely inadmissible." When Molotov insisted that Harriman submit the Soviet request to Washington, Harriman replied that he would do so, but he reminded Molotov that the "United States had been fighting the Japanese for four years and Russia had been in the war exactly two days." Molotov backed off after consulting Stalin and wanted only to be notified. It seemed that if Molotov's requests were accepted, then in exchange for agreeing to MacArthur, the Russians would have demanded a zone of occupation—for instance, Hokkaido, because Stalin mentioned that possibility to Hopkins. On August 14, 1945, the Japanese surrendered.[44]

Harriman still thought, even with the problems, that it was possible to deal with Russia. He returned to Moscow on October 4, 1945, after the London Council of Foreign Ministers. Byrnes had been angered by Molotov's "aggressive and arbitrary attitude." In exasperation, he relied on stalling, to which Molotov argued that the United States was trying to set itself up as "dictator of the world."[45] When Harriman visited Stalin in Agra, the dictator "complained that the Soviet government had never been consulted or even informed about policy decisions affecting Japan." Harriman protested. Stalin said it would be better "if the Soviet Union were to quit Japan than to remain there as a piece of furniture." It was the first time, as Harriman recalled, that Stalin suggested the Soviet Union might pursue a go-it-alone policy after the war. It dawned on him that "Soviet leadership had discussed and settled upon a new policy for the postwar period, a policy of increased militancy and self-reliance."[46]

It seemed to Harriman that after the London breakdown, Molotov's policy was to "seize the immediate situation to strengthen the Soviet position as much as possible through unilateral action." Such action had become "more marked." To recoup the situation, Byrnes instructed Harriman to propose a foreign ministers' meeting in Moscow for December. That conference, when convened, made slow progress. Byrnes saw Stalin. They settled on a tripartite commission to work out arrangements in Bucharest. Molotov agreed to a final text on an Allied council in Tokyo with MacArthur having the last and decisive word. Byrnes reported to Truman, "As a result of a long conference with Stalin yesterday afternoon, I now hope that we can make a forward step towards settling the Rumania-Bulgaria problems."[47]

On January 20, 1946, Harriman made his farewell call on Molotov and on the twenty-third called on Stalin for the last time. When Harriman asked Stalin about future U.S.-USSR relations, Stalin believed they "could find common ground." As to possible credits, Stalin asked Harriman whether the United States, as he supposed, would meet them halfway. "Stalin's question confirmed Harriman's belief that as late as January 23, 1946, the Soviet Government had not yet decided whether to press for a large American loan." Nor had Molotov raised the question with Byrnes. Harriman thought the United States was prepared to discuss it, but a settlement of the Lend-Lease account would have to be a part of the negotiations. Stalin agreed.[48] When Harriman reached Washington, he urged Truman and Byrnes for a "prompt resumption of serious negotiations with the Russians for a postwar credit but discovered that Byrnes had anticipated him by a day or two." A reporter asked him about Stalin's anti-Western February 9, 1946, speech, but he reminded the press that such speeches were directed internally. Harriman was out of the picture. Kennan awaited arrival of the new U.S. ambassador, Walter Bedell Smith. On February 22, Kennan answered the State Department's request for his views in a cable on February 2, 1946: "We should welcome receiving from you an interpretive analysis of what we may expect in the way of future implementation of these announced policies."[49]

• • •

Kennan referred to the effect of his "Long Telegram" on Washington's officialdom as "nothing less than sensational [and the] one that changed my career and my life in very basic ways."[50] He recognized that the capital was ready to receive his message. Probably, the president read it. Secretary of the Navy James Forrestal had it reproduced and made the Long Telegram required reading for thousands of his civil servants. In April 1946, Kennan transferred to Washington and became the first deputy for foreign affairs at Forrestal's newly opened brainchild, the National War College.[51]

Soviet policies referred to in Kennan's cable were those announced by Stalin and his colleagues in their preelection speeches: capitalism and communism were incompatible, and war between them was inevitable.[52] It had been obvious to Kennan when Byrnes replaced Stettinius that "in the present conference [Byrnes's] weakness in dealing with the Russians is that his main purpose is to achieve some sort of agreement, he doesn't much care what." He elaborated, "I had experienced unhappiness not only about the naïveté of our underlying ideas as to what it was we were hoping to achieve in our relations with the Soviet government but also about the methods and devices with which we went about achieving it." Byrnes's Moscow visit brought the "pot of my patience to boil over with relation to this area of our diplomacy, as it had boiled over with respect to so many others."[53] Differences with the Russians over peace treaties, forming East European governments, the unwillingness of the Soviet Union to adhere to the World Bank or the International Monetary Fund, and Byrnes's surrender in Moscow all contributed to his skepticism. He had already written an unfinished memorandum on the techniques for dealing with the Soviets—not to assume any common purposes or high-mindedness on their part, but only to consider what was in it for them.[54] Now, with Harriman out of town and Kennan in charge, he explained Russian behavior. Doc Matthews, director of the Office of European Affairs, and Elbridge Durbrow, chief of the Division of Eastern Affairs, had thought Stalin seemed to be saying cooperation was impossible and the United States had to be alert in counteracting Soviet propaganda and policies.[55]

Kennan wrote of the eight thousand–word Long Telegram that it was "all neatly divided, like an eighteenth century Protestant sermon, into five separate parts [and further] it reads exactly like one of those primers put out by alarmed congressional committees or by the Daughters of the American Revolution, designed to arouse the citizenry to the dangers of the Communist conspiracy." It had the advantage of timing—six months earlier or later, and it would have failed. That is, the New Dealers would have rejected it as interfering with their efforts at accommodation and the Trumanites for not being tough enough.[56] It had few, if any, memorable phrases—the best being: "The Soviet regime is a policy regime par excellence, reared in the dim half world of Tsarist police intrigue, accustomed to think primarily in terms of policy power."[57] The Long Telegram's primerlike organization gave it strength by being a schematic interpretation of the Soviet Union's characteristics, its origins, its official and unofficial projections, and how these would play out with U.S. policy. These categories were listed and each one expanded.

The Soviet Union believed, according to Kennan, that it was a beleaguered socialist state encircled by a hostile capitalist world. There could be no permanent peaceful coexistence. The USSR not only must exploit internal conflicts within each capitalist state but must also take advantage of the wars and rivalries they generated among themselves. By being "militarily powerful, ideologically monolithic and faithful to its present brilliant leadership," it was best able to prevent capitalist intervention and to use fellow travelers to keep capitalist states off balance. Kennan deduced that the Soviet Union would "advance relative strength" while reducing the "strength and influence, collectively as well as individually, of capitalist powers." It would exploit their difficulties, especially using "Democratic-progressive elements" within those states.

He made it clear this offensive was not shared, nor was it the "natural outlook" of Russians. "But party line is binding for outlook and conduct of people who make up apparatus of power—party, secret police and Government—and it is exclusively with these that we have to deal."[58] Kennan argued that their premises were false and arose out of "basic inner-Russian necessities which existed before recent war and exist today." They were built on an old Russian fear of the West, fear of foreign penetration, and a fragile psychological foundation. The Marxist dogma provided the fig leaf for justifying an "outside world as evil, hostile and menacing, but as bearing within itself germs of creeping disease and destined to be wracked with growing internal convulsions until it is given final coup de grace by rising power of socialism and yields to new and better world."[59] That and old Russian nationalism buoyed up the Soviet Union. Curiously, none of it conformed to fact and reality. Kennan wondered if anyone got an accurate picture of the outside world, especially Stalin himself. Contrary to Russian propaganda, the capitalist world could live in peace with itself.

Russia's far-flung apparatus was "highly sensitive to the logic of force" —withdrawing when confronted with superior power. As Kennan noted, "Gauged against Western world as a whole, Soviets are still by far the weaker force." And in a statement close to the later "X" article, he gave a first version of his "containment" theory: "Thus, if the adversary has sufficient force and makes clear his readiness to use it, he rarely has to do so. If situations are properly handled there need be no prestige engaging showdowns." Besides, the success of its internal power had not yet proved itself in the "supreme test of successive transfer of power from one individual or group to another." This would be complicated because the Russian people were so far removed from it and the party had ceased being "a source of emotional inspiration." Whatever propaganda it produced, it was "basically negative and destructive" and easily combated by constructive programs. It was necessary to "apprehend, and recognize for what it is, the nature of the movement [with] objectivity, and same determination" and the "public is educated to realities of Russian situation"—then the United States would prevail and not become like those with whom the United States was coping. Much depended on the "health and vigor of our own society." Otherwise, world communism fed on "diseased tissue." Courage and self-confidence in "our own methods and conceptions of human society" would see America through.[60]

The Long Telegram has been interpreted in many ways. Dean Acheson called it a "truly remarkable dispatch." Nevertheless, he also wrote that Kennan's recommendations "were of no help; his historical analysis might or might not have been sound, but his predictions and warnings could not have been better." Acheson concluded, "Minds in the Kremlin worked very much as George F. Kennan had predicted they would."[61] This was a curious evaluation, since the germ of a specific policy recommendation—containment—was in the Long Telegram: "Soviet power . . . does not work by fixed plans. It does not take unnecessary risks. Impervious to logic of reason . . . it is highly sensitive to logic of force. For this reason it can easily withdraw—and usually does—when strong resistance is encountered at any point."[62]

According to C. Ben Wright, the Long Telegram was "widely interpreted in official circles as a statement of United States policy, a switch from the 'wishful thinking' and optimism of the Roosevelt era." American Embassies were "very excited [by this] new line."[63] State Department officials such as Louis J. Halle believed there were "new intellectual moorings" for U.S. policy, and Joseph Jones saw in it a "stiffening of United States policy toward Soviet expansionism."[64] Ben Cohen thought it had "influenced departmental thinking."[65] Forrestal had allies in the anti-Rooseveltian line within the Truman White House, persons such as the chief of staff, Adm. William D. Leahy, and even Truman himself who, in January 1946, had told Molotov that he was not going to baby the Soviets. Byrnes praised the Long Telegram's "splendid analysis."[66] Harriman agreed.[67] There were those remaining holdovers from FDR's administration, who disagreed on the *turnaround* that Kennan was insisting on. Gen. Lucius Clay, the American military governor in Germany, disagreed with Kennan.[68] Another was Secretary of Commerce Henry A. Wallace, who delivered a speech at Madison Square Garden on September 12, 1946, "The Way to Peace." In it, Wallace declared that he was neither anti-Russian nor pro-Russian, but he thought the United States was "reckoning with a force which cannot be handled successfully by a 'Get tough with Russia' policy. 'Getting tough' never bought anything real and lasting—whether for schoolyard bullies or businessmen or world powers. The tougher we get, the tougher the Russians will get." The United States had to meet Russia halfway, which did not mean appeasement. Wallace called for "friendly peaceful competition."[69]

● ● ●

Only a year before the Long Telegram, in January 1945—and a little more than six months since he had returned to Moscow with Harriman—Kennan had fallen into a pit of despair. He wrote Chip Bohlen about leaving the service "as soon as this can be decently arranged after the termination of the war in Europe."[70] Bohlen had felt, during their previous discussions, that if his friend had shared his experiences in Moscow and Teheran, instead of being exiled in Lisbon and London, he would have had "more confidence in the pattern of things to come."[71] Kennan, so Bohlen then believed, would have had more optimism in the collaborationist and, frankly, "appeasement" approach of FDR to Stalin. That was not to be. As Kennan put it, "Six months of most intimate contact with Russian affairs have not changed anything in my conviction that Soviet political aims in Europe are not, in the main, consistent with the happiness, prosperity or stability of international life on the rest of the continent." Their aims were not "inspired by any concern for the preservation of western values, either spiritual or material." Rather than allow for any separate sources of integrity or unity in Europe, other than theirs, they would be prepared to inflict any amount of misery or evil. Not only were these Russian aims bluntly "inconsistent with the main currents of central and western European tradition but they are in conflict with our own interests."[72] As Kennan saw it, America had to preserve healthy democratic and capitalist states directly on the Atlantic and with similar countries behind them in central Europe. On the contrary, Russia was a "jealous Eurasian land power" that had to always seek its ultimate security by extending itself to the very shores of the Atlantic. This attitude was a product of its own tradition and environment. Its war effort had been so "masterful and effective," and, without it, the war could not have been won. Its reward would be at the expense of others: "I fail to see why we must associate ourselves with this political program, so hostile to the interests of the Atlantic community as a whole, so dangerous to everything which we need to see preserved in Europe." Kennan's solution was to divide Europe "frankly into spheres of influence" and confine each other to its own zone.[73]

Unfortunately, the United States not only refused to clarify its interests but also led Russia to believe the United Nations was a "disguised statute for the collaboration of the strong in the brow-beating of the weak." Thus, no positive programs were put forward for Europe. By not setting limits on Russian expansion or responsibilities, the United States endangered plans for Germany and Poland. Kennan lamented, "We have weakened into relative ineffectiveness out of a desire either to spite the British or to appease the Russians." That word—*appease*—came more and more into Kennan's depiction of FDR's Russian policy. In the name of wider collaboration, realities were settling borders in Eastern and central Europe: "We have had no appreciable influence over the conception or the execution of any of these settlements."[74] The Russians were doing "just as they please" and making it appear they had U.S. support: "In short, the sum total of our wisdom for the peace settlement in eastern and southeastern Europe has been to deliver the territory up without a murmur to the mercies of an uncertain and mistrustful Russia and to offer our sponsorship, in the form of a blank check, for whatever catastrophe might ensue." In Germany, U.S. influence amounted only to the "negative act" of destroying the Nazis. The cities, swollen with refugees, were starving, and "no tri-partite administration is going to save us from these difficulties."[75]

Though it was "late in the game," Kennan offered some suggestions: unify and play the West's assets "for their full value," "bury Dumbarton Oaks," don't freeze the status quo by relying on the UN, and don't commit to "some formal blanket engagement" to use U.S. forces to bolster the UN commitments: "Where the Russians hold power, there our world stops; beyond that line we should not try to lift our voices unless we mean business." Kennan urged acceptance of the complete partition of Germany, and then to develop a plan on a Western European federation, treating the U.S. zone as a separate issue, as also was the question of reparations.[76] He finished by admitting that he did not offer a "very happy program [as it] renounces—and for very good reason—all reliance on cooperation with Russia." If the United States continued FDR's "wishful thinking," it ran the risk of forfeiting even the barest minimum of security on the Atlantic seaboard.[77]

Bohlen's undated response, reproduced in his memoir, *Witness to History, 1929–1969*, defended FDR's policy: "I don't for one minute believe that there has been any time in this war when we could seriously have done very differently than we did."[78] He elaborated: "But the simple fact remains that if we wished to defeat Germany we could never have even tried to keep the Soviet armies out of Eastern Europe and Germany itself." Bohlen admitted FDR's Russian policy involved "no small risk." The Soviet Union was "one of the major factors in the world. Quarreling with them would be so easy, but we can always come to that." Kennan's constructive suggestions were, for Bohlen, "frankly naïve to a degree." Bohlen referred to the UN, tongue in cheek, as a "piece of paper" or "bits of paper." But in his memoir, he clarified this point: "To abandon the United Nations would be an error of the first magnitude." It would keep the United States internationally engaged, "without, as Kennan thought, committing us to use force when we did not want to."[79]

Bohlen's letter never deterred Kennan. Kennan wrote Harriman in February and again in March: the Russians would not be exporting surpluses from their occupied areas unless they could get "exclusive political dividends." The Russians, simply, would not "sit down at a table with us" and face the problem of European relief divorced from their national interest or the struggle for power. "I would not wish to have," he wrote, "any share of the responsibility for what will ensue if we—in deference to a chimera of Soviet collaboration which has no substance except in our wishful thinking—continue to pass up opportunities for prompt and effective action within our own sphere."[80] In March, Kennan saw no advantage to be gained in a "fruitless polemic with Molotov." His "tune had been set for him" by those who controlled Soviet policy.[81] By August 1945, Kennan still considered resigning. His resignation was not, as he wrote to Doc Matthews, director of European affairs of the State Department, "intended to be demonstrative, and reflects no bitterness or dissatisfaction with the Service as such. It does reflect certain impelling personal considerations, combined with a deep sense of frustration over our squandering of the political assets won at such cost by our recent war effort, over our failure to follow up our victories politically and over the obvious helplessness of our career diplomacy to exert any appreciable constructive influence on American policy at this juncture."[82]

Kennan continued fretting. He wrote his friend and colleague Elbridge Durbrow, chief of the East European Division, at the end of January 1946. By now his despair had reached its lowest ebb. His acute sense of frustration was over Russian matters. He had decided there was a "lack of understanding of the realities on the part of our public and in certain general deficiencies of our governmental system in the conduct of foreign affairs." Then came this devastating sentence: "I feel that before we can successfully face the problem of dealing with Russia, we will have to have an entirely different approach, perhaps not only to the problem alone but to the wider problems and techniques of our foreign policy in general."[83]

It was at this point he was asked for his opinion. He wrote the Long Telegram, sent on February 22, 1946. That broadside, as noted, changed everything. One of the best indicators of its impact was a letter to him from Henry Norweb, a former chief of mission in Portugal and currently ambassador to Cuba: "I want you to know," he wrote, "that it is about the best piece of political reporting I have seen in my thirty years in the Service."[84] By April, after Kennan had been recalled to Washington and assigned to the War College, he wrote a friend, "I have a feeling that some of the most dangerous tendencies in American thought about Russia have been checked, if not overcome. If we can now only restrain the hot-heads and panic mongers and keep policy on a firm and even keel, I am not pessimistic."[85] Kennan's despondency, in the wake of the Long Telegram, had quickly taken a 180-degree turn.

The summer of 1946, before Kennan had begun his duties at the National War College, he was asked by the Department of State to take a lecture tour out West to explain his views to prominent citizens and gauge their reactions. He related that both his audiences and their attitudes varied widely to his basic message: "Soviet-American antagonism might be serious without having to be resolved by war." Business leaders were the most realistic of his audiences, whereas academics were the most difficult.[86] The "hardest sledding," as he put it, "was with precisely those groups which devote most attention to foreign affairs, namely the academic circles and the groups organized for the specific purpose of studying and discussing international events." For most of these groups, collaboration with Russia had a "fine liberal ring about it," and it was not pleasant to be told about a "long, unpleasant process of setting will against will, force against force, idea against idea—through a long process of conflict and dispute rather than through a happy collaboration for common ends." He found certain scientists in Berkeley to be "as innocent as six year old maidens." He ended his report in a quandary about what to do with the "state of mind of liberal and academic people" on the eve of his return to take up his duties at the National War College.[87]

Kennan referred to his months at the National War College as "intensely enjoyable."[88] Outside of taking on administrative duties and participating in discussions and attending the lectures of his colleagues, he had given only four or five formal lectures, when he was asked by the Council on Foreign Relations in early January 1947 to give an informal talk, utilizing material he had revised for Forrestal. In his first lecture at the college, "Measures Short of War," delivered on September 16, 1946, he emphasized the notion that for such tasks, diplomatic in nature, to be successful, the United States must "keep at all times a preponderance of strength in the world." That strength was not just military, but it also relied on a country's internal strength: "National strength is a question of political, economic, and moral strength. Above all it is a question of our internal strength; of the health and sanity of our own society." Such measures could not be hit-or-miss, but used in a pattern of *grand strategy*.[89] On October 10, 1946, Kennan gave an analysis of the USSR's internal structure of power. He followed that on October 22 and December 10 with a two-part study of Soviet diplomacy. In a couple of revealing sentences, he made a swipe at FDR's approach, saying that some took Russian diplomacy for what it was not and alluding to the fact that hundreds of organizations and millions of people had been taken in by this "Trojan horse."[90] These were warm-up papers.

On January 24, 1947, Kennan gave a paper, "The Soviet Way of Thought and Its Effect on Foreign Policy." It became the forerunner of the "X" article and the substance of what had been the rewrite he had done for Secretary Forrestal. It was in this paper that he first used the terms *contained* and *containment* as shorthand for the new diplomacy he was trying to explain. After running through the ideological-historical and internal circumstances of Bolshevik methods, he assumed that no coexistence, at least in the minds of Russia's leaders, was possible because the outside or capitalist world was a hostile force. There could only be an "armistice" during periods of the ongoing struggle: "The problem of meeting the Kremlin in international affairs therefore boils down to this: Its inherent expansive tendencies must be firmly *contained* at all times by counter-pressure which makes it constantly evident that attempts to break through this *containment* would be detrimental to *Soviet* interests."[91] In his memoirs, he comments on the sensation the word created in the media: "The term 'containment' was picked up and elevated by common agreement of the press to the status of a 'doctrine,' which was then identified with the foreign policy of the administration. In this way there was established—before our eyes so to speak—one of the indestructible myths that are the bane of the historian."[92]

About the famous article itself, what exactly did it say and how was it said? It was a model of economy, of organization, of style. The editor, Hamilton Fish Armstrong, selected the key sentence from the piece and placed it at the masthead: "Summary: Soviet pressure against the free institutions of the Western world is something that can be *contained* by the adroit and vigilant application of counterforce at a series of constantly shifting geographical and political points, corresponding to the shifts and maneuvers of Soviet policy, but which cannot be charmed or talked out of existence."[93] There, bluntly stated, was Kennan's containment thesis. His elegant phrasing, reduced to one word, became a touchstone and shorthand for America's forthcoming global strategy. Kennan used one form or another of the word five times in the article. At first, it appeared after a series of adjectives meant to elaborate it: "long-term, patient but firm and vigilant *containment* of Russian expansive tendencies."[94] Its second use quickly followed at the start of the second part and provided the editor's summary statement. In the next paragraph, it was used for a third time in a sentence introducing eight Soviet weaknesses: "Let us bring this apocalyptic vision down to earth and suppose that the western world finds the strength and resourcefulness to *contain* Soviet power over a period of ten to fifteen years." What did that mean for Russia? Soviet Russia had weaknesses, which were the "seeds of it own decay, and that the sprouting of these seeds is well advanced." These internal weaknesses were total despotism, industrialization's terrible costs, war's destructiveness, the uncertainty of its younger generation, uneven industrialization, transference of power, and the hollowness of its political structure below the top party leadership. "If, consequently, anything were ever to occur to disrupt the unity and efficacy of the Party as a political instrument, Soviet Russia might be changed overnight from one of the strongest to one of the weakest and most pitiable of national societies"; it was the *Buddenbrooks* dynamic, that is, when a society, like a giant red star, shows its "greatest outward brilliance at a moment when inner decay is in reality farthest advanced."

The final uses of the magic word occurred closely together in the second paragraph of the fourth part as a strategic trumpet call for Kennan's global policy to be initiated: "Balanced against this are the facts that Russia, as opposed to the western world in general, is still by far the weaker party, that Soviet policy is highly flexible, and that Soviet society may well *contain* deficiencies which will eventually weaken its own total potential. This would of itself warrant the United States entering with reasonable confidence upon a policy of firm *containment,* designed to confront the Russians with unalterable counterforce at every point where they show signs of encroaching upon the interest of a peaceful and stable world."[95]

Containment was "unalterable counterforce"—unspecified, but assumed by others to be the full range of strength available if anywhere needed. If this active, rather than any passive, policy was brought to bear and built on the West's own internal strength, the strains produced on the USSR would cause it either to break up or gradually mellow. Either way, it would be a victory for the West, a generous Providence provided as a test of the West's crowning worth.

Well over half of the words of this article were devoted to a dark picture of the USSR and Marxism-Leninism. The ideology was pseudoscientific, nebulous, visionary, and impractical. The environment and specific circumstances in which Bolshevism grew bred a climate of "skepticism as to the possibilities of permanent and peaceful coexistence of rival forces." Such forces had to submit or be destroyed. The party alone knew the truth, and no restrictions could be placed on it. Its dictatorship had to be retained to rid itself of capitalism at home and abroad. Internal opposition was merely the agent of foreign capitalism. Perfecting the dictatorship required security, discipline, and economic monopoly to protect the socialist homeland from "implacable foreign hostility." Least of all, Kennan argued, could the Soviet rulers "dispense with the fiction by which the maintenance of dictatorial power has been defended." All this led to the contemporary political personality of Soviet Russia. The first characteristic was its belief in the "innate antagonism between capitalism and Socialism." That gave to it its "secretiveness, the lack of frankness, the duplicity, the wary suspiciousness, and the basic unfriendliness of purpose." These flowed from its basic nature. Its personality was the Kremlin's "infallibility" as the "sole repository of truth." Only brute facts, not words, could alter Soviet behavior. It was with such a beast the West had to deal and that called forth the doctrine of containment.[96]

•   •   •

Of all the themes expressed in the "X" article, containment far overshadowed the others. Yet it was Kennan's negative view of Russia, a view of Russia portrayed as the dark flip side of Western civilization, a crypto–Byzantine Orientalism, that had been most consonant with his readers and needed illumination. That dark vision was especially captured in his correspondence. It showed in his attack on FDR's policy of wartime collaboration and an effort on FDR's part to appease the Kremlin to gain its backing for a successful and long-lasting postwar settlement. Kennan and most of the rest of the Riga Boys took the position that collaboration with Russia was impossible and no amount of appeasement would satisfy the Russian drive for expansion and dominance. Kennan now became the leader in the charge to reverse FDR's policy.

Shortly after Kennan's article, Walter Lippmann, the well-known political pundit and journalist, published articles in the *New York Herald Tribune,* later collected as a book, *The Cold War: A Study in U.S. Foreign Policy.* In them he opposed, as FDR might have, Kennan's containment. He did so by suggesting an alternative to fencing in Soviet Russia, similar to what FDR might have had in mind if he had lived. For Lippmann, containment, what he thought to be the heart of the Truman Doctrine, as announced to Congress by President Truman on March 12, 1947, meant squandering power around the periphery of the Soviet Union in a kind of trench warfare instead of focusing on the Atlantic community, including its Mediterranean offshoot. The objective of policy should be to negotiate treaties with Germany and Austria that would include evacuation of non-European armies, even if that meant paying a ransom to Russia in the form of reparations, concessions, and trade agreements. The Red Army had defeated Germany; its removal could liberate Germany. Removal would restore the balance of power, which Lippmann considered the goal of czarist and Soviet diplomacy. "Our aim," he wrote, "will not be to organize an ideological crusade. It will not be to make Jeffersonian democrats out of the peasants of eastern Europe . . . but to settle the war and restore the independence of the nations of Europe by removing the alien armies —all of them, our own included."[97]

Kennan understood that Bolshevik goals varied from czarist ones, that Marxist ideology made a difference. Fanaticism turned Lenin and his colleagues into opportunistic leaders, giving them what Kennan called aggressive intransigence. His analysis began with Marxism-Leninism. He concluded that for Lenin, the "victorious proletariat . . . would rise against the remaining capitalist world"—capitalism was a menace to the socialist homeland and had intervened there, and, in Kennan's words, the Soviets cultivated the "semi-myth of implacable foreign hostility," or what came to be known as the doctrine of the two camps. Because of the "innate antagonism between capitalism and socialism," the Kremlin developed secretiveness, duplicity, suspiciousness, and unfriendliness. Kennan pointed to the backwardness of Russia and the problems of doctrine when a dictator made errors. What proved decisive in Kennan's critique was his analysis of the decay of the Stalinist system.[98] What Lippmann had ridiculed was his own interpretation of the most extreme form of containment—its militarization.

It should be noted that Kennan, after putting forward the idea, subsequently moved away from the most militant expressions of containment, while his successors at the State Department implemented them. "The diplomat who had done so much in 1946 to convince official Washington that the Soviets had to be contained—by the threat of force as well as political and economic pressure—felt by 1948 that he had created a monster."[99]

In a draft letter to Lippmann, a letter that Kennan decided not to send in April 1948, he defended himself from his most formidable critic. Kennan was at pains to dissociate himself from the Truman Doctrine, but he strongly supported the Marshall Plan.[100] "In these circumstances, I am a little nonplused to find myself sternly rebuked as the author of the 'Truman doctrine' and confronted with the Marshall Plan as an example of constructive statesmanship from which I might derive a useful lesson and improve my ways." He emphasized that Lippmann chose to "interpret the term 'containment,' as used in the X-article, in a military sense, and have talked of it as though it implied a readiness on our part to hold the Red Army at any point where it touches the free world." Rather, "The policy of containment related to the effort to encourage other peoples to resist this type of violence [third column stooge forces, not Russian invasion] and to defend the internal integrity of their own countries." War was inevitable only "if they let all of Europe go by default to the political onslaught which the Kremlin was conducting." Containment did not mean that "we had to be equally strong everywhere in a military sense." One had to concentrate on "isolated spots." Nor was containment meant as liberating Eastern Europe. "By 'containment' I meant holding Russian expansion, as far as possible, at the point it had reached to date, i.e., roughly the high water mark of the Soviet military advance during the recent war." Nor would emphasis on a single spot work, as Russia would move to another. In Eastern Europe, when police power went to indigenous communists, Kennan "knew for certain that the jig was up." The same applied to Manchuria and North China. The Kuomintang had not sufficient power to expel them. What of it?

Kennan "never said we would—or should—be able to hold equally everywhere." Nor was containment a "passive, negative policy." Russians had enough problems of their own to contend with, and, with firmness on America's part, they would defeat themselves. Their own internal contradictions would trip them up. "It is the Russians, not we, who cannot afford a world half slave and half free." Kennan threw the onus on the Russians, who drew the issue way back before World War I: "There is no more vicious nonsense than the theory which holds their enmity to us to be the result of our own doing." Kennan took Lippmann to task, especially, because he had "implied that somehow many of our problems might have been solved if we had talked more to the Russians. This was, of course, FDR's line to talk and, if you will, charm them." According to Kennan, those possibilities were limited. "Remember: these people are our enemies. This is no normal clash of national interest. They are our enemies not only by virtue of an intellectual and emotional conviction of some 50 years standing. They are our enemies because their whole structure of power has been founded on the theory of that enmity and would be unjustified—even criminal—without it." For Kennan, the Rooseveltian initiative had no chance. The United States must remain strong and await a communist collapse or mellowing.[101]

But what if the West became so strong that the only alternative for them was a forced collaboration or collapse? What if the United States threatened to so far outspend the Russians as to threaten them with bankruptcy? What if the United States could design and build weapons beyond the other side's scientific and technological abilities? What then?

This theme of irreconcilable enemies, where one must either collapse or mellow, goes forward in Kennan's later correspondence as a persistent theme. For example, in another never-sent draft letter to the *New York Times* in November 1950, he intended to remind Anne O'Hare McCormick that as the Red Army moved into Eastern Europe that "there was never the slightest reason to suppose that Moscow would fail to take advantage of this trend of military events for her political purposes; and we ourselves, far from raising any serious objection to it, aided and abetted it in many ways which in Moscow's eyes appeared to be sanction."[102] The following year Kennan wrote William Henry Chamberlin, formerly of the *Christian Science Monitor* and a distinguished former Moscow correspondent and author, candidly: "I feel you take the moral and political consequences of Yalta (which was, of course, only the culminating expression of a series of compounded blunders, all stemming from Roosevelt's complete miscalculation of the character and ambitions of the Soviet regime) too lightly."[103]

From Kennan's setting up of the U.S. Embassy in Moscow to the eve of his own ambassadorship there in 1952, he remained firm and consistent on the impossibility of collaboration and thought of it as "appeasement" in the worst sense of Neville Chamberlain's Munich, that is, as a nasty and cowardly act for which he had nothing but disdain and contempt.

Kennan's ambassadorship to the USSR and preemptory removal as persona non grata, from May to September 1952, did nothing to enhance his view of Russia. He often compared his departure to "Siberian" Kennan's expulsion: "You are of course quite right in pointing out that the cause of Russian freedom was the great and lifelong interest of my distinguished relative, the elder George Kennan. You will recall that at the outset of this Century Kennan was expelled from Russia as a penalty for this interest, his presence having become onerous to the Russian Government."[104]

That winter, Truman left office, and President Dwight D. Eisenhower's administration came to power. In January 1953, Kennan addressed the

Pennsylvania State Bar Association in Scranton. His remarks were the immediate cause of his dismissal from government service in 1953 by Secretary of State John Foster Dulles. He learned from his own associates at the Policy Planning Staff that one journalist had heard from another that the secretary "had now concluded that the latter [Kennan] was a very dangerous man: that he was advocating the admission of the Chinese Communists to the United Nations and a cessation of US military action at the 38th parallel." He continued, "Had my view been accepted, there would have been no advance by our forces to the Yalu, no Chinese intervention, but distinctly better prospects for an early termination of the conflict."[105]

About the Scranton speech, it simply rehashed Kennan's well-known ideas. He offered some caveats. For example, though justifying the Korean War, he hoped the sword would be used with "greatest reluctance." He took another swipe at FDR by saying, "Showing [Kremlin leaders] kindness and confidence had been tried, and it had failed signally." Also, he had reduced his list of ten principles of dealing with the Kremlin to only four: be strong, be coolheaded and deliberate, be ready to negotiate, and strive for domestic and international unity.[106]

By 1956, Kennan could look dispassionately at his expulsion from Russia and, shortly after that, from the State Department and, putting all that aside, begin a new life as a university professor at Princeton's Institute for Advanced Study. It was there he remained until his death in 2005. One major exception was when he became ambassador to Yugoslavia during President John F. Kennedy's administration. But his avocation, writing and teaching, now became his vocation. In that capacity, for almost the next fifty years, he produced an amazing amount of work in almost every genre, winning two Pulitzer Prizes and a National Book Award along the way. His gloomy orientation toward Russia remained, though sometimes moderated with détente and mixed with a little optimism. His condemnation of FDR's wartime policy remained. Both his productive longevity and his singular views served to keep American perceptions and policies toward Russia negative. He could gloat to himself when his predictions, like miracles, came true. And, since nothing succeeds like success, he lived to see the "Kennanization" of American foreign policy. It was a bolder and more aggressive policy than even he had intended. That newer version of containment came to be called "rollback," and its author was Paul H. Nitze.

7

Gray Eminence

Paul H. Nitze was an ever present shadow, or "gray eminence," who served eight consecutive presidents, from Harry S. Truman to Ronald W. Reagan. It all began for Paul Nitze in the early summer of 1940, when his friend James Forrestal of the "silent six"—FDR's administrative assistants—invited him to Washington, D.C., as his "secretary." Nitze wrote, "In this wholly illegal fashion, my career in Washington began."[1] He stayed there for five decades.[2] As deputy assistant secretary of state for economic affairs in 1949, he was assigned to aid Kennan on preparing the economic aspects of the ill-fated Palais Rose Conference held in Paris during May 1949 in the aftermath of the Berlin Blockade to discuss German and Austrian problems. He succeeded George F. Kennan as director of the Policy Planning Staff (S/P) on January 1, 1950, as "head of the division of ideas." It had just been learned in September 1949 that the USSR had detonated its first atomic bomb on August 29, 1949.[3]

The times, Nitze remarked, were ominous. There was Stalin's overtly anti-Western speech of February 9, 1946. He had revived the two-hostile-camps theory of an inevitable war between socialism versus capitalism. Also the People's Republic of China was established on October 1, 1949. The German Democratic Republic was created on October 7, 1949. In the following January, Russia's UN ambassador, Jacob A. Malik, walked out of the Security Council of the United Nations. On February 14, 1950, the USSR signed a Treaty of Friendship, Alliance, and Mutual Assistance with the PRC. British atomic scientist Klaus Fuchs was arrested for espionage that same February. Senator Joseph R. McCarthy (R-WI) made his first charges on February 9, 1950, at Wheeling, West Virginia, against 205 supposed communists in the Truman administration's State Department.[4] The times were perilous.

Nitze's policy making consisted in drawing up the NSC-68 document. It was the most authoritative statement on how Kennan's theory of containment could be used to build up U.S. and Allied forces to keep the USSR restrained and diminished. NSC-68 came about in the following way. Nitze took Kennan's place as head of the Policy Planning Staff at the beginning of 1950. Instead of Kennan's micromanaging of S/P, especially looking on his reports as "etched in steel," Nitze made each a "joint product," taking responsibility for "deciding the staff's position and for the wording of the final report." As Nitze relates, two problems confronted S/P: Soviet acquisition of an atomic device and consolidation of Mao's regime. He concluded, "We were on the verge of a fundamental change in the balance of power. The question was: How should we react to these developments?" Kennan felt nothing useful could be done on China to influence that problem. On the nuclear issue, "he believed that the time had come to put a halt to reliance on nuclear arms and to reopen negotiations with the Soviets on international control of atomic energy." Kennan opposed developing an H-bomb, even though prominent nuclear physicist Edward Teller believed it doable. After apt consideration, President Harry S. Truman asked if the Russians would be able to make it. Assured that they could, he gave the go-ahead to the H-bomb's development, referred to as the "super." Stalin had already done so three months earlier, in November 1949. What were, Nitze wondered, the national security implications of thermonuclear weapons?[5] On those possibilities, Nitze remained a hard-nosed pragmatist.

The decision to quicken the super's development began on November 18, 1949, when Truman created a special committee of the National Security Council to review the situation. It was the committee's report on January 31, 1950, favoring acceleration that prompted the president to direct NSC-68's strategic review. The draft study went out March 30 to top officials. Defense Secretary Louis Johnson circulated it to his senior staff. By then it had received the "strongest endorsement" by Robert A. Lovett, soon to be appointed deputy secretary of defense. The State-Defense Policy Review Group formed to examine these implications and worked intensively from mid-February 1950 until final submission of NSC-68 on April 14, 1950.[6]

Writing this report had fallen to S/P. Its conclusions were at first opposed by Johnson, who wanted to keep spending at thirteen billion dollars. Secretary of State Dean Acheson and S/P prevailed. Though the report contained no budget, Nitze estimated four to five yearly outlays of forty billion dollars a year.[7] He always contended that, as was often noted in opposition to NSC-68, 1954 was not the expected year of war with the USSR. It was the year of "maximum" danger. Besides, he believed that NSC-68 was not a sharp departure in U.S. policy. It provided details for what NSC-20/4, Kennan's product, called for: "timely and adequate preparation to combat internal and external Soviet moves that might jeopardize our security." Thus, NSC-68, which fathered yearly updates, called for "a stepped up level of effort to counter recent developments." In the final drafting of the report, Nitze was assisted by Chip Bohlen. He took a more conservative position than NSC-68, emphasizing the Russians were "most interested in maintaining their power base within the Soviet Union, that their second priority was maintaining control over their satellites, and that their ambitions for further expansion afield were only a third priority." Bohlen always claimed NSC-68 gave "too much emphasis" to Soviet expansion.[8]

• • •

NSC-68 expressed quintessential American Cold War policy. Its principal architect and author was Paul Nitze. Kennan had called for containment. Nitze's policy of "rollback" demanded reversing Soviet successes abroad.[9] Indeed, the negativism toward the USSR displayed in NSC-68, which earlier had been renewed by Kennan and the rest of Robert Kelley's boys from Riga like Loy Henderson and Chip Bohlen, was expanded by Nitze and Acheson into an all-consuming American phobia. With their growing view of the danger posed by the USSR, Nitze later remarked, "Truman, Acheson, Harriman, Bohlen, Kennan, Symington, Clifford, Conant and I were all in accord—as were the allies."[10] NSC-68 was the bridge between Kennan's "containment' and President Ronald Reagan's "evil empire."[11] An analysis of NSC-68 demonstrates this.[12]

By the end of World War II, the report started off, the earth's distribution of power had become bipolar between the United States and the USSR. NSC-68 argued that the Soviet Union "[is] animated by a new fanatic faith, antithetical to our own, and seeks to impose its absolute authority over the rest of the world."[13] Conflict, waged by both violent and nonviolent means, had become endemic, expedient, and terrifying, given the onset of weapons of mass destruction. The new polarized balance between the two superpowers was precarious: "Any substantial further extension of the area under the domination of the Kremlin would raise the possibility that no coalition adequate to confront the Kremlin with greater strength could be assembled." Further results of this would mean, according to NSC-68, "destruction not only of this Republic but of civilization itself." The report called this process the "Kremlin design," a phrase used more than a dozen times. The Kremlin would subvert or destroy the government machinery and social structure of the non-Soviet world and replace them with subservient ones, first dominating Eurasia's landmass and then confronting the United States as its principal enemy. America's "integrity and vitality must be subverted or destroyed by one means or another if the Kremlin is to achieve its fundamental design."[14]

These opening remarks set up a Manichaean dualism between the United States and the USSR, an either-or situation with nothing in between—an excluded middle. America was the only major threat to its achievement.

It was, in the opening words of the report, a fundamental struggle between freedom and slavery or, as it later intimates, between good and evil.[15]

The answer to such a drastic Soviet challenge by the United States was to "make ourselves strong" militarily, economically, and politically to "foster a fundamental change in the nature of the Soviet system, a change toward which the frustration of the design is the first and perhaps the most important step." Only by developing the West's "moral and material strength" would the Soviets accommodate and coexist. Force was only a last resort. Military power served to deter an attack. If it came to war, the report cited *The Federalist no. 28:* "The means to be employed must be proportioned to the extent of the mischief." The mischief may be very limited or global. The United States and its allies—the free world—must have at its disposal all available means to deter the threat on an entire spectrum from very limited conventional warfare to total thermonuclear. Otherwise, the United States would have to appease somewhere along the spectrum of intimidation rather than meet the intimidator with an appropriate response. NSC-68 looked at the growing Soviet means of intimidation it had at its disposal and proposed graduated reactions.[16]

The Soviet system was described as a militantly worldwide revolutionary movement, a "new universal faith" and a "model 'scientific society'"—the inheritor of czarist Russia's imperialism in the form of a totalitarian dictatorship. It would resort to war on calculations of practicality, otherwise employing violence, subversion, and deceit without regard to moral considerations. It was amoral and opportunistic.[17] In short, it was antihuman because it ran "counter to the best and potentially the strongest instincts of men." So it might prove "fatally weak." That meant it "cannot relax the condition of crisis and mobilization, for to do so would be to lose its dynamism, whereas the seeds of decay within the Soviet system would begin to flourish and fructify." Even with the total economic strength of the United States to the USSR at four to one, as well as in specific areas, though in scientific research an advantage was less clear, the report pointed out that the Kremlin focused its economy on war-making potential. It was reducing the gap and running on a near-maximum production basis. So America's greater capacity became more inoperative because of the USSR's concentrated efforts in the arms race. Given this object, the report suggested a potential scenario for 1950 on the basis of the USSR's excessive strength in conventional forces and its new atomic capability. Both served the USSR as a deterrent as well as an offensive projection of its power. The joint chiefs of staff considered the Soviet Union then capable of an initial attack that would overrun Western Europe, drive toward the Middle East, consolidate in the Far East, isolate Britain from the air and sea, and attack selected targets in North America. Afterward, it could simultaneously conduct further operations in all the above areas to compel surrender or destruction while strengthening its own air defenses. This frightening picture NSC-68 used as a way to call on a steady and long-term commitment by the West to increase its military strength to deter or delay the USSR. The report also spent time indicating what an atomic attack on the West might accomplish: laying waste to Britain and destruction of Western Europe's and North America's vital centers.[18]

Section VI of NSC-68, "U.S. Intentions and Capabilities—Actual and Potential," considered the current possibilities of the West to resist this scenario and painted a grim picture if the whole condition continued as it was and the West did not heed the full implications of containment. Accordingly, containment sought "by all means short of war to (1.) block further expansion of Soviet power, (2.) expose the falsities of Soviet pretensions, (3.) induce a retraction of the Kremlin's control and influence, and (4.) in general, so foster the seeds of destruction within the Soviet system that the Kremlin is brought at least to the point of modifying its behavior to conform to generally accepted international standards."[19] However, the cardinal point, NCS-68 argued, of the containment policy was that the United States must "possess superior overall power" alone or with allies. That superiority, once achieved and continually preserved, would both guarantee national security and provide the "indispensable backdrop to the conduct of the policy of 'containment.' Without superior aggregate military strength, in being and readily mobilizable, a policy of 'containment' [which is] in effect a policy of calculated and gradual coercion—is no more than a policy of bluff."[20]

With this statement, NSC-68 fully intended to flesh out Kennan's fuzzy notion of containment and get down to what it meant in specifics. It must, in Nitze's interpretation, be more than just "all means short of war," but rather consider in real dollars and cents, in military hardware, the "superior aggregate military strength" needed for the "calculated and gradual coercion" of the Soviet Union that was credible and not a bluff. When the bluff was called, as any realist knew it would be, the winning hand in military might was fully ready at an instant's notice. That is the heart and soul of NSC-68, what makes it qualitatively different from Kennan's containment. A calculated and gradual coercion was aimed at *rolling back* the Soviet Union until it relented or self-destructed. The report suggested a door be left ajar for the USSR's retreat in the face of the growing pressure of America's superiority. It figured in 1950 that the West would be able to conduct a sufficient military defense of the Western hemisphere but would be inadequate for Britain and the Near East and Middle East. If in two to three years, even shorter in an emergency, "the potential military capabilities of the U.S. and its allies would be rapidly and effectively developed, sufficient forces could be produced in order to deter war, or withstand an initial attack and stabilize supporting attacks, and retaliate with greater impact."[21]

The interesting feature of Part VII, "Present Risks," is that it created an either-or scenario because of what it attributed to the so-called Kremlin design. NSC-68 interpreted that "design" as an implacable system's seeking to "impose order among nations by means which would destroy our free and democratic system." What made this design sinister was that "the Kremlin's possession of atomic weapons puts new power behind its design, and increases the jeopardy to our system." Since the risks were of a "new order of magnitude," that is, of a "total struggle," it meant that "defeat at the hands of the totalitarian is total defeat. These risks crowd in on us, in a shrinking world of polarized power, so as to give us no choice, ultimately, between meeting them effectively or being overcome by them." The choice of some middle ground or accommodation was excluded. The United States and its allies would either prevail or go down; the same held for the other side. In the next paragraph, the Kremlin's design was called "evil." NSC-68 anticipated the eventual all-out efforts of achieving superiority by the Reagan administration to weaken and destroy the "evil empire." The military readiness of the United States and its allies also created choices short of global or total war in the efforts of the Kremlin to test the West's resolve at this or that point.[22]

In Section VIII, "Atomic Armament," perhaps the most important part of NSC-68, Nitze considered the uses of nuclear weapons and responded to critics. This oft-quoted section is important because the report talked about 1954—the "year of maximum danger"—as a possible target-date scenario for a nuclear exchange. That is because America's advantage would disappear and the USSR might inflict serious damage by a surprise nuclear attack. This has often been misinterpreted as a hard prediction. As Nitze pointed out, that was incorrect—a "misreading of the paper."[23] He noted that even though 1954 was considered the year of "maximum danger," that was only so because the "Soviets would have atomic weapons and delivery aircraft in sufficient number to threaten extensive (even unacceptable) damage to the United States."[24] No system of international control would be enough because there would be no way to verify it, and the time lapse might not be sufficient to retaliate. The report conceded that only if the Soviet Union moved substantially toward "accommodation and compromise" would such an arrangement be conceivable. It concluded, "It is impossible to hope that an effective plan for international control can be negotiated unless and until the Kremlin design has been frustrated to a point at which a genuine and drastic change in Soviet policies has taken place."[25] This did not sound likely in the 1950 report.

In Section IX, "Possible Courses of Action," four are listed: a continuation of current policies, isolation, war, and a rapid buildup. The first three were excused as ineffective or impossible. All four would take place within the backdrop of negotiation, but negotiation must have behind it a "force sufficient to inhibit a Soviet attack."[26] Even there, negotiations were planned so that proposals would have to be expected in advance of their acceptance. The report considered "radical change" in the Soviet design unlikely, and, therefore, the Kremlin's three major objectives would be difficult to meet: its effort to eliminate America's nuclear capabilities, prevent its mobilization of its superior potential, and get America's withdrawal from its Allied commitments.[27] To make negotiations more expedient than the use of force, the fourth course of action was necessary. Agreements would have to be enforceable, not susceptible of violation without detection, and effective countermeasures readied.[28]

Nitze considered but rejected both the present course and isolation because each reduced the United States to the limited sphere of its own hemisphere, shorn of its allies, trade, and communication with the rest of the world. Preponderance would shift to the Kremlin as it dominated Eurasia and threatened to crush the United States: "There is no way to make ourselves inoffensive to the Kremlin except by complete submission to its will. Isolation would in the end condemn us to capitulate or to fight alone and on the defensive. . . . Under this course of action, there would be no negotiation, unless on the Kremlin's terms, for we would have given up everything of importance."[29] A preventive war, as the report suggested, would be "unacceptable" and "repugnant" to Americans, unless as a counterattack to a Soviet blow about to be delivered.[30] NSC-68 concluded that only a rapid buildup of political, economic, and military strength was possible: "It is clear that a substantial and rapid building up of strength in the free world is necessary to support a firm policy intended to check and to *roll back* the Kremlin's drive for world domination." By rollback, the report meant "a situation to which the Kremlin would find it expedient to accommodate itself, first by relaxing tensions and pressures and then by gradual withdrawal."[31]

It was estimated, though not noted in the report, that a defense budget of forty billion dollars a year would be required for the next four to five years to meet all possibilities, especially local actions short of total war.[32] Short of a firm policy, appeasement meant defeat. NSC-68's proposals were costly but affordable. The report itself assumed the trend could be reversed, but it would require "significant domestic financial and economic adjustments."[33] The policy of rollback was finally announced, which meant the West would actively seek a process of forcing the Soviet Union to accommodate, withdraw, and make necessary changes in its system to frustrate its design for world domination.

Criticism arose over the costs. Though not stated in the NSC-68 report, Truman requested an ad hoc committee to make an estimate. Even Acheson had panicked. "Paul," he said, "don't you put that figure in this report. It is right for you to estimate it and tell me about it and I will tell Mr. Truman, but the decision on the amount of money involved should not be made until it is costed out in detail."[34] William Schaub, representing the Bureau of the Budget on the ad hoc committee, led the attack by questioning some of NSC-68's underlying thinking. According to Schaub, escalating military expenditures diverted resources from domestic needs. Such expenses were not productive. "For Schaub and the people at the Bureau of the Budget, the prospect of tripling military budgets was their worst nightmare come true."[35] Neither Hamilton Dearborn nor Leon Keyserling of the Council of Economic Advisors "thought that greater defense budgets would be catastrophic."[36] Scholar Samuel F. Wells Jr. cites Bohlen as giving the "most negative State Department response." That response was: "[NSC-68] tends, therefore, to over-simplify the problem and, in my opinion, leads inevitably to the conclusion that war is inevitable." The Soviets most wanted preservation of their system and would seek its extension only "without serious risk to the internal regime."[37] At that juncture, the whole issue remained deadlocked in early May. As one thoughtful student of the subject said, "By mid-June it seemed that the recommendations of NSC 68 were destined to be forgotten and ignored. Tripling defense budgets was too radical an idea."[38]

All this changed at 9:26 P.M. on June 24, 1950, when John J. Muccio, U.S. ambassador to South Korea, telegraphed the State Department from Seoul that North Korean forces had attacked the Republic of Korea. According to Wells, "The Korean War provided the necessary impetus for the adoption of the programs implicit in NSC-68. Had war not intervened, there is strong evidence that no major increase in defense spending would have won administration approval."[39] By then, the days of FDR's accommodation policies were finally, almost irrevocably, over. The most negative phase of America's love-hate relationship with Russia had begun. It was the culmination of a half century's worth of negativism toward Russia: the senior "Siberian" George Kennan's critique of the czarist government; Theodore Roosevelt's suspicions of Russian imperialism in the Far East; Wilson's quarantine of Soviet Russia; the bold realism of the boys from Riga and their "Riga Axioms"; the frustrations of William Bullitt, Laurence Steinhardt, and Adm. William Standley; and the junior George F. Kennan's policy of containment—all these perceptions and distortions now culminated most negatively in Nitze's rollback that, to one extent or another, prevailed to the end of the Soviet Union in 1991 and even beyond: "With George Kennan gone, his belief in a containment policy predicated on political and economic resistance to communism had no defenders. There was now remarkable unanimity in the State Department over the need to militarize containment. With few flourishes but undeniable finality, the Kennan era had ended."[40]

• • •

Paul Nitze's career stretched far beyond this incisive document, and over the years he made important theoretical and practical supplements to it. Its basic tenets remained and were to influence every president and secretary of state from Harry S. Truman and Dean Acheson to Ronald Reagan and George P. Shultz. That influence began almost immediately on the heels of NSC-68, because North Korea had invaded South Korea. As Nitze said, "I suspected—and had so warned repeatedly during the preparation of NSC-68—that the Soviets might be planning and did plan some kind of action, but where it would take place was difficult to foresee." Kim Il Sung, North Korea's communist leader, turned to Moscow for advice and aid. In hindsight, that the place was Korea seemed to Nitze the "inevitable consequence of a policy that from the beginning had been grossly shortsighted."[41] It flowed from the 1943 Cairo decision to divide the peninsula at the thirty-eighth parallel and reunify later. In 1947, those negotiations deadlocked, and Gen. Dwight D. Eisenhower, the army chief of staff, recommended withdrawal of U.S. forces from Korea, which by 1949 Truman had accepted.

Eisenhower's recommendation and later denial for removing U.S. troops from South Korea had a marked effect on Nitze: he switched his allegiance from being a Republican to a Democrat in 1952, charging the general with duplicity in blaming Truman and refusing to back Gen. George C. Marshall against Senator Joseph McCarthy's slander. Two days after the North Korean assault on the South, the president ordered Gen. Douglas MacArthur to provide air and sea support, agreeing with a UN resolution. On June 30, 1950, Truman also ordered American ground intervention, which had UN sanction. The S/P felt the Soviet Union was behind the attack but failed to prove it. During the first phase of the Korean War, from late June to mid-September, Truman replaced Louis Johnson with General Marshall as secretary of defense. The successful Inchon landing and counteroffensive began the second phase of the Korean War. Most important for Nitze, Truman was now convinced of NSC-68's approach and implemented it by bolstering U.S. conventional forces, strengthening strategic nuclear forces, and assisting allies. These decisions set the entire course of the Cold War as far as the United States was concerned. Perhaps it is a little simplistic to think that almost every later decision down to Nitze's concluding of the 1987 Intermediate Nuclear Force (INF) Treaty was a direct result of Nitze's NSC-68 document.[42] Yet there was no turning back. Whether Nitze was in or out of office, he was always close by for consultation and, if need be, objections—public or private.

By the spring of 1951, S/P believed that negotiated peace was possible. China's losses were immense, and Russia refused the full support of China. After failed feelers, Kennan spoke with the head of the Soviet UN delegation, Jacob A. Malik. Later, on June 23, Malik confirmed Soviet interest for an armistice, which would be conducted through the joint chiefs of staff, since China was not recognized by the United States. Nitze went to Tokyo to develop a negotiating position: location of the armistice line, return of prisoners, or the right to choose return. Negotiations were culminated early in Eisenhower's administration. The most important side effect of the Korean War was "to step up the pace of building what Acheson called 'situations of strength,'" especially if conflict with the Soviet Union proved unavoidable. All of this resulted in NSC-79, the war-aims paper.[43]

The first portion of NSC-79 dealt with military aims in a war with the Soviet Union: "radically reducing the Soviet Union's nuclear capability while minimizing losses to ourselves and our allies, the object being to shift the balance of remaining military power in our favor as a basis for negotiation of a settlement, not the capture of territory per se."[44] American policy toward Russia could be summed up as follows: "Our quarrel was with the Communist leadership, not the Russian people."[45] The Soviet Union would not be dismantled except for the Baltic states and the satellites. How, then, was the United States to deal with the rest of the world? Nitze rejected Pax Americana, world government, balance of power, or elements of all three. Rather, he favored a total elimination of Soviet nuclear weapons, turning all such weapons of all countries over to the UN, with a U.S. veto power, conventional armaments' cuts, and an ever varying dominant coalition of partners.[46]

The Korean War, according to Nitze, not only exposed U.S. military weakness but also showed that America's European allies needed strengthening. The April 1949 North Atlantic Treaty Organization's political objective was to restore confidence by treating a Soviet attack against any as an attack against all. Initially, it remained a paper alliance: "no command structure, no troops, and no immediate plans for acquiring any." Even its Medium-Term Defense Plan's needs were immense (one hundred ready and reserve divisions, eight thousand aircraft, and more than twenty-eight hundred ships). More serious was what to do about West Germany's participation. Until the Korean War, Acheson had enforced German demilitarization; now the question was not whether to militarize West Germany, but when? European fears of German remilitarization meant "creation of a European or NATO army, complete with an integrated command and supply system." Nitze headed a committee to solve the issue of paying for the plan, and produced the "Nitze Paper," or "Nitze Exercise," in which the United States filled the gap between what Europe could afford and actual costs. When the Truman administration ended, most of the major Cold War policies were in place because of the coordinated efforts of many persons, including an important role in these by Nitze. Though it was thought he might be retained as assistant secretary of defense for international security affairs, the new secretary, Charles Wilson, told him, "I'm having trouble over you because of your past associations." This meant difficult confirmation proceedings, especially after the problems that Bohlen incurred when nominated for ambassador to Moscow. Wilson went on to comment, "There were those who said I was the principal architect of much of Acheson's foreign policy, not merely an implementer of the policy." Nitze resigned and now became part of the loyal opposition.[47]

The loyal opposition meant being opposed to Secretary of State John Foster Dulles's doctrine of massive retaliation. In Dulles's words, "The basic decision was to depend primarily upon a great capacity to retaliate, by means and at places of our choosing."[48] Nitze thought Dulles's doctrine was a reversal of previous policy. "How, I asked, is the free world to decide the nature of its riposte to some act of aggression if the only sanction available is one that can be expected to result in the destruction of a major portion of its own factories and cities?" Nitze reasoned that massive retaliation remained only a declaratory policy. The action policy was graduated deterrence, that is, limiting wars to the minimum force necessary to deter and, if necessary, repel.[49]

To the notion that no one would win a nuclear war, Nitze thought there were two kinds of wins: In one, you ended the war only in a slightly better position than when it started. The other connotation was when one side ended in a much better position than the other. In an all-out nuclear war, "I would think it highly probable that one side or the other will 'win' the war and probably quickly [and] The winner may be in a hell of a mess but I think he will indubitably be the winner in that he will be giving orders to the loser and with no ifs, ands, or buts. And the winner in this sense will most probably go on to organize the world."[50] Even so, such a war of attrition, if neither side could win by blitzkrieg, would be hideous, and all measures had to be taken to prevent it. "Obviously if one cannot win in a blitzkrieg type war one must consider this alternative but the margin between accepting defeat without war and aspiring to victory in an attrition type atomic war is highly dubious."[51]

Nitze remained a proponent of graduated deterrence as well as defensive capability. In 1960, he could see no chance of moving toward such a posture. He gave a controversial paper at Asilomar, California. In it he proposed two alternatives: Class A and Class B capabilities. Class A put the

West in a position meaningfully to win nuclear war if deterrence failed; Class B was designed only to deny the other side's victory. Why not recognize Class B and not seek Class A? The problem was, the Soviets would continue seeking Class A, which compelled the West to do likewise. His Asilomar audience rejected that Class B suggestion.[52]

His years as an outsider ended when John F. Kennedy and Lyndon B. Johnson came to power.

• • •

Three main events constituted the Kennedy-Johnson years for Nitze: the Berlin Wall, Cuban missile crisis, and Vietnam War. During 1961–1968, both administrations had to deal with Soviet dictator Nikita S. Khrushchev, who seemed eager to come to terms with the West. Nitze considered Khrushchev a liar and bully: "Khrushchev continued to test our will and determination through threats and harassment in every way he could without forcing a major response from us."[53] When John F. Kennedy came into office in 1961, "he had already made the decision that a stated policy of reliance upon the prompt use of nuclear weapons was not only dangerous but a liability [and] ordered a reappraisal of our defense requirements, including our strategic plans and the nuclear and nonnuclear capabilities of our forces."[54] Nitze had favored this. Kennedy made him assistant secretary of defense for international security affairs, known in Washington, D.C., as the "little state department." The president wanted Nitze's office to be the "focal point in the administration for arms control."[55]

U.S. Ambassador to the USSR Llewellyn E. Thompson Jr. reported that Khrushchev was interested in meeting Kennedy, so the president wrote the Soviet premier in February 1961. Khrushchev agreed to a June 1961 meeting in Vienna. Kennedy found Khrushchev bellicose, which Thompson felt was par for the Russian.[56] Khrushchev assured Kennedy that he would not resume nuclear testing unless the United States did, which Nitze called a "cynical pledge." It was made just that when the first test-ban conference started in March, yet Soviet preparations for nuclear testing had begun and were initiated in August, when a 150-kiloton bomb, the most powerful ever detonated, was exploded. Besides, Khrushchev threatened to sign a separate East German peace treaty in December. That prior September, the United States and Britain had proposed an immediate ban on atmospheric testing and no on-site inspection. This, too, was rejected by Khrushchev as a "disservice to the cause of peace."[57] It was not until April 1962 that the United States finally carried out forty tests, together amounting to about 20 megatons, whereas the Soviets had done ten times that figure. Nevertheless, in April 1963, when Kennedy and Prime Minister Harold Macmillan again offered direct negotiations along similar lines to those of 1961,

Khrushchev responded with "recriminations, threats, and charges." In June, Khrushchev agreed to a Moscow meeting, and Kennedy sent Averell Harriman who, within ten days of negotiations, signed the Limited Test Ban Treaty on July 25, 1963, along the lines that had been proposed in 1961.[58]

When Khrushchev began massive nuclear testing, he opted to put pressure on Berlin. Acheson had warned that not only was this likely, but any communist takeover would fundamentally upset the European balance of power. Though not necessarily having the means to lift another blockade, the United States, according to Acheson, had to convince the Soviet Union that "loss of Berlin was more important to the United States than gaining it by force was to the USSR."[59] America would run greater risks than the Soviet Union. To counter further threats, Acheson suggested requesting large increases in the military budget, standby authority to call up the reserves, and tripling draft calls. Nitze believed the United States should not venture a war over Berlin or negotiate itself out of Berlin. The latter would simply obscure America's right to be there.[60]

Walter Ulbricht, communist East Germany's chief, retaliated by severely limiting exodus, which had already reached 3.5 million by mid-1961. Another 47,000 fled in the first twelve days of August. That action prompted construction of the Berlin Wall, at first barbed wire and rubble thrown up overnight on Sunday, August 12, 1961. Two East German and three Soviet divisions had covertly encircled Berlin, anticipating Allied retaliation to knock down the wall. That would give them an excuse to occupy the entire city. Khrushchev had recently guaranteed access, yet, if denied, there was no recourse but the single military plan. It called for massive retaliation. Secretary of Defense Robert McNamara asked NATO if its theater nuclear weapons could do anything short of a "prompt, full use of our strategic arsenal." NATO responded, "An initial nuclear exchange limited to targets in Europe was not what they had in mind."[61]

Because the allies were determined, Khrushchev realized that "maintaining our position in Berlin was more important to us than evicting us could possibly be to him." Two plans were considered: "Poodle Blanket" and "Horse Blanket." Each was a list of possible Soviet actions against allied access and NATO responses, the former being an abbreviated list, approved by Kennedy on October 23, 1961. The "Poodle" convinced NATO of a flexible response and resulted in the adoption of MC 14/3, "A Report by the Military Committee to the Defense Planning Committee on Overall Strategic Concept for the Defense of the North Atlantic Treaty Organization Area," on December 12, 1967. It consisted of a four-phased response: the first were various economic, maritime, and conventional military measures that escalated to the fourth phase, or "Horse," which included use of nuclear weapons.[62]

The second major event in the Kennedy-Johnson years was the Cuban missile crisis. Whereas in Berlin the allies might have to back down on the question of the wall due to an insufficiency of conventional military superiority, the reverse was true for Cuba. After the Bay of Pigs, Khrushchev had pledged that the Soviet Union would resist a U.S. attack on Cuba, but he had no intention of installing Soviet bases there. Yet in October 1962, there were not only about forty thousand Soviet troops in Cuba but also surface-to-air missiles and intermediate-range ballistic missiles (IRBMs). The Pentagon formerly had two contingencies against offensive missiles being placed in Cuba: an air strike alone or preceding an invasion. McNamara offered a third contingency: open surveillance and immediate blockade against offensive weapons. Nitze advised not blaming Fidel Castro, which would cast Khrushchev into the role of protector: "Better to accuse Khrushchev and not allow him to assume the role of innocent friend and protector of the small and weak."[63]

Why had Khrushchev decided on what Bohlen later called an "arrogant," "bellicose," "daring," and "dangerous" (*harebrained* was the term used by the Soviet Central Committee when it dismissed Khrushchev in 1964) scheme?[64] Perhaps, Bohlen and others speculated, Khrushchev thought the scheme would force the United States to settle the Berlin and German questions on Soviet terms, or Khrushchev believed he would stop Chinese charges that he had abandoned revolutionary Marxism, or he was confident in bullying Kennedy into accepting the Soviet's Cuban deployment, or it was a bargaining position to force U.S. Jupiter missiles out of Turkey.[65]

Nitze's thesis was that the Kremlin wanted to "consolidate its holdings around the periphery of the Soviet Union so that the USSR could dominate the Eurasian landmass. From there subsequent domination of Africa and Latin America through client states and direct coercion would be facilitated." What Nitze meant went back to his understanding of the Cold War as he had previously enunciated it in 1950 in the NSC-68 document. Then, the Soviets were striving for nuclear superiority and an enlarged naval control of the oceans. Over time, the free world would shrink to the boundaries of the United States, and, isolated in a unipolar world, America would have to give in to Soviet pressures. "This, I believed, was the Kremlin's grand design to achieve—patiently, over as much time as might be necessary—world domination without a nuclear shot being fired." The Cuban deployment was a quick and cheap way to shift the strategic balance of power in the USSR's favor.[66]

To prevent these various possibilities, McNamara suggested a range of escalating responses, starting at the lowest end of the scale. That end of the scale was a naval blockade limited only to offensive weapons. It could intensify into an air strike or invasion if it failed. If a Soviet ship had to be fired on, would the Kremlin respond by their submarines sinking U.S. ships or taking out U.S. missiles in Turkey, in Italy, or in other allied NATO countries? Though an air strike against Cuba would not be an attack against the Warsaw Pact, it would risk killing Soviet personnel. The blockade was called a "quarantine." Now, Nitze recalled, the United States had a distinct global nuclear superiority and an obvious conventional one in the Cuban area. Though the quarantine sought only to block added shipments of IRBMs, plans for other contingencies had to be made, that is, positioning supplies and troops as well as air support, both tactical and strategic, and placing antisubmarine barriers. Once in place, Kennedy made his Monday-evening speech on October 22, 1962, in which he announced that the quarantine would go into effect at 10:00 A.M., Wednesday, October 24.[67]

When the carrier *Essex* and its helicopters moved to intercept Soviet ships, sixteen of them were approaching the quarantine line and changed their course or stopped. Only a Third World country's ship, Lebanese under Soviet charter from Riga, was boarded, avoiding a direct confrontation.[68] Still, the missiles in Cuba had to be dismantled and removed, which UN Secretary-General U Thant offered to verify. Now, two letters were received from Khrushchev: the first on October 26 offered to dismantle or destroy the missiles already there in return for an end to the quarantine and a pledge not to invade Cuba; the second letter, the next morning, October 27, demanded removal of the Turkish Jupiter missiles in return for ridding Cuba of Soviet missiles. Though Nitze objected, Kennedy believed it better to eliminate obsolete Turkish missiles rather than risk war over Cuba and Berlin.[69] Kennedy responded to Khrushchev's first letter, agreeing to its terms. On November 19, Castro reluctantly allowed UN inspection due to Soviet pressure. The next day, the quarantine was lifted, and by December 6, Soviet IL-28 bombers had been crated and removed.[70]

The third major conflict in which Nitze participated during the Kennedy-Johnson period was the Vietnam War. Vietnam became to many Americans the proxy of the Soviet Union and, therefore, further magnified their distorted picture of Russia itself. In the fall of 1961, Kennedy sent Gen. Maxwell Taylor and Walter Rostow to Saigon to evaluate whether U.S. combat troops should be sent, and the general reported that South Vietnam could not be saved without introducing a U.S. military task force of 6,000 to 8,000 troops. McNamara believed that task force represented only a first installment of a much larger commitment. Taylor and Rostow cautioned against introducing U.S. troops and only doing so if it were necessary to prevent the fall of Saigon. It was at this point that Nitze "argued strongly against the introduction of U.S. combat forces into the war in Vietnam." As he put it, "There is no such thing as being a little pregnant."[71]

The year 1964 was Nitze's first as secretary of the navy. In the spring of

1965, he went to South Vietnam because the marines came under his jurisdiction. He returned pessimistic: "I told [McNamara] that I thought it
would take more than 200,000 men to accomplish our mission there, if we
were able to do it at all."[72] Nitze recommended withdrawal. In June 1965,
75,000 troops were there, and another 200,000 were requested by their commander, Gen. William C. Westmoreland. President Johnson asked Nitze
what the chances for success were. Nitze replied: "forty percent." Nevertheless, Johnson approved McNamara's request for 200,000. The Ameri-
canization of the war had then begun in the summer of 1965. Operation
Rolling Thunder, the aerial bombing of North Vietnam, had started the previous February. Both the ability of the North to recuperate, consistent with
Nitze's old study of World War II bombings, and Westmoreland's never-
ending requests for more troops dampened McNamara's confidence. In
March 1967, 471,616 U.S. troops were engaged, and Westmoreland asked
for another 200,000. McNamara now had second thoughts. In 1967, Johnson
offered the San Antonio formula to Hanoi—cessation of the naval and aerial bombardment of the North in exchange for serious discussions—but
these were emphatically rejected. By then, Nitze was deputy secretary of
defense. McNamara reported to Johnson in October 1967 that only slow
progress and stability could be attained, and he recommended a halt to
bombing the North. When Johnson showed the report to his so-called wise
men in November, they decided those actions would be playing into
Hanoi's hands and would demonstrate a lack of will. Thus, McNamara resigned, and he was replaced by Clark Clifford.[73]

On January 30, 1968, the Tet Offensive began in all major cities and
provincial capitals. The Vietcong was driven back, and it suffered enormous casualties. Hue held out nearly a month. Yet the North had won a
major political-propagandistic battle against almost 500,000 American
troops and a February request for another 206,000. Clifford had left the running of the department to Nitze, while he concentrated on the White House,
the war, Congress, and the press. In that role, Nitze remarked, "it was usually up to me to argue with him until I was hoarse on what I considered to
be the errors of his thinking on our course in Vietnam."[74] Nitze's advice
was a unilateral bombing halt, protection of South Vietnam's population,
integration of U.S. and Vietnamese forces with 50,000 more U.S. forces, and
negotiations. When Senator Eugene McCarthy won the New Hampshire
primary in March and Senator Robert Kennedy started running for president, change was in the air, even though Johnson still refused to stop the
bombings. As the Senate Foreign Relations Committee began its annual
hearings, Nitze was asked by Johnson to go to the Hill. He refused because
he could not back the recommendations and offered his resignation.
Though Clifford prevented his resignation, Johnson banished him from his

inner group. Paul Warnke was recruited to testify. At this point, faced with appearing himself, Clifford reversed his position on the war: "He led the opposition to our Vietnam policies and argued vehemently for disengagement as quickly as possible."[75]

The pace quickened as Johnson replaced Westmoreland with his deputy, Gen. Creighton Abrams. Johnson again met with his "wise men" on March 25–26, 1968. They gave him their judgment on the war: "Continued escalation of the conflict in Vietnam, intensified bombing of North Vietnam, and increased American troop deployments would not bring about a military solution. They recommended the president seek a political solution at the negotiating table."[76] This group, also known as the Clifford group, won the day. On March 31, 1968, Johnson announced he would not seek reelection. With Nixon's presidential victory, David Packard took over Nitze's responsibilities on January 30, 1969. Nitze remarked that the fateful decision of the summer of 1965 to escalate the Vietnamese War had had terrible repercussions: "The damage to our position in the world and to our strategic nuclear capabilities in relation to the Soviet Union was incalculable. It was during this period that the Kremlin laid the foundation for passing us in the strategic nuclear field."[77]

• • •

Paul Nitze's accomplishments in the seventies and eighties were threefold: negotiating and critiquing strategic arms limitation treaties (SALT I and SALT II), including the antiballistic missile (ABM) treaty; assisting in strategic arms reduction talks (START); and successfully concluding the INF Treaty. His main effort, as he put it, was to stabilize the nuclear arms race. In themselves, they represented a kind of distortion of U.S.-USSR relations to the level of the unthinkable—a potential nuclear hell. It was not pleasant for Nitze to think through the geography of a nuclear hell.

About the road to SALT I, which was finally signed in May 1972, it had become clear as early as 1956 that *Sputnik,* the first Soviet space probe, made it likely that developing Soviet intercontinental ballistic missiles (ICBMs) would threaten U.S. bomber bases before there could be significant retaliation. This resulted in enormous research and development expenditures from 1956 to 1962—approximately $48 billion a year to offset any Soviet advantage. By 1962, the strategic balance was reversed to America's advantage, which continued into the seventies. Already by the mid-1960s, each side sought different approaches to its strategic programs: the United States emphasized conventional forces to deter pressure on its allies and to improve the technology of its strategic forces with reliability, command and control, accuracy, penetration capability, and multiple independently targeted reentry vehicles (MIRVs). The Soviet Union decided to equal and exceed the United States in strategic missile launchers and throw weights. This rapid buildup, especially with their deployment of an ABM system, meant that the strategic balance would shift sooner rather than later in their favor.[78]

Because of the intense pace of the USSR producing 100 to 150 new ICBMs a year, countermeasures had to be taken by the early seventies. On that basis, Johnson wrote Premier Aleksei Kosygin in January 1967 about curbing the arms race, which set the stage for the Kosygin-Johnson summit at Glassboro in June 1967, where both sides agreed to further talks. A working paper for negotiations proposed freezing the number of strategic offensive missile launchers, limiting ABMs, and accepting unilateral verification. Nitze believed that throw weight (aggregate payload) was a more important measure than numbers because Soviet missiles and their silos were larger: "At some point in the future the United States might be faced with an enemy whose missiles were not only larger than, and therefore capable of carrying more warheads, but also as accurate as our own."[79]

As nothing happened by negotiations, Johnson, in January 1968, requested $1.2 billion to produce and deploy an ABM system and further funds for testing and placing MIRVs on the Poseidon and Minuteman missiles. In response, the Soviets proposed negotiations restricted to limiting strategic nuclear weapons and defenses against them. At the Nuclear Nonproliferation Treaty signing, on July 1, 1968, the United States announced early talks on limiting and reducing "offensive strategic nuclear weapons delivery systems as well as systems of defense against ballistic missiles."[80] Though Nitze backed up Clark Clifford, the secretary deferred these matters to him, and his position on negotiations was a non-zero-sum solution. Johnson was invited to Moscow for October 1968, but in August the USSR invaded Czechoslovakia, and Johnson canceled the trip. That pushed negotiations into the Nixon presidency. It appeared that Nitze's role was finished.[81]

Surprisingly, the new secretary of state, William Rogers, asked Nitze to be the ambassador to West Germany. Senator William Fulbright (D-AR) killed that over the issue of an earlier misunderstanding about evidence leading to the Gulf of Tonkin Resolution. Back in 1964, Nitze, as deputy secretary of defense, had testified before Fulbright's Foreign Relations Committee of the Senate that the North Vietnamese had attacked American ships and planes. The senator believed Nitze had deliberately produced false information to mislead the investigation.[82]

When the new authorization bill came up, Nitze joined the Committee to Maintain a Prudent Defense Policy to combat the anti-ABM campaign. The bill passed by a single vote, after the committee testified and circulated widely pro-ABM papers. During that debate, Nitze received another call from Rogers to serve on the SALT negotiating team, representing Secretary of Defense Melvin R. Laird. This put him in touch with President Richard

M. Nixon and his national security adviser, Henry Kissinger, whose book *Nuclear Weapons and Foreign Policy* he had panned in a review because Kissinger misunderstood the destructive power of a 50-kiloton bomb on a European battlefield.[83] In preparation for the first session of SALT, scheduled for Helsinki on November 17, 1969, Nitze put together the "Red Team" to assess Soviet aims and negotiating tactics. The joint chiefs of staff estimated that once parity was attained, the Soviets would cease building up their forces. However, the Red Team believed the Russians would see this as a confrontation to gain an advantage. Throughout, Nitze sought to stabilize the arms race within manageable limits. Whereas the two delegations agreed on no linkage to outside issues, Nixon thought otherwise. "I suspect," Nitze conceded, "that this was what was behind many of the concessions he made."[84]

Nixon decided on presenting two proposals: phased reductions or ceilings fitted to current levels and banning or limiting ABM. When talks resumed in Vienna, the Soviet delegation reacted negatively to the proposals, and things deadlocked. The United States dropped the inclusion of Soviet medium- and intermediate-range ballistic missiles in exchange for the Soviets excluding forward-based systems. Various ceilings were set.[85] The Soviets made no adequate concessions, and Nitze felt the administration was rushing into things. He wanted to negotiate each item, not offering a package but holding out for a quid pro quo. Instead, the administration opted for putting the entire package on the table to facilitate the Soviet delegation taking it to the Politburo for discussion. "As I suspected would happen, our gambit backfired. The Soviets pocketed each and every U.S. concession in our August 4 proposal and confirmed none of those expected of the Soviet side. . . . [H]aving already made substantial concessions, we had little left with which to bargain. It was a costly lesson—a mistake from which we were never able fully to recover."[86] A stalemate ensued. When negotiations resumed in Helsinki on November 2, 1970, the Russians sat tight, dismissing the August 4 points as inadequate. To break the stalemate, in December the Soviet delegation suggested negotiating a separate ABM treaty. In an exchange of notes between Nixon and Leonid Brezhnev, on May 29, 1971, they initially agreed to an ABM treaty and an interim or temporary freeze on offensive strategic missile systems until something permanent could be negotiated.[87]

The May accord did not relieve the stalemate. In January 1972, the Soviets approached Nitze on a possible compromise to limit the number of modern ABM radar complexes to a few specified areas such as national capitals, though the United States only wanted to protect its ICBM fields. Nitze suggested components rather than sites, those sites defending silos rather than cities, though national capitals were included. This set the stage for the Nixon-Brezhnev summit, scheduled for May 1972 and formalizing the Interim Agreement. Already, Henry Kissinger and the Soviet ambassador to the United States, Anatoly Dobrynin, had settled the submarine-launched ballistic missile (SLBM) issue. Since Nixon had no preference, they also would be included in the freeze once the status and number were fixed. As Nixon took off for Moscow on May 20, 1972, the press already was calling it the "historic" meeting with Brezhnev. After some tense last-minute negotiations, the final text was signed on the twenty-sixth. Nitze supported the SALT I Interim Agreement for congressional approval by joint resolution. Though it was not a formal treaty requiring the advice and consent of the Senate, this satisfied the 1961 Arms Control and Disarmament Act. In fact, Senator Henry Jackson (D-WA) incorporated an amendment stipulating that an eventual SALT II agreement would have to maintain the same strategic forces for both sides.[88]

Each party sought a more complete agreement in place of the interim, one that would limit offensive strategic nuclear arms, especially since ABM systems had been restrained. Negotiations resumed in Geneva in November 1972. A SALT II arrangement, according to Nitze, had to be based on equality in capabilities, increased stability, and an effort to restrain the costs and resources devoted to the arms race.[89] "We had conceded that the Soviet Union was entitled to an advantage for an indefinite time of some forty percent in the number of missile launchers and something better than double the average size, or throw-weight, of their missiles over ours."[90] According to Nitze, all the Soviets thought they now had to do was to limit other U.S. armaments, reduce U.S. nuclear support of its European allies, and stop further B-1 bombers and Trident programs: "The one-sidedness of their position made it difficult for me to see how an agreement could ever be reached." The result of this, if agreed to, would have left "all of NATO Europe at the mercy of Soviet conventional forces, backed by unrestrained numbers of Soviet medium-range, intermediate range, and tactical nuclear weapons."[91] Even Vladimir Semenov, head of the Soviet arms delegation, agreed with Nitze that the negotiations were going nowhere.

In May 1974, Nitze resigned from the arms-negotiating delegation after an unsuccessful attempt at becoming assistant secretary of defense for international security affairs, a position he had previously held. Secretary of Defense James Schlesinger had pressed Nitze to accept this post, but, as earlier with Fulbright, it was killed by Barry Goldwater even before it reached his Senate's Armed Services Committee. The senator blamed Nitze for spoiling his chances for the presidency by Nitze's counterattacking the senator's claim that the Democratic administration had weakened U.S. defenses by favoring the navy over the air force.[92] Nitze never intended to embarrass Kissinger and Nixon in their summit meeting with Brezhnev in

Moscow that May: "Whatever damage may have been done to the U.S. negotiating position was done by Nixon himself, not by others." Naturally, Nixon's "morally bankrupt and mortally wounded" presidency made the Soviets "reluctant to discuss substantive matters," and they quickly agreed to Kissinger's suggestion to negotiate a ten-year "replacement agreement" of the Interim Agreement. If agreed to, the "Soviets would have a preponderance of strategic offensive nuclear power [which] would leave Nixon's successors an almost hopeless task of negotiating an equal and stabilizing SALT III treaty."[93]

In November 1974, President Gerald Ford and Secretary of State Henry Kissinger signed the Vladivostok Accord with Brezhnev. Though setting ceilings on ICBMs, SLBMs, and heavy bombers, as well as on MIRVed missile launchers, it did not deal with either throw weights or forward-based systems. Nitze believed that, even if new programs were not factored in, the United States over a ten-year period would end with about half to a third of both the MIRVed and un-MIRVed missile throw weights, with only the bomber force remaining about equal.[94]

Kissinger's idea was to transform this accord into a SALT II agreement. Nitze's intention was to speak out as a private citizen against this possibility, which he saw as a "shift in the correlation of forces in their favor [with no] discernible effect in arresting the trend toward an increasingly large margin of Soviet offensive strategic superiority."[95] To counter this shift, he recommended deployment of 550 MXs (advanced technology ICBMs), Trident IIs in an appropriate number of Trident submarines, and B-1 bombers with strategic cruise missiles. Meanwhile, he favored quick fixes like deploying movable ICBMs and hardened capsules for Minuteman IIIs, among other things.[96]

At this time, Harriman recruited Nitze for the study group preparing democratic candidates for the 1974 and 1976 elections. That group's report, "Priorities for Defense, 1971–1981," was issued in April 1976. Unfortunately, as far as Nitze was concerned, it underestimated the needs in B-1s, Trident missile submarines, and a mobile ICBM force. As in 1950, when Nitze produced NSC-68, he emphasized the danger of the "growing imbalance and instability in the nuclear and conventional balance between the United States and its allies and the USSR."[97] In fact, it is amazing how consistent Nitze's views remained. To a friend in November 1976, he wrote, "Most of my thoughts on the subject of tactical nuclear postures and issues were formed during the period of the fifties. Even during the eight years that I was in the Pentagon during the sixties I failed to find persuasive evidence to change those basic views."[98] The same could be said about his views on conventional and strategic weapons, which became clear during Jimmy Carter's presidency.

Although Nitze supported Jimmy Carter in 1976 as a possible reincarnation of Kennedy, he "found his attitude toward politics grounded in a hortatory Wilsonian approach." Nitze believed that since Vietnam, America's conventional might and strategic posture "had deteriorated sharply."[99] With other experts, he was invited to Plains, Georgia, and the Pond House on Carter's estate. Carter had promised a cut of seven billion dollars in defense spending if elected. Contrary to the rosy picture painted by almost all the attendees, Nitze projected America's compromised position, remarks that were opposite to Carter's. The candidate asked him to prepare a paper, which eventually appeared as an article in *Foreign Affairs*, "Assuring Strategic Stability in an Era of Détente." It suggested that a fundamental shift was occurring in the strategic balance because the Soviets had achieved numerical parity and were pushing for technical improvements within the SALT agreement that would give them a potentially war-winning capability.[100] Whether or not Carter ever saw this article, it was not heeded. That fall, Carter rejected the so-called Team B report of Nitze and others, which postulated that the Soviet Union did not subscribe to America's concept of mutually assured destruction and that it appeared to be striving for fighting a nuclear war in which it would have a war-winning strategic posture, molding their doctrine and nuclear capabilities accordingly.[101]

As the question of SALT II came up, the press termed the Committee on the Present Danger (CPD) "cold warriors," "hawkish," and "representatives of the military-industrial complex."[102] An example was none other than Averell Harriman. In a *New York Times* article, Harriman was reported to have said, "Now Paul Nitze has the idea that they are planning a first strike. . . . I think that's paranoid, there's no evidence of it at all. To believe that this generation of Russians are [sic] willing to see their country destroyed—well, I can guarantee that isn't true." A few days later, Eugene Rostow, Walter's brother, came to Nitze's defense. The question, he pointed out, was not whether Russia was "about to commit a first strike [but whether] they are building-up so large a force that they can say (or hint) one day that we had better get out of the Mediterranean, or Europe, or confront us with a crisis in Greece or Norway or Korea or the Middle East, and back their demand with the implacable arithmetic of nuclear numbers." The Soviet buildup, as far as he and Nitze were concerned, threatened to "deter our deterrent. And that is why your comment as reported in the *Times* is so very wrong." When Harriman replied that he was not always wrong, Rostow answered, "You have indeed been right about the Russians on many occasions [but] I am worried about the orientation of the Carter Administration, very worried."[103]

A reporter for *Pravda*, Valentin Zorin, called Nitze the "hawk of hawks" and referred to a CPD analysis as "one of the most distorted, misleading and intellectually dishonest documents." Further, Zorin contended, "In this connection most action is by the so-called 'Committee on the Present Danger' and, on that Committee, by Paul Nitze who, by all evidence, possesses a pathologically deformed imagination regarding the Soviet Union's true intentions."[104] By September 1977, Carter had retreated to extending the SALT I Interim Agreement, pending conclusion of a SALT II, on the model of the Vladivostok Accord. That is, Carter's policies—cancellation of the B-1 bomber, indecision over the neutron bomb, and slippage on the Trident and MX programs, with his SALT II stance—did not bode well. There was a "tendency exemplified in them [that] was all too common to our SALT approach—a tendency to subordinate security policies to hopes of achieving arms control rather than to shaping arms control policies to our security needs."[105]

Carter succeeded in signing SALT II on June 18, 1979, to last until December 31, 1985. Though Nitze did not testify against SALT II, he urged changes and amendments. The Senate's Foreign Relations Committee voted nine to six in favor of it, but it attached twenty specific conditions, some requiring renegotiation. The Armed Services Committee voted ten to seven against the treaty, calling it unacceptable without major changes.[106] The Soviet invasion of Afghanistan in December 1979 allowed Carter to ask the Senate to stop consideration of it. Besides, he pledged a 3 percent real growth in military spending, reversing his previous stand. Though Carter and Brezhnev gave assurances of abiding by SALT II, the Soviets postponed reducing their launchers to 2,250 by the end of 1981. As Nitze remarked, "So not only did Carter fail to secure Senate approval; he failed to secure full Soviet compliance as well." By then, Paul Warnke had resigned as director of the Arms Control and Disarmament Agency in October 1978, though he and the Carter people had continued to believe that, in Rostow's words, "if we get mad enough, we can blow up Moscow and other cities, even if they have enough warheads in reserve to blow up New York and Washington by way of response. How sane men can believe such nonsense, in defiance of the arithmetic, passes my understanding."[107] In fact, Nitze admitted that Ronald Reagan's position on this issue in the 1980 campaign "accorded more closely with mine than did Carter's." If SALT II had been completely approved by the Senate, the Soviets would have used it as a basis for SALT III, thus prejudicing the results. It was better, as far as Nitze was concerned, to start with a "clean slate."[108] It remained for Ronald Reagan to clean the slate with a little help from Nitze. We will return to this cleaning in "Old Conclusions, New Beginnings."

part II
China

America's love affair with China, which reached low points only during the Boxer Rebellion (1898–1900) and Maoist period (1949–1972), is a riddle. After all, America and China are radically differing societies.

Oriental mystery combined with American missionary zeal played roles. So did U.S. economic and political expansion. China seemed a fertile field for religious conversion and progressive reform. Missionary work had President Woodrow Wilson's backing. Philosopher John Dewey represented progressivism. Edgar Snow was both adventurer and journalist. Fiction's evil Fu Manchu was countered by the cinema's Charlie Chan. And Wang Lung's earthy wife, O-lan, won the admiration of all who read Pearl Buck's romanticized picture of the Chinese in her novel *The Good Earth,* or saw the Academy Award–winning performance of Luise Rainer. China hands such as publisher Henry Luce defended Chinese eccentricities. Teddy White reported Chinese heroism during World War II. FDR backed Chiang Kai-shek and the Nationalists. He ditched Gen. Joseph "Vinegar Joe" Stilwell's hopes for reforming the generalissimo. FDR's special envoy Gen. Patrick Hurley and President Harry Truman's negotiator, Gen. George C. Marshall, failed to bring the Nationalists and communists together. American distortions turned sour.

The Chinese civil war destroyed Chiang's China and brought Mao Tse-tung to power. Those in the State Department who had favored cutting deals with Mao and dumping Chiang were purged by McCarthyites. It took an overbearing Russian policy toward China to bring Mao and President Richard Nixon together in 1972. President George H. W. Bush would not allow riots on Tiananmen Square (1989) to wreck America's special relationship with the People's Republic.

Today, the restored love affair continues, with Russia the odd person out. But lovers can quarrel, and they can find new partners. Tiananmen Square revealed those on either side who were not enthralled with the American-Chinese love affair. Problems over Tibet and Taiwan, with trade imbalances and dollar hoarding continue. The rise of Chinese power seemingly threatens America. What if there were another Tiananmen Square–type explosion? How would America and China react? Would Russia be interested in adding China to its list of those disenchanted with the West? To what extent would distorted mirrors contribute to bringing about such realignments?

It is useful, therefore, to trace the evolution of America's connection with China in the twentieth century and to look at China's mirrored reflections in America's looking glass more clearly. America's Chinese bonding, from the beginning to now, has rested on certain misconceptions and misunderstandings of China as perpetrated by a handful of people. It is worth looking at a sample of these persons' views, the images they have spun, and their future implications.

8

Missionary Diplomacy

Woodrow Wilson's diplomacy has been referred to as "missionary diplomacy," and perhaps in no instance is that term more appropriate than concerning his relations with China.[1] His views of, hopes for, and policy toward that country all bore a striking resemblance to the observations of "Old China Hands," particularly Rockhill and American missionaries in China. Although much has been written about Wilson's policy toward China, there is little about the origins of that policy, especially concerning the influence of Wilson's religious background and his acquaintance with American missionaries on that policy.[2]

When Presbyterian minister and China hand the Reverend Charles E. Scott wrote the president-elect on March 1, 1913, he was corresponding as a friend and observer on Chinese affairs.[3] He wrote about political and religious conditions, citing instances when the major powers were working against China. He condemned Russia and Japan and noted a great opportunity for the United States "to do vast good for China, and incidentally itself to reap very material advantages of all sorts, such as might be born of confidence in us & friendship for us." He suggested two acts. He regretted the American delay in recognizing the Chinese republic. He called for business leaders to lend money to Chinese Americans as individuals or as companies, but not as a government and urged American withdrawal from the proposed Chinese consortium. Such loans, according to Scott, "would forever take away the dread & fear in the hearts of the Chinese that the Government as such was trying to use its power to press them down for a land grab or special favors." Wilson appreciated these informative letters.[4]

Scott's views were typical of the missionaries in China. Wilson received the same information from S. I. Woodbridge, married to Wilson's first cousin Jeanie Woodrow. He wrote in July 1912 that China was in the throes of radical political change.[5] The missionaries, he said, were "in a position to furnish the awakened minds with solid thought and teach the people the meaning of true Christian altruism. It will take China many years to pull through this awful tangle of famine, floods and revolution with their attendant horrors, but with God's help she will do it, and we are telling them about God." Wilson thanked Woodbridge and wrote that "we think of you very often and it has been a great pleasure for us recently to have Casper [Woodbridge's son] in Princeton and learn through him of how things are going with you in China."[6]

It is, of course, difficult if not impossible to determine precisely the influence that missionaries, particularly Scott and Woodbridge, had on the pre-1913 attitudes of Wilson toward China. It is clear the missionaries provided most of Wilson's firsthand information about China and that Wilson's views about that country mirrored those of the missionaries. If nothing else, these opinions, combined with Wilson's own religious background, served to reinforce conclusions that he had come to from his own thinking.

• • •

As the administration began in 1913, the president faced three problems: whether to approve participation by American bankers in the Chinese consortium, whether to recognize the government of Yuan Shih-kai, and the choice of an American representative for China. The decisions in all three show the influence of religion and the missionaries.

Wilson came quickly to the first decision and withdrew official backing for the American bankers in a proposed six-power loan to the Chinese government. The statement, written by Wilson, though reviewed by his cabinet, appeared on March 19, 1913, and noted that the proposed loan touched "very nearly the administrative independence of China itself," particularly in expectation of government support, and possibly interference in the affairs of a country "just now awakening to a *consciousness* of its power and of its obligations to its people." That awakening, according to Wilson, was the most *significant*, "if not the most momentous," event of the generation. His statement concluded, "Our interests are those of the open door—a door of friendship and mutual advantage. That is the only door we care to enter."[7]

Wilson's decision disappointed some, but met with great approval from the missionaries. The Reverend Dr. Arthur J. Brown, secretary of the Board of Foreign Missions of the Presbyterian Church in the U.S.A., wrote of "the clearness of vision, breadth of statesmanship and high moral tone" that characterized Wilsonian foreign policy.[8] Scott added that the Chinese were gratified "beyond measure" at Wilson's action, and after Wilson's statement, "America & Americans have gone up above par with the Chinese. They feel that Americans are their only friends."[9] Similar expressions came from Z. C. Beals, secretary of the American Advent Mission Society, and James Sadler of the London Missionary Society.[10]

Wilson's policy was an outgrowth of his general views on foreign affairs. As Arthur Link has noted, "There is no reason to doubt that he thought he was acting in a moral capacity to save China from the designs of scheming European and American imperialism," designs, it might be added, about which missionaries had been writing him for some years.[11] This policy did gain confidence among the Chinese and placed American foreign policy on a higher plane of morality, but it did not prevent other nations from concluding the loan under conditions Wilson opposed. Wilson's action established an independent Chinese policy. This was also something that missionaries had called for, as they hoped China would follow the United States in the paths of righteousness.

The president at the same time was deciding the question of recognition of the government of Yuan Shih-kai. The Manchus had abdicated in February 1912, and the resulting Nanking and Peking governments had merged under Yuan's control. The Taft administration had tried to work in cooperation with the other powers concerning recognition, but the powers withheld recognition pending solution of the loan question. Wilson labored under no such constraint.

The president reached a decision almost as quickly as on the loan. He was aware of the pressure for recognition. Scott had written in favor, and Arthur Brown noted that "American prestige has suffered" because of the delay.[12] Bishop J. W. Bashford of the Methodist Church of Peking urged recognition, and had attempted to prod the Taft administration. He had written Assistant Secretary of State Henry Huntington Wilson: "I have not met a single American in China, save officials whose lips are sealed, without hearing complaints of the delay of our government in the recognition of the Republic."[13] Missionaries were joined in their call for recognition by doctors, merchants, lawyers, bankers, importers, exporters, manufacturers, and members of the American legation in Peking. The Chinese provisional government also indicated its desire for immediate recognition.[14] Wilson saw Yuan Shih-kai as the solution to internal instability and foreign aggression. Although he realized the new leaders might not introduce a true republican form of government, he thought other problems of more significance. The president had Secretary of State William Jennings Bryan telegraph the American chargé in Peking, E. T. Williams, to deliver a message of recognition upon the gathering of the Chinese National Assembly, and recognition took place with appropriate ceremonies on May 2, 1913.[15]

Wilson's decision seems to have been based in part on his hope that the new government would bring stability, a first step to a Christian state, and one that would aid the work of American missionaries and businessmen. Although some of the powers were not happy with Wilson's action, messages poured in from all over China.[16] Most Americans, including the missionaries, were delighted. Many believed, as did Scott, that people were hungry for a president like Wilson who would "summon them to heights of moral endeavor," for they wanted "to follow a President of vision, who is thoroughly religious with religion applied to life."[17]

Whereas the influences of Wilson's religious background and advice from missionaries were obvious in decisions relating to the loan and recognition, they were most apparent, perhaps, in his choice of a diplomatic representative for Peking. The president believed that the envoy to China should be of marked Christian character. He noted that "the thing most prominent in my mind is that the men now most active in establishing a new government and a new regime for China are many of them members of the Young Men's Christian Association (Y.M.C.A.), and many of them also men trained in American universities. The Christian influence, direct or indirect, is very prominently at the front and I need not say, ought to be kept there."[18]

One of the first candidates proposed for the position was William Jennings Bryan. Bishop Bashford campaigned to have the post raised to an ambassadorship, with Bryan as its first occupant. Bashford appealed to Bryan to "render a service which God would greatly bless and which the whole world would recognize."[19] Wilson's adviser, Col. Edward M. House, said he would try to persuade Bryan if Wilson desired.[20] Instead, Bryan was, of course, named secretary of state.

Wilson's choice seems to have been former Harvard president Charles W. Eliot. To House, in January 1913, the president-elect said that Eliot would be an ideal individual to help "uplift them in their general struggle to help themselves."[21] Wilson wrote to Eliot, "I am very much concerned that our representatives in China and Japan should be of the best quality the country affords. I believe that there is probably nothing more nearly touches the future development of the world than what will happen in the East and it ought to happen, so far as our influence extends, under the best possible guidance."[22] Bryan was disturbed because Eliot "was a Unitarian and did not believe in the divinity of Christ, and the new Chinese civilization was founded upon the Christian movement there."[23] Possible conflict between Wilson and Bryan, even before the new administration began, was averted when Eliot decided he was unable to accept.[24] Even so, the prominence given to religious considerations, the attitude of the candidate about religion and missionaries, is striking.

The next candidate appeared during the month before Wilson entered office. Wilson wrote Bryan, by this time selected as secretary of state, about the YMCA leader, John R. Mott, noting that "Mr. John R. Mott, whom I know very well and who has as many of the qualities of a statesman as any man of my acquaintance, is very familiar with the situation in China, not only that, but he enjoys the confidence of men of the finest influence all over the Christian world." Mott, Wilson said, was in China, and if he accepted, he could remain as minister.[25] In another letter, Wilson wrote that he wanted "exceptional men" for diplomatic posts. Mott, the president said, "of whom I wrote is one of a thousand." Bryan accepted Wilson's suggestion.[26] The post was offered to Mott on February 24, 1913, but the YMCA leader refused.[27]

Wilson was not willing to accept Mott's answer and began a campaign to change his mind. Wilson telegraphed Cleveland H. Dodge, Wilson's college classmate and old friend: "Feel it imperatively necessary Mott should go to China. Can you not bring proper pressure to bear on him from his most influential friends? I do not know where else to turn."[28] Dodge accepted and requested Edward C. Jenkins to help.[29] The latter telegraphed the president that he was asking others to cable Mott and wondered if Wilson had any instructions. The president did not, and asked only that a coded message be sent to Mott: "Feel that my duty to the public interest obliges me to urge reconsideration on your part. The interests of China and of the Christian world are so intimately involved."[30]

Mott agreed to reconsider, and the president said that Mott could retain his "posts of guidance" with the YMCA, taking such leaves as were necessary. Wilson told Mott that "I am eager to unite what you represent with what this government means to try to represent."[31] The president's campaign was not limited to private appeals. When a group of missionaries on furlough stated their support for Mott, "the President said he realized the influence that the missionaries had had in regenerating China and that he looked upon Mr. Mott as a man especially well fitted to serve the purposes of the administration because of his knowledge of the mission world."[32] Dodge wrote the president of a long cable he had sent to Mott, then in Korea.[33] All to no avail, as Mott again refused because of the press of his duties. Wilson was distressed: "Mott's decision was [a] great blow to me. I don't know when I have been so disappointed." But, as Dodge noted, the attempt to appoint Mott announced to the world, as nothing else could, the kind of policy Wilson intended to follow in dealing with China.[34]

Other names appeared in correspondence. Henry Morgenthau was mentioned for the post.[35] Dodge warned that some missionaries were urging a journalist, W. T. Ellis, but said he was of "very light calibre." Wilson agreed, saying he would seek a different sort of man.[36] Dodge suggested Professor Jeremiah W. Jenks of New York, but Wilson said he was going slowly on the matter.[37]

Meanwhile, Charles R. Crane put forth the name of sociology professor Edward A. Ross of the University of Wisconsin, author of *The Changing Chinese*.[38] Wilson was interested, but moved slowly, prompting Bryan to write that it was "quite important that we find a minister to China as soon as it can be conveniently done," particularly since recognition had already taken place. Bryan wondered if Wilson had found any reason for not appointing Ross and suggested former Missouri governor Joseph W. Folk. According to Bryan, Folk met all Wilson's characteristics and was "identified with the religious life of the nation, and would, I am sure, be acceptable to the missionaries."[39] Wilson had other ideas. Ross's name shortly appeared on a tentative list of diplomatic appointments, and Wilson began to make inquiries about him.[40] By the end of June, Ross was out of the running because, as Wilson put it, Ross's politics "turned out to be unsatisfactory."[41] Mott confirmed the president's decision by reporting that Ross was not a church member. He wrote that Ross's initial attitude toward the missions was "comparative indifference," and though he showed growing sympathy, Ross was more impressed with the practical work, "as that of the Young Men's Christian Association, than the work of the different denominations." Mott then recommended Ernest D. Burton of the University of Chicago, who recently made a tour of China and "formed a personal acquaintance with practically all of the leading missionaries of all the Churches working in China as well as with Government officials, Chinese educators and other prominent men."[42]

By this time Wilson had decided on another man, Paul S. Reinsch of the University of Wisconsin. Reinsch's name was first suggested by Crane in March, but for another position: "Think of Professor Paul Reinsch of Wisconsin for the post of Secretary of the South American States."[43] At the end of that month Bryan wrote to Wilson, "Have heard Reinsch highly spoken of, but do not know him personally, and do not know how much interested he may be in missionary work. Would like to talk with you about China."[44] In the ensuing months, as Ross lost ground, Reinsch's name was mentioned. In mid-June, Joseph E. Davies, chief of the Bureau of Corporations, urged Reinsch for Peking, and Wilson promised to "give earnest consideration" to him. The president wrote Bryan on June 25 about diplomatic vacancies and noted, "Professor Reinsch, of the University of Wisconsin, a great student of world politics and particularly oriental relationships, to China."[45]

• • •

Wilson invited Reinsch to Washington for a talk.[46] Reinsch had a national reputation as a political scientist. The son of a Lutheran minister, he was a sound religious man who believed that American missionaries, doctors, and educators contributed much to the American position in China. He was acceptable to the missionaries. He was known as an opponent of imperialism and a champion of self-development.[47] These facts made him, in the president's mind, an ideal choice for Peking. After a satisfactory conversation and after checking with both senators from Wisconsin, Wilson commissioned Reinsch on August 15, 1913. After thirty days of consultation, Reinsch left for Peking. On November 15, 1913, he relieved chargé Williams at the American Legation.[48] Normal relations between Washington and Peking had begun by August 1913.

The years of Wilson's administration saw reports of success of the work of the missionaries coming from all sources. Reinsch wrote of China: "Through the earnest efforts of two generations of Americans, our country has been able to achieve an enviable position of good will, trust and confidence among the Chinese people: Americans being widely active in educational, religious and benevolent work have impressed the Chinese with our feeling of friendliness." He called for financial support of China, as the Chinese were attempting to reform "their political methods and institutions largely in the direction of the experience and example of the United States."[49] His statements, and those of his first secretary, John V. A. MacMurray, confirmed Wilson's belief in the work of the missionaries and their ability to show the Chinese the correct path.

In the next years, this "normality" was shattered by a series of difficulties: the Twenty-one Demands; Yuan Shih-kai's attempt to return the monarchy; Yuan's death; the possibility of a new consortium, as well as American economic activities in China; and the Chinese problem at the Peace Conference at Paris, which produced the Shantung settlement. Throughout these crises, as well as in the more normal times, Wilsonian diplomacy derived from certain assumptions, especially the president's desire that America should serve mankind by example. The United States was to aid in the development of constitutional government in the world, and in China, missionary activity was one of the major means.[50] Wilson told Reinsch shortly before the latter left for Peking that the United States had "to do her share independently and to give specific moral and financial assistance" to China. Wilson, Reinsch noted, dwelled "more on the educational side and on political example and moral encouragement, than on the matter of finance and commerce."[51] To emphasize these beliefs, when Crane wrote of a reception for Reinsch at which Mott had talked to the new minister, Wilson answered that "it starts him out in just the right way, with just the right thoughts in his mind."[52]

Reinsch arrived at Shanghai on November 1, 1913, ready to institute Wilson's liberal and progressive agenda of maintaining the open door by encouraging democratic reforms and economic development. He set out for Peking on the third, reaching there on the sixth. He was to rely heavily on his "kitchen cabinet" of such persons as Roy S. Anderson and William H. Donald, the former a journalist and son of a missionary, the latter an Australian newspaperman, and his Ph.D. student, Stanley K. Hornbeck. Reinsch believed that the Chinese market offered a golden opportunity for American business and the United States could play a unique role in Chinese development. He was especially interested in ending spheres of influence.[53] Within weeks of settling in Peking, Reinsch had callers from the Chinese government: Premier Hsiung Hsi-ling and Minister of Posts and Communications Chow Tzu-ch'i. They feared Russian ambitions in Outer Mongolia and the Japanese in the eastern parts of Inner Mongolia. "The Chinese Government would like the United States," they urged, "to enlist the cooperation of Great Britain and Germany in opposing these schemes." They solicited American help in drafting a constitution for China. Could, they asked, the ambassador help China conclude contracts with Bethlehem Steel for shipping and with Standard Oil for developing the Shansi-Shensi oil fields as well as aid a tobacco monopoly with the British American Tobacco Company? Finally, they were interested in river and harbor improvement, especially the Huai River project.[54] It was a full menu of requests. A few days earlier, on November 24, he had been received by the president of the Chinese republic, Yuan Shih-kai.

This interview, as Reinsch called it, "was characterized by great cordiality" with the "dictator-president" of China: "[He] seemed to have a desire to impress me with his interest in and preference for republican principles of government." That is, he wanted a constitution, parliament, and an electoral law. Nevertheless, Reinsch pointed out, "his chief criticism of the existing Parliament was that it did not represent experience and the substantial interests of the country, but was composed, in large part, of young and inexperienced theorists." And the new constitution took for its starting points the "existing power of the Executive and does not give to Parliament the immediate control over executive action, such as was contemplated in the draft submitted by the Constitution Drafting Committee of Parliament." Thus, Reinsch noted, "[the president] demands a new election law and constitutional arrangement which will not fetter executive action." There was no sense of honest political opposition. In fact, "political opposition to the Head of the State is confused with disloyalty, or even treason, to the State itself." Reinsch concluded that this military man and his followers were most concerned with the "maintenance of authority."[55] In his autobiography, *An American Diplomat in China,* he quotes Yuan Shih-kai even more directly: "My opponents are disloyal. They would pull down my government."[56] Here was Reinsch, open-door diplomat and liberal, representing a democracy wishing to do good, yet feeling the "almost ruthless power of the man. Republican in title he was, but an autocrat at heart. All the glittering trappings of the empire he had preserved."[57] After the occasion of state, as Reinsch called it, he had a more informal interview. Yuan had, by then, expelled the Democratic Party from the parliament, and dismissed the parliament itself. Reinsch dwelled on Yuan's career: "His personal rule, his unscrupulous advancement to power, with the incidental corruption and cold-blooded executions that marked it, and his bitter personal feeling against all political opponents—these were not qualities that make for stable parliamentary government."[58] The new Chinese republic was, to put it simply, a military dictatorship. Almost as an afterthought, Reinsch wrote, "During the two and a half years from my coming to Peking until the time of his death, Yuan Shih-kai left the enclosure of his palace only twice."[59]

On one of those occasions, he went before daybreak to the Temple of Heaven to offer prayers, inaugurating the first Confucian ceremony: "The whole Chinese people hold the doctrines of Confucius most sacred." Yuan reintroduced this old state religion by decree on November 26, 1913. Foreign missionaries were "agitated" and believed this to be a "step backward."[60] By making the Prayer of Heaven on the day of the winter solstice, according to some, Reinsch was told that Yuan had edged toward resumption of the "imperial dignity." The Confucian revival came as new ways were being adopted. For instance, Chinese ladies came out in society for the first time, and elements of the West such as legislatures and constitutions made their tentative appearances. The Rockhills, who visited the new ambassador, bemoaned this fact, feeling that it would be better for the world not to meddle with China. As Rockhill noted, "She should be allowed to continue under her social system, a system which has stood the test of thousands of years; and to trust that the gradual influence of example would bring about necessary modifications."[61] Reinsch shared Rockhill's confidence in the Chinese people and China's vast human and natural resources. This was part of the perception that underlay American policy in China. The other part of the perception was that China was striving to model itself largely after the American example by creating truly representative political institutions. Reinsch put it this way: "But in China all liberal-minded, forward-looking men see in the United States a free government which they not only wish to emulate, but to which they look for interest, sympathy, and moral assistance."[62] Yet Yuan's government did all it could to thwart such persons: it dissolved the Kuomintang (Nationalist Party), arrested its leaders, and turned to the military governors for support. Even the rump parliament was dissolved, and in its place a central administrative conference with advisory capacity only was created.[63]

Reinsch, as a Wilsonian, saw U.S. policy as building the commerce of China, helping its organizational skills, and improving its rails. "No one," he wrote, "could have appreciated more highly than I did the important work done by American missionaries, teachers, and medical men, in bringing to China a conception of Western learning and life."[64] American policy should strive for a "united China, master of its own land, developing its resources, open to all nations of the world equally for commercial and industrial activity, should be the chief desideratum."[65] Here was, indeed, the broadest statement of the open door policy.

It seemed as if events conspired against this goal. The first was Yuan Shih-kai's efforts to become emperor and the Japanese seizure of Shantung. Even the Japanese opposed the new dynasty. With provincial disaffection, in March 1916 Yuan decreed that he would only retain the presidency. But even this became doubtful. In early June, Yuan died, and a major crisis was averted. His premature death again opened the way for the creation of a republic. The monarchical movement had failed. Sun Yat-sen, leader of the Nationalist Revolution of 1911, returned to Shanghai and for the next four years played an important role in Chinese politics, though the warlords drove him out of Canton in 1918. By 1920, China had a new constitution. Sun's situation in Shanghai was tenuous. During the early twenties, power there was among foreigners and warlords. Nevertheless, Sun was a vigorous spokesman for Chinese rights, argued against the militarists, and defended China against Japanese claims.[66]

In August 1917, Reinsch was informed that China would join the Allies in World War I. China had been persuaded to take this step on the assurance that the Great Powers would guarantee its political and administrative integrity. At the same time, these powers assured the Japanese that they would not effectively oppose whatever Japan might desire in China after the war. China received loans from the Japanese. Then, in a move that stunned Ambassador Reinsch, Secretary of State Robert Lansing signed the Lansing-Ishii note on November 4, 1917, which read in part: "The Government of the United States recognizes that Japan has special interests in China, particularly in the part to which her possessions are contiguous." That, Reinsch commented, "struck me in the face with stunning force, before I had time to weigh its meaning in relation to the remainder of the declaration."[67] For him, the United States had betrayed China. The Chinese responded by refusing to recognize agreements relating to China between other powers. Obviously, the Japanese were busy "cutting loose" Shantung. America seemed indifferent. Japan was creating for itself a special Monroe Doctrine in China. Its "arrangements in Shantung were made secretly, riding roughshod over Chinese rights and intended to sterilize in advance the enactments of the Peace Conference." Reinsch condemned Japan's policy. The ambassador spent four weeks in the United States to explain his actions, but to no avail. "I found it hard to believe," he remarked, "that President Wilson would be compliant to the Japanese demands, in view of the complete and insistent information the American Government had had from me and all other American officials in China as to what would result from such action." On June 7, 1919, Reinsch resigned. As far as Reinsch was concerned, President Wilson misunderstood Japanese intentions by lamely claiming the concession "conferred on Japan no political rights but only economic privileges." He left Peking on September 13, 1919.[68]

· · ·

Wilson had his own private channels of information about China. During the years he was in the White House, missionaries, particularly Scott and Woodbridge, kept the president informed about China. Much of the correspondence concerned routine matters. Wilson indicated confidence in Woodbridge by writing in July 1913 that he needed "information about the extra-territorial court of the United States at Shanghai and I do not know where to obtain it, except to trouble you to get it for me." The president had to appoint a judge, marshal and attorney, and hoped Woodbridge could learn "in what estimation the marshal and attorney are held, what sort of men they are, and how they are thought to perform their duties."[69] Woodbridge replied two months later that the present judge was universally respected, and "we are sorry he has resigned." Court attorney Dr. F. E. Hinckley did not receive the same praise, for the latter appointee had magnified his office "several diameters in excess," and was "a thorn in the flesh of Judge Thayer." Woodbridge thought Hinckley tactless and hoped Wilson would replace Thayer with someone who would maintain the "true dignity of the Supreme Court and dispose justice in a proper way."[70] Wilson forwarded this letter to Bryan, noting that it was very interesting. Bryan agreed, saying he would confer with the president about the appointments, and adding that "the attorney [Hinckley] does not seem to be a desirable man."[71] Someone else was appointed.

Wilson received information about YMCA activities in China. Lucius Hopkins Miller, chairman of the Princeton work in Peking, sent the president letters from Princeton men "regarding present conditions." Wilson read them with interest and profit.[72] One of the Princeton men in Peking, Robert R. Gailey, wrote on September 15, 1913, asking for a message for opening the new YMCA building in Peking on October 9. Gailey's letter arrived too late for such a message.[73] Later, in December 1914, Gailey wrote from Princeton. He called the president's attention to a Peking Night at Princeton. This program, held not only to arouse interest "in this particular enterprise of Princeton in Peking but stimulate all good healthy effort on behalf of the religious life of the University" featured many speakers. He pointed out that Princeton in Peking had established a lectureship "to present a modern, constructive and vital interpretation of the Christian Religion and its application to present day problems." Wilson replied, "May I not through you express to those gathered at that time my deep and lasting interest in the Princeton work at Peking and my earnest hope that it may be sustained and enlarged to the utmost."[74]

In October 1914, Sherwood Eddy of the YMCA's International Committee wrote from China. From Hunan, Eddy described the audiences of thousands of "Confucian students desiring to join Bible classes as inquirers, here in the capital of a province that was long the most bigoted in China." He described the difficulties missionaries had faced in Hunan before, and exclaimed, "What a contrast today!" The provincial governor approved of the meetings, sending a message of welcome as they arrived in Changsha, the capital of Hunan. Eddy noted that they preached against bribery, graft, dishonesty, and immorality, all of which had contributed to the weakness of China. China, Eddy believed, could be saved by the gospel. He asked Wilson, "As we go from city to city will you at home who believe in God pray today for this nation so suddenly and so marvelously open to the Gospel of Christ?" To the president it looked "as if the old empire were waking to a new life."[75]

Scott was the most frequent correspondent. In early 1914 he wrote of his work. He criticized the Chinese government, which was "perfectly rotten from bottom to top," and complained that American diplomats were lax in defending American citizens in China.[76] The next month, he again complained that the diplomats should work closely with the missionaries, for the latter understood the Chinese. He pointed to instances he felt showed that diplomats did not understand China. Wilson thanked Scott for writing "so fully concerning conditions in China."[77] Scott, on furlough, wrote from Holyoke, Massachusetts, on May 12, 1914, "You may or may not know that the Chinese Christian leaders in China have a genuine admiration for your Christian character & upright policies. It is a marvel to them that the ruler of a great nation should be a Christian & trying to deal righteously."[78] Later he wrote that he was forwarding a banner from Chinese Christian leaders. He noted the Chinese leaders "can never think with other than gladness that you are a Christian man and ruler; that you caused the United States to recognize the Chinese Republic; and to withdraw from what they consider to be the cynical, Egyptianizing, 'forced loan' of the kingly governments, intent only on humiliating and crippling China while they may."[79]

The First World War caused much trouble for Wilson in regard to China. Woodbridge noted, as early as August 15, 1914, that "the Chinese are taking much interest in this great war which affects the whole of Asia as well as Europe."[80] His words proved prophetic. The Chinese government hoped to keep the war out of the Far East by dissuading the belligerents from extending the war. The Japanese opposed this suggestion, as they hoped to take control of German extraterritorial interests in China. The Japanese plans became clear in January 1915, when they presented the Twenty-one Demands. Originally made in secret, they became public, and would have turned China into a Japanese protectorate.

Most Americans in China opposed these demands. The missionaries were outspoken. Bishop Bashford wrote in March 1915 that Wilson had asked him in 1911 to correspond "about Chinese matters of interest to the United States." Bashford was very concerned about the Japanese demands, as they affected the missions. He recounted what had happened to the missions in Korea once Japan took control. The bishop wrote that "Japan's attempt through threats of force and through her efforts to impose secrecy upon China to secure the control of this nation in the very nature of the case will lead her also to hinder, cripple and if possible destroy the work of Christian missionaries in China." Bashford hoped the president would let the Japanese know that the United States opposed threats "upon China compromising her dignity as a nation or in any degree infringing upon her sovereignty." He said that some missionaries were "willing to state the facts thus clearing our consciences before God and man, and to leave the consequences with Him who controls the destinies of men and of nations." Wilson thanked Bashford for "so illuminating a statement."[81] In a separate letter to Secretary Bryan, forwarded to the president, Bashford had gone into greater detail, writing that "these demands transfer the control of the commercial life of China and in substance the sovereignty of the nation to Japan, while maintaining in form the independence and integrity of the Chinese nation." He stressed the injury that the demands would cause to American commercial interests and the historic American policy in favor of Chinese integrity, noted the threat to security the Japanese could offer in the Pacific, and pointed to American moral obligations. "A firm policy at the present time," Bashford concluded, "will conserve interests of priceless value to humanity and will win lasting renown and the just gratitude of posterity for the statesmen who maintain it."[82]

Other missionaries expressed these views. Dr. John Leighton Stuart wrote Wilson on March 24, 1915, asking for an interview for himself, A. E. Cory of the Foreign Christian Missionary Society, R. F. Fitch of the Presbyterian Board of Foreign Missions, and John Gowdy of the Methodist Board of Foreign Missions. As Stuart wrote, "We have found ourselves sharing in a very oppressive sense of the gravity of this issue for China," adding that he thought they had information that might help the president. Wilson was unable to see the missionaries, but they did see Bryan, who relayed their views to the president.[83] Scott, in Philadelphia, wrote Wilson in response to the president's request for information about "Japanese aggression in the great Province of Shantung." Scott said that Japanese plans for Shantung were like those of the Germans, and "alarming reports (personal letters) come from missionary friends." According to Scott, the Reverend Dr. W. M. Haves, one of three American missionaries chosen by the Chinese government to help plan the new school system, had just written, "We have very grave fears. The Japanese seem determined to destroy China's independence." In his own missionary center of Tsingtao (Qingdao), Scott wrote that the Japanese were interfering with the missionaries' high school "in an effort to scare the teachers and drive away the pupils from this centre of Christian learning." He said he was not anti-Japanese but reflected the opinion of many observers "in the Far East, who, despite their alignments in the European War, feel there is less to fear from Germany in Shantung than from Japan."[84] Woodbridge discussed the aggressiveness of Japan and the Chinese response.[85]

Some missionaries did not act with restraint. A group of them telegraphed Wilson about conditions, asking that he release their telegram to the American people. Bryan opposed release of a communication attacking the Japanese government. Such a release would "put all of our Missionaries in Japan, as well as in China under suspicion and it will not help China because it will be regarded by Japan as an expression of China's animosity." Wilson agreed, believing the missionaries had been "unwise in giving it out themselves on the other side."[86] The president's refusal to heighten tensions by releasing the telegram was supported by Woodbridge, who wrote that the president had correctly "discouraged the meddling with oriental politics by certain missionaries."[87]

Whatever his disagreement with public statements of certain missionaries, the president was sensitive to their concerns and took pains to keep them informed. Secretary Bryan noted at one point in the controversy, "I had a talk with Bishop Bashford today and he is very deeply concerned about the situation in China. I told him, confidentially, what we had done and left very much relieved."[88] The president then came to the decision to announce opposition to any agreement "impairing the treaty rights of the United States and its citizens in China, the political or territorial integrity of the Republic of China, or the international policy relative to China commonly known as the open door policy."[89] The agreement between China and Japan signed in May 1915 preserved the autonomy of China, though Japan did gain large concessions. In this whole controversy Wilson and the missionaries exchanged opinions. Although it is impossible to determine the exact influence the missionaries had on Wilson, or whether his thinking resulted at least in part from his own religious background and attitudes toward foreign policy, it is clear that the opinions of the missionaries confirmed his own judgment. The missionaries realized the American people would not support military action against Japan but believed the president should go on record against the Japanese aggression. Wilson agreed.

• • •

In the summer of 1915, the president's attention left the Far East, turning to Europe and his reelection bid. The submarine crisis, the Russian revolutions, American entry into the war, and eventually the treaties of peace all consumed the president's time and interest in foreign affairs. China in the years beginning with 1915 became a secondary consideration. The president continued to receive reports from the diplomats in Peking and kept reading about China. He appreciated a copy of Scott's book, *China from Within,* and wrote that he hoped to read shortly "about a country which engaged my interest, I think, as much as any country in the world."[90] But the president concentrated his attentions on other areas.

The missionaries continued to keep the president informed, and Woodbridge in particular provided on-the-spot news. In January 1916, he commented, "The erstwhile President of this country is about to announce himself as Emperor of China, and with one stroke of his pen bring back the people to a monarchy." He saw politically troublesome times ahead for China. However, he went on, "so far as our spiritual work is concerned we have a glorious outlook[;] never was there more inquiry: never a better chance for one to let his light shine."[91] He praised Wilson's policy of keeping America out of the war. In a later letter he said, "You have made America the model for this great China by keeping us out of war. China is so beset with enemies now that I do not see how she can escape. Help China by a peace policy."[92] Woodbridge afterward wrote to express gratification over Wilson's reelection. The president's policies, he noted, had "gained the admiration of us all in China and the Chinese are a pro-Wilson tool." Woodbridge believed that America's best assets in China were the hospitals, schools, colleges, and printing presses manned by missionaries.[93] In September 1917, Woodbridge wrote of the "unhalcyon days" in China. Woodbridge was depressed about the political turmoil in China, and possible Japanese control of the country. Wilson, perhaps, summed up his reaction when he wrote, "You may be sure we are watching developments in China, so well as we can from this distance, with the greatest solicitude. I hope with all my heart that in the providence of God some permanent and beneficent results may be worked out."[94]

Woodbridge's views were corroborated by Scott, who in 1918 wrote two long letters to the president. He discussed the difficulty in getting to the annual mission meeting in Shantung in July because "practically everything in this province, as well as in Manchuria, is already in the hands of the Japanese Gov't." The Japanese ran the hotels, railroads, and the steamers, and charged excessive prices.[95] Next month, Scott wrote again, enclosing a detailed report on conditions in Shantung, as related to retardation of missionary activity by the Japanese.[96] The report, prepared for Arthur Brown, was a stinging indictment of the Japanese. Scott discussed "Japanese Hindrances," and said "to the minds of many the situation is becoming 'impossible' both for the Chinese church in this end of the province and for the foreigners ministering to it." The missionaries and the Chinese, particularly the Chinese Christians, were living in fear. Taxes were being increased, the Japanese taking over commerce of the area. A trick to put firms out of business, Scott wrote, was "the opening of all mails, and the taking out of checks therefrom so that money sent to Chinese and foreign firms does not reach them." Japanese authorities denied responsibility for such practices, but "they are the smoothest of liars, smiling when it suits their purpose and disdainfully contemptuous, brow-beating and cruel when people are inarticulate, or when their voices, raised in protest, are weak." The Japanese had moved from military to civil administration, "which style means permanent occupancy." Scott reported fifty thousand Japanese in Qingdao, and little regard for Chinese sovereignty. The Japanese boasted that "Shantung belongs to them." Scott compared the takeover of Shantung to the German occupation of Belgium and called for action to reverse the process.

The president was so alarmed by Scott's report that he sent it to Bryan's successor at the State Department (in 1915), Secretary of State Robert Lansing, asking for someone "familiar with Far Eastern Affairs and who is trustworthy" to "look carefully over the enclosed matter for me."[97] Lansing responded by enclosing a memorandum by Ransford S. Miller of the Far Eastern Division.[98] Concluding that although some details were based on hearsay, Miller noted that there was "a basis of truth to a number of the main charges against the Japanese administration in Shantung mentioned in the confidential report from Mr. Scott to his Mission Board." Miller thought that Scott's observations were colored by a strong anti-Japanese prejudice, but department sources confirmed that the Japanese "have from the outbreak of hostilities against the Germans in Qingdao acted in a high-handed manner against the Chinese in Shantung." Indeed, the Japanese were "in control of practically the whole Province," with plans for permanent occupation. Scott's report, and its State Department evaluation, did little to reassure the president.

By the time of the European Armistice in November 1918, it was apparent that China would be a major problem at the Peace Conference. And at Versailles, Wilson turned to consideration of Chinese affairs for the first time since the trouble over the Twenty-one Demands in 1915. Studying this problem, no doubt the president had the missionaries' views in mind. They had written about the "uplift" of China, talked about republican government in that country, and urged the giving up of spheres of influence. Since

1915, most of the missionaries had discussed the danger that Japan posed to China, and implored the president to safeguard Chinese interests. Their observations duplicated the views of the diplomats, especially Minister Reinsch and First Secretary MacMurray, both of whom made Japan a topic of their dispatches.[99] And the missionaries were supporting the president's beliefs. More sensitive to diplomatic complexities and to the limits of American power and interests in China, Wilson nonetheless based his thinking on a background similar to the missionaries and agreed, more than he disagreed, with their observations. Their opinions had certainly helped to shape his views when the president left for Europe on December 4, 1918.

China proved a difficult problem for the negotiators at Paris. The Japanese pressed for German rights in Shantung, recognition of a paramount position in eastern Asia, acceptance of wartime treaties with China, a declaration of racial equality, and control of the German islands in the North Pacific. The Japanese failed to get the statement on equality and gained only mandate control, through the League of Nations, of some of the German islands. The big stake was Shantung and a general solution of the Chinese problem. Wilson's advisers, along with his missionary correspondents, called for returning to China German rights in Shantung, but the Japanese insisted on those rights. After difficult negotiations, complicated by prior treaties between Japan and France and Great Britain, and a Japanese threat to boycott the treaty and the league, the Japanese won control of German economic rights in Shantung.[100] Wilson had opposed the claims, but saw the solution as a compromise.

Reaction heated up in both the United States and China. The Chinese refused to sign the peace treaty. Missionaries were shocked and called for a reversal of the settlement. Two of them, Scott and Woodbridge, wrote directly, expressing alarm. In a letter of July 1919, in which he enclosed a long report, Scott noted, "Political conditions in China, forced upon the Chinese by 'a certain power,' are desperate and daily more critical."[101] He hoped for "some authoritative, hopeful word" from Wilson regarding Shantung. Scott's long report was more specific. He began by saying, "Foreigners of all nationalities in China, businessmen and missionaries, as well as the Chinese, are alarmed beyond words at the rapid unfolding of the plans of Japan for military and economic conquest of China. Since Japan's 'diplomatic triumph' at Paris, she has thrown off the mask here of seeming to be China's friend and has revealed clearly her purpose." Describing Japanese behavior as arrogant, cynical, cruel, sinister, Prussian, brutal, aggressive, and cunning, Scott told of the twofold objective of Japanese propaganda in China: "to make the Chinese distrust and turn out American business and missionary work; and to convince the Chinese that their salvation consists in coming under the powerful protecting wing of Japan." He detailed the

Japanese takeover of Tsingtao, comparing Japanese actions there to earlier behavior in Korea.

Woodbridge, vacationing at Augusta, Michigan, wrote in similar tones in August, noting that his thirty-year experience convinced him that "Japan will *never* relax her hold on China."[102] It disturbed him that America had put its "imprimatur" on the Shantung agreement, for this would negate the work of the hospitals, colleges, printing presses, and missions, and put back the work of the church for years. He said Wilson's approval of the agreement had put him in a "terrible light in the eyes of four hundred millions of people." Referring to Japan as brutal and a "military, autocratic neighbor," he wondered, "how can we face those millions of disappointed, desperate Chinese people if you uphold the designs of those brute military despots?"

Had the president been interested in changing the Shantung arrangement, the opportunity passed, for Wilson left on his "swing around the circle," which was curtailed when he became ill, and back in Washington a thrombosis paralyzed Wilson's left side and virtually all presidential activity. Foreign affairs suffered because of a lack of leadership, and John V. A. MacMurray, by this time chief of the Far Eastern Division at the State Department, wrote that Wilson "has been so exclusively responsible for policies particularly in the realm of foreign affairs—the whole administration has been so much of a one man show—that his disability has paralyzed the whole executive. One has that queer feeling of a ship at sea with engines stopped."[103]

It soon became apparent the Japanese had tightened their control over Shantung. Reinsch, meanwhile, submitted his resignation in June 1919, effective September 15, seeing the outlook as discouraging, unless the United States was willing "to face the situation and to act." He believed that constructive forces in China had to be supported and that Washington should give attention to Chinese affairs. His work, he thought, had suffered because of lack of attention. Although Assistant Secretary of State Breckinridge Long disagreed, believing "attention has been given to China and has been continuous," it is hard to dispute Reinsch's contention.[104] Wilsonian diplomacy in regard to China had been crisis oriented.

Wilson's final activities in American-Chinese relations dealt with organizing a committee to relieve famine. Wilson appealed to Americans by noting, "To an unusual degree the Chinese people look to us for counsel and for effective leadership." As Roy Watson Curry has observed, "In many ways this was the summation of Wilson's career and policy-service to the welfare of mankind."[105] Thus, three factors stand out in American-Chinese relations, between 1913 and 1921: Wilson himself, the situation, and the tradition of American policy.[106] All three, but especially the first, contributed to the influence of religion and the missionaries on American policy toward China. Much of Wilson's policy was along traditional lines. He favored the open-door policy and believed that Japan might control certain economic rights in China, but not political sovereignty. Aspects of Wilson's policy were, however, different. The missionaries had more access to Wilson and more influence on him, both directly and indirectly, because of Wilson's background, than they had with previous presidents. Paul Varg has written, "No president was more sympathetic with the missionary movement than Woodrow Wilson, but he soon learned that he could not carry on foreign relations in accordance with the dictates of his missionary friends."[107] Varg is too harsh, for only over the Shantung settlement did the president find himself in disagreement with the missionaries. It is difficult to determine how much this similarity of views resulted from Wilson's own background and from his accepting the missionaries' advice, but the similarity is striking. However much Wilson's idealism seemed contradicted by the Lansing-Ishii and Shantung agreements, by the compromises at the Paris Conference, he was still willing to make whatever sacrifices were necessary to get the Versailles Treaty approved.

• • •

Missionary advice did not stop after Wilson's administration. It has been a persistent voice throughout most of the twentieth century. An outstanding example of this and, perhaps, its most vocal political voice was Dr. Walter H. Judd (1898–1994). His voice was the perfect model of a modern major Cold Warrior, ringing out in the halls of Congress from 1943 to 1963, where Judd served Minnesota's Fifth District in the Seventy-eighth through Eighty-seventh Congresses, and he became chair of the House Foreign Relations Committee. Most famously, he gave the keynote address at the 1960 Republican National Convention, and in 1981 he received the Presidential Medal of Freedom. What made him so interesting as an important congressman was his medical missionary career to China in the 1920s and 1930s. After a 1918 stint in the army and graduations from college and medical school, he served as a medical missionary and hospital superintendent in China for the American Board of Commissioners for Foreign Missions of the Congregational Church from 1925 to 1931 and again from 1934 to 1938.[108]

Japan's war against China brought Judd into politics. He had escaped from Japanese-occupied northern China in 1938. After starting a medical practice in Minneapolis while attached to the Mayo Clinic, he made speeches warning Americans about Japanese intentions. He testified before congressional committees and, after Pearl Harbor, ran for Congress in 1942. He became the voice of Generalissimo Chiang Kai-shek and his Republic of

China (ROC). Judd grew suspicious of Russian intentions and became a sharp critic of President Franklin D. Roosevelt's Yalta agreements. For instance, in a 1968 interview, he mentioned, "The Far Eastern Division [of the State Department] was loaded with people who were on the other side— who thought the Chinese Communists were 'agrarian reformers,' they were the better horse to back, Chiang's government wasn't good enough for us to support."[109]

By the time of the Cairo Conferences in late 1943, Chiang had reached his peak in international politics. Nevertheless, prominent Americans in Chungking, China's wartime capital, had come to the conclusion, especially such visitors as Vice President Henry Wallace, accompanied by John Carter Vincent, head of the Division of Chinese Affairs of the State Department, and Owen Lattimore, a prominent Sinologist and official of the Office of War Information, that Chiang should make peace with the communists, whom Wallace called "agrarian democrats." Judd criticized the Wallace report for being procommunist, as a biographer put it.[110] Further, Judd's biographer indicated that the congressman believed America's commander in chief in southeastern Asia, Gen. Joseph Stilwell, "depended for his political analysis almost exclusively on foreign service officers like John Paton Davies, John Stewart Service, Raymond Paul Ludden, and John K. Emmerson, who were convinced that the communists represented China's future."[111]

By 1947, Judd was harping in Congress on Nationalist China's importance in the Cold War: "As China goes, so will Asia." Abandoning China would mean, he believed, "we defeated Japan—and Russia won the war." Further, giving Russia a veto in the UN was also a blunder—even allowing the USSR into the world organization was the "climatic tragedy of President Roosevelt's life," a failed "grand design." "Russia hasn't used the veto once to block war," he commented. "She has used it over a score of times to block measures or decisions that were steps in the right direction of peace." If Asia fell to communism, Russia would gain "preponderance in territory, resources, and manpower." The fault for such an outcome would lie at the feet of a U.S. government playing the diplomatic games of "striped pants." Judd came out strongly for aiding Greece, Turkey, and Korea. Again, he blamed FDR: "At Yalta we sacrificed our principles and other people's rights and territories to get Russia to come into the United Nations." Finally, he faulted the U.S. failure to win in Korea because America's "star quarterback" Gen. Douglas MacArthur was fired. By the mid-1950s, Judd stoutly opposed admitting the People's Republic of China into the UN.[112]

Two domestic issues pestered this former medical missionary: first, the Alger Hiss case and, second, McCarthyism, though he protested Senator Joseph McCarthy's methods: "Anticommunism became the central crusade of his life."[113] In 1947, he joined the subcommittee of the Government Operations Committee, which removed 134 security risks in the State Department. In this capacity, he ran across Alger Hiss's name; he contacted Whittaker Chambers, then an editor for *Time* magazine. Chambers admitted his years as a communist agent who worked with Hiss. Hiss denied the Chambers connection. Judd further found that Hiss had been a China Section member of the State Department, able to "make China policy—build up the Communists and build down our ally—by selecting the [information] he passed on to his superiors, such as the reports of Service and Davies which were overwhelmingly favorable to the Communists. . . . Then people wonder why we lost China."[114] Along with the conviction of Hiss, who had served on FDR's Yalta delegation, for perjury, Hiss "categorically denied" before the House Un-American Activities Committee that he had been a communist spy and even filed a defamation suit against Chambers. Chambers had, at first, only accused Hiss of promoting communist policies in the U.S. government, and specifically denied any espionage until a second trial in which typed "Baltimore" documents (the kind of typewriter used) were discovered as, supposedly, part of Hiss's espionage work—the so-called pumpkin papers. Hiss was indicted on two counts of perjury, found guilty, and served forty-four months at the Lewisburg Federal Prison before his release in November 1954. Senator McCarthy made his famous Wheeling, West Virginia, speech two weeks after Hiss's verdict, in which he claimed that there were large numbers of communists and Soviet spies in the government and that he had a list of such persons. He never substantiated these wild charges, especially in the Army-McCarthy Hearings, and in 1954 the Senate censured him.[115]

It was also now that a group of Democrats and Republicans stood for an effective policy to aid the Nationalists rather than Red China. Judd was named an important member of the so-called China Lobby—a "loose conglomeration of persons and organizations which for various reasons are interested in China." However, according to one researcher, the China Lobby was composed of those, like Judd, who "passionately believe American policy to be wrong; who think that American withdrawal from China caused a needless break in the dike against the spread of communism."[116] With the "lobby," the "Committee of One Million" grew up. It opposed seating the People's Republic of China in the UN, while expelling the ROC. It obtained a million signatures on a petition and presented it to President Dwight Eisenhower on October 22, 1953. Judd was a member of its steering committee. In 1961, the UN General Assembly voted forty-five to thirty against the PRC's admission, without expelling the ROC. It was only in 1971 that the UN seated the PRC and expelled the ROC. That action ended the Committee of One Million.[117]

Until the end of his life, Judd actively supported Taiwan. He pointed out, for example, that the Shanghai Communiqué of 1972, signed by President Richard Nixon at the end of his historic China trip, was not a legal document and was never presented to the Senate. In 1978, President Jimmy Carter recognized the PRC and "derecognized" the ROC, which action Judd sharply criticized. Judd continued to opposed accommodation to communism, faulting President Ronald Reagan for his 1982 trip to the PRC and General Secretary Mikhail Gorbachev's 1987 visit to the United States. In 1989, he was encouraged by the Tiananmen Square protests. To show how doggedly persistent Judd remained as late as 1978, he insisted Chiang Kai-shek would "go down in history, in many respects, as the greatest man of this century. He's the one man who's been right on all the major issues."[118]

In the end, America overlooked Judd, the missionaries, and their constituencies to embrace Red China, even when events fulfilled Judd's predictions, such as Tiananmen Square and suppressing Falun Gong, the "mind and body cultivation" related to Buddhism. The Chinese Communist Party (CCP) cracked down on it in July 1999, even though human rights groups protested and the U.S. House of Representatives accused China of "unlawful harassment of U.S. citizens who practiced Falun Gong."[119] Today, unlike the heyday of Judd's right-wing anticommunism, traditional American sympathy for China blooms, and whatever wrinkles and warts contemporary China has, they are overlooked. Overlooking those wrinkles and warts after Wilson, things began with a somewhat unlikely candidate —neither a diplomat nor a sightseer, but the famous American philosopher John Dewey.

9

Pragmatist in China

America's most famous philosopher, John Dewey, and his wife, Alice Chipman Dewey, toured China from May 1, 1919, to July 11, 1921. They arrived in Shanghai at the invitation of some of his former students at Columbia University—Hu Shih, P. W. Kuo, and Chiang Monlin—to present lectures at universities and colleges in Peking, Nanking, and other cities.[1] His devotion to, and fascination with, China often mirrored the experiences of W. W. Rockhill, the missionaries, and Ambassador Paul S. Reinsch. Like them, he learned much from the Chinese, but he also taught them an American perception of the world. Unlike many of his contemporaries, he quickly came to understand and appreciate what was unique to China. He stopped preaching, started listening, and began learning about the immense complexity that was China.

Dewey was close to his sixtieth year, older than most of the Chinese intelligentsia. His most important Chinese doctoral student, Hu Shih, a professor at National Peking University, was still in his twenties and considered by some of his cohorts as a progressive, even a revolutionary. Dewey entered Hu's Chinese intellectual circles at, perhaps, their most crucial years when they asked: just what adaptations should China make to survive in the newly emerging world order? "He had acquired a feeling that his special mission in life was to teach men how to live and think in the new age of science, technology and democracy."[2] Behind him were already published his most influential works, *School and Society* (1899), *Democracy and Education* (1916), and *Reconstruction in Philosophy* (1919), the latter a result of his lectures recently delivered in Japan. He understood the moment's importance for China: "Simply as an intellectual spectacle, a scene for study and surmise, there is nothing in the world today—not even Europe in the throes of reconstruction—that equals China."[3] China had to be made over, or it could not endure. It had to condense into a century the progress of the rest of the world, or existing disorders would allow either Japanese domination or the Bolshevization of China.

When Dewey left China, he had spent two years, two months, and ten days there. He had given lectures on more than thirty topics, made speeches everywhere he visited, concerned himself with events then happening in China, and even wrote a report to the Ministry of Education. All of this made him more than just a simple visitor.[4] Before his arrival, none of his works existed in Chinese. "By the time of his departure in July 1921, however, there had been at least fifty articles about his ideas in journals of every persuasion, and translations began which continued throughout the 1920s."[5] The War Department made this comment about the famous philosopher: "Exceptionally good judgment and knowledge of general affairs. Particularly well informed on student movement and radical elements. A very careful and unemotional investigator."[6] Almost fifty years later, Dewey's daughter Lucy wrote, "The Chinese are a wonderful people, their consideration and generosity were boundless. Those two years are among the richest and most pleasant of my life and both my parents felt the same way."[7] Another daughter, Jane, said, "China remains the country nearest his heart after his own."[8]

• • •

The Deweys had arrived in Shanghai on April 30, 1919. His earliest letters home to his family were ordinary enough. There were no first impressions, he insisted, because "China hasn't revealed itself to our eyes as yet."[9] Immediately, he wrote his boss, Murray Butler, president of Columbia University, "On my arrival here I was met by [Dr. Hu Shih] from Peking as well as by educators from here and Nanking. They all feel that the present in [sic] quite a critical time in the educational and intellectual development of China, and that a representative of Western and especially American thought can be more useful now than at any other time for a long period."[10] His first impression of Shanghai was that it could be compared with Detroit. These early letters dealt with subjects other than the typical touristy things, except the greeting party of his former students: labor issues caught his attention, such as piecework, child exploitation, and poor wages. Also, he remarked about efforts to stop concubinage and plural marriage. To his dismay, the Chinese cared little about what outsiders thought of them. They were "noisy, not to say boisterous, easy-going and dirty—quite human in general effect."[11] Already the famous American philosopher and educator had toured a local school and, while visiting a department store, noted that the locals bought American-made goods over those produced in Japan.[12]

As for the Japanese, "The most impressive thing about their Chinese hatred for Japan is that it isnt [sic] loud and boisterous; it is just as much a matter of fact as the weather, and it is combined with great moral contempt."[13] Within a month, his first article appeared in the *New Republic*, "On the Two Sides of the Eastern Sea." His initial impressions were ones of enthusiasm, though based only on casual encounters and with little preparation. Two later scholars were critical of Dewey: "A man who laid claim to a scientific outlook that cautiously formulated statements on the basis of factual knowledge might have been more circumspect. Dewey was not."[14] Nevertheless, those exuberant remarks were often on the mark: "It is three days' easy journey from Japan to China. It is doubtful whether anywhere in the world another journey of the same length brings with it such a complete change of political temper and belief." He meant that in Japan "liberalism is in the air, but genuine liberals are encompassed with all sorts of difficulties especially in combining their liberalism with the devotion to theocratic robes which the imperialistic militarists who rule Japan have so skillfully thrown around the Throne and the Government." In contrast to that circumscribed Japanese liberal spirit, in China it turned out to be the "all-pervading power of Japan which is working as surely as fate to its un-hesitating conclusion—the domination of Chinese politics and industry by Japan with a view to its final absorption." Half-informed Americans mistook the former for the latter. The Japanese press and Baron Shimpei Goto, the "TR" of Japan and former mayor of Tokyo, reassured Americans there were not any "improper ambitions on the part of Japan. In China, they were taken as announcements that Japan has about completed its plans for the absorption of China, and that the lucubration preliminary to operations of swallowing are about to begin." Dewey complained that Americans had little idea of the state of affairs. "But that Japan and China should be so geo-graphically near, and yet every fact that concerns them appear in precise-ly opposite perspective, is an experience of a life time."[15]

The Deweys found themselves amid an upheaval known as the May Fourth Movement, intimately connected with specific events in Peking but also tied to the intricate developments that ensued. Students from thirteen colleges and universities congregated in Tiananmen Square, directly before the Forbidden City, and marched toward the foreign legations. They carried banners with the names of hated pro-Japanese members of the ruling cabinet written on them. That morning they had drawn up five resolutions: protest of President Woodrow Wilson's Shantung arrangement at Versailles, appeal to China's masses over its plight, a call for mass meetings, formation of a Peking student union, and a demonstration that afternoon against the Versailles Treaty's terms. That day they marched on the home of the minister of communications, the one responsible for large Japanese loans. Violent clashes followed. Consequently, they and some of their teachers tried to implement the remaining resolutions, including supporting coeducation. By June, delegates from more than thirty areas formed a

Student Union of the Republic of China. Mass support for the students came from merchants, business leaders, and workers. Periodicals and newspapers in the simple vernacular style sprang up. These reformers were patriots who sought to rejuvenate and unify China by ending warlordism, feudalism, and imperialism. Hu Shih played an important role in the May Fourth Movement as a follower of Dewey's "'ever-enduring process of perfecting' rather than perfection."[16] So, here were the Deweys, cast into the swirl of reform and revolution—what they called the "Peking tempest."[17]

One of his first letters, reporting on the May Fourth Movement, was dated May 12, 1919. The Japanese, he wrote, called it student pranks, but there was a nationwide boycott of Japanese goods and money. Beyond anti-Japanese protests, students discussed the subjection of women, China's domestic and educational backwardness, and its physical degeneration, political corruption, and lack of public spirit. Dewey called the soldiers, who were brought into the cities to quell the demonstrations, bandits.[18] The root of the current disturbances, Dewey thought, was the Versailles giveaway of Shantung to the Japanese. "American sentiment here hopes that the Senate will reject the treaty because it virtually completes the turning over of China to Japan." Japan already possessed Manchuria. In five or ten years, he believed, China would be under Japanese military domination, unless it was "Bolshevikized." In Dewey's conversation with Sun Yat-sen, the former president considered one of China's main weaknesses its inability to act for fear of making a mistake.[19]

In a long letter of May 13, 1919, Dewey stressed that the Chinese did not take advantage of their resources, but the Japanese did. They were in every town across China like a net closing in on fish. The cession of Shantung precipitated the May Fourth Movement, resulting in Chinese protests, strikes, and boycotts against the Japanese. The date of the Twenty-one Demands of Japan had now turned into an anniversary observed everywhere as the Day of Humiliation. General meetings and speech making occurred all over China. The United States, Dewey felt, should call the Japanese to account for their aggressive moves in China: "It is sickening that we allow Japan to keep us on the defensive and the explanatory, and talk about the open door, when Japan has locked most of the doors in China already and got the keys in her pocket." A corrupt military clique now controlled China and had sold it out to the Japanese.[20]

In mid-May the Deweys moved to Nanking (Nanjing), before pushing onto Peking at the beginning of June. They pointed out that Hangchow (Hangzhou) was the most prosperous of the strictly Chinese cities. By then, the Deweys thought the Chinese were the same as "dirty, poor miserable people anywhere." Nevertheless, they were cheerful but restrained by the "let-George-do-it" attitude, the one Sun referred to, which was the curse of

China. Even in Nanking there were fewer than a hundred schools, each having only a few hundred students. Technology there was primitive. Students had formed a patriotic league. The former examination halls were being torn down along with the old official system. The student movement had introduced a new political factor: "You heard nothing but gloom about political China at first, corrupt and traitorous officials, soldiers only paid banditti, the officers getting the money from Japan to pay them with, no organizing or cohesion among the Chinese and then the students take things into their hands, and there is animation and a sudden buzz."[21]

In that same period, Dewey wrote a long set of letters to his children. Although these letters often dealt with mundane matters such as tourism, cuisine, or the oriental lifestyle, he also touched on important current events there. For example, he wrote at length on Versailles and the Shantung question, which involved Japan in China and the question of the Chinese government and its military. In these problems, the United States, with its open-door diplomacy, had an interest. In fact, Dewey complained that President Woodrow Wilson had sent special agents to China to collect information. Even Wilson's friend Charles Crane, a former ambassador to China, was there, and the Chinese had counted a great deal on him. Quickly, however, "they seem to have lost enthusiasm for him." One of the papers, Dewey noted, had cynically referred to "Craniological optimism."[22]

Germany's Shantung concession, as complex an issue as it became, had resulted from two problems. The first was a weak and corrupt Chinese government—democratic and republican in name only. Its parliament was prorogued, its cabinet under reconstruction, its premier, Duan Qirui, was pro-Japanese. Japan, Dewey thought, probably had a secret deal with the Allies for Shantung as a price for its entering the war. President Wilson gave in to the Japanese on the flimsy excuse that Germany's Shantung concession was only a temporary expedient to mollify the Japanese. And Japan itself wanted a return of China's old imperial government until it was in a position to take China over itself. "It is just one more evidence of the failure of the Peace Conference to comprehend the excuses that Wilson is making for the concessions he has granted to the practical needs, as he calls them." Under pressure from British prime minister David Lloyd George and French premier Georges Clemenceau, Wilson agreed to transfer all of Germany's Shantung rights to Japan on April 30, 1919.[23] The political struggle in China had centered between the extreme military elements against a group of colorless moderates. In protest, China's delegates to the Paris Peace Conference had refused to sign the Versailles Treaty, but it would be imposed anyway. "You can't imagine what it means here," he wrote, "for China not to have signed. The entire government has been for it—the President up to ten days before the signing said it was necessary."[24]

The Chinese government could go on indefinitely without a cabinet and with no responsibility to react to public indignation as expressed in the May Fourth Movement. "The bulk of the nation is against this state of affairs, but with the support of foreigners and the lack of organization there is nothing to do but stand it and see the nation sold out to Japan and other grabbers." Meanwhile, the Japanese minister haunted both the president of China and the prime minister and every day reported to Tokyo that the Chinese delegation would sign. Even ordinary Japanese were not told the truth about their government's "fostering a weak and unrepresentative government here, and what a temptation to it a weak and divided China will continue to be, for it will serve indefinitely as an excuse for postponing the return of Shantung—as well as for interfering elsewhere." The Chinese army was a useless bunch of brigands and tuchuns (military governors) who were often in the Japanese pay. If allowed to continue, China would find itself in the same situation as Korea. Meanwhile, the new China was in its birth throes with the "kids . . . taking the lead in starting a big cleanup reform politics movement and shaming merchants and professional men into joining them." The "kids" were chanting American ideals, which the United States was too timid to demand, though it could use its power, financial resources, and food and raw materials to enforce. The "kids," so the military or Anfu clique running the government thought, were in the care of the university's chancellor, who was "morally responsible for the students taking an interest in politics—altho he himself is no politician—in fact his own interest is in esthetics and literature—Paris educated."[25] It might, Dewey thought, take a war between the United States and Japan to resolve China's problems with Japan.[26] "It was as if far-off events at Versailles and the mounting evidence of the spinelessness of corrupt local politicians," according to one historian, "coalesced in people's minds and impelled them to search for a way to return meaning to Chinese culture."[27]

Dewey's ideas fed into the swirling broth of revolutionary China. Hu Shih, Dewey's closest Chinese follower, originally was a close friend and collaborator of Chen Duxiu, founder of the Chinese Communist Party. Then, Dewey still believed that "there is as much danger of Bolshevizing China as there is of the farmers of Berks Co [Pennsylvania] turning Bols [Bolshevik]. But verything [sic] goes when it comes to propaganda. The only question left is the depths of human gullibility."[28] The following month he had to admit that Bolshevism was growing very rapidly in China, not Sovietism, but "a belief in revolution as the cure of both Japan and their won [sic] govt, and making use of the Russian revolutionary aid to bring it on—there is too much lamd [sic] owned by individualistic peasants for a real Russian Bolshevism and factory industry too undeveloped."[29] What he called "technical" Bolshevism had no chance, but "psychological" was "fairly intense in the educated minority, especially if they have not been educated abroad."[30] China was like Europe in the seventeenth century, and the rest of the world would not give it two hundred years to modernize. It would have to do it in the next fifty years.[31] He quoted a longtime foreign resident as saying, "In China the Renaissance, the reformation, the English, French and American revolution are all taking place simultaneously and in the same country."[32]

By August 1919, Dewey reported that an anguished Ambassador Paul S. Reinsch was leaving China, though Reinsch was well liked by the Chinese but disliked by the foreign community. Dewey speculated that he would be replaced by a business type. Nobody knew for certain why Reinsch resigned, though Dewey surmised that it had something to do with the Shantung compromise of Wilson: "It is the growing opinion that if the US backs down on either the Shantung issue or the Japanese consortium for reservation of Manchuria and Mongolia, it means the going back to the old policy of the partition of China, as China cant [*sic*] hold its own alone."[33] And Japan would keep the open door "bolted and barred much more than the Russians did."[34] About his own work in China, he lamented, "Whether I am accomplishing naying [*sic*] as well as getting a great deal is another matter. China remains a massive blank and impenetrable wall, when it comes to judgment."[35]

Dewey's students were usually in the modernist movement, and they saw him as a revolutionist in philosophy in that it should be an instrument for solving human problems. But the Russian Revolution had also made Marx and Lenin important collateral influences in China. This leftist leaning made Bertrand Russell popular in China as well. With Dewey's help, Russell and his mistress, Dora Black, came to China while the Deweys were there. Dewey thought that Russell was the greater influence on Chinese intellectuals. To astonished Chinese intellectuals, Russell criticized Bolshevism. Dewey believed Russell's stance fortunate for the Chinese, especially in Hunan, where the Bolshevists were idealized. When Russell fell ill for some months with pneumonia, the Deweys took Dora Black into their home for six weeks. Not only did the "Russells" not acknowledge any gratitude, but later Russell attacked pragmatism. Dewey was not hurt and believed the Englishman was, simply, anti-American. Russell's lectures appealed more to the radical elements in China, though they were frustrated by his insistence on praising the pacifist thought of Lao-tzu.[36] Some of their letters show a more bitter relationship than anti-Americanism. Russell wrote to a friend, "The Deweys are here, & got into trouble in America during the war for their liberalism, are as bad as anybody—American imperialist, hating England . . . & unwilling to face any unpleasant facts. In 1914,

I liked Dewey better than any other academic American; now I can't stand him."[37] Dora Black was even more candid: "Dewey has surpassed himself in the latest *New Republic* saying that all suggestions of America being concerned in Canton Port are pure lies. They do not print any [my?] remarks about the Shank [Shantung] concessions. B. [Russell] is now coming into the fray with the heavy guns. But it seems clear that Dewey is not as we hoped a fool, but a villain."[38]

Dewey was anti-British. He wrote a friend that China was a good place to study international politics: "I realize for the first time what is the real meaning of British Imperialism and how little English liberalism and democracy has [sic] touched foreign policies. . . . An American remarked the other day the entire foreign policy of Downing Street was dictated by British financial interest."[39] Shortly after the confrontation of the two philosophers, the *Weekly Review* for July 23, 1921, announced: "Two distinguished philosophers, who have been lecturing in China for some time, left Peking on Monday last on their way home, Dr. John Dewey, accompanied by Mrs. Dewey and Miss Dewey left in the morning, while Mr. Bertrand Russell, accompanied by Miss Black, left in the afternoon."[40]

Dewey reported that the Americans, most Chinese believed, liked to talk but do nothing. He cited Thomas Lamont, the financier of J. P. Morgan and Company, who spoke about the possibilities of investment and returned to the United States without doing anything.[41] Lamont had been interested in forming a banking consortium—the United States, Great Britain, France, and Japan. Dewey supported the idea because, he thought, it would curtail loans by imperial powers to gain concessions and spheres and, though less economic than political, might help preserve China's territorial integrity.[42] He came to believe that a consortium in China might not be all that bad and could be the salvation of China by protecting it from further exploitation.[43] By the end of 1920, he put this proposition forcefully: "There is but one end logically to the present political situation, and that's complete international foreign control of finance which means of course practically all governmental administration. Nothing happens logically in China however. One is often inclined to think that would have been better if China had been allowed to go to pot in its own way, and no foreigner had ever set foot in it. But 'ifs' that assume the non-existence of steam and electricity don't go far."[44] A few days later he went on to say, "The Consortium is the 'best thing' in sight for China, in fact the only thing in sight politically." But, even so, it was questionable whether it would ever function.[45] By March 1921, he was convinced the consortium was more political than financial. It was more anxious to protect old investments than make new ones.[46]

• • •

John Dewey's public pronouncements on China were many and sustained. He had developed a fascination with the Orient and its mystique. His lectures while in China from 1919 to 1921 revealed some of his earliest sentiments.[47] They were always well publicized, and his audiences often numbered more than a thousand at a time.[48] There was also an array of articles about China that he published while there and later.[49]

His various lectures, though topically diverse and varied in content, may be grouped into the following areas: social and political philosophy, the philosophy of education, the development of democracy in America, the relationship between democracy and education, trends in contemporary education, self-activity and self-government, social factors, and the history of philosophy.[50] They were important political and social statements, as they represented Dewey's first formulation based on pragmatism and its implications for China. On the one hand, these lectures revealed his interest in pluralism and guild socialism, while, on the other, they showed his concern over state capitalism and state socialism. Instrumentalism, the name his social philosophy went by, was not radical and not conservative, that is, it rejected both revolution and the status quo. Instead, he wrote, "we need the ability (and the disposition) to look for particular kinds of solutions by particular methods for particular problems which arise on particular occasions."[51] It was an incremental or cumulative process. As Dewey often said, it was "reconstruction," not "revolution." Dewey was also a pluralist in that he saw society as a collection of groups, where social conflicts arose between them due to inequities, that is, some groups "gained at the disadvantage of, or even by the suppression of, the interests of other groups."[52] The job of society, according to Dewey's social and political theory, was to "devise means for bringing the interests of all the groups of society into adjustment, providing all of them with the opportunity to develop, so that each can help the others instead of being in conflict with them."[53] Social reform, therefore, sought to harmonize group interests in a rational way. The role of the state was to mediate conflict between social groups. The ideal should be what he called "associated living" or "moral democracy." These societies were held together by consensus, not force. Dewey referred to this as "guild socialism"—by which he meant ones "centered on the concept of the welfare of the total society, and this, rather than individual profit, should be the criterion according to which economic organization and economic enterprises are judged."[54] Since this was not a fact but an ethical postulate, many Chinese intellectuals were not persuaded; indeed, it appeared to them irrelevant.[55]

It was Dewey's style, where appropriate, to refer to the relevant Chinese experience in each lecture. Often, though not necessarily, he put this near the end of each lecture. In the first cycle of lectures on social and political philosophy, when speaking on the function of theory, he noted the Chinese had early on recognized the importance of accepting a philosophy that provided a basis for a stable society. Nevertheless, in the modern world Confucianism resulted in rigidity instead of stability and interfered with progress.[56] When he was frequently asked where the Chinese should begin in reforming their society, his answer was to "start by reforming the component institutions of the society." He meant families, schools, and government at all levels by individuals collaborating with others. Progress would be their intelligent efforts in solving problems one by one, avoiding an instant, total reconstruction.[57] When speaking of the rise of privileged groups in society, he pointed out that often it was dominating ecclesiastical groups, though China was an exception, since there had never been a state religion. By contrast, in Western societies, especially America, material things and those who made money gained respect. The Chinese were critical of this aspect of American society.[58]

About social reform, Dewey considered that theorists in the past were wrong about the origins of social conflict, mistaking it as the "disparity between the interests of the individual, on the one hand, and of his society on the other [but] in our theory, social conflict is a matter of groups in conflict —and groups are, by definition social."[59] He used China as an example of this: family interests preceded those of the sons and younger brothers; their interests were seen as threats to social stability. To reform this condition required three phases: first, accepting the status quo; second, a phase of challenge; and, third, a reform movement going through an era of transition in which greater numbers attained power and were willing to make changes. Traditional theory deprived reformers of a framework and time to consider reform dispassionately and, instead, branded them as troublemakers and enemies.[60] Reform in China would be difficult because Chinese institutions exercised too tight a control over individual actions. "China tends to wait till the problem is upon her before making any plan at all."[61]

This waiting until the end, according to Dewey, was illustrated by the cycles of transition from one dynasty to another. Instead of fostering communication between social groups and associated living among them, one part of society was kept separated from another. The appearance of stability was maintained until near the end of a dynasty, but the onset of a new dynasty was accompanied by violence. That dynasty's first emperor was strong and enlightened, but his successors increasingly estranged themselves: "If the ruling families had encouraged associated living and profited from free communication with all sectors of their society, they would not have become so decadent and so unable to perform their functions as rulers."[62] In reorganizing Chinese society, its important resources—rails, highways, minerals, forests, trade, manufacturing—should not be subjected to a minority for its own exclusive interest. China's unique guild system might become the basis of its political organization. Developing a specific version of socialism, "rather than individual profit, should be the criterion according to which economic organization and economic enterprises are judged. This same concept should be our criterion as we deal with concrete problems which confront China today."[63]

Dewey believed that China did not have to go through every capitalist stage of development to reach a socialism unique to it. It need not go through "self-seeking individualism [but could] achieve social equality in one operation." The road there was through popularizing education, which would "provide all men with equal opportunities for self-development. . . . [I]ndustrialization of China is just now beginning; there is thus the chance for China to universalize education now, so that by the time it reaches full-scale industrialization it will also have achieved social equality."[64]

The second set of lectures Dewey gave was on a philosophy of education. He stressed that one of the goals of a democratic society was to provide an equal opportunity for each person to develop his or her full potentialities. This was, he thought, particularly important when things were in flux, as they were in contemporary China. Most important, "the aim of education, especially in democratic countries, is to create good citizens." Politically, that meant being a good neighbor and friend, contributing to and benefiting from others' contributions, producing rather than just sharing, being a wise consumer, and creatively adding to one's culture. To advance education in China, textbooks must be written in the spoken language of China. Such texts had to extend the range of a child's environment: "China faces an unprecedented and unparalleled opportunity to do this sort of thing in her schools . . . to speed up cultural exchange between East and West, and to select from Western culture for adaptation to Chinese conditions those aspects which give promise of compensating for the disadvantages which accrued from earlier contacts." This would not be easy, for the Chinese were not greatly interested in importing modern science or allowing intellectual freedom. Further, there was the age-old Chinese wisdom that "to know is easy; to act is difficult." But, as Dewey pointed out, "This is just the opposite of the experimental method, for in this method it is only after we have acted upon a theory that we really understand it." The next fifty years would be crucial for China, Dewey believed, because developing a material civilization would depend to a large extent on what the Chinese did about scientific education.[65]

The remainder of this series' lectures dealt with vocational training, with his well-known emphasis on this area: learning for living. The new leaders of China would have to plan for "social reconstruction in such a way that workers in the future will have full opportunity for intellectual development."[66] The Chinese had to "combine theory with practice; and the effective union of knowledge and practice is one of China's crying needs."[67] Because education was a process for Dewey, he would judge China not only by its schools and their effects but also by what went on outside the classroom—in the mines, fields, and factories.[68]

• • •

Many of Dewey's articles on China, appearing in various American contemporary newspapers and magazines such as the *New Republic* and *Asia*, were later anthologized. He was under contract with the former to do one article per month and the latter for six articles in total. At that time, "Herbert Croly and Walter Lippmann, as well as *The New Republic*'s owner, Willard Straight, stressed the crucial role of China in the future of the world."[69] Straight was a former China hand. If the letters were snapshots and first impressions, if the lectures were devoted to philosophical and educational matters, often referencing China, the articles were well-considered pieces aimed directly at gaining a wider public understanding of China. Concerning publishing in the *New Republic*, Dewey had this to say: "I get an opportunity for publication from them and fair pay and beyond that I want and expect nothing. Meantime the NR itself is doing more good than any other American publication; it maynt be much but its something [sic]."[70]

One of the earliest of these articles had already appeared in *Asia* in November 1919, "Transforming the Mind of China." Dewey marked the beginnings of modern China to the Boxer Rebellion of November 1899 to August 1900. It was the last effort of Old China to rid itself of foreigners and their influence. Its collapse meant that China had to live with the West—intellectually, morally, economically, financially, and politically. But China's living with the inevitable had to be active rather than patient passivity. "China learned in 1900 that she had to adjust herself to the requirements imposed by the activities of western peoples." There had to be a readjustment of China's "age-long customs, that she has to change her historic mind and not merely a few of her practices."[71] Since then, and especially after the Russo-Japanese War of 1904–1905, Japanese influence was enormous, the Chinese taking over Japan's administrative and educational techniques. The task was huge, and time was of the essence. Dewey worried that external forces would not stand by idly, but they would "invade and irritate and deflect and thwart till there is a final climax of no one knows what tragic catastrophe."[72]

This interference, Dewey worried, would come from those who were not prepared to understand the characteristics of Chinese institutions. Dewey saw the China he visited in 1919-1921 as a paternalistic democracy, where this "nominal republic" was dominated by a military clique that was maintaining itself through foreign loans and leasing or selling national property and authority. He was dismayed at the thought of some foreign guardianship or trusteeship for interim protection while China modernized, whether it would be Japan or other states or an international organization such as the League of Nations. He did think that if there were to be a successful guardian, it would have to confine its efforts to "stimulating, encouraging and expediting the democratic forces acting from within. And since such a task is almost entirely intellectual and moral, the guardianship is not necessary provided that China can be guaranteed time of growth protected from external attempts at disintegration." It would all have to be accomplished in the face of an impatient Western world that, "if it brings aid, also brings a voracious appetite."[73]

In December 1919, he published—again in *Asia*—"Chinese National Sentiment," anthologized as "The Growth of Chinese National Sentiment." He returned to the theme of China's encounter with the West. Old China, he claimed, was profoundly indifferent to the state and government. For a traditionally agrarian society, the farmers believed that governors, emperors, and mandarins were far away. Chinese politics was a survival of an original theocracy in which each province was a conglomeration of villages or "petty republics." They maintained a "static equilibrium," probably the most stable in history, though "rebellions overthrew dynasties." Indeed, the four thousand–year-old political life of China continued undisturbed.[74]

Then the outside world slammed into China with its battleships, artillery, railways, machinery, and chemicals. No longer could a complacent China absorb and gradually work these forces into its system. "China, a civilization, was confronted by a civilization which was organized as China was not, into national states. The consequences of this contact are written in every problem, internal as well as external, that occupies China to-day."[75] The Chinese had patriotism, or love of country; they had a sense of community. They had to become a nation, that is, have a political organization claiming sovereignty over their territory in the Western sense. Without that, they could not resist foreign encroachments, which occurred through finance—a conquest by banks and railways. China's modernization required foreigners, on whom it became dependent. This led to the partition of China and the scramble for empire there.[76]

How did Americans perceive their role in all of this? It was now, December 1919, that Dewey published in the *New Republic* a piece that he called "The American Opportunity in China," anthologized as "America and China," grouped with two later pieces, written in 1922 and 1926, on this same general topic. The average American, Dewey contended, regarded U.S. dealings with China complacently, imagining that the Chinese admired America and the Americans. After all, they had successfully initiated the open-door policy that, so they thought, arrested the further partitioning of China. The United States had returned the Boxer indemnity. These and other mild measures, Americans fancied, "secured for us the grateful confidence and respect of the Chinese." Never mind American treatment of Chinese immigrants on the Pacific coast or the exclusion act. Disagreeable thoughts could be put out of mind as "so much past history." But, Dewey asked, how far did the American perception of the Chinese attitude to the United States correspond with the facts?[77]

The facts were that many Chinese, Dewey explained, had the impression that American foreign policy was not very practical and that Americans lacked energy and persistence in their international relations. Americans were well disposed, but ineffectual in practice. For example, when the United States was making loans to its other World War I allies, China got nothing. Japan came forward, and, from that date, its hold on official Chinese circles began. Another example was the Hankow-Peking railway—a grandiose American scheme that collapsed. Dewey lamented, "The fact remains that the United States is the only great power that has nothing to show in China in achievement on a large scale [and this had] led educated and influential Chinese to feel that America could not be seriously counted upon."[78] Americans "readily emit large and good schemes, but are ineffectual when it comes to the test of action."[79] The excuse that Americans never had enough interest in the Far East to do substantial things did not hold up in the face of the Shantung sellout. Though the war showed America capable of decisive action, "unfortunately," continued Dewey, "the contrast between President Wilson's words and the concrete results of the Peace Conference—a contrast that circumstances make glaringly conspicuous in China—tends to restore the older idea about the United States."[80] In fact, Dewey contended, the United States was the only country with the necessary capital, executive experience, and engineering skills for big projects—projects that would still leave Japan with ample opportunities.[81]

By March 1922, in the *New Republic* article titled "America and Chinese Education," Dewey took exception to American missionary education, which had failed to create independent and energetic thought and produced only a "subservient intellectual type," one that a Chinese student leader characterized as slavish. So-called Young China had little sympathy with missionary efforts because they did not represent what China needed most from the West—its scientific method and freedom of inquiry. Such a newly created China would possess only Western knowledge and Western methods that could be independently employed to sustain it and not be a mere copy. As far as Dewey was concerned, "American influence in Chinese education should have something better to do than to train commercial, political and religious compradors." China did not need copies of American schools, but it did require schools supported by foreign funds and even partly manned by well-trained foreigners.[82]

In May 1926, in an article along the same lines titled "America and the Far East," in the *Survey Graphic*, he remarked, "In a true sense, our concern with China is parental rather than economic." The United States had gone to China "with advice, with instruction, with example and precept." Being in loco parentis, the United States was protective, but China was growing up rapidly and no longer wanted any kind of foreign guardianship or tutelage. The following decade would require a good deal of patience and understanding to alter that American parental role. Dewey warned, "If we cannot successfully make the change, the relationship of this country with the entire Far East will take a decided turn for the worse."[83]

In April 1920, Dewey turned his attention to China's legal system in an article originally published in *Asia* as "The New Leaven in Chinese Politics," and anthologized as "Justice and Law in China." Whereas Americans took for granted a regularized legal system and judicial procedure, in China there was almost no such guarantee or support, even though a certain peace and order prevailed. Rather, in China the law was enforced by private agencies and arrangements. "There is," Dewey asserted, "no confidence in government, no trust in the honesty, impartiality or intelligence of the officials of the State. Families, villages, clans, guilds—every organized group —has more confidence in the willingness of an opposed group to come to some sort of reasonable settlement than it has in the good faith or the wisdom of the official group."[84] This meant the Chinese government remained mostly personal, that is, a question of edicts, mandates, and decrees, not common or statuary law. For outsiders, it appeared that China was in a permanent state of lawlessness. There was a steady temptation for an "unscrupulous foreign power to carry on intrigues and bargains with provincial officials and politicians at the expense of the National State." Recent Chinese history was largely a series of foreign interventions, often fomented externally and resulting in extraterritoriality and concessions. Nevertheless, a process of legal codification was taking place, and Young China aimed at creating a government of and by laws.[85]

The year 1920 continued to be Dewey's most productive in writing about China for the American press. In May, he published in *Asia* an article titled "What Holds China Back," later called "Chinese Social Habits." In it, he answered that question. There were various social habits that held the Chinese back, including the lack of a stable government, Japanese intrigue and interference, being too pliant or easygoing, the ability to absorb difficulties and attain an equilibrium over long periods, a tendency to mind one's own business and not to interfere, and a fear of acting to avoid making mistakes. Of these, Dewey found the last one to be the most galling. He had already spent an evening with former president Sun Yat-sen, who had quoted an ancient Chinese sage: "To know is easy; to act is difficult." The Chinese did not act, Sun explained, because they were afraid of making mistakes and wanted to be guaranteed success in advance. "I am inclined to think," Dewey reflected, "the old sage was influential because his teaching was reinforced by effects of the ever-close and ever-thick environment." Dewey meant the enumerated Chinese social habits were the products of a long and continued population density whereby the mind was affected by constant living at close quarters that assumed the dimensions of a crowd.[86]

In June 1920, Dewey published in the *New Republic* a stunningly perceptive piece on China's political predicament, "China's Nightmare." In it, he blamed Russia for the original disintegration of China by the technique of conquest by railways and banking. Each Russian step was followed by demands for concessions and spheres of influence, which techniques other powers copied. The most successful imitator was Japan, which first set itself up as a defender of China's integrity against European aggression. But the Japanese militarist party believed that its destiny depended on getting sufficient control of China by keeping the Europeans restrained. "Japan's own policy became less and less defensive and more and more flagrantly offensive." American naïveté both to Russian diplomacy in China and its influence on Japan allowed the United States to fall an "easy victim" to Japanese propaganda. Most important, according to Dewey, "American ignorance secured almost universal approval for the Portsmouth treaty with its 'supplementary clauses' which in spite of their innocent appearance meant that the settlement was really a truce concluded at the expense of China's rights in Manchuria." Especially startling was Dewey's opinion that Russia's influence in China—whether czarist or commissarist—would, in the long run, predominate over Japan's.[87] Dewey lived to see Mao's victory.

Dewey published more articles on China in 1920 and sent a letter to the military attaché of the American legation in early December. The letter itself is an interesting piece, as it deals with the Bolshevik influence in China. In it, Dewey reversed himself and claimed that he had seen no direct evidence of Russian communism in China. He came to this conclusion because he had dealt with teachers, writers, and students, that is, those most susceptible because they were the groups most opposed to the old regime. The 1911 revolution had failed, they believed, because an intellectual change had to occur before democracy could be established. They were open to new ideas, especially socialism. Some even called themselves communists and thought highly of the Russian Revolution. Nevertheless, "I am absolutely certain they have nothing to do with the general tone and temper of radical thought in the country. . . . It is stimulated by the corruption and inefficiency of the government, and by the pro-Japanese character of the former cabinet." There was no leverage in China for a social revolution then. He decided, "The whole social and economic background of Bolshevism as a practical going concern is lacking."[88]

Dewey's remaining published pieces on China in 1920 dealt with Shantung and the reaction to it as well as an interesting article on Chinese industrialization. All were published that year in the *New Republic*. The first, "The Sequel of the Student Revolt," dealt with a disturbance between Chinese and Japanese in late November 1920 in Foochow (Fuzhou) which again inflamed public feelings, as had the original May Fourth Movement. Students and others demanded a cessation of all social and economic relations with Japan. It was feared that once the Japanese got a foothold in Fukien Province, it would go the way of Manchuria and Shantung. The student movement had prevented the signing of the Versailles Treaty, but it had not stopped further Japanese penetration of China. Its plans for internal reform—spreading democratic education, raising the standard of living, improving industries, relieving poverty—were at a standstill. And the literary revolution—making the vernacular the standard language for print —was already well under way before the May Fourth Movement. A national education conference resolved that all textbooks be composed in the colloquial language. Dewey believed that China now realized that it must also adopt the modes of thought and ideas that stood behind mere material progress.[89]

The second article, "Shantung as Seen from Within," made the point that Japan's Russian-style policy in China had awakened Chinese nationalism: "No nation has ever misjudged the national psychology of another people as Japan has that of China." America continually mistook Japanese policy in China for what had occurred in the industrialization of America. But the Japanese planned to stay: "*Given the frequent occurrence of such economic invasions, with the backing of soldiers of the Imperial Army, with the overt aid of the Imperial Railway, and with the refusal of Imperial officials to intervene, there is clear evidence of the attitude of intention of the Japanese government in Shantung.*"[90]

The third article, "A Political Upheaval in China," broke revolution in China into four parts: overthrow of the Manchus, prevention of Yuan Shih-kai's aspirations to be emperor, defeat of attempts to put the Manchu boy-emperor on the throne, and, finally, the May Fourth Movement in all of its manifestations.

Another article of 1920, "Industrial China," sought to separate the notions of China as "industrious" and "industrial." The Chinese were proverbially industrious, but they had only just begun industrialization. It was Dewey's hope that China could benefit from Western mistakes and make a smoother transition. He was not sanguine: "China is the land of problems so deadlocked and interlocked that one is constantly reminded of the Chinese puzzles of his childhood days."[91]

The main body of Dewey's Chinese articles, composing several hundred pages of materials beyond his lectures in the Far East, ended with another set appearing in 1921, one in 1922, and a last piece in 1925. Dewey published on January 12, 1921, in the *New Republic* an article he called "Is China a Nation?" which was later anthologized as "Conditions for China's Nationhood." China was not a nation in the European sense of the word, but it was becoming one. Certain things stood in the way: lack of public spirit; debt and foreign interference; provincial divisions, particularly between North and South; the lack of a middle class; and little industrialization. "China *is* another world politically and economically speaking, a large and persistent world, and a world bound no one knows just where [and furthermore] Japan cannot sit upon her chest forever." Dewey was unsure where China would land after crowding in the next half century literary, religious, economic, scientific, and political revolutions.[92] By May 1921, he had presented in *Asia* a piece he originally titled "Old China and New," republished as "Young China and Old." Dewey was candid in admitting that everyone's favorite indoor sport was saving China from itself if only this or that were done. Made over it must be, or it could not endure. Some international control of its finances, Dewey thought, would be necessary if further disintegration and complete dependency on Japan were to be avoided. Some international consortium might be essential. And, of course, introducing modern tools had to be accompanied with scientific ideas and methods.[93] In "New Culture in China," published in *Asia* in July 1921, Dewey repeated once more his call for "condensing into a century or so the intellectual, scientific, industrial, political and religious progress for which the rest of the world has taken several centuries."[94]

In January 1922, under the title of "As China Thinks," and revised as "The Chinese Philosophy of Life," Dewey focused on the importance of better understanding the psychology of other nations. Though he realized China's "long and obstinate resistance to modern methods [and] to open up her country" to the rest of the world, he had to concede that "there is much to be said for a combination of nations, a kind of economic-political consortium, which will force modern industrialism upon China, overcoming her obstinacy for her own good, not allowing sentimental considerations to stand too much in the way."[95]

In three separate pieces, under the heading of "The White Peril," published successively in April and November 1925 and in May 1928—the first two in the *New Republic* and the last in *Current History*—Dewey challenged whether America was going back on its traditional policy of "friendly detachment" toward China and "approaching a union or understanding with European policies of economic and political aggression." The U.S. State Department had to decide whether to engage in the regulation of China's internal affairs, contrary to the almost united will of the Chinese, or whether "it will have the courage and initiative to act in not merely a democratic but a decent way in permitting financial self-government to the Chinese government." It would, he had decided, be a fantastic nightmare to interfere. He ended: "She needs our help. But it must come by patience, sympathy and educative effort, and the slow processes of commerce and exchange of ideas, not by a foreign rule imposed by military force."[96]

• • •

According to Thomas Berry, the challenge for Dewey was to replace Confucian humanism with a democratic and secular-scientific world order, something even Sun Yat-sen could not accept. Sun and his followers rehabilitated Confucius for China's cultural heritage in order to save old Chinese virtues, discipline, and order. In this sense, Deweyism was undermined.[97] More recently, Robert W. Clopton and Tsuin-chen Ou introduced Dewey's Chinese lectures with an important article. For them, there was no doubt that "China was the one foreign country on which Dewey exercised his greatest influence, particularly in the field of education." They agreed that 1919 was the "most critical year" in China's modern history, the year Dewey arrived there—perhaps the "supreme moment of intellectual communication between China and America was about to take place when Professor Dewey, among the most renowned of American philosophers, arrived in China."[98] The authors listed several ways in which Deweyism powered Chinese educational reform, including the new school curriculum of 1923 and its revision in 1929. After 1949, even the communists declared that "the educational ideas of Dewey have dominated and controlled Chinese education for thirty years." They decided that "the Communist attack on Dewey is one good indication of the force of his impact on Chinese thought and education, and of the degree to which the Chinese Communists deem it necessary to extirpate his influence, root and branch."[99]

Dewey, like "Soviet Sam" Harper for Russian studies, helped make Sinology fashionable. As with the Russian experts, so also the Chinese specialists played an important role in creating popular perceptions of Russia and China. This was particularly true because China scholars such as Kenneth

Scott Latourette and especially John King Fairbank—two founders of Sinology in the United States—were drawn into the wider public discussion of Chinese affairs. Fairbank inaugurated regional interdisciplinary studies at Harvard, an inspiration for other programs. These two Sinologists, their students, and the institutions they represented played major parts in creating images of China in America. The U.S. government consulted them: during World War I Latourette and in World War II Fairbank. Each produced standard best-selling texts on China for their generations—Latourette's *Development of China* (1917) and Fairbank's *United States and China* (1948). Yet these two scholars, as representative of China specialists, offered a remarkable contrast, both in their lives and works.[100]

Latourette was born in 1884, attended Linfield College, and did his graduate work at Yale. He became interested in East Asia while taking courses from Frederick Wells Williams, son of Samuel Wells Williams, who had written *The Middle Kingdom* (1882–1883), the standard two-volume text on Chinese history of its day. Latourette received his master's degree in 1907 and his doctorate in 1909, his dissertation titled "The History of the Early Relations between the United States and China, 1784–1844." The following year he went to China as a faculty member for Yale-in-China at Changsa. In 1911–1912, he witnessed Sun Yat-sen's revolution, returning to the United States in 1912 due to ill health. Instead of a career as a Baptist missionary, he became an academic zealot for promoting Sinology. His writings were characterized by a pro-Protestant and Anglo-Saxon perspective, viewing the beneficial results of America's relations with China.

He began to fill a bibliographical vacuum in Asian studies: *The Development of China* (1917) and *The Development of Japan* (1918). His dissertation was published in 1917 under the same title. Though offered a State Department position in its Far Eastern section during World War I, he declined, but gave advice. In the 1920s, he taught most of Yale's courses on Asia. By 1934, he had published *The Chinese: Their History and Culture.* Also, he became active as a member of the International Board of the YMCA, worked with the International Missionary Council, and helped to form the World Council of Churches. His career peaked in the 1940s, in 1946 publishing for Macmillan *A Short History of the Far East,* and in 1948 he became the president of the American Historical Association. In 1952, at the request of the Institute of Pacific Relations, he published *The American Record in the Far East.*[101]

It was at the height of McCarthyism, and though never called to testify, he took a brave position: "The United States could not have prevented the communist victory on the mainland of China and was in no way responsible for it [and] it was nevertheless essentially the official position of the United States State Department."[102] Though Latourette retired in 1953, he served as president of the Far Eastern Association in 1955. Until his death in 1968, he remained confident that, despite China's problems, a new and better society would emerge. In an obituary, he was called the "optimistic" historian.[103]

Fairbank was born in 1907, just at the time Latourette was taking his advanced degrees at Yale. At first, he attended the University of Wisconsin in 1925, then transferred to Harvard in 1927 and was a Rhodes scholar in 1928. While at Harvard he fell under the spell of visiting English Sinologist Charles Kingsley Webster and read Hosea Ballou Morse's *International Relations of the Chinese Empire* while aboard ship on the way to Great Britain and study at Oxford. Morse encouraged Fairbank to study the Chinese Maritime Customs Service, resulting in his dissertation for Oxford in 1936. That resulted in a book, *The Origin of the Chinese Imperial Customs Service, 1850–1858*. This interest in China's diplomacy and institutions characterized Fairbank's career. In 1938, he began teaching at Harvard, where he criticized America's East Asian policies. In contrast to the reticent Latourette, he fully engaged in public debate and had an important influence on national opinion.[104]

World War II was a turning point for Chinese studies in America, which then got large endowments from the Rockefeller and Carnegie foundations. Fairbank served in the American Embassy at Nanking from 1945 to 1946, and he directed the U.S. Information Service during Gen. George C. Marshall's early efforts at mediation between Chiang Kai-shek and Mao Tsetung. He was a trustee of the Institute of Pacific Relations from 1946 to 1959. At the same time, he inaugurated a Chinese regional studies program at Harvard, inspiring other such programs at American universities. Yet the Cold War years were rough on Fairbank, as he was accused of being a communist.[105]

Despite this controversy, he wrote some of his best works: *The United States and China* (1948) and *Trade and Diplomacy on the China Coast* (1954). With Edwin O. Reischauer, he coauthored such books as *A History of East Asian Civilization* (1960) and wrote his own *China: The People's Middle Kingdom and the U.S.A.* (1967). He also took criticism from the "New Left." These were younger and more radical China scholars, who called him an "apologist for imperialism." Fairbank maintained that America inflated its own past, and the study of China gave Americans a more realistic assessment of itself. His chief focus remained diplomacy.[106]

Latourette had portrayed Sun Yat-sen's and Chiang Kai-shek's opponents as villains, whereas the two Nationalist leaders remained his heroes. Besides, he praised U.S. efforts to Christianize and democratize China. He admired Sun's and Chiang's Christian affiliations and their policy of the Three Principles: Nationalism, Democracy, and Livelihood. Latourette saw the communist domination of the mainland as a tragedy. Oppositely, Fairbank believed Western values should not be Chinese values. Such an approach was limited and too "cultural-bound." For Fairbank, the Western industrial and commercial revolutions were neither salutary nor inevitable for China. Fairbank found that no merchant class was able to develop independently of the state, which dominated commerce. From the Chinese point of view, the West was simply the latest barbarian invasion, akin to the Mongols and the Manchus. America's relations, like the previous "barbarians," were a disaster for China. Both the United States and China had to learn to coexist with their differing values. Whereas Latourette saw Chiang as a democrat, Fairbank thought of him as a Confucian, emphasizing the autocratic and bureaucratic nature of his government. Latourette's Chinese heroes became Fairbank's villains. "So while Latourette believed that the Western world had the answers to what he saw as political, physical, and moral degeneration in China, Fairbank suggests that China may have found a way to avoid the subtle and insidious forms of repression and exploitation indicative of more affluent societies."[107]

Latourette stated that the Chinese Communist Party, throughout its pre–World War II history, was under the Kremlin. Its ruling group came to power closely allied to Moscow. Fairbank believed there was collaboration for Soviet aid, never ideological agreement. Mao was not Moscow's puppet. Fairbank went so far as to maintain, "Soviet paramountcy in China even in the 1950s was no greater or more threatening than had been the British influence after 1860 and the Japanese after 1900, or the American in the 1940s."[108] For Fairbank, "Chiang's failure was due not so much to the communists who opposed him, but more to his unwillingness and inability to lead Chinese reform." His military command was a fiasco. Unlike Fairbank, Latourette continued to believe Chiang struggled against totalitarian aggressors. "The best-selling novelist, Pearl Buck, Time-Life Corporation, missionary reports such as those of Dr. Walter Judd, and the film industry all played important roles in promoting sympathetic attitudes toward China in its struggle against Japan and toward Chiang Kai-shek in his struggle against the communists." That climate of opinion moved a generation of Americans to believe they had a "prime responsibility" to determine China's destiny.[109]

Dewey had poked his nose into China to reform its educational system along the new lines he had pioneered for America. The others—missionaries, business leaders, politicians, and some scholars—would have liked to have made China Christian, capitalist, and democratic. All failed. When a brilliant journalist, Edgar Snow, suggested a radically different approach, he too was rejected by his fellow Americans.

10

Red Star over China

When Edgar Parks Snow reached China in 1928, it was already a thriving milieu of Western "China Hand" journalists. Peter Rand, whose father, Christopher, worked for the *New York Herald Tribune*, describes the origin of this journalistic hotbed. Its progenitor was Thomas F. F. Millard, a one-time drama critic for the *New York Times*, who had turned into a war correspondent. After covering the Russo-Japanese War of 1904–1905, he decided to stay on in China as the *Paris Herald*'s man in Shanghai. From there he influenced a generation of American opinion sympathetic to China. He was an ardent champion of the Chinese cause, eventually on the payroll of Nationalist China. "Edgar Snow, also from Missouri, and one of many, who came in Millard's wake to practice journalism in China, considered himself a direct heir to Millard's China Hand values."[1]

• • •

Much like "Siberian" Kennan and "Old China Hand" Rockhill, or Eugene Lyons, Snow was able to convey a sense of enchantment, literary imagination, and the magic of a "forbidden land" that still casts its romantic spell today.[2] One gets that sense especially from his diary, where he writes about the army of Zhu De (Chu Teh) finally arriving as a "great reunion" and refers to their "spirit & morale" as "they embraced, hugged, walked arm in arm all asking questions & talking at once." He remarks of treating "reactionary landlords" as "dealt with accordingly." He refers to repulsing the enemy as "What a day!" When he meets Zhu De, he calls him "the father of R.A. [Red Army] and he is so to speak."[3] To sell this amazing story, he once again emphasized that it was "exclusive, a world scoop —on a nine-year-old story that is still very much alive." About his "over 200 pictures," he, at least, wanted enough compensation to pay for what they had cost him. After all, he pointed out, "I did risk my neck to get them."[4]

In *Red Star over China*, the author became narrator. Snow himself noted there had been "no greater mystery" in the world than the story of Red

China. Guessing the world had many questions about Red China that needed answering, Snow started off with a bevy of them that he intended to ask while on his quest in Yanan (Yenan), capital of Red China—a place he had to be very carefully sneaked into—the place where Mao's communists had finally arrived after their six thousand–mile "Long March" from the South. Snow's questions fell into a handful of groupings: ideology, especially differences between Guomindang (Kuomintang or Nationalists) and Gongchandang (Kungch'antang or Communists), the nature of the Chinese Communist Party, ethos of the party, its leadership, its foreign advisers, its soviet, the structure of its society, the nature of the Red Army, and the consequences—if and when the Reds won the civil war with the Nationalists. Snow also wondered about the sincerity of its united-front program for getting together with the Nationalists in fighting the Japanese. The blockade of silence had lasted nine years. Snow intended to burst it wide open.[5]

When Snow finally reached the Red enclave at Pai Chia P'ing, he was greeted by a group of partisans, the An Tsai Red Guard. They had been warned of a foreign devil! He was approached by a "slender young officer" who addressed him in English, the "notorious" Zhou Enlai (Chou Enlai), for whose head Chiang offered eighty thousand dollars. Zhou made it plain that Snow, a noncommunist, was welcome and that he was free to "write about anything you see and you will be given every help to investigate the soviet districts."[6] From there Snow proceeded to Bao An (Pao An), where, as mentioned, he had met Mao Zedong (Mao Tse-tung), chairman of the Chinese People's Soviet Republic, soon after his arrival. Snow's first appraisal of Mao was of a "gaunt, rather Lincolnesque figure" with an "intellectual face of great shrewdness" and Snow felt a "certain force of destiny in Mao."[7] Snow was the first foreign journalist to interview him. The chairman's influence was greater than anyone's within Red China. Though he had "incisive wit" and "worldly sophistication," he loved the theater and "sat inconspicuously in the midst of the crowd."[8] Mao felt he could cooperate with President Roosevelt, but he regarded Hitler and Mussolini as "mountebanks." Mao knew philosophy, harbored strong proletarian class feelings against the capitalists, and was a tireless worker with an iron will. During Snow's four months in Yanan, he had a chance to check on many of Mao's assertions, and he found them to be correct.[9]

Snow repeatedly quizzed communist leaders about their policies. The long and the short of it was that they believed in agrarian revolution and an end to imperialism in China as the first necessary steps toward national independence and democracy. They viewed the Nationalist policy of "nonresistance" to imperialism, particularly to the Japanese, as bankrupt. However, in 1932 and again in 1933, they had offered to unite the Red Army to any other groups willing to fight the Japanese if they would guarantee a democratic, representative government with broad civil liberties. In other words, they would espouse a liberal program of anti-imperialism, antifascism, and antifeudalism. Once the war with Japan was victorious, they would invite legitimate foreign trade into China.[10]

On July 16, 1936, Snow interviewed Mao for the first time. His initial questions dealt with the Japanese war. Mao, he found, believed that the defeat of Japan would result in the end of foreign imperialism in China. Certain conditions would be necessary to beat the Japanese: a national and world anti-Japanese united front and revolutionary action by the peoples oppressed by Japan. If these conditions were met, the war would be short; otherwise, it would last a long time. Japan's strategy was to seize not only North China but also the lower Yangtze Valley and the southern seaports; its naval plans would coordinate with these by blockading China. That meant invading the Philippines, Siam, Indochina, Malaya, and the Dutch East Indies. To counter Japan's efforts, Mao emphasized that "the central point of the problem becomes the mobilization and unification of the entire Chinese people and the building up of a united front, such as has been advocated by the Communist Party ever since 1932."[11] A long war would bring Soviet aid and intervention and result in the restoration of all of China's lost territories. No restrictions would be placed on communist cooperation with the Kuomintang if the people were freely given the right to arm and organize themselves. The main strategy and tactic of such a war would be a "war of maneuvers, over an extended, shifting and indefinite front."[12] It would depend on a high degree of mobility with swift concentration and dispersal. There would be positional warfare only for "vital strategic points." As Mao put it, "China's sole hope of victory over Japan must rest ultimately on superior maneuvering of great masses of troops, divided into mobile units, and the ability to maintain a protracted defense over immense partisan areas."[13] All of this required avoiding great battles early on and equipping large numbers for partisan and guerrilla warfare. Snow, exhausted, concluded his first interview with Mao at past two o'clock in the morning.

After a dozen or so such nights, Snow finally got Mao to say something about himself. At the time it was new information, eagerly awaited by the outside world, which knew nothing personally about him. Actually, the fifty or so pages dedicated to Mao's personal story—the earliest biographical account—told more about China and the revolutionary movement than they did about Mao. He still remained a mystery. Concerning the defeat of the communist party in 1927, Mao blamed it on the urban-first policy, rather than on agrarian revolution, of his great rival, Chen Duxiu (Ch'en Tu-hsiu). Next, it was the fault of Mikhail Borodin, Comintern agent, who reversed his position from favoring radical land redistribution in 1926 to opposing it in 1927. Then, there was M. N. Roy, also of the Comintern, who only talked but had no concrete ideas. "Mao thought that, objectively, Roy had been a fool, Borodin a blunderer, and Chen an unconscious traitor."[14] Though Mao did not believe the 1927 counterrevolution could have been defeated, nevertheless, without the mistakes of Chen, Borodin, and Roy, the communists would have been better off in the South in a base that could not be destroyed. After the Nanking Uprising of August 1927, Chen was removed and hope abandoned for working anytime soon with the Kuomintang. The open struggle for power began. Mao initiated his program in Hunan: separate from the Kuomintang, organize the Red Army, confiscate property, set up an independent communist power, and organize soviets.[15] It was to the Red Army that much of Mao's and General Zhu De's efforts were devoted.

Mao's basic rules for the Red Army were obedience, no confiscations from the poor peasantry, and landlords' confiscated goods turned over to the Soviet government. Additional rules of good military behavior were later added. The new army's slogans were "retreat when the enemy advances," "trouble enemy encampments," "attack when the enemy retreats," and "pursue retreating armies." "The main tasks of the Red Army then," said Mao, "were the recruiting of new troops, the sovietization of new rural areas, and, above all, their consolidation under a thoroughgoing soviet power of such areas as already had fallen to the Red Army." At the First Soviet Congress of December 11, 1931, Mao had been made chairman of the Central Soviet Government. From then until the Long March, Mao had devoted himself only to government tasks, while Gen. Zhu De had worked extensively on the military. When Chiang's Fifth Extermination Campaign started in October 1933, preparations were made to head northwest, from Jiangxi (Kiangsi) to Yanan. The Long March began on October 16, 1934, and ended a year later. As Snow noted, "Mao made no reference to the important meeting of the Central Committee held at Tsunyi, which had elected him to the leadership."[16]

The Communists evacuated most of Jiangxi and large areas of Fujian (Fukien) and Hunan. There they had already redistributed land, lightened taxes, established collectives, and eliminated unemployment, opium, prostitution, child slavery, and forced marriages. However, as Mao said, "Revolution is not a tea party." Arrests, mass trials, and executions were carried out against landowners and various class enemies. Yet Snow refused to comment, excusing himself with the remark that his book was largely "limited to the range of an eyewitness." Anyway, it required "independent corroboration" and was now a matter for "academic interest." The Fifth Extermination Campaign failed, and within two years the Communists had "a remarkable comeback, seldom equaled in history," according to Snow.[17]

The most dramatic part of Snow's narrative was his account of the Changzheng (Ch'ang Cheng), or Long March—a trek of 368 days, covering six thousand miles, averaging roughly twenty-four miles per day. Its most compelling moments were bridging the great Dadu (Tatu) River and crossing the western grasslands. Along the path of this strategic retreat, they propagandized and played Robin Hood by their confiscations and distributions. Some had favored remaining in Sichuan (Szechuan) and reasserting influence south of the Yangtze, but most of the Politburo were determined to push on to the northwest. They arrived just below the Great Wall in northern Shaanxi (Shensi) on October 20, 1935.[18]

After discoursing on the plight of rural China, especially during the famine of 1929, which he had witnessed, Snow described soviet society as established by the Reds in the Northwest once they had come there. It was an area in transition, not one with true communism. Land distribution was the key, following Sun Yat-sen's injunction: "Land to those who till it." The Central Soviet Government, the party, and the Red Army proclaimed themselves a "democratic dictatorship of the 'rural proletariat.'"[19] Taxation was minimal, and it was entirely eliminated in new districts for the first year. The cooperative movement was "vigorously" pushed and "Saturday Brigades" of volunteers utilized. The Old China of opium, corruption, beggary, unemployment, prostitution, infanticide, and so forth was abolished. The economy was entirely geared for two functions: feed and equip the Red Army and uplift the poor peasantry. Illiteracy was attacked, and education was primarily political.[20] Snow got a chance to visit with farmers and factory workers. There were complaints, yet they melted away when peasants were asked to compare today with yesterday under the Nationalists and their White Army. In the factories, Snow noted they were all handicraft; there was no electric power. The aim was to make Soviet China completely self-sufficient. The arsenal hand-made everything and repaired damaged equipment. There were also cloth and uniform factories as well as a shoe and stocking factory. The workers got equal pay for equal work. Among the peasants and workers, the life Snow observed was healthy and hopeful. "It was hard," he related, "for an old China hand like me to believe, and I was confused about its ultimate significance, but I could not deny the evidence I saw."[21]

Snow was pressed by his hosts into spending time with the Red Army, which some called "irregulars," but the communists had them strictly divided into front units, independents, partisans, and peasant guards. He ended by devoting a large section of the book to military personnel and affairs. The Red Army was not, as many contended, a bunch of outlaws and malcontents. Rather, it was composed of young peasants and workers who fought for their homes, land, and country. General Joseph "Vinegar Joe"

Stilwell characterized their spirit by their officers not ordering their men to go ahead of them, but they themselves going ahead and asking to be followed.[22] Some 58 percent were of peasant origin, and more than 50 percent were party members. Most were literate. For their services, they received a portion of land. They called themselves "fighters," not "soldiers," and they followed Mao's disciplines for dealing with peasants—replace doors, roll up mattings, be courteous, return borrowed items, replace damaged articles, be honest, pay for purchases, and be sanitary. Their source of military supplies came from their enemy, since nothing arrived from abroad, especially not from the USSR. This was so even though 60 percent of the state's budget went to the army.[23]

After describing the personality of certain archetypical "red bandits" such as Peng Dehuai (Peng Teh-huai), Snow moved on to Peng's discussion of partisan warfare. The main reason for partisan warfare, Peng explained, was rural bankruptcy. This had been brought on by imperialism, landlordism, and war, especially the Japanese invasion. Partisan warfare could succeed only under the party's tactics, whose main principles were to avoid unequal battles, use surprise, make detailed plans, destroy the gentry, maximize flexibility, use decoy, and win peasant support. That last point was crucial: "The Red Army is a people's army, and it has grown because the people helped us."[24] For these partisan warriors, there were no camp followers, no prostitutes, and no opium. They were infused by their Lenin clubs with "revolutionary consciousness." As Snow said of Peng, "I sensed an immense inner spiritual pride in him about his connection with the Red Army. He had a pure feeling of religious absolutism about communism, and I believed he would not have hesitated, on command, to shoot any number of 'counterrevolutionaries' or 'traitors.'"[25] Men like Peng or Xu Haidong (Hsu Hai-tung), another famous red bandit, believed the "poor of China, the peasants and the workers, were the good people—kind, brave, unselfish, honest—while the rich had a monopoly of all the vices."[26] Xu explained that the White Terror had been so severe that everyone in his district who was named Xu was ordered to be killed. Of course, the Reds also used violence, only differing in their choice of class victims. Chiang Kai-shek commanded that wherever soviets had long been established, everyone was to be killed because "it was impossible to tell a Red bandit from a good citizen."[27] Snow rhapsodized about Zhu De, who had changed from a villainous White Guardist to a Red general of genius.[28]

Before bidding farewell to Red China, Snow examined Russian and Comintern influence. For these Reds, Lenin was godlike, and Stalin was the most popular foreign figure alive. This was so even though little or no help came from the USSR, and Stalin could be blamed for the 1927 failure: "The idea of having behind them a great ally—even though it was less and less validated by demonstrations of positive support from the Soviet Union —was of primary importance to the morale of the Chinese Reds. It imparted to their struggle the universality of a religious cause, and they deeply cherished it."[29] Snow was explicit about the 1927 crisis: it coincided with the Stalin-Trotsky struggle, when Stalin had become chiefly responsible for Comintern policy. The opposition had demanded communist separation from the Kuomintang. Stalin defended himself by "ridiculing as non-Marxist the Trotskyist contentions that the tactical line of the Comintern had been the main cause of the failure." Tactics could not substitute for the relation of class forces. Snow had to admit that after 1927 only a trickle of help was received, especially in comparison with fascist and American help to Chiang.[30]

Before departing Red China, Snow had one last interview with Mao. In it, Mao laid out the terms of rapprochement with the Nationalists. The seriousness of the Japanese aggression necessitated such a move. If Sun Yat-sen's Three Principles—Nationalism, Livelihood, Democracy—were maintained, the basis of a partnership could be made. Mao was willing, in such an alliance, to desist from civil war and the overthrow of the Nanjing government, to submit to the Nationalists' high command within a representative central government, to change the Red nomenclature to suit Nanjing, and to modify his agrarian policy.[31] After this interview in mid-October, Snow left Red China.

Before giving his final reflections on his Yanan experiences, Snow recounted the subsequent Sian Incident of December 1936. In a coup by northeastern troops (Manchurian Army) of the "young marshal," Zhang Xueliang (Chang Hsueh-liang), Chiang Kai-shek was captured and almost executed. The Reds, particularly Zhou Enlai, negotiated his release in return for an anti-Japanese Communist-Nationalist coalition. Through all of this, Snow maintained that "it fell to the lot of the Communists to persuade [the northeastern troops] that [Chiang Kai-shek's] life should be saved."[32] Snow commented about the long-range consequences of the Xi'an (Sian) Incident to his London editor, L. M. MacBride: "The effect of this, ultimately, will either force a fundamental revision of policy at Nanjing and the political unification of China on an anti-Japanese, democratic basis—or there will be deep civil war in the not distant future, very much like the situation in Spain."[33]

• • •

One cannot say the rest of Snow's life was anticlimactic. His subsequent books and articles are a testimony to his achievement as the foremost Western spokesman of Red China. President Richard M. Nixon acknowledged this in a personal letter to Snow on the eve of the president's departure to the People's Republic of China in February 1972: "I know how confining a hospital must be for a man of your energy and enthusiasm, and I can only hope that it will strengthen you to know that your distinguished career is so widely respected and appreciated."[34] Actually, the road for Snow from his classic book on China to that final recognition just before his death traveled through many difficult places.

Snow in 1937 may have at first thought that he had found a Chinese version of midwestern populism that mobilized China's public enthusiasm for the nation's good. Mao appealed to him as a Chinese Lincoln who was determined to give the Chinese a rough version of democracy. Nevertheless, he had to admit, and always maintained, the Chinese Reds were, indeed, red, and not just agrarian reformers.[35]

As he finished his book *Red Star over China* while working in Beijing (Peking) in July 1937, he could hear the approach of the Japanese Imperial Army. By July 7, the Japanese had fought at the Marco Polo Bridge; they had rolled on to Baoding (Paoting) by late September, and in December sank the U.S. gunboat *Panay* on the Yangtze River. China had become hot news, and everyone wanted to know more. The movie version of Pearl Buck's *Good Earth* and the publishing of Snow's *Red Star* made China a sympathetic country for Americans.[36] *Time* chose the generalissimo and his wife as the couple of the year 1937. An "age of admiration" had begun. Henrietta Herz, Snow's literary agent, appropriately changed Snow's title from *Red Star in China* to *over* China, and Snow not only immediately accepted the change but got Random House to publish his book earlier than scheduled. It came out on January 3, 1938, to protect his scoop. Buck's and Snow's books became the best loved of the decade.[37] Snow reflected that he was no "sinolog." In fact, he told American ambassador to Nanjing Nelson T. Johnson that Nanjing's anger at his reporting "now and then make me consider risking all on a 'literary' career—only to be drawn back to the stormy life of a political reporter by some satanic urge." Snow had, so he explained, "no intention of using the material I collected to 'attack' Nanjing, a project which, as such, has no interest for me." However, he believed in his "right as an American journalist to tell the truth as I have found it—just as a Chinese journalist is entitled to do in America."[38]

As one of his biographers wrote, "Snow favored the Chinese Communists, he romanticized them, and he did so with great force."[39] Agnes Smedley, a China Hand herself, wrote Snow from Yanan, "They all like you, are fond of you, and admire you,—both your work and your personality."[40] However, the book attracted some criticism. For instance, his notion that the Soviet movement and the Chinese Red Army began spontaneously under purely Chinese leadership challenged Moscow as the heart of Marxism. His emphasis on the fact that it was the Comintern's fault for the 1927 failures struck raw nerves among Stalinists. According to their representative, Heinz Shippe, who wrote under the pen name Asiaticus, the Chinese Communist Party would pave the way for socialist revolution only by joining the Nationalists and not by themselves. However much Snow revised and toned down some of his remarks, on these points he remained firm. Most disappointing for Snow was that the Communist Party of America boycotted his book even though General Yakhontoff's review in *New Masses* did not warrant that action. Snow pointed out that British communist Harry Pollitt favorably reviewed it, as did the *Labour Review*. "Well," wrote Snow, "I'm naturally puzzled to know why a book which is not considered too strong a stimulant for British and Chinese Communists should be regarded as dangerous thought for the Americans." But Snow answered his own query by noting that he had criticized the Comintern as a "bureau of the Soviet Union."[41]

Snow got especially angry at a review by Harry Paxton Howard. It cut to the core of his being: "I have had a lot of silly charges hurled at me, from being an agent of Moscow to being an agent of Wall Street, and have regarded them as too ridiculous to dignify by a reply. You called me no names, but something much more serious, used my book in connection with your own statement implying that the United Front was a surrender, that the Communists had abandoned the struggle for social revolution, etc. etc." He did not want his book used to slander the idealism of heroes.[42] One commentator later wrote that Snow's book "opened a window on the unknown and changed the thinking of millions."[43] Snow had given international credibility to the CCP. John K. Fairbank later called *Red Star* "an event in modern Chinese history."[44]

Snow returned to Yanan in 1939 for a ten-day stay. Zhou Enlai was away in Moscow. Russian advisers were instructing the Red Army. Mao's modest appearance led Snow to call him a "plain man of the people, the queer mixture of peasant and intellectual, the unusual combination of great political shrewdness and earthy common sense." Mao did not worry about a possible Russo-Japanese agreement. Whatever criticisms Snow had received from Stalinists like Heinz Shippe, Mao still defended him: "Snow came here to investigate our situation when nobody else would, and helped us by presenting the facts. You [Shippe] did not come. Even if he later did something which we detest, we will always remember that he did a great service for China."[45] Since Snow had been sharply, though mistakenly, criticized for presenting Mao as an agrarian reformer instead of an agrarian revolutionary, he asked Mao which it was. Mao answered, "We are always social revolutionaries, we are never reformists."[46] Snow was the last foreign journalist to visit Yanan for five years. Snow also emphasized that the Chinese communists could not then practice Marxism, but they were as much

Marxists as Christ's followers were Christians.[47] Snow returned home in 1940 with enough notes for another book, *The Battle for Asia*.

In this second successful book, Snow predicted a major war in Asia among the Great Powers. He wrote of the brutal Japanese attacks on China, and he forecast that deep social changes would result from this broadened war for China. Freda Utley, then still a Stalinist, again raised her former criticism that Snow had been wrong to call Mao a social revolutionary rather than a reformist. Even she recognized Snow's impeccable accounting of the situation in China. Reviewers agreed with her only on the single charge that Snow was a "sympathetic" observer of China. Snow realized that Americans probably did not understand much of what he wrote: "You could convince Americans that pyorrhea, body odor, halitosis, constipation and pimply skin threatened the security of their home, but wars were an Asiatic disease or a European disease."[48]

Snow interviewed President Franklin D. Roosevelt and came away with the same appraisal—that the president had only a shallow understanding and sympathy for the Chinese. Shortly after Snow had returned home, he wrote that aid to China, even if entirely to Chiang, meant the United States had intervened not only in the Sino-Japanese war but also in the internal politics of China. FDR's administration had supplied almost two hundred million dollars in aid to Chiang from late 1938 to March 1941. If nothing were done to strengthen Mao's guerrilla basis, Snow thought, "China will probably be lost until such time as the fortunes of the Japanese Empire suffer a reversal through major war elsewhere."[49] American pilots had helped with the so-called American Volunteer Group, more popularly known as the Flying Tigers. Therefore, in June 1941, Snow declared the United States would be at war with Japan within probably four months or before the end of the year. That war came as he had predicted.[50] During that war, Zhou Enlai complained to Snow that in the anti-Japanese united front, though it overcame many obstacles, certain circles of the Kuomintang still entertained the idea of "suppressing and annihilating the C.C.P." rather than using everything for the "anti Japanese national liberation war [and] annihilating the common enemy, Japan."[51]

• • •

It was now that Snow asked his various publishers to assign him to cover the war in Russia. Perhaps he had grown weary of the China beat.[52] He first went by way of Africa to India and eventually on to Russia, where in late 1943 the Battle of Stalingrad was about to begin.[53] Three books came from this new assignment; *People on Our Side*, *The Pattern of Soviet Power*, and *Stalin Must Have Peace*. These books sold well. Snow also was a sympathetic Russian observer. He believed as early as 1943 that the Soviets would also participate in Asia and that there and in Eastern Europe the USSR would exact a high price for its help. He understood that FDR was "reconciled to Soviet hegemony in Eastern Europe." As Snow asserted, America had to make some tough choices. Americans paid little attention to his "unpleasant predictions" on the necessity of accommodations. In December 1944, Snow wrote FDR about an important off-the-record conversation in Moscow that he had had with Maxim Litvinov, former commissar of foreign affairs and then ambassador to the United States. This conversation was so secret that Litvinov asked Snow not even to share it with America's ambassador to the USSR, W. Averell Harriman. "[Litvinov] was so frank that I believe you [FDR] may find something useful in these notes—especially in the paragraphs checked in red."[54] Snow, indeed, wrote the president's personal secretary, Grace Tully: "I would appreciate it if you would see that this memorandum reaches only the President, and that if that proves impossible it is promptly destroyed."[55]

In his autobiography, *Journey to the Beginning,* Snow commented on his conversation with Litvinov: he explained to his readers that his August 1944 letter to FDR, where he had written that ordinary Russians greatly appreciated America's Lend-Lease relief, wanted peace, and looked toward long-term cooperation with the United States.[56] But in Litvinov's conversation with him, Snow noted the former commissar also predicted an anti-Russian bloc in the postwar world. That is, sooner or later, the Anglo-Americans would want to reconstitute Germany with Poland as a springboard against Russia. He blamed this attitude on the British for their balance-of-power thinking, their ability to influence U.S. opinion, and their insistence on bringing back the old Polish crowd of the Becks and Sosnowskys—those who dreamed of recreating Poland's sixteenth-century empire. Litvinov also blamed the conservative wing of the Kremlin—the Molotovs and Vyshinskys. That crowd "saw little difference between Nazi imperialism and Anglo-American imperialism."[57] Snow's notes for FDR, seven pages, mispaginated by him as six, were made from the October 6, 1945, interview with Litvinov, and FDR's reply was dated January 2, 1945: "I am tremendously interested in those notes."[58]

The actual notes that FDR received differ not only in some details but also in various important respects from Snow's accounting of it in his published autobiography. In them, two additional topics were elaborated: first, the inability of the Soviets to deal well with the foreign press as well as with foreign diplomats, which they would come to regret as Russia's wartime achievements wore off; and second, the opportunity for postwar collaboration may already have been lost even before the Dumbarton Oaks Conference because a security system, which would cut across the balance-of-power and spheres-of-influence system, had not been agreed upon. As Litvinov suggested, "It meant permanent elimination of distrust, permanent cooperation, permanent solution of the German question, as against restoration of the British balance of power system, the maneuvering to get a bloc of powers into combination vs. the Soviet." In fact, Litvinov had suggested the four big powers handling security and a secretariat of small nations organized by regions. The only move that might restore some security organization was for FDR to convince Stalin: "I [Snow] suggested it was so important that it probably could be improved only on the level of talks between Roosevelt and Stalin when they met again. FDR agreed: 'THAT'S ABSOLUTELY THE ONLY WAY, IN FACT, TO IMPROVE MATTERS.'" It was Snow who had added the emphasis.[59]

Even by July 1945, after FDR's death in April, Snow was still expressing guarded optimism that America and Russia could get along.[60] Pragmatism would take over, and both sides would seek compromises. The Russophobes were mistaken to think the Kremlin wanted to take over Europe.[61] Russia's internal needs would dominate Stalin's policies. Of course, anything lying around loose would be sucked up by the Soviets to lighten the tasks of reconstruction at home,[62] "but if there's anything we really want, and insist on holding, and assume responsibility for controlling, Moscow will accept."[63] Shortly after FDR's death, Snow felt that President Harry S. Truman's toughest job would be to reestablish FDR's close ties with Stalin.[64] After all, the United States could not play "spheres of influence" and not expect the Russians to do likewise.[65]

"Americans," Snow's biographer noted, "were not prepared for the events he forecast in Eastern Europe and Asia."[66] Therefore, they blamed the messenger rather than the message. Hugh Cabot, chairman of the Russian War Relief, wrote Snow at the beginning of 1944, "The appalling ignorance of the American people in regard to Russia is an immediate and supremely urgent problem." He continued, "Failure will, I think, land us in the soup. We have consumed too damn much soup in the last fifteen years and the diet is not nourishing."[67] Snow had called for support of the Chinese communists as well as the Nationalists. He also recognized that accommodation with Moscow's demands in Eastern Europe would be necessary if peace were to be maintained. "The Kremlin," he suggested, "is not open to persuasion or conversion but it *is* open to bargaining." If true, that meant finding out what the Russians wanted as against what they would finally take. Snow challenged George F. Kennan's doctrine of containment: "Hopelessly muddled, the poor dope [USSR] begins to think that he is surrounded."[68] Freda Utley, by now a rigid conservative, sharply criticized Snow for hoodwinking the public. Snow was, in her estimation, a fellow traveler. Even Snow felt he was beginning to drag the conservative *Saturday Evening Post* to a more radical position, so he offered to resign. This time the *Post* rejected his offer.[69]

In 1949, after the Reds won the civil war, Chiang Kai-shek resigned and retreated to Taiwan with his Nationalist followers. As early as 1946, Snow had refused to go there for the *Post*, because he would have to take sides in "support of a regime and a policy with which I would be out of sympathy."[70] Snow reiterated his long-held views: the CCP was Marxist, would try to construct a communist society, and would be an independent ally of the USSR, which had neither anticipated nor run the Chinese revolution. Mao's victory revealed the end of the imperialist system, and its strength lay in a national liberation movement accompanied by real social and political reform.

Chiang's American supporters put Snow on their list of those who had sold out Nationalist China to the communists. Some of them even listed Snow as a former communist. When he wrote anti-Soviet articles, Utley thought he was reversing himself due to public pressure. Despite this assault on his person and views by the China Lobby and its sympathizers, Snow stuck to his guns: "American policy has offered little to countries whose primary pre-occupation or problem is not military defence against hypothetical Communist aggression from without but internal defence against the political consequences of profound poverty, industrial and scientific backwardness, and lack of capital and technique."[71] As his biographer notes, "Snow swam against the tide of public opinion. His defiance made him as unacceptable as his message that all was not evil in China."[72]

One thorn that persistently stuck into Snow's side was Maj. Gen. Patrick J. Hurley, FDR's former ambassador to China from 1944 to 1945. Hurley then had made the charge that many State Department officials supported the Chinese communists.[73] In 1947, Snow had written a series of articles for the *Post*, gathered into a small book titled *Stalin Must Have Peace*.[74] Snow argued that Stalin would bargain but not be bullied or persuaded. As Snow's biographer notes, "Snow wrote directly challenging the 'containment' policy taking shape. . . . Picking up a theme that would eventually become a keynote in his discussion of Communist China, he argued that the United States bore more responsibility for creating the climate of accommodation."[75] The unusually high volume of letters to the *Post* ran about half against Snow. Most prominent among them was the letter from Hurley, dated February 15, 1947. "Hurley reacted angrily to the reference, sending the editor, Ben Hibbs, an open letter protesting falsehoods in Snow's 'pro-Communist article.' He alleged that Snow's distorted account came from confidential reports 'given or sold to Communists by State Department officials.'"[76] Snow had used the general as a typical example of how Americans misunderstood the USSR. Hurley, Snow emphasized, had met with Stalin in April 1945 and had believed that Stalin would give the United States a free hand in China. Snow's biographer directly quotes Hurley's report to Washington: "Stalin agreed unqualifiedly to America's policy in China as outlined to him during the conversation."[77]

On February 28, 1947, Hurley responded directly to the editor's defense of Snow: "Your 'attitude' is more perplexing to me than Mr. Snow's falsehoods. In my opinion the historical reputation of *The Saturday Evening Post* would indicate that you should now either affirm the truth or admit the falsity of certain of Mr. Snow's statements which were published with your approval. You have done neither." Hurley maintained that he was opposed to "any agreements with Stalin or with anyone else giving any other nation or nations any extra-territorial or administrative rights in China." He went on to conclude his letter to Hibbs: "[Snow's] falsehoods are intended to pervert history and to smear me."[78] Getting no satisfaction from the editor, Hurley sent a long statement to the journal *Plain Talk,* what Hibbs referred to as "this bastard publication." Hibbs told Snow that he had "brushed Hurley off [and that] we stood behind you on this matter."[79] Hibbs stood fully and squarely behind Snow, writing to Hurley, "I realize that you probably will feel that I should accept your statements regarding this matter without further investigation, but, to be quite candid, I don't. I have known Ed Snow for many years, and I know he is a careful reporter who rarely makes mistakes."[80]

Snow substantiated his claim to Hibbs by suggesting he speak with John Davies, John Service, George Atcheson, John Carter Vincent, and Eddie Page. All but the last had been on Hurley's list of Chinese communist sympathizers when he quit! Averell Harriman and George Kennan could also have been named by Snow.[81] By the end of April, Martin Sommers of the *Post* reported to Snow that, though Hurley got "very legal and pompous," he had backed off.[82] Six months later, Freda Utley and Rose Wilder Lane made their accusations, as noted above. When later reflecting on this entire incident in 1955, Snow mused, "My editor called Hurley's bluff and refused to published [*sic*] a retraction, however, and nothing happened."[83]

• • •

Snow developed his own interpretation of the immediate post–World War II geopolitical structure of the world and the origins of the Cold War. He shared much in common with the well-known views of his fellow correspondent Walter Lippmann—the man who had popularized the term *Cold War.* Snow had written to Martin Sommers at the end of March 1947 to explain his take on the trend of events. Commenting on the Truman Doctrine, announced earlier that month, Snow called it an "incredible exhibition of scatterbrained proposals."[84] Lippmann, thought Snow, seemed to be looking over his shoulder. America had to invest large capital in Europe, as reparations would be insufficient compensation. This was especially true of

Russia. If America failed to pay the Russians enough, they would simply take everything they could out of Italy, Austria, and Germany, and the United States would, in the end, have to refinance these countries to save them from communism in the same way as Greece. Why, he believed, did it make any sense to go around the periphery of the USSR to support "tottering regimes of the moment" only to end up by further isolating Russia, bringing on increased militarization and an arms race? That was what Lippmann meant by treating Europe as a "single economic unit" and what Snow understood as an "organic policy." An investment in peace would be a lot cheaper than another war. In an almost exasperated tone, Snow blurted out his bottom line: "Would it not be more sensible to go direct to Moscow and ask how much they need to rebuild and what they will take in exchange for a) lower reparations and b) political and economic cooperation and c) demilitarization and disarmament and whatever in hell it is we want?"[85]

Two years later, writing retrospectively, Snow commented in greater detail. Referring to his 1947 book, *Stalin Must Have Peace*, he told an inquirer how the program he had suggested to "stabilize peace in a progressive world" might have worked and said, "Nothing has happened since then to make me think that the means I indicated would not have been worth trying, as the only alternative to the present situation."[86] He had been in Russia long enough to know the task was not a simple one, that is, "reconciling Soviet aims with the necessity for mutual tolerance and mutual help as the foundation of Russo-American amity."[87] Whereas he did not overestimate Russia's capacity to make peace, he admitted that he had overestimated America's capacity to seize the moment: "Because of our immensely greater real power, our responsibility was the greater."[88]

It was a great lost opportunity to balance U.S.-USSR power in the postwar era. The Marshall Plan, presented by Truman's secretary of state, George C. Marshall, and Commissar Vyacheslav Molotov's rejection of it, given to French foreign minister Georges Bidault and British foreign secretary Ernest Bevin in June 1947, liquidated that opportunity. Previously, he reasoned, it might have been possible to offer sufficient economic accommodation to weaken the hard-liners in the "extreme orthodox wing" of the Politburo. Such aid had to be conditioned by "concrete Soviet concessions to help stabilize peace and cooperation in measures for speedy European recovery."[89] With the creation of the Cominform, these events marked the triumph of the more "reactionary great-Russian national communists inside the Politburo." At the same time, the reactionaries triumphed in the United States. The Republican irreconcilables dissipated America's "remaining chances to exploit the Roosevelt legacy in Soviet-American relations."[90]

Even if the "opportunity" was only slight, it still was there. And that justified FDR's Soviet policy during the war, both at Teheran and at Yalta. FDR, according to Snow, never believed the Russians on their own initiative would seize the opportunity, but "very probably he did not anticipate that post-war America, and the leadership it would put in office, would prove incapable of comprehending it and of exploring it to the utmost in positive ways, while pursuing negative aims which would hasten its end." However, no alternative was left to the United States after the "declaration of war laid down by the Soviet Politburo at Warsaw, 1947." For Snow, to repeat, the greater guilt in this tragedy lay with the United States because of its vastly greater power, which bestowed on it the "graver responsibility."[91] Snow concluded by noting America's inept dealing with Russia, its bungling in Greece, and its "tragic and criminal mistakes" in China.[92]

Americans concentrated on who lost China, while Snow focused on the kind of society and government the communists had created. However cruel or just the Reds were, it made no sense for the United States to have a policy that ignored one-quarter of humanity. By 1960, he was at last able to go and see for himself what had been accomplished by Mao.[93] He spent four months there and was able to interview all of the top leadership. Zhou Enlai called Snow the greatest of foreign journalists and "our best friend abroad."[94]

This trip resulted in his tenth book, and the seventh of which he had written on China itself, titled, *The Other Side of the River: Red China Today*. This thick volume, even with its title later reversed, struggled to overcome immense American skepticism, yet it did not sidestep hard issues. Most important, Snow made it clear the Red Chinese were not about to crumble and that Mao, however powerful, was not Stalin. Errors were made, but the leadership had not abandoned the people. And whatever problems of the "Great Leap Forward," "There is no question that the material and cultural condition for the great mass of the *poor* people of China has been vastly improved."[95] Even though Snow talked of a "democratic dictatorship," what Lenin had called "democratic centralism," Snow realized the party had all the power. Nevertheless, he remained enthusiastic for China's improvements under Mao, though he disliked the Maoist cult. About the sharp decline in agriculture, amounting to what Western media were quick to label a famine, Snow felt that it was due rather to the party's poor planning and errors, not just Maoist excuses that blamed the weather and the Soviet Union. Yet even there, Snow had to admit that he could not get sufficiently good data. The food crisis was not, Snow realized, "the sum total of the revolution."[96]

During the fall of 1960, while still in China, he kept careful notes before writing a new book and selling his interviews. For instance, at the October 1, 1960, celebration of the Communist victory, he finally was told that he would have a chance privately to interview Mao Zedong, but it was then withdrawn because Mao was so busy. It was Zhou Enlai who, while greeting foreign dignitaries, heartily shook his hand and assured him that he would get his chance and told him to be prepared with questions. That was very reassuring to Snow, who had not met with them in twenty years.[97] In November 1960, he wrote Colston Leigh, owner of the Leigh Bureau of Lectures and Entertainments, of both his interest in doing lectures around the country and the importance of his trip to the PRC and of his interviews with the leadership there. The letter gave a recap of his recent career and highlights of his China trip; he would lecture about that. He had gone to China that June and remained there for five months. Not only had he been to many places where no noncommunist had ever been, but he had had three long on-the-record interviews with Premier Zhou Enlai and, intermittently, spent about eight hours with Chairman Mao Zedong. No one from the West had interviewed Mao for a decade and not even socialist journalists for many years. Now an exception was made because of Snow's old friendship as the first Western correspondent ever to have interviewed these leaders in 1936 and to have written a famous book about them. They respected his "honesty and integrity," though he held views contrary to theirs. Even the State Department had made an exception to him and allowed him passport validation as an author and writer rather than correspondent since the Chinese would have to reciprocate for a correspondent, which they refused to do. He could boast to Leigh of his forthcoming publication as well as articles for *Look* magazine, his cosponsor with Random House. Besides, he would be making radio and TV appearances with the fall promotion of his book.[98]

This book turned out to be large and difficult to read. In the introduction, Snow set out the case for his objectivity in this essentially eyewitness account of contemporary China. One controversial chapter, "Facts about Food," argued there had not been a famine from 1959 to 1962, as asserted in the Western press. "I realize," wrote Snow, "that belief in mass starvation in China is now so widespread as a result of cold-war press indoctrination that statements by actual eyewitnesses may be dismissed as wholly irrelevant."[99] In a letter to Mme. Gong Peng (Kung P'eng), head of the Information Department of the PRC's Foreign Office, he noted, "I have told people that there is no 'famine' in China but a food shortage owing to crop failure mainly caused by natural calamities; in former times it would have caused a famine but owing to effective rationing and distribution that would not happen now."[100]

He had questioned official Beijing's orthodoxy on the Korean War, spoken out against Soviet Russia and Sino-Soviet relations, and predicted that Yugoslavian leader Marshal Tito's heresy "marked the beginning of Communist heterodoxy and foreshadowed today's Sino-Soviet dispute."[101] By supporting the old regime in China—anticommunist parties, groups, politicians, and warlords—and, especially, not recognizing at least in principle that Taiwan belonged to mainland China, the United States forced the Chinese communists to "resign themselves to the terms of Russian alliance in self-defense [but in] any event, in the long run the Chinese Communist Party cannot and will not subordinate the national interests of China to the interests of the Kremlin."[102] Snow speculated that communism could be contained by other communisms, and not only by just its exact opposite, capitalism. Here was a clear recognition by Snow that a triangular diplomacy meant that communist China might align with capitalist America to thwart the USSR.[103] Zhou Enlai expressly told Snow that it was useless to discuss concessions to be made by China "unless the United States would agree to mutual rejection of the use of force in the settlement of Sino-American disputes *and* simultaneously recognize, *in principle,* the sovereignty of China over the Taiwan territories."[104]

The worst review of *The Other Side of the River* came in the *New York Times,* written by Michael Lindsay, a British professor at American University. Lord Lindsay had been a "fellow traveler" and adviser to the Red Chinese during World War II. Like Freda Utley, he had become disillusioned and, besides, had once blamed Snow for turning down an article he had written for the *Post.* Lindsay felt others had already covered Snow's topic and the interviews only revealed the leaders' concern to spend time with sympathetic persons who would excuse their mistakes. The book, for Lindsay, was not another scoop. Yet it sold a respectable twenty-one thousand copies. Snow wrote Mao Zedong in 1963 to tell him the book was "widely read and is still much in demand." This was so even though "reactionary papers and individuals attacked me, as was to be expected, as a Chinese Communist apologist." Further, he mentioned, "Many have expressed astonishment that facts and photos belie reports of widespread starvation, of people sullenly waiting to revolt, of China's intentions to conquer India, or launch a new holocaust."[105]

Americans still remained confused about China, and well-organized groups like the China Lobby had more than their share of negative influence. Naturally, such groups were anti-Snow.[106] The China Lobby of Alfred Kohlberg and his millions of dollars made from a previous textile trade with China supported the "Senator from Formosa," William F. Knowland (R-CA), and also Senator Kenneth Wherry (R-NE), who both would have liked to "lift up Shanghai and make it like Kansas City." Congressman William Judd, a former China missionary and member of the America-China Policy Association, part of the China Lobby, joined the critics of America's China policy—the policy, they believed, that had allowed Nationalist China to fall to the communists. They had discredited Secretary of State Dean Acheson's policy of "letting the dust settle in China." Congressman Styles Bridges (R-NH) accused Acheson of sabotaging the Nationalists and appeasing the Reds. The atmosphere created by the China Lobby had been so negative that Presidents Truman, Eisenhower, and Kennedy failed to react to Zhou Enlai's feelers. Acheson's "White Paper" had attempted to educate Americans on the venality of the Nationalists' regime, which, he maintained, had been beyond the power of the United States to save. Even George F. Kennan pushed the point that Mao was no "stooge of Stalin." Both Acheson and Kennan promoted "letting nature take its course in China." It seemed to Americans that Soviet control had been imposed upon China: "The image of a grateful China acknowledging the benevolent guidance of its American 'elder brothers' became impossible to sustain." The China Lobby believed that Washington's China policies were the consequence of "stupidity at the top—treason just below."[107] Indeed, one article, "The United States Sells China Down the Amur," maintained that the failure of Nationalist China resulted from Washington's betrayal of Chiang Kai-shek.[108] This interpretation explained China's loss and justified America's nonrecognition policy. It was, one expert suggested, a "product of the mutual needs of the American people and the China Lobby . . . to accept an extreme explanation of events in China."[109]

Some claimed that there was a "Red" China Lobby. On June 28, 1966, a congressman from Ohio, Ashbrook, maintained just that. Members of it were propagandists who were, according to the congressman, "an active, diligent coterie engaged in influencing American public opinion toward a softer posture on Red China." What the congressman meant by the Red China Lobby was "lecturers and journalists like Felix Greene and Edgar Snow, two leaders of what might be called the 'let's-not-be-beastly-to Mao' school of journalism." Ashbrook attributed to Snow the statement that Mao's section of China in 1944 "constitutes the closest approach to political, economic and social democracy that the Chinese have ever known." The Chinese communists were only "agrarian reformers." That old canard continued to plague Snow. For good measure, Ashbrook threw in several names such as Doak Barnett, John King Fairbank, and Hans Morgenthau as well as organizations such as the Asia Society, Association for Asian Studies, Americans for a Review of Far Eastern Policy, *New York Times,* National Council of Churches, Amalgamated Clothing Workers, and the United Auto Workers. Even Senators William Fulbright, Edward Kennedy, and George McGovern were supposed sympathizers.[110]

Snow made two last visits to China, one in 1965 and another in 1970. In each of these instances, his interviews were mangled in the press or simply hijacked. He was upset with the *New York Times,* which had chased him all over China to get the rights to publish, in full, his interviews with Mao and Zhou. Then, out of a clear blue sky, the *Times* turned them down on the excuse that Snow wanted too much for them.[111] He decided, "I had not fully realized how very nearly complete the monopoly is and how impossible it is to get publication for views or facts contrary to those dearly held by the owners."[112]

In the first of his last two visits in 1965, both Zhou Enlai and Mao Zedong pressed him about U.S. policy toward China. Were they looking for an opening to America? When Snow asked, Mao said no. However, the leadership was worried about the Soviet Union. In 1970, during his last visit, Zhou quizzed him intensely about negative U.S. policy and perceptions. "When Snow asked about the chances of new Sino-American initiatives, Chou replied that they invited him hoping to get the answer to that."[113] When pictures appeared of Snow and Mao side by side at Tian (T'ien) An Men Gate for the National Day celebrations, Beijing's *People's Daily* described Snow as the "friendly" American.[114] In his last time with Mao over a long breakfast that lasted past noon, Snow asked him about Sino-American relations. Mao replied that China was looking for ways of admitting Americans and that he would be happy to invite President Richard Nixon either as a tourist or as president.[115] In April 1971, the American table-tennis team was invited to China.[116] That allowed for Snow to release his last interview with Mao.[117] In July, Nixon appeared on television to tell Americans that his national security adviser, Henry Kissinger, had just returned from a secret visit to Beijing. The Chinese, indeed, had invited the president. Nixon accepted. At last, Snow's policies were vindicated. Snow died on February 15, 1972, just a few days before Nixon left for his stunning about-face trip to China.[118]

Snow was the model of that deep and abiding American sympathy for China, Red or White, that no twenty-three-year hiatus, 1949–1972, could eradicate. He was in a direct line of distinguished Americans from W. W. Rockhill to the present who have found the Chinese irresistible. No anti-Chinese policy could, for very long, buck that sentiment. Likewise, he was the direct opposite of Eugene Lyons and those who, from the elder Kennan to the present, mistrusted Russia, whether Red or White. The persistence of these opposing patterns—loving China and hating Russia—was most notable among journalists like Lyons and Snow, both preeminent specialists who were deeply immersed in Chinese and Russian cultures and fluent in those languages. Furthermore, it was not by accident that Lyons and Snow were polar opposites. They simply reflected American perceptions most acutely. Parenthetically, Snow also believed, like FDR, that accommodation with both Russia and China was possible. He attacked George F. Kennan's doctrine of containment and maintained that accommodation was a postwar necessity. He found himself at odds with people like Lyons, who became a Cold Warrior. There were other notable journalists who came to side with Snow, particularly Harrison Salisbury.

• • •

Harrison Salisbury's career was the reverse of Edgar Snow's: he went first to Russia as a correspondent in 1944 and then, after retirement, to China in 1972. However, the results were much the same.[119] In his memoir, he wrote, "I was more than forty years behind in getting to China." He had finally arrived there "at long last in 1972." How he got there was a story in itself. When Salisbury finally did arrive in China in 1972, China's premier, Zhou Enlai, apologized for the delay: "I'm sorry that we could not receive you earlier, but you are known as such a leading anti-Soviet champion, we were afraid it might upset our relations with Moscow." Salisbury insisted there was a "nub of truth" in Zhou's remark. Actually, after the 1989 Tiananmen Square incident, Salisbury became critical of the CCP. Since childhood, he had had China on the brain. Even since his mother had taken him to the "Chinaman's shop" in his hometown of Minneapolis, that "Chinaman's shop *was* China, a place of mystery, romance, excitement—exotic, a world which drew me like a magnet, so different from plain flat Minnesota." So also was his father's curio case with its bamboo opium pipe and tiny red and green embroidered shoes. "This was the China of my youth, and my imagination grazed over it endlessly, so endlessly that when I entered the writing seminar at the university, my first sketch was about the Chinaman and his shop."[120]

As luck would not have it, Salisbury tried as a journalist for United Press to get to China, he spoke with John Dewey's onetime student Hu Shih, he conversed with Henry Luce and his missionary father, and finally United Press sent him to cover World War II in London, North Africa, the Middle East, and Moscow. There, he became a well-known Russian expert. He met Edgar Snow and Anna Louise Strong. Through them, his China education proceeded, but he still had not arrived in China.[121] Through them, he met Mikhail Borodin, once Stalin's agent in China. After Strong's exile from the USSR in 1949 and her residence in China in 1958, Salisbury learned of Borodin's sad end and Strong's new career as a China apologist.[122] But still he remained in Moscow, residing at the Metropole Hotel's room 393–the very place where he had his great insight into America's and Russia's China paradox: Stalin had purged his Chinese experts and banned China from the Soviet media; at the same time, Senator Joseph McCarthy successfully purged America's Chinese specialists. Salisbury lamented that he—a non-expert on China—"could discern enough to suspect that something was rotten between the two big Communist countries. Is it not reasonable to expect that the president of the United States, his Secretary of State and all the other secretaries, intelligence analysts, members of the Senate, members of the House and assorted wise men would scent a faint clue?" He remarked that McCarthy was simply the poster child for Secretaries of State Dean Acheson and Dean Rusk.[123]

Salisbury decided that after Mao's two-month trip to Moscow in 1949–1950, after vanishing from the Russian media and being treated like a "petty petitioner," he would have "broken with Russia and gone over to the American side, had it not been for our ostentatious hostility." That was how General Secretary Nikita Khrushchev revealed it, and Salisbury wrote later in 1988, "I am inclined to accept Khrushchev's story." The treaty Mao and Stalin signed, after all, was only slightly broader than the one Stalin signed in 1945 with Chiang Kai-shek. The China card was America's to play, Salisbury contended, but President Truman feared the Republican war cry, "The Democrats Lost China."[124] Stalin was surprised at Truman's decision to defend South Korea, where he thought he could "squeeze Mao out like a pip from an apple." That inveigled "China into a war with the United States." According to Salisbury, Stalin "knew, as we didn't seem to understand, that Mao was his stubborn, implacable antagonist." The United States had "figuratively put out the eyes of our best China specialists. . . . We blinded ourselves and by so doing stumbled into two terrible wars—Korea and Vietnam—neither of which need have been fought." It took two of the most unlikely people—Nixon and Kissinger—to get it right in 1972 and "put us on the right track at last."[125]

So who lost China? Stalin did for Russia; McCarthy did for America. "The symmetry of Stalin's and McCarthy's 'loss of China' was so delicious, the ignorance so colossal, the implications so profound I can still hardly believe it."[126] Relations between Russia and China became so intense, the military buildup on either side of the border so great in the 1960s, that Mao could finally play the American card and invite the table-tennis players to China in April 1971, after hinting to Edgar Snow in the fall that Nixon was welcome.[127] The rest—Kissinger and Nixon—was history.[128] At last, Salisbury realized his childhood dream and saw, finally, the real China and not the image of an exotic place created in his childhood days in Minneapolis.

Whereas presidents, professors, diplomats, and journalists had made an impact on America's vision of China, it took a novelist to turn China into an everyday image in the American consciousness.

11

The Novelist and the Ambassador

Sun Yat-sen's 1911 revolution destroyed the Manchu regime, and he became the republic's first president. The question was whether he could sustain his creation. Warlords were swarming. The Chinese were suspicious of the West, though America remained the most favored nation; communism was still unknown; Japan was the most feared country. The failure of Sun's revolution was not yet clearly seen. Yuan Shih-kai (Shikai), the second president, dreamed of reinstituting an imperial system. Sun struggled for political unity. Both Sun and Yuan opposed Western militarism, imperialism, Japanese partitioning, and warlordism. When Yuan unexpectedly died in 1916, all but the mandarins were relieved. It was a fantastic era of selfish warlords and the Japanese gnawing away at Chinese territory.

In 1919, the New China Rising, instituted by the May Fourth Movement, stirred Chinese culture, especially among its literati. Two of its brightest lights, Chu Tu-hsiu (Chen Duxiu) and Hu Shih, persuaded their contemporaries to use vernacular Chinese, Pai (Bai) Hua. The intelligentsia's interests turned to classical Chinese novels, written five or more centuries earlier, for the first time. This was the backdrop against which Pearl S. Buck began her career as America's "Novelist of China."[1] It was, coincidentally, at the same time that a bright young man named Nelson T. Johnson began his long career in China under the care of that most quixotic of American ministers to China, W. W. Rockhill. Johnson was to become America's ambassador to China and a leading proponent of Chiang Kai-shek, while Buck became Chiang's critic. They offer a fascinating contrast because they both loved the Chinese but took opposite views of Chiang Kai-shek's chances to succeed over the Chinese communists.

• • •

As the poor and obscure daughter of Southern Presbyterian missionaries, Absalom (Andrew) and Carie Sydenstricker, Pearl began translating into English China's vernacular literary masterpiece, *Shui Hu Chuan [Zhuan]*,

(Water Margin), which she named *All Men Are Brothers*—a title she borrowed from the Confucian *Analects:* "Round the four seas, all men are brothers." Though it had been written in the fourteenth century, Chinese life had remained, almost until then, essentially the same. She was fluent in both Chinese and English, and she had in 1914 graduated from Randolph-Macon Woman's College. After that, she met a Cornell graduate, John Lossing Buck, and they married in 1917. At first, the Bucks lived in Nanhsuchou in rural Anhwei (Anhui), where John was an agronomist employed by the Presbyterian mission. It was here that Pearl began gathering information for her novels. In 1921, her daughter was born, a victim of phenylketonuria, resulting in mental retardation. That same year, her mother, earlier stricken by sprue, passed away, and Pearl went with her husband to Nanjing, where both taught at the university. In 1922, Pearl began writing a small manuscript, *The Exile,* which she sealed in a little box and hid in her cupboard.[2]

From then on, "The major goal of Buck's writings throughout her long career was to teach the western world about Asia, especially China, which she naturally knew and loved best." It allowed her to be "mentally bifocal" —the ability to look at each on its own terms.[3] Two Chinas, the Old and New, formed much material for her art. Her approach was documentary, focusing on environment, heredity, and the lifestyle of the lower classes. "Buck did more to bring the East and West closer together in empathy and understanding than any other previous writer."[4] The *Dictionary of Literary Biography* claimed, "She will be remembered for creating the best portraits ever drawn of life in China in the 1920s and 1930s.[5] G. A. Cevasco maintained that "of the more than 250 Western novelists who have used China as a backdrop, she is quantitatively and qualitatively the most outstanding."[6]

The next year, 1923, she wrote her first article, published in 1924 in the *Atlantic,* "In China, Too." The editors of *Forum* were impressed with that article and asked her to do one for them, also published in 1924 as "Beauty in China."[7] In the first, she compared the youth of America and Britain to China, especially with regard to relationships between men and women. Though she lived deep in China, she never saw the "barbarous sights whereof I read in the modern magazines." In China, it was a placid and well-regulated existence. Nevertheless, there was an undercurrent of change that troubled her. For instance, a neighboring girl had convinced her parents not to bind her feet because in the big cities like Beijing and Shanghai, the fashionable girls did not bind their feet any longer. Nor did they at her boarding school. Here was, Pearl remarked, change. This neighbor girl snidely noted her mother's lack of worldly experience and her father's clinging to a water pipe instead of smoking cigarettes, and hinted that she might attend a suffragist meeting. Only in China, she opined, were women so helpless; elsewhere they could do what they liked: "Her parents are too stupid about anything a little different from what they used to do." For Buck this was a heresy against traditional China, and she was breathless over it. She confessed to liking China's traditions and had to acknowledge that "these young upstarts are the beginnings of a new growth out of the decadent soil of an old civilization." There was a little sunlight let into the old courtyards—perhaps enlightenment and rationality were good things. As her biographer notes, Buck's views were being revised, and the stuffy start of this little essay gave way to her identifying with her neighbor's young daughter.[8]

In her second article, she complimented the beauty of America and Europe, but noted that it was "strange how I never thus think of the peoples of the earth without my thoughts leaving me and twisting about the world until they come to my adopted country, China." When someone told her that China was not as beautiful as Japan, she smiled and bided her time, knowing the beauty of China had to be discovered. It was not dainty like Japan, and its cities were ugly. From a mountaintop in Kiangsi (Jiangxi), she could see hundreds of streams and the mighty Yangtze River winding to the sea, clusters of trees, and rice fields glowing like jade. Though that picture seemed peaceful, if dropped into it, one would discover pollution and millions of miserable, underfed people—dirty, unkempt, and poor. Where, then, she asked, was China's beauty?

China's beauty was not in tourist places like the Forbidden City. Rather, "her beauty [is] those of old things, old places carefully fashioned with the loftiest thought and artistic endeavor of generations of aristocrats, and not like their owners, falling gently into decay." One could, for instance, see the great silk shops of Hangchow (Hangzhou). From these shops burst the splendor of a king's robe. China was old things, places fashioned from great thoughts with artistry from generation to generation, but now degenerating. Pearl regretted the despoiling of China by curio seekers and the lack of appreciation of her art by Chinese youth: "It is inevitable, of course, that in their distrust and repudiation of the past, they should apparently cast off the matchless art of old China and should rush out to buy and hang upon their walls many of the cheap vulgarities of the West." China's beauty, unlike the American landscape, was in its ancient arts and crafts. Unfortunately, it was the exclusive property of the rich. Buck believed that "unjust circumstances have deprived the poor of one of their basic rights."[9]

When in 1925 Sun Yat-sen died, Pearl and her husband went on sabbatical to Cornell University, where she worked on her master's degree and her husband on his doctorate. The highlight of the year at Cornell was the writing of her prizewinning essay titled "China and the West." It won first honors in the Laura Messenger Prize competition and a purse of two hundred dollars. As she recounted it, "The importance to me of this prize was more than money. It gave me confidence as a writer."[10] This essay was "an impressive combination of scholarship and analysis that traces the complex patterns of Western influence on Chinese society."[11]

The essay began in the sixteenth century and gave a close account of the past three centuries in which China defended its cultural integrity. She criticized China's treatment of females, due especially to Confucianism: "Any student of society [would admit] the inferior education given women and the inferior position of women had an evil effect on ancient China."[12] Such an education, she concluded, made women into servants instead of whole persons. She attacked the missionaries and their "unwise and dogmatic teachings [that reviled native culture as] heathen and irreligious because it was incompatible with a narrow view of religion." Yet they played an unintentional role in improving women's status by undermining traditional culture through establishment of modern schools and clinics as a part of the social gospel. She praised the achievements of Chinese art and philosophy, and she drew attention to China's growing antiforeign attitude and the collapse of the West's credibility, particularly American imperialism and racism: "In the Exclusion Act [China] sees the significance of a rising race feeling on the part of the white race and a determination to maintain supremacy on the grounds of color. She is being told anew by Japan and the Indians that the East must stand together in the final struggle which will eventually come against the white race."[13]

Buck used this essay as an address before the American Academy of Political and Social Science at Philadelphia on April 8, 1933, and, subsequently, published her address in its *Annual* in July of that year.[14] It contained a striking thesis: "It is natural at this time that the United States maintains her *negatively friendly* [beneficial] attitude, feeling remote from China's problems and puzzled by their complexity."[15] What she meant by this remark was that Americans had, through Secretary of State John Hay's open-door policy, refused to recognize any agreements between China and others that impaired the rights of Americans in China and did not recognize the political and territorial integrity of China. The open door, that is, "held in check the rapacity of other powers at a time when China was weak, and made the seizure of parts of China less profitable by compelling one nation to share the spoils with others." However "friendly" and "reservedly cooperative," and however much "real sympathy" American public opinion in its perception of China held, it never "crystallized to the point of direct aid to China." Therefore, as the Chinese said, the United States lacked a policy of positive action. It was "not completely beneficial" in that, according to them, "though it kept China integral, it did not prevent spheres of influence, the making of unjust treaties, and was concerned for itself in that it took "all the benefits of the unequal treaties, and that the only reason she did not pursue the same aggression as the other nations was because she did not have their need, having within herself sufficient territory and trade for the time."[16]

"Occidentalization," mostly from Great Britain and the United States, forced China, especially because of the Boxer Rebellion, to recognize that "her civilization was inadequate for modern conditions." However "valuable and beautiful," it was no longer useful: "Her leaders, smarting under the disgrace of her humiliation to the foreign powers, face everything and grimly decided that the only way to fight the West was to learn to use western weapons and to understand the western civilization, however inferior to their own it might in reality be." Buck predicted that China's military would be modernized, making the country strong. "China will assuredly influence the progress of the world in the next century and perhaps even in the next half century."[17]

In the summer of 1926, the Bucks returned to China with an adopted daughter of only three months old. By the spring of 1927, revolution broke out in Nanjing. Her neighbor provided hiding in a little half room because they were white and would be killed. Mobs ransacked Buck's house, snatching up anything but missing the little box holding manuscripts. Her hosts had even been to the Nationalist commander in chief to save their lives, but he told them that they would be killed by nightfall. As Pearl put it, "My sister and I lay clasping each other's hands, and then realizing that she had her husband, I turned to my father. He sat on a bench, his face calm, his spirit unmoved. I had never loved him as much or admired him more. As for the children, they were small and would never know. As for me, I would see that they went ahead of me." As loud feet passed and repassed the door, they were expecting it to burst open any minute. Suddenly, they heard a frightful noise, a thunder, rumbling over the roof. It came repeatedly, foreign cannons from warships on the river, though seven miles away. After a long time of bombings, Nationalist soldiers opened the door and ordered them to the university, where all white people were gathering. American consul John Davis directed the U.S. commander to await their arrival. They were saved. Pearl's family went to Nagasaki, but her sister's family traveled to Kobe, places where all remained for the better part of a year. They returned to Nanjing in 1927, where Chiang Kai-shek, having split from the communists, now made his capital.[18]

In a December letter home that year, Pearl reflected on China: "The hardest thing about living in China these days, however, is the spirit of disillusionment and despair which everywhere is growing." The Chinese were sad over Nationalist failures, which were already apparent and heartrending, especially their use of old military methods. There were heavy and illegal taxes, which were corruptly spent. The taxes were hard to bear, as were the returned students who believed that in modern education lay the salvation of China, though Buck complimented John Dewey's efforts to plan a university for each province, a high school in every county, and grade schools in all cities. Despair and disillusionment might be the beginning of a realization that China's troubles lay in the moral weakness of the upper classes and the peasantry's helplessness. Both the West's and the Nationalists' remedies had failed.[19]

One day, while perusing the shelves of Kelly and Walsh Booksellers in Shanghai, Pearl spotted a soiled writer's guide that had been published in London. It contained the names of two literary agents. One replied to her inquiry that fiction on Chinese subjects could not sell. The other, David Lloyd, asked to see samples of her writing, and so she sent him two stories published by *Asia Magazine*. Intrigued, he asked for her first novel, one she had hidden in the cupboard during the Nanjing insurrection. *East Wind, West Wind* made the rounds of editorial offices in New York for a year until finally the John Day Company accepted it: "It was [Richard Walsh] who had decided to publish my little book, since his editorial staff was equally divided for and against it and he had cast the deciding vote, not, he told me quite frankly, because he thought it a very good book, since he did not, but because he believed that he saw evidences there of a writer who might continue to grow." Lloyd had told her the manuscript had made the rounds, and if Walsh had declined it, it would have been withdrawn.[20]

East Wind, West Wind dealt with topics already broached in her master's essay. It is the story of the interracial marriage of a Chinese man to an American woman as seen through Chinese eyes. This reversal of the paradigm, in a first-person account by the Chinese sister, came as a shock to the intended Western audience. The narrator, a young Chinese wife, had already been exposed to the Westernism of her husband, a doctor trained in America. Though in love with her, the doctor will not allow his traditional Chinese wife to remain traditional. Her struggle is to adapt to his modern ways. The birth of their son makes this effort worthwhile for her, and through painful incidents, she continues her adoption of Western ways. The most painful incident is when her brother, also a Western-educated doctor, marries a white woman. The fictional narrator, Kwei-lan, tells of her mother's refusal to accept her American daughter-in-law and death over the pain that this crisis brings to a traditional and wealthy Chinese family. The father, though sympathetic to the American, in the end refuses to accept her and her biracial child. Kwei-lan's brother is disinherited. He has to make his way in medicine along with his sister's husband. Perhaps the biracial child, she muses, will resolve the conflict between the races.

Much of the novel's charm is in its deeply traditional Chinese awareness of the West within the newly acquired habits of Kwei-lan's husband and her brother, especially in Kwei-lan's estimation of her brother's American wife. Westernized Chinese elite are used to prepare the American reader for a different appreciation of the West from the insights of a traditional Chinese girl and her purposeful breaking of Chinese taboos. In the end, Kwei-lan tells her friend, "My Sister," that her husband keeps her face set to the future: "He says, we must let all that go, my Love! We do not want our son fettered by old, useless things. And thinking of these two, of my son and his cousin-brother, I know that my husband is right—always right." For her, that was a great admission because it had also broken her heart to see her mother die over the issue of the son's disobedience to his parents by keeping his American wife rather than accepting the Chinese bride promised since infancy.[21]

Almost immediately after publishing her first novel, Pearl returned to China. She recalled that her Nanjing house felt empty without her eldest daughter, whom she had left in the care of the Vineland Training School in New Jersey. She decided it was time for her to work on a second novel, a story that had already been clearly conceived in her mind. Pearl chose northern China as the scene and Nanking because she knew these areas and their people as she knew herself. She finished it in three months, typing the manuscript twice, and sent it to the John Day Company.[22] Walsh accepted the next novel, proposing three important suggestions: changing the title from *The Family of Wang Lung* to *The Good Earth*, several cuts in the back half of the novel to improve its pacing, and moving up the publishing date to March 2, 1931. The previous January, the Book of the Month Club had chosen it, insisting that it be rushed into print. It took America by storm.[23] Yet just below the novel's romantic surface, Buck's more realistic views of China lay hidden.

Some of Buck's most revealing writings about China are her own letters to her best friend from her college days, Emma Edmunds White. In August 1918, she described her tiny living quarters in remote Anhwei Province. She told of how oppressed she felt about her evangelistic work among women in the area because of "how awfully much there is to be done." This was true, for "I can't spend all of my time on the work, because I owe it to Lossing [Buck] to make his home cheerful and pleasant and be so myself."[24] By 1927, she and her husband had moved to Nanjing when Chiang Kai-shek was suppressing communists and warlords. It was a period of heightened antiforeignism. She commented, "We are running under a Chinese administration of committees, but I don't know whether or not it will pass muster."[25] About the fate of China, "We are fast approaching the crisis here with thousands of soldiers here—Fengtien—who are cordially hated by the people. We expect the South any day and only hope we will escape without a siege and a battle—but no one can tell." Her sister's house had been looted.[26] That crisis broke in mid-May. She wrote a moving account, the Nanjing Incident as previously mentioned, to her friend about "that terrible day in Nanking [and those] thirteen hours—in a tiny windowless room, listening to the shooting, and yelling and burning of houses around us." She had been rescued by her Chinese friends and the booming U.S. naval guns from warships on the Yangtze River.[27]

She blamed the "red influence" in the Nationalist Party. When Buck reflected on this event from her Japanese sanctuary, she told White that China would be unsafe for years, and missionaries, especially, had to be prepared "at any instant to run for their lives." She continued this theme after returning to Shanghai: "The atmosphere is *very* tense here now with threatened Communist outbreaks like the one in Canton constantly." Then she turned her attention to the Nationalists: "Of course among good and thinking Chinese there is terrible disillusionment over the corruption of the Nationalist leaders—Chiang Kai-shek for instance, made his fortune in banking." She told her friend never to come back to China, and, as for herself, "As long as I never have to get back to America [I can hide] somewhere in the country and be really quiet for a time out of this seething *mess* China has become."[28]

A year later in 1929, Buck was back in Nanjing to survey damages from those "terrible two days" and her wrecked house. The situation in China was desperate. "Everywhere one sees posters 'Down with the Kuomintang' —'Down with Chiang'—etc. There is indeed serious danger ahead—the danger of a *real* revolution—of the masses of common, ignorant people— You know them Emma!—rising up and demanding their rights as they did in Russia. Everywhere there are bandits—even just outside the walls of Nanking where we have *never* had bandits before!"[29] She knew there would be an "explosion" and the "young and half-baked" Nationalist government would not be able to handle it.[30]

From this point until her final departure from China in 1934, her picture of China remained the same: "Things are as usual here," she wrote, "war raging, bandits everywhere—Kuling impossible this year on account of Communists all around."[31] In 1931, the "Communists are thick about there [Yochow]."[32] A week later she said, "Our spring war is shaping up and looks serious. One doubts the ability of the government to start this time."[33] By the fall of 1931, she could mention, on top of all the internal strife and Nationalists' failures, "this aggression of Japan."[34] By early 1932, her picture was grim: "Everything seems very dark—complete disunion among the Chinese government officials, and rebellion among soldiers of the very army now opposing the Japanese." In Hunan, she communicated that "reports of Communists are rife."[35] Her early prediction about the communists proved clairvoyant for the long-term: "Communism, at least for a period, is inevitable in China."[36]

After Buck permanently settled in America, she told her friend Emma, "The China situation is bringing a good deal of pressure on me. I feel nothing justifies our getting into war, and are making Chinese enemies by saying so. But for twenty five years the Chinese have known this day would come and they have gone right on grafting and polluting money that should have been used for national defenses."[37] She had even sent a letter to the *China Critic*, published in April 1936, noting how Chinese intellectuals tried to paint the opposite picture of China as "all calm and content and teeming with fine philosophy and plenty for everybody [while avoiding] famines and bandits and Japanese in China."[38]

With all of her criticism, she busied herself with raising money for the Chinese. In the fall of 1940, she wrote, "My Chinese campaign keeps me busy and is going well. So little has been done for China. All the organizations have spent much and collected little. My campaign is spending little and collecting very well."[39] By 1944, she was pessimistic about the fate of China and the Chinese if they had to rely on America and the Americans.[40]

• • •

The period from mid-1932, when the Bucks returned to the United States, and November 1937, when she first received word that she had won the Nobel Prize in Literature, chronicled the rapid ascent of an unknown and obscure writer to celebrity status and then world fame as a Nobel laureate. Within less than a month after her return to Ithaca, Buck, as guest of honor, spoke at the Waldorf-Astoria to a star-studded audience of two hundred in the Jade Room. By October, *The Good Earth* was transformed into a play. Invited by Presbyterian women to speak on missionaries, she attacked their efforts as superstitious, arrogant, and cruel. By May of the following year, she resigned as a missionary amid sharp criticism. As early as 1931, she wrote to her brother Edgar, anticipating this attack: "Some of the missionaries think the book extremely wicked—one, I hear, won't 'have it in her house!' Holy hours!' And she continued, "The sex part seems to worry the missionaries very much, which astonishes me, since they must realize the Chinese point of view, which is to view sex as a perfectly natural part of life. I am sometimes exceedingly weary of missionaries and wish very much we need not be so much among them."[41] Already she and Eleanor Roosevelt had shared the same stage at Cornell University in February 1933, and, by the spring of 1936, she lectured in Washington, D.C., and was the dinner guest of the Roosevelts at the White House. A special treat was for Pearl to address the graduating class at her alma mater Randolph-Macon

Woman's College in 1933. At the same time she received her first honorary degree from Yale University. In the summer, she took a world tour to Europe and the Far East, arriving in Shanghai that October. An MGM movie crew was there in China filming *The Good Earth*, though the film was ruined, due to Chinese negligence or purpose, and had to be reshot in the United States. The film came out at the end of 1937 and, though significantly changed from the book and heavily romanticized, was a triumph, netting an Oscar for Luise Rainer as best actress. Pearl finished 1933 with her definitive translation of the Chinese classic *All Men Are Brothers*, and started off 1934 with publishing *The Mother*. In the fall she lectured at the University of Chicago and again at Yale, and at the beginning of 1935, her *Good Earth* trilogy came out as a boxed set with the completion of the second, *Sons*, and third in the series, *A House Divided*.

After her divorce from Lossing and her marriage to Richard Walsh, she took on the job of book review editor for his newly purchased and titled journal, *Asia*. In 1936, she published the biographies of her mother and father, *The Exile* and *Fighting Angel*, sold also in a boxed set as *Flesh and Spirit*. The previous year she had won the William Dean Howells Medal and was inducted into the National Institute of Arts and Letters of the American Academy. During this crowded decade, she became the nation's voice and conscience on China, and though deeply sympathetic to the common people, she was critical of China's elite and had reservations about the Nationalists and especially Chiang Kai-shek.

Although still in China at the time of her famous novel's publication, the cult of celebrity immediately changed Buck's life and with it popular American perceptions of China. It was the best-selling fiction for both 1931 and 1932. The critical response to it was virtually unanimous. Reviewers saluted the novel for rigorously avoiding stereotypes and for rendering Chinese life as recognizably human and even ordinary. Buck's novel did much to overcome typical prejudices. It was an engaging story, consisting of a brilliant treatment of its subject matter in the thematic terms of popular Chinese fiction.[42]

The story starts with a poor farmer, Wang Lung, told to take a wife by his father. It has been arranged that he would receive one of the slaves from the richest family in the village, the house of Hwang. Wang Lung seeks out the slave O-lan and brings her home, and she bears him two boys before famine overtakes his farm and forces them south by rail. They live as beggars in the great city by barely eking out a living through alms and rickshaw work. When revolution overtakes Nanjing, Wang dashes through a rich man's home with a mob and forces gold from a family member while his wife finds a bag of jewelry behind a loose brick. From this small fortune, Wang buys more and more land in the North until he becomes a rich farmer and, through wise management, is able to purchase the entire house of Hwang, its lands as well as its neighbors' property. His eldest son becomes a scholar, his second is a successful merchant in the grain trade, and the youngest son goes off to war and rises to an officer's rank. One daughter is brain damaged, whereas the other marries into a well-off family. Amid all that, Wang fights off a plague of locusts, a severe flood, and an army that quarters itself in his home—the old house of Hwang, which he has acquired.

Through natural disasters, the human story unfolds of the personal lives of the characters, essentially the family of Wang Lung and its vicissitudes and tribulations. On the surface, there is the constancy of his long-suffering wife and treachery of his uncle's family. Beneath, there is the heroic story of how this man of the soil is able to overcome all the obstacles put before him and make the best of his situation. The toughest obstacles are not big events but the personal ones—his relationship to O-lan, his immediate family, and his uncle. He falls a victim to his passions and ends by taking two concubines at different times. The first, Lotus, and her lady-in-waiting, Cuckoo, come close to destroying his first family, especially when his first son has an affair with Lotus and Wang makes him leave for further schooling in the South. His wife, O-lan, endures the shame, finally falls ill, and dies, to his great remorse.

Lotus becomes fat and lazy, and she and Cuckoo cause despair, though the latter often solves difficult problems for Wang. The uncle is a bandit leader of sorts, blackmailing his nephew into allowing his family to sponge off him. The uncle's son is a dangerous addition to the family and almost rapes Wang's daughter. He joins the army after marrying one of the farmer's slaves and returns with his military unit, almost ruining Wang. His second son's wife hates the first son's consort, and, of course, the boys hate each other. The youngest child, a brain-damaged daughter, requires great care. Even toward the end of Wang's life, he takes another younger concubine, Pear Blossom. Through all of this travail, Wang is able to prevail over his misfortunes by his own native shrewdness, often through the wise advice of O-lan. After her death, he is able to take advantage of his sons' skills, adding to his own cleverness. He triumphs as the new lord of the village and ends by successfully creating a wealthy bourgeois family, though his sons will not keep the land. Wang's life is the story of his strength of character prevailing over all obstacles.[43]

While still in China, news of her novel's success reached Pearl. A flood on the Yangtze River brought aid workers such as Will Rogers and his wife and Charles and Anne Lindbergh. Both couples praised her second novel. Such praise was welcomed, since no one near to her, not even her father, had read *The Good Earth* before she had sent it off to New York. However, the Southern Presbyterian mission board gave her a blistering rebuke because she had been so candid about life in China.[44] By the beginning of 1933, the Bucks were again in America on sabbatical. As the writer of a best-seller, there were dinners, parties, lectures, and other promotionals to attend to, thus making her life something of a whirl. It was now that a Chinese intellectual, Professor Kiang Kang, sent a letter to the *New York Times*, published with her response, on January 15, 1933. An editorial on the subject followed the next day.[45]

Kiang was critical of Buck's *Good Earth*. He believed that she had painted a cartoonist's caricature of China and not the real one, as he defined it. What if, he asked, a mandarin's ancestral portrait were painted in the Western style and instead of following convention, the artist did a half-black and half-white composition rather than either all color or all white or all black? Such a portrait could not be accepted. So also, he reasoned, with Buck's picture of Chinese life. "Very often," he wrote, "I felt uneasy at her minute descriptions of certain peculiarities and defects of some lowly bred Chinese characters." He concluded, "They may form the majority of the Chinese population, but they are certainly not representative of the Chinese people."[46]

Buck countered by noting that her novel was not an ordinary portrait. Such portraits were far from life and truth, that is, most Chinese people were "common" and not, at least in Kiang's view, representative. "One cannot but ask," she continued, "if the majority in any country does not represent the country, then who can?"[47] The others, whom Kiang thought symbolized China, were the cultural elite: "They want the Chinese people represented by the little handful of intellectuals, and they want the vast, rich, somber, joyous Chinese life represented solely by history that is long past, by paintings of the dead, by a literature that is ancient and classic."[48] The people would be counted as nothing and contemptuously spoken of as coolies and amahs, or servants. Instead, Kiang should be proud of commoners. In addition, about obscenity in her book, "only the narrowest sects of missionaries agree with him, and I suppose this fear of normal sex life is a result of some sort of training. I do not know. Suffice it to say that I have written as I have seen and heard."[49] As to whether her works were a service to China, she thought that only time would tell.

The *Times*'s editorial commented that Kiang's reference to ancestral portraiture gave his entire position away as elitist. On the other hand, "Mrs. Buck has enabled us to witness and appreciate that patience, frugality, industry and indomitable good humor of a suffering people, whose homes the governing intellectuals would hide from the sight of the world."[50]

That year, 1933, Pearl leisurely returned to China by way of Europe and Southeast Asia before heading back to her home in Nanjing. Along the way, she worked on her next novel in *The Good Earth* trilogy, *A House Divided*

(1931), which then followed the second, *Sons* (1932); in 1935, literary critic Malcolm Cowley called these three novels a "Chinese *Buddenbrooks*."[51] *Sons* deals with the fate of Wang's three boys, Wang the Elder, a scholar; Wang the Second, a merchant; and Wang the Tiger, a soldier. It describes Wang Lung's three sons' rejection of his life in the soil with their pursuits of scholarship (Wang the Landlord), commerce (Wang the Merchant), and soldiering (Wang the Tiger). All of them renounce their father's joy in the land, and they decline into decadence. The last novel in *The Good Earth* trilogy is *A House Divided*. Yuan, the Tiger's son, has returned home from his military training school in the South with the uniform of the revolutionary army. Much of the novel reduces to Buck's opinions and propaganda for China, especially blending the two dissimilar cultures of West and East—the recreation of Old China painfully, as pictured in the confusions confronting Yuan, who rejects an American and the West for a Chinese maid but accepts the West's scientific learning and modernity, even though his precious crop of foreign seeds fails in the floods. The "cause" of revolution is also rejected, though he vows that a new city and a new heaven will be created in China.

This ends the trilogy, although at the end of Buck's life, she worked on a fourth novel in that series, *Red Earth*. Malcolm Cowley, though he praised Buck's effort to create a Chinese *Buddenbrooks* in the style of Thomas Mann, believed that this last novel in the trilogy was inferior to the others and lost the original vigor of Wang Lung: "That vigor, first found in one figure, is dissipated, as time goes on, into many sons and many places. In *A House Divided* the vigor seems quite scattered." It was a novel, he thought, that "ought to be destroyed."[52] Paul A. Doyle was a little more favorable: "Yuan does not hold the same reader interest as did Wang Lung or even Wang the Tiger. Yuan does not come alive as a believable individual. None of the characters in *A House Divided* arouses any particular interest; and, while much happens, the events do not involve the reader in the action." Even so, the volume is significant in that it "studies the development of one young man's mind during a turbulent and crucial period of modern Chinese history and also probes the changes wrought in one family over a period of several generations."[53] Dody Weston Thompson wrote that in the sequels to *The Good Earth*, Buck's technical deficiencies dominated.[54]

• • •

By 1934, it was clear to Pearl that all white people would have to leave China because of China's unsettled situation and the growing communist influence. She visited Beijing, then back home to Nanjing, where she sorted out her things, and finally journeyed home to America.[55] It was now in 1936 that she published the biographies of her parents, though each book had been written earlier. These rightly became the "Nobel Prize biographies." *The Exile*, about her mother, Caroline or Carie, is a frank and honest portrait, though it is "flowery" and "too tender; too romantic for modern taste. Further, *The Exile* is at times too diffuse and repetitive; on occasion, it needs to be tightened; to be fixed more firmly on the main materials. This is, perhaps, because Buck admired Caroline profoundly and was so devoted to her. But, with all these obvious weaknesses, the portrait drawn of Caroline Sydenstricker remains imprinted in one's memory. And the character analysis is rendered with persuasive depth."[56]

Fighting Angel, the biography of her father, Absalom, is considered a masterpiece. Neither wordy nor repetitive as is *The Exile*, it is "taut and focused." Buck is less devoted to her father, less sympathetic. This objective picture develops in a "harsher, rougher fashion."[57] This is especially true in her graphic depictions of missionary life. "Besides a vividly realized portrait of a human being, there emerges from *Fighting Angel* a compelling delineation of the nineteenth-century type of crusader—the very essence of a rock-ribbed individualism, a fiery zeal which, depending upon the direction in which it was channeled, could produce a General Charles 'Chinese' Gordon, a John D. Rockefeller, a David Livingstone. Pearl Buck sees her father as a manifestation of a spirit that especially permeated America at a particular time."[58] And, most important, for the American perception of China, these two biographies present a remarkable portrait of China from the reign of the Dowager Empress through the Boxer Rebellion and on to the deaths of Carie and Absalom.

There are, however, some remarkable passages in both biographies that reflect the parents' and the daughter's perceptions of China and, perhaps, that of Americans, in general, of that time. Pearl relates that her mother, Carie, on first arriving in Shanghai, gazed at "heathen faces," and her thought was, "How dreadful they were to look upon, how cruel their narrow eyes, how cold their curiosity!"[59] When she reached the countryside, "They were not hard faced and cruel looking as the people had been in the city."[60] Her husband, Andrew (Absalom), "usually oblivious to all save the Work, noticed a hostility of scowling faces when he spoke in the streets or when he tried to give away his tracts."[61] One night, warned by her amah that they would be killed, Carie asked if they really would do it. The amah answered, "All these people you have been kind to, all these people—not one of them will dare to help you. If they came forward they too would be killed."[62]

Despite all of that, Carie came to love her Chinese friends, "forgetting as she did so easily their differences in race and background."[63] Perhaps the most dramatic moment for her was the time during the Boxer Rebellion when the old empress, by secret royal edict, ordered all foreigners killed.

She and the children left, and ten months passed before they returned. Afterward, it was the most peaceful time in China for Carie, even though Sun's revolution made it difficult for Manchus, who were slaughtered, as Chinese custom dictated: "These years were a time of unprecedented peace in China. The retribution that had fallen upon the country after the attempt to expel the foreigner in the Boxer Rebellion had left the people stricken with a sense of their own weakness and the power of the foreigner for a few brief years was strong as it was not before and has not been since."[64] The Chinese saw behind the "foreign devils" their warships, guns, and "swift and ruthless soldiery."[65] Carie caught sprue, a tropical disease of the digestive tract, in 1915 and died in 1921.

Curiously, there is much less of China in Pearl's biography of her father. This portrait focuses on the singular figure of Andrew. Though he tried in every way—from his clothing to his speech, as well as his family's—to be Chinese, "none of them made him in the least Chinese."[66] He had gone there young, and he died there old. As his daughter wrote, "He had seen the Chinese people as few white men ever have—in the most intimate moments of their own lives . . . as a nation in the cycle of their times—he had seen the reign of emperors and the fall of empire, revolution and the rise of a republic and revolution again."[67] Yet in all of this "intimacy," his biography reflected little of his perception. As Pearl noted, he wrote only a twenty-five-page autobiography, which she stretched to three hundred pages in her biography of him. It was, in this case, "the story of his soul, his unchanging soul." She went on to observe, "There was nothing in it of empires or emperors or revolutions or of all the stir of changing human times. There was no reflection upon the minds or manners of men or any subtlety of philosophies."[68] Pearl had to get all of that from his family. His life was, in her opinion, "a manifestation of a certain spirit in his country, and his time."[69] It was a spirit of certainty and intolerance and zealousness. Like Rockhill, he mastered many languages, especially Chinese, becoming a recognized scholar and translator of the New Testament from its original Hebrew and Greek into Chinese. He had gone to college and met and married Carie, and they went off to China to spend the rest of their lives.

Even that evangelical movement was one of Christian imperialism, both spiritual and physical in that each denomination had its own territory. "One of the astounding imperialisms of the West," Pearl commented, "has been the domination over the Chinese of Methodists, Presbyterians, Baptists, and what not, to the number of well over a hundred different types of the Protestant Christian religion alone."[70] Andrew worked his territory, a space larger than Texas, and grew to love the Chinese better than whites.[71] Carie decided to stop following him around China, and made her home in one place. As she told him, "You can preach from Peking to Canton, but I and these little children will never go with you anymore."[72]

The eight years before the Boxer Rebellion of 1900 were the most dangerous in their mission. "The Chinese," Pearl wrote, "have always been distrustful of foreigners, not only foreigners from other countries but even people of their own nation from other provinces or regions."[73] A "slow storm" arose over China. When the storm broke, several missionaries were killed. Carie and the children left, but Andrew stayed on. "He would," she wrote, "have been amazed if anyone had told him that the Chinese had the right to protest the presence of foreign missionaries upon their soil."[74] He survived, though his family prayed, "God, please keep our father from the Boxers." After the Boxers, a strange, ominous peace reigned for eight "triumphant" years. After a sabbatical, they all returned to a new China, one made by Sun Yat-sen's revolution. Andrew allied with it. He hated the old empress, "Jezebel," as he called her. Besides, Sun was a Christian.[75]

As her father grew old and her mother died, Pearl cared for him at her home in Nanjing. And he lived long enough to see the beginnings of Bolshevism in China, though he believed the Chinese would never accept it. They all lived through the storming of Nanjing, after hiding in a Chinese neighbor's mud hut, when other white people were slaughtered. Foreign gunboats, as previously mentioned, saved them, and Absalom (or Andrew) went off to Korea for a year of evangelical work there. Pearl returned after a year, and her father came back to die there. "The end came happily and quickly that summer. The heat had made him very faint, and so quite willingly he agreed to go up the river to the Lu Shan Mountains to his other daughter." Pearl concludes, "We buried the pearly shell upon the mountain top."[76]

Absalom died before his daughter's novel had received acclaim in America, remaining "one of the most popular novels of the twentieth century."[77] It should be recalled that the 1937 film version starred Paul Muni as Wang Lung and Luise Rainer in her Oscar-winning best-actress performance as O-lan; Karl Freund received an Oscar for his cinematography. It was, as one movie book called it, a story of "famine, plague and the fight for survival in China [and] one of the greatest films Hollywood ever made."[78] Another movie book wrote, "Mammoth Pearl Buck novel recreated in detail, telling the story of greed ruining lives of simple Chinese farming couple."[79] Though the movie ended with O-lan's death, the novel continued to near the time of her husband's demise twenty years later. The Nationalist government disliked the film and "accidentally" destroyed the prints before they could reach America, after which MGM refilmed it on a Hollywood back lot. Buck was amazed at how well Rainer could play a Chinese woman. Rainer told her that she had, simply, watched a Chinese woman daily, whom she had hired from the set for that purpose. Though Buck thought the film overly romanticized the novel, she was content to go along with MGM's sentimentality.[80] That same year, 1937, another film about the mysterious Orient also captured the American imagination, *Lost Horizon.* That film re-created British author James Hilton's tale of five people stumbling into a remote Tibetan land where "health, peace, and longevity reign." It starred Ronald Colman and was directed by Frank Capra.[81]

Buck's Nobel Prize acceptance speech in Stockholm, on December 12, 1938, focused on the Chinese novel by defending her own approach to fiction. "But it is," she said, "the Chinese and not the American novel which has shaped my own efforts in writing." She meant the indigenous, classical Chinese novel, not the modern one.[82] She could say this with absolute authority because she had already done the first complete translation and published a thousand-page work, *Shui Hu Zhuan* (Water Margin), or, as earlier noted, *All Men Are Brothers.*[83]

In her speech, she claimed that the Chinese novel had always been separated, as such, from literature, which had been the domain of scholars. Novels, it was thought, were documents of social significance. Therefore, Buck continued, the Chinese novel was the peculiar product of the common people. It was written in the popular vernacular, Pai hua (Baihua), or simple talk, not the classical language, Wen-li (Wenyanwen). When Buddhism came to China from India, the monks also preferred the vernacular. As Buck said, "They put their religious teachings into the common language, the language which the novel used, and because the people loved story, they took story and made it a means of teaching."[84] Such a genre arose from an oral tradition, and its essential feature emphasized character. These tales were so popular that even emperors sent spies as "imperial ears" to hear and write them down. The novels were always more important than the novelists, hence the novelists remained largely unknown: "From such humble and scattered beginnings, then, came the Chinese novel, written always in the vernacular, and dealing with all which interested the people, with legend and with myth, with love and intrigue, with brigands and wars, with everything, indeed, which went to make up the life of the people, high and low."[85]

The three greatest of these so-called anonymous novels were *Shui Hu Zhuan, San Kuo [Guo],* and *Hung [Hong] Lou Meng;* the first were between the Yuan and Ming dynasties in about the fourteenth century, the third in the Qing dynasty of the eighteenth century. Buck called these works "the vindication of that literature of the common people, the Chinese novel. They stand as completed monuments of that popular literature, if not of letters." These were masterpieces such that, as the Chinese said, the "young should not read *Shui Hu* and the old should not read *San Kuo.* The young might be so charmed as to become robbers, while the old could be led into deeds too vigorous for them." The first was a monumental document of Chinese life and the latter of war and statesmanship, whereas the last, *Hong Lou Meng,* was the document of family life and human love.[86]

The aspect of these novels that Buck stressed in her speech was their profound and sublime development of the imagination of a great and democratic people. It was a raw instinct that created *"the arts,"* but not the same that produced art. She was on the side of creation, not production. "In this tradition of the novel have I been born and reared as a writer." Like the Chinese novelist, "I have been taught to want to write for these people." For her, the story belonged to the people.[87]

In 1933, when Richard Walsh took over as editor of a slick journal called *Asia,* he turned it into a serious and scholarly one because he believed that America was ready for well-written pieces on the Far East.[88] Writing in its pages and elsewhere, Buck embodied the conscience of Americans toward China. Perhaps not since William Woodville Rockhill had an American, commanding so thorough an understanding of the Chinese, made her views available to a large audience through her popular fiction and nonfiction.

In May 1943, Pearl wrote an important article for *Life* magazine, "A Warning about China." She had asked *Life*'s and *Time*'s owner and editor, Henry Luce, to publish it because she feared that "certain dark possibilities now looming in China will materialize and cause undue disillusionment and pessimism about China over here. . . . I have endeavored to prepare a background, in this article for whatever comes."[89] It was a problem for Luce, himself the son of American missionaries to China, to publish her article. He could go along with greater military aid and a better understanding for China. Even Chiang's greatness and the charge that America was throwing away a nation he could countenance. But Chiang's conservative bureaucracy, oppressive silencing of free speech, flagrant corruption, and the whole question of how effective Chiang could be in the future if he did not deal with the current evils troubled Luce. Such disturbing problems brought forth the "Private Memorandum on Pearl Buck's Article on China" to Luce's senior staff. On the one hand, he did not want to be considered as having misled Americans because of oversentimentality, but, on the other hand, "being considerably, if not fully, aware of the faults or evils in Chinese administration, I would naturally welcome anything that can be done to improve the actual situation."[90] Nevertheless, would her article do more harm than good by replacing indifference with confusion? "Now, let the general approval of China be open to widely conflicting views, involving the basic integrity of the leaders of China, and I hate to think of the hash that can be made out of the situation from both left and right." On the Left were FDR, labor, and radicals; on the Right were Colonel McCormick of the *Chicago Tribune* and Wall Street capitalists, but "we believe in truth." Moreover, ordinary Americans were still at the "laundryman" stage of opinion. The real question revolved around American opinion of the Chinese government, of which not 10 percent had any knowledge, except of the generalissimo and Madame Chiang (of the wealthy Soong family). "So the actually semantic question turns on Chiang and the Soongs. If we want to talk straight, isn't that the real point?" China's struggle was for modernity, and for sixteen years both of them had led that struggle, for better or worse. These were tough questions, he emphasized, but why not give them the benefit of the doubt?[91]

In that article finally published by Luce, Pearl Buck reinforced the positive image of Nationalist China and Chiang Kai-shek. However, she also noted some problems, such as corruption and oppression. Madame Chiang's visit to the United States, Pearl wrote, exhibited a new Chinese, one of intelligence, charm, and goodwill. But her presence and her manifest abilities were not enough, because Americans knew so little of China and the war. America's failure was not helping China sufficiently, so China could help the United States. It was a necessity. American friendship was overly sentimental and required a "dose of common sense"—not condemnation, not adoration. Of course, the American fear was that China would make a separate peace with Japan. Certain oppressive elements around Chiang Kai-shek might betray him. His personal efforts might not be enough. Such elements had silenced even Madame Sun Yat-sen (the sister of Madame Chiang), and they had control of the Secret Service. There were, in a word, good and evil forces around Chiang. The people wanted democracy, but they were voiceless. Yet they still believed in Chiang and held him as a symbol and center of unity. They needed weapons to fight Japan and to learn the techniques of modern democracy. Opening Burma and restoring transportation to supply China was crucial. Not doing so was due to the feeble effort of the British. Japan was not a "secondary" enemy. China's national people's war, stagnated by isolation, was turning cynical. Official corruption corroded the people's faith. America had to figure out how to overcome these difficulties. Otherwise, the United States would be throwing China away to the Japanese. No one, Pearl maintained, wanted outright civil war. Conflicts between the Kuomintang and the Chinese Communist Party were due to forces around China and not the result of Chiang himself. It was through America's defaults, not theirs, that China was being discarded.[92]

• • •

Whatever China's problems in 1943, and they were severe, previous U.S. relations with China had not been altogether satisfactory, nor had they been sufficiently pragmatic or realistic enough to avert or ameliorate the Sino-Japanese War in 1937. From the end of 1929 to 1941, America's immediate relations were under the supervision of Minister Nelson T. Johnson, whose position was upgraded in 1935 to ambassadorial rank. He succeeded John Van Antwerp MacMurray in 1929. Johnson's Chinese experience was profound and long-standing. He first came to China in 1907 as a student interpreter. In two years, he completed his language training and was sent to Mukden. After a year there, he went to Harbin with the rank of deputy consul general. Then he served in various Chinese posts before he was detailed to the Department of State in Washington, D.C., in 1925, as chief of the Division of Far Eastern Affairs, where he worked closely with Secretaries of State Frank Kellogg (1925–1929) and Henry Stimson (1929–1933).[93]

A more intimate view of Johnson is gained from his letters home, starting when he was a student translator. For instance, in a letter to his sister Betty, he told of assisting a Chinese magistrate: "The worst tasks are the inquests when we have to sit over the body of some man who has died a violent death or otherwise. Ugh!" He already believed that a "republic will no doubt be established in this oldest of old countries."[94] Johnson admired both Yuan Shih-kai and Sun Yat-sen, and he was amazed the two got along. All efforts were being made to unite North and South China, though "China has never before been able to unite on anything." They were a nation "without any public spirit." During World War I, he looked forward to "when China has won her place in the world, extraterritoriality has gone and we shall have to look to the protection of Chinese law in our rights." Nevertheless, China "seems awakened as she never has been in the past to her real weakness." But he still despaired for the "Chinese as a nation." Only competition for China outside China and the Japanese threat seemed to hold it together: "Conditions in China just at present do not look at all promising." In 1916, he noted China's rejoicing at the death of Yuan Shih-kai and the general sense that he had committed suicide. A consistent theme of Johnson's was that Americans did not understand China: "There is no doubt but that English and American public officials and merchants are sadly at sea with regard to conditions in China."[95]

Johnson spent most of the 1920s in Washington, D.C., in 1921 serving for the Washington Naval Conference, returning to the Far East in the aftermath of the Japanese earthquake of 1923 as an inspector for the District of Eastern Asia, and then back to Washington as chief of the Division of Far Eastern Affairs and, finally, assistant secretary of state.[96] In 1926, he wrote then minister to China John Van Antwerp MacMurray that China seemed to be "gradually disappearing before our eyes." He continued, "History, I am afraid, will record that Chinese would-be nationalists did what the United States tried to prevent, namely, divided China. One looks for Jeffersons and Franklins capable and unselfish enough to bring these people together."[97] The Nanjing Incident outraged Johnson, who complained, "Why does not General Chiang establish in the eyes of the world the fact that he is the man which all of his admirers claim that he is by an outright cleaning of the Nanking matter without marring the situation by insisting on negotiations."[98] This situation for Minister MacMurray had become untenable by mid-1929, because he was against any U.S.-China treaty revisions, particularly the distrust between MacMurray and the Chinese foreign minister, C. T. Wang, over the issue of extraterritoriality. That led to Johnson's replacing MacMurray in 1929.[99]

In 1930, Johnson noted the growing communist menace: "The situation in regard to these so called communists is very serious. They appear to increase in numbers and their activities have been purely destructive thus far." He pointed out that by 1931 Chiang Kai-shek had created a "real revolution in the Government [and] succeeded in eliminating Hu Hanmin from the Government." Chiang had to depend on "his military prestige and his promise to the people of a Bill of Rights to gain the good will of the People's Conference." Moreover, that relied to a great deal on "the effectiveness with which he is able to handle the communist situation in Kiangsi [Jiangxi] and Hunan." The Nationalists continued to press the question of extraterritoriality. But the West played tough in what Johnson called "gunboat diplomacy." About a dinner with C. T. Wang, he mused, "I would have given a good deal to have know [sic] what was passing through C. T. Wang's mind while we were at dinner last evening, a dinner that included both the British and American Admirals. It all looked like the old gunboat policy with a vengeance." Johnson especially feared "stirring up the people to acts of anti-foreignism unless we agree to give up completely and without strings our extraterritorial privileges before hand."[100]

Manchuria was aflame in a war of extermination, and "the whole business is of course ludicrous for everyone knows that the whole thing was engineered by the Japanese and that the puppet government presided over by the pathetic little Pu Yi would disappear into thin air were the Japanese to withdraw their army." That "whole business" made his "blood boil [and] I have no brief for the Chinese who have mismanaged their country most terribly. I feel certain that I could write an indictment against them far more convincing than any that the Japanese have thus far produced." He predicted the embers from Manchukuo, the new Japanese name for Manchuria, would smolder and then "all blaze up in a terrible flame." And that would lead to the "birth of a new and strong nation here in China."[101]

In May 1935, Johnson was happy to hear that FDR planned to keep him in China and "make an Embassy out of this mission." As he put it, "Of course I want to remain on. This is the most interesting part of our diplomatic or consular world and I would not like to leave it now."[102] On September 16, 1935, he presented his letter of credence "as the first American Ambassador to China."[103] Later, after the Marco Polo Bridge incident brought on the Sino-Japanese War and occupation of the Yangtze and Yellow River valleys, he wrote Secretary of State Cordell Hull, "There is no apparent evidence that this intellectual leadership and what is left of its armed forces are prepared to capitulate and make peace."[104] In an undated letter to the secretary, he added, "The Government is more united under Chiang and there is a feeling that the future is not entirely hopeless due to the recent failure of Japanese arms at Hsuchow."[105] In November 1938, he told his sister that the fall of Canton practically had shut China off from the outside world.[106] He was already preparing his escape from Chungking (Chongqing) over the Burma Road.

In February 1939, Johnson informed FDR directly about China. He praised the Nationalist government and the leadership of Chiang Kai-shek. Japanese intentions to conquer all of China and their accompanying cruelties had "done more to unite the people of China behind the National Government and Chiang, who symbolizes the Chinese desires for an independent national existence, than anything else and I feel that the Japanese Army has commenced something which it cannot finish." The United States had not only to lead but also to put teeth in its leadership and prevent Japan from taking everything west of the 160th meridian. That meant "we should do what we can to assist and encourage the Chinese in their fight for an independent national existence."[107] It was at the very time, as Johnson became a major spokesperson favoring Chiang and the Nationalist cause, that he was featured on the cover of *Time* and in the lead article.[108]

On December 9, 1941, Johnson was thrilled with FDR's speech declaring war on Japan. He spent the remaining years of the war in Canberra, Australia, as ambassador. From there, he praised Gen. Joseph Stilwell's efforts to retake Burma, noted Ambassador Patrick Hurley's failure to get the Nationalists and Communists to compromise, and quoted journalist Frazer Hunt's caricature of FDR as the "Great Sailor King." Especially, he emphasized, "Chiang is not going to sacrifice his friends at the behest of foreigners. His prestige with his own people would suffer too much."[109]

After his retirement in 1952, Johnson became an advocate for Nationalist China. In an interview with the Columbia Oral History Project in 1954, just before his death, he spoke of how he once admired FDR, who had overcome being a cripple to dominate his world, but noted, "There came a time when I became acquainted with men like this fellow who went off to Columbia—Lauchlin Currie—and one or two people like that, who came to me as very close to Mr. Roosevelt, when I lost a good deal of my admiration for him. And when I finally discovered what had happened at Yalta, I lost a terrible amount of respect."[110] FDR struggled over what to do about China and, in the end, took neither Buck's nor Johnson's advice: to drop or keep Chiang Kai-shek. Instead, he and his successor, Harry S. Truman, tried to work out a compromise between Chiang and Mao Zedong. That effort failed. It is important to see how it failed and what the consequences were.

12

The President and the Generalissimo

It remains to be discovered where and how President Roosevelt's views and policies on China were formed. Herbert Feis, diplomat and historian, offered an explanation. He noted that Prime Minister Winston Churchill in December 1941 found, paradoxically, "extraordinary significance of China in American minds, even at the top, strangely out of proportion. I was conscious of a standard of values which accorded China almost an equal fighting power with the British Empire, and rated the Chinese armies as a factor to be mentioned in the same breath as the armies of Russia." Churchill thought this "judgment foolish," in Feis's words, and he told FDR, "American opinion overestimated the contribution [and that he felt it was] a wholly unreal standard of values." It was that same December, nevertheless, that they agreed the European war must come first. As Feis pointed out, "The President was at pains to make sure Chiang Kai-shek would feel that his ideas and wishes had been kept well in mind; and that China was counted on to have a real and inner part in the proposed arrangements [but] one which could [be made] important by its effort."[1]

At the Quadrant Conference of August 1943 in Quebec, FDR designated Secretary of State Cordell Hull to, as Feis put it, "mark the path toward the future United Nations Organization in which both China and the Soviet Union were to be formative participants." Of course, China had to become a well-governed and strong ally through averting civil war by political compromise between the Kuomintang and the CCP. The former would institute wide-ranging reforms. It had become increasingly evident that Chiang's mounting requests for aid—money, matériel, men—could not be met if the war in Europe was won first. Diplomatic promises could be made, especially when it was necessary to bolster Chinese morale to keep them in the war. Feis asserted, "Some corrective for the fears weighing on Chungking (Chongqing) was, the American government concluded, much needed." That corrective was a diplomatic prescription: "to have China written in among the great powers that were to guide the world after the war. The President and the Secretary of State carried this purpose into a series of conferences at Moscow, Cairo, and Teheran."[2] China would gain back its lost territories and be among the four Great Powers guaranteeing the postwar peace, especially stability in East Asia.

China's foreign minister, T. V. Soong, was asked to be at, but not involved in, the Quebec Conference, even though Chiang requested equal footing as a member of all Allied agencies. Especially, he wanted membership on the combined chiefs of staff and Munitions Assignment Board. The conference rejected these requests. Instead, as redress, "China was to be one of the four originating great powers, the Soviet Union another." FDR, Churchill, Hull, and his opposite, Foreign Secretary Anthony Eden, had discussed China's role and liked it; Moscow objected. Hull then went to Moscow for the foreign secretaries' meeting of October 18–30, 1943. Hull pushed hard. He told Molotov, "In my judgment it would be impossible to omit China from the Four-Nation Declaration. My Government believes that China has been in the world picture as one of the Big Four for the prosecution of the war."[3] Molotov reluctantly agreed. The Chinese ambassador to Moscow was quickly located, and the Moscow Four Power Declaration signed on October 30, 1943.[4]

Robert Dallek, writing a quarter century after Feis, also noted how "distinctly unenthusiastic" Churchill and Eden were about FDR's China ideas. Roosevelt, Dallek related, worried that if China collapsed, it would "play havoc with postwar plans." He went on to comment that in 1942 the United States gave up its extraterritorial rights in China, and in March 1943, when Eden was in Washington, "he found the President insistent on the idea that China be treated as a major force in world affairs." China, FDR pleaded, was a potential world power. Dallek concluded, "The President urged the inclusion of China as one member of a Four-Power executive committee which 'would make all the more important decisions and wield police powers' in a postwar peacekeeping body."[5]

More recently, Townsend Hoopes and Douglas Brinkley traced the origins of the so-called Four Policemen terminology. As early as January 1, 1942, when the Soviet and Chinese ambassadors joined FDR and Churchill at the White House for signing the declaration by the United Nations, "first by the four major powers," it reflected, they wrote, "FDR's ingrained belief in the rightful primacy of the strong [and] The President now privately referred to these major powers as the Four Policemen, and this distinction between great and small nations quickly became a fundamental element of all U.S. postwar planning." By February 1942, the plan had evolved into a United Nations Authority of the twenty-six nations, which signed the previous January's declaration with control in a Provisional Armistice Administration of the four powers, plus five regional representatives. "The [Undersecretary of State Sumner] Welles group," they noted, "recommended a 'security commission' made up of the Four Policemen, who would provide all of the forces needed for keeping the peace; it would operate under the general authority of the executive committee." The authors cited an article by Forest Davis in the *Saturday Evening Post* of April 10, 1943, in which Davis quoted FDR's public use of the term *Four Policemen:* at Teheran, FDR told Stalin there would be an "enforcement body, composed of Four Policemen, with authority to deal swiftly with any emergency of threat to the peace." Stalin was unimpressed. Like Churchill and Eden, he doubted China's ability to be a world power, and he proposed a separate committee for Europe. The final evolution of the Four Policemen, the authors explained, came with a suggestion by Hull's assistant Leo Pasvolsky, "One was to merge the Four Policemen (which under FDR's conception were to constitute a separate entity) with the larger (ultimately eleven-nation) Security Council. The other was to assign exclusive jurisdiction for security matters to that council."[6] In all of this, China kept its place, thanks to FDR's persistence, whatever doubts he had come to have about China or Chiang.

• • •

The Cairo Conferences, coded Sextant I and II—between FDR, Churchill, and Chiang Kai-shek—represented "China's Hour," its "watershed."[7] As hard as President Roosevelt tried, he failed to convince Churchill at Cairo, or Stalin at Teheran, that Nationalist China counted in winning the war against Japan or maintaining the peace afterward. FDR admitted to his son Elliott: "Who is there in China who could take Chiang's place? There's just no other leader. With all their shortcomings, we've got to depend on the Chiangs."[8] Sextant I symbolized the high tide in America's positive image of China, summoning FDR's illusory policy, however short-lived, for within a week at Sextant II, the Second Cairo Conference, China fell from its apogee to its nadir. What had befallen China?

To see the calamity of how China crashed from Sextant I to Sextant II, it is necessary to look at the preceding Moscow Conference of Foreign Ministers and the Teheran Conference sandwiched between Sextant I and II. By Sextant II, it was clear the luster had worn off Chiang's medals. America could win the Pacific war without China. Among the Big Three, it seemed no one but FDR believed in China's fighting ability. British disbelief and Russian cynicism finally convinced FDR that China under Chiang was only a paper tiger.

As early as August 10, 1943, Stalin proposed a "meeting of the responsible representatives to fix a place and date for a future conference" of the Big

Three. The others agreed, and Stalin insisted on August 24 that it be of a "practical preparatory character" so the questions studied by them could be presented for final decision when the heads of state met.[9] Secretary of State Cordell Hull noted that FDR had already made four unsuccessful attempts to meet with Stalin directly. However, in August the Soviet press suddenly suggested a meeting of the foreign ministers, and that had led the president and Prime Minister Winston S. Churchill to ask Stalin whether he concurred. He did: "I consider it necessary to revert to my proposal that the range of questions to be discussed by the representatives of the three powers should be determined in advance and the proposals selected which are to be studied by them and presented to our Governments for final decision."[10] There was some concern about Hull going to Moscow due to his health and age; other places were mentioned. If Moscow, FDR hinted, that meant Undersecretary Sumner Welles might have to go. Hull strenuously opposed Welles. FDR relented. Hull wrote, "The President cabled Stalin on September 24, saying that on further consideration he was most anxious that I attend in person the meeting with Mr. Molotov and Mr. Eden."[11]

It was at this Moscow meeting of the foreign secretaries that Hull was able to persuade the Russians to include China in the Four-Nation Declaration, a statement calling the United Nations into existence by the four Great Powers—the United States, Great Britain, Russia, and China. As Hull explained, he had been disappointed that Molotov had rejected China because "China had no interest in European matters and consequently should be left out." However, "The President and I believed, on the contrary, that China had a rightful place in such a declaration [because] her population was larger than those of the other three put together, she had vast potentialities if her people could be united, she had been fighting against the major Pacific enemy for more than six years, and after the defeat of Japan she would be the principal strictly Asian Power." He added that being excluded would damage China psychologically.[12]

The run-up to FDR's decision to include China, reluctantly accepted by the British, was the relinquishment of America's extraterritorial rights in China. Back in 1937, the United States had issued a memorandum to the British asking for negotiations on this point; they finally responded in April 1942. Hull signed the treaty on January 11, 1943, and it was ratified by the Senate in May. At the same time, the House passed the Fulbright Resolution, which favored creating a world organization. At conferences with FDR, it was agreed that Hull should "make every effort to secure both British and Russian agreement to China's participation in a four-power arrangement." The four were soon referred to as the "Four Policemen." Hull later wrote, "China was too important a factor, both now and in the future, both because of herself and of her influence in British India, to be alienated."[13] Churchill thought of China as not "representing a great world Power. Certainly there would be a faggot vote on the side of the United States in any attempt to liquidate the British overseas Empire."[14] Added to British reluctance, there was Molotov's flat rejection of China at the Moscow Conference: China was, the Russians believed, weak, dependent, unable to play an equal part, uninterested in European affairs, and unacceptable to Europeans. Molotov, in fact, "made quite a lot of trouble—trouble lasting a week, and ending only after dark hints that unless he gave in the American government might not be able to continue to cooperate with the Soviet Union."[15]

At the conference, beginning October 19 and ending with a secret protocol on November 3, the foreign ministers covered a wide range of subjects besides the Four-Power Declaration: treating Germany and Italy; policies toward Sweden, Turkey, and Persia; and, especially, the Russian query concerning the cross-Channel invasion of France as well as Arctic convoys. For the Americans, the all-important Four-Power Declaration was signed on October 30, after securing quick agreement to have China's Russian ambassador, Foo Ping-shueng (Fu Bing Chang), hastily sign even though Molotov had been certain that Chongqing's permission could not be granted that quickly.[16]

For the Chinese aspect of the conference, Hull's account is the most pertinent. Right from the first regular meeting on October 19, according to Hull, Molotov expressed a "willingness to put this point [Four-Nation Declaration] back on the agenda." It had not been included because "it was not clear to his Government from the correspondence with the British and American Governments whether it was to be omitted or not, and, if we desired, this point could receive further consideration." Hull proposed that it be point 2 on the formal agenda.[17] It was not until the third session on October 21 that the Four-Nation Declaration was discussed, along with the cross-Channel invasion of France. The British foreign secretary, Anthony Eden, strongly supported the declaration's principles, as did Molotov, though he objected to China because, "if [China] were included it would probably be impossible to get her adherence in time to sign the document during the conference." Hull had already taken the precaution to get Chinese approval of the draft statement. During a break, Hull emphasized, "For [China] now to be dumped out on her face by Russia, Great Britain, and the United States in connection with the Declaration would create in all probability the most terrific repercussions, both political and military, in the Pacific area."[18] Hull appealed to negative American opinion also. At that, Molotov allowed the declaration to be put off. At the fourth session, Molotov "now said he had no objection to the inclusion of China as an original signatory [however,] I felt that [Russia] was really against the admission of China and therefore sought to postpone an action." So Hull volunteered to communicate the text to the Chinese. Hull told Fu Bing Chang that China had to seize the opportunity and make a quick reply. For Hull's energy and persistence, FDR cabled him on October 28: "I am made very happy by your splendid achievement in putting this through. I know the China part of it was due to your personal insistence." At the last formal session on October 30, the "three foreign ministers and the Chinese Ambassador signed the Four-Nation Declaration." The Chinese ambassador personally thanked Hull, and Generalissimo Chiang Kai-shek "was delighted with the results of the Moscow Conference." Hull finished: "And China, too, would be one of the charter members by virtue of her signature of the Four-Nation Declaration. Had I not persisted in the effort to get China in as one of the original signatories, her claim to permanent membership on the Security Council of the United Nations would not have been so solid."[19]

Perhaps attitudes had been assuaged when Stalin made it known to Hull at the final banquet on October 30 that he could inform the president that after the Allies destroyed Hitler, the USSR would join in defeating Japan. Hull was "astonished and delighted."[20]

All along, the Moscow Conference had been conceived as preparatory to a meeting of the Big Three in the near future. Indeed, the discussions and protocol were all addressed to FDR, Churchill, and Stalin. But one problem remained: where to meet? While thrashing out that question, FDR suggested that he and Churchill gather at the Pyramids with their technical staffs to work out details of the second front, while also asking Generalissimo Chiang Kai-shek to join them for a few days. FDR even suggested inviting Molotov, which Churchill vehemently opposed. Nor was he keen about the generalissimo. Nevertheless, they each retained good spirits. When Teheran could not be agreed on initially, Churchill suggested to FDR that he read Saint Matthew, chapter 17, verse 4: "Then answered Peter, and said unto Jesus, Lord, it is good for us to be here: if thou wilt, let us make here three tabernacles; one for thee, and one for Moses, and one for Elias." Roosevelt replied, "I like the idea of three tabernacles. We can add one later for your old friend Chiang."[21]

Stalin remained fixed on Teheran, rather than Basra or tabernacles in the desert. The president finally succumbed to the idea of Teheran, and Stalin forbade Molotov from attending the first Cairo meeting, as it might compromise Soviet-Japanese relations. "Whereupon the President gave in. He did so probably because he concluded that he could not achieve his main purposes unless he talked with Stalin himself; possibly also because this message persuaded him that Stalin's reasons were meritorious."[22] For FDR, it was important the "Combined Chiefs of Staff should meet in Cairo before any contact was made with the Russians or the Chinese, whose presence in Cairo had been so strongly urged by him."[23]

Churchill's account of the first Cairo Conference is brief and almost excludes mention of Generalissimo and Madame Chiang Kai-shek. Yet it provides interesting atmospherics. FDR's advisers had suggested Khartoum or Malta, but, neither having suitable accommodations, Churchill stuck to Cairo, and FDR "brushed all objections aside." The prime minister reached Alexandria on the HMS *Renown* and then flew to the Pyramids. Chiang and his wife were already there. The president came aboard his plane *Sacred Cow* from Oran to Tunis, met with Gen. Dwight D. Eisenhower, and the next day went on to Cairo, having previously crossed the Atlantic on the USS *Iowa*. Churchill met Chiang for the first time and was favorably impressed with the generalissimo, who "stood at the height of his power and fame. To American eyes he was one of the dominant forces in the world. He was the champion of 'the New Asia.'" Nevertheless, Churchill complained that FDR took an "exaggerated view" of the Asian sphere and wasted time in long closeted conferences with Chiang. To Churchill's disgust, the "Former Naval Person" recognized that the "Chinese business occupied first instead of last place at Cairo."[24] That characterized the prime minister's feelings about China.

Though Harry Hopkins, the president's personal adviser, left no views of the Cairo Conference, his biographer, Robert E. Sherwood, claims to "have given a faithful reflection of them." Cairo's news factor, as Sherwood put it, was "color—the pyramids, the Sphinx and the extremely chic costumes of Madame [Chiang] Kai-shek, about which the correspondents could write much more skillfully than Hopkins could."[25] About military talks, ANAKIM, the overall plan to drive the Japanese out of Burma and reopen land communications with China, was passed: Gen. Joseph W. Stilwell would lead a ground operation in the North, while Adm. Lord Louis Mountbatten would direct a large amphibious operation in the South, especially against the Andaman Islands in the Bay of Bengal (BUCCANEER). On the latter, hedging on committing his own ground forces until Japanese supply lines were cut, Chiang insisted, "Burma was the key to the whole campaign in Asia. After he had been cleared out of Burma, the enemy's next stand would be in North China and, finally, in Manchuria. The loss of Burma would be a serious matter to the Japanese and they would fight stubbornly and tenaciously to retain their hold on the country."[26]

• • •

It is necessary to pause here and recount the "Stilwell episode." Teddy White, *Time*'s correspondent in Chongqing, had returned to China older and wiser. His first assessment of "Vinegar Joe" happened when he had called on him in New Delhi. Lt. Gen. Joseph Warren "Vinegar Joe" Stilwell commanded U.S. forces in the China, Burma, and India (CBI) theater. The general, Teddy recounted, had been thrust into Chinese politics because his command of troops ended by being a lesser responsibility than his setting a policy where none had existed. White's first evaluation came from the general himself: "The trouble in China is simple," said Vinegar Joe. "We are allied to an ignorant, illiterate, superstitious, peasant son of a bitch." Sent to placate the generalissimo, the army's China expert found, among other peccadilloes, Chiang's cousin embezzling U.S. military supplies. "No fighting army," White recounted, "could be created in China without changing the politics of China." President Roosevelt, it seemed to White, had considered China a great power only to soothe public opinion. In reality, he assigned China low priority, and it became only a military matter for a military man, "with no one reaching beyond combat considerations to the problems of politics and policy." Stilwell was the first commander handed a policy assignment disguised as a combat mission: he was to modernize and retrain China's armies into a fighting force that could break through Burma and join America's Pacific assault on Japan. Chiang's generals stole their soldiers' pay, food, and equipment. It soon became obvious to Stilwell that "China had a government [that] did not govern; [he] came to the awful conclusion that the government of China had to be changed if it was to be made useful to America—even if its chief of state must be shoved aside."[27]

White's second assessment concerned Stilwell's feud with Brig. Gen. Claire Chennault of Flying Tiger fame. Both men despised each other personally, but their actual argument was over conceptual differences about the war. Chennault believed in airpower absolutely. He convinced Chiang, who wanted to reserve his best troops for fighting the communists rather than the Japanese; further, Chennault got FDR to promise him sufficient planes to destroy Japan. "Chennault and the Chinese in Washington thus became palace allies at the White House to overturn the strategy of Chennault's nominal superior, theater commander Stilwell." Vinegar Joe believed that Chennault's forward air bases in Kweilin (Guilin) and farther north could not be held, because if Chennault's air strikes punished the Japanese severely, they would "protect their entrails by striking at the American air bases in East China—and the Chinese armies defending those bases simply could not hold." This is what eventually happened.

Nevertheless, FDR decided in favor of Chennault in May 1943. "At the game of palace politics," White noted, "Stilwell was hopelessly outsmarted." Though White had previously advocated airpower, he came to Stilwell's position because China was more than just a platform to launch airpower against Japan: "What if the purpose of war is not just to 'get the enemy,' but to defend what one sets out to defend as well? What if the preservation of a plateau of resistance depends as much on politics as on armies? What if those politics are more important than immediate combat opportunities? What if you lose what you began to defend by the manner of winning? [Stilwell was] trying to find a responsible government to deal with—a task that should not be forced on generals in uniform."[28]

The test over Stilwell versus Chennault and the very viability of Chiang's government came to a head when the Japanese began the ICHIGO offensive in early spring 1944. They moved their forces from three staging points —from Hankow (Hankou) southward, from Canton eastward, and from Burma northward—all driving at Chennault's forward bases. "As Stilwell predicted, Chennault had punished the Japanese too much; and Chiang could not provide ground cover for Chennault's bases." Now it was not just Stilwell complaining of Chiang's "incompetence, decay and graft," but Washington as well.

FDR could not order Chiang's removal, but the president could ask him to step aside and let Stilwell command all Nationalist armies, which FDR did on July 6, 1944. Chiang stalled; FDR sent Donald Nelson, former chair of the War Productions Board, and Patrick J. Hurley, former secretary of war under President Herbert Hoover. As John Paton Davies, the embassy's second secretary, later wrote, "The president had dispatched a preposterous series of plenipotentiaries to China—[Lauchlin] Currie, [Wendell] Willkie, [Henry] Wallace, [Donald] Nelson, and Hurley—undermining the ambassador's [Clarence Gauss's] position as the only personal representative of the president." They were to negotiate Chiang into a mere figurehead. By early September, they got Chiang to agree only in principle.[29]

Stilwell flew to Chennault's forward air base at Guilin on September 14 and ordered it blown up with all the supply dumps of materials so painfully flown over the Himalayas, the so-called Hump. "So much," quipped White, "for the Chennault-Chiang strategy of a year earlier." Nevertheless, Chiang demanded that Stilwell fly his Burma troops to East China to save the situation. Oppositely, Stilwell called for Chiang's personal two hundred thousand reserves fighting the communists in the North to rescue the East China front. Stilwell radioed Gen. George C. Marshall, who was then with FDR at the Octagon Conference in Quebec, that the generalissimo would not "listen to reason, merely repeating a lot of cock-eyed conceptions of his own invention." On September 18, 1944, FDR, with Churchill's approval, ordered Chiang to put Stilwell in charge or face "possible catastrophic consequences [and for] this you must yourself be prepared to accept the consequences and assume the personal responsibility." That message, White recounts, was to be delivered by Stilwell personally, which he gleefully did on September 19, 1944: "No more enthusiastic messenger could have been chosen than the four-star general who had suffered so long from the duplicity and false courtesies of Chiang Kai-shek." It turned out to be a Pyrrhic victory for Stilwell. A week later, Chiang took FDR's challenge head-on: either he or Stilwell would have to go. White remarked that a personal disaster for Chiang might have been good for China, but "one cannot expect any political leader to accept castration, however necessary for the good of the country." The stalemate between Chiang and FDR lasted about a month, from September 25 to October 19, 1944, when FDR finally relieved Stilwell of his command and ordered him home immediately. In that month's interim, both Hurley and Vice President Henry A. Wallace met and sided with Chiang.[30]

There is probably a good deal of truth to White's contention that FDR's alter ego, Harry Hopkins, had leaked to his friend T. V. Soong that FDR would give in to Chiang. Hopkins sided with Chennault, who was close to the Kuomintang. Besides Chennault, journalist Joseph V. Alsop and T. V. Soong flooded FDR with Chiang's biased side of the issue. Hopkins was critical of Stilwell's testy intransigence and favorable to Chennault. Finally, though Stilwell probably had the "right" on his side, he was a nuisance, and many times Roosevelt, according to FDR's White House speechwriter playwright Robert Sherwood, had come close to ordering his recall.[31]

There was an important lesson to be learned, and White came to understand it, though America did not then, and may not even now: "Stilwell was the first American to insist that our interests required political elimination of a major foreign chief of state. This policy perplexes me with its arrogance. However, paradoxically I know, in Stilwell's case, that he was absolutely right. It would have been better for China, for America and for the world had Chiang been removed from China's leadership in time. There might then have been some hope of a Chinese leadership more humane, less hostile, just as effective yet more tolerant than the one that succeeded Chiang."[32] When White read *Time*'s account, which faulted Stilwell and glorified Chiang, he labeled it the "worst bit of journalism I have ever seen in America."[33]

Since FDR and his military advisers believed the Chinese front was essential, they were willing to give "Peanut," as Stilwell derisively called Chiang, the benefit of the doubt. The Japanese were eventually defeated from attacks in the Pacific, not from Southeast Asia, and no decisive U.S. battles were fought on Asia's mainland. Admirals Ernest J. King and Adm. Chester W. Nimitz proved right in their thinking that sea power in the Pacific would win the war; Generals Marshall, Henry H. Arnold, MacArthur, and Stilwell disagreed and, as events turned out, were wrong. FDR supported the ANAKIM formula. But within ten days after the generalissimo's departure from Cairo on November 28, it was apparent that "American forces had started to strangle Japan from the Pacific, in the last six months of the war, that the first trucks started to roll over the Ledo or Stilwell road from Burma into China. By then it was too late to matter much."[34] More important, Stalin's promise to enter the war against Japan, confirmed within days at Teheran, further obviated the necessity of ANAKIM and associated operations in Southeast Asia—Stilwell's little-known but important story about Chiang and FDR. The devil, unfortunately, was in the details of this story.

● ● ●

One of the best sources for the diplomatic bargaining between the United States, Britain, and China at the two Cairo Conferences and their spillover at Teheran with Russia may be found in the published Stilwell Papers.[35] According to Vinegar Joe, it appeared that the United States, Britain, and China had agreed to a three-pronged attack on the Japanese: an amphibious assault in South Burma with British troops, the Chinese X-force attacking North Burma, and the Chinese Y-force with Americans driving on East Burma from Yunnan. It had fallen to General Stilwell to work out the details. Chiang Kai-shek finally, but reluctantly, consented; he still wanted more American aid. The generalissimo and his wife left Cairo for Chongqing and a hero's reception before the Teheran Conference, instead of staying for the second round at Cairo directly after Teheran.[36]

Stilwell had arrived in Cairo on Saturday, November 20, 1943. The "G-mo" or "Peanut," Stilwell's derisive nicknames for Chiang Kai-shek, came in on the evening of November 21, as did Churchill. That evening Stilwell made the rounds by seeing Chiang as well as the generals—George C. Marshall, Patrick J. Hurley, and Brehon B. Somervell. He complained that FDR did not like him calling Chiang "Peanut," but then he cruelly referred to FDR as "Rubberlegs," because of his irritation with FDR, who "gave away every opportunity to drive a bargain with Chiang Kai-shek for Chinese military performance." This was "a horrid mockery of Roosevelt's infirmity that appeared only once or twice again in the diary."[37] The president's plane landed the following morning, November 22, and that afternoon Generalissimo and Madame Chiang Kai-shek and Churchill paid courtesy calls. A preliminary conference of the prime minister, president, and their staffs met that evening.[38]

The following morning, November 23, Chiang met with FDR, Churchill, and their staffs. During that time, the joint chiefs convened, and in the afternoon the combined chiefs met and discussed the plan for the Burma campaign. Stilwell's diary revealed his frustrations: "G-mo phoned. 'Do not present proposals.' Message the G-mo would come. Then he wouldn't. That he would. Christ. [British Chief of Staff Alan] Brooke got nasty and

King got good and sore. [Finally,] Chinese came. Terrible performance."[39] The record simply indicates that Soviet and Chinese representatives should be there "only when the Combined Chiefs of Staff were discussing the problems of the particular fronts in which each was interested."[40] Stilwell presented a memorandum at the afternoon session on what operations could be mounted without overly competing for specialized equipment or in conflict with operations in other theaters: assist in North Burma; develop a land route to China; train and improve Chinese combat effectiveness; intensify bombing Japan, Formosa, and the Philippines and deny Japan the Formosa Straits and the South China Sea; and recapture Canton and Hong Kong. To do all of that required three additional infantry divisions, a supply program for equipping the Chinese, and moving U.S. troops in India to China after capturing North Burma; attack Shanghai—also Formosa, if needed.[41]

The twenty-third was, no doubt, a most intense day. The official record indicates that the Chiangs and the Chinese generals made a courtesy call on FDR that morning, followed up with a Chiangs-Hurley meeting discussing Teheran and the pending plan for Asia. The Chiangs then attended a plenary meeting at eleven o'clock. It was here that Chiang insisted on "vigorous naval operations." According to him, "Burma was the key to the whole campaign in Asia. After [the Japanese] had been cleared out of Burma, the enemy's next stand would be in North China and, finally, in Manchuria." Burma would be a "serious loss," and the Japanese would fight "stubbornly and tenaciously to retain their hold on the country."[42] That afternoon at the meeting of the combined chiefs of staff, Marshall took a critical look at China's performance: the generalissimo seemed more interested in obtaining large numbers of American transport aircraft while at the same time being reluctant to form and commit ground forces. He held back training Chinese troops at Ramgarrh or agreeing to habilitation of the Yunnan force. The most recent proposals had somewhat changed the generalissimo's mind.[43] Chiang finally decided not to attend this meeting, but his generals did. They entered the meeting at half past three and gave a "terrible performance," according to Stilwell. He noted that "Brooke was insulting. I helped them out. They were asked about the Yoke and I had to reply. Brooke fired questions and I batted them back."[44] It was Adm. Lord Louis Mountbatten, Supreme Allied Commander, South-East Asia Command, who pointed out that the "success of our efforts to open the land route to China was dependent on the successful operation of the Yunnan Force in coordination with the British attacks." Stilwell backed this up with an optimistic appraisal of making up shortages in Chinese personnel, supported by tactical aircraft.[45]

Dated November 22, probably delivered on the twenty-third, there was a memorandum for FDR's use by John Paton Davies Jr., second secretary of the U.S. Embassy in Chungking and political adviser to Stilwell. In it, he cautioned against using American troops to help re-create "the colonial empires of the British and their Dutch and French satellites." He predicted that only friction and misunderstanding would result. The Chinese would welcome a plan based on China itself. He also noted that the Chinese army was corrupt and ineffective except when under U.S. guidance. That meant giving Stilwell "bargaining power." Taking North Burma to open a land route to China was valuable, but not turning south to help the British. He concluded: "Our main interest in Asia will lie to the East from whence we can strike directly and in coordination with other American offensives at the center of Japan's new Empire."[46] Davies had foreseen British criticism of Chiang's objectives.

On the evening of November 23, FDR hosted a dinner for Generalissimo and Madame Chiang Kai-shek, who both remained afterward until eleven. Though no official record was kept of this meeting, the Chinese made brief notes, and the president's son Elliott also put down some of his father's remarks the next morning on topics not covered in the Chinese memorandum: formation of a coalition government in China, British rights in Shanghai and Canton, the use of American rather than British warships in pending operations, and the future status of Malay, Burma, and India.[47] The following morning, November 24, Elliott and his father chatted about China, the Chiangs, and Cairo. What, asked Elliott, did his father think of the generalissimo? "He knows what he wants, and he knows he can't have it all." FDR believed that he had learned more about the war that was not being fought by talking with the Chiangs than he had in four hours with the combined chiefs. According to the Chiangs, Chinese troops were not trained and had no equipment. Yet he was disturbed about why Chiang tried so hard to "keep Stilwell from training Chinese troops. And it doesn't explain why he keeps thousands and thousands of his best men up in the northwest—up on the borders of Red China." He realized the difficulty of supply, especially over the Hump, the shortage of landing craft, and the resistance of the British. Of Stilwell, FDR remarked, "I can't think what would be happening in China, if it weren't for him." Then, candidly, he opined about China's importance to the war effort: "Actually, of course, the job in China can be boiled down to one essential: China must be kept in the war, tieing [sic] up Japanese soldiers."[48]

The Chinese record of after-dinner remarks on the twenty-third indicates a much more ambitious conversation. FDR brought up his Four Policemen idea: "China should take her place as one of the Big Four and participate on an equal footing in the machinery of the Big Four Group and in all its decisions." About a postwar Japan, Chiang believed the Japanese should decide on the retention of the emperor, but China should not play a leading role in Japan's occupation. Japan should pay reparations to China and re-store its territories. Korea should be granted its independence and In-dochina helped toward that goal. Chiang proposed a China-U.S. Joint Council of Chiefs of Staff, or China's participation in the existing Britain-U.S. Council of Chiefs of Staff. Finally, they discussed the economic recon-struction of China, which "would require United States financial aid in the form of loans, etc., and also various types of technical assistance."[49]

On the morning of Wednesday, the twenty-fourth, the combined chiefs of staff met with FDR and Churchill—the Chinese were not present. This was Churchill's chance to make his case for enlarging the Mediterranean theater, especially the capture of Rhodes. "It might be better," he insisted, "to bring back from the Southeast Asia Theater to the Mediterranean suf-ficient landing craft for an attack on Rhodes. Thus the sequence would be, first Rome then Rhodes." He was none too excited about Asia, commenting, "It seemed that the Generalissimo had been well satisfied with the discus-sion held the previous day. There was no doubt that China had wide aspi-rations which included the re-occupation of Manchuria and Korea."[50] He was wrong about Korea.

At a luncheon that afternoon with the Chiangs, Stilwell, and General Marshall, Vinegar Joe noted in his diary that Marshall "talked a streak dur-ing lunch, and afterward G-mo held forth on the plans. Not much hope for United States troops. Peanut first said he'd go to meeting and then reneged, telling me to tell them his views."[51]

That conference of the combined chiefs of staff was held on the afternoon of the twenty-fourth. It had been suggested that a united chiefs of staff be created, that is, one including Russian and Chinese commanders. The com-bined chiefs, British and American, rejected this because Russia and China were not fighting the same enemies and would be unable to take a global outlook.[52] They should be invited only when the combined chiefs were dis-cussing Russian or Chinese issues or at special conferences devoted to them alone. After conversing about the agenda for Teheran, the chiefs turned to Southeast Asian operations. General Marshall opened the discussion by outlining the generalissimo's objections to the current plan. It would, Chiang thought, lead to heavy losses and maybe defeat. He would go along with only the following stipulations: first, that an amphibious operation be carried out simultaneously and synchronized with a land attack in Burma —against the Andaman Islands; second, that all the advancing columns be aimed at a line running east and west through Mandalay, with Mandalay being occupied; third, Yunnan troops (the Y-force) should not advance be-yond Lashio; fourth, the plan should include the entire conquest of Burma, with Rangoon as an objective and the Mandalay-Lashio line as only the first stage; and fifth, that whatever the needs of the land and sea campaigns, that the airlift to China over the Hump not drop below ten thousand tons per month. As Gen. Chen Shang (Shang Zhen), chief of the General Office and of the Foreign Affairs Bureau of the National Military Council of China, noted: "The Generalissimo was most insistent with regard to the maintenance of the air lift to China."[53]

Criticisms of the generalissimo's conditions were rife among the chiefs. Marshall complained that he had presented only a first stage—the recapture of Burma—and that it was much less dangerous than what Chiang wanted, especially the generalissimo's insistence on a naval assault in the Bay of Bengal. Mountbatten added that the advance had to end when the monsoon broke. Brooke agreed that the Allies were committing to the recapture of all Burma and there could be no holding halfway, that is, finally there would be an airborne attack on Rangoon and amphibious operations. Either Burma would have to be finished or the alternative would be to give up that campaign altogether and try to open the Malacca Straits. Admiral King thought Bangkok could be substituted for the straits. It was Mountbatten who stressed logistical difficulties in dealing with Chiang's demands: "It was illogical to demand in the same breath that this extensive plan should be carried out and a 10,000 ton air lift to China maintained."[54] He added that Chiang's required tonnage had never been achieved and, furthermore, that small reductions below the target might be necessary to allow the plan to take place. After all, the generalissimo himself had told him that he would consider sympathetically small reductions below the ten thousand–ton target. "It was essential," he thought, "that the Chinese should make up their minds whether to insist on a 10,000 ton lift to China or whether they wished his present operations carried out."[55] China could not have it both ways: ten thousand tons *and* land operations to open the Burma Road. As Marshall pointed out, "The present campaign was designed to open the Burma Road, for which the Chinese had asked, and that the opening of the Road was for the purpose of equipping the Chinese Army." There could be no misunderstanding. Unless the road were opened, supplies could not be increased to China since no further equipment or aircraft could be spared from the United States due to commitments elsewhere.[56] As Stilwell had indicated, it was Mountbatten's turn to fix it up with the generalissimo.

The afternoon of the following day, Thursday, November 25—Thanksgiving Day—Admiral Mountbatten reported to the combined chiefs on his meeting the previous day with Chiang: "The Generalissimo insisted that the alternative plan of campaign should be carried out, the plan for which, in fact, the resources were not available and which demanded an additional 535 transport aircraft." Then the leader of Nationalist China abruptly reversed himself and gave his "enthusiastic and personal support to the less extensive plan being put into effect, the Generalissimo acceded but said that first the Combined Chiefs of Staff must be asked formally to provide the aircraft necessary for the more extensive plan." He also insisted that the amphibious operation had to be carried out simultaneously with the land operation in North Burma. When Churchill explained to him that the amphibious operation did not affect the land battle, Chiang contradicted the prime minister, indicating that "it would draw off part of the enemy air forces available." When told that only eighty-nine hundred tons over the Hump could be supplied for the six months of the operation's course, the "generalissimo had demanded that the full 10,000 tons per month should be made available." With all the reservations of Chiang Kai-shek, the combined chiefs required that Mountbatten "would draw up a paper for submission to the Generalissimo with a view to getting the latter's written agreement to the Burma operations now contemplated."[57]

Late that afternoon, Stilwell noted in his diary: "With George [Marshall] to see F.D.R., who said Peanut had agreed [to the Burma plan]."[58] Actually, it was much more complicated, as Hopkins sent for Stilwell at nine thirty that evening to tell him, as Vinegar Joe put it, that "G-mo as of 6:00 P.M. does not like the plan [for Burma]. My God. He's off again."[59] Stilwell thought his and Marshall's meeting with FDR was sterile. The president seemed to pay little attention and broke into the conversation with remarks about the Andaman Islands, on which he intended to put heavy bombers. When Stilwell painted a gloomy picture about the Chinese reneging on their agreements, FDR promised to press the generalissimo. Marshall believed "there was pressure on the President to give the Generalissimo something to show as a result of his trip [and] Roosevelt had made it clear the United States intended eventually to equip ninety Chinese divisions."[60] Sometime between that late-afternoon meeting on the twenty-fifth and FDR's departure for Teheran early on the twenty-seventh, he cut a deal with Chiang: "It was probably at this meeting [late afternoon on the twenty-fifth] that Roosevelt gave Chiang the promise . . . of a considerable amphibious operation across the Bay of Bengal within the next few months."[61]

Madame Chiang met with FDR on the twenty-sixth, accompanied by Mountbatten and, presumably, spoke about her husband's attitude toward proposed operations in Southeast Asia. Whatever pleasantries they might have exchanged, the generalissimo met again with American generals late that morning. He still demanded ten thousand tons per month over the Hump, "regardless of any demands which might be made on the equipment to support necessary operations in the South East Asia Command." They called attention to Mountbatten's requirements for the next seven months and that it might be more realistic to estimate eighty-nine hundred for that period. Chiang stated, "His requirements and those of Lord Mountbatten in the South East Asia Theater should be divided and that they should be handled as separate items." When the impossibility of his demands was explained, he said "he would accept the figures given to him with the understanding that the ATC [Air Transport Command, the Hump line] would devote its best endeavors to securing the greatest possible increase in the tonnage."[62] The combined chiefs met that afternoon. Gen. Sir Alan Brooke, chief of the British Imperial General Staff, believed that it might be necessary to put off Operation Buccaneer, the assault on the Andaman Isles. But the Americans had been gotten to by FDR. Admiral King said that "the land campaign in Burma was not complete without the Operation." General Marshall "believed that the suggestion that putting off Operation Buccaneer would shorten the war was an overstatement. The American Chiefs of Staff were most anxious that Buccaneer should be undertaken. They had gone far to meet the British Chiefs of Staff views but the postponement of Buccaneer they could not accept." In fact, if BUCCANEER had to be postponed, "this would need to be taken up with the President and the Prime Minister."[63]

FDR and Churchill met for a final time with the Chiangs for tea late on the afternoon of November 26 for more than two hours. They framed a communiqué that was not to be released until Stalin approved it after the Teheran Conference. "Chiang is reported as having agreed to every point that he had rejected the day before."[64] Even Hopkins spent another three hours that evening with the Chiangs, talking about the return of Outer Mongolia.[65] Stilwell remarked about the accomplishments of that last working day at Cairo: "Peanut went into his song and dance. We talked him down. He wants Louis [Mountbatten] to keep his hands off the ATC. Must have his 10,000 [tons a month over the Hump]. Finally said O.K."[66] Things looked good: "Such was the situation when Churchill and Roosevelt with their key advisers departed for Tehran, and the Generalissimo prepared to go to Chungking. For the first time in the war, the Prime Minister, the President, and the CCS [combined chiefs of staff] had met the Generalissimo and endeavored to secure a binding agreement from him." But, as Lord Mountbatten said, "they have been driven absolutely mad, and I shall certainly get far more sympathy from the former in the future."[67]

• • •

At 7:07 A.M. on Sunday, November 27, 1943, the president's plane took off from Cairo for Teheran and the first meeting of the Big Three. He covered the 1,310 miles between six and seven hours, arriving at three o'clock local time. After Cairo I, could FDR sell Stalin on the new role of China in the postwar world, manage an all-out assault on Hitler for Stalin, and simultaneously mount offensives in Burma for Chiang and the eastern Mediterranean for Churchill? It was a tall task that pitted FDR's charm against the wily Churchill and the stubborn Stalin.

As soon as FDR arrived, he was invited by Stalin to stay at the Soviet compound, next to the British Embassy, and he accepted. The president brought up the Cairo Conference, and Chiang Kai-shek at his first private meeting with Stalin. "Marshal Stalin remarked that the Chinese have fought very badly but, in his opinion, it was the fault of the Chinese leaders." The next great question after the second front had now appeared: whether diversionary operations such as Burma could be carried on either simultaneously or closely connected with OVERLORD, the projected Allied landing in northern France. After lightly touching on other subjects such as France and Indochina, Stalin left.[68] Only just that morning, the joint chiefs of staff had spoken with enthusiasm about operations in the Andaman Islands, or Rhodes. General Marshall believed Churchill would try hard to cut out BUCCANEER, push for Rhodes, and, if that were successful, press for Greece. Nevertheless, the chiefs already recognized the shortage of landing craft.[69]

Perhaps responding to the sting of Stalin's words in their first conversation, FDR again pleaded the Chinese cause: keep them in the war by an expedition in North Burma and Yunnan as well as Andaman and Bangkok. The result would be the opening of the road to China for supply and getting in a position to bomb Japan. He then spoke of the war's most important theater, Europe, and the cross-Channel operation set for May. Stalin, in one bold move, swept aside the necessity of China in the Pacific and dismissed the Mediterranean theater, the Balkans, and Turkey. The only essential place, first and foremost, was northern France, even though "he had not meant to convey the impression that he considered the North Africa or Italian operations as secondary or belittle their significance since they were of very real value."[70]

That afternoon, November 29, FDR and Stalin again met privately. After asking Stalin for Allied airfields in the USSR for the purposes of shuttle bombing, which Stalin approved, the president brought up the Chinese question. This time any immediate operation in Southeast Asia was missing. Instead, FDR worked on China's place in a future world organization as one of the "Four Policemen." Stalin countered with a regional alternative, since he believed that the European nations would never allow China such a role. Besides, he remained dubious about that level of Chinese participation. Even FDR had to recognize the weakness of China, but he thought China would be important in the future.[71] By the time of the final luncheon on December 1, both the president and the prime minister focused on OVERLORD; it should not suffer due to actions in other theaters, though FDR had not completely closed out Burma from the realm of possibility.[72]

The president returned to Cairo in the early afternoon of Thursday, December 2, 1943. FDR's commitments to China would have to be squared with Stalin's insistence on OVERLORD's priority, a May target date, and the Soviet leader's promise to declare war on Japan immediately after Germany's defeat. Roosevelt found himself in an awkward position. Churchill had never accepted BUCCANEER, and Stalin thought of it as a Chinese diversion. Churchill clung to Rhodes only if he could cajole Turkey into declaring war against the Axis. Otherwise, operations in the eastern Mediterranean were off. This was Churchill's quid pro quo: no Rhodes, no Andaman. FDR persisted. Over dinner on December 3 with the prime minister, he insisted on the "Andaman Islands operation and emphasized that promises made to Chiang should be fully carried out."[73]

The morning of December 4, at a meeting of the combined chiefs, Churchill attacked the whole notion of BUCCANEER. First, he paraded out Stalin's promise that the Soviet Union "would make war on Japan the moment Germany was defeated. This would give us better bases than we could ever find in China, and made it all the more important that we should concentrate on making Overlord a success." Second, OVERLORD transcended all other operations. That meant ANVIL, the operation against southern France, should be as strong as possible to divert Germans from concentrating against Allied bridgeheads in Normandy. Third, he was "astounded" at the demands for BUCCANEER, which now required fifty-eight thousand men to capture an island with only five thousand Japanese defenders. In his words, "In the face of Marshal Stalin's promise that Russia would come into the war [against Japan], operations in the Southeast Asia Command had lost a good deal of their value; while on the other hand their cost had been put up to a prohibitive extent." Fourth, the May target date for Operation Overlord made it impossible to find the necessary landing craft unless it were postponed by two to four weeks to allow for new construction to reach Britain. Hence, BUCCANEER might be left until after the monsoon season. Sir Alan Brooke chimed in, "It would be better to employ all the Buccaneer resources to strengthen up the European front." The president still held out: "We had a moral obligation to do something for China and he would not be prepared to forego the amphibious operation, except for some very great and readily apparent reason."[74] Stalin's demands proved to be the great exception.

That afternoon the combined chiefs met without the president or prime minister. Brooke emphasized that at Teheran it was agreed with Stalin that the "main effort against Japan should be made in the Pacific. He was frankly disturbed with regard to present ideas on operations in Southeast Asia." The chiefs wrangled over the question of Southeast Asia: "TARZAN," the India-based portion of the Southeast Asia attack on Japan, would not be carried out; the Chinese would advance nowhere, but then they were an "unknown factor" anyway. In Sir Andrew Cunningham's opinion, "The capture of the Andamans was not worth the candle, except as a stepping-stone to a southward advance."[75]

When the combined chiefs met on the fifth, FDR was reduced to arguing about how solid Stalin's word was: "Suppose Marshal Stalin was unable to be as good as his word; we might find that we had forfeited Chinese support without obtaining commensurate help from the Russians." This statement was made in the face of mounting British attacks, led by the prime minister himself. Churchill was "disturbed" at the growth in resources required for BUCCANEER; it could be postponed until after the monsoon; BUCCANEER would not materially influence China's continuation in the war, which depended more on supplies over the "Hump"; commando raids would be sufficient; tell Chiang that Mountbatten wanted more, rather than less, forces: "If the Generalissimo expressed surprise and threatened to withhold the Yunnan forces, we should say that we would go on without them." Finally, there was the killer argument: "We could not get away from the fact that we should be doing wrong strategically if we used vital resources such as landing craft on operations of comparatively insignificant importance, instead of using these resources to strengthen up Overlord and Anvil, where it looks like we are working to a dangerously narrow margin."[76]

Roosevelt met with his joint chiefs late that afternoon, and he finally decided to bite the bullet and abandon the Andaman Islands plan—and Southeast Asia in general. He sent Churchill a laconic message: "Buccaneer is off."[77] On the following day, the president admitted to Stilwell, "We're at an impasse. I've been stubborn as a mule for four days but we can't get anywhere, and it won't do for a conference to end that way. The British just won't do the operation, and I can't get them to agree to it."[78] Elliott Roosevelt's take on this was that beating the Nazis first would allow FDR to give priority to China. Stilwell remained negative about Chiang: "Vinegar Joe voiced his dissatisfaction with the politics of the Generalissimo, and made the point that Chiang was storing up all his strength to use against the Chinese Communists after the war."[79]

This necessitated the following telegram to Chiang Kai-shek, sent on the fifth and received on the sixth: "Conference with Stalin involves us in combined grand operations on European continent in late spring giving fair prospect of terminating war with Germany by end of summer of 1944. These operations impose so large a requirement of heavy landing craft as to make it impracticable to devote a sufficient number to the amphibious operation in Bay of Bengal simultaneously with launching of TARZAN to insure success of operation."[80]

The generalissimo replied on December 9, saying the pledge to launch an all-out offensive in the Pacific had been altered by a "radical change" of policy. Nevertheless, he was "inclined to accept your recommendation. You will doubtless realize that in so doing my task in rallying the nation to continue resistance is being made infinitely more difficult." Then, without blinking, he asked for a billion gold-dollar loan, the doubling of the number of aircraft, and increasing the air transportation over the Hump to twenty thousand tons. His threat was that he would abandon the Chinese theater to the Japanese, and, thus, China could fold.[81]

China had moved into the shadows: "No sooner was China recognized as a great power than the promise to Chiang Kai-shek was broken just as if he had been only the Sultan of Morocco. China's mistrust of the West deepened and Western confidence in Chiang plummeted as a result of their mutual contact."[82] By putting a monetary price on continuing the war, China caused Washington's disenchantment. Both Secretary of the Treasury Henry Morgenthau and Ambassador Clarence Gauss opposed the loan, as China, they thought, had no way of effectively using it. China had already made a fiasco of the 1942 loan. Morgenthau told FDR to reject a new loan. Chiang responded by declaring that the United States should pay at the official rate for the cost of constructing airfields in Chengtu (Chengdu) for the B-29 bombing program. The United States was outraged. Through other interim financial arrangements, the airfields were built, and the B-29s flew until the Japanese counterattack. Support for Chiang waned in the United States, and other ways for defeating Japan were seriously considered—especially by sea.[83]

Herbert Feis, then an economic adviser for international affairs to the State Department, later wrote that the president had "urgent business" with Chiang Kai-shek. FDR was aware of Chinese carping about being neglected, particularly in terms of equipment deliveries over the Hump. FDR believed that the Chongqing government might drop out of the war and, as well, that an explanation of global strategy might improve Chinese morale. Hence, the promise of an increase of military aid "over the Hump" to ten thousand tons per month and a strategy to drive Japan out of Burma, open the Burma Road, and make an amphibious attack on the Andaman Islands pleased Chiang, especially if his participation was minimal, and even though, as indicated, this soon was proved unnecessary. FDR gave in to the British because he "could not deny the bearing of these reasons, but he was much distressed at the idea that the *whole* plan for Burma on which he had agreed with Chiang Kai-shek might be upset; and that possibly the Generalissimo might be so hurt and discouraged that China might virtually stop fighting."[84] As for Churchill, he knew General Marshall was disappointed and Stilwell resentful. "About Chiang Kai-shek's reaction, he was not much concerned."[85] And Chiang did complain that these promises were not being kept. Nevertheless, Chiang had a lot to be happy over: at Moscow, China became an original signatory of the Four-Nation Declaration, by which it had a spot on the Executive Council of the future world organization, and at Cairo, confirmed at Teheran, "China was deeded vast areas, great potential influence, and top responsibilities." All this had been achieved because the American official mind believed China capable of greatness and a reliable friend of the West. China was deemed up to the unity necessary in order to rule over vast new domains.[86]

Yet when all was said and done, China's "Hour at Cairo" was short-lived, according to Barbara Tuchman. The Chinese had seen Cairo as a chance to gain status and territory. Momentarily, they had. The Moscow Conference confirmed the former, Cairo the latter. "Chiang Kai-shek was thus at last the acknowledged equal of Churchill, Roosevelt and Stalin, and his status was about to be made visible by his presence at Cairo."[87] Tuchman believed that FDR was determined to make Cairo a success from the Chinese point of view: "He wanted to lay the ground for settlement of Sino-Soviet relations and of the Kuomintang-Communist schism, so likely to disturb the postwar order."[88] At Teheran, he told Stalin that the one essential was to "keep China in the war tying up Japanese soldiers." And remember that to his son Elliott he said, "With all their shortcomings we've got to depend on the Chiangs."[89] Yet on November 20, when Stilwell arrived in Cairo, the U.S. Marines had landed in the Gilbert Islands, marking the beginning of the end for the need of China in the war against Japan. Chiang himself was overconfident of FDR granting him anything, as he told Mountbatten: "The President will refuse me nothing. Anything I ask, he will do."[90] However, no sooner had Chiang arrived home than a telegram came announcing the cancellation of BUCCANEER. Chiang retaliated by putting a high price on his cooperation, asking for a one billion–dollar loan, double the number of aircraft, and tons over the Hump. As noted, Morgenthau had rejected the loan, insisting that China should do its share of the fighting, and FDR had then sent Morgenthau's memorandum on to Chiang with some "placating assurances of goodwill."[91] Chiang responded by demanding something in the neighborhood of eight hundred million dollars for constructing B-29 airfields in Chengdu; the United States was not rich enough to fight with Chiang.

By various compromises, the fields were built, and the planes flew. From this time on, U.S. support for Chongqing diminished. Excluding these opinions of Churchill, Hopkins, Feis, and Tuchman, the actual conference record, text and pictures, records as a resounding success for China. The Chinese mystique remained. Even another journalist of genius, Teddy White, could not shake it.

13

Luce's Man in Chungking

For Theodore H. "Teddy" White, *it*—meaning China and all of that—started simply enough.[1] Teddy chose Harvard's Yenching Institute as a Chinese studies protégé of John K. Fairbank.[2] The "Chief" as Teddy called Fairbank, insisted on the Twenty-one Demands of Japan on China in 1915 as his senior essay. On graduation, Teddy won a Frederick Sheldon Traveling Fellowship, which took him to Europe and the Far East. He wrote "mailers" on commission for the *Boston Globe*. The Chief had told Teddy to sell editors on the idea that correspondents in China should read Chinese: "You have had the training in Chinese that none of these boys have had and can tell them you are good, the language is hard."[3] Now Teddy would sell himself, first to Nationalist China and then to press lord Henry R. "Harry" Luce.

• • •

For the first few months in China, Teddy made Shanghai his base of operations while he searched about to be a "floater"—an anonymous foreign reporter for American newspapers. In a long letter to Harvard's Dean Hanford at the end of July 1939, which he also sent to the Chief, White summarized his Chinese experiences. He mused that Chongqing was a city on a rock at the confluence of the Yangtze and Kialin (Jialin) rivers. From just 200,000 inhabitants, it had swollen to 750,000. These refugees lived in bamboo shacks and were perfect targets for Japanese incendiary bombings, which followed the foggy season from autumn to spring. On May 4, 1939, the bombings started: "There cutting across the skies in one single straight line, wing tip to wing tip were 27 Japanese planes." After a minute, unopposed except for antiaircraft guns, Teddy witnessed "the most effective and disastrous bombing of any town in world history." Before then, he wrote, he had journeyed to Beijing and Manchuria, where he detested Japanese arrogance and the Legation Quarter's lifestyle: "It is only after a sojourn that one realizes that the glitter is false; that life here is empty, and that this entire society functions still only by the grace of the Japanese army." He had, he told his Harvard dean and Fairbank, visited burned-out Shanghai. In Chongqing, his reporting had to be "strained through the sieve" of Chiang Kai-shek's Ministry of Propaganda. His work had an "Alice-in-Wonderland quality." There were three years of Chinese heroism, but "there is inefficiency in this war that makes on [sic] go white with rage [so that] I cannot get used to seeing unarmed men thrown to death beneath the wheels of a mechanized juggernaut."[4] Already, White was critical of the Nationalist regime.

On January 5, 1939, White announced to a friend that, because of his reporting of his trip to Shansi (Shanxi), he was now employed permanently in Chongqing by both *Time* and Reuters. He also noted the fall of Nanjing and the split with the Kuomintang and Chinese Communist Party due to the effort of Chiang Kai-shek to wipe out the Red's Eighth Route Army.[5] In April he wrote a retrospective letter to his family explaining his work for the China Information Service, which kept the entire Western world informed of news from China: "[White was to] turn out the proper stories to elicit the proper and desired response in all the various circles who are so important to China, the American liberal crowd, the missionairy [sic]–Red Cross–Philanthropy gang, the commercial men of money etc., etc., etc.,—there were a lot of queer tasks that I would be responsible for." The job required churning out propaganda, and that made him uncomfortable. He could tell his family the truth, but they could reveal nothing.[6]

Curiously, on June 2, 1939, in a late letter answering his family's letters of April and May, he further explained his new relationship with *Time:* he had met John Hersey, a "young milking lad," who, though "green," had the "right kind of parents," the "right kind of luck," the "right kind of school," and, therefore, "is going to become Far Eastern Editor of the magazine *Time.*" The point was that "John Hersey is here now looking for a correspondent who will live in Chungking and work for *Time* and just send political analyses home from time to time." His friends suggested him to Hersey, even though he worked for the Chinese government.[7] By August, he had finally concluded that the KMT was "black with corruption and inefficiency." He put the matter squarely: "Never was there a purer cause in a fouler vessel, than the cause of the Chinese people in the hands of the Kuomintang government."[8] The cause of the Chinese against Japan led Teddy to praise the KMT in his reporting for *Time* even when he knew Chiang Kai-shek's regime was rotten to the core. For instance, in October he told Gen. Ch'en Ch'ien that he was "extremely happy to tell the people of America of the splendid successes of the Chinese armies in southeast Shansi and the conditions of fighting there."[9] It must be admitted that he worked under severe censorship and any reporting of the truth would have quickly been censored or ended his career.

From August to November 1939, Teddy went on an expedition to North China and wrote his breakaway article on the Shanxi war front for *Time*. In a long letter home in mid-November, he gave a strictly personal account of his journey, a trip that for the first time took him into the real China and away from a big city where he was surrounded by European and West-ernized Chinese and on purely Chinese transport. In fact, he went by train, horseback, and bus. "Day after day," he wrote, "we rode through scenes of utter and complete desolation." Nevertheless, he noticed, "I was traveling as an American journalist on the war front, and the name of America is a key to every door of China." In fact, signs reading "Welcome to the Amer-ican Journalist, Mr. Theodore H. White [and] Chinese is America's Good Friend" greeted him.[10]

In December, White decided to quit working for Holly Tong of the Cen-tral Publicity Board of the Ministry of Information. With Tong and the Chi-nese personal patronage system, he could go on forever, but the allure of reporting solely for *Time* was too great. As he told Tong, here was an op-portunity to work for America's leading newsmagazine and a valuable ex-perience for his career. Besides, the money was important to him and his family. A clean break was now essential so his readers would not find his name attached to two masters. On December 21, 1939, Tong accepted his resignation, effective January 1, 1940.[11] He had offered to triple his salary if he wrote for no others, namely, *Time* and the Australian Broadcasting Commission. The censorship was awful, especially the story he had on the treacherous Russian activities in the Northwest. At that point, "the long arm of the Chinese government reached down and grabbed me by the scruff of my neck and said, No!" Tong had cautioned him that Russian aid to the KMT could not be jeopardized. He decided that it was "daman [*sic*] difficult to write the truth."[12]

Already by October 1939, his feelings about Nationalist China had cooled, though he remained pro-Chinese. For *Time*, initially, he could write honest-ly and accurately: "TIME's philosophy is that it is the man that makes the news. It's one with which I don't quite agree—but, Lord God, when I think of the men who direct China, their weaknesses, peculiarities, stupidities; and of the relation of their weaknesses, their stupidities, their prejudices to the fate of the people they direct; then I'm almost convinced that TIME's phi-losophy of man in relation to history is right."[13] For instance, he referred to "Old Daddy Kung" as that "old, fat, double-chinned, pot-bellied bastard." H. H. Kung was vice president of the executive Yuan, chairman of the cen-tral bank, chairman of the industrial cooperatives, brother-in-law of the *gis-simo* (Chiang Kai-shek), and minister of finance. He was not necessarily dishonest, but he could not make up his mind and was the "weakest-willed" of all the government's leaders. Further, he was "surly, mean-natured and vain." White apologized for bursting into a diatribe, but "there are half-a-dozen men like him in Chungking who in their totality make up China's greatest danger—complacency in high places; stupidity; sloth." Or take the National Military Council: "No collection of bureaucrats with less competence ever afflicted the struggle of a great people for life." Curiously, he remained positive but cynical about Chiang: "He's been a first-class butcher in his time. Cruel and ruthless. Stubborn as a mule. A man less tough, less convinced of his own destiny than Chiang would have cracked long ago—but Chiang, he carries on." White lamented that China could win the war in only one of two ways: first, give the people the land and beat the Communists at their own game; second, pray for foreign help. Since Chiang would not do the former, the latter was his only hope, and it had better arrive quickly.[14]

White's war story, slicked up by Hersey, he titled "Eagles in Shansi," and it appeared in *Time* on December 18, 1939. Hersey began by calling White's dispatch the least noticed yet most important of the entire war because the Chinese had managed to roll down on the Japanese and slaughter two thousand. Shanxi was the key to coal, the future Pennsylvania of China. Hersey complimented White's Harvard training as well as the brave Chinese soldiers, whether Nationalist or Communist. This report was especially graphic of the Japanese rape of the Chin Valley and Japan's failing morale. Fitting nicely into Luce's own views, Teddy inferred that China had progressed from a fourth- to a second-rate army. Hersey, directly quoting White, noted, "The present Chinese Army has spirit. It glows. The men are willing to die. They mix and tangle with the Japanese with a burning hate that is good."[15] Increasingly, "Despite wickedness White saw in Chiang's government, he continued to equivocate and even ignore reality in his news reports while his doubts were expressed in his private correspondence. [White wrote] 'As for China, the longer one stays here the more confused one gets. . . . One sees behind the good and heroic, to see the corruption, graft, intrigue, administrative stupidity, cowardice and greed of the officials. And one begins to doubt.'" Emily Hahn, Teddy's contemporary China journalist, thought that Teddy was a leading Chinese expert who could be trusted, but, "then, I thought that his reports were too highly colored by what he wanted to see rather than what he actually saw."[16]

On April 18, 1941, Teddy received the biggest news: "HENRY LUCE AND WIFE SCHEDULED ARRIVE IN CHUNGKING MAY SIXTH REMAINING THROUGH MAY THIRTEENTH KNOW YOU WILL DO ALL POSSIBLE BUT ESPECIALLY URGE YOU UPDATE LUCE CURRENT SITUATION SOON AFTER ARRIVAL STOP." Teddy had mixed feelings about having the "big boss" around because they might disagree politically, and it would be hard for him to keep his mouth shut.[17] A few days later, he wrote his sister that he did not think that he could get along with *Time* because he did not like their news policy or general politics, but he would stay on until the Luces came. He was anxious to write the real story of China, not the book he had sent to Random House: "I'm not writing a Communist apologetic as [Hugh] Deane and Snow have done; nor a Kuomintang tract as I did myself last year." In addition, he predicted that America would be at war within a year.[18] First, he had to sell himself to Luce, whom some persons now referred to as another "Citizen Kane." Harry and Claire Booth Luce arrived in Chungking on May 6, 1941, and White's miracle happened. Two days before Luce left, he asked White to pack up and return with him as Far Eastern editor of *Time*. He had become Luce's "fair-haired" journalist.[19]

Luce, like Pearl Buck, was a mishkid (child of missionaries) who had been born on April 3, 1898, in Tengchow (Dengzhou), China, the son also of Presbyterian missionaries. Teddy's boss during most of his China years was Harry Luce. In 1961 Luce, cofounder of *Time* in 1923, was described as "the giant of twentieth-century American journalism." He served as editor in chief of all Time, Inc., publications until 1964, when he resigned and remained editorial chair.[20] In the 1930s and 1940s, Luce became a powerful media mogul. His publications provided an integrated view of the world not found elsewhere. By 1941, Luce enterprises took in forty-five million dollars.[21] One in five Americans read a Luce journal in 1940, and he commanded the favor of both journalists and readers.

Until 1940, Luce's publications conveyed contradictory views. This changed as Luce turned toward policy, especially China and Chiang. His publications now presented news revealing Luce's opinions. His magazines ridiculed opponents and championed Luce's foreign policies. According to White, "No restraint bound him in using his magazines to spread the message of his conscience."[22] Luce viewed Nazi Germany with fright. America could not be isolationist. The United States had to accept armed intervention in Europe and dominate the postwar world, which Luce referred to as the "American Century."[23] Luce questioned Russia's intentions. *Time* fostered a Cold War consensus. Critics of America's containment, on the Left or the Right, were roughly treated. Luce told a congressional committee, "I do not think there can be a peaceful coexistence between the Communist empire and the free world."[24]

When they arrived in San Francisco, he turned to White and said he was to call him "Harry," and, in turn, White became "Teddy." Luce's office door, he announced, was not open to everyone, but their offices were never closed to him. That summer and fall Teddy learned the byways of Luce's publishing empire. "Luce insisted the pattern of the world, his reporters and his magazine all conform to the pattern his perception traced over random events." His pattern for China was stubbornly pro-Chiang Kai-shek. Then, one Sunday afternoon, Japan bombed Pearl Harbor; Teddy would be back in Asia as *Time*'s war correspondent.[25] White had left Asia for one year—summer 1941 to summer 1942. While in New York City, Teddy "put aside his grave doubts" and wrote exaggerations of the Nationalist government and Chiang as one who made "magic strides" toward democracy.[26] The years 1942–1944 changed all of that braggadocio.

By November 1942, he had been to Honan (Henan) and reported on its disastrous famine. He had, through the good offices of Mme. Sun Yat-sen, been to see Chiang Kai-shek, who denied everything, though Teddy had pictures to prove it. He wrote a friend in July 1943, "I've had my ass eaten out in Chungking for the Honan famine story I wrote last February. The whole government has been on my tail ever since—I'm almost an outcast. Rumor has it that either T. V. [Soong] or Madame Chian [*sic*] herself has asked Mr. Luce to have me replaced or sacked. Such are the rewards of journalistic honesty."[27] The Chinese government's censorship had become so restrictive that Teddy wrote Chiang himself objecting to it in the spring of 1944.[28] He often found sanctuary with Gen. Joseph W. Stilwell, but after the general's recall in October 1944, he wrote his mother and sister that "General Wedemeyer has the finest mind of any staff officer I ever met, and I think he'll make things hu, [*sic*]. I don't transfer loyalties easy, but this guy is good."[29]

In early 1944, Luce appeased his China critics by publishing a heavily edited article of Teddy's as "Life Looks at China" in the May 1, 1944, issue of *Life* magazine. *Life* would not abandon Chiang, as White had suggested but, instead, would praise him.[30] In White's memoir, *In Search of History*, he reviewed the heated "colloquy" between them that finally resulted in publishing White's article. It was the last time that Luce let him comment on Chiang's China, but not on Chiang himself. White had flown back to New York City to convince Harry that "we must now, finally, tell the truth about China, for Chiang Kai-shek was doomed unless he could be shocked into reform by America." Luce's argument, as White stated it, was "whether redemption was possible for the sinner or whether America (meaning *Time-Life-Fortune*) must cast him out." Their "intellectual volleying," as Teddy put it, he quoted from extensively. Luce's bottom line, according to Teddy, was that "though Chiang's government was wicked, it was less wicked than the Japanese or than Stalin's Communism; and that in Chiang lay our hope." White further stated that only after he had returned to China "was I persuaded by facts, murder, execution and incompetence that Chiang was no longer a useful vessel either of American or Christian purpose."[31]

Actually, there was much more to the dialogue between Teddy and

Harry than White chose to relate later in his memoir, *In Search of History*. On April 3, 1944, Luce told White, "You have written undoubtedly the most important article about China in many years, perhaps ever. And perhaps few important articles ever published will prove to be more important for America." The compliment, Luce insisted, was "not for the sake of apple-sauce," but because it was impossible not to say it and because it placed a heavy responsibility on the editor: Luce was both editor in chief and, like it or not, a China expert. "And so I will have to undertake to argue with you on some points of your article—probably at no point whatever concerning your reporting, but at one or two important points of your thesis."

He commented by making five points. First, Luce blamed most of the corruption, inefficiency, and lack of reform on conditions imposed by Chongqing due to the war. "War has had the effect of stultification: in politics as in life." Second, the legend of Chinese civilization should not be romanticized. "However defined or located in time and space, Chinese civilization is, by almost any standard of value, one of the supreme achievements of post-Cro-Magnon man." One should not view China only through the point of view of 1940–1944 Chongqing but see its entire tapestry. Third, it was wrong to ascribe all virtue to the "Chinese peasant—common man —and give practically no credit at all to Leadership [specifically] To ignore as you do the immense toil of countless reformers which centered finally in the crisis-leadership of Chiang Kai-shek, is surely to overlook objective phenomena which History is not yet ready to write off." Fourth, Luce excused Chiang's book, *China's Destiny*, which attacked foreigners, as something "to be well slapped for the unchristian spirit he exhibited in writing it as he did in the first place." Yet there was something in it that had to be "sympathetically understood—and that is the effort of Chinese to discover the moral basis of their Reconstruction not in the morality of the West, but in their own, as they think, indigenous morality," He found it "very strange to be defending the cause of Confucius." Most, nevertheless, "who knew China knew that however perfect Chinese civilization might be in philosophic essence, it had fallen into a very sad and crude state of corruption, gross superstition and dishonor." China required a "profound reformation from stem to stern." The spirit of reform in China was a "spill-over" of evangelical zeal from the West. The schizophrenia of the West—Christianity and progress—brought reform while it exploited China. China asserted "Chinese-ism [that is] wholeness of its own in an appeal to Confucius [and] Of course this appeal can become nothing more than a tool of reaction. It may close the door to the very universalism of which Confucius was so great a prophet." Finally, fifth, it was not America's job to order the KMT to come to terms with the CCP.[32]

Teddy responded by taking up Luce's points. He agreed the war, especially the effects of the blockade and inflation, "have basically affected the political equations in Chungking." Nevertheless, White insisted he was trying to distinguish between what was "irremediable" due to the blockade and what was "remediable": "The political situation, however, is different. Here there are a number of alternatives and I believe the one that the Kuomintang has chosen is wrong. I think the political situation is remediable and I wish to set it apart." About the legend, Teddy believed it to be true and not legend, and he asked for space to enlarge that section. Of leadership, he could not name liberals without the fear that they would be severely punished as "America's running dogs [and] I would be putting the kiss of death on them." But he could cite Chiang's greatest contribution to China—the unification of the nation. About Confucius, China could not cast him out even if it wished to do so: "What China must do is to realize that the west is not merely playing with barbarian tricks, but that the west is far more than that—the west is Christian ethic and morality, the west is Greek intellectual inquiry, the west is Hebraic conscience, the west is Anglo-Saxon democracy, the west is Roman Law. . . . [O]ther civilizations that interlock with us must understand us and try to cut out their gears to fit—otherwise there is friction." For Luce's last point, Teddy did not feel the KMT had to make concessions or yield to the CCP. Rather, "if the Kuomintang goes consistently more reactionary they will force everyone in society . . . into the hands of the Communists." To save his government, Chiang had to give China liberty, reorganize landholdings, and grant basic democratic rights. Otherwise, the Communists and the people would, by promise or reality, "go over to Uncle Joe."[33] After much haggling, Teddy commented, "I pushed Luce as far as he would go (publishing that Chiang's Kuomintang combined 'the worse features of Tammany Hall and the Spanish Inquisition') and he restrained my angers, still heated by the Honan famine, as far as I could let myself be restrained."[34]

The actual article by White, "*Life* Looks at China," appeared in *Life* on May 1, 1944.[35] What Luce had termed perhaps the most important article ever written on China had been significantly altered by the editor in chief and his court magician, Whittaker Chambers. They spared Chiang any direct criticism. Teddy's attack was redirected to the "CC clique" of the Chen brothers and a "sycophantic court interested in poisoning his mind and feeding his prejudices [though] he is a man of great intelligence."[36] Luce and Chambers were also responsible for the Chiang apologetics that excused away the generalissimo's vitriolic book, *China's Destiny*, and its attacks on foreign powers and Western influence, with all of its technological tricks. Myths, like Fu Manchu, Confucian nobility of spirit, and the cynicism of Chongqing's "fascist gang," were swept away. Though a land of peasants, they had justifiable pride in their civilization and greatness, which was no myth. For the past thirty years, the Nationalists had restored China's unity by beating back the warlords and communists. The Japanese war was responsible for the blockade, transportation breakdowns, an exorbitant grain tax, runaway inflation, and corruption—though not for the political deadlock in Chungking: the Nationalists insisted on oppression rather than freedom in a period they labeled "political tutelage." The tutelage accounted for a "crumbling away of loyalty to the regime."[37] Though Chiang may have been at fault, which was indirectly hinted at by White, he could be forgiven because "Chiang bears on his shoulders an enormous burden of personal work."[38] The Communists had been "gaining in influence and power [like Tito, while] concurrently within the Nationalist Party a progressive deterioration has set in which makes the ultimate test of strength difficult to determine."[39] The situation was complicated because of a "great and unknown factor: what is the relationship of the Chinese Communist Party to the Soviet Union?"[40] Until that was resolved, how could their "democratic protestations" be assessed? The article concluded that Chiang was "the symbol of China at war, the man whom even the Communists recognize as the only possible leader."[41] The Chinese people, the article insisted, "possessed an affection for America which is one of our greatest assets in foreign affairs." Therefore, it concluded, the United States had a "real obligation [to aid China] on a scale far greater" than before.[42]

After returning to China in the summer of 1944, White became so disenchanted with *Time* that in late 1944 he hung a sign over his Chongqing Press Hostel desk that said, "What is written in this office has no relation to the things that appear in *Time* magazine."[43] In his memoir, he wrote dramatically, "I found that decay had moved faster than even I had anticipated, that the Japanese were destroying what remained of the East China front, and that Stilwell was to be sacrificed. Luce had my full report of the Stilwell crisis in hand when he let the story of the crisis be edited into a lie, an entirely dishonorable story."[44] *Time*'s Stilwell article, "Crisis," appeared in its November 13, 1944, issue, written by Fred Gruin and edited by Chambers. About that article, which marked a turning point in the Harry-Teddy relationship, White wrote, "America must choose, was the message of the story —to support Chiang or yield China to Russia. The story had the tone of apocalypse and, as usual with apocalyptical stories, had the forces and the future all wrong."[45]

Teddy had correctly characterized the Chambers-Luce cover story on Stilwell in *Time*. Stilwell's recall had been used as a cover for *Time*'s message, or what the article called the "basic situation." Stilwell's dismissal was not only an "embarrassing episode [but a] blunder of the first magnitude." Washington, through General Stilwell, Ambassador Gauss, and FDR's personal representatives—Vice President Henry Wallace, Donald

Nelson, and Patrick Hurley—had lectured Chiang Kai-shek on the "urgent need to cooperate with Russia and the Chinese Communists." All of that, according to *Time,* had pushed the ever patient generalissimo too far. He had swallowed his pride when he could not be trusted with Lend-Lease and complained privately that he was being treated as an American "slave" and "thief." Representative Walter H. Judd (R-MN) had words to the effect that "no self-respecting head of state could countenance such an ultimatum." Judd further remarked, "Stilwell did not make the mistake. He was merely the goat of personal government in Washington. We had to back down from an impossible position in which we should never have put ourselves." That, however, did not make the general a pleasant "Uncle Joe"—he was not named "Vinegar" for nothing.

After absolving Chiang and halfheartedly excusing Stilwell, *Time* got at what it termed the "basic situation": "Stripped to the bare facts, the situation was that Chungking, a dictatorship ruling high-handedly in order to safeguard the last vestiges of democratic principles in China, was engaged in an undeclared civil war with Yenan, a dictatorship whose purpose was the spread of totalitarian Communism in China." Only leftists and left-echoing liberals such as Brooks Atkinson (the *New York Times*), Edgar Snow, Agnes Smedley, and their like criticized Chiang and excused Mao. The truth of the CCP was exposed by a disillusioned Chinese Communist called by his alias as "Wild Artichoke" (Wang Shih-wei). His best exposé was of the CCP's bloody fratricidal civil war in Kiangsu. Blockading the CCP was as important as fighting the Japanese because "Yenan is also a war front. If Chiang relaxed the blockade, perhaps all of China would ultimately be lost to the democratic cause."

Time's article, "Crisis," ended on a sobering note from Walter Lippmann's famed book *U.S. Foreign Policy: Shield of the Republic,* in which the journalist maintained that two countries were essential to America's survival and the United States would have to go to war if their existence was threatened: Great Britain and China. If the blockade of Yenan were lifted, the CCP might replace the KMT and, then, turn to Russia rather than America. The apocalyptic note was clear: "If the rift in U.S.-Chinese relations were not quickly repaired, both China and the U.S. would be the losers. For China, the loss might be great. For the U.S. it might be catastrophic."[46]

That *Time* story threw Teddy into a rage. He cabled Luce that if the account of it that he read were true, he would have to resign. Luce fired back, "Keep you shirt on until you have full text of Stilwell cover story." But the published story proved even worse. Then Teddy sent a long letter to Luce noting that neither the KMT nor the CCP was democratic and the United States needed the support of those who could be of the greatest aid against the Japanese, especially if American troops had to land on the Chinese coast in preparation for attacking Japan. Helping Chiang only committed the United States to "meddling" in a civil war, and the United States would come out the loser anyway. Teddy's letter broke down into a two-page introduction and another twenty-seven-page rebuttal of the *Time*'s Stilwell cover story, with the caveat that Harry had to tell him what *Time*'s policy was so that "I honestly know whether I can honestly remain with you." And, he added in his own handwriting just before sending this very important letter off, "I hope with all my heart we are not too far apart for reconciliation."[47]

Teddy admitted that although the KMT was inefficient and corrupt, it still retained the support of its army and the United States; though the CCP was sanctimonious, ignorant of the outside world, and kept social distinctions, it also maintained a one-party democracy and had tremendous potential power. There was, especially, no proof whatever of Russian aid. Teddy was very irritated with *Time*'s handling of the whole Stilwell issue: he had to be sacrificed for Chiang to keep the blockade of Communist Yanan, because it represented an imminent danger of taking over all China and would be a tool of Russia. Teddy called such reasoning a fundamental error to justify the blockade. Those troops had been needed to save South China from the ICHIGO offensive, for which South China had paid dearly. Yet Teddy agreed partly with Walter Judd, who was quoted as saying that FDR's ultimatum was wrong, not that all U.S. military support would be withdrawn if Stilwell was not made commander in chief. Stilwell himself could no longer tolerate an unreformed KMT, but no one ever referred to Chiang as a thief, even though *Time* prominently quoted Chiang as making that accusation of the United States. But everyone could see Lend-Lease goods being sold on the black market. No one had been able to talk with the CCP, until the Dixie Mission, sent to Yanan by Stilwell to investigate the CCP, and then no one urged the CCP to accept Chiang's compromise, except for Hurley. As far as Teddy was concerned, there was more democracy in Yanan than in Chongqing, if one used the term generously. About the informant "Wild Artichoke," he had been free to publish, more than could be done in Chongqing, and rather than disappearing, he was in a tuberculosis sanitarium. In the end, Teddy wanted to remain friends with Harry, but he was not going to keep apologizing for *Time*.[48]

It was now that *Life* published White's most controversial piece, "Inside Red China," hitting the newsstands on December 18, 1944. It also was heavily edited to avoid condemning Chiang, who was spared. His advisers were pilloried. If he could reform his government, Americans would adopt him. Even the editor's lead-in to White's article indicated the Japanese ICHIGO offensive threatened to cut China in half and, therefore, the "U.S. government has been urging Generalissimo Chiang Kai-shek to accept the Communists' help in a united campaign to stop the Jap invader."[49] With this left-handed apology by editor in chief Luce out of the way, White's article began.

Teddy laid his article's groundwork by giving the impression of Yanan as a place filled with resolve, organization, and efficiency. "The people within this tiny gobbet of loess are the eyes, ears, nerves, and tentacles of the Communist war against Japan."[50] Behind the Red armies, there was a base of popular peasant support because their social structure was reorganized by reducing rents from 40 percent to 20 percent. Further, "you treat him [peasant] like a man, ask his opinion, let him vote for his local government and police, let him vote himself a reduction of rents, let him vote an army and militia—if you do all that you have given him a stake in society."[51] With typical optimism, Teddy maintained, "The Communists feel that if all adults of all classes are given a vote the Party can retain control of the masses and that, therefore, democracy is precisely the best medium for the three-fold development of China itself, of the Communist Party and of the masses."[52] Most important, the ferocity of the Communist war effort versus the Japanese made the Reds popular. As White put it, "They offered the peasants protection, and they offered resistance, the only possible outlet for the terrible, quenchless hatred of the Chinese peasant for the Japanese soldier."[53]

Luce answered that support for Chiang was nothing more than aiding Churchill's fight against Hitler.[54] In February 1945, another one of his stories was so thoroughly edited by Chambers that not a single word of his survived. Finally, in April he was told to stop all political reporting for four or five weeks and restrict himself to "colorful yarns."[55] He decided to continue with *Time* only to hold his credentials as a war correspondent.[56]

After that, an aide-mémoire was drawn up between the dueling star journalist and his editor in chief by Allen Grover, a Luce deputy and sometime go-between mediator.[57] Grover wrote Teddy, "As Harry says, an aide memoire can be a useful thing in human relations. I hope this is such a one. . . . Whether or not you and Time Inc. can get along may depend now and then on getting specific agreements on specific points." There had to be a "mutual agreeableness of behaviour."[58]

Teddy received the aide-mémoire in mid-November 1945 from Grover: "After discussing with Harry Luce the various problems raised by your desire to speak and write on China in the next few months, Harry made the following suggestions which I relay to you." There were three: First, there was to be a three-cornered discussion with Harry, Teddy, and a pro-Chiang journalist, Charlie Murphy. As Grover stated, the conference's purpose was to "criticize, debate, deny, tear apart whatever case is made for the Central Government or for any aspect of American policy in China on which you may disagree with Murphy or Luce." Murphy would then write a piece to be published by *Life*. Second, after Murphy's publication, Teddy either would enter directly into a "colloquy" with Luce on U.S. policy in China or could submit a candid piece of his own frank views, but "he does ask that after you have done the first draft you will accord him the privilege of making whatever points he wants to make." And, third, Luce requested that for four to six weeks Teddy was to refrain from dwelling on the "failures of the National Government in 1944" publicly.[59] White responded on November 16, 1945; he considered that a "fair proposition." Further, "As I understand it, after Murphy publishes, I submit my draft, talk it over very earnestly with Harry himself, then publish an uncensored version of what I consider to be the real situation in China."[60] He understood incorrectly.

White sent a memo to Tom Mathews, managing editor of *Time*, well after its Stilwell cover issue of November 13, 1944. He now understood that the "China Policy" of *Time* over the past year since the Stilwell cover's "turning point" had become "indistinguishable from the official propaganda of the Kuomintang party. In no other instance in world politics have we identified ourselves so undiscriminatingly [sic] with one man and one party, neither in Russia, Britain, South America, or at home." He then summarized *Time*'s China policy: it never criticized Chiang in any way; it printed Chiang's promises as if they were facts; it failed to note noncommunist independent democratic elements that opposed Chiang; it "kissed off" Chiang's brutality—concentration camps, secret police, tortures, and severe censorship while simultaneously attributing those faults to the communists; it ignored Chiang's starvation policies, his press gangs and corrupt conscription system, and his unfair tax collection; and it held that it was necessary to support Chiang to avoid the Russian supported CCP and, thus, spread the "Red bogey" throughout *Time*'s China columns—even though "there has never been during the war the slightest military aid from one to the other, nor the slightest evidence of organizational direction from Moscow."

Only one side of China's story had been presented: "It is my belief that the picture of heroism and glory is only true if it is balanced by a factual presentation of the other side of the ledger." For a balance to be achieved, White suggested taking the following steps: first, a strict adherence to the facts; second, while acknowledging the KMT as the government of China, list its "sins of error and commission," especially comparing its promises against the realities of Chinese life; third, recognize the "historic sympathy and community of interests that link China and America as enduring friends"; fourth, dissociate *Time*'s assessment of the CCP with its evaluation of the American Communist Party; and fifth, if civil war erupted, *Time* "should report it not as a crusade either for democracy or against Communism [but] as a tragedy of world dimensions which American [*sic*] can view with sorrow, taking the side of neither one group or the other."[61]

Luce celebrated the end of the war with his first two postwar issues of *Time*'s cover—one of Douglas MacArthur and the other of Chiang Kai-shek. He asked Teddy to write the Chiang story; Teddy refused. Luce accused White of political partisanship and ordered him home. White left China on September 18, 1945, flying across the Hump, India, Africa, and the Atlantic. Arriving in New York, he saw his first task as writing a book that explained what was happening in China. He asked his fellow China correspondent Annalee Jacoby to coauthor it. "I was determined to be the first with the story of the inevitable collapse of Chiang Kai-shek—even if it meant full clash with *Time* and Harry Luce."[62]

In White's memoir, he reports on the ending of his relationship with Time, Inc., just as *Thunder Out of China* was completed and he was sending a copy of it to Luce: "not for censorship, but for courtesy's sake—and without breaking stride reported for reassignment as foreign correspondent at the *Time* magazine offices." Some weeks later, they met. As Teddy noted, "The session was highly emotional [Luce] was terribly angry." Hersey, he recounted, had already told Luce to his face that "there was as much truthful reporting in *Pravda* as in *Time* magazine."[63] Luce called White and Hersey "ingrates." He wanted to know whether White would accept any assignment, but he refused to tell White what that would be, though White had asked for Moscow. Luce continued to insist on whether White would accept any assignment offered. He gave White one week to answer. On Friday, July 12, 1946, White replied: No! Luce, though away on vacation, had expected that answer. He officially replied to Teddy in a letter dated June 29, 1946 by sacking him.[64]

White returned to work for *Life* only after Luce passed away in 1967. In 1951, Luce visited Teddy in Paris and had a "long, warm chat."[65] Nevertheless, each still maintained that he had been right all along about China.

• • •

That 1946 book, *Thunder Out of China,* written with fellow *Time* journalist Annalee Jacoby, was a best-selling commentary about politics, revolution, and why "America should get out of China, *now,* should let China find its own way into the future, by itself."[66] White and Jacoby boldly set out their view that "China must change or die."[67] In their introduction, they indicated that while crushing Japan, "America's war had cut blindly across the course of the greatest revolution in the history of mankind, the revolution of Asia." American military technicians beat Japan but did not understand the politics involved. Japan's defeat did not bring peace. The peace of Asia and American security depended on understanding that "both victory and peace rested on the measure with which the strength of the people could be freed from feudal restraints." According to the authors, only General Stilwell comprehended that fact, which his policy strove to support, and which was why he was relieved. Chiang, the Japanese, and the allied technicians misunderstood the war. When Chiang tried to preserve the old fabric of society, he was unable to defeat the Japanese, and powerless to preserve his own authority. Even America "could not recapture for him the power that had been his in the first glorious year of the war of national resistance."[68]

Historian Barbara Tuchman thought, along with Robert Sherwood, that FDR was willing to cashier Stilwell because Chiang would appoint another American general. Marshall opposed the recall, but "an unofficial version of the President's attitude was conveyed by [Harry] Hopkins to [H. H.] Kung at a dinner party and immediately telegraphed to [T. V.] Soong on October 1." Consequently, Kung's telegram noted that since it concerned China's sovereignty, FDR would comply with a request for Stilwell's recall. As Tuchman concluded, "This was what Chiang and Soong had been waiting for and all they needed."[69]

Stilwell was formally relieved on October 24 by Gen. A. C. Wedemeyer and on November 17 Ambassador Clarence Gauss by Maj. Gen. Patrick Hurley. Any effort to court the Reds was thrown away by Hurley: "It was," the authors remarked, "the course of American diplomacy during the year 1945 that finally convinced the Chinese Communists that America was a hostile power."[70] From criticizing Hopkins and FDR, the authors focused on Hurley.

Hurley had failed, in the authors' opinion, in all three of his assignments: first, to secure American authority over the Chinese Nationalist army; second, to promote harmony between Chiang and Stilwell; and third, to make peace between the Kuomintang and the Communists. On the last of these, in November 1944, the Reds were willing to sign agreements granting them U.S. military aid, but they would not turn their armies over to Chiang in exchange for only one proffered seat on the Nationalist Defense Council in return for a one million–man army. In other words, "The Communists would accept no solution that left China governed by the will of one man; Chiang would accept no solution that challenged his complete authority."[71]

Thunder Out of China ended with two important observations: first, peace between Chiang and Mao would have ensued if Stilwell's recommendations had been followed; and second, the year before victory, America had been in the position of an arbiter, but now it was reduced to a partisan to save Chiang. In October 1945, at a conference between Chiang and Mao, the latter rejected Chiang's compromise, the one supported by Hurley and Wedemeyer. It would have required, according to the authors, submission to Chiang's demand for "full Kuomintang control over the areas in debate to the Communist submission to the old bureaucracy, the old landlords and gentry, in every county and village. It meant high taxes again, high interest rates, and the brutality of the old village gendarmes." At the end of November, Hurley resigned, leaving behind a bankrupt policy in which America was a partisan in a civil war rather than judge in a dispute, and the choice was either Chiang or Mao to the exclusion of any middle way. In addition, it ranged Russia against the United States in Asia, because Mao was forced into the Soviet camp.

When Gen. George C. Marshall arrived as Hurley's replacement, he arranged a truce in January 1946 to form a multiparty interim government. In April 1946, when he returned, that compromise had also collapsed. Chiang's gamble to hold Manchuria also failed. He continued to maintain that peace would come only with the submission or surrender of the communists. By late summer, the CCP refused. "Marshall co-opted a wise and dignified American missionary, Dr. J. Leighton Stuart, to be ambassador as his fellow envoy. Within a few weeks the two men issued a joint statement admitting the failure of their diplomacy and declaring that it was a seeming impossibility to arrive at any peaceful solution agreeable to both parties."[72]

Thunder Out of China sold well over a half-million copies. One of its earliest reviewers, a China expert, called it a "brilliant and important book."[73] Even politicians and statesmen, the reviewer declared, "have been obliged to take account of its impact on public opinion in this country and in China." The review, for instance, noted President Truman's December 18, 1946, statement clarifying U.S. policy as well as Secretary of State George C. Marshall's announcement of the termination of America's efforts at mediation. According to the reviewer, "This rapid series of events, whether coincidental or not, has substantiated the basic contentions of the book under consideration relative specifically to the reactionary tendencies within the Kuomintang and the grotesque ineptitudes of past American policy." He called the book a "masterpiece of reporting" and at times reaching to "literary heights." The reviewer faulted White and Jacoby only for not crediting the Kuomintang's past contributions, but he went on to say that as a universal dictum, their following statement could not be controverted: "China must change or die." In addition, Donald G. Tewksbury pointed out that the book's policy recommendations were deeply in conflict "with certain trends in American life than [they] revealed in the book." The reviewer concluded by calling the book "a forceful and poignant plea for justice for the Chinese people."[74]

In less than a year after General Stilwell died of cancer in 1946, his widow asked White to edit her husband's diaries. "White was amazed and shocked at the contents of Stilwell's diaries."[75] Stilwell had used such epithets as

"Peanut" and the "crazy little bastard" to describe Chiang. By editing these diaries, White realized that he would not reenter China as long as Chiang ruled. Their publication, *The Stilwell Papers,* made waves similar to those of *Thunder Out of China.* Some reviewers considered White a leftist, a fellow traveler, even a communist. White's old Harvard mentor John K. Fairbank called the publication a thoroughgoing castigation of Chiang, whereas Richard Watts of the *New Republic* thought it a significant addition to the China story.[76]

• • •

Maj. Gen. Patrick J. Hurley's role as FDR's "personal representative" in the Stilwell crisis was to mediate differences and stabilize the Chinese military situation—perhaps also arrange military unity with the Reds—in the summer of 1944. It is worthwhile, briefly, to repeat this story, but from Hurley's vantage point. In this role, he became a major critic of White. His appointment came about because of Vice President Henry Wallace's trip to Chongqing in the spring of 1944 to promote KMT-CCP negotiations. Wallace had urged FDR to send someone to convince Chiang to reform and move toward a united front with the Reds. Hurley's appointment originated in the War Department with Secretary of War Henry Stimson. FDR had wanted Hurley to reconcile Chiang with Stilwell as well as to be Ambassador Gauss's replacement. Hurley did not arrive in Chongqing until September 7, 1944. He knew little about the issues involved but rushed ahead anyway, completely failing in the reconciliation of General Stilwell to Generalissimo Chiang Kai-shek. He then proceeded to his next task—reconciling Generalissimo Chiang Kai-shek to Chairman Mao Zedong.

On November 7, 1944, Hurley arrived unannounced in Yanan. On that day, he had sent a telegram to FDR informing him that he was taking advantage of a previous invitation by the CCP to come there. It would, he wrote, be a brief trip to see whether there was any basis for a KMT-CCP agreement. He carried with him a draft "Basis for Agreement" worked out with Chiang: unification of forces under the central government, support of Sun Yat-sen's principles, army ranks and pay would be the same, and all parties would be given legal status.[77] He had already failed to make peace between Stilwell and Chiang; now he attempted the same feat between Chiang and Mao. Hurley, White noted, disliked being instructed on China, and worse, he betrayed White's private conversation with Mao—about no agreement being possible—to both Washington and Mao, and both subsequently rejected him, Washington eventually accusing him as one of those who lost China.[78] Nevertheless, in three days of negotiating, Hurley got the Communists to sign a facetious draft document as a basis for discussions with Chiang, which Zhou Enlai would conduct: "The Americans were promising to abolish Chiang's government and replace it with a coalition government in which their [communist] armies, their [communist] government, would qualify for the guns they wanted." Zhou flew to Chongqing to negotiate and obtain Chiang's signature to the Hurley document, but it was a hopeless mission, and in less than a month, Zhou returned to Yanan.[79] The key phrase in that document, aside from lip service to a "Coalition National Government" and a long third section outlining a Chinese version of the American Bill of Rights, was that "the supplies acquired from foreign powers will be equitably distributed."[80]

Both Chiang and Mao agreed in principle to Hurley's five points as a basis for talks: unify the military, recognize Chiang as both president and military leader, support democracy and Sun's three principles, legalize the Chinese Communist Party, and create one army with equal treatment of all soldiers. To Hurley's chagrin, Chiang would not meet the communist demand for a true coalition government with full and meaningful participation and freedom to seek support throughout the country. Short of these, the communists would accept recognition of the various governments they had established and American military supplies.[81]

Hurley's trip to Yanan on November 7, 1944, did succeed in getting Mao's signature to a revised five-point counterplan: coalition, reform, a United National Military Council, military supplies equally distributed, and legalization of the communists and others. Two additions were inserted: promote progress and utilize the American Bill of Rights. Chiang declined these because the "agreement would ultimately amount to giving the government to the Communists; Hurley said he disagreed."[82] Chiang again offered more counterproposals: incorporate the Red Army, provide equal treatment, legalize the Communist Party and grant it a place on the National Military Council, and create a democratic state on Sun's principles. He expected communist support in the war and postwar. He also demanded complete control of the communist troops immediately.[83]

On November 17, 1944, FDR had Hurley formally replace Gauss as ambassador. Hurley presented a three-point proposal to Zhou Enlai: promote democratic processes, give communist representation on the National Military Council, and require the communists to turn over all of their armies. On December 8, these items were rejected. Zhou cited the unwillingness of Chiang to end one-party rule and accept coalition government.[84] Chiang called this rejection a ruse. After this denial, the Reds' position hardened: they were unwilling to negotiate until the KMT released political prisoners, withdrew their northern blockade of Shansi (Shanxi), abolished all repression, and ended all Secret Service activities. When Gen. Robert McClure, Wedemeyer's chief of staff, made a proposal for military cooperation with the Reds, Mao and Zhou suggested they go to Washington to negotiate;

Marshal Zhu De sought twenty million dollars of U.S. aid directly through the Foreign Service officers, but all these attempts only heightened Hurley's paranoia.[85]

Foreign Servicemen such as John Paton Davies, John Emmerson, Raymond Ludden, and John Service thought Hurley was too inflexible and that a deal could be cut solely with Mao: "Hurley found their 'relationship' to the Embassy exasperating, but the content of their reports often more so."[86] Their dispatches suggested the strength, efficiency, and honesty of the communists and their support by large numbers of Chinese. Oppositely, they called Chiang corrupt, inefficient, and lacking popular support. In a memorandum, Davies called again for more effort.[87]

For Hurley, "Such reports represented defeatism and, in his view, accounted in part for the impasse in late December."[88] In January 1945, Hurley contacted Mao and told him that Chiang wanted to reorganize his war cabinet by allowing significant communist representatives, plus other more liberal reforms. Zhou returned to Chongqing on January 24, but all of this amounted only to an offer of a troika of an American officer under Chiang and placed in charge of Red armies, including a communist to advise the generalissimo, with a war cabinet of seven to nine, containing all parties. Yet the American representative was attached to Chiang, thus tying the Reds to Chiang indirectly. Zhou rejected this. Through all of these failures, FDR continued to support Hurley. Russian entrance in the Far East would make the CCP more "truculent" and Chiang's situation even more difficult. Perhaps this was why FDR "supported Hurley, even though he received plenty of contrary advice through the State Department."[89]

What was the real history of China, then? When Ambassador Hurley arrived in Washington for consultations in March 1945, he was greeted by a February report done by his Chongqing staff in his absence. The ever suspicious ambassador thought of it as a stab in his back. His staff argued that achieving unity between the KMT and the CCP through diplomacy was an important goal, but increased military and economic aid might make Chiang even more reluctant to compromise. Especially, "The Generalissimo . . . needed to be told, not asked, regarding U.S. aid to the CCP, and this would force him to terms quicker than anything else."[90] Such a policy, they maintained, would gain everyone's cooperation and keep the CCP in America's rather than the USSR's orbit. Hurley's anger at what he believed a disloyal act resulted in getting these officers reassigned or transferred, even though they continued to press for a more flexible policy. Davies kept insisting that a politically bankrupt regime should not be supported. It would be better to try to win the Chinese communists over to the American side.[91]

It should be noted that during 1949 while John Service reported to the

Foreign Service personnel, "Hurley . . . suggested publicly that I gave the Communists the text of this memorandum. This is entirely untrue." Besides, he never suggested ditching Chiang and that the memo was solely for Stilwell.[92] Even Hurley saw the CCP as something less than communists, and Davies believed them to be opportunists. Service considered them democrats. Many thought them to be agrarian reformers, even though journalists such as James Bertram, Agnes Smedley, Freda Utley, and Edgar Snow cautioned that they were committed Marxists-Leninists. The "U.S. Ambassador and the officers thought reconcilable two irreconcilable forces."[93]

After FDR's death in April 1945, the State Department's policy became vague. On the one hand, it counseled fixity of purpose, and on the other hand, it suggested that Hurley maintain flexibility. Pursuant to this, Hurley got the Reds to agree to resume negotiations in late June 1945. A seven-man committee flew to Yanan in early July and returned with a communist demand calling off the National Congress and, instead, holding a political conference of all parties.[94] Realizing the USSR's importance in sorting out the China tangle, Hurley had stopped in Moscow and received Stalin's assurances in agreeing to a free democratic China under Chiang, though cautioned by George F. Kennan and Averell Harriman that Russia would "cooperate with whatever side seemed best to serve her interests."[95] Stalin had agreed at Yalta to such a policy. To affirm further Stalin's intentions, Harry Hopkins met with Stalin from May 26 to June 6, 1945, and he received the same commitment. Truman was delighted. He wrote Hurley, "Stalin has made to us a categorical statement that he will do everything he can to promote unification under the leadership of Chiang Kai-shek."[96] Harriman also affirmed this. Hurley was then allowed to inform Chiang of the Yalta agreements and Stalin's intentions on June 15, to which the United States would adhere strictly. Nevertheless, T. V. Soong negotiated the Treaty of Friendship and Alliance with the Soviets, and Stalin demanded and got by August 14, 1945, joint railway ownership in Manchuria, a free port at Dairen (Dalian), and the use of Port Arthur. In return, Stalin renewed his promises made at Yalta to Hopkins and Harriman.[97]

Simultaneously, reports of rising conflict between the CCP and KMT spread as each side raced to occupy areas evacuated by the Japanese and secure their weapons. Hurley arranged a face-to-face meeting of Chiang and Mao in late August and personally flew to Yanan to fetch the chairman and Zhou Enlai. Mao's demands on September 3, 1945, amounted to a political partitioning of China at the Yangtze. Russia's invasion of Manchuria had strengthened Mao's hand. Truman's reaction was to promise Chiang aid in order to gain peace and security in areas formerly occupied by the Japanese, but that aid should not be diverted. That proved to be a fatuous request. Wedemeyer, backed by Secretary of the Navy James Forrestal and

Secretary of War Robert Patterson, argued for supporting Chiang and raising U.S. involvement in China's civil war. Washington was not ready for
that. The rapidly collapsing situation encouraged Hurley to resign, though
both Truman and Byrnes initially resisted. Criticism of Hurley mounted in
the press and Congress. At the end of November, Hurley resigned. His letter of resignation emphasized that a section of the State Department supported communism, which astonished Byrnes and Truman.[98] The president passed Hurley's letter of November 26, 1945, around to his cabinet
and said, "'Look what this son-of-a-bitch has done to me.'" Truman accepted his resignation with a blunt letter of six lines.[99]

On the following day, November 27, 1945, the president appointed Gen.
George C. Marshall as his special envoy to China with the personal rank of
ambassador. He succeeded the following year in getting the two sides,
Chiang and Mao, together. Marshall attended many meetings, but by
midyear, he could see there was no reconciliation in sight. He returned and
told Truman about the situation. From then on, America had no China policy except "let the dust settle." In 1947, Wedemeyer went on a fact-finding
mission, hoping to succeed where Marshall failed. His report faulted the
Nationalists. China policy drifted. Gauss remarked that it would have been
better to abandon the Nationalists and support the communists; Truman
flew Nationalist troops to Chinese coastal cities to displace the Japanese,
but that was a mistake. John Carter Vincent, at the China Desk of the State
Department, said that policy gave the impression of supporting the Nationalists. When the dust had settled, Mao was in control of China and
Chiang reduced to Taiwan.[100]

Hurley's resignation letter was a sharp indictment of State Department
officials who, according to Hurley, had "openly advised the Communist
armed party to decline unification of the Chinese Communist Army with
the National Army unless the Chinese Communists were given control."[101]
These same diplomats had "continuously advised the Communists that my
efforts in preventing the collapse of the National Government did not represent the policy of the United States."[102] He reiterated that throughout this
time the "chief opposition to the accomplishment of our mission came from
the American career diplomats in the Embassy at Chungking and in the
Chinese and Far Eastern divisions of the State Department."[103] His shifting
of the blame of his own failures was clear: "A considerable section of our
State Department is endeavoring to support communism generally as well
as specifically in China." He ended his diatribe by calling for the complete
reorganization because the "Hydra-headed direction and confusion of our
foreign policy in Washington during the late war is chargeable to the weakness of our Foreign Service."[104] It was incumbent upon the administration
to undertake a "complete reorganization of our policy-making machinery

beginning at the lower official levels." This would prevent America's foes from "defeating American policies and interests [due to] a weak American Foreign Service."[105]

Hurley's personal vituperations and accusations did not stop there. Teddy White appeared before the Committee on Foreign Relations of the Senate in its "Investigation of Far Eastern Policy" on December 10, 1945. Hurley claimed, "American policy in China was to uphold the Government of the Republic of China; that the career men were opposed to that, and were supporting the attempts of the armed political Communist party in China to overthrow the government; and they [documents Hurley submitted or asked for] will sustain that contention."[106] Chairman Tom Connally (D-TX) opened by reading a letter stressing the "extraordinary gravity of the charges made by former Ambassador to China, Patrick J. Hurley." That letter—sent by White, Richard Watts Jr., Eric Sevareid, Annalee Jacoby, and Jack Belden—wanted American journalists to go on record as "testifying to the complete integrity and conscientious devotion to American interests of the career diplomats whom Mr. Hurley so indiscriminately attacks." Hurley, they maintained, "disagreed with them, and he got rid of them. By doing so, he deprived himself and the State Department of American sources of information that his predecessors had found both valuable and objective." White appeared before the committee with their full support.[107]

Connally told White, "It has been testified here by General Hurley that these two gentlemen [George Atcheson and John Service] who were career men, were engaged in sabotaging the U.S. policies and efforts in China."[108] What did White know of that? White's entire testimony hinged on his maintaining, "I know of no attempt whatsoever to sabotage General Hurley's policies in China by any career officer of the State Department."[109] White's point was that he knew these men well; he had lived with them day and night in "discomfort and danger," so he was aware of what they thought. He could testify that those men fought zealously to create a "united, democratic China." He stated, "I do not think it would be possible for any member of the press in Chungking to be unaware of any conspiracy or of any attempt to sabotage Ambassador Hurley."[110]

Senator Arthur H. Vandenberg (R-MI) questioned White's qualifications as a witness "to determine whether or not that was their point of view, and whether or not they were encouraging their own point of view." White replied at length, based on "whether or not any officer or any reporting observer of the State Department should temper his reports to agree with the opinions or prejudices of his superiors." Such persons would, in White's opinion, be useless and dangerous. He wanted, especially, to testify on behalf of John Service, because he knew him best.[111] Service worked on the orders of Stilwell; he reported the facts. As White put it, "If their opinions differed with those of General Hurley, that is regrettable; they reported the facts as honestly as it can be done." Service had a brilliant record and went to Yanan. White's bottom line was, even more vividly in his own words, "I do not believe it would be possible in Chungking for a man to attempt to conspire with the 'Communist armed party' as General Hurley calls it, in an attempt to overthrow the Government of Chiang Kai-shek, without the press corps knowing of it." White concluded about Service: "I am absolutely sure he was not conspiring with anybody to overthrow our Government. He was reporting the facts as he saw them."[112]

When asked by Vandenberg whether Lend-Lease, if extended to the CCP, would have made the Nationalist government fall, White replied unequivocally, "No, sir; I do not believe so." Then Vandenberg and White argued over whether holding such an opinion was inimical to American interests or whether it was to "report on what he has seen and on what he knows of China. An employee's superiors can either accept or reject his recommendations, but he must report, as an intelligence officer, himself, the situation as he sees it." Vandenberg disagreed and again charged that White was not in a position to "say whether or not these gentlemen were or were not loyal to the service when they were doing the thing you say they ought to do. That is for us to decide." White replied, "I am not trying to transgress upon your prerogatives, sir. I am merely saying that to the best of my belief and knowledge these men were serving their country as honorably as they possibly could, that they were reporting the truth, that no one of them ever attempted to sabotage, undermine, or overthrow the Government of Chiang Kai-shek." Vandenberg continued to believe that it might be White's opinion, but it was "hearsay" as far as the hearing was concerned.[113]

When Senator Warren R. Austin (R-VT) suggested White was merely corroborating the opinion of Service, Teddy disagreed: "No, sir. There is a charge leveled against these men that they were attempting to overthrow the Government of Chiang Kai-shek, and that they were attempting to sabotage American policy; and I am coming here and offering to testify that these men did not do so."[114] When Senator Alexander Wiley (R-WI) asked if these men disagreed with Hurley about what American policy was, Teddy replied, "Never, once! Never, once!" All had concluded, Hurley also, that an "agreement could be reached in China by the various parties on the basis of a full coalition government, and in which the parties would subordinate their armies. . . . [E]very one of us, I believe, in China . . . believed that that is the best policy to be applied."[115] A landing on the Chinese coast was projected in 1944, and that would have required Chinese communist help, White maintained. But Hurley failed to secure that help. If he had succeeded, and only then, Lend-Lease would have been supplied. That was the policy all were in favor of, including Hurley. White again underlined the theme that had brought him to Washington: "All of us know the people who are under attack, and we wanted a chance to proclaim in public our faith in their loyalty and in their honesty and in their good service for our Government. That is, we feel that these men, who underwent hardship, were really ordered into danger by our Government, should not be hauled up in public and so attacked without somebody speaking in their defence."[116]

• • •

White's testimony illustrates the confusion and bitterness over America's wartime policy toward China, which was dominated by strategies of the early period of the conflict. Because of America's Pacific orientation, major efforts were undertaken in 1943 to make China a great power. That required improving China's military substantially, but the war in Europe prevented full implementation. The perplexity in America, resulting from according China Great Power status, given its actual military weakness, further increased because of two views on the Kuomintang. It was recognized that Chiang Kai-shek's government lacked unity and was militarily weak. He was excused due to the Japanese war, China's need for armaments, and America's inability fully to supply China's needs. The United States, according to Luce and the "Asia Firsters," should do everything to strengthen Chiang and increase his prestige even at the expense of its European commitments.[117] Oppositely, there were those, like White, who thought that Chiang had failed to get the support of China's masses. The Kuomintang, it seemed, wanted to leave China's military supplies and great power status to the United States while it prepared an inevitable conflict with the Chinese communists.[118]

Chiang Kai-shek symbolized America's personification of China. Whether America underestimated China's real goals, the Asia Firsters believed American policy was sabotaged by the treasonous activities of some Americans and that led to the fall of Chiang to Mao Zedong in China's civil war. In August 1949, the State Department published a white paper explaining its failed policies. Secretary of State Dean Acheson, in his letter to President Truman accompanying the white paper, wrote, "The unfortunate but inescapable fact is that the ominous result of the civil war in China was beyond the control of the government of the United States. A decision was arrived at within China, if only a decision by default."[119] Acheson was a Europeanist. He had read *The Good Earth* and the Luce publications and been impressed by Generalissimo and Madame Chiang and the fact that they were Christians, but he had also read Teddy White. The China Lobby of Alfred Kohlberg and his millions of dollars from his former textile trade with China supported the "Senator from Formosa," William Knowland, and Senator

Kenneth Wherry, who both would have lifted up Shanghai to make it Kansas City. Congressman Walter Judd, the former China missionary, joined them as a member of the America-China Policy Association, part of the China Lobby. They credited Acheson with a policy of "letting the dust settle in China." In fact, Congressman Styles Bridges accused Acheson of sabotaging the Chinese Nationalists and appeasing Russia. Probably, Acheson would have recommended recognizing Communist China, and feelers actually came in from Zhou Enlai to the State Department. However, the atmosphere created by the China Lobby was too negative. Acheson attempted to educate the American public with a white paper. The white paper gained only a sound bite in the newspapers: the communist victory was "beyond the control" of the United States. George F. Kennan agreed and pushed the point that Mao was no "stooge" of Stalin. Acheson and Kennan promoted the American policy of "letting nature take its course in China."[120]

In October 1949, the Chinese Communists established a government, and Chiang Kai-shek fled to Taiwan. It seemed to Americans that Soviet control had been imposed upon China: "The image of grateful China acknowledging the benevolent guidance of its American 'elder brothers' became impossible to sustain."[121] Common goals such as China's cooperation with its former allies, stabilizing the Far East, and maintaining U.S. prestige in Asia collapsed. The Asia Firsters exploded at the Truman administration: they believed that Washington's China policies were the consequence of "stupidity at the top—treason just below."[122]

An article, "The United States Sells China Down the Amur," maintained that Nationalist China's collapse resulted from Washington's betrayal of Chiang Kai-shek.[123] This interpretation some Americans used to explain the loss of China and justify their policy toward the Chinese People's Republic. The China Lobby did not invent this interpretation. Rather, that explanation was the "product of the mutual needs of the American public and the China lobby . . . a predisposition among the American people to accept an extreme explanation of events in China."[124]

Once, when reflecting on Luce's influence with David Halberstam, White claimed, "The history of the world would've been changed" if Luce had honestly covered China. In addition, "We would've avoided two wars with Asia. . . . There would've been no Korean War, there would've been no Vietnam War."[125] It took a couple of gurus—Nixon and Kissinger—to make that change; they changed the world. Meanwhile, during the fifties and sixties, U.S. policy toward the PRC remained static. But American images of mainland China took a negative turn.

14

Gurus

The Chinese People's Republic was proclaimed on October 1, 1949, though the full occupation of the mainland by the People's Liberation Army was not completed until May 1950. From then to February 27, 1972, when President Richard Nixon signed the Shanghai Communiqué, a hiatus in Sino-American relations occurred.[1] Two courses of action appeared for the United States. The first was to try to upset communist rule in China. The second was to consider China a "potential Yugoslavia," allowing for eventual recognition and even support. Acheson had indicated, "If Peking should move away from Moscow, she would find America receptive; if she moved closer to Moscow, she would find America hostile, even to the point of using armed force."[2]

In early 1950, Senator Joseph McCarthy contributed to the anticommunist hysteria over the "loss of China." John K. Fairbank called the period an "open season on China specialists." The resulting investigations, he believed, ranged from conscientious concern to political opportunism. A senatorial subcommittee focused on the Institute of Pacific Relations (IPR). The subcommittee claimed "an IPR conspiracy to influence State Department policy makers under Democratic administrations in favor of the Chinese communists."[3] Two specialists were especially attacked—Owen Lattimore for perjury, but a federal court threw out his indictment in 1955, and John S. Service, cleared six times by the State Department Loyalty Board and eventually sacked, but in 1957 reinstated by order of the Supreme Court. Fairbank inferred, "The chief significance of Joseph McCarthy was that he was tolerated so long by those Americans who approved his stated aims but not his methods and yet out of fear were willing to countenance his methods."[4]

Increasingly, the United States pursued a two-Chinas policy. In 1957, China proposed cultural exchanges, but the United States responded with the demand that the PRC renounce force in the Taiwan Straits, whereas the PRC demanded formal recognition of its sovereignty over Taiwan. Nothing changed during President Kennedy's administration. A threatened landing by the Kuomintang on the mainland was vetoed by the United States.[5] In the later 1960s, with the onslaught of the Vietnam War, "China was seen as an increasingly dangerous enemy, the new center of revolutionary communism, and the source of subversive contagion, as Russia had been in the earlier days." These U.S. policies proceeded despite Zhou's arguments for peaceful coexistence and the fact that China's nationalism appeared increasingly more important than its communism. It was at this point that President Richard Nixon and his national security adviser, Henry Kissinger, entered the picture, and the Soviets began putting hostile pressure on the PRC.[6]

Nixon's earliest mention of a change in policy toward the PRC, while a presidential aspirant, was published in a 1967 article by *Foreign Affairs* as "Asia after Viet Nam." He still spoke about Asian "nations in the path of Chinese ambitions"; however, he also wrote about coming to "grips with the reality of China."[7] Here, at last, was a significant movement forward from the once card-carrying member of the China Lobby and former Red baiter. After being nominated in 1968 by the Republican Party for the presidency, he gave an interview to *U.S. News and World Report* on August 9, 1968. He insisted, "We must not forget China. We must always seek opportunities to talk with her, as with the USSR [and] must not only watch for changes. We must seek to make changes."[8]

With his changed attitude and just after being elected, he had already planned to direct foreign policy from the White House rather than from the State Department. Nixon decided that his choice of a national security adviser was crucially important, though, as he later admitted, "I made my choice in an uncharacteristically impulsive way." He knew Henry Kissinger had served as Nelson Rockefeller's foreign policy guru. Nixon arranged to meet Kissinger at his transition office on November 25, 1968. He realized from reading Kissinger's book *Nuclear Weapons and Foreign Policy* that "we were very much alike in our general outlook in that we shared a belief in the importance of isolating and influencing the factors affecting worldwide balances of power." Both saw Vietnam as a short-term policy problem, but in the long term, "I mentioned my concern about the need to re-evaluate our policy toward Communist China, and I urged him to read the *Foreign Affairs* article in which I had first raised this idea as a possibility and a necessity." Kissinger agreed and suggested the National Security Council as developing the best policy options. On that note, then and there, Nixon decided on Kissinger as his national security adviser. Two days later he appointed him. Nixon later reflected, "The combination was unlikely—the grocer's son from Whittier and the refugee from Hitler's Germany, the politician and the academic. But our differences helped make the partnership work."[9]

• • •

In Nixon's inaugural address on January 20, 1969, he alluded to the Chinese by saying that no people should live in "angry isolation."[10] After that, he ordered a complete review of U.S. policy toward China to be carried out by the National Security Council. He wrote Kissinger, "I think we should give every encouragement to the attitude that this Administration is exploring possibilities of rapprochement with the Chinese—privately plant the idea."[11] Kissinger informed the secretaries of state and defense and the director of the Central Intelligence Agency on February 5, 1969, that the NSC's Interdepartmental Group for East Asia would do it, and the "study should incorporate alternative views and interpretations of the issues involved."[12] The NSC's Interdepartmental Group for East Asia's report, "United States–China Policy" (NSSM-14) was completed April 29, 1969. It constituted the first important and official analysis of the Chinese situation for Nixon.

Although China was not an immediate threat to the United States, according to the report, all of Asia could "feel the weight of China's looming mass, and others believe China has a claim to great power status, including representation in the UN Security Council." The United States had a special concern about China because of its "mystique" that distorted America's vision as well as its adversarial relationship since the Korean War. The report considered the "nature of the Chinese 'threat' to U.S. interests and the possible range of U.S. objectives and options in our relations with China." The current hostility had resulted from ideological divergences, national objectives, and U.S. defense commitments in Asia. These causes would continue because, it was considered, the communist dictatorship would remain and China's military capacity would increase, even though there might be some moderation in a post-Maoist era. Other Asians were uneasy about China's objectives. These factors would increase the likelihood of recognition of the PRC by other states. Beijing wanted recognition, accommodation, and modeling after itself—in other words, "to be treated as a major world power and as a primary source of revolutionary ideological leadership, and to gain control of Taiwan." Its objectives were limited by agricultural problems, political confusion, and having only a defensive military capability except near its borders. Although the United States was committed by treaty to Taiwan's defense, it had made no obligations requiring the Republic of China's consent to changing U.S. relations with the PRC. This report, cautious at its beginning, later hinted at a possible major shift in the Far Eastern four-power relationships of the United States, USSR, Japan, and China, although it seemed unlikely under Mao: "A future Chinese leadership may seek, through the manipulation of its relations with these three states, to achieve limited rapprochement with one or more of them."[13]

Any change in U.S.-PRC relations would cause a greater accommodation of states around China's periphery, not necessarily for the United States. About the UN, keeping the PRC out was already problematical, as members thought one-quarter of humanity should be represented, though the ROC should also be there. If there were no prospects for attitudinal changes in the PRC's leadership, then policy options for the United States would be "meager and bleak." Current antagonisms would not be indefinite. Therefore, U.S. objectives could be more flexible: deter aggression; avoid alliances between the PRC and other major states directed against the United States; sustain U.S. influences in East Asia; obtain the PRC's acceptance and co-operation with other Asian countries; achieve relaxation of tensions, especially in arms control, disarmament, and normalizing U.S. political and economic relations with the PRC; resolve Taiwan's status and access to Taiwan; and encourage Taiwan's economic growth.

On normalization, the report directed its readers to tab F: "Diplomatic Contacts to Relations with the PRC." It expanded on Nixon's idea in his *Foreign Affairs* article of bringing the PRC into the mainstream of world politics. The question asked was: "At what level should contact and relations be maintained with the PRC?" It ran through the advantages and disadvantages of the current policy and offered alternatives. At present, the report continued, there were no formal diplomatic or consular relations, only the Warsaw meetings between ambassadors. Though temporarily discontinued, embassy officials did gather, and a revival of the former was being sought to the 134 meetings held since 1954. The first alternative was to await Beijing's initiative to renew or expand contacts. The problem with this was that it was too passive but, the report noted almost in passing, an important point: it "reassures Soviets that U.S. is not developing Sino-U.S. entente against the USSR." Though a straw in the wind or even a casual comment, this was exactly what was to become the most crucial outcome of the Nixon-Kissinger breakthrough to the PRC.

Another possibility was to increase the frequency of talks, allowing the United States to take the initiative. Though this was considered unlikely to get a favorable response, it might provide Beijing with an indication that the United States accepted de facto Peking's position on the mainland. The last alternative considered a foreign ministerial meeting and other higher-level ones, which would open access to the PRC's top levels—a major effort to negotiate Sino-American differences. Again, vis-à-vis the USSR, the report recognized that it would tend to "equalize U.S. treatment of the PRC and the USSR and might increase U.S. flexibility in dealing with both." It was considered a long shot. The United States could propose establishing some kind of "permanent reciprocal representation in Peking and Washington and, if accepted, it would strengthen a détente in Sino-American relations." Curiously, this was seen, if developed, as occurring "during a period of sharp Sino-Soviet tension, [it] stimulates major reassessment by the USSR of Soviet policies toward both the U.S. and the PRC with possible deterioration in U.S.-USSR relations." Exactly the opposite happened and should have been perceived in the report as an advantage to put pressure on the USSR.

The rest of the report adopted a tone of suggesting that little could result in the short run and that only a post-Maoist leadership might be willing to consider a more moderate line in dealing with the United States, but noting—again almost in passing—that "China's leaders probably genuinely feel threatened by a U.S.-USSR-Japan-India 'encirclement.'" This led the Maoist leadership to a siege mentality and probably contributed to a "rigid and defiant stance vis-à-vis the three other major powers in the area." Only a second generation of Chinese leadership might see advantages in a rapprochement with one or more of the three. But the report warned, "Under present circumstances, however, U.S. efforts to exploit Sino-Soviet tensions to pressure the Soviets or entice Peking most probably would result in a worsening of relations between the U.S. and either or both China and the Soviet Union." The report dismissed the geostrategic possibility of triangular diplomacy and poured cold water on it. Yet to everyone's surprise, events swiftly moved exactly in that direction. Rising PRC-USSR hostility, springing from armed conflict along the Manchurian-Mongolian border, may have been the catalyst stimulating things.[14]

The clashes along the Ussuri River in the spring of 1969 may have provided the occasion the report had rejected as impossible. "Ironically," as Kissinger wrote, "it was heavy-handed Soviet diplomacy that made us think about our opportunities." The Russian ambassador to Washington, Anatoly Dobrynin, first raised the issue, adding gory details. Kissinger remarked how the incident "must have shaken the Chinese," and he was intrigued with how unexpected events could have a major impact. The conflict on the Sino-Soviet border continued through April and into May. Kissinger was aware that a Russian invasion of the PRC could tip the geopolitical balance and the mere threat offered an opportunity for China to "reenter the diplomatic arena and that would require it to soften its previous hostility to the United States."[15]

Kissinger analyzed NSSM-14 because of a group discussion on May 15. He found the report treated China's foreign relations bilaterally and that "no reference was made to the global implications of Sino-Soviet tensions and the opportunities for us in triangular relationship." He challenged its "excessive emphasis on China's ideology [and] ignored China's role in the power equation." Finally, he questioned Kremlinologists who asserted that improving U.S.-PRC relations might damage U.S.-USSR diplomacy. In a separate report made to Nixon, he wrote of the "growing obsession of the Soviet leaders with their China problem [and that it could be] turned to our advantage." So Nixon and Kissinger intensified their efforts at contacting Beijing.[16]

Kissinger sliced right down the middle of the NSSM-14 report by suggesting a mix of the two alternative policies: "harshness and restraint." There would be both deterrence and limited efforts to persuade the Chinese to change their policies. If this were followed, then the questions would be whether current U.S. policy was the best possible mix, and, if not, what were the alternatives—more deterrence or more reduction of tensions? Even if the latter, he was ginger, remarking that it would be a "'*Gradual Movement* towards a Reduction in Tension'; *and* not that the option be re-worked to reflect this gradual movement." The gradual movement would be in phases or steps, the first being a continuation of the current military policy with minor political adjustments, then steps to bring trade into balance with that of the USSR, and last lifting travel restrictions. Further studies would elaborate loosening trade controls and alternative UN scenarios.[17]

In July, Nixon made a round-the-world trip, intending to leave "visiting cards for the Chinese at every stop." He told leaders in Indonesia and Thailand that he would reject Soviet calls for some Asian collective-security scheme, emphasizing, "A condominium is out of the question." Nixon was especially candid with Presidents Yahya Khan of Pakistan and Nicolae Ceauşescu of Romania. To the former, for example, he said that "Asia could not 'move forward' if nations as large as China remained isolated."[18] The United States would not be a party to isolating the PRC, and he asked Yahya to tell the top Chinese leadership what he had said. In Romania, he rejected an Asian security pact. Kissinger in August visited the Pakistani ambassador to Washington, Agha Hilaly, and asked him "to establish a secure channel for communicating between the U.S. and the PRC." The ambassador's brother was the Pakistani envoy to China, and his sister had been Kissinger's student at Harvard. Nixon required that channel to be the single confidential point of contact for any further discussions with China.[19]

By August, there were rumors of further bloody clashes on the Sino-Soviet border. Things became so tense that Nixon at an NSC meeting on August 14 declared the United States could not allow China to be "smashed." Kissinger remarked, "If a cataclysm occurred, Nixon and I would have to confront it with little support in the rest of the government—and perhaps the country —for what we saw as the strategic necessity of supporting China."[20] Though by October, the PRC had backed down and called for border negotiations, the "underlying tensions could not be reversed by procedural agreements." By then, Yahya had passed to the PRC information about U.S. willingness to improve relations. Washington removed its patrol of the Taiwan Straits in November and emphasized U.S. interest in talks.[21] In December, the PRC released two Yankee yachtsmen who had recently strayed into Chinese waters. In Warsaw, U.S. ambassador Walter Stoessel exchanged words with the Chinese chargé in an attempt to trigger a start of the talks there. When these became too public, things were moved from the State Department to the White House's so-called back channels. "By the end of 1969, it was apparent that China, too, had made a strategic decision to seek rapprochement with us, even while it fended off the Soviet Union by resuming an intermittent dialogue on the border dispute."[22]

The most productive of these back channels was through the Pakistani ambassador to Washington, Agha Hilaly. As early as October 1969, Kissinger had "indicated that the Pakistanis might communicate with the communist Chinese informally of U.S. intentions to pull out two destroyers from the Taiwan Straits."[23] As the president of Pakistan, Agha Yahya Khan, explained to the Chinese ambassador to his country, the "U.S. is interested in normalizing relations with Communist China and a gesture was withdrawing two destroyers from the Taiwan Straits." He based what he said on a conversation with Nixon in August. Though the Chinese ambassador called this double-talk, Yahya insisted that this message be conveyed to Premier Zhou Enlai. On December 13, the PRC ambassador related China's appreciation to Yahya and freed the two American yachtsmen. In addition, Zhou planned a visit to Pakistan, and the Warsaw talks resumed. President Yahya could tell Zhou when he visited Pakistan that the United States was serious, and, Kissinger added, "If they want to have these conversations in a more secure manner than Warsaw or in channels that are less widely disseminated within the bureaucracy, the President would be prepared to do this."[24] Hilaly met Kissinger again on December 23, and Kissinger noted that Nixon wanted to stay in communication with Yahya. Thus, the Pakistani back channel would continue. These conversations also provided a way to get the talks out of the State Department's hands.[25]

On February 11, 1970, Kissinger made it known to Maj. Gen. Vernon Walters, army and defense attaché in Paris, that the president was ready to establish a more secure channel than Warsaw—even though Stoessel had chased down China's envoy and, on Kissinger's orders, suggested a renewal of the Warsaw talks—in "matters of the most extreme sensitivity."[26] The Warsaw Rounds reopened at their 136th meeting on February 20, 1970, after a two-year pause. Stoessel, at this first resumed meeting, not only suggested "talks at a higher level might be held [but] even went further putting forward the idea of sending a representative to Peking or to Washington for discussion." Lei Yang, the Chinese envoy, replied, "If the U.S. wished to send a representative of ministerial rank or a special presidential envoy to Peking for further exploration of the fundamental principles of relations between the U.S. and the PRC, the Chinese would be prepared to receive him."[27] Both envoys indicated that talks might also occur through other channels. Kissinger's take on this Warsaw session to Nixon was that the Chinese had "picked up that element in our negotiating position which would be the most dramatic development in terms of the effects on the outside world." He meant the Soviets would be "taken aback" by a U.S. envoy in Beijing, the ROC would react adversely, and opinions elsewhere would question U.S. motives. But the PRC would also face public relations problems with an imperialist in Beijing and with their inflexible stand on Taiwan, especially if their position resulted in a U.S. walkout, thus encouraging the USSR to "believe that Chinese explorations of the U.S. option had failed and that the Chinese now had to face the Soviets on their own." Otherwise, a positive response had to be made and great care exercised in selecting a U.S. envoy to Beijing. He believed current negotiations paralleled the 1955 situation when the PRC desired friendly relations, but not the United States.[28]

Simultaneously, the Pakistani back channel showed vigor. Ambassador Hilaly met Kissinger on February 22 with a letter from President Yahya, assessing China's thinking about PRC-U.S. relations: they no longer saw Vietnam as a problem. The United States and the USSR were not in collusion against China. The PRC's actions to U.S. overtures would be "very measured and cautious steps," and negotiations would be "hard and difficult." Expansion of the Vietnamese conflict, in their view, had lessened, and war between the United States and the PRC seemed remote. In response, Kissinger indicated the United States could control press speculation and, therefore, preferred to avoid formal diplomatic means and instead use "a direct White House channel to Peking which would not be known outside the White House and on which we guarantee total security."[29]

At this stage, another back channel was opened through Kissinger's friend Jean Sainteny, a French businessman who had spent many years in Vietnam, who had known Ho Chi Minh personally, and was playing a role to facilitate Kissinger's secret negotiations with the North Vietnamese. Kissinger sent the American military attaché General Walters to Sainteny with a secret message for the PRC and emphasized, "No one, other than the President, myself and General Walters is aware of it." Sainteny was to inform no one, with the exception of President Georges Pompidou. That message in draft opened with the reference to "recent events," meaning the Pakistanis and Warsaw, and that a reliable channel needed to be opened:

"If the Government of the People's Republic of China desires talks that are strictly confidential, the President is ready to establish such a channel directly to him for matters of the most extreme sensitivity." Their purpose was for improving Sino-American relations, known only to Nixon and Kissinger. Initial contact by them would be through Walters, who would relay messages to Kissinger. Kissinger would be prepared to come to Paris and meet with whomever the PRC designated.[30] The text of the final message read as follows:

> The United States had no aggressive intentions concerning Communist China. On the contrary, we would like to establish regular relations with her, recognizing our differences in ideology. We have no interest in establishing military bases in Vietnam, and we believe a peace that takes into account everyone's interests in that area can be achieved. Dr. Kissinger is prepared to talk to a person of stature on the Communist Chinese side if this can be done secretly. The Chinese can reply by getting in touch with Major General Vernon Walters, Senior U.S. Military Attaché, American Embassy, Paris. No one but the President is aware of this message and the Chinese reply should be through General Walters and nobody else.[31]

Again, on June 15, 1970, Kissinger gave Walters another message, similar to the above, wishing to continue the Warsaw Rounds, but pleading for a back channel to maintain complete secrecy: "If the Government of the People's Republic of China desires talks that are strictly confidential and not known by other countries, the President is ready to establish an alternative channel directly to him for matters of the most extreme sensitivity."[32] Their purpose was improvement of relations. The channel could be activated through Walters, and, then, a high-level representative of Nixon's would come to Paris or some other convenient location.[33] Around September 12, 1970, Kissinger reported to Nixon that Walters had still not been able to deliver the message of June 15, though he had tried. Another channel had been attempted through the Dutch, to no avail. There was no choice but to wait and see.[34] Nixon jotted at the bottom, "K—should you not try again on your Walters contact with the Chinese in Paris? Or do we have an offer outstanding?"[35] While Kissinger was in Paris later that month, Sainteny reported that his conversations with Ambassador Huang Chen (Huang Zhen) got nowhere, though he would try to arrange something.[36] Parenthetically, at this time, the Chinese sent a subtle message of their own. The famous journalist Edgar Snow appeared at Mao's side on Tiananmen Square and reviewed the annual anniversary parade on China's National Day, October 1, 1970. It was a first. No American had ever been so honored.

At a meeting with Yahya in the Oval Office, Nixon suggested to the Pakistani president that he should tell the Chinese when he visited Beijing that the United States believed, "It is essential that we open negotiations with China. Whatever our relations with the USSR or what announcements are made I want you to know the following: (1.) we will make no condominium against China and we want them to know it whatever may be put out; (2.) we will be glad to send [Robert] Murphy or [Thomas E.] Dewey to Peking and to establish links secretly." Besides, when Yahya said the Chinese thought the United States was referring to a hotline, the president said, "No, that wasn't what he meant; he was willing to send ambassadors." About secret links, Kissinger was after communications less visible than Warsaw, so the parties could say what was on their minds. The president would consider sending Kissinger or some other high-level contact.[37]

The topic of this conversation was followed up on October 27 with a similar chat with President Nicolae Ceauşescu of Romania, who was then visiting Washington. Kissinger told him the United States wanted to establish political and diplomatic communications with the PRC, free of outside pressures and confined to the White House. Nixon believed there were no more clashing interests. Ceauşescu promised to convey this to China.[38] Interestingly, neither the secretary of state nor the State Department itself was informed of this talk through the Romanians, though they leaked the information to the USSR. "This resulted in the odd situation in which the foreign ministries of China, Pakistan, Romania, and the Soviet Union all knew about the American initiative to China, but the United States' State Department did not." Sainteny also asked if he should further pursue a contact in the Paris embassy of the PRC, citing the importance of Ambassador Huang Chen, a veteran of the Long March and a Mao confidant.[39]

While Nixon continued to bide his time, the NSC staff studied various aspects of a relationship with the PRC by establishing a China Policy Group. This interagency group considered the whole range of China initiatives as well as the entire UN membership question. The State Department had to be content with one more examination of options, their advantages and disadvantages.[40] However, the important initiative that finally achieved a breakthrough occurred through the Pakistanis. On December 9, 1970, Ambassador Hilaly met with Kissinger and reported Zhou Enlai's comments directly:

> This (meaning the reply) is not from me [Chou En-lai] alone but from Chairman Mao and Vice Chairman Lin Piao as well. We thank the President of Pakistan for conveying to us orally a message from President Nixon. China has always been willing and has always tried to negotiate by peaceful means. Taiwan and the Straits of Taiwan are an inalienable part of China

which have now been occupied by foreign troops of the United States for the last fifteen years. Negotiations and talks have been going on with no results whatever. To discuss this subject of the vacation of Chinese territories called Taiwan, a special envoy of President Nixon's will be most welcome in Peking. [Zhou Enlai said, in the course of the conversation:] We have had messages from the United States from different sources in the past but this is the first time that the proposal has come from a Head, through a Head, to a Head. The United States knows that Pakistan is a great friend of China and therefore we attach importance to the message.[41]

Kissinger immediately drafted Nixon's reply on December 10, which the president approved, to be conveyed to Zhou Enlai through the Pakistanis. Nixon made the following points: he welcomed the PRC's positive response to receive a high-level representative in Beijing to discuss not just Taiwan, where U.S. forces were being progressively reduced, but also other steps to improve relations at the earliest possible moment. Hilaly expanded on both Kissinger's and Nixon's comments on December 16. Nixon gave his message for delivery to President Yahya and explained it with Kissinger, elaborating that an initial meeting might be held in Rawalpindi and, since the Chinese wondered who might attend, suggested Ambassador Murphy or Thomas E. Dewey or Ambassador David Bruce or himself. If the latter, he would come under cover, secretly, by paying a visit to Vietnam and, then, arranging a halt in Pakistan to meet with a Chinese representative.[42]

On January 11, 1971, Romanian ambassador Corneliu Bogdan carried a message from Zhou Enlai, which suggested the only issue was Taiwan, that the PRC was prepared to receive a special envoy, and that Nixon himself would also be welcomed in Beijing. This message had also been reviewed by Mao and Lin Piao. Nixon noted at the bottom of the memorandum from Kissinger, "I believe we may appear too eager. Let's cool it—wait for them to respond to our initiatives."[43] Kissinger heard from Sainteny that he had delivered his message to the Chinese ambassador, who received the note with reserve but transmitted it to Beijing. At the end of January, Bogdan was received in the White House on the eve of his departure for home. He asked if there was something new, and Kissinger told him that not just Taiwan but the whole range of issues should be discussed—and the United States would not agree in principle on Taiwan ahead of time. Simultaneously, the State Department still labored on dry reports such as NSSM-106, dated March 6, 1971.[44]

April brought a surprise. On the sixteenth the American table-tennis team was in Japan for the thirty-first World Table Tennis Championships. It received an invitation from the Chinese team to come to China. *Time* hailed it as "the ping heard round the world." The team of nine players, four officials, and two sponsors entered the PRC from Hong Kong as the first group of Americans officially allowed into China since the communist victory in 1949. The world was "suddenly transfixed by the spectacle of ping-pong diplomacy." At a banquet in the Great Hall of the People on April 14, Zhou Enlai announced, "You have opened a new chapter in the relations of the American and Chinese people. I am confident that this beginning again of our friendship certainly meets with majority support of our two peoples."[45] Ray S. Cline of the Bureau of Intelligence and Research of the State Department labeled it "Peking's People's Diplomacy." There was a shift "timed to influence opinion in the U.S. and other countries to press for China policy changes favorable to Peking." Nevertheless, the State Department claimed, "Through people of this type, Peking will hope to win propaganda benefits while avoiding the tough substantive issues which would inevitably arise in governmental discussions or visits by high-level U.S. personages." The State Department still remained far away from NSC initiatives. On that same day, April 14, Nixon announced easing trade restrictions.[46]

A crucial message was received from Zhou Enlai through the Pakistanis, dated April 21, 1971, and delivered by Hilaly to Kissinger on April 27. Though it still emphasized that Taiwan was the sticking point, it reaffirmed the necessity for direct discussions between high-level responsible persons: "Therefore, the Chinese Government reaffirms its willingness to receive publicly in Peking a special envoy of the President of the U.S. (for instance, Mr. Kissinger or the U.S. Secretary of State or even the President of the U.S. himself) for direct meeting and discussions."[47] Such a meeting could be arranged through Yahya. In addition, Brig. Gen. Alexander Haig, for Kissinger, sent a package to Walters, via courier to Paris. The letter to Walters enclosed Kissinger's note to the PRC for Sainteny to deliver. Kissinger asked Sainteny to arrange a meeting between Walters and the PRC ambassador at which Walters would deliver the note offering to establish a secure channel, and Kissinger would come to Paris for direct talks with whomever the PRC designated. It was obvious the crucial moment had arrived to select someone to go to Beijing.[48]

Kissinger maintained, "'Originally, there was no thought of sending me.'" The thought occurred to him. Nixon had toyed with him on this issue."[49] A good example of this was the telephone conversation between Nixon and Kissinger on the evening of April 27, 1971. The president suggested the American ambassador to France, David Bruce, who was the chief negotiator on Vietnam. Then he thought of Nelson Rockefeller, but Kissinger countered, "He wouldn't be disciplined enough, although he is a possibility." Nixon asked, "How about Bush?" Kissinger replied, "Absolutely not, he is too soft and not sophisticated enough." Kissinger suggested Elliot Richardson, but, again, he mused, "He wouldn't be the right thing." The president agreed that Richardson was "too close to us and [I don't think it would set well with Rogers]." Though the Chinese, Nixon thought, would consider Rockefeller important and could help out for the domestic situation, he added, "No, Nelson is a wild hare running around." Kissinger believed he could keep him under control. Kissinger reemphasized that "Bush would be too weak." The president agreed. If Rockefeller went, he could be backed up by Haig, who was, Nixon considered, "really tough." The conversation then drifted back and forth between selecting Ambassador Bruce or a Rockefeller-Haig combination, with no decision being made. At one point, Kissinger made the following interesting observation: "The difference between them [Chinese] and the Russians is that if your [*sic*] drop some loose change, when you go to pick it up the Russians will step on your fingers and the Chinese won't. I have reviewed all the communications with them and it has been on a high level. . . . The Russians squeeze us on every bloody move and it has been stupid." Nixon agreed.[50] Other names were put forth by Nixon, "musing about a long list of possible envoys who could make the trip [for instance,] Henry Cabot Lodge." Kissinger later mentioned that "Rogers's name had not come up. Nixon remembered otherwise [and] later recounted with some amusement, that Kissinger rolled his eyes upward." Nixon finally announced: "Henry, I think you will have to do it." Kissinger was immensely relieved.[51]

On April 28, 1971, an oral message was delivered to Ambassador Hilaly, then transmitted to the PRC ambassador in Rawalpindi by President Yahya on May 1. In this communication, Nixon thanked Zhou Enlai for his constructive message of April 21 and promised an early formal response. There was also a separate text of Yahya's personal views, stressing Nixon's interest in handling negotiations himself until a government-to-government channel was finally established.[52] On May 10, at last, came Nixon's message, delivered to Hilaly by Kissinger, to be transmitted to the PRC: "In order to prepare the visit by President Nixon and to establish reliable contact with the leaders of the Chinese People's Republic, President Nixon proposes a preliminary *secret* meeting between his Assistant for National Security Affairs, Dr. Kissinger and Premier Chou En-lai or another appropriate high-level Chinese official." The purpose would be to set an agenda for Nixon and "begin a preliminary exchange of views on all subjects of mutual interest." The precise details of Kissinger's trip would be worked out through the good offices of President Yahya Khan. The important communication finished on this note: *"For secrecy, it is essential that no other channel be used. It is also understood that this first meeting between Dr. Kissinger and high officials of the People's Republic of China be strictly secret."*[53]

Anticipating a positive Chinese reply in preparation for a trip to the Far

East, Kissinger secretly met the American ambassador to Pakistan, Joseph Farland, at Palm Springs. He revealed Nixon's commitment to meet with the Chinese leadership. Plans were laid to open a special navy communicator in Karachi to expedite a back channel directly through Farland to China, as Pakistani couriers were becoming cumbersome. Kissinger discussed a proposed covert itinerary to hide his secret trip to China, with Yahya acting as his host. Kissinger would be in Beijing. "I would," Kissinger indicated, "probably require about 24 hours with the Chinese and would plan on meeting in three separate sessions."[54] A White House aircraft, prepositioned in Pakistan, would allow his larger arrival plane to remain parked. On May 20, Farland gave Yahya Nixon's message that no Soviet negotiations would be directed against the PRC, and, furthermore, "Mr. Kissinger is prepared to include this issue and related questions on the agenda of the proposed meeting with the designated representative of the People's Republic of China."[55] Yahya agreed to provide clandestine arrangements, including a cover story that Kissinger was "on an extensive sightseeing tour of mountain area with an overnight at president's guest house."[56] On May 9, Kissinger used the Karachi naval channel to announce that he would serve as the personal envoy of Nixon. "On June 2 the reply came back that Kissinger would describe as 'the most important' since World War II: Zhou Enlai approved his trip and expressed Chairman Mao's 'pleasure' at the prospect of receiving President Nixon sometime soon thereafter." The "Message from Premier Zhou En Lai to President Nixon" was dated May 29, 1971, but probably arrived on June 2, while Nixon was hosting a state dinner. Kissinger sent a message to interrupt the president, and the two retreated to the Lincoln Sitting Room, opened a bottle of old Courvoisier, and took two snifters. "Let us," said Nixon, "drink to generations to come who may have a better chance to live in peace because of what we have done."[57]

The message of the Chinese premier expressed Mao's pleasure that Nixon was "prepared to accept his suggestion to visit Peking for direct conversations with the leaders of the People's Republic of China." Mao looked forward to having "direct conversations [in which] each side would be free to raise the principle [sic] issue of concern to it." For China, Zhou continued, that was Taiwan and the Taiwan Straits area. As for Kissinger, Zhou welcomed him in advance, preferably between June 15 and 20 in Beijing. He could come in a Pakistani Boeing or a special Chinese plane; the entire trip would take three to four days. He concluded, "If secrecy is still desired the Government of the Peoples Republic of China will on its part guarantee the strict maintenance of secrecy." As for details, Yahya could arrange them. The message closed, "Premier Chou En Lai warmly looks forward to the meeting with Dr. Kissinger in Peking in the future."[58]

Kissinger and his special assistant, Winston Lord, drafted Nixon's reply. Nixon not only looked forward with "great pleasure" to his forthcoming discussions but appreciated the "warm welcome" extended by Zhou Enlai to his personal representative, Dr. Kissinger. Nixon proposed Kissinger's arrival for July 9 and departure for July 11, via a Pakistani Boeing aircraft from Islamabad to Peking. Kissinger did not need his own telecommunications equipment; he would arrive with four staff members, and he was "authorized to discuss all issues of concern to both countries preliminary to President Nixon's visit to China." Again, it was emphasized that the strictest secrecy was essential until afterward, when a joint communiqué would be possible.[59] Kissinger handed this message to Ambassador Hilaly on June 4. Although Nixon ordered Kissinger not to put his own name on any of the posttrip announcements, he considered this ridiculous and ignored the order.[60]

To avoid conservative criticism, which might scuttle the whole enterprise, elaborate precautions were taken. When on July 1 Kissinger left for a fact-finding tour of Asia, he brought along his aides—John Holdridge, Winston Lord, Dick Smyser, and David Halperin—and his Secret Service agents, who wore fedoras and sunglasses. On the side trip, only Lord, Holdridge, Smyser, and the two Secret Agents went; the others were ornaments at the guesthouse. A ruse of pretended sickness secluded Kissinger, but the embassy doctor did not go to Hill Station, as the "principal traveller is relaxing, feeling better, wishes to be left alone, will call if doctor needed."[61] Further, "he will also ask for sick pills to lend credibility to the change in plans."[62] The overt schedule had to be concurred by overt channels.[63]

Kissinger and Haig met with Nixon in the Oval Office and role-played Kissinger's forthcoming conversations in Beijing. Nixon insisted on no names to be announced for the visitors to the PRC afterward. On Taiwan, "he wished him not to indicate a willingness to abandon much of our support for Taiwan until it was necessary to do so." Nixon insisted that Kissinger refer to the issue of one versus two Chinas only once rather than threaded throughout. With respect to the UN, Kissinger was to ask for the PRC's point of view. Kissinger should tighten the talks on Vietnam. He was to emphasize the threat of Japan's future orientation. The United States, the president believed, should not appear to be dumping allies, especially Taiwan: "The President stated that he wanted a somewhat heavier emphasis on the Soviet threat [by referring to facts, for example,] tell the Chinese that we note that there are more Soviet divisions on the Chinese border than those arrayed against all the NATO pact countries." Kissinger was to build on three Chinese fears: first, what Nixon might do in Vietnam if the stalemate continued; second, the threat of a resurgent and militant Japan; and, third, the danger of the Soviet Union on their flank.[64]

On July 1, 1971, Kissinger departed on his fact-finding tour of Asia. Because other jets had already been commandeered, Kissinger left with a windowless communications plane from the Tactical Air Command. No reporters came, and the story was stuck deep in the July 10 papers. The *New York Times* described him as "feeling slightly indisposed." Instead of going to Nathia Gali, as announced in the *Times,* a decoy motorcade went there while Kissinger secretly boarded a Pakistani Boeing 707 with his three aides, Lord, Smyser, and Holdridge, and two Secret Service men, John Ready and Gary McLeod. They landed in Beijing just after noon on Friday, July 9, 1971. Shortly thereafter, Kissinger shook Zhou Enlai's hand, and for the next two days they held many hours of discussions with each other, some sessions lasting seven or more hours. Though they only had to settle on Nixon's arrangements, their talks ranged widely, especially on their mutual distrust of the USSR. After Kissinger rested, his first meeting started at 4:35 P.M. The agenda each day covered eleven items, in sequence, each day through to the last day, July 11. The first agenda item between Kissinger and Zhou, starting that first afternoon, was under the heading of "General Philosophy: U.S. and Chinese Foreign Policy and Relations," and then they proceeded through each item, breaking at 7:55 P.M. for dinner and then meeting at 9:40 P.M., continuing to 11:20 P.M. Kissinger turned up with his fat binders of briefing books, whereas Zhou Enlai arrived with a single sheet of paper.[65]

•   •   •

The July 9, 1971, discussions were wide ranging. In these exchanges, the flow of conversation between Kissinger and Zhou fell loosely under four headings: the introductory remarks of greetings and agenda settings; the Taiwan problem; the Vietnamese-Indochina issues; and philosophical-geopolitical questions. Zhou took on the role of a grand inquisitor, demanding either answers or resolutions to essential problems that separated China from America. Kissinger became the dexterous counterpuncher, often offering up ways out of seemingly impossible dead ends and, on occasion, displaying toughness when confronted by an impasse, where compromise was not in the offing. Later, when Winston Lord reviewed the "Memcon" of the July 9 conversation between the two principals, in his comments, dated July 29, he thought the Chinese premier came across "very impressively," but also that his boss acquitted himself well. "One is struck again just how 'searching, sweeping, and significant' these talks were." More pointedly, "[Zhou] is perhaps a little more rhetorical, without being nasty, than we remember him." Zhou played more on history, but he noted that Nixon was not responsible for mistakes he inherited. Though tough on Taiwan, he was "relatively restrained" on Indochina, and a little too preoccupied with Japan.[66] Kissinger remembered Zhou as "one of the two or three most impressive men I have ever met." He gave off an air of "controlled tension, steely discipline, and self-control [and he also displayed] extraordinary graciousness."[67]

In their first half hour, Zhou set the tone when Kissinger referred to China as "mysterious." Zhou contradicted him. Taken aback, Nixon's man confessed that the premier was certainly right: "We had to build confidence; to remove the mystery. This was his fundamental purpose with me, as was mine with him." There were converging interests, not goodwill, that brought America and China together. To put it another way, "It was not personal friendship with Chou but a commonly perceived danger that fostered the elaboration of our relationship."[68] Zhou never went pawn grubbing; he was a pure power politician. Kissinger commented, "Neither side asked the other to do what its values or interests prohibited. Thus ensued a conversation whose easy banter and stylized character, as if it were a dialogue between two professors of political philosophy, which nearly obscured the fact that the penalty of failure would be continued isolation for one side and sharpened international difficulties for the other."[69] The presidential visit became a subsidiary matter. Zhou agreed with Nixon's Kansas City speech of July 6, that is, in the broader context of the United States to the world: the Chinese were a creative, productive, and one of the most capable people, and that was why it was "essential that this Administration take the first steps toward ending the isolation of Mainland China from the world community." Five economic superpowers—the United States, Western Europe, Japan, the Soviet Union, and the PRC—would determine the structure of peace. Zhou rejected "superpower" designation. China would not play that game. Kissinger reflected, "It was both true and prudent; China needed us precisely because it did not have the strength to balance the Soviet Union by itself."[70]

They settled the one practical item quickly, Nixon's forthcoming trip. For the rest, they could "spend their time enjoying conceptual discussions." Most important, "The mutual interests they discussed mainly involved their shared distrust of the Soviets." Kissinger showed the Chinese "supersecret intelligence about Soviet military actions and communication intercepts of Soviet installations on the Chinese border."[71]

The Memcon of their first meeting played out differently. It all started with easy chatter about Edgar Snow and the story in *Life* of his interview with Mao. Kissinger opened by suggesting the order of business and laying some groundwork on mutual Asian concerns and world peace. He set out a seven-point agenda and cautiously added an eighth, "I know you are concerned about collusion, or what you call collusion, of other countries against you." Kissinger assured him that the United States "will never collude with other countries against the People's Republic of China, either with our allies or with some of our opponents." America would "strive to avoid this." This question of collusion, or what came to be termed "condominium," came up again in some detail after the dinner break. It started with Kissinger being pressed about Korea and responding, as he had previously argued, about Washington's presence in Taiwan: the issue of U.S. military presence would be gradually solved as America withdrew from Asia, including Japan. Kissinger tried to show how his adopted country had spread over the world. After World War II, there was a vacuum in Europe. Against its inclinations, Washington was driven by both a military doctrine that communism had to be promptly dealt with instead of festering as fascism had until it was almost too late and also with liberal elements, zealots for social welfare, to improve the economic progress of nations, even before they had adequate political organization. Nixon thought the defense of faraway countries was primarily their own responsibility, and he would use American power only to "intervene primarily when a super-power threatens to establish hegemony" over weaker countries. Zhou understood, "There is another super-power." Kissinger replied, "Here? To the north?" A dialogue ensued:

> *PM Chou:* Yes. We don't believe that super-power will be able to control the world. It will also be defeated as it stretches out its hand so far. You are feeling difficulties now, and they too will also feel difficulties. They are just now following after you.

> *Dr. Kissinger:* With all respect, I think they triggered us, they caused our actions. Even today their constant probing makes it very hard to have a real settlement with them.[72]

The friendly banter turned serious as Zhou picked up on Kissinger's agenda. The premier prefaced his remarks with emphasis on coexistence, equality, and friendship. On the latter, he recalled, "Chinese and American peoples are friendly toward each other. This was true in the past and will be true in the future." After the new China appeared and after the Bandung Conference, exchanges ceased, and sixteen years of fruitless meetings followed, all 136 of them in Warsaw; the crux of the issue was whether now there was an intention to solve problems, not peripherals but fundamental ones. That introduction led him to Taiwan. From the Chinese revolution and civil war onward, it was the touchiest subject. Kissinger revealed how agonizing that topic was: "one of the most painful meetings of my career" occurred on July 1, 1971, the very day of his "Polo I" departure. ROC envoy James Shen came to his office to see about preserving Taiwan's seat at the next UN meeting. He was opposed to a dual seating plan devised by the State Department. Kissinger explained, "No government less deserved what was about to happen to it than that of Taiwan,"[73] Now the president's national security adviser had to deal with the whole Taiwan issue, brought bluntly before him by the premier.

Zhou maintained that Taiwan was the crucial issue to be resolved, and it had been brought on by a change in Washington's position shortly after the start of the Korean War. Before then, the United States had considered Taiwan an internal Chinese matter: "And, therefore," Zhou continued, "the U.S. declared that it wouldn't interfere in China's internal affairs and would leave the Chinese people to settle internal questions." After the Korean War broke out, "you surrounded Taiwan and declared the status of Taiwan was still unsettled. Even up to the present day the spokesman of your State Department still says that this is your position." That meant, according to Zhou, "if this crucial question is not solved, then the whole question will be difficult to resolve." He considered that all other Sino-American questions seemed to rest on this one, and they would have to wait until this was satisfactorily solved. If the PRC was the sole legitimate government of China, then the United States could not make any exceptions, and it must withdraw all its armed forces and dismantle all its military installations. All treaties between the United States and the Republic of China were illegal.[74]

The NSC chief agreed with the premier's historical review, and then he proceeded to Taiwan's linkage to Indochina. If the Korean War had not occurred, Taiwan would probably be a part of the PRC. "For reasons which are now worthless to recapitulate, a previous Administration linked the future of Korea to the future of Taiwan, partly because of the U.S. domestic opinion at the time."[75] Developments since then created "some principles of foreign policy for us." Kissinger divided the question into two parts: the military situation and the political evolution between the ROC and the PRC. Of the first, some symbolic steps already were taken—for example, ending the Taiwan Straits patrol, removing a squadron of air tankers, and reducing the military advisory group by 20 percent. He recognized these steps were only symbolic, but they indicated the direction of Washington's intentions. Two-thirds of the American military presence was related to "activities in other parts of Asia," while one-third was connected to Taiwan's defense. The United States was prepared to remove the former within a specified brief period after the war in Indochina. As to the latter, "We are prepared to begin reducing our other forces on Taiwan as our relations improve, so that the military questions need not be a principal obstacle between us."[76]

America did not advocate a one-China solution, a two-Chinas solution, or a one China–one Taiwan solution. Rather, Nixon insisted the political evolution of Taiwan would likely be in China's direction. The president was firm on these principles. There were certain necessities that had to be observed. That rankled Zhou, who asked, "What necessities?" Kissinger maintained that Washington should not be forced into formal declarations, which would have no practical effect, but the United States would not stand in the way of a basic evolution. Zhou repeated the PRC's position, but because of Kissinger's admission of no two Chinas or one China or one Taiwan, Zhou opened the door a crack: "This shows that the prospect for a solution and the establishment of diplomatic relations between our two countries is hopeful." Kissinger slipped himself and Nixon through that narrow opening. He underlined that the PRC could count on those principles, so Zhou asked what about the time left to Nixon in his first and, perhaps, second term—could Nixon discuss with Mao the establishment of diplomatic relations, assuming equality and reciprocity despite the years of estrangement? Kissinger insisted that recognition had nothing to do with Nixon's reelection but was based on Nixon's "lifelong conviction that there cannot be peace without the participation of the PRC." When Kissinger asked the premier if Nixon's meeting with Mao depended on recognition or whether the two could be separated, Zhou replied that they could be parted.[77]

Kissinger suggested the military question could be settled if the war in Southeast Asia were ended within Nixon's first term, and an evolution of the Taiwan issue left to the second term. When Zhou asked about a Taiwanese independence movement, he said the United States did not support it. Zhou attached great importance to that statement. About the PRC's recognition, he had to be honest and candidly told the premier there was no possibility of it within the next few years. About Indochina, Kissinger insisted the time had come to make peace, but the settlement had to be consistent with America's honor and self-respect. Actions in Laos and Cambodia were not, he maintained, aimed at China. Nixon was ready to set a specific date for complete withdrawal. But to reach such a deadline, an overall settlement had to include a cease-fire in all of Indochina, release of prisoners, and respect for the Geneva Accord. Demands for reparations were not consistent with honor, but voluntary aid might be given once peace was made. A final political solution in South Vietnam after America's withdrawal could be left to the Vietnamese alone, without external interference. Differences now versus 1954 and 1957 were political history—as between Dulles's missionary zeal versus Nixon's realism.[78]

The premier insisted on all foreign troops out of Southeast Asia and Vietnam left alone to resolve its own fate. Kissinger agreed. After some quibbling about the role of advisers, Kissinger noted that it was not likely the United States would return from ten thousand miles away. When the premier complained that the United States was responsible for enlarging the war, Nixon's envoy sidestepped the issue: "That is history, and our problem now is how to end it." Zhou urged the best way was to end it forthrightly and leave. Kissinger, miffed, replied, "I have stated our views and don't believe I need to repeat them." At that they broke for dinner.[79] No one wanted the Peking duck to cool.

The Vietnamese problem continued over dinner. Zhou remarked that even if there were a cease-fire and a U.S. withdrawal, those in power would have to be either removed by democratic elections or overthrown. Nixon's NSC adviser approved the former. Zhou did not believe in the forthcoming elections. Kissinger noted the North Vietnamese wanted the United States "both to withdraw and get rid of the government of [South] Vietnam. To do both of these is impossible." Table talk drifted to the coup in Phnom Penh, which, Kissinger insisted, "was not of our doing; it was unfortunate. We did not want Sihanouk overthrown. Why should we lie? What difference does it make now? We were negotiating with North Vietnam at that moment. The coup ruined negotiations that we were conducting and that we wanted to succeed." Formal conversations resumed at 9:40 P.M.[80]

The first day's discussions wound down with further comments about Vietnam, especially the conditions of withdrawal and more geopolitical talk. Zhou referred to Nixon's recent Kansas City speech on July 6. Nixon had said the United States should not concentrate all of its energies on Vietnam, which it had for the past ten years, and should begin to look at things from a global perspective. "One can say in all frankness," the premier continued, "that if it were not for the help given the South Vietnamese puppets, the Saigon regime would have collapsed long ago." Why, he wondered, must the United States leave a "tail" there? "So I cannot quite understand what you mean by wanting to leave a tail there, although you reaffirmed moments ago your complete withdrawal." When Kissinger asked what Zhou meant by a "tail," the premier replied, "the Thieu regime." Kissinger endeavored to state clearly the U.S. position. No negotiations would mean a long and slow withdrawal, and the Saigon government would be strengthened in the interval. But was not that a conditional withdrawal? Zhou asked. Again, Kissinger elaborated that the United States did not want to maintain a specific government and would restrict its support of the current government, but "what we cannot do is to participate in the overthrow of people whom we have been allied, whatever the origin of the alliance." If that government was unpopular, it would soon be overthrown after U.S. withdrawal, and if that was the case, America would not intervene. During withdrawal, Washington would abide by internationally set guidelines for stipulated limits on military aid for a specified time period of, say, eighteen months or so.[81]

As an aside, Zhou raised the question of removing U.S. troops from South Korea, which Kissinger said would evolve naturally, as in Japan and Taiwan. From that point, the conversation dealt with geopolitics—triangular diplomacy and the USSR—and ended at 11:20 P.M. They met again on the tenth to clarify details on Nixon's visit about dates, who would be invited, to settle on an announcement regarding Kissinger's visit, as well as agree on another visit for him in October.

On his return trip to the United States, Kissinger wrote a long memorandum, dated July 14, for Nixon, giving a candid evaluation of the entire experience. His remarks divided into fourteen sections. They revealed keen appreciation of the trip: "My two-day visit to Peking resulted in the most searching, sweeping and significant discussions I have ever had in government." In more than twenty hours of discussions, he had managed to set a summit meeting before the following May, candidly covered important issues between the United States and PRC in detail, and had established a "major new departure in international relations [and] have laid the groundwork for you and Mao to turn a page in history."[82] About Nixon's later "thunder out of China," his national security adviser's communiqué of July 15 made all the noise. Kissinger neatly put it, "We all agreed with Chou En-lai that the announcement now firmly scheduled for the following Thursday at 10:30 P.M. Washington time, would 'shake the world.'"[83] Once shaken, the world would not need reshaking by Nixon's encounter with Mao. The great realignment, diplomatically referred to as triangular relations, had been accomplished by Kissinger and Zhou. Global relationships were transformed.[84]

Kissinger recounted how relaxed the atmosphere and conversations were and how constructive as between equals—so unlike those held with the Soviet Union. Both he and Zhou were contemptuous of the USSR. The Chinese, urbane and at ease, contrasted with the "self-conscious sense of hierarchy of Soviet officials." Zhou attacked imperialism, including the Soviet brand, as retold by Kissinger: "[There was] the specter of big power collusion, specifically of being carved up by the U.S., the USSR, and Japan; [there was his] contempt of the Indians, [his] hatred for the Russians and apprehension over the Japanese, the disclaimer that China is, or would want to be, a superpower like the Russians and we who have 'stretched out our hands too far.'"[85]

"There was," Kissinger emphasized, "none of the Russian ploymanship, scoring points, rigidity or bullying. They did not turn everything into a contest." There was no maneuvering for petty gains. When Kissinger mentioned how the Russians had put out their own English translation, differing from the Americans', of the May 20 Strategic Arms Limitation Treaty, Zhou "showed obvious contempt" and noted the Chinese would "never resort to such a gambit." When the discussion turned toward the actual date of a summit, Zhou wished for a time after Nixon's Soviet summit, but Kissinger explained the problem to Zhou, and he "was willing to be flexible because [as Kissinger explained] this is a significant sign (and perhaps the most significant) of the Chinese worries about their confrontation with the USSR." Kissinger was often explicit about Zhou's resentment of Russia: "He showed deep bitterness against Russia and contempt for their petty tactics."[86]

About the Chinese, behind their "elaborate correctness and courtesy [they were] extremely tough on substance and ideological in their approach but their dealings were meticulous." Zhou was, according to Kissinger, matter-of-fact, clear, eloquent, at home in philosophy or historical analysis, genial, urbane, and considerate, and he had a "refreshing sense of humor." He concluded, "In short, Chou En-lai ranks with Charles de Gaulle as the most impressive foreign statesman I have met." When Zhou made an "extremely tough presentation" before lunch on the second day, Kissinger "responded very toughly" and with a "deliberately brusque point-by-point rebuttal," stopping only to eat. Then, during lunch, "Chou's geniality returned." Kissinger cited a certain tension in Zhou and his compatriots. He thought the Cultural Revolution was an "anguishing period" for them, and he noticed a "moral ambivalence" and a "certain brooding quality" and "schizophrenia" in Zhou's presentations and the "jagged rhythm" in drafting the announcement. These were, he reflected, "men in some anguish. Yet their long history of past suffering gave them an inner confidence that was reflected in a certain largeness of spirit." There was always the ambivalence of Beijing's position on its support of Hanoi without wishing to jeopardize a chance of improving Sino-American relations. The exile from Nazi persecution had skated through all this "turmoil under heaven" and handed the grocer's son a Beijing summit.[87]

Kissinger chuckled over little incidents that lent charm to the drama. The first was that he left his extra pair of shirts in Pakistan and had to make do with John Holdridge's—a six-footer and former West Pointer. Then there was the possible interference of *New York Times* reporter James Reston, whose visit coincided with his in Beijing. Zhou gleefully delayed Reston's train from Shanghai. Reston actually ended up hospitalized in Peking for an appendectomy. He was so near, yet so far, from the scoop of a lifetime. When Kissinger deplaned in Pakistan, his security was almost blown because his Chinese gifts of Mao's collected works and photos of the historic trip could not be concealed. Finally, there was that nostalgic remark of the ever proper Marshal Teh (Zhu) when, on their way to Beijing's airport, the marshal recounted how he, as a Nationalist officer, ran off to join Mao and endure the Long March. None of that little band "ever dreamed of seeing victory in their lifetimes. They thought their struggle was for future generations." As they reached the boarding ramp, the marshal said, "Yet here we are and here you are."[88]

By now Kissinger and his small staff agreed with Zhou—the announcement of Kissinger's secret trip and its purpose would "shake the world." Nixon awaited his national security adviser's arrival at El Toro Marine Corps Station at 7:00 A.M. on July 13. Kissinger had cabled his mission's success while on his way to Teheran, using the code word "Eureka." From 7:20 to 9:30 A.M., Nixon debriefed Kissinger. Kissinger and Lord prepared a four hundred–word announcement of seven minutes that Nixon made at Burbank's NBC television studio. They repaired to Perino's restaurant for a celebration with crab legs and a 1961 bottle of Chateau Lafite Rothschild.[89]

With that, America entered an era of triangular diplomacy: "Equilibrium was the name of the game. We did not seek to join China in a provocative confrontation with the Soviet Union. But we agreed on the necessity to curb Moscow's geopolitical ambitions." Washington had no reason to be involved in the Moscow-Beijing ideological dispute, and it had a "moral and political obligation to strive for coexistence." What the United States could not tolerate was Soviet aggression against China. If that succeeded, "the whole weight of the Soviet military effort could be thrown against the West." Kissinger called this newly assumed American position a balancing act on a tightrope. The U.S.-PRC relationship could not overcome Soviet paranoia and had to assure China against any Soviet-American collusion. Mao put it succinctly: America must not "stand on China's shoulders" to reach Moscow.[90]

To prepare Nixon's road trip to Beijing, it required a second journey by Kissinger, Polo II, undertaken in October. Chinese preparations necessitated purging the top military, including Lin Piao (Biao), in September. Kissinger left for Beijing on October 16, testing the route Nixon would travel in February. Zhou toasted Kissinger on October 20, emphasizing the trip's purpose to continue political discussions and settle technical aspects of the president's itinerary. Now, said Zhou, China should no longer be considered a "mystery." The test of Kissinger's visit, he believed, "would be our ability to arrange the Presidential trip, advance further our political rapprochement, and begin to agree on a communiqué." Trip arrangements were easy, review of world events took twenty-five hours, and another fifteen were devoted to the Shanghai Communiqué. The bland draft devised by Kissinger Zhou scotched, declaring the U.S. approach unacceptable. Rather, it would be a statement of disagreements between the two parties, without making propaganda or humiliations, and contain a section devoted to common positions, especially a paragraph including the U.S.-PRC objections to "hegemony." Kissinger introduced that label as a euphemism for Soviet expansionism. A compromise was also reached on Taiwan by a Kissinger formula: "The United States acknowledges that all Chinese on either side of the Taiwan Straits maintain there is but one China. The United States Government does not challenge that position." Kissinger remarked, "I do not think anything I did or said impressed Chou as much as this ambiguous formula which both sides were able to live [with] for nearly a decade."[91]

Brig. Gen. Alexander Haig, Kissinger's deputy, took a brief trip to Peking in early January to finalize technicalities of the president's journey. Briefing books were prepared for Nixon as well as talking points. Finally, on February 21, 1972, Nixon arrived, stepped off the airplane, and gave Zhou the historic handshake, symbolically reversing Dulles's 1955 snub, when he had refused a similar handshake at the Geneva Conference. No sooner had they finished lunch than Chairman Mao requested the president's presence, to be accompanied by Kissinger and Lord. Nixon barred Secretary of State William P. Rogers and Assistant Secretary of State Marshall Green. Kissinger had to admit about Mao, "I have met no one, with the possible exception of Charles de Gaulle, who so distilled raw, concentrated willpower." Kissinger recounted that Mao greeted Nixon by taking the president's hand in both of his. When Nixon proposed several countries requiring attention, Mao insisted those be dealt with by Zhou, while only philosophical questions should then be discussed. Mao indicated a preference for conservative leaders and told Nixon he had "voted for you during your election." About his own reactionary group, they had fled in an airplane bound for Outer Mongolia. It crashed. Nixon recounted his long road from Red baiter to Peking promoter, while Mao assured Nixon that China threatened neither Japan nor South Korea. Major issues, Mao insisted, should be settled before smaller ones. Taiwan was subsidiary, the chairman maintained. The international situation was the crucial one, and he meant the Soviet Union. It was clear China would not intervene in Indochina militarily. Mao went beyond ideology to the "absolute primacy of geopolitics." Of the sixty-five minutes spent with Mao, half were devoted to translating.[92]

Much, according to Kissinger, depended on their assessment of Nixon's determination to act parallel with them in maintaining the balance of power, what he called "the real purpose of their opening to us." Its formal expression was the Shanghai Communiqué. Lord and Kissinger labored over it for more than twenty hours. They finally had to make some last-minute changes in words, such as *prospect* for *premise* in the paragraph on Taiwan and *part* rather than *province* in referring to Taiwan. An acceptable draft was only held up by the State Department—mostly on trivial points, which angered Nixon to such a degree that he stormed about the guesthouse at Hangchow (Hangzhou) in his briefs. The Chinese translation was more generous than the original English draft. The Nixon administration had adjusted to a "world fundamentally different from our historical perspective." By contrast, America's romance with China had ended because that China "no longer existed, if it ever had." And the new perception had now become a reality.[93] Rather than compromising positions, each side used separate paragraphs to state its differences with the other. For instance, on Vietnam the Chinese supported the Vietnamese peace proposal, while the United States reaffirmed Nixon's position. However, in two important areas both sides agreed: neither nation "should seek hegemony in the Asia Pacific region and each is opposed to efforts by any other country or group of countries to establish such hegemony." The second agreement was about Taiwan: Zhou demanded American withdrawal and firmly opposed any "two Chinas" formula. The United States acknowledged Chinese on either side of the straits agreed there was one China and Taiwan was a part of it. Further, the United States reaffirmed a peaceful settlement of the Taiwanese question by the Chinese and affirmed its objective of eventually withdrawing its military from there.[94]

Both Kissinger and Nixon made it clear Taiwan was not abandoned. The United States planned to stay in South Korea and Japan. Though not stated, it was clear the United States would also remain in the Philippines. All in all, it was each man's—Nixon's and Kissinger's—greatest triumph. On February 27, 1972, at a farewell dinner held in Shanghai, Nixon said it best: "This magnificent banquet marks the end of our stay in the People's Republic of China. We have been here a week. This was the week that changed the world."[95]

Two presidents were the direct beneficiaries of the changed world, Ronald Reagan and George H. W. Bush.

Old Conclusions, New Beginnings

Not until the Reagan-Gorbachev era was accommodation again taken up seriously. Diplomatically, President Ronald Reagan played the part of the wartime FDR, and General Secretary Mikhail Gorbachev reenacted the role of Stalin at Teheran and Yalta, that is, both were genial compromisers. In their own unique ways, Stalin and Gorbachev needed America. In return, FDR promoted Teheran and Yalta, whereas Reagan initiated the Geneva, Reykjavik, Washington, and Moscow summits. Stalin, with the aid of the Teheran and Yalta conferences, survived Hitler; Gorbachev, with the Reagan summits, gained breathing room for perestroika and glasnost. The question was: how were Reagan and Gorbachev able to accomplish by accommodation what no others had since FDR and Stalin? The promise of Yalta had been lost; with the Reagan-Gorbachev summits, the promise was renewed.

The Chinese Tiananmen Square calamity of 1989 almost ended the Nixon-Kissinger opening of China, saved only by President George H. W. Bush's sending of a high-level mission of National Security Adviser Brent Scowcroft and Deputy Secretary of State Lawrence Eagleburger to Beijing to rebuild confidence. By 1991, with the Soviet Union's disintegration and the simultaneous renewal of Sino-American relations after Tiananmen Square, some old Cold War conclusions still remained, but new beginnings of finding common ground were taking shape: confrontation was giving way to accommodation with Russia; realism was replacing idealism with China. Russia was emerging from "Siberian" Kennan's distortion, and China was something more than "Old China Hand" Rockhill's exotic land of the lamas.

• • •

Reagan began his presidency as a hard-liner. In March 1983, Reagan gave two memorable speeches, one to the National Association of Evangelicals on March 8, which was convening in Orlando, and the other a nationally televised address to the nation on March 23. In the first, after delivering his standard litany of conservative values, he launched into a morality play on good and evil. As author Frances Fitzgerald pointed out, this was not the first time Reagan used the word *evil* when considering the USSR: "In a speech at West Point in May 1981, for example, he had referred to the assembled cadets as a 'chain holding back an evil force.'"[1] She went on to suggest Reagan had trip-wired the whole eschatology of Armageddon for these evangelicals as derived from the biblical books of Ezekiel and Revelation. They had been identifying the Soviet Union since the Bolshevik Revolution as an evil empire headed by the Anti-Christ.[2] The phrase as used by Reagan occurs toward the end of his speech: "So, in discussions of the nuclear freeze proposals, I urge you to beware of the temptation of pride—the temptation of blithely declaring yourselves above it all and label both sides equally at fault, to ignore the facts of history and the aggressive impulses of an *evil empire,* to simply call the arms race a giant misunderstanding and thereby remove yourself from the struggle between right and wrong and good and evil."[3]

He pointed out that Marxism-Leninism rejected morality based on the supernatural and recognized as moral only what furthered its cause. He asked these evangelicals to pray for those who lived in "totalitarian darkness." And he finished by calling the real crisis facing Americans as a spiritual one, testing the nation's "moral will and faith."[4]

The second memorable speech that month was his televised "Address to the Nation on Defense and National Security," delivered on March 23, 1983. In it, he first detailed the enormous Soviet military buildup over the past twenty years. Meanwhile, America's defenses had atrophied. Besides, a freeze would make America only less, not more, secure by preventing modernization. Again, at the end of his speech, in which he had already enumerated his list of the Soviets' standard threats, as in the previous one, he shocked his viewers with an announcement known before to only a few of his closest advisers.[5] It was a last-minute insertion in one critical paragraph: "What if free people could live secure in the knowledge that their security did not rest upon the threat of instant U.S. retaliation to deter a Soviet attack, that we could intercept and destroy strategic ballistic missiles before they reached our own soil or that of our allies?"[6] The specter of retaliation or mutual threat was a "sad commentary on the human condition" and could be viewed only as "fostering an aggressive policy." Therefore, he was initiating long-term research on what he called his Strategic Defensive Initiative (SDI) so the threat of strategic nuclear missiles could be eliminated.[7] The press immediately labeled it "Star Wars," and the address itself as Reagan's "Darth Vader speech." This notion of an antimissile shield, wrote Fitzgerald, was "surely Reagan's most characteristic idea."[8]

Reagan played up the theme of a "security shield" in his second inaugural on January 21, 1985.[9] On March 8, 1985, Reagan went to the hospital to have a polyp removed from his intestine. On March 10, General Secretary Konstantin Chernenko died, and Vice President George H. W. Bush and Secretary of State George P. Shultz and team went to Moscow for the funeral and to meet the new general secretary, Mikhail S. Gorbachev. Back in October, when William Clark had resigned as Reagan's national security adviser, his place was taken by Bud McFarlane. During 1984, McFarlane's team developed its four-point agenda: end the use of force, eliminate nuclear arms, improve bilateral relations, and promote human rights. Now Reagan and Gorbachev began an exchange of letters, and soon the new general secretary invited Reagan to Moscow. After some maneuvering, they decided to meet in Geneva in November 1985. A new era had begun.

In their first private meeting of November 19, 1985, Reagan made it clear to Gorbachev that "countries do not mistrust each other because of arms, but rather countries build up their arms because of the mistrust between them." Gorbachev replied, "The Soviet Union recognized the role of the U.S. in the world, and wished it no harm." Reagan countered that it was not people who created arms but governments. Gorbachev maintained that the central issue was ending the arms race and finding a formula for doing so. Reagan again turned to the question of mistrust and the need to remove its causes.[10] For Lou Cannon, Reagan's biographer, the immediate breakthrough was that both men found something likable in the other. Though this first encounter was scheduled for only fifteen minutes, it lasted sixty-four minutes. Cannon insisted that for Reagan, first impressions were important. "There was a warmth in his face and his style," Reagan later stated, "not the coldness bordering on hatred I'd seen in most senior Soviet officials I'd met until then."[11] Reagan had touched on the heart of the American problem with Russia for almost a century, since "Siberian" Kennan: a deeply negative perception of mistrust. Somehow that had to be cleared away, even if it began first only at the top, between the two leaders themselves.

In their first plenary session later that morning, Reagan returned to the theme of mistrust, while Gorbachev called for increased trade by offering the USSR as a great market for U.S. goods rather than as a potential outlet for the U.S. military-industrial complex's production and storage of weaponry. Each man gave a litany of the other country's sins. Cannon called it the standard Cold War rhetoric each was at some point expected to elaborate. There was some substance as each leader drew his own line in the sand. Reagan brought up the fact that the USSR had been a great wartime ally, but, due to its mistrust of America, it had thrown away FDR's attempts to bridge the gap between the two alternative systems, capitalism and communism. When the United States was the sole possessor of the bomb, it did not use its threat to gain advantages over the USSR. Reagan concluded, "Most of these times the United States did not get cooperation from Gorbachev's predecessors." It got the opposite results in terms of mistrust because of the vast Soviet military buildup. "The President said that now the two sides have come to this meeting he had said frankly why the American people had fears. Maybe not fears of war, but that the Soviet Union could acquire such an imbalance of strength that it could deliver an ultimatum." That mistrust could be relieved only by deeds: "But deeds can relieve mistrust, if we can go on the basis of *trust*, then those mountains of weapons will shrink quickly as we will be confident that they are not needed." Given sufficient trust, both sides could do research on SDI—not even knowing if such a system could ever work—and share their results with everyone, so "no one would have a fear of a nuclear strike." A shield would also prevent a madman from starting a nuclear holocaust.[12]

The conversation had gotten hot. It was Reagan who suggested that it was time for the two of them to take a walk and get a little fresh air. It was a brisk November afternoon, and they soon retreated to the boathouse, where a roaring fire had been prepared. Cannon, leaning on Reagan's own estimation, believed the president's invitation to cool off and the ensuing private fireside chat and return walk were the key moments at the summit, especially when the president got ahead of his delegation and suggested future summits in Washington and Moscow, to which Gorbachev readily agreed.[13]

The boathouse conversation focused on a single subject, the one that usually troubled the Russians: SDI. It remained the core issue; it never went away. It already was the most objectionable feature at the second plenary. Now Gorbachev had a chance to go one on one with Reagan. Reagan handed him an envelope of materials that stressed a 50 percent reduction in strategic offensive arms as a seed for negotiating, and Gorbachev admitted that was a good starting point. But he pointed out that in January, it had been agreed this would be negotiated with a halting of an arms race in space. Reagan's standard rejoinder by then was that SDI was strictly a defensive weapon, not a part of the arms race, and its technology would be shared among the other nuclear powers. Be that as it may, Gorbachev answered, even when talking about intermediate-range nuclear forces (INFs), what about other than land-based systems and the separate French and British systems? Gorbachev wanted to know whether Reagan subscribed to the narrow or broad interpretation of the ABM Treaty. Reagan belonged to the latter because any laboratory system would have to be tested to know in practice whether such a weapon worked; it would, he reiterated, be shared by all. "The worst thing he could imagine was for any one country to acquire a first strike capability." Even so, Gorbachev queried, it was already declared that nuclear weapons would never be used—was not that enough? The president said he believed him, but what about after they were gone? Gorbachev, "with some emotion," asked what the purpose was of deploying a weapon as yet unknown and unpredictable. Verification would always be unreliable due to the weapon's maneuverability and mobility, even if called defensive; it would always be regarded as an added threat. "If the goal was to get rid of nuclear weapons," he asked, "why start an arms race in another sphere?" Each side could refrain, open its laboratories, and start the process of a 50 percent reduction of its offensive weaponry.

Reagan stuck to insistence on the space shield that reminded him of the First World War and poisonous gas, which each side rendered useless with its gas masks. The mutually assured destruction doctrine would be, likewise, rendered useless because each side now would have the impenetrable shield. Gorbachev, finally, said he believed him personally, but politically "could not possibly agree with the President with regard to this concept [and he] would urge the President jointly with him to find a way of formulating guidelines for their negotiators with a view to stopping SDI." If both sides deployed layer after layer, Gorbachev warned, "only God himself would know what they were." It was only then, as they strolled back from the boathouse, that Reagan suggested the future summits and Gorbachev agreed.[14] That was the major breakthrough.

Reagan returned home and wrote Gorbachev. In his letter he suggested negotiators focus on ways to eliminate first-strike possibilities, and he offered to cooperate in helping the USSR get out of Afghanistan. Almost at the same time, Secretary of State George P. Shultz proposed to Ambassador Anatoly Dobrynin that Gorbachev come to Washington the following June. It was only a month later that Gorbachev responded to these initiatives. He still demanded a ban on what he considered SDI to be, a space-strike weapon, and he disputed the claim of a Soviet advantage in first-strike weapons.[15] In a January publicized message to Reagan, he proposed a three-stage elimination of nuclear weaponry, 50 percent, followed by further reductions, and then including other nuclear powers. "Everything was conditioned on an immediate moratorium on nuclear testing and banning 'space-strike weapons' from the start."[16]

Gorbachev's "new thinking" was a little slow in coming. In February, he called on Anatoly Chernyaev to become his assistant for foreign affairs. Chernyaev was, perhaps, the most critical of traditional Soviet diplomacy. Like Gorbachev, he believed something new had to be done: improve agriculture and create work incentives, replace Brezhnev's people, let Polish leader Gen. Wojciech Jaruzelski solve his own problems, renounce the

Brezhnev doctrine, get out of Afghanistan, remove SS-20s from Europe, shift from a militarized economy to a civilian one, free dissidents, and allow refuseniks and Jews to leave.[17] Yet Gorbachev was cautious and clung to some of the "old thinking." For instance, he still believed in the so-called narrow interpretation rather than the "broad interpretation" of the 1972 ABM Treaty. The former prohibited testing and developing any ABM components, whereas the latter assumed the right to conduct research, testing, and development, but not deployment. And Reagan kept writing to him, even offering to "enter into an agreement to liquidate and ban all offensive ballistic missiles before any strategic defenses would be deployed." These proposals were ignored, and Gorbachev continued railing against the "militarization of space."[18] The stalemate continued into the summer. Finally, Gorbachev suggested a late September or October summit in Reykjavik, Iceland. He needed to get Reagan to ease the burden of Soviet military expenditures necessary to keep pace with the United States and, therefore, allow his domestic reforms to continue.

When they met on October 10, 1986, both Reagan and Gorbachev agreed the central issue was a strategic arms proposal. Already Reagan had picked up the Russian proverb "Doveryai, no proveryai" (Trust, but verify). Seeking to "sweep Reagan off his feet," Gorbachev proposed a 50 percent overall reduction of strategic arms; he dropped the counting of French and British INFs and offered removing his from Europe. He wanted continuation of the narrow interpretation of ABM for at least another ten years, that is, only research and testing in laboratories, a prohibition on all antisatellite weapons, and a ban on nuclear testing. Reagan countered with a call for eliminating all strategic offensive weapons, ridding Asia as well of INFs, and replacing the ABM Treaty with one that allowed the broad interpretation, explaining why SDI did not fit an offensive definition. After further argument, they reached reasonable accord on everything except SDI. As Ambassador Jack Matlock admitted, "Progress came to a complete halt when the two went over the tediously familiar ground of SDI and the ABM Treaty. The exchanges seemed almost a replay of Geneva, except that Reagan was now suggesting a complete elimination of all ballistic missiles before strategic defenses could be deployed. Gorbachev would not move off his demand that SDI research be confined to laboratories and that the United States commit itself not to withdraw from the ABM Treaty for ten years."[19] As they got closer and closer to making "the most sweeping commitments in history to reduce mankind's most destructive weaponry," Gorbachev dug in his heels on the make-or-break issue: "We may as well go home and forget about Reykjavik," he said. Reagan lost patience and blurted out, "Oh, shit!" He was dumbfounded: "Can you really mean that you would turn down an historic opportunity because of a single word?" The word Reagan had in mind was *laboratories*. Gorbachev replied, "But for us it's not the word that counts, it's the principle."[20] And with that, Reykjavik failed.

By 1987, Gorbachev began to focus on the narrow interpretation rather than getting Reagan to sign off on only laboratories for SDI. Also, he realized that his domestic reforms depended on an arrangement with Reagan and time was not on his side. Furthermore, he came to understand that Britain's and France's INFs were not important because there was not going to be a war with either of them. Margaret Thatcher drove home the point that the West had a legitimate fear of the traditional worldwide communist goal. And finally, "parity" only meant creating a Soviet-style bloated military-industrial complex in which, as Gorbachev noted, "we are stealing everything from the people and turning the country into a military camp."[21] When Shultz visited Moscow in April 1987, he found Gorbachev was willing to conclude an INF treaty, leaving the remaining problems for another time. Perhaps more important, he now realized that with Shultz, "maybe for the first time, . . . I was dealing with a serious man of sound political judgment." The way to a summit in Washington for December 1987 was clear: Reagan's goals now fitted Gorbachev's needs for "perestroika," or restructuring the Soviet economy.[22]

• • •

Vice President George H. W. Bush succeeded Reagan to the presidency in 1989. A Reaganite diplomacy remained intact. The Tiananmen Square protests of that year were a series of demonstrations led by students, intellectuals, and labor activists in the People's Republic of China between April and June. Although the protests lacked a unified cause or leadership, participants were critical of the ruling Chinese Communist Party and voiced complaints ranging from minor criticisms to calls for a full-fledged democracy and establishing broader freedoms. The demonstrations centered on Tiananmen Square in Beijing, but large-scale protests also occurred in cities throughout China, which stayed peaceful throughout the protests. In Beijing, the resulting military crackdown on the protesters by the PRC government left many civilians dead or injured. It was against this background that President George H. W. Bush sent two high-level missions to the PRC —one in July and the other in December—to assure the Chinese leadership the United States would mind its own business, no matter what Congress, the public, or even what the president himself might publicly say or demand. These two missions were conducted by Gen. Brent Scowcroft, head of the National Security Agency, and Lawrence Eagleburger, deputy secretary of state.[23]

Congress prodded the administration, and limited sanctions were imposed on June 6: stopping the sale of military items, suspension of visits between U.S. and Chinese military leaders, and a review of requests for asylum by Chinese students studying in the United States. Even so, Bush stated, "I don't want to hurt the Chinese people. I happen to believe that commercial contacts have led, in essence, to this quest for more freedom." Bush further reduced the sanctions' significance by stating, "Now is the time to look beyond the moment to important and enduring aspects of this vital relationship for the United States." Various sanction bills were introduced in Congress, and on June 20 hearings were held, forcing the administration to announce an effort to postpone World Bank and other new multilateral development loans and to suspend "participation in all high-level exchanges of Government officials with China." Though a more thorough review was promised, no further sanctions were imposed, and Bush began backing off of those that were already decreed.[24]

By early July, so the Human Rights Watch claimed, the Bush administration began publicly to reverse itself. Unknown to the public, the president decided to send a secret mission to Beijing, consisting of his national security adviser, Gen. Brent Scowcroft, and Deputy Secretary of State Lawrence Eagleburger. Bush sent a letter to Deng Xiaoping suggesting the mission, and Deng agreed. Scowcroft and Eagleburger left Washington before dawn of June 30, and their air force plane was refueled in flight. They were in Beijing for twenty-four hours, saw Deng, and returned. A memo titled "Themes" laid out the mission's talking points in advance. It stressed Bush's priorities in maintaining the Sino-American relationship, and separated these priorities from those of Congress and the public at large. It underlined long-term versus immediate events. Especially, Bush was at pains to have Scowcroft and Eagleburger emphasize a hands-off policy in point 8: "How the [government of the PRC] decides to deal with those of its citizens involved in recent events in China is, of course, an internal affair. How the [U.S. government] and the American people view that activity is, equally, an internal affair. Both will be governed by the traditions, culture, and values peculiar to each."

According to James Mann, the "Themes" document revealed just why the first Scowcroft-Eagleburger mission was "worthy of such remarkable secrecy." First, it was an appeal for China to moderate repression and ease the crackdown, though Bush's incoming ambassador, James Lilley, told Scowcroft and Eagleburger frankly, "They're going to get these guys, one way or another." Second, the mission hoped to reopen Bush's direct channel to Deng, who had refused earlier to take Bush's messages and phone calls. As Douglas Paal, a China expert on the NSC staff, said, "If you don't talk to Deng, and he's running the country, you're not talking to anyone that matters."[25]

Another message was that the sanctions would not be serious or long lasting, but were necessary to relieve public and congressional pressure on Bush. After all, it was only minutes prior to testifying before Congress that Secretary of State James A. Baker III told Bush he intended to announce sanctions. He would add to the already-mentioned end on the military relationship applying to arms and officers a freeze on World Bank and other financial lending and the suspension of all high-level contacts. That announcement by Baker surprised Scowcroft, who was already planning his first mission to Beijing at the initiative of Bush himself. Eagleburger was included at Baker's insistence because the secretary, according to Mann, not wishing to turn Chinese relations over to the NSC and Scowcroft, "had insisted that Scowcroft take a senior State Department official with him, and Deputy Secretary of State Eagleburger was assigned to go along."[26]

Finally, "Themes" explained that long-term relationships were crucial and short-term ones were to be "managed." Mann speculated, "The Scowcroft mission may well have aimed at telling Deng that despite the differences over the Tiananmen crackdown and the American sanctions, the United States wanted to continue its security cooperation with China against the Soviet Union—and particularly to keep in operations the clandestine intelligence facilities in China that monitored Soviet missile and nuclear tests." Mann also considered that the mission entailed certain consequences: since Bush mainly wanted to preserve the relationship ante-Tiananmen, he had to assure Deng that he should not take seriously whatever the president said or did in public. The NSC, not State, would now mainly deal with China. These provisions meant a certain divide within the administration because Bush himself would handle the daily details between the United States and the PRC. Those daily details between June 30–July 1 and December 10–13, the dates of the two Scowcroft-Eagleburger missions, marked a steady erosion of the sanction regime from July to December.[27]

The president sent Deng a personal and private letter, and, by June 25, 1989, Deng had replied in kind and agreed to the mission, pledging complete secrecy. As Baker put it, "The Chinese must be made to understand that while [Bush] was committed to maintaining the relationship, he was personally dismayed by the violence and could not in good conscience allow a return to normalcy until the repression ceased."[28] Secrecy had to be maintained, or else congressional hard-liners such as Senator Jesse Helms (R-NC), head of the Foreign Relations Committee, would label the administration as appeasers. Even James Lilley was recalled from Beijing and told face-to-face of the mission to avoid incriminating cables. The mission, Baker continued, spent a day in Beijing and returned: "They reported back to the President that the Chinese had been as inscrutable as ever. The leaders complained bitterly about the sanctions and repeated their ritual insistence that the United States was meddling in their internal affairs."[29] Eagleburger told

Baker, "'They never said so directly, but I think the smarter ones absorbed the message that we can do a lot more for them when they aren't killing their own people.'"[30]

On June 24, Bush got a personal response from Deng, accepting the mission. Bush wanted to get the best expert who knew Deng, and that was Brent Scowcroft. Bush also proposed Eagleburger.[31] The plan was to have an "over-the-top" flight in an unmarked plane, refueled in the air, landing at some Chinese base. The emissaries took off from Andrews Air Force Base at 5:00 A.M. on June 30 in a C-141 cargo plane. President Yang Shangkun himself had to clear it from almost being shot down. They arrived at 1:00 P.M. on July 1, parked in the old terminal building used by Nixon, and went straight to the Diaoyutai State Guest House. The following morning they arrived at the Great Hall of the People where they were received by Deng, Li Peng, Vice Premier Wu Xueqian, and Foreign Minister Qian Qichen. Scowcroft gave a detailed account of that meeting, with close attention to Deng's long monologue: Bush, Deng said, was his friend because his words were trustworthy. But the current impasse could not be resolved "from the perspective of being friends." It was a state issue. "The United States . . . on a large scale had impinged upon Chinese interests and had injured Chinese dignity." China would persist in punishing the instigators and would "never allow outsiders to interfere in their internal affairs, no matter what the consequences." Besides, outside opinion was based on rumors and exaggerations.[32] The United States must understand that the CCP won China after twenty-five years of warfare and would brook no interference. "There is no force whatsoever that can substitute for the People's Republic of China represented by the Communist Party of China."[33]

Scowcroft's rebuttal laid out the president's position that China and the United States were friends on a series of points: their basic interests were the same, each respected the fundamental diversity of the other, both sides benefited strategically against the Soviet Union and also by increased world stability, the relationship was good economically in bilateral trade (more than ten billion dollars), and, finally, the American people's admiration for China increased as the Chinese government encouraged reform. Unfortunately, the June events on Tiananmen Square jeopardized this evolving friendship because Americans viewed this tragedy from a perspective of their own tradition of freedom. Each side must remain true to its own traditions, not interfering in the other's internal affairs. Scowcroft played his last card faceup by showing that Bush was so anxious to preserve the relationship that he was willing to "manage events in a way which will assure a healthy relationship over time." That meant, according to Scowcroft, opposing stiffer sanctions by Congress on China.[34]

How faithful had Scowcroft been to carrying out the points of the

"Themes" document? Those talking points insisted on the benefits of the strategic relationship, especially for the USSR; peace and stability in the world partly due to Sino-American cooperation; its economic viability; that each side must respect the other's internal matters by keeping hands off; and that Bush would continue to be as prudent as possible in maintaining the relationship against hostile and critical voices in the United States. Scowcroft had successfully followed the underlying intention of the "Themes" document to the letter: Bush would continue treating China as if the bloody June demonstrations in Tiananmen Square had never happened, because the overall relationship between China and the United States was more important to each side than the human rights issues involved. They were, as the Chinese maintained and Bush agreed, solely an internal matter. If the U.S. Congress and public disagreed, Bush would do whatever was necessary to mute, even reverse, that criticism to keep China in the U.S. fold. The coming months between the first mission of July 1 and the second mission of December 10–13 illustrated this commitment by Bush and its general acceptance by the Chinese leadership.

Bush's retrenchment continued in early July. He amended his sanction regime in order to allow the sale of three Boeing jets previously banned because of their Honeywell navigation systems, and a shipment of a fourth plane was scheduled. Also, Honeywell was permitted to repair defective systems on similar planes already purchased by China. Defiantly, the Senate approved by an 81 to 10 vote on July 14 of the previous House sanctions as well as called for postponement of Export-Import Bank loans and a review of all bilateral trade agreements, including MFN status, and opposed loans to China by international financial institutions. In November, both the House and the Senate passed legislation sponsored by Rep. Nancy Pelosi (D-CA) waiving the requirement that Chinese students holding J-1 visas return home for two years upon completion of their studies in the United States. Bush pocket vetoed this legislation and instead issued an executive order to the same effect on December 1. Bush reportedly gave a private message to former president Richard Nixon to share with the Chinese leadership on his four-day visit to Beijing, starting on October 28, 1989. Topping all of this off, Scowcroft and Eagleburger made a second visit to Beijing on December 10–13, 1989, that was to be made public.[35]

News of the second Scowcroft-Eagleburger mission and the public revelation of the first came as a shock to Americans. It all happened in this way, as Secretary of State James Baker later put it: "In December, the President sent Scowcroft and Eagleburger back to Beijing. Unfortunately, this trip ignited a new controversy after the Chinese allowed news coverage of the toasts at a dinner in the Great Hall of the People." Baker went on to explain that he had mentioned to TV anchorman David Brinkley on December 10, "This was the first time we'd had high-level officials go to China since the massacre. A week later, the first Eagleburger-Scowcroft trip was reported by TV network CNN. The secrecy of that first mission was so absolute that I literally had forgotten about it during the broadcast to my subsequent embarrassment."[36] CNN, according to Mann, had probably gotten wind of the first mission because the Chinese forwarded to the Pentagon the bill in Chinese for refueling the mission's C-141 air force plane, and the Pentagon had to call in its translators. Through this, word of the first mission gradually leaked out.[37]

About the content of the second mission, Scowcroft wrote that, unlike before, they had no need this time to remain secret.[38] In these talks, each side put forward its complaints, and Scowcroft covered the Bush-Gorbachev meeting at Malta. "The second meeting with Qian [Qichen, foreign minister] was a private one. We hammered out the terms of a 'road map' of reciprocal moves to take us gradually but steadily toward normalization." There was mention of a visit to the United States by General Secretary Jiang Zemin and a lifting of sanctions. By January 1990, the House override of the veto was 390 to 25, but in the Senate on January 25, the override failed by a 62 to 37 vote, a close call for the Bush policy. However, the whole process of normalization was so slow. China did not explain, and this tardiness one could only speculate about.[39]

Within weeks of Tiananmen Square, Bush had made concessions to the Chinese: he had allowed the U.S. Export-Import Bank to resume loans to American companies for business in China and had approved the export of Hughes Aircraft satellites for launching in China. The first, in itself, granted the China National Offshore Oil Corporation $9.75 million. Later, because the Cold War was winding down in 1989 with the fall of the Berlin Wall, on February 7, 1990, Eagleburger testified before the Senate Foreign Relations Committee about the old rationale of the anti-Soviet policy that had pushed the United States toward China. The new justification, said Eagleburger, was that China might sell weapons of mass destruction overseas. China was strategically important to the United States because of its threat to sell these weapons, and if it stopped exporting them, it would have less strategic importance. Beijing had an incentive "if not to act in menacing ways, at least always to appear to be on the verge of doing so."[40]

Russia and China continue to perplex Americans with distorted mirrors, even after Reagan's Russian accommodation and Bush's realism toward China. The persistence of old conclusions—negative to Russia and positive to China—prevents the new beginnings sought by them. Even a casual look at two recent reports by an influential policy-shaping organization tends to confirm the suspicion that old attitudes die hard.

Afterword

It is interesting to note how persistently the image of distorted mirrors continues into the twenty-first century. For instance, the Council on Foreign Relations in 2006 published *Russia's Wrong Direction: What the United States Can and Should Do*. Though the council talks of accommodation and the importance of Russia, it continues to sustain a century of negativism toward Russia by focusing on "Russia's growing authoritarianism," which it sees as undermining a potential cooperation that has to be based on democracy as a prerequisite. Only such a "modern and effective state" could cooperate successfully. The long and short of it is, as this report contends, "The United States and its allies should not belittle Russia by subjecting it to double standards but show respect by holding Russia to higher ones." At the same time, the United States is to exert pressure to get Russia to limit its exports as instruments of coercion and ease its pressure on its neighbors. The report even suggests helping organizations in Russia to support "free and fair" elections. Bureaucratic authoritarianism and overreliance on energy exports are Russia's twin problems, even though a middle class seems to be emerging with the latent creation of a civil society. But it is all fragile: "Yet taken as a whole, the balance sheet of the past five years is extremely negative."[1]

Problems continue. There is corruption, and the so-called dictatorship of law has resulted in dissolving Yukos Oil and the trial and imprisonment of its chief, Mikhail Khodorkovsky. At the same time, the Kremlin's power grows as it controls the "commanding heights." The Duma weakens, with Putin's party, United Russia, running it. Thus, "High levels of corruption, ineffective institutions, and the centralization of power" make it difficult to predict Russia's future.[2] Divisive issues also split Russia from the West —NATO expansion, abrogation of the ABM Treaty, Iraq and Iran, and Chechnya, to name a few. Perhaps the only remaining areas of cooperation are in counterterrorism, energy security, and nonproliferation. The report outlines what a partnership might consist of: mutual confidence without hidden agendas and one-sided advantages. And the report worries about a growing geopolitical partnership between Russia and China.[3]

Democracy, for this report, is the wedge issue. Only the Russian people can change that; nevertheless, "how Western leaders talk about democracy can make a difference." Pressure on Russia through the old G7 (Group of Seven) and withholding World Trade Organization (WTO) membership can be used as well as perpetuating, or not, the NATO Russian Council. This gets to the council's recommendations: continuing nonproliferation and nuclear cooperation; keeping up with counterterrorism efforts; transparency on energy policies; promoting WTO for Russian accession, if it works to liberalize the Russian economy, as well as graduating Russia from the Jackson-Vanik Amendment (a 1972 trade act denying MFN status to countries without market economies that restrict emigration rights, a yearly waiver granted to the PRC, but not the Russian Federation); and environmental cooperation. The 2008 presidential elections in Russia are one key cause, and, therefore, the United States needs to win public commitments to "open, constitutional, and pluralist bases to reverse the practices described above." That means stopping attempts to block candidates and parties, retributions, and news domination.[4]

Criticisms of this report were included within the report. For instance, one critic believed that making authoritarian trends the wedge issue would be ineffective and counterproductive. Others thought that closing various clubs to Russia was an "empty gesture—annoying Moscow without influencing it." Further, American policy would be better off if it cold-bloodedly realized that the "United States and Russia have real differences and conflicts but that they can cooperate when they have shared goals." The United States did that with the USSR, so why not with post-Soviet Russia?[5]

As to China, what, might we ask, has been gained in the almost twenty years since 1989 in U.S.-China relations? Was the Bush administration or its critics essentially right about how to proceed with the PRC to gain greater cooperation as well as broader human rights in China? A current China Task Force of the Council on Foreign Relations assesses this in its report number 59: *U.S.-China Relations: An Affirmative Agenda, a Responsible Course,* dated 2007. "No relationship will be as important to the twenty-first century," contends the Council on Foreign Relations report, "as the one between the United States, the world's great power, and China, the world's rising power."[6] China's development is "shifting the geopolitical terrain and contributing to uncertainty about China's future course." The "engagement" policy of the past thirty-five years needs a strategy, according to the task force, "focused on the integration of China into the global community and finds that such an approach will best encourage China to act in a way consistent with U.S. interests and international norms."[7] The task force maintains that the United States should be "creating and taking advantage of opportunities to build on common interests in the Asia-Pacific region and as regards a number of global concerns."[8] The policy of engagement, supported in 2004 by 59 percent of the American public against alarmist polemics, has allowed the U.S.-China relationship to be transformed from antagonism to dialogue and often cooperation, where China itself changed, becoming integrated in various multinational organizations, such as the World Trade Organization, Association of Southeast Asian Nations Regional Forum, and Asia-Pacific Economic Cooperation. Instead of standing militarily aloof, it has joined the Nuclear Nonproliferation Treaty, the Chemical Weapons Convention, and the Nuclear Suppliers Group; agreed to abide by the limits of the Missile Technology Control Regime; and signed the Comprehensive Nuclear Test Ban Treaty.

The task force mentions Tiananmen Square and the American response with sanctions and human rights concerns, but notes that two years later the Cold War rationale had collapsed, ending the strategic-triangle justification that gave Nixon his cause for engagement. That shifted the emphasis to nonproliferation, trade, and regional security. "Despite the overall success of engagement in helping to shape China's interests in ways desired by the U.S. government, U.S. political support for engagement is under strain."[9] On the one hand, some say that China's strategic interests are not compatible with the United States and that the United States is not sufficiently protected, while, on the other hand, there are those who call economic engagement a form of appeasement. Sources of uneasiness are China's economic challenge, its lag on human rights, its effort to displace U.S. influence, and its military modernization, all while America is heavily involved in Iraq and Afghanistan and China is becoming more powerful and assertive.[10]

The task force believes that "China's overall trajectory over the past thirty-five years of engagement with the United States is positive. Growing adherence to international rules, institutions, and norms—particularly in the areas of trade and security—mark China's global integration." But there are still divergences: the best way to pursue nonproliferation, respect for human rights—political liberty, free speech, religious freedom—and what the limits on sovereignty should be to protect a nation from outside intervention when it "grossly violates international norms (e.g., Sudan)."[11]

The tenor of the task force report, with some exceptions, supports the Nixonian policy, the one the former president asked then-president George H. W. Bush to sustain in a phone call on the night of June 3, 1989. That was when Bush took the extraordinary step of sending his national security adviser, Gen. Brent Scowcroft, and Baker's deputy secretary of state, Lawrence

Eagleburger, to Beijing on a top-secret mission, repeated publicly the following December. Now, almost two decades later and with much public and congressional hand-wringing, President George W. Bush continued accommodation. With or without sanction regimes of one sort or another, whether it is termed appeasement, that policy of Nixon's has won in the long term and been productive of some positive results. It has not been free of faults, and it has been less productive of human rights.

So where is the United States? The long march through the twentieth century, from "Siberian" Kennan to Ronald Reagan, from "Old China Hand" Rockhill to George H. W. Bush, demonstrates just how persistent perceptions of Russia and China are. Both reports from the Council on Foreign Relations continue the same old stereotypes and build their recommendations on them: negative to Russia and positive to China. After a century, not much has changed. When the authors interviewed General Scowcroft and former Secretary of State Eagleburger, they were amazed to find the same views as the council's: China was headed for a democratic future; Russia was relapsing into authoritarianism.

On September 15, 2006, one of the authors, Eugene P. Trani, published an op-ed piece in the *International Herald Tribune*. It is the other bookend to his 1984 piece quoted in the preface, and it is titled "Criticize but Don't Exclude."[12] It concludes this book with our essential point about Russia and China, and it is quoted in full below:

> The Moscow and St. Petersburg I traveled to this summer stand in stark contrast to the Russia depicted by the media and politicians in the United States.
>
> The Russia I visited was one of growing prosperity and innovation, progressive education and an economic strength not based exclusively on oil and gas.
>
> It was a Russia uniquely positioned to forge solid partnerships for the war on terrorism, nuclear nonproliferation and energy—all vital issues for America.
>
> But Russia intends to achieve its economic goals, even if that means doing so without the United States. The Bank of Russia made several announcements in 2005 that heralded the increasing role of the euro in its exchange-rate strategy. I observed in many Russian hotels that currency markers were in rubles and euros, not in dollars.
>
> This sidestepping of America is apparent in other pivotal arenas. Russia has taken an active interest in the expanding Chinese market, and in connecting its security strategy to China's expanding power.
>
> Russia is in a unique position, geographically and politically, to meet

China's rapidly growing demand for energy, natural resources and timber. And China provides Russia with a ripe market for high-tech weapons.

In a 2005 article in the Beijing Review, the Russian ambassador to China, Sergei Razov, wrote of bilateral relations with China as being "at the highest level in history," citing their first joint military maneuvers and rapidly growing trade, the volume of which exceeded $29 billion in 2005.

Razov also discussed the ten-fold increase in Chinese students in Russia over the past decade—that when the number of Chinese students applying to U.S. universities has drastically decreased.

Russia's deepening relations with China have already created alarming vulnerabilities.

In 2005, Russia and China attempted to restrict access by the United States and NATO to Central Asian air bases, despite the critical role of these bases for military and humanitarian operations in Afghanistan—an effort that Russia previously supported.

If the United States continues to criticize Russia, Russian-Chinese relations over the next 10 years could lead to a regrouping of world powers and possibly a new Cold War.

But if the United States moved to full engagement with Russia, it could realize considerable policy and economic gains. For a model, America need look no further than its foreign policy with China—like Russia, a nuclear-armed nation with a long history of authoritarian government.

China also does not always play by America's rules. But while the State Department recently announced sanctions against Russia for the alleged selling of restricted items to Iran, the Department of the Treasury gave China only a slap on the wrist in May over its currency manipulation in flagrant disregard of U.S. law.

Last April, President George W. Bush welcomed President Hu Jintao to the United States, saying, "The United States and China are two nations divided by a vast ocean yet connected through a global economy that has created opportunity for both our peoples."

America's failure to bestow the same recognition on Russia as it has on China could end up relegating the United States not only to the other side of the ocean, but to the other side of a new kind of iron curtain.

Yes, Russia is a less democratic nation than it was under Boris Yeltsin. Yet forcing a political reform agenda on Vladimir Putin not only runs the risk of failure, but of alienating Russia to such an extent that possibilities for positive engagement will be lost.

A more plausible policy toward Russia would be to take more of an "agree to disagree" stance on certain issues, such as Russia's relations with other post-Soviet states, and to remain unequivocal about the emerging authoritarianism, while embracing Russia's emerging economic liberalism.

Crafting a Russian relationship around areas that are mutually advantageous would give the United States a better chance of fostering political liberalism in Russia.

America's policy of isolating Russia may not only fail, but it may also force Russia to create its own world without the United States—a world that really would head in the wrong direction.

notes

1. See, for instance, Peter G. Filene, *Americans and the Soviet Experiment, 1917–1933,* and Ralph B. Levering, *American Opinion and the Russian Alliance, 1939–1945,* on the Russian side, and T. Christopher Jespersen, *American Images of China, 1931–1949,* and Patricia C. Neils, *China Images in the Life of Henry Luce,* on the Chinese side. For historiographical problems, see opening paragraphs of the Bibliography.

2. Filene, *Americans and the Soviet Experiment,* 2, 4.

3. Levering, *American Opinion and the Russian Alliance,* 6; Alec M. Gallup, *The Gallup Poll Cumulative Index: Public Opinion, 1935–1997* (for Russia see 468–74, for China 91–93). See also http://brain.gallup.com; under the heading "Russia," 1,601 items are listed, and for China 536 items are found. An interesting release closer to our analysis was March 8, 1967, "Public Softening Views on Russia." Gallup noted Americans were "far less antagonistic to Russia today than a decade ago [because of a] dramatic shift in attitudes toward Red China." Highly unfavorable opinions had declined since 1957 from 71 to 48 percent. By 1967, Americans believed Red China was the greater menace. In 1961, opinion had been five to three against Russia. Whereas in 1961, only 32 percent believed China was the greater menace, it had grown to 71 percent in 1967. See *The Gallup Report* (March 8, 1967) or go to http://brain.gallup.com and search Russia, checking the date for March 8, 1967.

4. Filene, *Americans and the Soviet Experiment,* 5, 2.

5. In the case of Russia, see, for instance, Eugene Anschel, ed., *The American Image of Russia, 1775–1917,* and for China, Arthur H. Smith, *Chinese Characteristics.*

6. Paul Kennedy, *The Rise and Fall of the Great Powers: Economic and Military Conflict from 1500–2000,* 41–70.

7. For the original interview, see *Reference News* (Beijing), May 20, 1984; for the op-ed, see Eugene P. Trani, "China the Friend vs. Russia the Foe: Different Perceptions Can't Help but Affect Shape of Foreign Policy," *Kansas City Star,* July 8, 1984.

8. As to the op-ed in *International Herald Tribune,* see Eugene P. Trani, "Criticize, but Don't Exclude," *International Herald Tribune,* September 15, 2006.

Introduction. Distortions in the Looking Glass

1. See Donald E. Davis and Eugene P. Trani, "Roosevelt and the U.S. Role: Perception Makes Policy," where we deal with public opinion and Kennan's influence on TR.

2. George Kennan (hereafter GK) to R. Smith, June 16/28, 1885, GK Papers, box 6, Library of Congress (hereafter LC).

3. Kennan, *Siberia and the Exile System*, 1:74–83, 95, 160.

4. Ibid., 187.

5. Ibid., 288, 348–49.

6. Ibid., 8, 16, 19, 20, 25, 122, 125, quote on 17.

7. Smith to GK, October 9, 1885, and R. W. Gilder to GK, October 15, 1885, GK Papers, box 1, LC.

8. Kennan, *Siberia*, 2:168ff, 184, 194n, quotes on 189, 199, 200.

9. GK to Smith, October 26, 1885, GK Papers, box 6, LC.

10. Kennan, *Siberia*, 2:372–74.

11. Ibid., 420, 422, 424, 428–29; R. Smith to GK, March 26, 1886, GK Papers, box 1, LC for quote.

12. Kennan, *Siberia*, 430, 431.

13. GK to Gilder, November 3, 1888, Century Company Papers, box 53, New York Public Library. As to Isabel Hapgood's criticism of Kennan, see Anna M. Babey, *Americans in Russia, 1776–1917: A Study of the American Travelers in Russia from the American Revolution to the Russian Revolution*, 20; and Norman E. Saul, *Concord and Conflict: The United States and Russia, 1867–1914*, 290. An interesting take is Martin E. Malia, *Russia under Western Eyes: From the Bronze Horseman to the Lenin Mausoleum.*

14. We use Pinyin for Chinese romanization, except for familiar names in Wade-Giles, and both are usually given at first mention.

15. Peter Hopkirk, *Trespassers on the Roof of the World: The Secret Exploration of Tibet*, 74–75.

16. William Woodville Rockhill (hereafter WWR) to Alfred E. Hippisley, December 17, 1889, Series I, item 2086, William Woodville Rockhill Papers, Houghton Library, Harvard University (hereafter WWRP, HLHU).

17. George F. Kennan, *American Diplomacy, 1900–1950*, 31.

18. The open-door notes are nicely summarized in Robert H. Ferrell, *American Diplomacy: A History*, 224–27 (quote on 227). For more on the state of the field, see Warren I. Cohen, ed., *Pacific Passage: The Study of American–East Asian Relations on the Eve of the Twenty-first Century.*

19. For a short review of Rockhill's career, see the *Dictionary of American Biography* and Paul A. Varg, *Open Door Diplomat: The Life of W.W. Rockhill*. A newer version of this is Peter Stanley, "The Making of an American Sinologist: W. Rockhill and the Open Door."

20. A. Whitney Griswold, *The Far Eastern Policy of the United States*, 74. "Rockhill composed the actual drafts of the open door notes themselves [and later did] so much to launch the United States on its new policy" (82).

21. Theodore Roosevelt to Mrs. Rockhill, January 15, 1915, item number 2284, WWRP, HLHU.

22. Henry Adams to WWR, March 10, 1896, Series I, item 19, WWRP, HLHU; TR to WWR, February 12, 1896, Series I, item 2270, WWRP, HLHU.

23. TR to WWR, February 17, 1896, Series I, item 2271, WWRP, HLHU; WWR to C. W. Campbell, April 3, 1896, and to Gen. James H. Wilson, October 24, 1896, WWR Letterbook, vol. 2, WWRP, HLHU.

24. Adams to WWR, August 24, 1898, Series I, item 24, WWRP, HLHU; September 15, 1898, Series I, item 25, WWRP, HLHU; John Hay to WWR, August 31, 1898, Series I, item 1051, WWRP, HLHU; TR to Charles McCauley, March 9, 1899, Series I, item 2272, WWRP, HLHU.

25. WWR to Hay, August 3, 1899, Letterbook, vol. 4, WWRP, HLHU.

26. Hay to WWR, August 7, 1899, Series I, item 1054, WWRP, HLHU; WWR to Hippisley, August 18, 1899, Series I, item 2105, WWRP, HLHU (emphasis added); WWR to Alvey A. Adee, August 19, 1899, Letterbook 4, HLHU, WWRP.

27. Hay to WWR, August 24, 1899, Series I, item 1005, WWRP, HLHU; WWR to Adee, August 19, 1899, Letterbook 4, WWRP, HLHU; WWR to Hippisley, August 26, 1899, Series I, item 2106, WWRP, HLHU.

28. WWR to Hippisley, August 28, 1899, Series I, item 2109 A., WWRP, HLHU.

29. WWR to Hippisley, August 29, 1899, Series I, item 2108, B., WWRP, HLHU.

Chapter 1. "Soviet Sam" and the Émigrés

1. Samuel N. Harper (hereafter SNH), *The Russia I Believe In: The Memoirs of Samuel N. Harper, 1902–1941*, 6–9, quotes on 9 and 10.

2. William R. Harper to SNH, January 16, 1904, box 1, f. 6, Samuel Harper Papers, Special Collections, University of Chicago. All SNH letters are found in this collection unless otherwise noted.

3. SNH, *Russia I Believe In*, 67–90.

4. SNH to Charles Crane, June 21, 1916, box 3, f. 5.

5. Milton Browner, "Crane and Harper Tell Why New Russia Will Succeed," March 22, 1917, box 3, f. 12.

6. This attitude may be seen in such items as "Address to the National Geographic Society," March 30, 1917, box 32, f. 44, or SNH to Nicholas Murray Butler, April 19, 1917, box 3, f. 16.

7. SNH MSS, "Address to American-Russian Chamber of Commerce, Chicago, Illinois," March 28, 1917, box 32, f. 44.

8. SNH MSS, "1914–1917," box 34, f. 36.

9. SNH to Crane, March 18, 1917, box 3, f. 12; SNH to James Keeley, April 18, 1917, box 3, f. 16. See also SNH to Nicholas M. Butler, April 19, 1917, box 3, f. 16.

10. SNH, "Address to National Geographic Society," March 30, 1917, box 32, f. 44.

11. SNH to Paul Milyoukov, April 12, 1917, box 3, f. 15; Robert Lansing, *War Memoirs of Robert Lansing, Secretary of State*, 351.

12. SNH to Jean Jules Jusserand, April 21, 1917, box 4, f. 1.

13. SNH MSS, "February Revolution," box 32, f. 49.

14. Donald E. Davis and Eugene P. Trani, *The First Cold War: The Legacy of Woodrow Wilson in U.S-Soviet Relations,* 37; SNH, *Russia I Believe In,* 99.

15. SNH to Roger H. Williams, [April 1917], box 3, f. 13.

16. SNH, *Russia I Believe In,* 100–101.

17. Ibid.,107–8. It is interesting that as late as the beginning of May, Harper had criticized the "wild rumors" spread by American correspondents in Petrograd, and he put "little stock in their 'sensational' comments" (SNH to Richard Crane, May 1, 1917, box 4, f. 3).

18. SNH to R. Crane, July 23, 1917, box 4, f. 9.

19. Draft for "The Spirit of the Russian Revolution," box 60, f. 23. "Lenin and his ideas," Harper said, "are discredited" (SNH to Eugene Prince, July 12, 1917, box 4, f. 9).

20. SNH to Harry Pratt Judson, December 14, 1917, box 4, f. 15; SNH to William Phillips, December 14, 1917, box 4, f. 15; SNH to Walter Lippmann, January 18, 1918, box 4, f. 18.

21. SNH, *Russia I Believe In,* 126–31.

22. U.S. Senate Documents, vol. 4, *A Memorandum on Certain Aspects of the Bolshevist Movement in Russia,* 66th Cong., 2d sess., 1920.

23. "Memo on the Discipline of the Russian Communist Party," 1920, box 23, f. 13.

24. "Introduction to the Harper Papers," 11, 10; "Selected Materials for Memoirs," box 77, f. 2.

25. SNH, *Russia I Believe In,* 131.

26. Ibid., 197–98.

27. SNH to Chapin Huntington, October 4, 1918, box 6, f. 1. See also William Appleman Williams, *American-Russian Relations, 1781–1947,* 152–53, concerning Batolin and Harper's interest in this project.

28. On demoralization, see SNH to Breckinridge Long, March 22, 1920, box 7, f. 20; for the quote, see SNH to Long, April 10, 1920, box 7, f. 21.

29. SNH to Bernard Pares, May 6, 1920, box 7, f. 24.

30. For Harper's leave from the State Department, see SNH to Allen J. Carter, April 17, 1921, box 9, f. 8; and for the department's reorganization, see Carter to SNH, May 8, 1921, box 9, f. 10.

31. SNH to R. Crane, May 1, 1921, box 9, f. 10.

32. SNH to W. C. Huntington, April 24, 1922, box 10, f. 1.

33. SNH to Poole, October 10, 1922, box 10, f. 7; SNH to Boris Bakhmetev, November 11, 1920, box 10, f. 8; SNH to Ariadna Tyrkova-Williams, April 14, 1923, box 10, f. 21; SNH to Pares, April 14, 1923, box 10, f. 21; SNH to Pares, January 14, 1924, box 11, f. 6.

34. SNH to Bakhmetev, October 2, 1924, and SNH to Don Brodie, October 2, 1924, both in box 11, f. 23.

35. See his letters to Mikhail Karpovich, December 15, 1925, and to Brodie, December 26, 1925, both in box 12, f. 13.

36. "Introduction to the Harper Papers," 14.

37. SNH, "Three Months in the Soviet Union," box 60, f. 1.

38. Ibid., 1.

39. Ibid., 6.

40. SNH, *Russia I Believe In,* 6.

41. SNH, "Three Months in the Soviet Union," 12.

42. George S. Moyer, *The Attitude of the United States towards the Recognition of Russia,* 150–51.

43. "Secretary of State Kellogg's Declaration of Policy of April 14, 1928," *New York Times,* April 15, 1928, as quoted in *American Policy towards Russia since 1917: A Study of Diplomatic History, International Law, and Public Opinion,* by Frederick Schuman, 352.

44. Assistant Secretary of State William R. Castle to Mr. Carter, March 13, 1931, State Department (hereafter SD), Record Group (hereafter RG) 59, roll 1, National Archives (hereafter NA).

45. Editorial, *New Republic* 70 (March 30, 1932): 165; Jerome Davis, "Capitalism and Communism," 68.

46. Castle to Carter, March 30, 1932, SD, RG 59, roll 1, NA; Francis R. Walsh to Franklin Roosevelt, October 28, 1933, SD, RG 59, roll 1, NA; Robert Durham to Robert F. Kelley, December 4, 1933, SD, RG 59, roll 1, NA.

47. Felix Cole to the secretary of state (hereafter SS), November 27, 1931, SD, RG 59, roll 1, NA.

48. Charles C. Hart to SS, September 20, 1933, SD, RG 59, roll 1, NA.

49. Cole to SS, June 5, 1931, SD, RG 59, roll 1, NA.

50. Castle to Carter, March 13, 1931, SD, RG 59, roll 1, NA.

51. Schuman, *American Policy,* 290.

52. Marriner to Castle, February 13, 1931, SD, RG 59, roll 1, NA.

53. Hollace Ransdell, "Mr. Fish Down South," 30; Conrad Seiler, "The Redmongers Go West," 347.

54. Edmund Wilson, "Foster and Fish," 162.

55. Hamilton Fish, "The Menace of Communism," 58. For a discussion of the minority report, see "Outlawing of Reds: A National Menace," 1.

56. SNH, *Russia I Believe In,* 158.

57. Preston Kumler to SNH, January 28, 1928, box 13, f. 15.

58. Kumler to SNH, January 30, 1928; SNH to Kumler, February 2, 1928, both in box 13, f. 15.

59. SNH, *Russia I Believe In,* 156.

60. SNH, *Civic Training in Soviet Russia,* xi–xii.

61. Most notably there was Merle Fainsod of Harvard and John Hazard of Columbia University.

62. Ibid., xvii, 15, 33, 39, 366, 381.

63. Translation of I. M. Pavlov's review from *Izvestiia,* November 14, 1929, box 14, f. 27.

64. SNH, *Russia I Believe In,* 156.

65. SNH to Prince Mirsky, October 11, 1928, box 13, f. 33.

66. Ibid.; "Lecture on Bolshevism," ca. 1930, box 31, f. 5.

67. "Lecture on Bolshevism."

68. SNH, *Russia I Believe In*, 242.

69. Ibid., 245.

70. SNH, "Selected Notes, 1937–41," box 76, f. 20.

71. Ibid.; "Selected Notes for Press Release," April 19, 1938, box 20, f. 20.

72. SNH, *Russia I Believe In*, 246–48.

73. "Introduction to the Harper Papers," 14.

74. SNH, *Russia I Believe In*, 268.

75. SNH, memo, "American-Soviet Relations," box 76, f. 4.

76. Ant. Florovsky, "The Work of Russian Émigrés in History (1921–27)."

77. Harold H. Fisher, ed., *American Research on Russia*, 23–25; Robert F. Byrnes, *Awakening American Education to the World: The Role of Archibald Cary Coolidge, 1866–1928*, 8, 53, 143.

78. R. Byrnes, *Awakening American Education*, 43, 67, 139.

79. Not only did the number of university students increase, but the composition of the student body changed as well. Jews, presuming an interest in their roots in the Russian past, came to make up 40 percent of the students at Columbia and 20 percent at Harvard (Stephen Steinberg, *The Academic Melting Pot: Catholics and Jews in American Higher Education*, 9).

80. Martin E. Malia, "Michael Karpovich, 1888–1959," 60–71; R. Byrnes, *Awakening American Education*, 108.

81. Malia, "Michael Karpovich, 1888–1959," 63.

82. R. Byrnes, *Awakening American Education*, 108.

83. Bakhmetev to George Vernadsky, May 23, 1939, Boris Bakhmetev Papers, Bakhmetev Archive of Russian and East European History and Culture, Columbia University (hereafter BP, CU).

84. Editor's preface to Michael Florinsky, *The End of the Russian Empire*, vii.

85. *New York Times*, January 31, 1940; September 20, 1953; October 14, 1981.

86. Michael Florinsky, *Toward an Understanding of the USSR: A Study in Government, Politics, and Economic Planning*, 70, 232.

87. *US/USSR Textbook Study, Project: Interim Report, June 1981*, Howard D. Mehlinger, director (Bloomington). The Soviet-authored section of the report notes that of the twenty-five grade-seven to grade-eleven geography, world history, and U.S. history textbooks examined, "the majority . . . call V. I. Lenin 'Nickolai Lenin.'" Florinsky refers to Lenin as "Nicholas" in the 1939 edition of *Toward an Understanding of the USSR* (84) but changed to "Vladimir" in the 1951 edition (9). To be fair, Florinsky rarely used a given name in his references to Lenin; he prefaced Lenin's name in citations with the initial N. On the tone of Soviet coverage, see Marvin Hershel Berman, *The Treatment of the Soviet Union and Communism in Selected World History Textbooks, 1920–1970*, 153–54.

88. Bakhmetev to Edward M. House, March 11, 1919, and to DeWitt Clinton Poole, April 23, 1923, BP, CU. Bakhmetev advised the United States to insist upon the following conditions before entering into any relations with the Soviets: the

Russian government must renounce revolutionary propaganda outside Russian borders, the Russian army must be demobilized, the Russian government must demonstrate that it enjoyed the confidence and support of the people, and the Russian government must pledge to make no political or economic agreement that would interfere with Russia's "free and unhampered development" (Bakhmetev to Poole, February 13, 1922, BP, CU).

89. Bakhmetev to Vernadsky, October 14, 1937, and to Mikhail Karpovich, October 27, 1942, BP, CU; Arthur P. Mendel, ed., *Political Memoirs, 1905–1917,* vi–vii.

90. Stephen F. Cohen, *Rethinking the Soviet Experience: Politics and History since 1917,* 6 (Merle Fainsod quote) (see also 150n7).

91. Ibid., 11–12, 161n22; Fisher, *American Research on Russia,* 2; Cyril E. Black and John M. Thompson, eds., *American Teaching about Russia,* 13, 52.

Chapter 2. The Boys from Riga

1. For the exchange of artists and the special terminology, see Norman E. Saul, *Friends or Foes? The United States and Russia, 1921–41,* 105, 117–21, 136–45, 157–8, 200–204, especially chapters 4 and 5 for an extraordinary account of cross-cultural themes.

2. "Autobiographical Sketch," n.d., box 9, f. 1, Robert F. Kelley Papers, Georgetown University; "Robert F. Kelley: Soldier-Scholar-Diplomat," n.d. (probably June 3, 1976, *Washington Post*), box 5, f. 1, Loy W. Henderson Papers (hereafter LH), Library of Congress (hereafter LC); Loy W. Henderson to F. L. Propas, February 5, 1977, box 15, f. Post-Retirement Materials, LH, LC.

3. Daniel Yergin, *Shattered Peace: The Origins of the Cold War and the National Security State,* 18–41. We are indebted to Daniel F. Harrington's excellent analysis of Yergin's "Riga Axioms" hypothesis in his article "Kennan, Bohlen, and the Riga Axioms," 423–37.

4. Frederic L. Propas, "Creating a Hard Line toward Russia: The Training of State Department Soviet Experts, 1927–1937," 215; Kelley quoted in Foy D. Kohler and Mose L. Harvey, eds., *The Soviet Union, Yesterday, Today, Tomorrow: A Colloquy of American Long Timers in Moscow* (Miami: University of Miami Press, 1975), 164.

5. Kohler and Harvey, *Soviet Union,* 167, 203.

6. Saul, *Friend or Foe?* 255, 256; Gumberg writing to Ray Robins, March 13, 1931, as quoted by Saul. Saul believes that Kelley would remain opposed, though yield to accommodation. Saul comments: "It is truly unfortunate that Kelley, America's main State Department expert on Russia and a genuinely erudite scholar, if there ever was one in the State Department, had such hostile, prejudiced views toward the Soviet Union" (256n8).

7. Propas, "Creating a Hard Line," 222; Marin Weil, *A Pretty Good Club: The Founding Fathers of the U.S. Foreign Service,* 53.

8. Yergin, *Shattered Peace,* 26.

9. Henderson to Maurice B. Conway, September 5, 1971, box 15, f. Post-

Retirement Correspondence, LH, LC. Charles E. Bohlen also agreed. See his *Witness to History, 1929–1969,* 271; and historians W. A. Williams, *American-Russian Relations,* especially chap. 5; and Davis and Trani, *First Cold War,* 200–206.

10. Loy W. Henderson, *A Question of Trust: The Origins of U.S.-Soviet Diplomatic Relations; The Memoirs of Loy W. Henderson,* 41, 43, quote on 46.

11. Henderson, *Question of Trust,* 50–51, 57, 60, 66, 75, 79, 117.

12. Natalie Grant, "The Russian Section: A Window on the Soviet Union," 109–11.

13. Ibid., 112. Grant notes one report by Packer as receiving a "special commendation" for excellence: it reviewed the Fifth Congress of the Communist International (Comintern), of perennial interest to policy makers in Washington because of fears of communist interference in American domestic affairs.

14. Ibid., 114, 115; Propas, "Creating a Hard Line," 219–20, 222. On Lehrs, see Saul, *Friends or Foes?* 12.

15. George F. Kennan, *Memoirs, 1925–1950,* 83. Although there is an absolute dearth of Riga materials in *Foreign Relations of the United States* (hereafter *FRUS*), a very few managed to slip through, such as Hugh Martin's. Kennan also reported on the problem of American citizens in Russia, especially those who took Soviet citizenship and then decided to return but were refused by Soviet authorities. As far as the State Department was concerned, they ceased being U.S. citizens. For Kennan, see *FRUS, 1932,* 3:521–26. As to the Riga Legation-Consular materials, they constitute thirty-five boxes at the National Archives in College Park, Maryland (hereafter NARA, CP). This is a largely untapped source.

16. Bohlen, *Witness to History,* 10–11, 13, 39.

17. Henderson, *Question of Trust,* 144, quotes on 145, 147. As to Borah's resolution, see *FRUS, 1924,* 2:683; and Committee on Foreign Relations, United States Senate, 68th Congress, 1st sess., pursuant to Senate Resolution 50, declaring that the Senate of the United States favors recognition of the present Soviet government in Russia (pt. 2, 159, 227ff).

18. Henderson, *Question of Trust,* 147–49, quotes on 149, 156–57. On the issue of trade, see the refusal of floating German loans in the United States to be used to advance credits to the USSR. See *FRUS, 1926,* 2:906–10; and *FRUS, 1927,* 3:652–53.

19. Henderson, *Question of Trust,* 159–61, quote on 160; Secretary of State Frank B. Kellogg to Senator Butler, February 23, 1928, *FRUS, 1928,* 822. The secretary maintained that the United States did not object to long-term credits, if the financing did not involve the sale of securities to the public and would look with disfavor on the flotation of a loan in the United States or use of U.S. credit if advanced to a regime that had repudiated its obligations to the United States and its citizens (825).

20. Henderson, *Question of Trust,* 162–68, quotes on 162, 165.

21. Ibid., 173–78, quotes on 175, 178.

22. Ibid., 181–98.

23. Ibid., 203; Stimson to Borah, September 8, 1932, as quoted by Henderson in ibid., 204; ibid., 213–15.

24. Evan Young to SS, March 9, 1920, RG 84, Records of Foreign Service Posts: Latvia (hereafter RFSP:L), vol. 009, "American Mission, Riga, Gade, and Young," 800, 1920, NARA, CP.

25. Poole to the Undersecretary of State, March 20, 1920, Information Series C, no. 49, Russia no. 16, "Memorandum on the Bolshevist or Communist Party in Russia and Its Relations to the Third or Communist International and to the Russian Soviets," 3. This pamphlet is included in ibid.

26. See the front piece to Robert F. Kelley's *Report*, "Documents Setting Forth the Attitude of the Soviet Government Towards the United States," June 15, 1927, RG 84, RFSP:L, vol. 218, NARA, CP.

27. Ibid., 44–47, quote on 47.

28. Ibid., 47–49, 51, quotes on 52, 53, 55, 56–57.

29. Ibid., 59–69, quotes on 61, 64, 65, 66, and 69.

30. For Steklov, see ibid., 73 (or *Pravda*, March 27, 1923). As to Hughes's remarks, see *FRUS, 1923*, 2:755–58.

31. See Kelley's *Report* of June 15, 1927, 74 (or *Pravda*, May 26, 1923), RG 84, RFSP:L, vol. 218, NARA, CP.

32. Ibid., 75 (or *Pravda*, June 19, 1923).

33. Ibid., 76, 77, 80.

34. Ibid., 80, 82, 83, 84.

35. Ibid., 87, quotes on 90, 92, and 94.

36. Ibid., 96–99.

37. Quotes from F. W. B. Cole to SS, December 17, 1924, "Signs of Opposition," RG 84, RFSP, American Legation—Riga, Cole, 800R, vol. 043, no. 843, December 17, 1924, NARA, CP; vol. 044, no. 2032, March 31, 1924 (inclusive for the month of April, in part), NARA, CP.

38. Ibid.

39. Cole to SS, January 22, 1927, no. 1303, vol. 074, RG 84, RFSP:L (Russian) American Legation: Riga—Cole, 800R—Communist Party, 1927, NARA, CP.

40. SS to Amlegation [American Legation], Riga, September 19, 1928, vol. 082, RG 84, RFSP:L, American Legation: Riga, Coleman, 020R-713R, NARA, CP.

41. Cole to SS, June 12, 1928 and June 25, 1928, vol. 082, RG 84, RFSP:L, American Legation: Riga, Cole 020R-713R, no's. 5376 and 5408, NARA, CP.

42. Cole to SS, January 9, 1930, vol. 110: RG 84, RFSP:L, American Legation: Riga-1930, 800R, NARA, CP.

43. Henderson to SS, June 12, 1930, no. 7039, vol. 110, RG 84, RFSP:L, American Legation: Riga, 1930, 800R; Cole to SS, December 15, 1930, no. 7372, in ibid., NARA, CP.

44. Kennan, *Memoirs, 1925–1950*, 50, 52. See also C. Ben Wright's dissertation commenting on this memorandum that trade was considered mutually unprofitable with Russia over a long period, "George F. Kennan, Scholar-Diplomat, 1926–1946," 32–34.

45. Kennan to SS, April 5, 1933, dispatch no. 1270, p. 1, vol. 161, RG 84, RFSP:L, American Legation, Robert Peet Skinner, 010-R to 800-R, General-Confidential, NARA, CP (hereafter dispatch no. 1270). Please see also chapter 6, "Mr. X."

46. Ibid., 1, 2 (emphasis added).

47. Ibid., 4–5, 10.

48. Ibid., 14, 18–19, quotes on 15, 16.

49. Ibid., 22–24, quotes on 21, 23.

50. Ibid., 43–66, 70–76, quotes on 66, Kennan's comment on 67.

51. Ibid., 79.

52. Ibid., 80–88, quote on 83.

53. Ibid., 84, 85, 86; see also 87–98.

54. Kennan, *Memoirs, 1925–1950*, 50.

55. Mostly German engineers accused of sabotage, spying, and put on trial in May 1928. Five were sentenced to death, forty-four sent to prison, and four acquitted (Robert Conquest, *The Great Terror: Stalin's Purge of the Thirties*, 730–31).

56. Kennan, *Memoirs, 1925–1950*, 52; *FRUS: The Soviet Union, 1933–1939*, 34–35.

57. Kennan to SS, April 5, 1933, dispatch no. 1270, 49–50.

58. Kennan, *Memoirs, 1925–1950*, 52, 53, 54, 55.

59. *FRUS: The Soviet Union, 1933–1939*, 8.

60. RG 84, RFSP:L, American Legation: Riga, MacMurray, vols. 186 and 187, 1935 and 1936, respectively, RFSP, NARA, CP.

61. See vol. 124.6, and especially dispatches dated October 2 and 10, 1939, John Wiley to SS, Riga, Latvia Legation and Consulate, General Records, 1936–1939, RG 84, RFSP, NARA, CP.

62. See both Saul, *Friends or Foes?* 319–20; and Kennan, *Memoirs, 1925–1950*, 84–85, quotes on 84.

63. Kennan, *Memoirs, 1925–1950*, 84.

Chapter 3. Assignment in Utopia

1. Whitman Bassow, *The Moscow Correspondents: Reporting on Russia from the Revolution to Glasnost*, 87–88, quote on 348, and see 349.

2. SNH, *Russia I Believe In*, 16, 18, 44–45, 51.

3. Walter Lippmann and Charles Merz, "Test of the News," 2.

4. Christopher Lasch, *The American Liberals and the Russian Revolution*, 74, 43. See also *New York World*, February 22, 1918.

5. *New York World*, November 4, 1917; Lasch, *American Liberals*, 75.

6. Lasch, *American Liberals*, 77.

7. *New York World*, February 22, 1918.

8. Lasch, *American Liberals*, 80–81.

9. George F. Kennan, *Russia Leaves the War*, 264–74.

10. Leonid I. Strakhovsky, *American Opinion about Russia, 1917–1920*, 62.

11. Isaac Don Levine, *Eyewitness to History*, 39, 44.

12. Robert Lansing to David Francis, November 2, 1917, *Papers Relating to the Foreign Relations of the United States, 1918, Russia*, 1:217.

13. Levine, *Eyewitness to History*, 45, 46.

14. Ibid., 49; *New Republic*, February 2, 1918.

15. Lasch, *American Liberals*, 143, quote on 144.

16. *New York Times*, January 28, 1918, as quoted in Kennan, *Russia Leaves the War*, 352.

17. *New Republic*, August 4, 1920, 12–13.

18. *New York Times*, January 28, 1918, 10.

19. Ibid., 11.

20. Neil V. Salzman, *Reform and Revolution: The Life and Times of Raymond Robins*.

21. Isaac Deutscher, *The Prophet Armed: Trotsky, 1879–1921*, 346–404.

22. Davis and Trani, *First Cold War*, esp. 90–99.

23. Bassow, *Moscow Correspondents*, 29.

24. Ibid., 33–40.

25. Ibid., 46. See all S. J. Taylor, *Stalin's Apologist: Walter Duranty, the New York Times's Man in Moscow*. Duranty has been under attack for covering up Stalin's brutal enforced famine in South Russia in 1932, when Duranty won the Pulitzer Prize. He even once called Stalin the "greatest living statesman." See Charles Leroux, "Bearing Witness," *New York Times*, June 25, 2003. After reconsidering the award, the Pulitzer committee decided Duranty should keep it (David D. Kirkpatrick, "Pulitzer Board Won't Void '32 Award to *Times* Writer," *New York Times*, November 22, 2003).

26. Barrow, *Moscow Journalists*, 55–57, quote on 57.

27. Ibid., 58–60, quote on 65.

28. SNH, *Russia I Believe In*, 233–34, 235.

29. See R. H. S. Crossman, ed., *The God That Failed*.

30. Eugene Lyons, *Assignment in Utopia*, 8, 9, 10, 21–38.

31. Ibid., 45, quote on, 48.

32. Ibid., 79–80, quote on 93, 96–98.

33. Ibid., 110, 115–18, 120–21, 131–32, quotes on 114, 133.

34. Ibid., 169, 201, quotes on 147, 196.

35. Ibid., 203, 204–5, 208–11.

36. Ibid., 227, quotes on 228, 231.

37. Ibid., 241, 254, 275, 276, 287–88, quotes on 276, 280, 288.

38. Ibid., 288–90, 291–92.

39. Ibid., 264–65.

40. Ibid., 383–84.

41. Ibid., 385–89, quotes on 387, 388, 389. The entire typescript of the actual press release of the interview may be found in box 6, f. 21, Lyons Papers, Hoover Institute. The actual typed letter signed by Stalin, dated November 26, 1929, declining an interview is in the Lyons Papers, University of Oregon Archive, as is the original typed and corrected copy of the interview itself, also signed by Stalin, November 22, 1930. A photocopy was sent to authors by courtesy of the university's archive.

42. "Stalin Interview," *New York Telegram*, November 24, 1930, box 19, Selections from Second Scrapbook, Lyons Papers, Hoover Institute.

43. Lyons, *Assignment in Utopia*, 391–92.

44. Ibid., 322–23, 337, quotes on 323, 329, 338–39, 358.

45. Ibid., 423, 434–37, quotes on 418–19, 428–29.

46. Ibid., 455, 461, quotes on 461–64. For Fyodor Dostoyevsky, check *The Brothers Karamazov* (Baltimore: Penguin Books, 1958), 1:287–88.

47. Lyons, *Assignment in Utopia*, 477, 478–79.

48. Ibid., 491, quotes on 485, 490. Lyons, in a note, explains that Walter Duranty and the *New York Times* had to swallow their words about "it is a mistake to exaggerate the gravity of the situation; the Russians have tightened their belts before to a far greater extent than is likely to be needed this winter." They had to change their estimate to at least two million dead through "malnutrition," though later they "tried crudely to deny [their] own estimate" (541). The story of Walter Duranty has been taken up, as mentioned above by Taylor, in *Stalin's Apologist*. This book, it appears, has started a campaign among mainly Ukrainians to rescind Duranty's 1932 Pulitzer Prize. See, for instance, Charles Leroux, "Bearing Witness," *Chicago Tribune*, June 25, 2003.

49. Lyons, *Assignment in Utopia*, 545, quotes on 541, 542, 547.

50. Ibid., 557.

51. Ibid., 579. See also Bassow, *Moscow Correspondents*, 68–69.

52. Lyons, *Assignment in Utopia*, 581, 606, quote on 583.

53. Bassow, *Moscow Correspondents*, 109, quotes on 350, 112, 117.

54. Ibid., 117, 121, 125, 135, 156, 159, 205, 208–9, 211, 333ff.

55. For the full story of Daniloff, see his *Two Lives, One Russia*.

56. Ibid., 33.

57. Ibid., 34, 65–70, 81, quotes on 13, 36, 65, 70, 107, 109. See also Marquis de Custine, *Empire of the Czar: A Journey through Eternal Russia* (New York: Doubleday, 1989).

58. Daniloff, *Two Lives, One Russia*, 231, 70, quotes on 117, 125, 137, 191.

59. Ibid., 260, quotes on 202, 205, 266. Daniloff has updated his story: *Of Spies and Spokesmen: My Life as a Cold War Correspondent*.

60. Bassow, *Moscow Correspondents*, 349.

Chapter 4. Honeymooners

1. That position is neatly summarized by a letter sent by Secretary of State Henry L. Stimson to longtime advocate of recognition, Senator William E. Borah (R-ID), September 8, 1932: "In the Far Eastern situation the United States was making a fight of world-wide importance for the integrity of international obligations . . . of good faith and the sacredness of keeping international promises. . . . If under these circumstances and in this emergency we recognized Russia in disregard of her very bad reputation respecting international obligations and in disregard of our previous emphasis upon that aspect of her history, the whole world would . . . jump to the conclusion that our action had been dictated solely by political expedience" (*FRUS: The Soviet Union, 1933–1939*, 1–2).

2. Edward M. Bennett, *Recognition of Russia: An American Foreign Policy Dilemma*, 88, and note 2 on that page where the author cites a number of FDR's letters indicating his ambiguity on this subject.

3. Robert Paul Browder, *The Origins of Soviet-American Diplomacy*, 74–75.

4. Edward Bennett, *Franklin Delano Roosevelt and the Search for Security*, 6–7.

5. "Roosevelt Confers," *New York Times,* July 26, 1932, 1.

6. Walter Duranty, *I Write as I Please,* 320. See also Taylor, *Stalin's Apologist,* 184.

7. Bennett, *Roosevelt,* 7. A typical example of opposition to recognition from otherwise well-wishers was a letter from Mrs. Lowell F. Hobart, vice chair of the American Coalition of Patriotic Societies, who wrote to FDR on December 17, 1932: "These people are 'at war' with us, and being so, is it not a mistake to make believe that we are friends with them? Particularly would it be troublesome to have them established in an embassy with all its privileges, prerogatives and immunities. . . . The promise by the Soviet government not to engage in propaganda would not be binding on the Third International and would mean nothing" (Official Files [hereafter OF], box 2, f. 220: Russia, 1932–1933, FDR Library and Archive, Hyde Park, New York [hereafter FDRHP]).

8. Bennett, *Roosevelt,* 23.

9. Frank Freidel, *Franklin D. Roosevelt: A Rendezvous with Destiny,* 172. Beatrice Farnsworth, biographer of William C. Bullitt, thought that it was not completely clear why FDR wanted to recognize Russia. She assesses his motives as follows: break with the Republican twenties; end unnatural relations; by strengthening Russia, FDR would "bring pressure on the outer flanks of both Japan and Germany," especially halting Japanese aggression; and boosting trade to help the American economy (*William C. Bullitt and the Soviet Union,* 89–90).

10. B. Farnsworth quotes FDR from Morgenthau's *Diaries* (*Bullitt,* 92).

11. Yergin, *Shattered Peace,* 20–21; John Richman, *The United States and the Soviet Union: The Decision to Recognize,* 89.

12. Kelley to Phillips, September 25, 1933, in *FRUS: The Soviet Union, 1933–1939,* 14.

13. "Memorandum by the Assistant Secretary of State" (Moore), October 4, 1933, in ibid., 15.

14. Cordell Hull, *The Memoirs of Cordell Hull,* 1:297. The secretary leaned on Robert Kelley's advice. See Browder, *Origins,* 106; and "Memorandum by the Chief of the Division of Eastern European Affairs" (Kelley), July 27, 1933, in *FRUS: The Soviet Union,* 6–11. Bullitt's addition included a clause that recognition not be retroactive to November 7, 1917 ("Memorandum by the Special Assistant to the Secretary of State" (Bullitt), October 4, 1933, in ibid., 16–17).

15. As quoted in B. Farnsworth, *Bullitt,* 93.

16. Ibid., 93–94.

17. Quoted in ibid., 86.

18. Ibid., 87.

19. Browder, *Origins,* 104.

20. B. Farnsworth, *Bullitt,* 94.

21. Ibid., 94–95.

22. "President Roosevelt to the President of the Soviet All-Union Central Executive Committee" (Kalinin), October 10, 1933, *FRUS: The Soviet Union, 1933–1939,* in 17–18.

23. "The President of the Soviet All-Union Central Executive Committee (Kalinin) to President Roosevelt," October 17, 1933, in ibid., 18.

24. William Phillips to FDR, October 10, 1933, OF, box 2: OF 218a–218b, f. Russia 1933, FDRHP.

25. Browder, *Origins,* 141. The exchange of eleven letters between FDR and Litvinov constitute Appendix D of Browder's book, *Origins,* 227–38. As to the so-called gentleman's agreement, see *FRUS: The Soviet Union, 1933–1939,* 26–27, where the less precise is phrased: "The Soviet Government will pay to the Government of the United States on account of the Kerensky debt or otherwise a sum to be not less that $75,000,000 in the form of a percentage above the ordinary rate of interest on a *loan* to be granted to it by the Government of the United States or its nationals" (emphasis added).

26. R. Walton Moore, "Memorandum as to the Russian Conversations," November 10, 1933, R. Walton Moore Papers, box 18, f. Russia, November 1933, FDRHP. A month later, Moore wrote Phillips on December 7, 1933: "The effort to work out a plan of disposing of the Russian debt problem, to be submitted for his consideration, has had almost daily attention since Mr. Bullitt's departure, being in charge of a group composed of Messers Kelly [*sic*], Hacksworth, Wiley and myself. . . . The situation is being carefully explored with the hope that a plan can be devised not involving the employment of the funds or credit of our Government with a minimum resort to that expedient" (ibid.).

27. "Reply of the President of the Soviet All-Union Central Executive Committee (Kalinin) to the American Ambassador in the Soviet Union (Bullitt), at Moscow," December 13, 1933, in *FRUS: The Soviet Union, 1933–1939,* 50.

28. As quoted in B. Farnsworth, *Bullitt,* 110, from "Bullitt to the Acting Secretary of State," January 4, 1934, in *FRUS: The Soviet Union, 1933–1939,* 59.

29. B. Farnsworth, *Bullitt,* 110, 113.

30. "Bullitt to the Acting Secretary of State," January 4, 1934, in *FRUS: The Soviet Union, 1933–1939,* 55–62.

31. "Bullitt to the Acting Secretary of State," December 24, 1933, in ibid., 54.

32. "Bullitt to the Acting Secretary," January 4, 1934, in ibid., 61.

33. "Bullitt to the Secretary of State," February 10, 1934, in ibid., 63.

34. Beatrice Farnsworth takes the following view: "That Bullitt accepted Stalin's assurances at face value seems indicated by his report to the State Department that in order to 'avoid the jealousy' of colleagues he had arranged with Litvinov to make known to the press merely that he had been at Vososhilov's and that 'Stalin had dropped in'" (*Bullitt,* 114). However, that the "misunderstandings," "fundamental divergence," "ambiguous debt arrangement," and "Litvinov's reservations regarding Comintern propaganda" seemed a good indication that Bullitt was willing to endure growing hostility rather than play the chump (115). For further consideration of Bullitt as a tough pragmatist, see Michael Cassella-Blackburn, *The Donkey, the Carrot, and the Club: William C. Bullitt and Soviet-American Relations, 1917–1948.*

35. For first two quotes, see Bullitt to Hull, March 28, 1934, in *FRUS: The Soviet Union, 1933–1939,* 71, 74. For the last quote, see B. Farnsworth, *Bullitt,* 119.

36. Bullitt to Hull, March 28, 1934, in *FRUS: The Soviet Union, 1933–1939,* 74.

37. Bullitt to Hull, March, 15, 1934, in ibid., 67. For Beatrice Farnsworth's evaluation, see *Bullitt,* 119.

38. B. Farnsworth, *Bullitt,* 120.

39. Bullitt to Hull, February 10, 1934, in *FRUS: The Soviet Union, 1933–1939*, 63–65. Bullitt had managed to visit with the Soviet Union's first ambassador to Washington on February 10, 1934, and Troyanovsky followed the "gentleman's agreement" as well as remarks made to Bullitt by Stalin and others during his first days in Moscow. The specific draft referred to here is that included in the note of Hull to Bullitt, April 7, 1934, which was dated February 20, 1934 (in ibid., 78–79).

40. Bullitt to Hull, March 15, 1934, in ibid., 66–67.

41. B. Farnsworth, *Bullitt,* 126.

42. Hull to Bullitt, March 19, 1934, in *FRUS: The Soviet Union, 1933–1939*, 68.

43. Ibid.

44. Bullitt to SS, April 2, 1934, in ibid., 76.

45. See the draft proposal in SS to Ambassador, April 7, 1934, and Ambassador to SS, April 8, 1934, in ibid., 78–79.

46. Bullitt to SS, April 28, 1934, and Moore to Bullitt, April 28, 1934, President's Secretarial File (hereafter PSF), box 49, f. Diplomatic: Russia, 1934–1935, FDRHP.

47. Moore to FDR, May 8, 1934, ibid.

48. FDR to Bullitt, May 14, 1934, and Bullitt to FDR, May 18, 1934, PSF, box 50, f. Russia: Bullitt, William C., 1933–1936, FDRHP.

49. Bullitt to FDR, August 5, 1934, PSF, box 49, f. Diplomatic: Russia, 1934–1935, FDRHP.

50. John Wiley to Bullitt, August 16, 1934, Wiley Papers, box 2, f. Diplomatic Files: Russia, 1934–1935, FDRHP.

51. FDR to R. Walton Moore, August 31, 1934, in *FRUS: The Soviet Union, 1933–1939*, 139.

52. Moore to FDR, August 29, 1934, in ibid., 138.

53. Moore to Bullitt, September 7, 1934, in ibid., 142.

54. Bullitt to FDR, September 8, 1934, PSF, box 50, f. Russia, Bullitt, William C., 1933–1936, FDRHP.

55. "Personal Observations of Ambassador William C. Bullitt on Conditions in the Soviet Union," October 2, 1934, PSF, box 49: Diplomatic: Russia, 1934–1945, f. 1934, FDRHP.

56. Henderson, *Question of Trust,* 261, 351, quote on 350.

57. FDR to Bullitt, April 21, 1935, PSF, box 50, f. Russia: Bullitt, William C. 1933–1936, FDRHP.

58. For the remark about Konstantin Oumansky, see Bullitt to FDR, March 4, 1936, in ibid. His new assignment is in a letter from FDR to Bullitt, April 21, 1936, also in ibid.

59. *FRUS: The Soviet Union, 1933–1939:* for Fischer, 220; for Litvinov, 221–22; for Bullitt's conclusions, 224.

60. Ibid., 224–25, quotes on 224, 227.

61. Ibid., 244–45 on justification, 246–57 on Bullitt's advice, quotes on 247–48, 253.

62. Ibid., 289, quote on 291.

63. Ibid., 289–91, quotes on 291.

64. Ibid., 291–93, quotes on 292, 293.

65. Ibid., 294–296, quote on 296.

66. B. Farnsworth, *Bullitt*, 126–54.

67. Ibid., 173.

68. Ibid., 175.

69. George F. Kennan, *Memoirs, 1925–1950*, 80–81.

70. Ibid., 82. Also see B. Farnsworth, *Bullitt*, 232–33n17.

71. Cassella-Blackburn, *Donkey*, esp. 127.

72. H. W. Brands, *Inside the Cold War: Loy Henderson and the Rise of the American Empire, 1918–1961*, 79. Two good studies of the purge are Weil, *Pretty Good Club*, 93; and Mary E. Glantz, *FDR and the Soviet Union: The President's Battle over Foreign Policy*, 33.

73. Two important but cautious exceptions are Yergin, *Shattered Peace*: "Conventional Cold War history, like the Riga School itself, has portrayed Davies as naïve, muddle-headed, and dishonest—a dangerous, meddling fool. That view is inaccurate" (32–33). Yergin goes on to say that Davies was sent to Moscow not to report on the facts but to win Stalin's confidence (33). The other was David Mayers in his book *The Ambassadors and America's Soviet Policy*, where he makes the following point: "Largely as a result of his book (and the movie gave added emphasis), most historians have accepted the charges against Davies leveled by Kennan and Bohlen" (119). Mayers adds that scholars used the same critique against FDR as "evidence of the president's incompetence (or worse) in the international field" (ibid.). Mayers credits Davies with a keen evaluation of the Soviet role in the European balance of power.

74. Thomas R. Maddux, "American Diplomats and the Soviet Experiment: The View from the Moscow Embassy, 1934–1939," 469.

75. Richard H. Ullman, "The Davies Mission and United States–Soviet Relations, 1937–1941," 220 (FDR quote). See also Elizabeth Kimball Maclean, "Joseph E. Davies and Soviet-American Relations, 1941–43."

76. George F. Kennan, *Memoirs, 1925–1950*, 82.

77. Ibid., 83.

78. Bohlen, *Witness to History*, 44.

79. Ibid., 44–45.

80. Ibid., 45.

81. Ibid., 51.

82. Joseph E. Davies, *Mission to Moscow*, 238.

83. Bohlen, *Witness to History*, 52.

84. Ibid.

85. Ibid., 56.

86. Ibid., 123. Generally, however, the film is given three stars, and one critic said, "A fine, well-played movie adaptation from the book" (Steven H. Scheuer, ed., *Movies on TV and Videocassette, 1992–1993*, 698).

87. Henderson, *Question of Trust*, 321. For Faymonville's influence, see Glantz, *FDR and the Soviet Union*, 30–33.

88. Henderson, *Question of Trust*, 392.

89. Ibid., 316.

90. Ibid., 394.

91. Ibid., 385.

92. Ibid., 412.

93. Ibid., 412.

94. Ibid., 413.

95. Ibid., 413–14, quote on 414.

96. Ibid., 415, quote on 417.

97. Ibid., 417.

98. Ibid., 456.

99. Ibid., 457.

100. Ibid., quotes on 421, 422.

101. Ibid., 473–74.

102. Mayers, *Ambassadors*, 124.

103. As quoted in Henderson, *Question of Trust*, 545.

104. Ibid.

105. Bohlen devotes a chapter to this in his memoir, *Witness to History*, 67–84.

106. Henderson, *Question of Trust*, 520, 521.

107. Ibid., 521.

108. Ibid., 524; Mayers, *Ambassadors*, 126.

109. Bohlen, *Witness to History*, 88, 89.

110. Joseph E. O'Connor, "Laurence A. Steinhardt and American Policy toward the Soviet Union, 1939–1941," 21–66.

111. Mayers, *Ambassadors*, 127–28.

112. As quoted in ibid., 115.

113. Ibid., 118.

114. Ibid., 121.

115. Ibid., 138.

116. Ibid., 155.

117. Ibid., 157–59.

118. See Hull, *Memoirs*, 2:972–73, where he embodies reciprocity in six points.

119. Ibid., 967.

120. Quoted in O'Connor, "Steinhardt and American Policy," 180–81.

121. Ibid., 181; J. E. Davies, *Mission to Moscow*, 475–97.

122. Harold Ickes, *The Secret Diary of Harold Ickes*, 3:593.

123. Robert W. Sherwood, *Roosevelt and Hopkins: An Intimate History*, 294.

124. Ibid., 296.

125. Ibid.

126. Ibid., 297.

127. Ibid.

128. Ibid., 298.

129. Ibid.

130. Ibid.

131. Ibid., 300.

132. Ibid., 306.

133. Ibid., 307–8.

134. Ibid., 308.
135. Ibid., 309.
136. Ibid.
137. Ibid.
138. Ibid., 311.
139. Ibid., 311–12.
140. Ibid., 331.
141. Ibid., 317.
142. Ibid., 318.
143. Ibid., 322–31 for the whole report, quote on 330.
144. Ibid., 334.
145. Ibid., 331–32.
146. Ibid., 333.
147. Ibid.

Chapter 5. Chums

1. Winston S. Churchill, *The Hinge of Fate*, 475.

2. Harriman interview, "Events Leading up to the Beaverbrook Mission to Moscow," October 18, 1953, box 872, f. recollections, 1953–54, W. Averell Harriman Papers (hereafter WAH), LC. Daniel Yergin goes so far as to say that Hopkins laid the foundations of the Grand Alliance (*Shattered Peace*, 50).

3. Harriman interview, "Comments on Langer and Gleason, on the Beaverbrook Mission," October 19, 1953, box 872, f. recollections, 1953–54, WAH, LC.

4. Harriman interview, "Beaverbrook Mission," October 21, 1953, box 872, f. recollections, 1953–54, WAH, LC. In his book with Elie Abel, *Special Envoy to Churchill and Stalin, 1941–1946,* Harriman makes special note of this: "Certain of the Americans in Moscow appeared to look upon Harriman as an interloper and his mission as an exercise in futility" (84).

5. Harriman and Abel, *Special Envoy*, 87.

6. Harriman interview, October 21, 1953, boxes 641–42, WAH, LC.

7. Ibid.

8. Harriman and Abel, *Special Envoy*, 92.

9. Ibid., 94.

10. Ibid., 100–101.

11. William Standley and Arthur Ageton, *Admiral Ambassador to Russia*, 63.

12. Ibid., 69.

13. Ibid., 111.

14. Ibid., 117.

15. Ibid., 163.

16. Ibid., 195.

17. Ibid., 202.

18. Ibid., 205.

19. Ibid., 208, quotes on 209, 214, 219.

20. Ibid., 249, quote on 305.

21. Ibid., quotes on 305, 309.

22. Ibid., 314.

23. On Faymonville, see Joseph O. Baylen and James S. Herndon, "Col. Philip R. Faymonville and the Red Army, 1934–43"; and John Daniel Langer, "The 'Red General': Philip R. Faymonville and the Soviet Union, 1917–52."

24. Standley and Ageton, *Admiral Ambassador to Russia,* quote from 341; see also 342–48 for reaction.

25. Ibid., quotes from 351–52.

26. Ibid., 356, 358, chap. 22.

27. Herbert Feis ms, esp. chaps. 1–4, p. 3, box 872, f. Feis, WAH, LC.

28. Ibid., quoting from W.F. (war files), 25.

29. Ibid.

30. Secretary of State Edward R. Stettinius Jr., Hull's replacement, maintains that Harriman "had a unique assignment at Moscow. There was nothing, during the war, quite like it. His task was totally different from that of a mere ambassador. He was the over-all co-ordinator of both the civilian and military matters in Moscow" (*Roosevelt and the Russians: The Yalta Conference,* 95).

31. Kathy Harriman to Mary Fisk, August 30, 1944, box 6, f. Kathy to Fisk, WAH, LC.

32. Harriman and Abel, *Special Envoy,* 237.

33. FDR to Marshal Stalin, November 8, 1943, in *Correspondence between the Chairman of the Council of Ministers of the USSR and the Presidents of the USA and the Prime Ministers of Great Britain during the Great Patriotic War of 1941–1945,* 105. See also Stalin's reply, November 10, 1943, in ibid., 105.

34. Harriman and Abel, *Special Envoy,* 235, 236–37, 238–40, 239–40, 241–42.

35. Harriman interview, Harvard 1970, p. 309, boxes 641–42, f. Oral History, WAH, LC.

36. Ibid.

37. Simon Sebag Montefiore, *Stalin: The Court of the Red Tsar,* 466.

38. Bohlen, *Witness to History,* 139.

39. Ibid., 140, quote on 141.

40. Harriman and Abel, *Special Envoy,* 265.

41. Montefiore, *Stalin,* 466. See also Chapter 13 for the Cairo-Teheran conferences, especially dealing with China.

42. Harriman and Abel, *Special Envoy,* 267.

43. Montefiore, *Stalin,* 467.

44. Harriman and Abel, *Special Envoy,* 268.

45. Ibid., 268 for first quote, 269; for second quote, see Bohlen, *Witness to History,* 143.

46. Harriman and Abel, *Special Envoy,* 270–71; Bohlen, *Witness to History,* 144–45.

47. Montefiore, *Stalin,* 468.

48. Ibid., 469.

49. Bohlen, *Witness to History,* 145, quote on 146.

50. Ibid., 148.

51. Ibid., 274.

52. For declaration quote, see Harriman and Abel, *Special Envoy*, 283; for Bohlen's quote, see *Witness to History*, 52–53.

53. FDR to Stalin, December 4, 1943, and Stalin to FDR, December 6, 1943, in *Correspondence*, 111–12.

54. Harriman and Abel, *Special Envoy*, 285.

55. Ibid., 345.

56. Ibid., 345, 347, 356–57. (Churchill recounts his percentages offer to Stalin in *Triumph and Tragedy*, 196–97.)

57. Ibid., 362.

58. Ibid., 362, 383–84, 388.

59. Yergin, *Shattered Peace*, 42.

60. Ibid., 43ff.

61. Churchill, *Triumph and Tragedy*, 336.

62. Anthony Eden, *The Reckoning*, 593–94.

63. David Dilks, ed., *The Diaries of Sir Alexander Cadogan*, 704–9.

64. James F. Byrnes, *Speaking Frankly*, 22.

65. Ibid., 48.

66. William D. Leahy, *I Was There*, 298.

67. Ibid., 307.

68. Ibid., 313.

69. Ibid., 321.

70. Stettinius, *Roosevelt and the Russians*, 13.

71. Ibid., 25.

72. Ibid.

73. Ibid., 26.

74. Ibid., 30.

75. Ibid., 62.

76. Ibid., 73.

77. Ibid., 203.

78. Ibid., 104, 188.

79. Ibid., 267.

80. Bohlen, *Witness to History*, 180. (See also *FRUS, 1945: Conferences at Malta and Yalta*).

81. Ibid., 179.

82. Stettinius, *Roosevelt and the Russians*, 102–11.

83. Bohlen, *Witness to History*, 181.

84. Ibid., 182.

85. Ibid.

86. Ibid., 185.

87. Stettinius, *Roosevelt and the Russians*, 121–34.

88. Bohlen, *Witness to History*, 189. The full text of that letter appears on pages 188–91.

89. Ibid., 192.

90. Sherwood, *Roosevelt and Hopkins*, 821–22.

91. Bohlen, *Witness to History*, 193.

92. Stettinius, *Roosevelt and the Russians*, 189–222.

93. Bohlen, *Witness to History*, 223–49.

94. Stettinius, *Roosevelt and the Russians*, 251–78.

95. Bohlen, *Witness to History*, 201. See also John Lewis Gaddis, *The United States and the Origins of the Cold War, 1941–1947*, 73.

96. Harry S. Truman, *Memoirs*, 2:349; Dean Acheson, *Present at the Creation: My Years in the State Department*, 753.

97. See the interesting essays in Klaus Larres and Kenneth Osgood, eds., *The Cold War after Stalin's Death: A Missed Opportunity for Peace?*

98. An interesting continuation of American ideological aims in Russia began with "Siberian" Kennan and the so-called Free Russia movement, which continued in one form or another into the twentieth century. An excellent account of this is David S. Foglesong, *The American Mission and the "Evil Empire": The Crusade for a "Free Russia" since 1881.*

99. Hans J. Morgenthau, "Changes and Chances in American-Soviet Relations," 429; Richard V. Allen, *Peace or Peaceful Coexistence?* 178, 184.

100. Dwight D. Eisenhower, *Mandate for Change*, 506–27, 529, 530.

101. For an interesting discussion of this, see Alan M. Bell, *Imaging America: Influence and Images in Twentieth-Century Russia*, 180ff.

102. See Kenneth Osgood, "The Perils of Coexistence: Peace and Propaganda in Eisenhower's Foreign Policy," 27–48.

Chapter 6. Mr. X

1. Walter L. Hixson, *George F. Kennan: Cold War Iconoclast*, 35.

2. George F. Kennan, "The Soviet Way of Thought and Its Effect on Foreign Policy," in *Measures Short of War: The George F. Kennan Lectures at the National War College, 1946–47*, ed. Giles D. Harlow and George C. Maerz, 128 (emphasis added).

3. Hixson, *Kennan*, 40.

4. Hamilton Fish Armstrong to George F. Kennan (hereafter GFK), January 10, 1947, box 28, f. 6, GFK Papers (hereafter GFKP), Seeley Mudd Manuscript Library (hereafter SMML), Princeton University (hereafter PU).

5. GFK to Armstrong, February 4, 1947, in ibid.

6. Armstrong to GFK, March 7, 1947, in ibid.

7. GFK to John T. Connor, March 10, 1947, in ibid.

8. Byron Dexter to GFK, April 14, 1947, in ibid.

9. Armstrong to GFK, May 15, 1947, in ibid.

10. Arthur Krock, "A Guide to Official Thinking About Russia," *New York Times*, July 8, 1947, 22.

11. Hixson, *Kennan*, 43. For a comparison of "Siberian" Kennan and George F. Kennan, see Donald E. Davis and Eugene P. Trani, "A Tale of Two Kennans: American-Russian Relations in the Twentieth Century," 31–55.

12. GFK, *Memoirs, 1925–1950*, 84, 85, 86, 180.

13. Ibid., 180.

14. GFK to Harriman, September 18, 1944, box 28, f. 1944, GFKP, SMML, PU.

15. "Recollections of Mr. Harriman," p. 333, box 872, f. 2, Recollections, WAH, LC.

16. GFK, *Memoirs, 1925–1950*, 503–5.

17. Ibid., 506–9.

18. Ibid., 510–31, quotes on 514, 515, 530, 531.

19. Ibid., 532–33.

20. Ibid., 536–38, long quote on 540.

21. Ibid., 541.

22. Ibid., 543–44, quote on 545.

23. FDR to the Secretaries of State, War, and the Navy (April or May 1943), box 309: Aid to Russia, f. 2, pt. 2, Sherwood Collection (hereafter SC), Franklin D. Roosevelt Papers (hereafter FDRP), Franklin D. Roosevelt Presidential Library (hereafter FDRPL). See also Weil, *Pretty Good Club*, 139.

24. GFK, *Memoirs, 1925–1950*, 543.

25. As quoted from the 1996 CNN television program, *Cold War*, http://www .cnn.com/SPECIALS/cold.war/episodes/01/interviews/kennan.

26. GFK, "The Shattering of the Rooseveltian Dream," May 1965, box 21, item 141–III, GFKP, SMML, PU.

27. Ibid.

28. Harriman and Abel, *Special Envoy*, 447.

29. Ibid., 448.

30. Ibid., 448, 449.

31. Ibid., 452, 453.

32. Ibid., 454, quote on 457.

33. Ibid., 457.

34. Ibid., 458, 459.

35. For a good accounting of the Davies-Churchill meeting, see Robert H. Ferrell, *Harry S. Truman: A Life*, which refers to it as a "soon-forgotten irritation" (202).

36. Harriman and Abel, *Special Envoy*, 463.

37. Ibid., 463, 464, 467. As to Putin's remarks and the authors' critique of them, see *Time*'s "Person of the Year" issue, December 31, 2007–January 7, 2008, 48; and Eugene P. Trani and Donald E. Davis, "Time Magazine Missed an Opportunity," *Richmond Times-Dispatch*, January 12, 2008.

38. Harriman and Abel, *Special Envoy*, 468–69, 471, quotes on 473, 475.

39. Ibid., 476, quote on 488.

40. Ibid., 481, 482–83.

41. Ibid., 484, 486, 487.

42. Ibid., 490, 491.

43. Ibid., 493–95.

44. Ibid., 498–501, quote on 500.

45. Ibid., 508.

46. Ibid., 514–15.

47. Ibid., 519, 526.

48. Ibid., 533.

49. Ibid., 546; Cable 861.00/2–1246, as quoted in Kenneth M. Jensen, ed., *Origins of the Cold War: The Novikov, Kennan, and Roberts "Long Telegrams" of 1946*, 69.

50. GFK, *Memoirs, 1925–1950*, 294.

51. Ibid., 295, 298. Historian Robert H. Ferrell, though conceding the "Long Telegram"'s powerful effect on Truman, nonetheless downplays its direct influence on the president (*Truman*, 248, 429n4). David McCullough agrees on its immediate effect (*Truman*, 491). Alonzo L. Hamby disagrees (*Man of the People: A Life of Harry S. Truman*, 346), as does Wilson D. Miscamble, *George F. Kennan and the Making of American Foreign Policy, 1947–1950*, 27.

52. Joseph Stalin, "Speech Delivered by J. V. Stalin at a Meeting of Voters of the Stalin Electoral District, Moscow, February 9, 1946," from the Pamphlet Collection of J. Stalin, *Speeches Delivered at Meetings of Voters of the Stalin Electoral District, Moscow*, 19–44. In this speech Stalin argued that World War II did not break out accidentally but was a result of the capitalist world "split into two hostile camps, and war breaks out between them" (22). Furthermore, the "Soviet social system has proved to be more viable and stable than the non-Soviet social system, that the Soviet social system is a better form of organization of society than any non-Soviet social system" (27). Ronald Grigor Suny in *The Soviet Experiment: Russia, the USSR, and the Successor States* notes, "Though the speech was a fairly conventional statement of the Soviet interpretation of the causes of war, it was read by many in the West as an aggressive statement of Soviet hostility to the West. Supreme Court Justice William O. Douglas called the speech the 'declaration of World War III'" (350).

53. GFK, *Memoirs, 1925–1950*, 287, 290. No doubt, Kennan thought, this request for his opinion was an "anguished cry of bewilderment that had floated over the roof of the White House from the Treasury Department on the other side" (293).

54. Ibid., 291–92.

55. *FRUS, 1946: Eastern Europe—the Soviet Union*, 6:695n.

56. GFK, *Memoirs, 1925–1950*, 294–95.

57. GFK, "Long Telegram," in Jensen, *Origins of the Cold War*, 28.

58. Ibid., 18, 19.

59. Ibid., 20, 21.

60. Ibid., 29–31.

61. Acheson, *Present at the Creation*, 151, 196.

62. GFK, "Long Telegram," in Jensen, *Origins of the Cold War*, 29. This quote and comment are singled out in C. Ben Wright, "Mr. 'X' and Containment," 9.

63. Wright, "George F. Kennan," 411.

64. Ibid., 412, as quoted by Wright.

65. Ibid., 413, as quoted by Wright.

66. Hixson, *Kennan*, 31.

67. Mayers, *Kennan*, 100.

68. Ibid.

69. Henry A. Wallace, "The Way to Peace," September 12, 1946, Madison Square Garden, New York, http://newdeal.feri.org/wallace/haw28.htm.

70. GFK to Bohlen, January 2, 1945, box 28, f. 1945, GFKP, SMML, PU.

71. Ibid.

72. Ibid.

73. Ibid.

74. Ibid.

75. Ibid.

76. Ibid.

77. Ibid.

78. Bohlen, *Witness to History*, 176.

79. Ibid.

80. GFK to Mr. Ambassador, February 24, 1945, box 23, item 35, GFKP, SMML, PU.

81. GFK to Mr. Ambassador, March 8, 1945, box 23, item 36, ibid.

82. GFK to H. Freeman Matthews, August 21, 1945, box 28, f. 1945, ibid.

83. GFK to "Durby" (Elbridge Durbrow), January 21, 1946, box 28, f. 1946, ibid.

84. Henry Norweb to GFK, March 25, 1946, box 28, f. 7, ibid.

85. GFK to Bruce Hopper, April 17, 1946, box 28, f. 7, ibid.

86. GFK, *Memoirs, 1925–1950*, 299.

87. GFK to George Russell, circa September 1946, box 28, f. 7, GFKP, SMML, PU.

88. GFK, *Memoirs, 1925–1950*, 304.

89. Harlow and Maerz, *Measures Short of War*, 14, 16.

90. Ibid., 66, 74.

91. Ibid., 121, quote on 128 (emphasis added).

92. GFK, *Memoirs, 1925–1950*, 356.

93. GFK, "The Sources of Soviet Conduct," as taken from http://www.foreign affairs.org/19470701faessay25403/x/the-sources-of-soviet-conduct.html (emphasis added).

94. Ibid., at the start of the last paragraph of part 2 (emphasis added).

95. Ibid. (emphasis added).

96. Ibid.

97. Walter Lippmann, *The Cold War: A Study in U.S. Foreign Policy*, 36. Two interesting reports on the mood of Moscow in the last years of Stalin are by Harrison E. Salisbury, *American in Russia* and *Moscow Journal: The End of Stalin*.

98. GFK, "Sources of Soviet Conduct," 566–82.

99. See Acheson, *Present at the Creation*, chap. 25 and pt. 3. For the quote, see Walter Isaacson and Evan Thomas, *The Wise Men: Six Friends and the World They Made*, 435. On liberalization and cultural infiltration, see Walter L. Hixson, *Parting the Curtain: Propaganda, Culture, and the Cold War, 1945–1961*.

100. GFK to Lippmann, April 6, 1948, box 17, item 7, GFKP, SMML, PU.

101. Ibid.

102. GFK to Anne O'Hare McCormick, November 15, 1950, box 29, f. 1950, GFKP, SMML, PU.

103. GFK to William Henry Chamberlin, October 20, 1951, box 29, f. 1951, GFKP, SMML, PU.

104. GFK to Gregoire Alexinsky, December 3, 1952, box 29, f. 1952, a–n, GFKP, SMML, PU.

105. GFK, *Memoirs, 1925–1950*, 496.

106. "Address by the Honorable George F. Kennan before the Mid-winter Din-

ner Meeting of the Pennsylvania State Bar Association at the Casey Hotel, Scranton, Pennsylvania, Friday, January 16, 1953, at 9:00 p.m., e.s.t.," box 2, item 21, GFKP, SMML, PU.

Chapter 7. Gray Eminence

1. Paul M. Nitze with Ann M. Smith and Steven L. Rearden, *From Hiroshima to Glasnost: At the Center of Decision, a Memoir,* 7 (hereafter referred to as Nitze, *Memoir*).

2. Ibid., ix.

3. Ibid., 11, 13, 16, 86; for quote, see John B. Keogh to Nitze, March 17, 1951, box 29, f. 10, Paul Nitze Papers (hereafter PN), LC] Special permission is required to use Nitze's papers, and some boxes remained closed.

4. Paul Nitze, "The Development of NSC 68," 172. See also Samuel F. Wells, "Sounding the Tocsin: NSC 68 and the Soviet Threat," 117. On February 8, 1950, Nitze himself presented a paper, "Recent Soviet Moves," which is printed in *FRUS, 1950,* 1: 145. He points out that the USSR is committed to defeating the United States, not immediately, but shows a "greater willingness than in the past to undertake a course of action, including a possible use of force in local areas, which might lead to an accidental outbreak of general military conflict."

5. Nitze, *Memoir,* 85–91, quotes on 85, 86, 87. At the 104th meeting of the NSC on October 11, 1951, Truman said, "He now knew that the Soviets respected nothing but force, and would talk and negotiate only in the face of force." See also box 136, f. 5, PN, LC.

6. State-Defense Policy Review Group, Record of Meetings with Oppenheimer and Conant, *FRUS, 1950,* 168–82.

7. Nitze to Edward S. Flash Jr., May 9, 1960, box 136, f. 6, PN, LC. Though NSC-68 contains no cost analysis, Nitze states, "We on the Policy Planning staff developed a pretty clear idea in our own minds as to the order of magnitude of the programs . . . something of the size of forty to fifty billion dollars a year" (RG 218, CCS 381 U.S. [1-31-50], sec. 4, as found in box 136, f. 6, PN, LC).

8. Nitze, *Memoir,* 94–98, quotes on 97, 98.

9. For Kennan's views, see NSC 20/4, in *FRUS, 1948,* I, pt. 2, 662ff.

10. Nitze, "Development of NSC 68," 171.

11. NSC-68 "portrayed the Soviet Union in a far more dismaying light than Kennan's Long Telegram" (Strobe Talbot, *The Master of the Game: Paul Nitze and the Nuclear Peace,* 55). This is explained by Robert W. Tufts: "What the paper called for can be stated in a very simple argument. The Soviet Union, we argued, would devote resources to building up an atomic capability to go with its conventional capability. This would lead to a dangerous military imbalance unless the United States developed conventional capabilities to go with its atomic capabilities. The result, if we were successful, would be a military balance favorable to our interests in successful containment . . . in time bring[ing] about the 'mellowing' NSC-68 saw as the success we looked for" (Tufts to Steven Reardon, April 14, 1989, box 136, f. 6, PN, LC).

12. As noted in David Callahan, *Dangerous Capabilities: Paul Nitze and the Cold War*, "In these books *[FRUS]*, dozens of Nitze's memorandums have been reproduced, and from them it was possible to document in detail Nitze's thinking on nearly every major national security issue from 1949 through early 1953" (510). See these documents in Department of State, *Papers Relating to the Foreign Relations of the United States.* Check the Bibliography for complete listings.

13. This quote and the remainder are from a complete Web posting of the document: http://www.r-three.com/nsc68-1-4.htm. However, most of this document appears in Kenneth W. Thompson and Steven L. Rearden, eds., *Paul H. Nitze on National Security and Arms Control*, 5–31. See also *FRUS, 1950*, 1:235–92, for NSC-68 —the entire document.

14. See Thompson and Rearden, *Nitze on National Security*, 5–7, quotes on 6, 7. See also Tufts to Reardon, April 14, 1989, where Tufts comments on the language used in NSC-68: "The purple prose was intended to make as strong a case as possible for the kind of preparedness we thought was needed" (box 136, f. 6, PN, LC). Callahan claims that NSC-68 saw the comparison between the U.S. and the USSR as "between good and evil" (*Dangerous Capabilities*, 117). Talbot also asserts that "NSC 68 stressed the offensive nature of the threat [and depicted it as] near-term and potentially military" (*Master of the Game*, 56, 57).

15. Thompson and Rearden, *Nitze on National Security*, 15.

16. Ibid., 10–11. Callahan makes the point that NSC-68 postulated that "there could never be true coexistence between the United States and the Soviet Union" (*Dangerous Capabilities*, 116). In a similar analysis, Talbott says that, according to NSC-68, "Peace must now be waged in much the same way that war had been waged in the past-by amassing and deploying military power" (*Master of the Game*, 54–55).

17. See Section V of NSC-68, "Soviet Intentions and Capabilities," as found on http://www.r-three.com/nsc68-1-4.htm.

18. Ibid.

19. Ibid.

20. Ibid.

21. Ibid.

22. Thompson and Rearden, *Nitze on National Security*, 14–16.

23. Nitze, *Memoir*, 97. However, Talbott does not quibble with this estimate: "Yet, on the advice of the Air Force, the authors of NSC 68 concluded that the Soviet Union already had aircraft of sufficient range to reach the United States and that by mid-1954, it would be able to drop a hundred bombs on the United States, enough to 'strike swiftly and with stealth' and 'seriously damage this country'" (*Master of the Game*, 56).

24. Nitze, *Memoir*, 97.

25. See http://www.r-three.com/nsc68-1-4.htm.

26. Thompson and Rearden, *Nitze on National Security*, 18.

27. Ibid., 19.

28. Ibid., 20.

29. Section IX, "Possible Courses of Action," Part C, "The Second Course—Isolation," http://www.r-three.com/nsc68-1-4.html.

30. Ibid.

31. Thompson and Rearden, *Nitze on National Security,* 24 (emphasis added). See also Melvyn P. Leffler, *The Specter of Communism: The United States and the Origins of the Cold War, 1917–1953,* 93–94, 96–97, 103, 105. This theme is expanded in Leffler, *A Preponderance of Power: National Security, the Truman Administration, and the Cold War.*

32. Thompson and Rearden, *Nitze on National Security;* Nitze, *Memoir,* 96. The sum of forty billion dollars per year for each of the next four to five years was Nitze's estimated cost, though Acheson advised against mentioning it in the report. Naturally, the secretary told the president. As Acheson said, "The purpose of NSC-68 was to so bludgeon the mass mind of 'top government' that not only could the President make a decision but that the decision could be carried out" (*Present at the Creation,* 374).

33. Thompson and Rearden, *Nitze on National Security,* 23, 25, quote on 31.

34. Quoted in Callahan, *Dangerous Capabilities,* 120.

35. Ibid., 122.

36. Ibid. On this budget issue, see also Wells, "Sounding the Tocsin," 135–36, where Willard L. Thorp, assistant secretary for economic affairs, is cited as complaining that we are not closing the economic gap and that the United States invested twice as much as the USSR in 1949 on defense: $16.2 billion compared to $9 billion. And also pages 137–38, where cost estimates varied from $5.2 billion in FY 1951 to $7.5 billion in FY 1955. Cost estimates were interrupted because of the Korean War, and on September 29, 1950, the NSC adopted the study's conclusions, approved by Truman the next day (138). Nitze himself recalled that "Leon Keyserling consistently advocated the view that we could afford programs of the size contemplated on economic grounds and that it was largely a politico-military question as to whether we needed such programs for security" (Nitze to Flash, May 9, 1960, box 136, f. 6, PN, LC).

37. As cited in Wells, "Sounding the Tocsin," 136.

38. Callahan, *Dangerous Capabilities,* 123.

39. Wells, "Sounding the Tocsin," 139.

40. Ibid. See also Gaddis, "NSC 68 and the Soviet Threat Reconsidered," where he notes the widening concept of the balance of power in NSC 68 to include "such intangibles as intimidation, humiliation, or even loss of credibility." He also credits NSC 68 with a "way to increase defense expenditures without war, without long-term budget deficits, and without crushing tax burdens . . . to live with temporarily unbalanced budgets" (166). However, he sharply criticizes NSC-68's implying the "ability to generate resources needed to match commitments" because "the simple presence of a Soviet threat alone is deemed sufficient to make all interests endangered vital. The consequences of this shift in thinking were more than procedural: they were nothing less than to transfer to the Russians control over what United States interests were at any given point" (167–68).

41. Nitze, *Memoir,* 101–2. As to the so-called correlation of forces and accurate predictions, Nitze points to his spring meeting with Alexander Sachs, an economist and man who had introduced Einstein to FDR, who "thought that Moscow

was naturally cautious, and would try to minimize risks by acting through a satellite. He predicted a North Korean attack upon South Korea sometime late in the summer of 1950" (Nitze, "Development of NSC 68," 174).

42. Nitze, *Memoir*, 103–6.

43. Ibid., 117.

44. Ibid., 119.

45. Ibid.

46. Ibid., 119–20.

47. Ibid., quotes on 121, 123, 147; see also 125–26.

48. Ibid., 151.

49. Ibid. 152.

50. Nitze to James E. King, October 24, 1955, box 29, f. 15, PN, LC.

51. Nitze to Peter Ogloblin, May 9, 1956, box 35, f. 11, PN, LC.

52. Nitze, *Memoir*, 170–74.

53. Ibid., 207; see 182, 186–87, 191, 202 for Nitze's negative appraisal of Khrushchev.

54. Ibid., 195.

55. Ibid., 182.

56. Ibid., 186. See also Arthur M. Schlesinger Jr., *A Thousand Days: John F. Kennedy in the White House*, 358–74.

57. Ibid., 187, quote on 189.

58. Ibid., 191–94, quote on 191.

59. Ibid., 197.

60. Nitze to Lippmann, October 26, 1959, box 32, f. 5, PN, LC.

61. Nitze, *Memoir*, 201–2.

62. For this document, see http://www.nato.int/docu/stratdoc/eng/a680116a .pdf.

63. Nitze, *Memoir*, 215, quote on 217.

64. Bohlen, *Witness to History*, 495.

65. Nitze, *Memoir*, 219.

66. Ibid., 221–22, quotes on 221.

67. Ibid., 226–29.

68. Ibid., 230–31.

69. Ibid., 232–33. For Nitze's role in the ExComm of the NSC for the crucial October 27 meeting, see the entire transcript in McGeorge Bundy and James G. Blight, "October 27, 1962: Transcripts of the Meetings of the ExComm." Nitze reported that U.S. Ambassador Raymond Hare (to Turkey) thought it would be "anathema" for the Turks to have the Jupiter missiles removed. Nitze felt it was a NATO decision involving whether to "denuclearize NATO." Therefore, he recommended dealing only with the Cuban crisis and reserving all other questions for later. To this suggestion, JFK replied, "I don't think we can—if this an accurate [*sic*]—and this is the whole deal—we just have to wait—I don't think we can take the position— [and further on] they're [Jupiter missiles] not militarily useful, number 1. Number 2, it's going to—to look to any man at the United Nations or any other rational man it will look like a very fair trade" (35–36). Though Nitze persisted (39), JFK finally

adopted the suggestion first broached by columnist Walter Lippmann in the *Washington Post* on Thursday, October 25, 1962, that is, a swap of Cuban for Turkish missiles.

70. Nitze, *Memoir*, 235.

71. Ibid., 256.

72. Ibid., 258.

73. Ibid., 265, 270. See also the revelations of Harrison E. Salisbury's *Behind the Lines: Hanoi, December 23, 1966–January 7, 1967.*

74. Ibid., 275.

75. Ibid., 279.

76. Ibid.

77. Ibid., 281.

78. Ibid., 285–87.

79. Ibid., 290.

80. Lyndon B. Johnson, *The Vantage Point: Perspectives on the Presidency, 1963–1969*, 485.

81. Nitze, *Memoir*, 291–92.

82. Ibid., 293, esp. note 3.

83. Ibid., 295–98. For Nitze's review, see "Limited Wars or Massive Retaliation?" 40. Callaghan records that Nitze "savaged" the book. Check Callaghan, *Dangerous Capabilities*, 166.

84. Ibid., 304. See also Richard M. Nixon, *RN: The Memoirs of Richard Nixon*, 369–70.

85. Nitze, *Memoir*, 310.

86. Ibid., 311–12.

87. Ibid., 312–13.

88. Ibid., 317–32.

89. Ibid., 335.

90. Ibid., 336.

91. Ibid., 336–37.

92. Ibid., 339–40.

93. Ibid., 341. Henry Kissinger takes an opposite view of this. He suggests a kind of conspiracy between Nitze, Schlesinger, and Senator Henry Jackson in an effort to distance themselves from Nixon. See Henry Kissinger, *Years of Upheaval*, 1151–55. Kissinger believed their reasoning behind objections to SALT II was wrong: "Schlesinger's June 3 letter paralleled one by Paul Nitze [June 14, resignation letter] to the President. Nitze . . . argued that any agreement that permitted the Soviets more than 200–300 MIRVed ICBMs was strategically intolerable because a larger number would put America's land-based strategic forces at risk. It was the fallacy of many SALT opponents to ask arms control negotiations not simply to stabilize the arms race but to solve all our strategic dilemmas as well" (1155). Kissinger complains of the "broad innuendos—in public statements and hints by Senator Jackson, by Paul Nitze, by retiring Chief of Naval Operations, Elmo Zumwalt, and in press commentary—warning against excessive concessions" (1175).

94. Nitze, *Memoir*, 344.

95. Ibid., 345.

96. Ibid., 345–46.

97. Ibid., 347.

98. Nitze to Dr. Donald G. Brennan, November 27, 1974, box 19, f. 1, PN, LC.

99. Nitze, *Memoir*, 348.

100. See *Foreign Affairs* (January 1976), reprinted in Thompson and Rearden, *Nitze on National Security*, 181–209.

101. Nitze, *Memoir*, 352.

102. Ibid., 359.

103. The article is Graham Hovey, "Gov. Harriman: Salty Views on SALT, Etc.," *New York Times*, October 9, 1977. For Rostow's first letter, see Eugene V. Rostow to Harriman, October 12, 1977; for Harriman's response, Harriman to Rostow, October 24, 1977; and, finally, Rostow to Harriman, November 1, 1977, box 37, f. 14, PN, LC. At this time, both Nitze and Rostow were very active in the Committee on the Present Danger. In fact, Rostow wrote Nitze, "I suppose that on foreign policy problems you and I are about as close as any two people can be in outlook, style, formation, tone, and substance" (August 5, 1980, box 73, f. 2, PN, LC).

104. "Valentin Zorin Criticizes Campaign to Poison U.S.-USSR Relations," October 21, 1978, *International Affairs-USSR*, a clipping as found in box 74, f. 5, PN, LC.

105. Nitze, *Memoir*, 360.

106. Ibid., 363.

107. Ibid., 364; Rostow to Kissinger, October 12, 1978, box 37, f. 14, PN, LC.

108. Nitze, *Memoir*, quote on 365.

Chapter 8. Missionary Diplomacy

Sections of this chapter first appeared as an article by Eugene P. Trani in 1971, reprinted in Chinese in 2005: "Woodrow Wilson, China, and the Missionaries, 1913–1921," *Journal of Presbyterian History* 49 (1971): 328–351, reprinted in *Chinese in Religion and American Society* (Shanghai) 3 (2005): 281–314. Since 1971, some important works have appeared on this subject, especially John K. Fairbank, ed., *The Missionary Enterprise in China and America*; Kathleen Lodwick, *The Chinese Recorder Index: A Guide to Christian Missions in China, 1867–1974*; and James Reed, *The Missionary Mind and American East Policy, 1911–1915*.

1. This term has resulted from Arthur Link's descriptions of Wilson's diplomacy. See Link's *Wilson: The New Freedom*, the second volume of the definitive biography of Wilson; and *Wilson the Diplomatist: A Look at His Major Foreign Policies*.

2. A general treatment of Wilson's China policy is Roy Watson Curry, *Woodrow Wilson and Far Eastern Policy*. An account of the first term of the Wilson administration is Tien-yi Li, *Woodrow Wilson's China Policy, 1913–1917*, whereas Russell H. Fifield, *Woodrow Wilson and the Far East: The Diplomacy of the Shantung Question*, concentrates on the Versailles peace conference. The standard work on the origins of Wilsonian diplomacy is Harley Notter, *The Origins of the Foreign Policy of Woodrow Wilson*, but Notter's study does not deal with China in any detail. Finally, there is

Paul Varg, *Missionaries, Chinese, and Diplomats: The American Protestant Missionary Movement in China, 1890–1932*, but this is a general study.

3. Scott to Woodrow Wilson (hereafter WW), March 1, 1913, Wilson Papers (hereafter WP), LC.

4. WW to Scott, April 15, 1913, WP, LC.

5. S. I. Woodbridge to WW, July 6, 1912, WP, PU.

6. WW to Woodbridge, August 5, 1912, J. S. Woodbridge Collection, copy in PU.

7. Wilson statement, March 19, 1913, WP, LC. For the best discussion of the decision-making process that brought this statement, see Link, *Wilson: The New Freedom.* See also Curry, *Woodrow Wilson;* and Tien-yi Li, *Woodrow Wilson's China Policy.*

8. Arthur J. Brown to WW, March 20, 1913, WP, LC.

9. Scott to WW, May 31, 1913, WP, LC.

10. Z. C. Beals to WW, March 29, 1913, and James Sadler to WW, March 21, 1913, WP, LC.

11. Link, *Wilson: The New Freedom*, 286.

12. Scott to WW, March 1, 1913, and Brown to WW, March 20, 1913, WP, LC.

13. Bishop J. W. Bashford to Henry Huntington Wilson, January 20, 1913, 893.00/634, State Department Records (hereafter SDR), NA, as cited in Tien-yi Li, *Woodrow Wilson's China Policy*, 67.

14. E. T. Williams, Peking, to William Jennings Bryan, March 28, 1913, SDR, NA, as cited in Tien-yi Li, *Woodrow Wilson's China Policy*, 70.

15. Bryan to Williams, April 6, 1913, SDR, NA, as cited in Tien-yi Li, *Woodrow Wilson's China Policy*, 72–77.

16. See, for example, the message from Yen His-Shan, governor of Shansi, to WW, May 7, 1913, and the many similar telegrams, in WP, LC.

17. Scott to WW, May 31, 1913, WP, LC.

18. WW to Bryan, February 51 [*sic*], 1913, Ray Stannard Baker Collection, LC.

19. James Kerney, *The Political Education of Woodrow Wilson*, 288–89; Bashford to Bryan, March 20, 1913, 893.00/634, SDR, NA, as cited in Tien-yi Li, *Woodrow Wilson's China Policy*, 16.

20. Edward M. House to WW, February 1, 1913, WP, LC.

21. House Diary, January 17, 1913, as cited in Curry, *Woodrow Wilson*, 36.

22. WW to Charles Eliot, January 20, 1913, Baker Collection, LC.

23. Charles Seymour, *The Intimate Papers of Colonel House*, 105.

24. Eliot to WW, January 27, 1013, WP, LC.

25. WW to Bryan, February 51 [*sic*], 1913, Baker Collection, LC.

26. WW to Bryan, February 14, 1913, and Bryan to WW, February 17, 1915, Baker Collection, LC.

27. Tien-yi Li, *Woodrow Wilson's China Policy*, 18.

28. Cleveland H. Dodge to WW, March 8, 1913, and WW to Dodge, March 10, 1913, WP, LC.

29. Dodge to WW, March 10, 1913, WP, LC.

30. Edward C. Jenkins to WW, March 14, 1913, and WW to Jenkins, March 17, 1913, WP, LC.

31. WW to John R. Mott, March 21, 1913, WP, LC.

32. *Boston Herald,* March 27, 1913, as cited in Curry, *Woodrow Wilson,* 41.

33. Dodge to WW, March 28, 1913, WP, LC.

34. Dodge to WW, April 1, 1913, enclosing telegram from Mott to Dodge, ca. April 1, 1913, and WW to Dodge, April 5, 1913, WP, LC.

35. George Mason La Monte to Joseph P. Tumulty, March 29, 1913, WP, LC.

36. Dodge to WW, April 1, 1913, and WW to Dodge, April 5, 1913, WP, LC.

37. Dodge to WW, April 8, 1913, WP, LC; and WW to Dodge, April 10, 1913, Dodge-Wilson Collection, PU Library.

38. Charles Crane to WW, April 8, 1913, and WW to Crane, April 10, 1913, WP, LC.

39. Bryan to WW, June 2, 1913, WP, LC.

40. WW list of diplomatic appointments, ca. June 4, 1913, WP, LC.

41. WW to Bryan, June 25, 1913, WP, LC.

42. Mott to WW, July 3, 1913, WP, LC.

43. Crane to WW, March 21, 1913, WP, LC.

44. Bryan to WW, ca. March 1913, and WW to Bryan, June 25, 1913, WP, LC.

45. WW to Joseph E. Davies, June 10, 1913, and WW to Bryan, June 25, 1913, WP, LC.

46. WW to Paul S. Reinsch, June 30, 1913, Reinsch Papers (hereafter PSR), Wisconsin State Historical Society, Madison (hereafter WSHS]).

47. A good article on Reinsch's service as minister to China, as well as his background before the appointment, is Noel H. Pugach, "Making the Open Door Work: Paul S. Reinsch in China, 1913–1919."

48. WW to Senators Isaac Stephenson and Robert La Follette, July 31, 1913, WP, LC.

49. Reinsch to WW, October 5, 1914, attached to WW to William G. McAdoo, November 9, 1914, William G. McAdoo Papers, LC.

50. Ray Stannard Baker, *Woodrow Wilson: Life and Letters,* 6:61.

51. Paul S. Reinsch, *An American Diplomat in China,* 63.

52. Crane to WW, October 1, 1913, and WW to Crane, October 3, 1913, WP, LC.

53. Noel H. Pugach, *Paul S. Reinsch: Open Door Diplomat in Action,* chap. 4.

54. "The American Minister with the Premier and Minister of Posts and Communications," November 27, 1913, box 2, PSR, WSHS.

55. Reinsch to State Department, no. 17, December 1, 1913, box 2, PSR, WSHS.

56. Reinsch, *American Diplomat,* 1.

57. Ibid., 1–2.

58. Ibid., 3.

59. Ibid., 6.

60. Ibid., 23. Reinsch quotes Yuan.

61. Ibid., 31. Reinsch quotes Rockhill.

62. Ibid., 42.

63. Ibid., 42–47.

64. Ibid., 64.

65. Ibid., 66.

66. Ibid., 187, 192–93, 201; Jonathan D. Spence, *The Search for Modern China,* 297–99.

67. Reinsch, *American Diplomat,* 286–87, 299, quotes on 307.

68. Ibid., 313, 321, 328, 334, 364–66, 379, 384, quotes on 315, 333, 359, 378.

69. WW to Woodbridge, July 16, 1913, J. S. Woodbridge Collection, copy in PU Library.

70. Woodbridge to WW, September 12, 1913, WP, LC.

71. WW to Bryan, October 3, 1913, and Bryan to WW, October 3, 1913, WP, LC.

72. Lucius Hopkins Miller to WW, July 14, 1913, and WW to Miller, July 15, 1913, WP, LC.

73. Robert R. Gailey to WW, September 15, 1913, WP, LC.

74. Gailey to WW, December 3, 1914, and WW to Gailey, December 4, 1914, WP, LC.

75. G. S. Eddy to WW, October 5, 1914, and WW to Eddy, December 9, 1914, WP, LC.

76. Scott to WW, March 4, 1914, WP, LC.

77. Scott to WW, April 8, 1914, and WW to Scott, April 25, 1914, WP, LC.

78. Scott to WW, May 12, 1914, WP, LC.

79. Scott to WW, July 7, 1914, and July 10, 1914, and WW to Scott, July 14, 1914, WP, LC.

80. Woodbridge to WW, August 15, 1914, WP, LC.

81. Bashford to WW, March 12, 1915, WP, LC.

82. Bashford to Bryan, March 12, 1915, enclosed in Bryan to WW, April 19, 1915, WP, LC.

83. J. Leighton Stuart to WW, March 24, 1915, WP, LC.

84. Scott to WW, April 8, 1915, WP, LC.

85. Woodbridge to WW, August 14, 1915, WP, LC.

86. Bryan to WW, April 15, 1915, and WW to Bryan, April 16, 1915, Wilson-Bryan Correspondence, vol. 4, SDR, NA.

87. Woodbridge to WW, August 14, 1915, WP, LC.

88. Bryan to WW, April 27, 1915, Wilson-Bryan Correspondence, vol. 4, SDR, NA.

89. Bryan to Ambassador in Japan, May 11, 1915, *FRUS, 1915,* 146. The best analysis of the American policy in this controversy is in Arthur Link, *Wilson: The Struggle for Neutrality, 1914–1915,* the third volume of Link's biography of Wilson. See also Curry, *Woodrow Wilson;* and Tien-yi Li, *Woodrow Wilson's China Policy.*

90. WW to D. B. D. Warfield, October 30, 1917, WP, LC.

91. Woodbridge to WW, January 28, 1916, WP, LC.

92. Woodbridge to WW, October 7, 1916, WP, LC.

93. Woodbridge to WW, November 17, 1916, WP, LC.

94. Woodbridge to WW, September 11, 1917, WP, LC; WW to Woodbridge, August 21, 1917, J. S. Woodbridge Collection, copy in the PU Library.

95. Scott to WW, September 14, 1918, WP, LC.

96. Scott to WW, October 7, 1918, enclosing report for the Reverend Dr. A. J. Brown, ca. October 7, 1918, WP, LC.

97. WW to Lansing, November 22, 1918, WP, LC.

98. Memo of Ransford S. Miller, November 26, 1918, enclosed in Lansing to WW, November 26, 1918, WP, LC.

99. For an analysis of Reinsch's views, see Pugach, "Making the Open Door Work."

100. See Fifield, *Woodrow Wilson and the Far East,* for the most complete analysis of the negotiations.

101. Scott to WW, July 26, 1919, WP. LC.

102. Woodbridge to WW, August 26, 1919, WP, LC.

103. MacMurray to Roland S. Morris, February 7, 1920, Roland Morris Papers, LC, as cited in Curry, *Woodrow Wilson,* 295.

104. Reinsch, *American Diplomat,* 382; Reinsch to WW, June 7, 1919, 123R271/101, and Breckinridge Long to Lansing, August 5, 1919, 123R271/105, SDR, NA.

105. Curry, *Woodrow Wilson,* 308.

106. Ibid., 311.

107. Varg, *Missionaries, Chinese, and Diplomats,* 146.

108. For two short biographies, see http://www.infoplease.com/biography/us/congress/judd-walter-henry.html and http://en.wikipedia.org/wikiWalter_Judd.

109. "Interview with Walter H. Judd on Dwight D. Eisenhower," August 29, 1968, in *Walter H. Judd: Chronicles of a Statesman,* ed. Edward J. Rozek, 12.

110. Quoted in Lee Edwards, *Missionary for Freedom: The Life and Times of Walter Judd,* 97–98.

111. Ibid., 100.

112. Rozek, *Walter H. Judd,* 116, 122, 138, 142, 143, 147, 159; see also 168.

113. Edwards, *Missionary for Freedom,* 159.

114. Quoted in ibid., 160–61.

115. See http://en.wikipedia.org/wiki/Joseph-McCarthy.

116. Edwards, *Missionary for Freedom,* 205, quoting from Ross Y. Koen, *The China Lobby in American Politics,* 27ff.

117. Edwards, *Missionary for Freedom,* 205, 213, 215.

118. Rozek, *Walter H. Judd,* 276.

119. See http://en.wikipedia.org/wiki/Falun_Gong.

Chapter 9. Pragmatist in China

Abbreviations used in this chapter include: DNA-1 (Archives I, Textual Archives Services Division, National Administration, College Park, Maryland; ICarbS (Special Collections, Morris Library or Dewey Center (see note 6 below), Southern Illinois University–Carbondale); NNC-Ar (Columbia University Archives and Columbiana Library, New York); TLS (Typed Letter Signed, Columbia University Archives); TxU-R (Rare Books and Special Collections, Tarlton Law Library, University of Texas–Austin); VtU (University of Vermont Archives).

1. Robert W. Clopton and Tsuin-Chen Ou, introduction to *John Dewey: Lectures in China, 1919–1920,* 3.

2. Thomas Berry, "Dewey's Influence in China," in 191–201, quote on 200.

3. Ibid., Berry quotes Dewey, 200–201.

4. Anonymous, "Dewey in China," f. China, Center for Dewey Studies, Southern Illinois University, Carbondale.

5. Barry Keenan, *The Dewey Experiment in China: Educational Reform and Political Power in the Early Republic*, 11.

6. War Department to whom it may concern, June 14, 1921 (DNA-1, 06413), in *The Correspondence of John Dewey*, vol. 2, *1919–1939* (these letters may be found on the disks by their accession numbers); original, Central Files, Columbia University Archives and Columbiana Library. All of the Dewey correspondence has been gathered on these disks, which are available from InteLex or at the Dewey Center, Southern Illinois University, Carbondale.

7. As quoted in George Dykhuizen, *The Life and Mind of John Dewey*, 200.

8. As quoted in Steven C. Rockefeller, *John Dewey: Religious Faith and Democratic Humanism*, 357.

9. John Dewey and Alice Chipman Dewey, *Letters from China and Japan*, 147.

10. John Dewey (hereafter JD) to Murray Butler, May 3, 1919 (NNC-Ar, 04068), *Correspondence* (Dewey's letters are full of his own typos).

11. Dewey and Dewey, *Letters from China* 150–56, quote on 156.

12. Ibid., 159–60.

13. JD to children, May 9, 1919 (ICarbS, 03903), *Correspondence.*

14. Oscar Handlin and Lilian Handlin, introduction to *Reconstruction in Philosophy and Essays, 1920: The Middle Works of John Dewey, 1899–1924*, by Dewey, xviii.

15. JD, "On the Two Sides of the Eastern Sea," in ibid., 174–79, quotes on 174, 175, 178. This article first appeared in *New Republic* 19 (1919): 346–48.

16. Spence, *Search for Modern China*, 310–16.

17. Dewey and Dewey, *Letters from China*, 161.

18. Ibid., 161–65.

19. Ibid., 166–69, quote on 166.

20. Ibid., 171–81, quote on 179.

21. Ibid., 182–203, quotes on 184, 193; the remaining letters in this volume, from June to early August, were sent from Peking.

22. JD to children, June 10, 1919 (ICarbS, 03910), *Correspondence.*

23. For Treaty of Versailles, check colonial matters, in Pt. IV. German Rights and Interests Outside Germany, II. China, Section VIII. Shantung: Articles 156–58, http://avalon.law.yale.edu/imt/partiv.asp.

24. Dewey and Dewey, *Letters from China*, 217, 228–29, 238, 256, 258, quotes on 266 and 282.

25. JD to Wendell T. Bush, August 1, 1919 (TLS, 05019), *Correspondence.*

26. Dewey and Dewey, *Letters from China*, 279, 294–95, quotes on 284, 301.

27. Spence, *Search for Modern China*, 312.

28. JD to Albert C. Barnes, January 15, 1920 (ICarbS, 0491), *Correspondence.*

29. JD to children, February 17, 1920 (ICarbS, 03586), *Correspondence.*

30. JD to Barnes, September 12, 1920 (ICarbS, 04102), *Correspondence.*

31. Ibid.

32. JD to Dewey family, April 11, 1920 (ICarbS, 03916), *Correspondence.*

33. JD to children, August 25, 1920 (ICarbS, 03569), *Correspondence.*

34. JD to children, November 19, 1919 (ICarbS, 03472), *Correspondence.*

35. JD to John Jacob Coss, January 13, 1920 (NNC-T, 04882), *Correspondence.*

36. For this analysis, see Jay Martin, *The Education of John Dewey: A Biography,* 316, 324–25; Keenan, *Dewey Experiment,* 32–33; and Alan Ryan, *John Dewey and the High Tide of American Liberalism,* 205.

37. Bertrand Russell to Ottoline Morrell, February 21, 1921 (TxU-R, 08295), *Correspondence.*

38. Dora Black Russell to C. K. Ogden, October 20, 1921 (International Institute of Social History, 10449), *Correspondence.*

39. JD to James H. Tufts, February 23, 1921 (VtU, 07207), *Correspondence.*

40. *Weekly Review,* July 23, 1921, 402.

41. JD to family, April 11, 1920 (ICarbS, 03916), *Correspondence.*

42. Robert B. Westbrook, *John Dewey and American Democracy,* 254.

43. JD to Barnes, May 30, 1920 (ICarbS, 04095), *Correspondence.*

44. JD to C. Barnes, December 5, 1920 (ICarbS, 04113), *Correspondence.*

45. JD to C. Barnes, December 29, 1920 (ICarbS, 04115), *Correspondence.*

46. JD to C. Barnes, March 13, 1921 (ICarbS, 04120), *Correspondence.*

47. As to the lectures, his former student Hu Shih translated these lectures, originally delivered in English, into Chinese and, then, from the Chinese back into English. Dewey had planned to revise and expand them, but never got around to that project. Therefore, these lectures are in the form of Hu Shih with an updating by Robert W. Clopton and Tsuin-chen Ou for the purposes a new publication in 1973. See Dewey, *Lectures in China,* 31–44.

48. Typically, they appeared as notices in *Millard's Review of the Far East*—for example, "Dr. John Dewey, the Columbia exchange professor at Peking University, who is now in Shanghai, addressed the members of the Shanghai Chinese Y.M.C.A. on Wednesday night on 'Elements of Citizenship'" (June 5, 1920).

49. Many of Dewey's articles have been conveniently collected in two books: *Characters and Events: Popular Essays in Social and Political Philosophy,* 1:193–323; and *Reconstruction in Philosophy,* 12:22–76, 53–55.

50. The first two topics have been completely rendered in this edition, whereas the latter six are abstracted. See Dewey, *Lectures in China,* 45–303, 309–27.

51. JD, "The Function of Theory, in ibid., 53.

52. JD, "Social Reform," in ibid., 73.

53. Ibid., 72.

54. JD, "Socialism," in ibid., 124.

55. Maurice Meisner, *Li Ta-Chao and the Origins of Chinese Marxism,* 107–8. This entire discussion of Dewey's social and political philosophy owes a great deal to the admirable analysis of Westbrook, *Dewey and Democracy,* esp. 244–50.

56. JD, "The Function of Theory," in *Lectures,* 48, 50.

57. JD, "Science and Social Philosophy," in ibid., 62–63.

58. JD, "Social Conflict," in ibid., 67–69.

59. JD, "Social Reform," in ibid., 73–74.

60. Ibid., 75–81.

61. JD, "Criteria for Judging Systems of Thought," in ibid., 88.

62. JD, "Communication and Associated Living," 93, quote on 98.

63. JD, "Classical Individualism and Free Enterprise," 115; "Socialism," 123–24, quote on 124.

64. JD, "The Right of Individuals," 154–55, in ibid.

65. JD, "Work and Play in Education," 199; "The Cultural Heritage and Social Reconstruction," 211–12, 215; "The Development of Modern Science," 235; "Science and Education," 259, quotes on 210 ("The Cultural Heritage and Social Reconstruction"), 216 (ibid.), and 247 ("Science and Knowing"), all in *Lectures*.

66. JD, "Vocational Education," 284, in ibid.

67. JD, "Self-Activity and Self-Government," 318.

68. Sidney Hook, *John Dewey: An Intellectual Portrait*, 181.

69. Gary Bullert, *The Politics of John Dewey*, 91.

70. JD to Barnes, March 28, 1920 (ICarbS, 04123), *Correspondence*.

71. JD, "Transforming the Mind of China," in *Characters and Events*, 1:285.

72. Ibid., 290.

73. Ibid., 290, 292, quotes on 294, 295.

74. Ibid., 222–23, 224, 226–27.

75. Ibid., 228.

76. Ibid., 230, 232–33, 235–36.

77. Ibid., 296.

78. Ibid., 297–99, quote on 299.

79. Ibid., 300.

80. Ibid., 301.

81. Ibid.

82. Ibid., 304–6, 308, quote on 307.

83. Ibid., 309–11, quotes on 309, 311.

84. Ibid., 244, quote on 246–47.

85. Ibid., 249–53.

86. Ibid., 211–21, quote on 220.

87. Ibid., 193–98, quotes on 196.

88. JD to Colonel Drysdale, December 1, 1920, published as "Bolshevism in China: Service Report," in *Reconstruction in Philosophy*, by Dewey, 24:253–55, quotes on 254, 255.

89. Dewey, *Middle Works*, 22–26.

90. Ibid., 28–40, quotes on 33 and 38.

91. Ibid., 65–70 and 7 1–76, quote on 75.

92. JD, *Characters and Events*, 1:237–43, quote on 240–41.

93. Ibid., 255–69.

94. Ibid., 284.

95. Ibid., 203.

96. Ibid., quotes on 316, 317, 323.

97. See Berry, "Dewey's Influence in China," 202, and Clopton and Ou, introduction to *Lectures in China*, by Dewey, 26 (both fully cited above).

98. Clopton and Ou, introduction to *Lectures in China*, by Dewey, quotes on 1 and 5, the latter where the authors quote Father Berry's article, 206.

99. Ibid., 22–25, quotes on 26 and 28.

100. Latourette's papers are at Yale University Library, Divinity Library Special Collections and comprise 169 manuscript boxes; Fairbank's archive is at Harvard University Archives and makes up 272 manuscript boxes. For their indexes and biographical notes, see http://webtext.library.yale.edu/xml2html/divinity.003.con .html, and for Fairbank, consult http://oasis.lib.harvard.edu/oasis/deliver/~hua 2704.

101. For Latourette's biographical notes, see preface notes to his archive and http://en.wikipedia.org/wiki/Kenneth_Scott_Latourette.

102. For this quote see page 45, as well as for much of the material in this section, we are indebted to the excellent dissertation by Patricia C. Neils, "China in the Writings of Kenneth Scott Latourette and John King Fairbank."

103. "Latourette: Optimistic Historian," obituary, *Christian Century* 86 (January 1969): 69–70. He also wrote a fine autobiography, *Beyond the Ranges*.

104. For more biographical information, see http://en.wikipedia.org/wiki/ John_Fairbank.

105. Neils, "Writings of Latourette and Fairbank," 46.

106. Ibid., 52–60, quote on 52. See also Fairbank's memoir, *China Bound: A Fifty-Year Memoir*.

107. Neils, "Writings of Latourette and Fairbank," 71–117, quote on 119.

108. Ibid., 155.

109. Ibid., quotes on 208, 209.

Chapter 10. Red Star over China

1. Peter Rand, *China Hands: The Adventures and Ordeals of the American Journalists Who Joined Forces with the Great Chinese Revolution*, 25.

2. Ibid., 158.

3. Edgar Snow (hereafter ES), *Diary*, December 3, 1936, and also selections from October 28–30, 1936, f. 10, Snow Papers (hereafter SP), University of Missouri at Kansas City (hereafter UMKC).

4. ES to L. M. MacBride, December 26, 1936, f. 10, SP, UMKC.

5. Snow, *Red Star over China*, 35–39. His clandestine entry is told in the first footnote to this chapter on page 419, and in the remaining chapters of part 1 and the first chapter of part 2.

6. Ibid., 67–70, quote on 70.

7. Ibid., 89, quotes on 90.

8. Ibid., 89–90, quotes on 92, 93.

9. Ibid., 94–96.

10. Ibid., 97–105.

11. Ibid., 109.

12. Ibid., 111.

13. Ibid., 112.

14. Ibid., 163.

15. Ibid., 164–65.

16. Ibid., 172–73, 174, quotes on 176, 178, 180, 181n.

17. Ibid., 185, quotes on 186.

18. Ibid., 190–206. For a full accounting of the Long March, see Harrison E. Salisbury, *The Long March: The Untold Story.*

19. Ibid., 219, quotes on 220.

20. Ibid., 230–37.

21. Ibid., 241–53, quote on 253.

22. Snow considered Stilwell an outstanding commander who spoke and read Chinese, and a man who had a "sharp, inquiring, and analytical mind and was anything but the conventional time-serving staff officer." However, he was given "formidable tasks to accomplish with ridiculously inadequate means and vacillating support both from Chiang Kai-shek and from Washington." He understood the necessity of reform and reorganization. Most revealing, Snow faults the "intrigue amounting to treason by Chennault and his coterie [and, therefore] it was never realistic to suppose that there was any chance of saving Chiang Kai-shek by the time Stilwell arrived on the scene" (ES to John N. Hart, February 29, 1960, f. 41, SP, UMKC). See also Edgar Snow, *Journey to the Beginning,* 151–52.

23. Snow, *Red Star over China,* 257–62, 173 for eight disciplines.

24. Ibid., 276.

25. Ibid., 283, quote on 284.

26. Ibid., 295.

27. Ibid., 300.

28. Ibid., see chap. 4, pt. 6.

29. Ibid., 352, quote on 353.

30. Ibid., 358–60, quote on 358.

31. Ibid., 366–67.

32. Ibid., 387; for details of the Sian Incident and its repercussions, see 373–409. In a very provocative epilogue written in 1944, Snow insisted that the movement launched in 1928 had by then turned into a "crusade" and that no "arbiters" of China's destiny could deny that it spoke for "vast multitudes" (418).

33. ES to MacBride, January 5, 1937, f. 11, SP, UMKC.

34. Quoted in John Maxwell Hamilton, *Edgar Snow: A Biography,* 280.

35. This question ended up getting Snow into a stew. Freda Utley, a former Marxist turned reactionary, claimed that Snow had always maintained in the thirties that the Chinese Reds were nothing more than agrarian reformers when he knew all along they were dyed-in-the-wool communists. That made him, for Utley and her friends, either a communist or a fellow-traveling apologist. In the spring of 1948, Utley began a crusade to get Snow removed from the editorial board of the *Saturday Evening Post.* Ben Hibbs, editor of the *Post,* wrote Snow: "I think you did see the vicious and untrue article which Freda Utley wrote about you for *Plain Talk,* but I doubt that you know about what followed." He then explained that a certain *Post* contributor, Rose Wilder Lane, circulated the Utley article to prominent people in order to "'get rid of this Communist,' meaning you." Though Snow offered to resign, the *Post* kept him on. Nevertheless, the attack forced Snow to cover Western Europe for the *Post,* and drop the Far East. When

Snow called for the United States to accept the fall of Nationalist China, oppose the French in Indo-China, and assist newly independent countries from colonialism, the *Post* finally accepted his resignation in 1953. Hamilton, *Edgar Snow: A Biography*, 190–91). See also Hibbs to ES, March 26, 1948, for the above quote in f. 23, SP, UMKC. See also ES to Hibbs, April 5, 1948, f. 23, SP, UMKC, and Hibbs to ES, April 12, 1948, f. 23, UMKC, where Hibbs writes, "Your work is so valuable to us that Marty [Martin Sommers] and I are always glad to stand up and do battle for you. We want you to continue with us because you are a damned good correspondent" (f. 23, SP, UMKC). It was not until 1958, however, that Snow finally cleared up the "agrarian reformer" myth that Utley had herself spread, when he wrote a letter to *New York Times* (ES to editor, November 12, 1958, f. 38, SP, UMKC) pointing out her own endorsement of that view back in 1939 in her book *China at War* (251).

36. As concerns Pearl Buck, Snow wrote to her husband, Richard Walsh, editor of *Asia* magazine, on the occasion of her winning the Nobel Prize for Literature: "My warmest congratulations to Pearl Buck, for an honor that was certainly fully and richly deserved. In my opinion, we all owe a great debt to her for opening up the Western mind to a new conception of the Chinese people and a more accurate and more honest one than any fiction had ever given." According to Snow, Buck's work made it possible for him and others to find an audience. See ES to Richard Walsh, February 24, 1939, f. 14, SP, UMKC.

37. Hamilton, *Edgar Snow: A Biography*, 75–85.

38. ES to Ambassador H. E. Nelson Trusler Johnson, February 6, 1937, f. 11, SP, UMKC.

39. Hamilton, *Edgar Snow: A Biography*, 87.

40. Agnes Smedley to ES, April 19, 1937, f. 11, SP, UMKC.

41. ES to Earl Browder, March 20, 1938, f. 12, SP, UMKC.

42. ES to Harry Paxton Howard, May 30, 1938, f. 12, SP, UMKC.

43. Hamilton, *Edgar Snow: A Biography*, 86, 96, author quotes Arch Steele on 90.

44. Ibid., 94.

45. Ibid., 114, first quote on 115 and second on 116; see also ES to Jim Bertram, December 13, 1939, f. 15, SP, UMKC.

46. Hamilton, *Edgar Snow: A Biography*, 116.

47. Ibid., 117–18.

48. Ibid., 125–27, quote on 127. As to Snow's Asian judgments, see Edgar Snow, *The Battle for Asia*, esp. 81–91, 241–52.

49. ES to Walsh, April 2, 1940, f. 16, SP, UMKC.

50. Hamilton, *Edgar Snow: A Biography*, 124–25, 126, 127 for first quote, 128–29, 130, 133–34, 136.

51. Chou En-lai to ES, May 18, 27, 1942, f. 18, SP, UMKC.

52. In his autobiography, Snow talks about a certain "flagging of morale and mental fatigue" and returned home by February 1941 (*Journey to the Beginning*, 241).

53. Ibid., 277.

54. ES to FDR, December 28, 1944, f. 19, SP, UMKC.

55. ES to Grace Tully, December 28, 1944, f. PSF: Diplomatic Correspondence:

Russia, 1945, PSF, Franklin D. Roosevelt Library (hereafter FDRL), Hyde Park, New York (hereafter HP).

56. Snow, *Journey to the Beginning*, 310–11.

57. Ibid., 312–17, quote on 314.

58. FDR to ES, January 2, 1945, f. PSF: Diplomatic Correspondence: Russia, 1945, PSF, FDRL, HP.

59. ES to FDR, *Strictly Confidential* (Memorandum), Moscow, October 6, 1944, and FDR's response, January 2, 1945, f. PSF: Diplomatic Correspondence: Russia, 1945, PSF, FDRL, HP. Snow did not believe that FDR became disillusioned with the Russians, remarking, for instance, that the last meeting with Stalin was the best (*Stalin Must Have Peace*, 127).

60. ES to Saxe Commins, July 21, 1945, f. 20, SP, UMKC. In his book *Stalin Must Have Peace*, he says that after FDR's death, U.S. foreign policy was more and more determined by generals and admirals on the basis of "strategic necessities" for a possible war with the USSR (31).

61. "Russia would not promote proletarian revolutions in Europe where it meant jeopardizing continued co-operation with the United States" (Snow, *The Pattern of Soviet Power*, 25).

62. "It was hard to believe the Red Army would, indefinitely, refuse to help itself to booty to recoup Soviet losses" (ibid., 30).

63. ES to Commins, July 21, 1945, f. 20, SP, UMKC.

64. Hamilton, *Edgar Snow: A Biography*, 136–44, 146, quotes on 150, 151, 154.

65. ES to Commins, November 10, 1945, f. 20, SP, UMKC.

66. Hamilton, *Edgar Snow: A Biography*, 156.

67. Hugh Cabot to ES, February 25, 1944, f. 19, SP, UMKC.

68. Hamilton, *Edgar Snow: A Biography*, 168, 171, quotes on 176. For the actual "hopelessly muddled" quote, see Snow, *Stalin Must Have Peace*, 86. Snow also talks about Americans as "atomic warriors," meaning atomic diplomacy to thwart Soviet intentions (ibid., 88ff, 122, 140–41): "our policy of atomic armament, aimed primarily at Russia" (160).

69. Ibid., 177, 179–80.

70. ES to Hibbs and Sommers, August 12, 1946, f. 23, SP, UMKC.

71. Hamilton, *Edgar Snow: A Biography*, 188, 198–99, 201, quote of Snow on 210–11.

72. Ibid., 217.

73. Ibid., 170–71. Harriman noted that when Hurley quit in November, he accused seven Foreign Service officers with favoring the Chinese communists, the opening salvo in the "melancholy chapter of 'Who lost China?' witch hunt in Washington" (Harriman and Abel, *Special Envoy*, 522).

74. For the *Post* articles: "Why We Don't Understand Russia," February 15, 1947, 18–19; "How It Looks to Ivan Ivanovich," February 22, 1947, 23; "Stalin Must Have Peace," March 1, 1947, 25. All these articles, plus a separate concluding chapter by Snow, were collected into a slim volume published by Random House under the title *Stalin Must Have Peace*, also in 1947, with an introduction by Martin Sommers, adapted from his *Post* article "Why Russia Got the Drop on Us," *Saturday Evening Post*, February 8, 1947, 25. Though the *Post* editors disagreed about whether to pub-

lish the three-part series, Hibbs decided in their favor and wrote an accompanying open letter, "To Generalissimo Stalin and Other *Post* Readers," *Saturday Evening Post*, February 15, 1947, 19.

75. Hamilton, *Edgar Snow: A Biography*, 176.

76. Ibid., 178, quoting directly from Hurley's open letter.

77. Ibid., 178–79 as quoted by Hamilton from Hurley's report (see also 319n39). Hurley illustrates typical misunderstanding by Americans of Russian intentions. In *Stalin Must Have Peace,* Snow sums up the extent of Hurley's misunderstanding when he "assured Truman that he had the Chinese Communists in his pocket—till political explosions after V-J Day demonstrated they were anywhere else but" (p. 34).

78. Hurley to Hibbs, February 28, 1947, f. 24, SP, UMKC.

79. Hibbs to ES, March 11,1947, f. 23, SP, UMKC.

80. Hibbs to Hurley, March 4, 1947, f. 24, SP, UMKC.

81. ES to Hibbs, March 17, 1947, f. 23, SP, UMKC, and attached a sample letter from ES to Hurley, dated March 17, 1947, that Hibbs had requested Snow send directly to Hurley, but, on second thought, told Snow not to send.

82. Sommers to ES, April 24, 1947, f. 23, SP, UMKC.

83. ES to J. L. McCully Jr., June 27, 1955, f. 33, SP, UMKC.

84. ES to Sommers, March 29, 1947, f. 23, SP, UMKC.

85. Ibid.

86. ES to Raymond A. de Groat, September 26, 1949, f. 25, SP, UMKC.

87. Ibid.

88. Ibid.

89. Ibid.

90. Ibid.

91. Ibid.

92. Ibid.

93. As early as 1951, the Chinese extended an invitation for Snow to visit the PRC, but he had declined at that time due to commitments elsewhere. In 1953, he began inquiries as to another invitation. See ES to Yang Han-seng and Lee Sheh, September 29, 1953, f. 37, SP, UMKC.

94. Hamilton, *Edgar Snow: A Biography*, 219, 221, 223–24, quote of Chou on 225.

95. Ibid., 236, 229–31, quote of Snow on 231.

96. Ibid., 231–36, quote of Snow on 236.

97. ES, "Notes," October 2, 1960, f. 41, SP, UMKC.

98. ES to Colston Leigh, November 28, 1960, f. 43, SP, UMKC.

99. Edgar Snow, *The Other Side of the River: Red China Today*, 619.

100. ES to Mme. Kung P'eng, March 31, 1961, f44, SP, UMKC.

101. Snow, *Other Side*, 4.

102. Ibid., 6–7.

103. Ibid., 7.

104. Ibid., 9.

105. ES to Mao Tse-tung, May 10, 1963, f. 48, SP, UMKC.

106. Hamilton, *Edgar Snow: A Biography*, 242–46.

107. The so-called white paper is State Department, *United States Relations with China, with Special Reference to the Period 1944–1949*, State Department Publication 3573, xvi. For important comments on Acheson's role, see Isaacson and Thomas, *Wise Men*, 474–77. As to the China Lobby, see Koen, *China Lobby*, 14–15.

108. William R. Johnson, "The United States Sells China Down the Amur."

109. Koen, *China Lobby*, 23.

110. *Congressional Record*, House, June 28, 1966, 13,933–38.

111. See the exchange between Snow and Harrison Salisbury: ES to Salisbury, January 30 and February 8, 1965, where in the latter Snow says, "All right, as long as we both know, for the record, that the question of price had nothing to do with the *Times* rupture of discussions, unconditionally, and curtly refusing any explanation, concerning purchase of my China reports" (both are in f. 59, SP, UMKC). In a letter of April 12, 1965, Snow told Salisbury that "I can't recall ever having been subjected to such a series of experiences" (f. 60, ibid.). Here he was referring to the overall rejection of his interviews by the U.S. media, or the vast editing, which he had strictly contracted against.

112. ES to Kung P'eng, March 9, 1965, f. 59, SP, UMKC.

113. Hamilton, *Edgar Snow: A Biography*, 255, and quote on 267.

114. Edgar Snow, *The Long Revolution*, 4.

115. Ibid., 189. Also see ES to Chairman Mao, May 16, 1971, f. 81, where Snow discusses the Nixon trip and the remark about welcoming Nixon as either a tourist or as president. With Nixon's withdrawal of large numbers of U.S. troops from Vietnam, the "Chinese responded on October 1 with what was meant to be the decisive 'signal' to Nixon. Chairman Mao invited Edgar Snow, the American journalist and author of the famous *Red Star over China* to stand beside him on the reviewing platform at celebrations in Peking of the twenty-first anniversary of the founding of the PRC. Unfortunately no one in the U.S. government realized this *was* a signal" (Spence, *Search for Modern China*, 629).

116. As to the "master stroke" of the table-tennis team, see ES to Ambassador Huang Hua (PRC to Canada), April 14, 1971, f. 81, SP, UMKC.

117. Snow, *The Long Revolution*, 9–12.

118. Hamilton, *Edgar Snow: A Biography*, 268–69, 272, 273–75, 277, 279, 282. In November and December 1971, Snow still contemplated going with the Nixon visit to cover the story. See ES to Arnoldo Mondavori (Snow's Italian publisher), November 16, 1971, and ES to Shag (Huang Hua?—PRC ambassador to the UN), December 6, 1971, f. 84, SP, UMKC.

119. For brief biographical sketches, see http://en.wikipedia.org/wiki/Harrison _Salisbury, http://www.answers.com/Harrison%20Evans%20Salisbury, and http://media-server.amazon.com/exec/drm/amzproxy.cgi/MjgwIPZ98yM2m MPzbyRt2k6j.

120. Harrison E. Salisbury, *A Time of Change: A Reporter's Tale of Our Time*, 196, 197.

121. Ibid., 198–99.

122. Ibid., 204–10.

123. Ibid., 214, 215.

124. Ibid., 218, 219.

125. Ibid., 220, 221.
126. Ibid., 228.
127. Ibid., see chap. 23.
128. Ibid., 258.

Chapter 11. The Novelist and the Ambassador

1. For the most complete bibliography of works by and about Pearl S. Buck, see Lucille S. Zinn, "The Works of Pearl S. Buck: A Bibliography," 194–208.

2. See http://english.upenn.edu/Projects/Buck/biography.html.

3. *New York Times*, September 16, 2004.

4. Ibid.

5. As quoted in http://bookrags.com/printfriendly/?p=lins&u=Pearl-S.-Buck.

6. G. A. Cevasco, "Pearl Buck and the Chinese Novel," in *Asian Studies*, 444.

7. Peter Conn, *Pearl S. Buck: A Cultural Biography*, 75–78.

8. Ibid., 75; Pearl S. Buck (hereafter PSB), *My Several Worlds: A Personal Record*, 162–67, where she quotes the first entire essay.

9. PSB, *Several Worlds*, 167–75, where she quotes the second entire essay, and, for Conn's comment, see his *Buck*, 77–78.

10. As quoted in Theodore F. Harris, *Pearl S. Buck: A Biography*, 126–27.

11. Conn, *Buck*, 80. It contains reference to almost 150 sources (393n87). It was written under the alias of David F. Barnes (393n88).

12. As quoted in ibid., taken from p. 18 of Buck's essay.

13. As quoted in ibid., 82, taken from the end of Buck's essay.

14. PSB, "China and the West," winner of the Laura Messenger Prize of two hundred dollars at Cornell University in 1926 for best essay on an international subject; part of this essay was used in an address given before the American Academy of Political and Social Science at Philadelphia, April 8, 1933 (118–31). As quoted in Zinn, "Works of Buck," 201.

15. PSB, "China and the West," 131.

16. Ibid., 130.

17. Ibid., 128.

18. PSB, *Several Worlds*, 207–25, quote on 213.

19. Ibid., letter reprinted on 229–31, 252, quote on 230.

20. Ibid., 231, 239, 250.

21. PSB, *East Wind, West Wind: The Saga of a Chinese Family*.

22. PSB, *Several Worlds*, 250.

23. Peter Conn, introduction to *The Good Earth*, by Buck, xi.

24. PSB to Emma Edmunds White, August 29, 1918, Emma White Papers, Lipscomb Library, Randolph-Macon Woman's College (hereafter LLRMWC), Lynchburg, Virginia.

25. PSB to White, March 7, 1927, in ibid.

26. Ibid.

27. PSB to White, May 19, 1927, in ibid.

28. PSB to White, January 4, 1928, in ibid.

29. PSB to White, January 4, 1929, in ibid.

30. Ibid.

31. PSB to White, May 26, 1930, in ibid.

32. PSB to White, January 20, 1931, in ibid.

33. PSB to White, January 27, 1931, in ibid.

34. PSB to White, September 24, 1931, in ibid.

35. PSB to White, February 24, 1932, in ibid.

36. PSB to White, May 21, 1932, in ibid.

37. PSB to White, October [?], 1937, in ibid.

38. PSB, "Friends and Enemies of China," *China Critic*, 69, and found in Buck's personal archive at Perkasie, Pennsylvania (see n. 41 below).

39. PSB to White, October 31, 1940, in White, LLRMWC.

40. PSB to White, October 16, 1944, in ibid.

41. PSB to Edgar Sydenstricker, May 5, 1941, box 1: Pearl S. Buck Correspondence, 1931–39 (A–L), f. 2: correspondence, 1931, Sydenstricker Family Letters, RG 1, Series 2, Archives of the Pearl S. Buck House, Pearl S. Buck International (hereafter PSBI).

42. Conn, *Buck,* 123–24, 126, 129, 131–32.

43. PSB, *The Good Earth,* 360 pp.

44. PSB, *Several Worlds,* 261–62.

45. Ibid., 269–78.

46. Ibid., 279.

47. Ibid., 280.

48. Ibid.

49. Ibid., 281.

50. Ibid., 282.

51. Malcolm Cowley, "Wang Lung's Children," 24–25.

52. Ibid., 25.

53. Paul A. Doyle, *Pearl S. Buck,* 68–69.

54. Dody Weston Thompson, "Pearl Buck," 1004.

55. PSB, *Several Worlds,* 336.

56. Doyle, *Pearl S. Buck,* 80–81.

57. Ibid., 81.

58. Ibid., 84.

59. PSB, *The Exile,* 98–99.

60. Ibid., 100.

61. Ibid., 155.

62. Ibid., 156–57.

63. Ibid., 194.

64. Ibid., 262.

65. Ibid., 263.

66. PSB, *Fighting Angel: Portrait of a Soul,* 9.

67. Ibid., 10.

68. Ibid., 11.

69. Ibid., 12.

70. Ibid., 71.

71. Ibid., 128–29.

72. Ibid., 138.

73. Ibid., 145.

74. Ibid., 163.

75. Ibid., 195–211.

76. Ibid., 300–301.

77. Conn, introduction to *The Good Earth*, by Buck, xi.

78. Scheuer, *Movies on TV and Videocassette*, 418.

79. Leonard Maltin, *2006 Movie Guide*, 506.

80. PSB, *Several Worlds*, 394–95.

81. Maltin, *2006 Movie Guide*, 776.

82. PSB, "The Chinese Novel," http://nobelprize.org/nobel_prizes/literature/laureates/1938/buck-lecture.html.

83. Conn, *Buck*, 317.

84. PSB, "Chinese Novel."

85. Ibid.

86. Ibid.

87. Ibid.

88. Conn, *Buck*, 159–60.

89. Pearl Buck to Henry R. Luce, March 3, 1943, *Time* Archives, as quoted in Neils, *China Images*, 104.

90. Henry R. Luce, "Private Memorandum on Pearl Buck's Article on China," March, 1943, *Time* Archives, as quoted in ibid., 105.

91. Ibid., 105–6.

92. PSB, "A Warning about China," 53–54, 56.

93. Russell D. Buhite, *Nelson T. Johnson and American Policy toward China*, 6–12.

94. Nelson Johnson to Sister, January 14, 1912, box 1, f. 3, Nelson T. Johnson (hereafter NTJ) Papers, Special Collections and Archives, James Branch Cabell Library, Virginia Commonwealth University (hereafter VCU).

95. For these four quotes, see NTJ to Father, September 8, 1912, to Dad, August 1, 1915, to Father, June 9, 1916, and to Dad, June 25, 1916, box 1, ff. 3, 6, and 7, NTJ Papers, VCU.

96. Stanley K. Hornbeck, "Nelson Trusler Johnson: An Appreciation," January 8, 1955, box 3, f. Writings about or by NTJ, NTJ Papers, VCU.

97. NTJ to John Van Antwerp MacMurray, June 24, 1926, 4:1925–26, NTJ Papers, LC.

98. NTJ to R. S. Norman, June 29, 1927, 6:1927: M–Z, NTJ Papers, LC.

99. NTJ to MacMurray, July 8, 1929, box 38, f. July 8–18, 1929, MacMurray Papers, SMML, PU. It should be noted that there is a considerable amount of material on the Nanjing Incident and its resolution scattered through boxes 31, 34, and 38.

100. Quotes are from the following: NTJ to Dad, August 5, 1930, to Dad, March 3, 1931, and to Dad, April 14, 1931, box 1, f. 8: October 1929–June 1932, all in NTJ Papers, VCU.

101. NTJ to Dad, July 23, 1932, January 8, 22, 1933, in ibid.

102. NTJ to Dad, May 21, 1935, box 1, f. 10, NTJ Papers, VCU.

103. NTJ to Dad, September 16, 1935, in ibid.

104. NTJ to SS, February 3, 1938, f. 11, in ibid.

105. NTJ to SS, State, n.d., in ibid.

106. NTJ to Betty, November 20, 1938, in ibid.

107. NTJ to Mr. President, February 27, 1939, box 37, f. 1939: N–P, NTJ Papers, LC.

108. See *Time* for December 11, 1939. Johnson's views, of course, paralleled those of *Time*'s editor, Henry Luce. (See chapter 13.)

109. These items occurred in a series of letters: NTJ to Betty, March 19, October 29, November 5, and December 24, 1944, and the quote in February 18, 1945, box 1, f. 11, NTJ Papers, VCU.

110. NTJ interview, 15, side 2, November 24, 1954, box 3, f. Writings about or by Nelson T. Johnson, in ibid.

Chapter 12. The President and the Generalissimo

1. Herbert Feis, *The China Tangle: The American Effort in China from Pearl Harbor to the Marshall Mission*, 11 (Churchill), 12 (Feis).

2. Ibid., 87, 95.

3. Hull, *Memoirs*, 2:1282.

4. Feis, *China Tangle*, 98–99. See Harley Notter, *Postwar Foreign Policy Preparation, 1939–1945*, 553, for the actual declaration.

5. Robert Dallek, *Franklin D. Roosevelt and American Foreign Policy, 1932–1945*, 389.

6. Townsend Hoopes and Douglas Brinkley, *FDR and the Creation of the UN*, 46, 50, 74, 100, 115.

7. See Barbara Tuchman, *Stilwell and the American Experience in China, 1911–45*, the heading to her chap. 16, p. 396. Charles F. Romanus and Riley Sunderland in the volume on the China-Burma-India Theater, *Stilwell's Command Problems*, title their second chapter, p. 49, "Sextant: The Watershed." Both books convey the idea that this was the best both U.S. perception and policy ever got toward China. It was too good to be true, and it quickly faded in the light of reality.

8. Elliott Roosevelt, *As He Saw It*, 154.

9. *FRUS, 1943: General*, 1:513, 515.

10. Ibid., 515. See also Hull, *Memoirs*, 2:1252.

11. Hull, *Memoirs*, 2:1255. See also *FRUS, 1943: General*, where FDR tells Stalin, "I am most anxious that Secretary Hull attend in person in the meeting with Mr. Molotov and Mr. Eden" (530), to which Stalin replied, "I share your opinion concerning the desirability of the personal attendance of the Secretary of State, Mr. Hull, at the forthcoming conference of the representatives of the three Governments" (531).

12. Hull, *Memoirs*, 2:1256–57.

13. Ibid., 1257–65, quotes on 1265.

14. Churchill, *The Hinge of Fate*, 562.

15. Herbert Feis, *Churchill, Roosevelt, Stalin: The War They Waged and the Peace They Sought,* 210. In fact, the Russians had rejected the entire notion of a four-power declaration, that is, point one of the proposed agenda. When it was finally accepted, it became point 2. See *FRUS, 1943, General,* 535.

16. For a quick survey of the Moscow Conference, see Winston S. Churchill, *Closing the Ring,* 277–99.

17. Hull, *Memoirs,* 2:1279.

18. Ibid., 1282.

19. Ibid., 1299, 1302, 1307, 1317; additional materials on 1301, 1306. The substance of the conference is covered in detail in *FRUS, 1943: General,* 513–749; the protocols of it are found on 749–81.

20. Hull, *Memoirs,* 2:1309.

21. Churchill, *Closing the Ring,* 307, quoting messages of October 14–15, 1943.

22. Feis, *Churchill, Roosevelt, Stalin,* 243.

23. Churchill, *Closing the Ring,* 317.

24. Ibid., 326–29, quotes on 328. No records were kept of the FDR-Chiang conversations, with the exception of some brief Chinese notes to one of them.

25. Sherwood, *Roosevelt and Hopkins,* 738, quote on 736.

26. *FRUS, 1943: Conferences at Cairo and Tehran,* 314.

27. Theodore H. White, *In Search of History: A Personal Adventure,* 138–47, quotes on 140, 142, 144.

28. Ibid., 147–51, quotes on 147, 149, 150–51.

29. John Paton Davies Jr., *Dragon by the Tail: American, British, Japanese, and Russian Encounters with China and One Another,* 342.

30. T. White, *In Search of History,* 174–86, quotes on 174, 175, 176, 177, 179.

31. Sherwood, *Roosevelt and Hopkins,* 705.

32. White, *In Search of History,* 186–87.

33. *Time,* November 13, 1944, and the quote as cited in Robert E. Herzstein, *Henry R. Luce, "Time," and the American Crusade in Asia,* 45.

34. Sherwood, *Roosevelt and Hopkins,* 739.

35. Joseph W. Stilwell, *The Stilwell Papers,* chap. 8.

36. Ibid., 242–44.

37. Tuchman, *Stilwell and the American Experience,* 398.

38. *FRUS, 1943: Cairo and Tehran,* 293–94. Though Chiang, his wife, and three Chinese generals are mentioned, it is doubtful that they attended (308).

39. Stilwell, *The Stilwell Papers,* 245.

40. *FRUS, 1943: Cairo and Tehran,* 306.

41. Ibid., 370–71.

42. Ibid., 314.

43. Ibid., 317–18.

44. Stilwell, *The Stilwell Papers,* 245.

45. *FRUS, 1943: Cairo and Tehran,* 321–22.

46. Ibid., 371–72.

47. Ibid., 323.

48. Roosevelt, *As He Saw It,* 142–43.

49. *FRUS, 1943: Cairo and Tehran*, 323–25.

50. Ibid., quotes on 332 and 334.

51. Stilwell, *The Stilwell Papers*, 246.

52. *FRUS, 1943: Cairo and Tehran*, 336–38.

53. Ibid., 338–42, quote on 342. (The points are summarized on p. 344 by Stilwell.)

54. Ibid., 338–39, quote on 342.

55. Ibid., 342.

56. Ibid., 343.

57. Ibid., 347–48.

58. Stilwell, *The Stilwell Papers*, 246.

59. Ibid.

60. Romanus and Sunderland, *Stilwell's Command Problems*, 64. FDR and Chiang had met at five o'clock, and though no official record was kept, Hopkins's comment seemed correct, that is, "the Generalissimo met again with the President and reversed himself on every point" (65).

61. *FRUS, 1943: Cairo and Tehran*: "According to Ehrman [John Ehrman, *Grand Strategy*, 5:165), this promise was given before November 26. Alanbrooke [Arthur Bryant, *Triumph in the West: A History of the War Years Based on the Diaries of Field Marshal Lord Alanbrooke, Chief of the Imperial General Staff*, 63] recollected the promise as having been given 'on the first day of our Cairo meetings,' but this appears unlikely" (350).

62. *FRUS, 1943: Cairo and Tehran*, 351, quotes on 354, 355.

63. Ibid., 364–65.

64. Editors' comment, ibid., 366.

65. Ibid., 367.

66. Stilwell, *The Stilwell Papers*, 247.

67. Romanus and Sunderland, *Stilwell's Command Problems*, 65.

68. *FRUS, 1943: Cairo and Tehran*, 483–86.

69. Ibid., 477–82.

70. Ibid., 487–91.

71. Ibid., 529–33.

72. Ibid., 587.

73. Ibid., 674.

74. Ibid., 675–81, quotes on 675, 676, 679, 680.

75. Ibid., 686–704, quotes on 687, 700, 702, 703.

76. Ibid., quotes on 706, 709, 710.

77. Ibid., 725 as recounted in an editorial note, but see also Churchill, *Closing the Ring*, 352, where the actual FDR quote is found.

78. Stilwell, *The Stilwell Papers*, 251.

79. Roosevelt, *As He Saw It*, 207–8.

80. *FRUS, 1943: Cairo and Tehran*, 803.

81. Romanus and Sunderland, *Stilwell's Command Problems*, 74–75.

82. Tuchman, *Stilwell and the American Experience*, 409.

83. Ibid., 409–14. Details of the mission to Washington by Dr. H. H. Kung,

China's financial minister, may be found in Henry Morgenthau's diary (*Morgenthau Diary (China)*, 936–37, 1037, 1181, 1199, 1205).

84. Feis, *Churchill, Roosevelt, Stalin*, 250.

85. Ibid., 251.

86. *FRUS, 1943: Cairo and Tehran*, 448.

87. Tuchman, *Stilwell and the American Experience*, 397.

88. Ibid., 400.

89. Quoted in ibid., 401.

90. Quoted in ibid., 404.

91. Ibid., 410–11.

Chapter 13. Luce's Man in Chungking

1. T. White, *In Search of History*, 13–17, quote on 17.

2. Theodore H. White (hereafter THW) to Fairbank, July 9, 1937, box 1, f. 2, Papers of THW, Pusey Library, Harvard University (hereafter THW, PL, HU).

3. Fairbank to THW, August 24, 1937, box 1, f. 2, THW, PL, HU.

4. THW to Dean Hanford, late July 1939, box 1, f. 8, THW, PL, HU.

5. THW to F. I. Smith, January 5, 1939, box 1, f. 13, THW, PL, HU.

6. THW to Mom, Gitty, and Borjy, April 24, 1939, box 1, f. 17, THW, PL, HU.

7. THW to Mom, June 2, 1939, box 1, f. 19, THW, PL, HU.

8. THW to Mom, Gitty, and Bobby, August 19, 1939, box 1, f. 20, THW, PL, HU.

9. THW to Gen. Ch'en Ch'ien, October 16, 1939, box 1, f. 21, THW, PL, HU.

10. THW to Mama, Gladys, and Bobby, November 16, 1939, box 1, f. 21, THW, PL, HU.

11. On patronage, see THW to Mama, Gitty, and Borjy, December 10, 1939; on quitting, see THW to Dr. Tong, December 18, 1939, and Tong's acceptance, December 21, 1939, box 1, f. 22, THW, PL, HU.

12. THW to Fairbank, November 28, 1939, box 2, f. 6, THW, PL, HU.

13. THW to Fairbank, October 1939, box 2, f. 23, THW, PL, HU.

14. Ibid.

15. THW, "Eagles of Shansi," *Time*, December 18, 1939, http://www.time.com/time/magazine/printout/0,8816,763085,00.html.

16. Emily Hahn, *China to Me*, 142.

17. White included the telegram in THW to Mama, Gladys, and Bobby, April 19, 1941, box 2, f. 26, THW, PL, HU.

18. THW to Gladys, April 25, 1941, box 2, f. 26, THW, PL, HU. His unpublished Kuomintang tract for Random House was titled *Ploughshares into Swords*.

19. First quote from THW, *In Search of History*, 133, and second from Joyce Hoffmann, *Theodore White and Journalism as Illusion*, 46.

20. Charles Moritz, ed., *Current Biography Yearbook*, 273–75, quote on 273.

21. Robert T. Elson, *The World of Time, Inc.*, 1:447–48.

22. THW, *In Search of History*, 126.

23. See Henry Luce, "The American Century," in *The Ideas of Henry Luce*, ed. John K. Jessup, 105–20.

24. U.S., Congress, Senate, Government Operations Committee, Subcommittee on National Policy Machinery, Organizing for National Security, Hearings, 86th Cong., 2d sess., 1960, 923.

25. THW, *In Search of History*, 133–37, quotes on 132, 133, 135.

26. Hoffmann, *White and Journalism*, 47.

27. For the reference to Mme. Sun, see THW to Mme. Sun, November 26, 1942, box 4, f. 20; for Chiang's denial, check THW to Till and Peg, June 1, 1943, box 4, f. 11; the quote is from THW to Quinn, July 12, 1943, box 4, f. 12, all in THW, PL, HU.

28. TWH to Chiang Kai-shek, [June to July] 1944, box 4, f. 25, THW, PL, HU.

29. THW to Mama and Gladys, January 17, 1945, box 4, f. 31, THW, PL, HU.

30. Herzstein, *Crusade in Asia*, 42.

31. THW, *In Search of History*, quotes on 217, 218.

32. Luce to THW, April 3, 1944, box 3, f. 21, THW, PL, HU.

33. THW to Luce, April 4 or 5, 1944, box 3, f. 21, THW, PL, HU.

34. THW, *In Search of History*, 217.

35. THW, "Life Looks at China." It has been anthologized in Edward T. Thompson, ed., *Theodore H. White at Large: The Best of His Magazine Writing, 1939–1986*, 96–110.

36. Thompson, *White at Large*, 109.

37. Ibid.

38. Ibid.

39. Ibid., 106–7.

40. Ibid., 108.

41. Ibid., 109.

42. Ibid., 110.

43. David Halberstam, *The Powers That Be*, 79.

44. THW, *In Search of History*, 218.

45. Ibid., 219.

46. For the Judd quotes and Artichoke, see *Time*, November 13, 1944, http://www.time.com/time/printout/0,8816,801570,00.

47. THW to Luce and David Hulburd, November 29, 1944, Mss 65, Series XIX, box 511, f. 2, copy by courtesy of the Mansfield Library, K. Ross Toole Archives/Special Collections, University of Montana.

48. Ibid.

49. Hoffmann, *White and Journalism*, 52; for quote, see THW, "Inside Red China," *Life*, 39.

50. THW, "Inside Red China," 39.

51. Ibid., 40, quote on 46.

52. Ibid., 46.

53. Ibid., 40.

54. THW, *In Search of History*, 219.

55. Ibid., 220.

56. Ibid., 221–22.

57. Thomas Griffith, *Harry and Teddy: The Turbulent Friendship of Press Lord Henry R. Luce and His Favorite Reporter, Theodore H. White,* 142.

58. Allen Grover to THW, October or November 1945, box 3, f. 21, THW, PL, HU.

59. Grover to THW, November 14, 1945, box 3, f. 21, THW, PL, HU.

60. THW to Grover, November 16, 1945, box 3, f. 21, THW, PL, HU.

61. THW to Tom Mathews, n.d., box 3, f. 21, THW, PL, HU.

62. THW, *In Search of History,* quotes on 251 and 252.

63. Ibid., 257.

64. Luce to THW, June 29, 1946, box 3, f. 21, THW, PL, HU.

65. As quoted in Hoffmann, *White and Journalism,* 87.

66. THW, *In Search of History,* quotes on 255, 265.

67. THW and Annalee Jacoby, *Thunder Out of China,* 298.

68. Ibid., quotes on xiii, xv, xvi.

69. Tuchman, *Stilwell and the American Experience,* 498. Furthermore, as previously noted, White's and Jacoby's contention about Harry Hopkins is also alluded to in Sherwood, *Roosevelt and Hopkins,* 705.

70. White and Jacoby, *Thunder,* 221–42, quote on 242.

71. Ibid., 255.

72. Ibid., 280–96, quotes on 287, 296.

73. Donald G. Tewksbury, "Review of *Thunder Out of China,*" 58–59.

74. Ibid.

75. Hoffmann, *White and Journalism,* 77.

76. Ibid., 78–79.

77. General Hurley's draft as corrected by Wang Shih-chieh and Gen. Chang Chih-chung, October 28, 1944, and see also Hurley to FDR, November 7, 1944, in *FRUS, 1944,* vol. 6, *China,* 666–67.

78. Memorandum by Gen. Patrick J. Hurley, November 8, 1944: "Theodore White, correspondent for *Time* and *Life,* told me that he had just talked to Chairman Mao and Mao had told him that there was not any possible chance of an agreement between him and Chiang Kai-shek. . . . White's whole conversation was definitely against the mission with which I am charged" (ibid., 673–74).

79. Buhite, *Johnson,* 207–14, quote on 213.

80. Revised draft by the Chinese Communist Party representative, "Agreement between the National Government of China, the Kuomintang of China, and the Communist Party of China," November 10, 1944, in *FRUS, 1944,* vol. 6, *China,* 687–88.

81. Russell D. Buhite, *Patrick J. Hurley and American Foreign Policy,* 166.

82. Ibid., 171.

83. Ibid., 172.

84. Ibid., 175–76.

85. Ibid., 180, 186.

86. Ibid., 181–82.

87. "Memorandum by the Second Secretary of Embassy in China" (Davies), November 15, 1944, in *FRUS, 1944,* vol. 6, *China,* 696.

88. Buhite, *Hurley*, 183.

89. Ibid., 184–85, quote on 187.

90. Ibid., 189.

91. Ibid., 193–94, 196.

92. John S. Service to Division of Foreign Service Personnel, October 19, 1949, in *FRUS, 1944*, vol. 6, *China*, 712–14.

93. Buhite, *Hurley*, 199–201, quote on 202.

94. Ibid., 212–19.

95. Ibid., 222.

96. Ibid., 224.

97. Ibid., 225–30.

98. Ibid., 230–72.

99. Ferrell, *Truman*, 316.

100. Ibid., 316–17.

101. "The Ambassador of China (Hurley) to President Truman," November 26, 1945, in *FRUS, 1944*, vol. 6, *China*, 723.

102. Ibid.

103. Ibid.

104. Ibid., 724.

105. Ibid., 725–26.

106. United States Senate, Committee on Foreign Relations, Hearings, *Investigation of Far Eastern Policy*, 300.

107. Ibid., quotes on 310–12.

108. Ibid., 314.

109. Ibid., 314–15.

110. Ibid., 315.

111. Ibid., 316.

112. Ibid., 317–18.

113. Ibid., 319.

114. Ibid., 320.

115. Ibid., 321.

116. Ibid., 322–24, quote on 325.

117. Walter H. Judd, *Congressional Record*, 79th Cong., 1st sess., vol. 91, pt. 2 (March 15, 1945), 2294–2302.

118. PSB, "A Warning about China"; Edgar Snow, "Sixty Million Lost Allies"; Darrell Berrigan, "Uncle Joe Pays Off"; E. O. Hauser, "China Needs a Friendly Nudge"; *New York Times*, October 31, 1944, 1, 4; Edgar Snow and Mark Gayn, "Must China Go Red?"; Samuel Lubell, "Vinegar Joe and the Reluctant Dragon"; Lubell, "Is China Washed Up?"

119. State Department, *United States Relations with China, with Special Reference to the Period 1944–1949*, State Department Publication 3573. See Dean Acheson's letter of transmission to President Truman, July 30, 1949, iii–xvii.

120. Ibid., xvi. See also Isaacson and Thomas, *Wise Men*, 474–77.

121. Koen, *China Lobby*, 14.

122. Ibid., 15.

123. W. Johnson, "Sells China Down the Amur."

124. Koen, *China Lobby*, 23.

125. As cited in Herzstein, *Crusade in Asia*, 250.

Chapter 14. Gurus

1. *United States Relations with China*, xvi.

2. Ibid., xvi–xvii, and for quote, see Franz Schurman and Orville Schell, *Communist China: Revolutionary Reconstruction and International Confrontation, 1949 to the Present*, 295.

3. John K. Fairbank, *The United States and China*, 351–52.

4. Ibid., 352–53, quote on 353.

5. See *New York Times*, June 27, 1962.

6. Schurman and Schell, *Communist China*, 303–5, quote on 303. Throughout the period, 1949–1969, the United States maintained "listening posts" in Taiwan and Hong Kong. See Theodore Shackley, *Spymaster: My Life in the CIA;* and Harrison E. Salisbury, *Orbit of China*, 7–25.

7. Richard M. Nixon, "Asia after Vietnam," 121.

8. As quoted in Henry Kissinger, *White House Years*, 164.

9. Nixon, *RN*, 340–41.

10. For Nixon's first inaugural, see http://www.yale.edu/awweb/avalon/presiden/inaug/nixon1.htm.

11. Richard Nixon (hereafter RN) to Henry Kissinger (hereafter HAK), February 1, 1969, box 1032, f. Cookies II, Nixon Presidential Materials Project, National Security Council (hereafter NSC) Files, Files for the President—China Materials, Nixon Presidential Papers (hereafter RNPP), NARA, CP.

12. HAK to SS, Secretary of Defense, and Director of the CIA, February 5, 1969, box H-037, f. Review Group China NPG (pt. 2), RNPP, NARA, CP.

13. NSSM 14, "United States–China Policy," April 29, 1969, box H-037, f. 2: Review Group China NPG (pt. 2), RNPP, NARA, CP.

14. Ibid.; Walter Isaacson, *Kissinger: A Biography*, 336.

15. Kissinger, *White House Years*, quotes on 172 and 177

16. Ibid., 178–79.

17. Summary Paper on NSSM 14, f. 2: Review Group China NPG, pt. 2, May 15, 1969, box H-037, Nixon Presidential Materials Project, Kissinger Office Files, August 1969 to August 1974, RNPP, NARA, CP.

18. Kissinger, *White House Years*, 180.

19. Ibid., 183.

20. Ibid.

21. Ibid., 186–87.

22. Ibid., 188–89, quote on 190.

23. Harold H. Saunders, Memcon between Agha Hilaly and Kissinger, December 19, 1969, box 1031: Nixon Presidential Materials Project—NSC Files—Files for the President—China Materials (hereafter China Materials), f. 1: Ex-

changes Leading Up to Kissinger's Trip to China, December 1969–July 1971, RNPP, NARA, CP.

24. Ibid.

25. Ibid., December 23, 1969. See also Isaacson, *Kissinger: A Biography*, 337.

26. "Direct and Indirect Specific Messages between the U.S. and PRC," box 1031: China Materials, f. 2, NARA, CP.

27. Amembassy Warsaw to SS, February 20, 1970, box 1031: Nixon Presidential Materials Project, f. 1: Exchanges Leading up to Kissinger Trip to China, December 1969–July 1971, RNPP, NARA, CP.

28. HAK to RN, February 20, 1970, in ibid.

29. HAK to RN, February 23, 1970, box 1032: Nixon Presidential Materials Project, f. Cookies II (Chronology of Exchanges with the PRC, February 1969–April 1971), NSC Files, Files for the President—China Materials, RNPP, NARA, CP.

30. HAK to Jean Sainteny, n.d. (probably April 1970), box 1031: China Materials, f. 1: Exchanges Leading up to Kissinger Trip to China, December 1969–July 1971, RNPP, NARA, CP.

31. "Message to Be Passed to the Chinese," May 3, 1970, box 1031, f. 3, in ibid.

32. "Message to Be Delivered by Major General Vernon A. Walters to the Chinese Communist Government," June 15, 1970, box 1031, f. 3, in ibid.

33. Ibid.

34. HAK to RN, ca. September 12, 1970, Document 1, National Security Archive (hereafter NSA), "The Beijing-Washington Back-Channel and Henry Kissinger's Secret Trip to China, September 1970–July 1971," National Security Archive Electronic Briefing Book no. 66, edited by William Burr, February 27, 2002. See http://www.gwu.edu/~nsarchive/NSAEBB/NSAEBB66/#docs.

35. Ibid.

36. Memcon, HAK and Jean Sainteny, September 1970, Document 2, NSA.

37. Memcon, RN and Yahya, October 25, 1970, Document 3, NSA.

38. HAK to RN, October 31, 1970, Memcon with President Ceauşescscu on October 27, 1970, Document 4, NSA.

39. The quote is from Isaacson, *Kissinger: A Biography*, 339. See also W. R. Smyser to HAK, Letter from your Friend in Paris; and Other Chinese Miscellania, November 7, 1970, Document 5, NSA.

40. Memorandum for Dr. Kissinger, November 18, 1970, box H-177, f. 4: "Study of UN Membership, Etc.," RNPP, NARA, CP.

41. HAK to RN, "Memorandum on the Chinese Communist Initiative," ca. December 10, 1970, Document 6, NSA.

42. Memo by Hilaly, "Record of a Discussion with Mr. Henry Kissinger on [*sic*] the White House," December 16, 1970, Document 7, NSA.

43. HAK to RN, January 12, 1971, "Conversation with Ambassador Bogdan, Map Room on January 11, 1971," NSA, Document 9, NSA.

44. Memcon by David Halperin, NSC staff, Bogdan-HAK Meeting, January 29, 1971, Document 10, and Smyser to HAK, "Message from Sainteny," January 18, 1971, Document 11, both in ibid. For NSSM 106, see box H-176, f. NSSM 106, RNPP, NARA, CP.

45. Isaacson, *Kissinger: A Biography*, 339, and "Ping-Pong Diplomacy (April 6–17, 1971)," http://www.pbs.org/wgbh/amex/china/peopleevents/pande07.html.

46. For the quote, see Ray Cline to Acting Secretary Irwin, Intelligence Brief, "Communist China/U.S.: Peking People's Diplomacy: A 'New Page' in Sino-American Relations," April 14, 1971, Document 13, and "Statement by Nixon on Travel and Trade with the PRC," April 14, 1971, both at the NSA.

47. "Message from Zhou Enlai to RN," April 21, 1971, received April 27, 1971, responding to RN's December 16, 1970, Document 17, NSA.

48. Isaacson, *Kissinger: A Biography*, 339.

49. Ibid.

50. "Record of Nixon-Kissinger Telephone Conversation Discussing Zhou's Message and Possible Envoys to China," April 27, 1971, Document 18, NSA.

51. Isaacson, *Kissinger: A Biography*, 339–40.

52. Alexander Haig, "Extract of a Memcon," May 5, 1971, Document 20, NSA.

53. Message from Nixon to Zhou, via Hilaly, May 10, 1971, Document 23, NSA.

54. HAK to RN, "Meeting with Ambassador Farland on May 7, 1971, May 15, 1971," Document 22, NSA

55. HAK to Farland, enclosing message to PRC on SALT announcement, May 20, 1971, Document 24, NSA.

56. Farland to HAK, May 23, 1971, box 1031: China Materials, f. 1: Exchanges Leading up to Kissinger Trip to China, December 1969–July 1971, RNPP, NARA. See also "Message from Farland to Kissinger," May 22, 1971, Document 25, NSA.

57. Isaacson, *Kissinger: A Biography*, 340.

58. "Message from Zhou to Nixon, May 29, 1971, with commentary, conveyed by Hilaly to White House," Document 26, NSA.

59. "Message to the Government of the People's Republic of China, from Nixon to Zhou, given to Hilaly on June 4, 1971," Document 28, NSA.

60. Isaacson, *Kissinger: A Biography*, 342.

61. "Message from Kissinger to Farland, late June 1971, on Travel Arrangement," Document 32, NSA.

62. Karamissines to "Immediate Isalmabad," June 30, 1971, box 1031: China Materials, f. 1: Exchanges Leading up to Kissinger Trip to China, RNPP, NARA, CP.

63. Ibid.

64. Memorandum for the President's Files, "Meeting between President, Dr. Kissinger, and General Haig, Thursday, July 1, Oval Office," July 1, 1971, Document 33, NSA.

65. Isaacson, *Kissinger: A Biography*, 343–45, quote on 343.

66. Memcon, Kissinger and Zhou, July 9, 1971, 4:45–11:20 P.M., with cover memo by Lord, Document 34, NSA.

67. Kissinger, *White House Years*, 745.

68. Ibid., 746.

69. Ibid., 747, quote on 748.

70. Ibid., 749.

71. Isaacson, *Kissinger: A Biography*, 345.

72. Memcon, "Kissinger and Zhou, July 9, 1971, 4:35–11:20 P.M., with cover memo by Lord, July 29, 1971," Document 34, NSA.

73. Ibid.; for quote, see Kissinger, *White House Years*, 733.

74. Memcon, "Kissinger and Zhou, July 9, 1971, 4:35–11:20 P.M., Document 24, NSA.

75. Ibid.

76. Ibid.

77. Ibid.

78. Ibid.

79. Ibid.

80. Ibid.

81. Ibid.

82. HAK to RN, "My Talks with Chou En-lai," July 14, 1971, Document 40, NSA.

83. For the two quotes, see Kissinger, *White House Years*, 754, 755.

84. HAK to RN, "My Talks with Chou En-lai," July 14, 1971, Document 40, NSA.

85. Ibid.

86. Ibid.

87. Ibid.; Kissinger, *White House Years*, 750.

88. Kissinger, *White House Years*, 753–55.

89. Ibid., 755, quote of announcement on 759–60.

90. Ibid., 763–66.

91. Ibid., 777, 780, 781, 783.

92. Ibid., 1051, 1054–55, 1058, 1060–63.

93. Ibid., quotes on 1066, 1077, 1083, 1089, 1090, 1095. The complete text of the Shanghai Communiqué may be found on 1490–92.

94. We have paraphrased a summary of the Shanghai Communiqué done by Stephen E. Ambrose, *Nixon: The Triumph of a Politician*, 515–16.

95. For this quote and analysis, see ibid., 516–17. For an entirely different take on the Nixon-Kissinger Chinese initiative from what might have been Mao's view, see Jung Chang and Jon Halliday, "Nixon: The Red-Baiter Baited," chap. 54 of *Mao: The Unknown Story*, where the major impression is that Mao got everything and gave almost nothing. The authors are convinced that Kissinger and Nixon were the ones who were "baited": over UN membership at Taiwan's expense, military intelligence, and technology. As they put it: "Mao was being given a lot, and on a platter" (570).

Old Conclusions, New Beginnings

1. As quoted in Francis Fitzgerald, *Way Out There in the Blue: Reagan, Star Wars, and the End of the Cold War*, 25.

2. Ibid., 26.

3. President Reagan's speech before the National Association of Evangelicals, March 8, 1983, http://www.presidentreagan.info/speeches/empire.cfm (emphasis added).

4. Ibid. (emphasis added).

5. Fitzgerald, *Way Out There*, 19.

6. "Address to the Nation on Defense and National Security," March 23, 1983, http://www.atomicarchive.com/Docs/Missile/Starwars.

7. Ibid.

8. Fitzgerald, *Way Out There*, 38.

9. Reagan's second inaugural, January 21, 1985, http://www.reaganfoundation.org/reagan/speeches.

10. "Memorandum of Conversation," First Private Meeting, Geneva, November 19, 1985, box 3, f. 1 (8510141), Executive Secretariat, NSC System Files, Reagan Presidential Library (hereafter RPL), Simi Valley, California.

11. Lou Cannon, *President Reagan: The Role of a Lifetime*, 673.

12. Ibid.; "First Plenary Meeting," Geneva, November 19, 1985, box 3: Executive Secretariat, f. 1, NSC System Files, RPL, Simi Valley, California.

13. Cannon, *President Reagan*, 675.

14. Second Private Meeting, box Executive Secretariat, f. 8510141, NSC System Files, RPL, Simi Valley, California..

15. Jack F. Matlock Jr., *Reagan and Gorbachev: How the Cold War Ended*, 170, 172.

16. Ibid., 178; see note at bottom of page.

17. Ibid., 179–80.

18. Ibid., 184; see 186 on narrow and broad interpretations.

19. Ibid., 207, 211, 213, 218–19, 220–21, 222, quote on 224.

20. Ibid., quotes on 232, 234, 235.

21. Ibid., 238–39, 242, 245, 248–49, 251–53, quote on 254.

22. Ibid., 259, quote on 260. For an interesting take on the Cold War and especially the important roles of Reagan and Gorbachev in ending it, see Melvyn P. Leffler, *For the Soul of Mankind: The United States, the Soviet Union, and the Cold War*. A valuable discussion of this book is Anna Kasten et al., "A Roundtable Discussion of Melvyn Leffler's *For the Soul of Mankind: The United States, the Soviet Union, and the Cold War*," in *Passport*.

23. Much of this material was gathered by the authors in an interview with Gen. Brent Scowcroft and former secretary of state Lawrence Eagleburger on May 30, 2007, in Washington, D.C.

24. Human Rights Watch, "China," http://hrw.org/reports/1989/WR89/China.htm.

25. For the "Themes" document, check NSA, "Tiananmen Square, 1989: The Declassified History," document 33, http://www.gwu.edu/~nsarchiv/NSAEBB/NSAEBB16/documents34-01-06.htm. See also James Mann, *About Face: A History of America's Curious Relationship with China, from Nixon to Clinton*, 207.

26. Mann, *About Face*, 205–9, quote on 206.

27. James A. Baker III (with Thomas M. DeFank), *The Politics of Diplomacy: Revolution, War, and Peace, 1989–1992*, 109.

28. Ibid.

29. Ibid., 109–10.

30. Ibid., 110.

31. George H. W. Bush and Brent Scowcroft, *A World Transformed*, 104.

32. Ibid., 105–7, quotes on 106, 107.

33. Ibid., 109.

34. Ibid., 108.

35. J. Baker, *Politics of Diplomacy*, 113.

36. Ibid., 113.

37. Mann, *About Face*, 223.

38. Bush and Scowcroft, *World Transformed*, 174.

39. Ibid., 174–79, quote on 175.

40. Mann, *About Face*, 227–28, quote on 228.

Afterword

1. Council on Foreign Relations, *Russia's Wrong Direction: What the United States Can and Should Do*, 5, 6, 7, 16; see also 10, 13.

2. Ibid., 18, quotes on 19, 21.

3. Ibid., 24–26, 30, 33.

4. Ibid., 37–38, 39–40, 57, 62–63.

5. Ibid., 72, quote on 74.

6. Council on Foreign Relations, *U.S.-China Relations: An Affirmative Agenda, a Responsible Course*, xi, http://www.cfr.org/content/publications/attachments/China Task Force.pdf.

7. Ibid.

8. Ibid., xii.

9. Ibid., 3–4, quote on 4.

10. Ibid., 5–6. (In May 2007, the Associated Press asserted that China's foreign assets grew by 57 percent in 2006 to a total of $662 billion. Its assets abroad rose 33 percent to $1.6 trillion. Its liabilities were up to 21 percent, or $964.5 billion. Two-thirds of these assets were in the form of reserves in other currencies—$1.1 trillion. China also had $82.4 billion in direct investments, $229 billion in securities, and $242 billion in loans owed to Chinese lenders.)

11. Ibid., 7.

12. Eugene P. Trani, "Criticize, but Don't Exclude," *International Herald Tribune*, September 15, 2006, 8.

bibliography

American attitudes toward Russia and China in the twentieth century, to be inclusive, necessarily command vast bibliographies and historiographic disputes. The authors' selective approach, focusing on certain individuals, is only suggestive of a larger picture. It necessarily leaves out many works. Some might argue that it is already too inclusive. If the authors had written their story differently, that is, structured it chronologically or thematically, then other works would be listed. They admit to omissions and commissions in their bibliography.

For those seeking other bibliographic and historiographic trends, check John Lewis Gaddis, *We Now Know: Rethinking Cold War History*, or Warren I. Cohen, ed., *Pacific Passage: The Study of American–East Asian Relations on the Eve of the Twenty-first Century*.

The authors have, within the range of their selections, gone to archival sources; these speak for themselves. Researchers have already plundered some, while others offered new areas of investigation. We have placed an asterisk beside those manuscripts. Out of that smaller grouping, we would like to cite the mammoth collection in Record Group 84, Diplomatic Post Records, Riga, Latvia, Legation and Consulate, Russia Series, at the National Archives and Record Administration, College Park, Maryland.

Manuscripts

Washington, D.C.
Georgetown University
    Robert F. Kelley Papers
Library of Congress
    Ray Stannard Baker Collection
    Charles Bohlen Papers

Bainbridge Colby Papers
Herbert Feis Papers
W. Averell Harriman Papers*
John Hay Papers
Loy Henderson Papers*
Nelson T. Johnson Papers*
George Kennan Papers
Robert Lansing Papers
Henry R. Luce Papers
William G. McAdoo Papers
George von Lengerke Meyer Papers
Roland Morris Papers
Paul M. Nitze Papers*
Theodore Roosevelt Papers
Elihu Root Papers
Woodbridge Collection
Woodrow Wilson Papers
National Archives, NARA (College Park, Maryland)
Henry Kissinger Papers*
Record Group 59, microfilm
Record Group 84, Diplomatic Post Records
Riga, Latvia, legation
Riga, Latvia, consulate, Russian Series
Record Group 218
Richard Nixon Papers (Presidential Materials Project)
Ronald Reagan Papers, Simi Valley, California*

Other

Carlisle Barracks, Pennsylvania
Philip R. Faymonville Papers
Robert L. Walsh Papers
Center for Dewey Studies, Carbondale, Illinois
John Dewey Papers
Columbia University
Boris Bakhmeteff Papers
Harry S. Truman Library, Independence, Missouri
Harry S. Truman Papers
Clifford, Clark. "American Relations with the Soviet Union: A Report to the President by the Special Counsel to the President." September 24, 1946. Naval Aide file.

Hoover Institute, Stanford University, Palo Alto, California
  Stanley Hornbeck Papers
  Eugene Lyons Papers and University of Oregon, materials sent to authors by courtesy of the archive*
Houghton Library, Harvard University, Cambridge
  W. W. Rockhill Papers
Hyde Park, New York
  Harry L. Hopkins Papers
  Isador Lubin Papers
  R. Walton Moore Papers
  Henry M. Morgenthau Jr. Diary, microfiche
  President's Soviet Protocol Committee
  Franklin Delano Roosevelt Papers
India Office, London
  Curzon Papers
Mansfield Library, University of Montana (letter sent to authors by courtesy of the archive)
  Mike Mansfield Papers
Massachusetts Historical Society, Boston
  Henry Cabot Lodge Papers
New York Public Library
  Century Company Papers
Perkasie, Pennsylvania
  Pearl S. Buck Papers
Pusey Library, Harvard University, Cambridge
  Theodore White Papers
Randolph-Macon Woman's College, Lynchburg, Virgnia (now Randolph College)
  Emma Edmonds White Papers
Seeley G. Mudd Manuscript Library, Princeton University
  George F. Kennan Papers
  John Van Antwerp MacMurray
  United Service to China Papers
  Woodrow Wilson Papers
University of Chicago
  Samuel Harper Papers
University of Missouri, Kansas City
  Edgar Snow Papers
Virginia Commonwealth University, Richmond
  Nelson T. Johnson Family Papers
West Branch, Iowa
  William Castle Papers

Herbert Hoover Presidential Papers
Henry L. Stimson Diary, microfilm
Wisconsin State Historical Society, Madison
Paul S. Reinsch Papers

Public Documents

Congressional Record. House, June 28, 1966.

Congressional Record. Vols. 13 and 91.

Department of State. *Papers Relating to the Foreign Relations of the United States: The Soviet Union, 1933–1939.* [Hereafter cited as *FRUS.*] Washington, D.C.: GPO, 1952. For the entire list of publications, see http://www.state.gov/r/pa/ho/frus/c4035.htm.

————. *FRUS, 1899.* Washington, D.C.: GPO, 1901.

————. *FRUS, 1900.* Washington, D.C.: GPO, 1902.

————. *FRUS, 1901.* Washington, D.C.: GPO, 1902.

————. *FRUS, 1904.* Washington, D.C.: GPO, 1905.

————. *FRUS, 1915.* Washington, D.C.: GPO, 1924.

————. *FRUS, 1918: Russia.* Vol. 1. Washington, D.C.: GPO, 1931.

————. *FRUS, 1923.* Washington, D.C.: GPO, 1938.

————. *FRUS, 1924.* Vol. 2. Washington, D.C.: GPO, 1939.

————. *FRUS, 1926.* Washington, D.C.: GPO, 1941.

————. *FRUS, 1927.* Vol. 3. Washington, D.C.: GPO, 1942.

————. *FRUS, 1928.* Vol. 2. Washington, D.C.: GPO, 1943.

————. *FRUS, 1932.* Vol. 2. GPO, 1948.

————. *FRUS, 1943: Conferences at Cairo and Teheran.* Washington, D.C.: GPO, 1961.

————. *FRUS, 1943: General.* Washington, D.C.: GPO, 1963.

————. *FRUS, 1944: China.* Vol. 6. Washington, D.C.: GPO, 1967.

————. *FRUS, 1945: Conferences at Malta and Yalta.* Washington, D.C.: GPO, 1955.

————. *FRUS, 1945: The Far East—China.* Vol. 7. Washington, D.C.: GPO, 1969.

————. *FRUS, 1946: Eastern Europe—the Soviet Union.* Vol. 6. Washington, D.C.: GPO, 1969.

————. *FRUS, 1948: The Far East—China.* Vols. 7–8. Washington, D.C.: GPO, 1973.

————. *FRUS, 1948: UN—General.* Vol. 1. Pt. 2. Washington, D.C.: GPO, 1976.

————. *FRUS, 1949: The Far East—China.* Vols. 8–9. Washington, D.C.: GPO, 1978, 1974.

————. *FRUS, 1950: East Asia and the Pacific.* Vol. 6. Washington, D.C.: GPO, 1976.

————. *FRUS, 1950: National Security Affairs—Foreign Economic Policy.* Washington, D.C.: GPO, 1977.

————. *FRUS, 1953: China and Japan.* Vol. 14. Washington, D.C.: GPO, 1985.

Gaimusho, Komura. *Gaikoshi.* 2 vols. Tokyo, 1953.

Judd, Walter H. *Congressional Record.* 79th Cong., 1st sess., vol. 91, pt. 2, March 15, 1945, 2294–2302.

Ministry of Foreign Affairs. *Sbornik diplomaticheskikh dokumentov kasaiushchikhsia peregovorov mezhdu Rossieiu i Iaponieiu o zakliuchenii mimago dogovora 24 maia–3 oktiabria.* St. Petersburg, 1906.

State Department. *United States Relations with China, with Special Reference to the Period 1944–1949* ["China White Paper"]. State Department Publication 3573. Washington, D.C.: GPO, 1949.

U.S. Dispatches from U.S. Ministers to Russia, 1808–1906. Record Group no. 59, National Archives.

U.S. Senate. "Memorandum on Certain Aspects of the Bolshevist Movement in Russia." In *U.S. Senate Documents.* 66th Cong., 2d sess., 1920, vol. 4.

U.S. Senate, Committee on Foreign Relations. *McCarthy Hearings.* 81st Cong., 2d sess., 1951.

U.S. Senate, Committee on Foreign Relations, Hearings. *Investigation of Far Eastern Policy.* Monday, December 10, 1945, 300–325. Chairman Senator Tom Connally. 79th Cong., 1st sess.

U.S. Senate, Government Operations Committee, Subcommittee on National Policy Machinery. *Hearings: Organizing for National Security.* 86th Cong., 2d sess., 1960.

U.S. Senate Documents. 68th Cong., 1st sess., pursuant to Senate Resolution 50, pt. 2. Washington, D.C.: GPO, 1925.

Microfilm

State Department. Record Group 59, roll 1. National Archives, Washington, D.C.

Newspapers, Journals, Magazines

American Naturalist
Annals of the American Academy of Political and Social Science
Asia Magazine
Asian Studies
Associated Press

Bulletin of Bibliography
Century Magazine
Chicago Tribune
China Critic
China Monthly
Christian Century
Collier's
Current History
Foreign Affairs
Foreign Affairs: Far Eastern Survey
Harper's Weekly
International Affairs: USSR
International Herald Tribune
International Security
Izvestiia
Kansas City Star
Life
Millard's Review of the Far East
New Republic
New York Herald Tribune
New York Telegram
New York Times
New York World
Outlook
Pravda
Prologue
Record Herald
Reporter
Richmond Times Dispatch
Russian Review
Saturday Evening Post
Slavic Review
Slavonic Review
South Atlantic Quarterly
Survey Graphic
Time
U.S. News and World Report
Washington Post
Weekly Review
World Affairs

Other Sources

"Accepting Soviet a Peril, Says Fish." *New York Times*, February 26, 1933, 6.

Acheson, Dean. *Present at the Creation: My Years in the State Department*. New York: W. W. Norton.

"A.F.L. Fights Drive for Soviet Accord." *New York Times*, February 22, 1933, 17.

Allen, Richard V. *Peace or Peaceful Coexistence?* Chicago: American Bar Association, 1966.

Ambrose, Stephen E. *Nixon: The Triumph of a Politician*. New York: Simon and Schuster, 1989.

Anderson, Lewis Flint. "George Kennan." In *Dictionary of American Biography*, 331–32. New York: Charles Scribner's Sons, 1932.

Anderson, Martin, et al., eds. *Reagan in His Own Hand*. New York: Simon and Schuster, 2001.

Anschel, Eugene, ed. *The American Image of Russia, 1775–1917*. New York: Frederick Ungar, 1974.

Askew, William. "An American View of Bloody Sunday." *Russian Review* 11 (January 1952).

Axtell, Silas B. *Russia and Her Foreign Relations*. Philadelphia: American Academy of Political Science, 1928.

Babey, Anna. *Americans in Russia, 1776–1917: A Study of the American Travelers in Russia from the American Revolution to the Russian Revolution*. New York: Comet Press, 1938.

Baker, James A., III. *The Politics of Diplomacy: Revolution, War, and Peace, 1989–1992*. New York: G. P. Putnam's Sons, 1995.

Baker, Ray Stannard. *Woodrow Wilson: Life and Letters*. 8 vols. Garden City, N.Y.: Doubleday, Page and Co., 1927–1939.

Ball, Alan M. *Imagining America: Influence and Images in Twentieth-Century Russia*. Lanham, Md.: Rowan and Littlefield, 2003.

Barth, Gunther. *Bitter Strength: A History of the Chinese in the United States*. Cambridge: Harvard University Press, 1964.

Bassow, Whitman. *The Moscow Correspondents: Reporting on Russia from the Revolution to Glasnost*. New York: Paragon House, 1989.

Baylen, Joseph O., and James S. Herndon. "Col. Philip R. Faymonville and the Red Army, 1934–43." *Slavic Review* 34, no. 3 (September 1975): 483–505.

Bayor, Ronald H. *Neighbors in Conflict: The Irish, Germans, Jews, and Italians of New York City, 1919–1941*. 2d ed. Urbana: University of Illinois Press, 1988.

Beale, Howard K. *Theodore Roosevelt and the Rise of America to World Power*. New York: Collier Books, 1967.

Becker, Carl L. *Modern History: The Rise of a Democratic. Scientific, and Industrialized Civilization.* New York: Silver, Burdett, 1935.

Bemis, Albert Farwell. "Social and Economic Problems in Russia." *Annals: Some Aspects of the Present International Situation.* Philadelphia: American Academy of Political Science, 1928.

Bemis, Samuel Flagg, ed. *The American Secretaries of State and Their Diplomacy.* 10 vols. New York: Alfred A. Knopf, 1929.

Bennett, Edward M. *Franklin Delano Roosevelt and the Search for Security.* Wilmington, Del.: Scholarly Resources, 1985.

———. *Recognition of Russia: An American Foreign Policy Dilemma.* Waltham, Mass.: Blaisdell, 1970.

Beresford, Charles William de la Poer. *The Break-Up of China: With an Account of Its Present Commerce, Currency, Waterways, Armies, Railways, Politics, and Future Prospects.* 1899. Reprint, Wilmington, Del.: Scholarly Resources, 1972.

Berman, Marvin Hershel. *The Treatment of the Soviet Union and Communism in Selected World History Textbooks, 1920–1970.* Ann Arbor: School of Education, University of Michigan, 1976.

Berrigan, Darrell. "Uncle Joe Pays Off." *Saturday Evening Post,* June 17, 1944, 20–21.

Berry, Thomas. "Dewey's Influence in China." In *John Dewey: His Thought and Influence,* ed. John Blewett. New York: Fordham University Press, 1960.

Bishop, Donald G. *The Roosevelt-Litvinov Agreements: The American View.* Syracuse: Syracuse University Press, 1965.

Bishop, Joseph Bucklin. *Theodore Roosevelt and His Time.* 2 vols. New York: Charles Scribner's Son's, 1920.

Black, Cyril E., and John M. Thompson, eds. *American Teaching about Russia.* Bloomington: Indiana University Press, 1959.

Bohlen, Charles E. *Witness to History, 1929–1969.* New York: W. W. Norton, 1973.

"Borah Argues Gains in Link with Soviet." *New York Times,* March 4, 1931, 1.

Brands, H. W. *Inside the Cold War: Loy Henderson and the Rise of the American Empire, 1918–1961.* Oxford: Oxford University Press, 1991.

———. *TR: The Last Romantic.* New York: Basic Books, 1997.

———, ed. *The Selected Letters of Theodore Roosevelt.* New York: Cooper Square Press, 2001.

Briley, Carol Ann. "George Elsey's White House Career, 1942–1953." Master's thesis, University of Missouri, Kansas City, 1976.

Browder, Robert Paul. *The Origins of Soviet-American Diplomacy.* Princeton: Princeton University Press, 1953.

Bryant, Arthur. *Triumph in the West: A History of the War Years Based on the*

Diaries of Field Marshal Lord Alanbrooke, Chief of the Imperial General Staff. Garden City, N.Y.: Doubleday, 1959.

Buck, Pearl S. "China and the West." *Annals of the American Academy of Political and Social Science* 168 (July 1933).

———. *East Wind, West Wind: The Saga of a Chinese Family.* 1930. Reprint, Kingston, R.I.: Moyer Bell, 2004.

———. *The Exile.* New York: John Day, 1936.

———. *Fighting Angel: Portrait of a Soul.* New York: P. F. Collier and Son, 1936.

———. *The Good Earth.* New York: Pocket Books, 1994.

———. *A House Divided.* 1934. Reprint, Kingston, R.I.: Moyer Bell, 1984.

———. *The Mother.* 1934. Reprint, Kingston, R.I.: Moyer Bell, 1984.

———. *My Several Worlds: A Personal Record.* New York: John Day, 1954.

———. *Sons.* 1932. Reprint, Kingston, R.I.: Moyer Bell, 1984.

———. "A Warning about China." *Life,* May 10, 1943, 53–56.

Buckingham, Peter H., ed. *America Sees Red: Anti-communism in America, 1870s to 1980s: A Guide to Issues and References.* Claremont, Calif.: Regina Books, 1988.

Buhite, Russell D. *Nelson T. Johnson and American Policy toward China.* East Lansing: Michigan State University Press, 1969.

———. *Patrick J. Hurley and American Foreign Policy.* Ithaca: Cornell University Press, 1973.

Bullert, Gary. *The Politics of John Dewey.* New York: Prometheus Books, 1983.

Bundy, McGeorge, and James G. Blight. "October 27, 1962: Transcripts of the Meetings of the ExComm." *International Security* 12, no. 13 (Winter 1987–1988): 30–92.

Burke, Kenneth. "Boring from Within." *New Republic* 65 (February 4, 1931).

Busch, Noel. *T. R.: The Story of Theodore Roosevelt and His Influence on Our Times.* New York: Reynal, 1963.

Bush, George H. W., and Brent Scowcroft. *A World Transformed.* New York: Alfred A. Knopf, 1998.

Byrnes, James F. *Speaking Frankly.* New York: Harper and Brothers, 1947.

Byrnes, Robert F. *Awakening American Education to the World: The Role of Archibald Cary Coolidge, 1866–1928.* Notre Dame: University of Notre Dame Press, 1982.

Callahan, David. *Dangerous Capabilities: Paul Nitze and the Cold War.* New York: Harper Collins, 1990.

Cannon, Lou. *Governor Reagan: His Rise to Power.* New York: Public Affairs, 2003.

———. *President Reagan: The Role of a Lifetime.* New York: Public Affairs, 2000.

Cassella-Blackburn, Michael. *The Donkey, the Carrot, and the Club: William*

C. Bullitt and Soviet-American Relations, 1917–1948. Westport, Conn.: Praeger, 2004.

Cevasco, G. A. "Pearl Buck and the Chinese Novel." *Asian Studies* 4, no. 3 (December 1967): 444.

Chamberlin, William Henry. *The Russian Enigma: An Interpretation by William Henry Chamberlin.* New York: Charles Scribner's Sons, 1944.

———. *Russia's Iron Age.* Boston: Little, Brown, 1935.

Chambers, Whittaker. *Witness.* Chicago: Regnery Gateway, 1952.

Chan, Gordon H. *Friends and Enemies: The United States, China, and the Soviet Union, 1948–1972.* Stanford: Stanford University Press, 1990.

Chang, Iris. *The Chinese in America: A Narrative History.* New York: Viking, 2003.

Chang, Jung, and John Halliday. *Mao: The Unknown Story.* New York: Anchor Books, 2005.

Churchill, Winston S. *Closing the Ring.* Boston: Houghton Mifflin, 1951.

———. *The Hinge of Fate.* Boston: Houghton Mifflin, 1951.

———. *Triumph and Tragedy.* New York: Bantum Books, 1962.

Clancy, Tom. *The Bear and the Dragon.* New York: G. P. Putnam's Sons, 2000.

Cohen, Stephen F. *Failed Crusade: America and the Tragedy of Post-communist Russia.* New York: W. W. Norton, 2001.

———. *Rethinking the Soviet Experience: Politics and History since 1917.* New York: Oxford University Press, 1986.

Cohen, Warren I., ed. *Pacific Passage: The Study of American–East Asian Relations on the Eve of the Twenty-first Century.* New York: Columbia University Press, 1996.

Colton, Ethan T. *The XYZ of Communism.* New York: Macmillan, 1931.

Conn, Peter. *Pearl S. Buck: A Cultural Biography.* Cambridge: Cambridge University Press, 1996.

Conquest, Robert. *The Great Terror: Stalin's Purge of the Thirties.* New York: Macmillan, 1973.

Cooper, Hugh L. "Observations of Present-Day Russia." *Annals: Some Aspects of the Present International Situation* 138 (July 1928).

Council on Foreign Relations. *Russia's Wrong Direction: What the United States Can and Should Do.* Independent Task Force Report no. 57. New York: Council on Foreign Relations, 2006.

———. *U.S.-China Relations: An Affirmative Agenda, a Responsible Course.* Independent Task Force Report no. 59. New York: Council on Foreign Relations, 2007.

Correspondence between the Chairman of the Council of Ministers of the USSR and the Presidents of the USA and the Prime Ministers of Great Britain during the Great Patriotic War of 1941–1945. Honolulu: University Press of the Pacific, 2001.

Cowley, Malcolm. "Wang Lung's Children." *New Republic* (May 10, 1939): 24–25.

Crossman, R. H. S., ed. *The God That Failed.* New York: Harper and Row, 1950.

Curry, Roy Watson. *Woodrow Wilson and Far Eastern Policy.* New York: Bookman Associates, 1957.

Custine, Marquis de. *Empire of the Czar: A Journey through Eternal Russia.* New York: Doubleday, 1989.

Dallek, Robert. *Franklin D. Roosevelt and American Foreign Policy, 1932–1945.* New York: Oxford University Press, 1979.

Daniloff, Nicholas. *Of Spies and Spokesmen: My Life as a Cold War Correspondent.* Columbia: University of Missouri Press, 2008.

———. *Two Lives, One Russia.* Boston: Houghton Mifflin, 1988.

Davies, John Paton, Jr. *Dragon by the Tail: American, British, Japanese, and Russian Encounter with China and One Another.* New York: W. W. Norton, 1972.

Davies, Joseph E. *Mission to Moscow.* New York: Pocket Books, 1943.

Davis, Donald E., and Eugene P. Trani. *The First Cold War: The Legacy of Woodrow Wilson in U.S.-Soviet Relations.* Columbia: University of Missouri Press, 2002.

———. "Roosevelt and the U.S. Role: Perception Makes Policy." In *The Treaty of Portsmouth and Its Legacies,* ed. Steven Erickson and Allen Hockley, 62–74. Lebanon, N.H.: University Press of New England, 2008.

———. "A Tale of Two Kennans: American-Russian Relations in the Twentieth Century." In *Presidents, Diplomats, and Other Mortals,* ed. Garry Clifford and Theodore A. Wilson, 31–55. Columbia: University of Missouri Press, 2007.

Davis, Jerome. "Capitalism and Communism." *Annals of the American Academy of Political and Social Science: Elements of a Foreign Policy* (July 1931).

———. *The Russian Immigrant.* New York: Macmillan, 1922.

Dean, Vera Michaels. *The United States and Russia.* Cambridge: Harvard University Press, 1948.

Dennett, Tyler. *John Hay: From Poetry to Politics.* New York: Dodd, Mead, 1933.

———. "President Roosevelt's Secret Pact with Japan." *Current History* 21 (October 1924–March 1925).

———. *Roosevelt and the Russo-Japanese War.* Gloucester, Mass.: Peter Smith, 1959.

Deutscher, Isaac. *The Prophet Armed: Trotsky, 1879–1921.* Oxford: Oxford University Press, 1954.

Dewey, John. *Characters and Events: Popular Essays in Social and Political Philosophy.* Ed. Joseph Ratner. 2 vols. New York: Henry Holt, 1929.

———. *The Correspondence of John Dewey.* Charlottesville, Va.: InteLex, 2001, 2005.

———. *Individualism Old and New.* New York: Capricorn Books, G. P. Putnam's Sons, 1962.

———. *John Dewey: Lectures in China.* Ed. Robert W. Clopton and Tsuin-Chen Ou. Honolulu: University Press of Hawaii, 1973.

———. *Reconstruction in Philosophy and Essays, 1920: The Middle Works of John Dewey, 1899–1924.* Ed. Jo Ann Boydston and Bridget A. Walsh. Vol. 12 of 27 vols. Carbondale: Southern Illinois University Press, 1988.

———. *Works.* Ed. Jo Ann Boydston et al. 17 vols. Carbondale: Southern Illinois University Press, 198–1990.

Dewey, John, and Alice Chipman Dewey. *Letters from China and Japan.* Ed. Evelyn Dewey. New York: E. P. Dutton, 1920.

Dictionary of American Biography. New York: Charles Scribner's Sons, 1932.

Dilks, David, ed. *The Diaries of Sir Alexander Cadogan.* London: Cassell, 1971.

Documents diplomatique français. Paris, 1930–1959.

Doyle, Paul A. *Pearl S. Buck.* Boston: Twayne, 1965.

Durant, Will. *The Tragedy of Russia: Impressions from a Brief Visit.* New York: Simon and Schuster, 1933.

Duranty, Walter. *I Write as I Please.* New York: Simon and Schuster, 1935.

Dykhuizen, George. *The Life and Mind of John Dewey.* Carbondale: Southern Illinois University Press, 1973.

E. G. "Sons." *Pacific Affairs* 6, nos. 2–3 (February–March 1933).

Eden, Anthony. *The Reckoning.* Boston: Houghton Mifflin, 1965.

Edwards, John, Jack Kemp, et al. *Russia's Wrong Direction: What the United States Can and Should Do.* Independent Task Force Report no. 57. New York: Council on Foreign Relations, 2006.

Edwards, Lee. *Missionary for Freedom: The Life and Times of Walter Judd.* New York: Paragon House, 1990.

Ehrman, John. *Grand Strategy.* London: Her Majesty's Stationery Office, 1956.

Eisenhower, Dwight D. *Mandate for Change.* Garden City, N.Y.: Doubleday, 1963.

Ellis, Ethan. *A Short History of American Diplomacy.* New York: Harper and Brothers, 1951.

Elson, Robert T. *The World of Time, Inc.* 2 vols. New York: Atheneum, 1968–1973.

Esthus, Raymond A. *Double Eagle and Rising Sun: The Russians and Japanese at Portsmouth in 1905.* Durham: Duke University Press, 1988.

Fairbank, John K. *China Bound: A Fifty-Year Memoir.* New York: Harper and Row, 1982.

————. *The United States and China.* Cambridge: Harvard University Press, 1979.

————, ed. *The Missionary Enterprise in China and America.* Cambridge: Harvard University Press, 1974.

Farnsworth, Beatrice. *William C. Bullitt and the Soviet Union.* Bloomington: Indiana University Press, 1967.

Farnsworth, Robert M., ed. *Edgar Snow's Journey South of the Clouds.* Columbia: University of Missouri Press, 1991.

Fausold, Martin L., ed. *The Hoover Presidency: A Reappraisal.* Albany: State University of New York Press, 1974.

Feis, Herbert. *The China Tangle: The American Effort in China from Pearl Harbor to the Marshall Mission.* Princeton: Princeton University Press, 1953.

————. *Churchill, Roosevelt, Stalin: The War They Waged and the Peace They Sought.* Princeton: Princeton University Press, 1957.

Ferrell, Robert H. *American Diplomacy: A History.* New York: W. W. Norton, 1959.

————. *Harry S. Truman: A Life.* Columbia: University of Missouri Press, 1994.

Feuerwerker, Albert. *The Foreign Establishment in China in the Early Twentieth Century.* Ann Arbor: University of Michigan Press, 1976.

Fifield, Russell H. *Woodrow Wilson and the Far East: The Diplomacy of the Shantung Question.* New York: Thomas Y. Crowell, 1952.

Filene, Peter. *Americans and the Soviet Experiment, 1917–1933.* Cambridge: Harvard University Press, 1967.

Fischer, Louis. *Why Recognize Russia? The Arguments for and against the Recognition of the Soviet Government by the United States.* New York: Jonathan Cape and Harrison Smith, 1931.

Fish, Hamilton. "The Menace of Communism." *Annals of the American Academy of Political and Social Science* 156 (July 1931).

Fisher, Harold H., ed. *American Research on Russia.* Bloomington: Indiana University Press, 1959.

Fitzgerald, Francis. *Way Out There in the Blue: Reagan, Star Wars, and the End of the Cold War.* New York: Touchstone, 2000.

Florinsky, Michael T. *The End of the Russian Empire.* New Haven: Yale University Press, 1931.

————. *Russia: A History and an Interpretation.* 2 vols. New York: Macmillan, 1953.

————. *Toward an Understanding of the USSR: A Study in Government. Politics, and Economic Planning.* New York: Macmillan, 1939.

————. "World Revolution and Soviet Foreign Policy." *Political Science Quarterly* 47, no. 2 (June 1932): 204–33, 248–53.

Florovsky, Ant. "The Work of Russian Émigrés in History, 1921–27." *Slavonic Review* 7, no. 19 (June 1928): 216–19.

Foglesong, David. *The American Mission and the "Evil Empire": The Crusade for a "Free Russia" since 1881*. New York: Cambridge University Press, 2007.

"Forms 'Paul Reveres' to Fight School Reds." *New York Times,* April 9, 1933, 6.

Forrestal, James. *The Forrestal Diaries*. Ed. Walter Millis. New York: Viking Press, 1952.

Freidel, Frank. *Franklin D. Roosevelt: A Rendezvous with Destiny*. Boston: Little, Brown, 1990.

Gaddis, John Lewis. "NSC 68 and the Soviet Threat Reconsidered." *International Security* 4, no. 4 (Spring 1980): 164–70.

———. *Russia, the Soviet Union, and the United States: An Interpretive History*. New York: McGraw-Hill, 1978.

———. *The United States and the Origins of the Cold War, 1941–1947*. New York: Columbia University Press, 1972.

———. *We Now Know: Rethinking Cold War History*. New York: Clarendon Press, Oxford, 1997.

Gallup, Alec M. *The Gallup Poll Cumulative Index: Public Opinion, 1935–1997*. Wilmington, Del.: Scholarly Resources, 1999.

Gallup, George. "Public Softening Views on Russia." *Gallup Report,* March 8, 1967.

Gelfand, Lawrence, ed. Introduction to "Herbert Hoover and the Russian Revolution, 1917–20," by Eugene P. Trani. In *Herbert Hoover: The Great War and Its Aftermath, 1914–23*, ed. Lawrence E. Gelfand. Iowa City: University of Iowa Press, 1979.

Ginzberg, Benjamin. "Science under Communism." *New Republic* 69 (January 6, 1932): 209.

Glantz, Mary E. *FDR and the Soviet Union: The President's Battle over Foreign Policy*. Lawrence: University Press of Kansas, 2005.

Gooch, G. P., and Harold Temperley. *British Documents on the Origins of the War, 1898–1914*. London, 1926–1938.

Grant, Natalie. "The Russian Section: A Window on the Soviet Union." *Diplomatic History* 2, no. 1 (January 1978): 107–15.

Griffith, Thomas. *Harry and Teddy: The Turbulent Friendship of Press Lord Henry R. Luce and His Favorite Reporter, Theodore H. White*. New York: Random House, 1995.

Griswold, A. Whitney. *The Far Eastern Policy of the United States*. New Haven: Yale University Press, 1962.

"The Growing Figure of Russia in International Trade." *Christian Century* 49 (June 22, 1932): 789.

Guild, Curtis. "Russia and Her Emperor." *Yale Review*, no. 4 (July 1915): 712–22.

Gwynn, Stephen, ed. *The Letters and Friendships of Sir Cecil Spring Rice: A Record.* 2 vols. New York: Houghton Mifflin, 1929.

Hahn, Emily. *China to Me.* Boston: Beacon Press, 1988.

Halberstam, David. *The Powers That Be.* New York: Alfred A. Knopf, 1979.

Hamby, Alonzo L. *Man of the People: A Life of Harry S. Truman.* Oxford: Oxford University Press, 1995.

Hamilton, John Maxwell. *Edgar Snow: A Biography.* Baton Rouge: Louisiana State University Press, 2003.

Harbaugh, William Henry. *Power and Responsibility: The Life and Times of Theodore Roosevelt.* New York: Farrar, Straus, and Cudahy, 1961.

Harcave, Sidney. *First Blood: The Russian Revolution of 1905.* New York: Macmillan, 1964.

Harlow, Giles D., and George C. Maerz, eds. *Measures Short of War: The George Kennan Lectures at the National War College, 1946–47.* Washington, D.C.: National Defense University Press, 1991.

Harper, Samuel N. *Civic Training in Soviet Russia.* Chicago: University of Chicago Press, 1929.

———. "Revolution in Russia." *Harper's Weekly,* February 1916, 132.

———. *The Russia I Believe In: The Memoirs of Samuel N. Harper, 1902–1941.* Ed. Paul V. Harper with the assistance of Ronald Thompson. Chicago: University of Chicago Press, 1945.

Harper, Samuel N., and Ronald Thompson. *The Government of the Soviet Union.* New York: D. Van Nostrand, 1949.

Harriman, W. Averell, and Elie Abel. *Special Envoy to Churchill and Stalin, 1941–1946.* New York: Random House, 1975.

Harrington, Daniel F. "Kennan, Bohlen, and the Riga Axioms." *Diplomatic History* 2, no. 4 (Fall 1978).

Harris, Theodore F. *Pearl S. Buck: A Biography.* New York: John Day, 1969.

Hauser, E. O. "China Needs a Friendly Nudge." *Saturday Evening Post,* August 26, 1944, 28–29.

Heilbronner, Hans. "An Anti-Witte Diplomatic Conspiracy, 1905–1906: The Schwaneback Memorandum." *Jahrbucher fur Geschichte Osteuropas* 14 (September 1966).

Henderson, Loy W. *A Question of Trust: The Origins of U.S.-Soviet Diplomatic Relations; The Memoirs of Loy W. Henderson.* Stanford: Hoover Institution Press, 1986.

Herzstein, Robert E. *Henry R. Luce, "Time," and the American Crusade in Asia.* Cambridge: Cambridge University Press, 2005.

Hills, Carla A., Dennis C. Blair, et al. *U.S.-China Relations: An Affirmative*

Agenda, a Responsible Course. Independent Task Force Report no. 59. New York: Council on Foreign Relations, 2007.

Hixson, Walter L. *George F. Kennan: Cold War Iconoclast.* New York: Columbia University Press, 1989.

———. *Parting the Curtain: Propaganda, Culture, and the Cold War, 1945–1961.* New York: St. Martin's Press, 1997.

Hoffmann, Joyce. *Theodore White and Journalism as Illusion.* Columbia: University of Missouri Press, 1995.

Hoff-Wilson, Joan. "A Reevaluation of Herbert Hoover's Foreign Policy." In *The Hoover Presidency: A Reappraisal,* ed. Martin L. Fausold. Albany: State University of New York Press, 1974.

Hook, Sidney, *John Dewey: An Intellectual Portrait.* Amherst, N.Y.: Prometheus Books, 1983.

Hoover, Herbert. *The Ordeal of Woodrow Wilson.* New York: McGraw-Hill, 1958.

Hoopes, Townsend, and Douglas Brinkley. *FDR and the Creation of the UN.* New Haven: Yale University Press, 1997.

Hopkirk, Peter. *Trespassers on the Roof of the World: The Secret Exploration of Tibet.* New York: Kodansha International, 1982.

Hough, Richard. *The Fleet That Had to Die.* New York: Viking, 1958.

Hovey, Graham. "Gov. Harriman: Salty Views on SALT, Etc." *New York Times,* October 9, 1977.

Howe, M. A. DeWolfe. *George von Lengerke Meyer.* New York, 1920.

Hull, Cordell. *The Memoirs of Cordell Hull.* 2 vols. New York: Macmillan, 1948.

Hundley, Helen. "George Kennan and the Russian Empire: How America's Conscience Became an Enemy of Tsarism." http://www.wwics.si .edu/topics/pub/ACF2BO.pdf.

Ickes, Harold. *The Secret Diary of Harold Ickes.* 3 vols. New York: Simon and Schuster, 1953–1954.

Isaacson, Walter. *Kissinger: A Biography.* New York: Simon and Schuster, 2005.

Isaacson, Walter, and Evan Thomas. *The Wise Men: Six Friends and the World They Made.* New York: Simon and Schuster, 1986.

Jensen, Kenneth M., ed. *Origins of the Cold War: The Novikov, Kennan, and Roberts "Long Telegrams" of 1946.* Washington, D.C.: United States Institute of Peace Press, 1993.

Jespersen, T. Christopher. *American Images of China, 1931–1939.* Stanford: Stanford University Press, 1996.

Jessup, John K., ed. *The Ideas of Henry Luce.* New York: Atheneum, 1969.

Johnson, Lyndon B. *The Vantage Point: Perspectives on the Presidency, 1963–1969.* New York: Holt, Rinehart, and Winston, 1971.

Johnson, Paul. *Modern Times: The World from the Twenties to the Nineties.* New York: Harper Perennial, 1992.

Johnson, William R. "The United States Sells China Down the Amur." *China Monthly* 8 (December 1947): 412–15, 425–27.

Karpovich, Michael. *Imperial Russia, 180–1917.* New York: Holt, 1932.

———. *Russia: A History and an Interpretation.* 2 vols. New York: Macmillan, 1953.

Keenan, Barry. *The Dewey Experiment in China: Educational Reform and Political Power in the Early Republic.* Cambridge: Harvard University Press, 1977.

Kennan, George [Siberian]. *Siberia and the Exile System.* 2 vols. New York: Century, 1891.

———. "The Sword of Peace." *Outlook,* October 14, 1905.

Kennan, George F. "America and the Russian Future." *Foreign Affairs* 29, no. 3 (April 1951): 35–70. (Reprinted in *American Diplomacy, 1900–1950.* New York: Mentor, 1951.)

———. *American Diplomacy, 1900–1950.* New York: Mentor, 1951.

———. *Memoirs, 1925–1950.* Boston: Little, Brown, 1967.

———. *Memoirs, 1950–1963.* New York: Pantheon Books, 1972.

———. *Russia Leaves the War.* New York: W. W. Norton, 1958.

———. "The Sisson Documents," *Journal of Modern History* 27, no. 2 (June 1956): 130–54.

———. *Sketches from a Life.* New York: W. W. Norton, 1989.

———. "The Sources of Soviet Conduct." *Foreign Affairs* 25, no. 4 (July 1947): 566–82. (Reprinted in his book *American Diplomacy, 1900–1950.* New York: Mentor, 1951.)

Kennedy, Paul. *The Rise and Fall of the Great Powers: Economic Change and Military Conflict from 1500 to 2000.* New York: Random House, 1987.

Kerney, James. *The Political Education of Woodrow Wilson.* New York: Century, 1926.

Keylor, William R. "Post-mortems on the American Century." *Diplomatic History* 25, no. 2 (Spring 2001): 317–27.

Kirkpatrick, David D. "Pulitzer Board Won't Void '32 Award to *Times* Writer." *New York Times,* November 22, 2003.

Kissinger, Henry. *Diplomacy.* New York: Simon and Schuster, 1994.

———. *White House Years.* Boston: Little, Brown, 1979.

———. *Years of Upheaval.* Boston: Little, Brown, 1982.

Koen, Ross Y. *The China Lobby in American Politics.* New York: Harper and Row, 1974.

Kohler, Foy D., and Mose L. Harvey, eds. *The Soviet Union, Yesterday, Today, Tomorrow: A Colloquy of American Long Timers in Moscow.* Miami: University of Miami Press, 1975.

Krock, Arthur. "A Guide to Official Thinking about Russia." *New York Times*, July 8, 1947, 22.

Langer, John Daniel. "The 'Red General': Philip R. Faymonville and the Soviet Union, 1917–52." *Prologue* 8, no. 4 (Winter 1976): 209–21.

Lansing, Robert. *War Memoirs of Robert Lansing, Secretary of State*. New York: Bobbs-Merrill, 1935.

Larres, Klaus, and Kenneth Osgood, eds. *The Cold War after Stalin's Death: A Missed Opportunity for Peace?* Lanham, Md.: Rowman and Littlefield, 2006.

Lasch, Christopher. *The American Liberals and the Russian Revolution*. New York: Columbia University Press, 1962.

Laserson, Max M. *The American Impact on Russia: Diplomatic and Ideological, 1784–1917*. New York: Macmillan, 1950.

Latourette, Kenneth S. *Beyond the Ranges*. Grand Rapids: Erdman, 1967.

Leahy, William D. *I Was There*. New York: McGraw-Hill, 1950.

Lee, Ivy. "Relationships to the Russian Problem." *Annals: Some Aspects of the Present International Situation* 138 (July 1928).

Leffler, Melvyn P. *For the Soul of Mankind: The United States, the Soviet Union, and the Cold War*. New York: Hill and Wang, 2007.

———. *A Preponderance of Power: National Security, the Truman Administration, and the Cold War*. Stanford: Stanford University Press, 1992.

———. *The Specter of Communism: The United States and the Origins of the Cold War, 1917–1953*. New York: Hill and Wang, 1994.

"Legion of Honor Urged for America." *New York Times*, April 13, 1933, 14.

Lensen, George Alexander. *The World beyond Europe: An Introduction to the History of Africa, India, Southeast Asia, and the Far East*. Boston: Houghton Mifflin, 1966.

Lepsius, J., et al., *Die Grosse Politik der Europaischen Kabinete, 1871–1914*. 40 vols. Berlin, 1922–1927.

Leroux, Charles. "Bearing Witness." *New York Times*, June 25, 2003.

Levering, Ralph B. *American Opinion and the Russian Alliance, 1939–1945*. Chapel Hill: University of North Carolina Press, 1976.

Levine, Isaac Don. *Eyewitness to History*. New York: Hawthorn Books, 1973.

Libbey, James K. *American-Russian Economic Relations, 1770's–1990's: A Survey of Issues and Literature*. Claremont, Calif.: Regina Books, 1989.

Link, Arthur. *Wilson: The New Freedom*. Princeton: Princeton University Press, 1956.

———. *Wilson: The Struggle for Neutrality, 1914–1915*. Princeton: Princeton University Press, 1960.

———. *Wilson the Diplomatist: A Look at His Major Foreign Policies*. Baltimore: Johns Hopkins University Press, 1957.

Link, Perry, and Andrew J. Nathan, eds. *The Tiananmen Papers.* Comp. Zhang Liang. New York: Public Affairs, 2002.

Lippmann, Walter. *The Cold War: A Study in U.S. Foreign Policy.* New York: Harper and Row, 1972.

Lippmann, Walter, and Charles Merz. "Test of the News." A supplement to *New Republic* 23, pt. 2, no. 296 (August 4, 1920).

Lodwick, Kathleen. *The Chinese Recorder Index: A Guide to Christian Missions in China, 1867–1974.* Wilmington, Del.: Scholarly Resources, 1986.

Lubell, Samuel. "Is China Washed Up?" *Saturday Evening Post,* March 31, 1945, 20, 93–94.

———. "Vinegar Joe and the Reluctant Dragon." *Saturday Evening Post,* February 24, 1945, 9–11.

Lukacs, John, ed. *George F. Kennan and the Origins of Containment, 1944–1946: The Kennan-Lukacs Correspondence.* Columbia: University of Missouri Press, 1997.

Lyons, Eugene. *Assignment in Utopia.* New York: Harcourt, Brace, 1938.

———. *The Red Decade: The Classic Work on Communism in America during the Thirties.* 2d ed. New York: Arlington House, 1970.

Maclean, Elizabeth Kimball. "Joseph E. Davies and Soviet-American Relations, 1937–41." *Diplomatic History* 4, no. 4 (Fall 1980): 73–94.

Maddux, Thomas R. "American Diplomats and the Soviet Experiment: The View from the Moscow Embassy, 1934–1939." *South Atlantic Quarterly* 74, no. 4 (Autumn 1975): 468–87.

Malia, Martin E. "Michael Karpovich, 1888–1959." *Russian Review* 19, no. 1 (January 1960): 60–71.

———. *Russia under Western Eyes: From the Bronze Horseman to the Lenin Mausoleum.* Cambridge: Harvard University Press, Belknap Press, 1999.

Maltin, Leonard. *2006 Movie Guide.* New York: Signet Books, 2005.

Mandelbaum, Michael. *The Ideas That Conquered the World: Peace, Democracy, and Free Markets in the Twenty-first Century.* New York: Public Affairs, 2002.

Mann, James. *About Face: A History of America's Curious Relationship with China, from Nixon to Clinton.* New York: Vintage Books, 1998.

Martin, Jay. *The Education of John Dewey: A Biography.* New York: Columbia University Press, 2002.

Matlock, Jack F., Jr. *Reagan and Gorbachev: How the Cold War Ended.* New York: Random House, 2004.

Mayers, David. *The Ambassadors and America's Soviet Policy.* New York: Oxford University Press, 1995.

McCullough, David. *Truman.* New York: Touchstone, 1992.

McKinzie, Richard M., and Eugene P. Trani. "The Influence of Russian Émigrés on American Policy toward Russia and the USSR, 1900–1933, with Observations on Analogous Developments in Great Britain." *Coexistence: A Review of East-West and Development Issues* 28, no. 2 (June 1991): 215–51.

Meisner, Maurice. *Li Ta-Chao and the Origins of Chinese Marxism.* Cambridge: Harvard University Press, 1967.

Melvin, Shelia. "Pearl's Great Price." *Wilson Quarterly* (Spring 2006).

Mendel, Arthur P., ed. *Political Memoirs, 1905–1917,* by Paul Miliukov. Ann Arbor: University of Michigan Press, 1967.

Meyer, Mike. "Pearl of the Orient." *New York Times,* March 5, 2006, Book Review Section, 23.

Mills, Walter, ed. *The Forrestal Diaries.* New York: Viking Press, 1951.

Miscamble, Wilson D. *George F. Kennan and the Making of American Foreign Policy, 1947–1950.* Princeton: Princeton University Press, 1992.

Montefiore, Simon Sebag. *Stalin: The Court of the Red Tsar.* New York: Alfred A. Knopf, 2004.

Morgenthau, Hans J. "Changes and Chances in American-Soviet Relation." *Foreign Affairs* 49, no. 3 (April 1971): 429–41.

Morgenthau, Henry. *Morgenthau Diary, China.* Vol. 2. Washington, D.C.: GPO, 1965.

Morison, Elting E., et al. *The Letters of Theodore Roosevelt.* 8 vols. Cambridge: Harvard University Press, 1951.

Moritz, Charles, ed. *Current Biography Yearbook.* New York: H. H. Wilson, 1961.

Morris, Edmund. *Theodore Rex.* New York: Random House, 2001.

Mowry, George E. *The Era of Theodore Roosevelt and the Birth of Modern America, 1900–1912.* New York: Harper and Row, 1962.

Moyer, George S. *The Attitude of the United States towards the Recognition of Russia.* Philadelphia: University of Pennsylvania, 1926.

Neils, Patricia C. *China Images in the Life and Times of Henry Luce.* Savage, Md.: Rowan and Littlefield, 1990.

———. "China in the Writings of Kenneth Scott Latourette and John King Fairbank." Ph.D. diss., University of Hawaii, 1980.

Nelson, Anna Kasten, et al. "A Roundtable Discussion of Melvyn Leffler's *For the Soul of Mankind: The United States, the Soviet Union, and the Cold War.*" *Passport: The Newsletter of the Society for Historians of American Foreign Relations* 39, no. 2 (September 2008): 24–34.

Ninkovich, Frank. *The Wilsonian Century: U.S. Foreign Policy since 1900.* Chicago: University of Chicago Press, 1999.

Nitze, Paul H. "The Development of NSC 68." *International Security* 4, no. 4 (Spring 1980): 170–76.

———. "Limited Wars or Massive Retaliation?" *Reporter* 17, no. 3 (September 5, 1957).

Nitze, Paul H., with Ann M. Smith and Steven L. Rearden. *From Hiroshima to Glasnost: At the Center of Decision, a Memoir.* New York: Grove Weidenfeld, 1989.

Nixon, Richard M. "Asia after Vietnam." *Foreign Affairs* 46, no. 1 (October 1967): 11–25.

———. *RN: The Memoirs of Richard Nixon.* New York: Simon and Schuster, 1978.

Notter, Harley. *The Origins of the Foreign Policy of Woodrow Wilson.* Baltimore: Johns Hopkins University Press, 1937.

———. *Postwar Foreign Policy Preparation, 1939–1945.* Publication 3580. Washington, D.C.: Department of State, 1949.

O'Connor, Joseph E. "Laurence A. Steinhardt and American Policy toward the Soviet Union, 1939–1941." Ph.D. diss., University of Virginia, 1968.

Osgood, Kenneth. "The Perils of Coexistence: Peace and Propaganda in Eisenhower's Foreign Policy." In *The Cold War after Stalin's Death: A Missed Opportunity for Peace?* ed. Klaus Larres and Kenneth Osgood. Lanham, Md.: Rowman and Littlefield, 2006.

"Outlawing of Reds: A National Menace." *New York Times,* January 18, 1933, 1.

Parry, Albert. "Charles R. Crane, Friend of Russia." *Russian Review* 6, no. 2 (Spring 1947): 20–36.

Petro, Nicolai N. "Russia as Friend, Not Foe." *Speaking Freely (Asia Times Online),* 2007. http://www.atimes/Central_Asia/IB17Ag02.html.

Pringle, Henry F. *Theodore Roosevelt: A Biography.* New York: Harcourt, 1931.

"The Progress of the World." *American Monthly Review of Reviews* 32, no. 4 (October 1905): 390.

Propas, Frederic L. "Creating a Hard Line toward Russia: The Training of State Department Soviet Experts, 1927–1937." *Diplomatic History* 8, no. 3 (Summer 1984): 209–26.

Pugach, Noel H. "Making the Open Door Work: Paul S. Reinsch in China, 1913–1919." *Pacific Historical Review* 39 (1970): 157–75.

———. *Paul S. Reinsch: Open Door Diplomat in Action.* Milwood, N.Y.: KTO Press, 1979.

Rand, Peter. *China Hands: The Adventures and Ordeals of the American Journalists Who Joined Forces with the Great Chinese Revolution.* New York: Simon and Schuster, 1995.

Ransdell, Hollace. "Mr. Fish Down South." *New Republic* 67 (May 20, 1931).

Reagan, Ronald. *An American Life.* New York: Pocket Books, 1990.

"Redmongers Go West." *New Republic* 64 (November 12, 1930): 347.

Reed, James. *The Missionary Mind and American East Policy, 1911–1915.* Cambridge: Harvard University Press, 1983.

Reinsch, Paul S. *An American Diplomat in China.* Garden City, N.Y.: Doubleday, Page, 1922.

Richman, John. *The United States and the Soviet Union: The Decision to Recognize.* Raleigh: Camberleigh Hall, 1980.

Rockefeller, Steven C. *John Dewey: Religious Faith and Democratic Humanism.* New York: Columbia University Press, 1991.

Rockhill, William Woodville. *Explorations in Mongolia and Tibet.* Washington, D.C.: Smithsonian Institution Press, 1893.

————. *The Land of the Lamas: Notes on a Journey through China, Mongolia, and Tibet.* London: Longmans, Green, 1891.

Romanus, Charles F., and Riley Sunderland. *Stilwell's Command Problems.* Washington, D.C.: U.S. Government Printing Office, 1956.

Roosevelt, Elliott. *As He Saw It.* New York: Duell, Sloan, and Pearce, 1946.

"Roosevelt Confers on Russian Policy." *New York Times,* July 8, 1932, 1–2.

Rosen, Baron Roman R. *Forty Years of Diplomacy.* 2 vols. London: George Allen and Unwin, 1922.

Rozek, Edward J., ed. *Walter H. Judd: Chronicles of a Statesman.* Denver: Grier, 1980.

"Russia and America Strike Hands." *New Republic* 77 (November 29, 1933): 62.

Ryan, Alan. *John Dewey and the High Tide of American Liberalism.* New York: W. W. Norton, 1995.

Salisbury, Harrison E. *American in Russia.* New York: Harper and Brothers, 1955.

————. *Behind the Lines: Hanoi, December 23, 1966–January 7, 1967.* New York: Harper and Row, 1967.

————. *The Long March: The Untold Story.* New York: Harper and Row, 1985.

————. *Moscow Journal: The End of Stalin.* Chicago: University of Chicago Press, 1961.

————. *Orbit of China.* New York: Harper and Row, 1967.

————. *A Time of Change: A Reporter's Tale of Our Time.* New York: Harper and Row, 1988.

Salzman, Neil V. *Reform and Revolution: The Life and Times of Raymond Robins.* Kent: Kent State University Press, 1991.

Saul, Norman E. *Concord and Conflict: The United States and Russia, 1867–1914.* Lawrence: University Press of Kansas, 1996.

————. *Distant Friends: The United States and Russia, 1763–1867.* Lawrence: University Press of Kansas, 1991.

————. *Friends or Foes? The United States and Russia, 1921–1941.* Lawrence: University Press of Kansas, 2006.

————. *War and Revolution: The United States and Russia, 1914–1921.* Lawrence: University Press of Kansas, 2001.

Schaller, Michael. *The United States and China in the Twentieth Century*. New York: Oxford University Press, 1979.

Scheuer, Steven H., ed. *Movies on TV and Videocassette, 1992–1993*. New York: Bantam Books, 1993.

Schlesinger, Arthur M., Jr. *The Cycles of American History*. Boston: Houghton Mifflin, 1986.

———. *A Thousand Days: John F. Kennedy in the White House*. Boston: Houghton Mifflin, 1965.

Schulz, George P. *Turmoil and Triumph: My Years as Secretary of State*. New York: Charles Scribner's Sons, 1993.

Schuman, Frederick. *American Policy towards Russia since 1917: A Study of Diplomatic History, International Law, and Public Opinion*. New York: International Publishers, 1928.

Schurman, Franz, and Orville Schell. *Communist China: Revolutionary Reconstruction and International Confrontation, 1949 to the Present*. New York: Random House, 1966.

Seiler, Conrad. "The Redmongers Go West." *New Republic* 64 (November 12, 1930): 347.

Seymour, Charles. *The Intimate Papers of Colonel House*. 4 vols. Boston: Houghton, Mifflin, 1926–1928.

Shackley, Theodore. *Spymaster: My Life in the CIA*. Dulles, Va.: Potomac Books, 2005.

Sherwood, Robert W. *Roosevelt and Hopkins: An Intimate History*. New York: Enigma Books, 2001.

Simes, Dmitri K. "Losing Russia: The Costs of Renewed Confrontation." *Foreign Affairs* 86, no. 6 (November–December 2007): 38–52.

Smith, Arthur H. *Chinese Characteristics*. Safety Harbor, Fla., 2001. (First published 1890).

Smith, Tony. *America's Mission: The United States and the Worldwide Struggle for Democracy in the Twentieth Century*. Princeton: Princeton University Press, 1994.

Snow, Edgar. *The Battle for Asia*. New York: Random House, 1941.

———. *Journey to the Beginning*. New York: Random House, 1958.

———. *The Long Revolution*. New York: Vintage Books, 1973.

———. *The Other Side of the River: Red China Today*. New York: Random House, 196–1962.

———. *The Pattern of Soviet Power*. New York: Random House, 1945.

———. *Red Star over China*. New York: Grove Press, 1968.

———. "Sixty Million Lost Allies." *Saturday Evening Pos,* June 10, 1944, 12–13.

———. *Stalin Must Have Peace*. New York: Random House, 1947.

Snow, Edgar, and Mark Gayn. "Must China Go Red?" *Saturday Evening Post*, May 12, 1945, 9–10.

Soule, George. "Hard-Boiled Radicalism." *New Republic* 65 (January 21, 1931): 261.

Spargo, John. *Russia as an American Problem.* New York: Harper and Brothers, 1920.

Spence, Jonathan A. *The Search for Modern China.* New York: W. W. Norton, 1990.

Stalin, Joseph. *Correspondence between Stalin, Roosevelt, Truman, Churchill, and Atlee during WWII.* Honolulu: University Press of the Pacific, 2001.

———. *Speeches Delivered at Meetings of Voters of the Stalin Electoral District, Moscow.* Moscow: Foreign Languages Publishing House, 1950.

Standley, William, and Arthur Ageton. *Admiral Ambassador to Russia.* Chicago: Regenery Press, 1955.

Stanley, Peter. "The Making of an American Sinologist: W. Rockhill and the Open Door." *Perspectives in American History* 2 (1977–1978): 419–60.

Steffens, Lincoln. *The Autobiography of Lincoln Steffens.* New York: Harcourt, Brace, and World, 1958.

Steinberg, Stephen. *The Academic Melting Pot: Catholics and Jews in American Higher Education.* New York: McGraw-Hill, 1974.

Stekol, Harry. *Through the Communist Looking Glass.* New York: Brewer, Warner, and Putnam, 1932.

Stettinius, Edward R., Jr. *Roosevelt and the Russians: The Yalta Conference.* Garden City, N.Y.: Doubleday, 1949.

Stilwell, Joseph, *The Stilwell Papers.* Ed. Theodore White. New York: William Sloane Associates, 1948.

Stoessinger, John G. *Nations in Darkness: China, Russia, and America.* New York: McGraw-Hill, 1990.

Strakhovsky, Leonid I. *American Opinion about Russia, 1917–1920.* Toronto: University of Toronto Press, 1961.

Sulzberger, Cyrus L. *A Long Row of Candles: Memoirs and Diaries, 1934–1954.* New York: Macmillan, 1969.

Suny, Ronald Grigor. *The Soviet Experiment: Russia, the USSR, and the Successor States.* New York: Oxford University Press, 1998.

Talbot, Strobe. *The Master of the Game: Paul Nitze and the Nuclear Peace.* New York: Alfred A. Knopf, 1988.

Taylor, S. J. *Stalin's Apologist: Walter Duranty, the New York Times's Man in Moscow.* New York: Oxford University Press, 1990.

Tewksbury, Donald G. "Review of *Thunder Out of China.*" *Far Eastern Survey* 16, no. 5 (March 12, 1947): 58–59.

Thatcher, Margaret. *The Downing Street Years.* New York: Harper Collins, 1993.

Thayer, Charles. *Bear in the Caviar.* Philadelphia: Lippincott, 1950.

———. "A West-Pointer Looks at Russia." *Forum* (May 5, 1934).

Thompson, Dody Weston. "Pearl Buck." In *American Winners of the Nobel*

Prize, ed. Warren G. French and Walter E. Kidd. Norman: University of Oklahoma Press, 1968.

Thompson, Edward T., ed. *Theodore H. White at Large: The Best of His Magazine Writing, 1939–1986.* New York: Pantheon Books, 1992.

Thompson, Kenneth W., and Steven L. Rearden, eds. *Paul H. Nitze on Foreign Policy.* Lanham, Md.: University Press of America, 1989.

———. *Paul H. Nitze on National Security and Arms Control.* Lanham, Md.: University Press of America, 1990.

———. *Paul H. Nitze on the Future.* Lanham, Md.: University Press of America, 1991.

Thorson, William B. "American Public Opinion and the Portsmouth Peace Conference." *American Historical Review* 3, no. 3 (April 1948): 439–64.

Tien-yi Li. *Woodrow Wilson's China Policy, 1913–1917.* New York: Twayne, 1952.

Tompkins, Pauline. *American Relations in the Far East.* New York: Macmillan, 1949.

Trani, Eugene P. "Criticize, but Don't Exclude." *International Herald Tribune* (September 15, 2006): 8.

———. "Herbert Hoover and the Russian Revolution." In *Herbert Hoover: The Great War and Its Aftermath, 1914–23,* ed. Lawrence Gelfand. Iowa City: University of Iowa Press, 1979.

———. "Russia in 1905: The View from the American Embassy." *Review of Politics* 31, no. 1 (January 1969): 48–65.

———. *The Treaty of Portsmouth: An Adventure in American Diplomacy.* Lexington: University Press of Kentucky, 1969.

Trani, Eugene P., and Donald E. Davis. *The First Cold War: The Legacy of Woodrow Wilson in U.S.-Soviet Relations.* Columbia: University of Missouri Press, 2002.

———. "Roosevelt and the U.S. Role: Perception Makes Policy." In *The Treaty of Portsmouth and Its Legacies,* ed. Steven Erickson and Allen Hockley, 62–74. Lebanon, N.H.: University Press of New England, 2008.

———. "A Tale of Two Kennans: American-Russian Relations in the Twentieth Century." In *Presidents, Diplomats, and Other Mortals,* ed. Garry Clifford and Theodore A. Wilson, 31–55. Columbia: University of Missouri Press, 2007.

Trani, Eugene P., and Richard D. McKinzie. "The Influence of Russian Émigrés on American Policy toward the USSR, 1900–1933, with Observations on Analogous Developments in Great Britain." *Coexistence: A Review of East-West and Development Issues* 28, no. 2 (June 1991): 215–51.

Trani, Eugene P., and David L. Wilson. *The Presidency of Warren G. Harding.* Lawrence: Regents Press of Kansas, 1977.

Travis, Frederick F. *George Kennan and the American-Russian Relationship, 1865–1924.* Athens: Ohio University Press, 1990.

Trotsky, Leon. "Russia and World Revolution." *New Republic* 76 (November 1, 1933): 328.

Truman, Harry S. *Memoirs.* 2 vols. Garden City, N.Y.: Doubleday, 1955–1956.

Tuchman, Barbara. *Stilwell and the American Experience in China, 1911–45.* New York: Grove Press, 1985.

Tucker, Robert W. "An Inner Circle of One: Woodrow Wilson and His Advisors." *National Interest* 51 (Spring 1998): 3–26.

Uyehara, Cecil H. *Checklist of Archives in the Japanese Ministry of Foreign Affairs.* Tokyo, 1868–1945, and Washington, D.C.: GPO, 1954.

Ullman, Richard H. "The Davies Mission and United States–Soviet Relations, 1937–1941." *World Politics* 9, no. 2 (January 1957): 220–39.

U.S./USSR Textbook Study Project: Interim Report, June 1981. Howard D. Mehlinger, dir. Bloomington, Ind., 1981.

Utley, Freda. *China at War.* London: Faber and Faber, 1939.

Varg, Paul A. *Missionaries, Chinese, and Diplomats: The American Protestant Missionary Movement in China, 1890–1932.* Princeton: Princeton University Press, 1958.

———. *Open Door Diplomat: The Life of W. W. Rockhill.* Urbana: Illinois Studies in the Social Sciences, Illinois University Press, 1952.

Vernadsky, George. *A History of Russia.* New York: Bantam Books, 1967.

Walder, David. *The Short Victorious War.* New York: Harper and Row, 1973.

Walsh, Fr. Edmund A., Jr. "Fr. Walsh on Russia." *Commonweal* (May 5, 1933).

Weil, Martin. *A Pretty Good Club: The Founding Fathers of the U.S. Foreign Service.* New York: W. W. Norton, 1978.

Wells, Samuel F. "Sounding the Tocsin: NSC 68 and the Soviet Threat." *International Security* 4, no. 2 (Autumn 1979).

West, Philip. *Yenching University and Sino-Western Relations, 1916–1952.* Cambridge: Harvard University Press, 1976.

Westbrook, Robert B. *John Dewey and American Democracy.* Ithaca: Cornell University Press, 1991.

White, John Albert. *The Diplomacy of the Russo-Japanese War.* Princeton: Princeton University Press, 1964.

White, Theodore H. *In Search of History: A Personal Adventure.* New York: Harper and Row, 1978.

———. "Life Looks at China." *Life,* May 1, 1944, 98–110.

———. "Inside Red China." *Life,* December 8, 1944, 39–40, 42, 44, 46.

White, Theodore H., and Annalee Jacoby. *Thunder Out of China.* New York: William Sloane Associates, 1946.

Williams, Oakley, trans. and ed. *Prince Billow and the Kaiser.* London: Thornton Butterworth, 1932.

Williams, William Appleman. *American-Russian Relations, 1781–1947.* New York: Rinehart, 1952.

Wilson, Edmund. "Foster and Fish." *New Republic* 65 (December 24, 1930): 162.

Wilson, Joan Hoff. *Ideology and Economics: U.S. Relations with the Soviet Union, 1918–1933.* Columbia: University of Missouri Press, 1974.

Wilson, Woodrow. "A Draft of an Essay." In *The Papers of Woodrow Wilson,* ed. Arthur S. Link et al. 69 vols. Princeton: Princeton University Press, 1966–1993.

———. *The Papers of Woodrow Wilson.* Ed. Arthur S. Link et al. 69 vols. Princeton: Princeton University Press, 1966–1993.

Worthington, Chauncey Ford, ed. *Letters of Henry Adams, 1892–1918.* Boston: Houghton Mifflin, 1938.

Wright, Arthur F. *Buddhism in Chinese History.* Stanford: Stanford University Press, 1959.

Wright, C. Ben. "George F. Kennan, Scholar-Diplomat, 1926–1946." Ph.D. diss., University of Wisconsin, 1972.

———. "Mr. 'X' and Containment." *Slavic Review* 35, no. 1 (March 1976).

Yarmolinsky, Abraham, trans. and ed., *The Memoirs of Count Witte.* London: William Heinemann, 1921.

Yergin, Daniel. *Shattered Peace: The Origins of the Cold War and the National Security State.* Boston: Houghton Mifflin, 1977.

Zinn, Lucille S. "The Works of Pearl S. Buck: A Bibliography." *Bulletin of Bibliography* 36, no. 4 (October–December 1979): 194–208.

index

About the Foreword Author

Thomas R. Pickering began his four-decade-long career in the Foreign Service after graduating with a B.A. from Bowdoin College and an M.A. from Tufts University. His assigned ambassadorships included the countries of Jordan, Nigeria, El Salvador, Israel, India, and Russia. Mr. Pickering also served as special assistant to Secretaries of State William P. Rogers and Henry Kissinger, and from 1997 to 2001, he was Undersecretary of State for Political Affairs. Mr. Pickering was awarded the distinction of Career Ambassador, the highest honor in the U.S. Foreign Service. To honor his contributions to U.S. diplomacy, the U.S. Department of State Foreign Affairs Fellowship Program was renamed the Thomas R. Pickering Foreign Affairs Fellowship Program. In retirement, he chairs the American Academy of Diplomacy.

About the Foreword Author (Russian edition)

Dr. Vyacheslav Nikonov, Molotov's grandson, is the founder and president of the Polity Foundation, which is involved in numerous projects and works closely with such organizations as the World Bank and the Carnegie Endowment. Dr. Nikonov holds a Ph.D. in history from Moscow State University and is the author of five books and numerous articles. He served in the Russian State Duma from 1994 to 1996 and chaired the Subcommittee for International Security and Arms Control.